Adolescent Sexuality in Contemporary America

The Sorensen Report

Adolescent Sexuality in Contemporary America

Personal Values and Sexual Behavior Ages Thirteen to Nineteen

ROBERT C. SORENSEN

Introduction by Paul Moore, Jr.

A Note on the Methodology by Jiri Nehnevajsa

Consultants

Herbert I. Abelson, Ph.D.
Iris Bruel, Ph.D.
Dana J. Harman
The Right Reverend Paul Moore, Jr.
Jiri Nehnevajsa, Ph.D.

Published by The World Publishing Company
Published simultaneously in Canada
by Nelson, Foster & Scott Ltd.

First printing—1973

Library of Congress cataloging in publication data

Sorensen, Robert C
Adolescent sexuality in contemporary America.

1. Youth—sexual behavior. I. Title.
HQ27.S67 301.41'75 72-11510
ISBN 0-529-04820-5

WORLD PUBLISHING
TIMES MIRROR

Contents

Part II. Personal Values and Sexual Attitudes: Building Blocks for Sexual Behavior

Part III. Sexual Behavior

Tables of Information

Technical Appendix

Acknowledgments

I am thankful to many for the inspiration, counsel, and valuable assistance they have given me in this undertaking.

My immediate associates to whom I am immensely indebted for every manner of effort are Thomas R. Kemm and Florence Tonjes. Carmiah Frank also was very helpful. They marshaled their minds, their skills, and their energies against a wide (and sometimes wild) variety of challenges that sometimes never seemed to stop. At times we would labor all night to meet a crisis only to face another the next morning. Without Tom Kemm in particular, carrying out this study would have been impossible.

Our depth interviewers were helpful in enabling us to perceive and develop our initial hypotheses. I thank them all but most especially acknowledge the brilliant and perceptive work of Leah Linsky.

Our sample design and field interviewing associates, Response Analysis Corporation, performed a superior job of implementing a series of difficult assignments. Their supervisors and employees were vital to the success of the survey.

I thank Dr. Allen Chapman, former dean of the Graduate School of Business at C. W. Post Center of Long Island University, and Lou Ziccardi, postmaster at the Center, for their help and encouragement.

I want to acknowledge the competence and kindness of my publisher and its staff. My editor, Peter Ritner, was generous, faithful to my ideals, and a true believer in the outcome of this project from the beginning.

To the young people who answered our questions and to their parents who gave us permission to ask them I offer my thanks and congratulations for their willingness to cooperate in illuminating our minds and our hearts.

My consultants have been helpful and hardworking. The computer operation with its hundreds of thousands of data entries could not have been accomplished without the skill of Dana Harman. The contributions of Dr. Iris Bruel, Dr. Jiri Nehnevajsa, and Dr. Herbert Abelson have been many.

Most important of all are my wife and three children, who have been loving, understanding, and helpful to me throughout this project.

Introduction

To open this book is to enter the tender and loving, fearful and intensely personal lives of our young people. Although the form of Sorensen's book is that of a sociological survey, the content is as exciting as a novel. Like a good novel, it reveals the mysterious life of the human spirit in its formative years, and it treats conflicts of values and their resolution. Some of the quotations move one to tears, others to compassionate laughter. Beneath the fragments of experience and the cold statistics lies perhaps the deepest tension of American life, and certainly the most crucial misunderstanding between generations.

Strangely enough, such a survey has never been made before. Kinsey and others have studied sexual behavior; moralists have explored the ethical content of various views on sexuality; anthropologists have compared sexual mores. But until Sorensen carried out this study, no one had specifically attempted to relate the sexual behavior to the sexual values of adolescents in the United States. The manner in which this difficult task was accomplished is equally noteworthy; the author has taken every measure to protect the privacy and psychic vulnerability of his subjects. The concern shown in this book for adolescent sensibilities contrasts sharply with the clumsiness, even brutality, of some parental behavior reflected in the interviews.

I read the book as a bishop deeply concerned about the changing sexual ethic of our day, as a pastor who continues to counsel many young people, and as a father of nine children ranging in age from ten to twenty-one. I found no absolute guidance in the book but gained much more insight than I would have anticipated. Now, a glance at what I found.

"It's just more of a love thing," says a girl about her sexual relationship with another girl. A bizarre example to pull out, you might think, but yet it is a significant one. Throughout the study, sex from the adolescent's view comes through as a combination of love, kindness, and mutual enjoyment between persons. The use of either women or men as sex objects is downgraded. Abusing or even using another for purely selfish sexual reasons is a rare thing among adolescents.

This is not to say that there is a pattern of total selflessness, although this may rank high as a goal; but, rather, the attitude reflected in the remark, "It is nice to have sex with a friend," is typical. The most common view was reflected in the simple statement, "Sex is OK if you love."

Let me point out a few more values which impressed me. Tolerance of sexual behavior of others as long as both partners want to experience it is really the value of charity. For instance, in this sampling there was considerable tolerance for homosexuality, although few admitted homosexuality. Statements such as, "I never would do it, but it is OK for them if they like it," show a tolerance for others consistent with a relatively strong code for oneself.

Mutuality seems more important to the young, as the author summarizes: "It isn't 'I love you and you love me,' but rather 'I love *us*.' "

I mention these values to demonstrate that a strong value system exists among adolescents, despite the fact that it differs from the value system of their parents and of much of the culture which surrounds them.

Certainly the values described above—charity expressed in tolerance, the importance of mutuality, the unwillingness to use another—are the same as those found in Judeo-Christian ethics and have much in common with the traditional values of our culture. In many cases their behavior is more moral, it seems to me, than the behavior of much of the older generation. The sex-object motif of advertising, the hostility and dishonesty within many marriages, the criticism of others' behavior while being less than moral oneself are examples of this.

Thus, I do not judge the adolescents' attitudes and behavior reflected here as more immoral or amoral than adults'. Rather, the conflict seems to center around the institution of marriage, which many young people feel to be a legal gimmick and see as a destructive institution for many people. I would say monogamy (outside as well as inside marriage) still holds a high respect, but the closed marriage of two people who no longer love each other is deeply resented. Young people, then, are painfully, fearfully, joyfully working out their own moral codes still based on Judeo-Christian ethics but articulated in codes they feel more appropriate for their own culture.

If this is so, the misunderstanding and hypocrisy of the generation gap on this subject is even more tragic. Some children are staying away from their parents' church partly because they think the church teaches that sexual joy is sinful, and they experience it as positive and loving. Barriers arise between parents and children because of the virtual impossibility of communicating on this subject. Often it is the parents' sexual fear which intervenes in natural communication; at other times, it seems to stem from parental uncertainty. Perhaps parents intuitively agree with their children, but cannot bring themselves to say so because of the behavior they were taught.

Those children who run away from home tend to be children who need their parents but feel rejected. This is another example of the tragic generation gap which often stems from sexual misunderstanding.

It seems to me that the years ahead will see the forging of a new sexual morality based on the commandment of love. How the churches and society in general will deal with this change is most important. I do not say that sentimental identification with adolescent views is called for. I do not say that the institution of marriage is outmoded. But I do say with great urgency that open dialogue must increase and that young people's moral views should be respected as such even when one differs strongly with them. Such respect will help break down the separation, fear, and tragedy which the generation gap now engenders and will increase respect for the more traditional views in response.

One cannot prophesy where we will be twenty years hence, but it is no small wonder that sexual behavior, which lies at the center of human experience, would change when the whole environment has changed. Margaret Mead has said that we are aliens in our culture while our children are the natives. It is they, not we, who must work out the heavy responsibility of human life in a fearful age.

After studying this book, I am even more confident that the patterns and morals our children determine will be loving, personal, and responsible. However, we can contribute to their creativity by making our own wisdom, our successes, and our failures available to them in candid dialogue. By giving them loving understanding, we can help them develop their emotional natures and help protect them from the disasters that any pioneering must risk.

I hope more studies will be encouraged by this sensitive survey done by Sorensen, because we have only begun to scratch the surface. As a parent and as a pastor, I need all the insight I can find so that I can be more confident in my own contribution to the kinds of exciting growth evidenced in the interviews in this book. I am sure other readers will feel the same and be grateful for the important step that this study represents.

Sex and values are inextricably intertwined; unless they are studied together both will be distorted.

PAUL MOORE, JR.
Bishop of New York
The Protestant Episcopal Church

I. Objectives: What This Study Is All About

What makes sex so vital for most people is not how good it feels, but the many ways sex feels good and the many personal needs it satisfies. There is no physical activity that consumes more of our thinking and emotional time. Without sex, there would be no outlet for many very satisfying forms of self-fulfillment and self-indulgence. Sex gives so much pleasure—even to think or talk about—that it becomes to a certain extent a medium of communication.

Sex is a life force that begins to express itself in all of us before adolescence. As infants and small children we became aware of our sex organs and sex differences without calling them sex. But beginning with adolescence, the power to have sex emerges to influence why young people think and do many things. The young person begins thinking sexually and doing sexual things on purpose.

When adolescents adopt certain beliefs and forms of behavior in response to their sexual desires, we call this *adolescent sexuality*. Adolescent sexuality is important because it greatly influences what young people think and do in all aspects of their lives. It is an energy or life force that is a supremely important personal resource to many adolescents today. Although it is a subject clouded with superstitions about what young people want and although there is very little current research that is accurate about young people, we can learn much about adolescent sexuality through serious research.

We began this study with three basic goals about how it would be conducted:

1. We wanted to study young people from the time in their lives that sexuality begins to assert itself: from the ages of thirteen through nineteen. We wanted to avoid captive audiences, whether in classrooms or hospitals or the army or in jail, and go directly to a representative sample of young people throughout the United States whether they have had any sexual experience or not. We wanted to achieve wholehearted cooperation from adolescents coming from households that differ very little from other households in all of the major characteristics we could measure.

2. We wanted to find out directly from young people themselves why they think and act as they do in sexual matters. There are only two ways to do this, and we did our study in both ways. First, adolescents were interviewed in depth about their attitudes and behavior. Throughout this book, with only names concealed, we repeat verbatim what young people told us about virginity, love, masturbation, abnormal sex, and many other things. We have hundreds of hours of tape on which we recorded young people's thoughts. Then, armed with what we learned in our depth interviews, we tested our findings against the most representative sample of thirteen to nineteen year olds in the United States that we were able to obtain. We asked them questions which they took anywhere from ninety minutes to three hours to answer.
3. We developed techniques of questioning so that adolescents would be frank and honest, telling the truth about themselves and telling it in detail. And we accomplished full confidentiality for all adolescents cooperating with us.

We feel that there are important uses to which we can put our findings. The last thing society needs is unnecessary confrontations between adolescents and adults based on misunderstandings and ignorance. Young people in contemporary America are often misunderstood for their sexual morals, their conception of love, and what they want from marriage and the family. Is adolescent sexuality deliberately promiscuous and antisocial? Do most young people *not* believe in love, and do they support sexual immorality? Must adolescents and adults be pitted against each other because of how they view each other's concepts of sex? If parents knew how, they could open up communications with their children about sex and love which have been lost to a multitude of families in recent years.

A study was required that would go directly to youth—in depth and on a national basis—and ask them questions point-blank. Do they favor promiscuity, a society without morals? Do they want to live within the system? Do young people want marriage and, if so, under what circumstances? What do they think can be accomplished by education, the law, and the church?

Most important of all, we wanted to learn what meaning life holds for adolescents and whether sex plays any significant part in making their lives more meaningful.

1.
How This Study Was Planned and Carried Out

If my son is willing to talk with you about sex, then you've done something I haven't been able to do. He won't talk with me about much of anything.

Father of a fifteen-year-old boy who gave us permission to interview his son

This is not *a test. There are no "right" answers and no "wrong" answers. But we are counting on you to give* truthful *answers about what you believe and what you do. Some of the questions are very personal, but to make sure that you can feel completely free and honest in what you say, the interviewer will tell you about the foolproof system we are using to make sure that these questionnaires remain* absolutely confidential *in every way.*

Instructions on front page of this study's questionnaire

1.1 Paucity of research about youthful sexual behavior and personal values

1.2 Basic research policy decisions

Need for objectivity

Need for both attitudinal and behavioral information

Need for multiple data-collection techniques

Problems of questionnaire development

Need for studying a wide variety of adolescents

Inclusion of younger adolescents

Inclusion of adolescents without sexual experience

Inclusion of married adolescents

Adolescents residing in institutions

The "invisible" adolescent

Need for obtaining parental consent

1.3 Conducting the national survey

1.4 Unique problems and their solutions

Obtaining parental authorization for interviews

Nature of parental concerns

Techniques for obtaining parental consent

Obtaining adolescent respondent cooperation

Nature of adolescent concerns

Techniques for obtaining cooperation

Learning the truth from adolescents

1.5 American adolescents: who they are

A description of our sample of American adolescents and its comparison with the U.S. 1970 Census of Population

The value of any study depends largely on the methods used in carrying it out. Methods must be valid and reliable, capable of producing the kinds of information required, and clearly explicable to all participants in the study. In this study an additional goal has been to develop and use methods that we could easily explain both to those whom we interviewed and to our readers.

This chapter describes the methods we developed and used in studying adolescent sexuality. Several months were spent in testing various methods and deciding which ones would be workable. Many useful techniques of social research had to be rejected because they were not applicable either to our objectives or to the unique problems we faced. Sometimes it was necessary to invent new techniques.

1.1 Paucity of research about youthful sexual behavior and personal values

Some of the most innovative social research of the last thirty years has been in the field of sex. We read and reviewed much of it; we are grateful to these earlier researchers and to the people who cooperated with them.

Considering that sex is front-page news in the minds of most young people, the absence of more systematic meaningful research about adolescent personal values and sexual behavior is itself a unique state of affairs in our society.

Certainly the question of adolescent sex has not been ignored. The pioneering Kinsey research on male and female sexual behavior in the late forties and early fifties is world famous. Studies have been recently conducted in some communities by the Institute for Sex Research (founded by Alfred Kinsey and his colleagues at Indiana University), SIECUS (Sex Information and Education Council), the YWCA, and other groups. A few scholars in the fields of sociology and psychology have examined communication among young people and premarital sexual permissiveness. A comprehensive study of sexual attitudes and behavior of teen-agers was carried out in England during the mid-sixties by a group headed by Michael Schofield. In 1971 a survey dealing with sexual intercourse, use of contraception, and pregnancy among older teen-agers was taken by the Institute for Survey Research at Temple University for the President's Commission on Population Growth and the American Future.

Some of these scholars and their studies will be referred to in this report. But the drastically changing folkways and mores of adolescent sexuality have undercut much of the usefulness of earlier data in understanding youthful sexual behavior today, even though it would be inaccurate and unfair to assert that the few studies of five and ten years ago are obsolete.

In the United States the absence of any recent nationwide study relating personal values and sexual behavior raises doubts about data obtained from studies involving a few young people, a few schools, or a few communities. When we consider the different ages, socioeconomic backgrounds, and geographic location of American adolescents, we realize there is no basis for assuming that all young people are alike in sexual attitudes and behavior. Moreover, studies of captive groups can at best only satisfy special interests. Many questions about American adolescent society as a whole cannot be answered in studies published about such groups as 122 air force recruits, 600 students of a West Coast university, VD patients, 45 delinquent girls in a southern reformatory, 192 students in an introductory psychiatry course at the University of Hawaii—despite the quality of their research and scholarship.

What are the reasons why more has not been learned about the sexual lives of young people?

1. To most American adults sexual behavior is a question of personal morality. Many adults dismiss consideration of how to deal with teen-age sexuality as a matter only of "common sense," which often closely corresponds with their own prejudices and parental inhibitions. Until recently, organized philosophy and theology generally ignored the relationship between man's personal values and his sexual instincts. Many clergymen equated sex with sin and sought nothing of its humanity.

   Any scholar whose findings challenged the conventional moralities concerning sex was almost certain to be disliked by those who demanded that people live by conventional moralities. In the post–World War II years Kinsey and his colleagues were castigated for disseminating information and assuming society would want to acknowledge hard facts about adult sexual behavior in its laws and institutions.

2. Only recently have many social scientists accepted the area of sexual behavior as a valid field of professional research. The vocal minority who censured Kinsey in the fifties included some social scientists who viewed sex as little more than a biological phenomenon. Pioneers in sex research were called sexologists—a vague label for persons who studied sexual behavior. Many social scientists enjoyed the satisfaction of knowing that Kinsey was by training a zoologist. "After all," a sociologist once told me, "I have no interest in the animal behavior of human beings." These thoughts echoed the assumptions of the twenties and the thirties that sex was an appropriate subject for the pathologist or criminologist who was interested in deviant behavior or possibly for the anthropologist who might seek contemporary parallels with Malinowski's *The Sexual Life of Savages.* Who else (the question ran) but prostitutes, criminals, and psychiatric patients would have sex lives meriting serious study?
3. Young people are not easy to study, and their sexuality is no exception. The reasons for this are explored later in this chapter, and they have heretofore been sufficiently great to discourage the kind of research on which this report is based. The fact that this is the first nationwide study of its kind in the United States may well be the best proof of this difficulty.

1.2 Basic research policy decisions

1.2.1 Need for objectivity

Having reviewed the relatively small amount of accurate information available about adolescent sexuality and having sampled the much larger amount of misinformation and uninformed speculation in circulation, it became clear that objectivity would be a primary goal of our study.

To be objective is to search out, measure, and report on the truth as it exists. If we can understand what we learn, so much the better. No point of view dominated the content of our questions, and no conclusion was reached in advance of our findings. It is not easy to be objective about either young people or sex. Almost everyone has well-developed opinions about both. Efforts to observe and evaluate young people may influence the very facts we seek to discover. In addition, many people in our society, some knowingly and others unconsciously, regard adolescents with such great emotion—be it envy, affection, or hatred—that their powers of observation are badly impaired.

In conducting this study, we were interested only in learning how and why adolescents behave as they do sexually. We want to make the reader think, and so we are not concerned with what the reader thinks. No one can feel assured that he will find comfort for his fears or support for his beliefs in this report.

In pursuit of objectivity, we established the following ground rules early in the project:

1. This study is neither for nor against young people; it is only *about* young people. We have no interest in influencing readers to understand the young person's point of view or to consider the potential contribution of young people to our society. Neither do we suggest that readers condemn the attitudes and behavior of young people. We seek only to understand and explain adolescent sexuality in a period of rapid change.
2. This study is *about* sexuality. It is neither for nor against sex, and it certainly is not an effort to glorify sex. Nothing is omitted from our research because it is sensational, but neither has any effort been made to feature the sensational.
3. Finally, in the interest of complete objectivity, we chose not to consult the people who had already studied young people and sex. In carefully reviewing all of the literature, it became obvious that the variety of different opinions is virtually as large as the number of people who hold them and the points of view are as many as the fields from which they come. It therefore seemed best to make our own judgments about what to ask, what to report, and what meaning to give our findings.

1.2.2 Need for both attitudinal and behavioral information

Sexual behavior is obviously an essential ingredient of adolescent sexuality and is inextricably linked with sexual attitudes and beliefs. We cannot fully understand why a person has certain beliefs unless we know whether he behaves consistently with his reported attitudes. Even though two young people may share the same belief, they have different sexual selves if one literally acts out his beliefs and the other behaves in a quite different way. Thus, we rejected the approach, taken by many past studies of young people, that is typified by the following instruction quoted from one of them: "Please keep in mind that we are not interested in your behavior or in your acceptance of other people's behavior, but in the values and standards which you personally hold."

At the same time, our study could not deal exclusively with behavior, because behavior—studied as an isolated phenomenon—is by no means a true measure of sexuality among adolescents. As Ira Reiss puts it:

> Behavior may be just as deceiving as attitude. Behavior in the sexual sphere may result from many cross-pressures and may involve what the individual fully accepts or what he almost fully rejects. An individual may do only what he accepts or he may do more or he may choose to do less by not indulging at all, even when he thinks it is right to do so. Thus, behavior is no more a "real" measure of sexual relationships than is attitude.*

Thus, the scope of this study was defined to include *both* adolescent sexual behavior and the attitude, or value, patterns underlying and closely interrelated with this behavior.

1.2.3 Need for multiple data-collection techniques

Two basic methodological tools are available to the survey researcher for collecting attitudinal and behavioral data: the personal interview and the self-administered questionnaire. In many ways the personal interview has significant advantages over the self-administered questionnaire, particularly in exploring intensively a wide range of questions in an area that most people regard as highly sensitive and personal. A competent interviewer is thoroughly familiar with the types of information being sought and is highly skilled in the subtle techniques of eliciting such information from reluctant or inarticulate respondents, as well as from those who are open and talkative. If a respondent does not understand a question, a skilled interviewer can paraphrase it in more meaningful terms; if a respondent gives vague or incomplete answers, a skilled interviewer can probe to clarify or expand such answers. Such a skilled interviewer can gather more useful material in a personal interview than could ever be obtained from a rigidly structured questionnaire.

But the advantages of the personal interview carry with them potential disadvantages when one is seeking to collect highly standardized and statistically quantifiable data from a large sample of respondents who are widely dispersed across the entire country. No two interviewers are alike; it is impossible to standardize the personalities and questioning mannerisms of the many different interviewers who must be involved in a nationwide survey. Even if the same questions are asked by all interviewers, inflections, speech mannerisms, and nonverbal cues (such as facial expressions or unconscious gestures) vary widely from interviewer to interviewer. When one is dealing with such a highly sensitive subject as sex, variations among interviewers can have a major effect upon the answers given, and such an effect can detract significantly from the reliability of statistical measures obtained from survey data.

It was therefore decided that this study should make use of *both*

* Ira Reiss, *The Social Context of Premarital Sexual Permissiveness* (New York: Holt, Rinehart and Winston, 1967), p. 11.

personal interviews and self-administered questionnaires, using each of these techniques for the specific purposes to which it is best suited.

Initially, a few highly trained interviewers conducted lengthy personal interviews to determine, from a small but heterogeneous sample of young people, what these young people thought most important about their sexuality, what vocabulary they used in discussing their sexual behavior, and what attitudes and values they expressed about their feelings, beliefs, and experiences. These interviews were recorded in their entirety on tape cassettes, with each respondent's full knowledge and advance consent. A total of 143 tape-recorded interviews were obtained, some of them three hours in length. The author interviewed an additional fifty-seven young people either alone or in groups during the developmental stages of this study.

The interviewers were *not* provided with a list of standardized questions for which they were to seek standardized answers. Instead, they worked from a subject outline, or interview guide, which simply indicated the types of subject matter to be discussed with the adolescent respondent. Every effort was made to encourage spontaneity on the part of respondents, giving them maximum opportunity to say what they wanted to say in the way that they wanted to say it. In some cases, this effort for spontaneity and informality was so successful that respondents—expecting formally stated direct questions—did not realize that the "interview" had begun until it was almost finished.

The 200 personal interviews provided us with invaluable understanding of the many different ways in which adolescents view their sexuality. We learned much about the language and emotions in which they express these views. Above all, these interviews gave us insight into the wide variety of behavioral and attitudinal patterns found in the adolescent population and enabled us to formulate numerous hypotheses about the complex ways in which these patterns might be interrelated. As we listened to the tapes and developed new insights into the kinds of subjects to explore and the kinds of hypotheses to research further, we continually revised the subject outlines on which subsequent interviews were based.

As vital as these tape-recorded personal interviews were, however, they did *not* provide us with quantifiable statistical data about *how many* adolescents participated in certain behavior or held certain attitudes and beliefs. To determine the number and kind of adolescents who fit into each behavioral and attitudinal pattern revealed by our initial interviews, we required a different data-collection approach. We needed a standardized questionnaire that could be administered to young people all over the country so that we would have responses that could be projected reliably to the entire adolescent population under study. Thus we could report hard statistical findings as well as narrative generalizations.

1.2.4 Problems of questionnaire development

In designing this standardized questionnaire for our national survey, one of our most difficult decisions was whether or not we should use questions and attitude scales that other researchers (Kirkendall, Christensen, Reiss, Kinsey, Schofield, and others) have used in the past several years. Too often, in research on any subject, the researcher likes to formulate his own questions rather than use the fine techniques of other researchers. The questions and scales used in earlier studies had already proved their value; moreover, by using them we could compare responses given in 1972 with those recorded in earlier studies.

We found it difficult to decide, and action on the question was temporarily postponed until we completed our review of the literature, our informal talks with young people, and our preliminary personal interviews. It was to our advantage that we waited. We found that some concepts investigated in the older studies (for example, "thrift," "chastity") are sufficiently obsolete that they are not understood by today's typical adolescent. Many words used in earlier tests are not current, and new words have come into being to describe some aspects of sexual behavior.

Thus, we decided to use our own questions and interview-scaling techniques. Our consultant, Dr. Iris Bruel, a clinical psychologist specializing in adolescent behavior, gave invaluable insights and techniques in this phase of our study.

Having made this difficult decision, we were immediately faced by one that was even more difficult and that caused the most argument and discussion among us. This decision involved the choice of content for the questionnaire. To ask or not to ask: that was the question.

Our knowledge of which areas we wanted to research was an invaluable guide in our decisions about what to ask. But our review of the literature on human sexuality, together with listening for hundreds of hours to our personal-interview tapes, convinced us that every answer leads to new questions. A seemingly simple subject such as attitudes toward masturbation can produce enough data for an entire chapter if not a small book. As full as this study may seem, we were compelled to whittle down drastically the number of things we were prepared to learn about adolescent sexuality. If one thinks of what we believed would be practical to explore as the numerator and what we actually wanted to learn as the denominator, the corresponding fraction would be 1/10,000.

Accordingly, we established three criteria to help us decide what questions to include in our questionnaire.

1. Constant and careful consideration was given to the sensitivities of adolescent respondents. While we omitted no subject of consequence in our exploratory depth interviews (where the decision about what to ask and how to ask it could be entrusted to a sensitive and responsible interviewer), there were certain questions that we considered too sensitive for unselective exposure to some younger or less mature adolescents in the national sample. Such exceptionally sensitive questions, dealing with oral sex, anal sex, and intercourse with animals, were stricken from the last draft of our questionnaire.
2. The incidence of some types of sexual behavior is very low, so low that a sample of ten thousand cases would be necessary to bring out even a handful of responses to some questions. Unless the absence of such behavior would be considered significant, questions we believed would bring these results were omitted from the questionnaire. (On the other hand, if we wanted to learn the details of this kind of behavior, respondents were interviewed in depth about it in the personal depth interviews.)
3. Questionnaires designed for self-administration do not lend themselves to the inclusion of questions that require open-ended responses. Answers to questions that involve a chain of reasoning (for example, "Why didn't you go further with a boy on your first date?" or "Why do you believe you are impotent?") are examples of this. When such questions are included in a self-administered questionnaire, the results are difficult to interpret with precision because respondents vary widely in their ability to articulate their answers and in their willingness to write them down with the necessary fullness and clarity.

   A soundly designed self-administered questionnaire must offer, for each question, meaningful but tightly structured alternative answers which can be checked off or filled in by respondents with a minimum of effort. Questions that could not be adapted to this type of format were excluded from the national study. We do not feel that a significant amount of information was lost by excluding qualitative questions, if only because of the wealth of qualitative material already available to us from the personal-interview tapes.

In addition to deciding which questions to include, a further consideration involved the sequential relationship between attitude and behavior questions. A fundamental purpose of this study was to learn the extent to which behavior and attitudes are interrelated and, above all, to learn about the respondent's attitudes independent of his or her behavior. It was difficult to decide how best to sequence our questions to achieve these goals. Should respondents be asked about their attitudes concerning sexual intercourse, for instance, and then be asked whether or not they have had sexual intercourse? Or should the order be reversed, with people being asked about their intercourse behavior first and only then being asked about their attitudes?

The disadvantages of asking people about their behavior first are clear. We risk throwing off some people and losing their cooperation in giving truthful answers to the remainder of the questionnaire. Accordingly, we decided not to ask people about their behavior each time we asked them about their attitudes. Instead we intermixed attitudinal and behavioral questions throughout the questionnaire.

Great care was taken to avoid an accusatory flavor in any question. We tried to eliminate surprise as an element of the questioning process, always seeking to let the kind of behavior we were talking about evolve from one phase to the next rather than suddenly asking a surprise question. Thus, for example, no one would be asked what he did after he had sexual intercourse unless he had already been asked whether or not he had in fact had any experience with sexual intercourse and his answer to this question had been yes. Because we were interested in learning whether the respondent knew anything about certain sex practices, we made it possible for the boy or girl to indicate lack of knowledge without having to appear ignorant or naive.

Separate questionnaires (reproduced in the Technical Appendix) were prepared for male and female respondents, with many of the questions being common to both. These questionnaires were used with respondents at all age levels. Both male and female questionnaires were pretested for good taste and comprehension and to learn whether adolescents deemed any question an invasion of privacy. Pretesting demonstrated that understanding of language and concept was not primarily a function of age and that even the youngest and most naive adolescents were unlikely to be offended or embarrassed by any of the material in the questionnaire. Some older respondents felt that some of the questions were written for younger adolescents; some younger respondents felt that some of the questions were written for people older than themselves. But no one expressed inability to understand the questions.

1.2.5 Need for studying a wide variety of adolescents

A meaningful study of adolescent sexuality in contemporary America must reflect, to the greatest extent practicable, the attitudes and behavior of *all* American adolescents. The data must represent, in proper proportion, the views and activities of young people from all sections of the country, from rural areas and small towns as well as cities and suburbs, from all racial and religious subgroups of the population.

To obtain the data from a representative sample that would also meet these requirements is a matter of no small difficulty. Later in this chapter, as well as in the Technical Appendix, we discuss in greater detail the stringent measures taken to assure the adequacy of our national sample. Before these measures could be implemented, however, a number of decisions had to be made about the categories of young people that should or should not be included in the population to be studied.

1.2.5.1 Inclusion of younger adolescents

The interviews and questionnaires upon which this study is based reflect the attitudes and behavior of young people between the ages of thirteen and nineteen.

From the beginning we wanted to interview younger as well as older adolescents. A major factor in our mind was the scarcity of attitudinal and behavioral data about the younger adolescent. We wanted to learn the age at which adolescents first begin to have explicit attitudes about sex and engage in specific kinds of sexual behavior. We believed that the earlier period of sexual feelings and perceptions was as important to register as the reactions of the older and more experienced adolescent.

Inevitably, problems resulted from this decision. Some parents disliked having younger children interviewed because of what the children might learn from the interview, even though they might give their permission more freely for their older children to be interviewed. We, too, were concerned about the sensibilities of younger adolescents, and we did not want to disturb their sensitivities or naiveté. The risk of a larger refusal rate on the part of the younger adolescent was clear, and it was also possible that the younger person would have more concern with the confidentiality of the questionnaire. As it turned out, however, younger adolescents in the thirteen-to-fifteen age-group are very well represented in the sample (see Section 1.5).

Nonetheless, after weighing all the factors over several months and after pretesting younger adolescents with our depth interviews, we decided to cover the entire spectrum of adolescence.

1.2.5.2 Inclusion of adolescents without sexual experience

This study is first of all about adolescents and then about their sexual attitudes and behavior. It was decided at the outset that we would understand sexual experience better if we understood the ground in which it begins: sexual *in*experience. Therefore, adolescents were selected for our study on a basis independent of the nature and amount (if any) of their sexual experience.

A sizable number of those adolescents interviewed had no sexual experience whatsoever; many others had only beginning sexual experience. Because we included the sexually inexperienced in our study, we have cast some light on the circumstances under which virginity is maintained or lost. We have also learned about the sexual hopes and fears of the sexually inexperienced, the real and imagined pressures they feel, and why some young people remain inexperienced longer than others.

By studying all adolescents rather than only the sexually experienced, we have also been able to discover the differences between the two groups and thus learn more about how sexuality and the process of growing up contribute to each other.

1.2.5.3 Inclusion of married adolescents

One question that concerned us was whether or not to include married, divorced, or widowed adolescents. Thousands of adolescents are, of course, married, and the number of divorced adolescents is increasing.

The married adolescent is certainly different from the single adolescent: the sexual relationship in marriage usually brings new habit patterns, new perceptions of self and sexual partner, and new personal values.

We decided to include data on the few married young people who were present in the national sample. Their number is very small, too small to identify their attitudes and behavior separately with acceptable accuracy. At the same time, we believed that they should not be omitted; they have attitudes and sexual experiences as do other adolescents and to omit them from the overall national statistics would introduce an unnecessary sampling bias.

Several married adolescents, moreover, were included in our personal interviews, and in a few cases we have quoted these married adolescents when their responses illustrate particular points.

1.2.5.4 Adolescents residing in institutions

An often overlooked fact is that there are many adolescents who do not reside in the ordinary types of dwelling places that the census bureau defines as "housing units." Such adolescents present a particularly difficult problem from the standpoint of survey research sampling, because it is difficult to assure their proper proportionate representation.

A certain number of adolescents are living under institutional conditions in jails, reformatories, hospitals, or mental institutions. Among younger adolescents there are also those who live away from home at church or preparatory schools. Among older adolescents there are those in military service and those who reside in college dormitories. Such "institutionalized" adolescents were unrepresented in our national sample, just as their adult counterparts are almost invariably unrepresented even in the most definitive surveys of the general adult population.

College students who live at home or off campus in houses, apartments, or other permanent, noninstitutional structures were of course represented appropriately in our national sample (as described in the Technical Appendix). A reasonable number of our interviews were conducted with college students living both on and off campus, including those living in college dormitories. While we regret the loss in our national sample of the tiny percentage accounted for by those college students who live in dormitories, we do not believe that this omission has a detrimental effect on this study. In any case, one reasonable objection to the inclusion of such students is that many of them have been interviewed repeatedly about sex and other personal matters, which may well have rendered many of them blasé when confronted with interviews of this sort.

1.2.5.5 The "invisible" adolescent

While college students who live on campus represent a highly visible but statistically very small segment of the total adolescent population of America, there is another segment—probably as large and with possibly even more influence on social change—who are for all intents and purposes virtually "invisible."

Making up this segment of the adolescent population are the runaways (of which there are hundreds of thousands every year), the drifters, the wandering transients who often migrate with the seasons. They can, if one searches carefully for them, be found living in Volkswagen buses along the roadside, in makeshift beach or forest shelters, or as transitory visitors in communes, crash pads, or private homes.

No one, not even the Bureau of the Census, has ever successfully attempted to enumerate this population segment, for many of its members—particularly the runaways—work very hard and with surprising ingenuity at maintaining their invisibility. Yet no well-traveled person who is a serious observer of the youth scene can fail to notice that the number of such young people seems to have increased over the last several years. Their disproportionate influence upon changing adolescent mores results from the fact that they are frequently if not constantly "on the move"; they spread their ideas and values to relatively large numbers of their more stably rooted contemporaries.

Because of their living circumstances, these "invisible" adolescents are overlooked by all surveys based upon area probability samples. We did, however, make unusual efforts to establish contact with such young people, obtaining from them over a dozen interviews, as well as eighteen questionnaires. The data from these questionnaires were integrated with that obtained in the national survey, so while this "invisible" segment of the adolescent population is admittedly underrepresented it is not unrepresented in our findings.

1.2.6 Need for obtaining parental consent

Initial pretesting efforts confirmed our belief that we should seek the written consent of each adolescent we interviewed and, if he lived at home, the written consent of one of his parents. We wanted to be fair to the parents and respondents. We did not want parents to find out about the interview only after it was concluded, or to interfere with the interview while it was going on. We did not want to put any adolescent respondents in difficulty with parents who might accuse them of not having sought parental permission for the interview. We did not want any parent or adolescent to believe that the latter was somehow compelled or tricked into granting the interview or filling out the questionnaire or that the nature of the subject matter had not been clearly announced in advance. And we did not want permission to be granted by parent or child unless both clearly understood the need for the child's privacy concerning the questions and his responses to them, as well as the mechanism by which we assured absolute confidentiality.

We know of no other nationwide study among adolescents where both parental and adolescent written permission have been obtained in advance of the interview. This policy was costly in time, effort, and money, but we are satisfied that we followed a highly professional and ethical procedure.

1.3 Conducting the national survey

Over several months we discussed the nature and requirements of our project with a number of different interviewing organizations. Several of them regarded the subject of adolescent sexuality as being too sensitive for their interviewers to handle. We eliminated some other interviewing organizations from consideration because their sampling techniques were inadequate to assure a representative sample of the adolescent population or because their interviewer-training and supervision practices could not have dealt with our many unique problems.

Eventually our quest narrowed down to Response Analysis Corporation, a national survey research organization headquartered in Princeton, New Jersey. The national sample employed by this organization consists of 200 city or suburban neighborhoods and rural locations, in 103 areas throughout the entire continental United States and selected in accordance with accepted principles of area probability sampling. After careful technical evaluation we concluded that households located in these areas and individually selected in accordance with Response Analysis Corporation's standard random procedure would yield findings that could, with a high degree of confidence, be statistically projected to the entire population under study.

In addition, we were impressed by the fact that Response Analysis Corporation's national interviewing staff was not unfamiliar with the problems of obtaining sensitive data from adolescent respondents. Not long before, the organization had conducted for the National Commission on Marijuana and Drug Abuse a large-scale survey about public attitudes toward marijuana and its use by adolescents. In the course of this survey several hundred self-administered questionnaires dealing with this extremely sensitive topic had been successfully obtained from youthful members of scientifically selected sample households.

In January 1972 Response Analysis Corporation began its work with us conducting a survey in 2,042 households randomly selected from within their 200 sample areas. In each household found to contain at least one person between the ages of thirteen and nineteen, the interviewer sought to obtain a signed parental consent form that would permit us to talk with the young people (see the following section of this chapter). This initial effort was successful in approximately 60% of the households, and during the next several weeks additional signed consent forms were obtained after recontacting reluctant parents by mail or telephone. In addition, on a case-by-case basis, we decided to reclassify as eligible for inclusion in our national study those adolescent respondents in sample households not living under parental supervision or control.

In late March and early April Response Analysis Corporation interviewers sought out the eligible adolescent respondents and obtained the cooperation of almost 80% of them in completing the self-administered questionnaires. This unusually high rate of questionnaire recovery was undoubtedly owing in large part to the credible assurance of anonymity and confidentiality that we gave each respondent. The credibility of these procedures can perhaps best be conveyed by the following statement which appeared prominently on the front of each questionnaire:

> *Please remember:*
> You are in complete charge of handling this questionnaire. The interviewer is remaining only to answer questions that you may have about the meaning of words or instructions that may not be clear to you. *Neither the interviewer nor anyone else who knows who you are will ever see the answers that you give.*
>
> You can make sure of this for yourself simply by doing the following three things as soon as you have finished filling out the questionnaire:
>
> 1. Immediately put the questionnaire in our postage-paid return envelope.
> 2. Seal the envelope yourself.
> 3. Go with our interviewer to the nearest mailbox, and mail the envelope. (If you prefer to have the interviewer mail it for you, he or she will be glad to do that. Either way, it will come directly to our Research Office.)

The data from 411 questionnaires were converted to machine-readable form, in which they accounted for a total of almost 300,000 separate data entries for computer processing. This critical operation yielding several thousand pages of statistical tabulations was conducted under the supervision of Dana J. Harman, our data-processing consultant. This computer output was used in preparing the Tables of Information* and as source data for many of our conclusions in the text.

This brief discussion of our national survey can convey only a general impression of its technical scope and complexity. It is intended primarily for the general reader, as assurance of the professional effort and expertise which went into safeguarding the validity, reliability, and projectability of our findings. The more technically inclined reader and those interested in details of survey research methodology will find much of interest and value in the Technical Appendix.

* The reader is urged to use the 530 Tables of Information (pp. 377–456). They are constantly referred to throughout the book, so that the reader can immediately examine the documentation for the conclusions drawn. The tables can also be read with profit by themselves.

1.4 Unique problems and their solutions

1.4.1 Obtaining parental authorization for interviews

Most parents expressed little or no concern about their children participating in this study. Many thought the experience would be a healthy or interesting one for their children. Others expressed the belief that the results of the study would reveal information valuable to both parents and children.

The characteristics of parents cooperating and not cooperating are summarized in the Technical Appendix. It is shown there that the households where parental consent was received do not differ in any measurable criteria from those households where parental consent was not received.

1.4.1.1 Nature of parental concerns

Expressions of parental concern varied considerably. Some parents wanted more details about the study or the author, and these facts were freely provided, except that under no circumstances were the contents of the blank or filled-out questionnaire shared with parents. A few parents wanted to add to or edit the questionnaire filled out by their children after they had completed it. Some said they were reluctant to sign any document on any subject. Others did not want to authorize an interview with their children without first seeking their permission.

The mother of an eighteen-year-old girl said: "It wouldn't matter to me, but she wouldn't want to." A mother of a seventeen-year-old boy: "I'd rather not put him on the spot. I think it's probably a good idea. But he doesn't have the time; he's so involved in sports." These parents volunteered their own willingness but dismissed their children's willingness before asking the children or permitting the interviewer to explain the survey to them.

Some people said no, and gave no reason. Others mentioned illness, emotional disorder, absence, or inability to understand on the part of their children. One mother whose older daughter had run away from home two years before was unable to talk about anyone or anything else.

But when there was concern, the largest amount of concern was expressed about the possible effects of the interview on the child. Some parents mentioned that their children's participation in the study would be irrelevant because their children are not involved in sex. The underlying thesis in this parental argument is best seen in statements such as the following: "My fourteen and twelve year old are always either at school or at home where there is no opportunity for sex play. If they don't have sex, you don't need to talk about it with them."

A rejoinder to this mother that the absence of sexual behavior or attitude was also significant information to us did not sway her. Her children would not be interviewed about "irrelevancies."

"Our child is too busy thinking about other things and playing with his friends, so what would he know about the subject," said a father who would not give permission for interviewing his thirteen-year-old boy. "Why don't you go to kids who know what they are talking about, maybe in the inner cities we keep hearing about," he added, with a slight touch of snobbery, suggesting that his boy was not only free of sex but insulated from it.

A Missouri housewife's son had just turned thirteen and "really doesn't know anything. He probably couldn't answer the questions and wouldn't understand them."

"The opinions of minors don't count," declared one father.

But obviously the line was thinly drawn between the attitudes of parents who felt their children were unconcerned with sex and a second group who believed their children would be disturbed or hurt by such an interview.

"No," said one Georgia mother. "I don't want her interviewed. They might put some ideas in her head she don't know about. No, with a capital N!"

Another mother said her daughter "isn't qualified at this time for such a study. Perhaps when she is older."

One Texas mother said, "I think sex is rammed down kids' throats these days. My kids [two boys] have sex education in school. They go to church and are well adjusted. I just don't want to subject them to something like that. It is unnecessary as far as I can see. They don't need to know, talk, study so much about sex. Leave it alone and the kids will be better off."

"Why should my thirteen year old have to learn things she never heard about from some stranger?" asked a young mother who had two older daughters. She preferred her daughter to acquire what she called "graded knowledge" in the classroom and from her friends under conditions when "my girl will be better prepared to understand these things because the situation will call for it instead of just suddenly hearing about these things from some interviewer."

"Lord," said one man, "I don't know whether I want my boy to talk to your people or not. Is he just going to ask me another bunch of questions about topics I'm already having trouble talking about?"

One woman was very much aroused in this vein: "Don't tell me my boy won't be dirtied by this kind of talk," she indignantly told an interviewer. "At fifteen, they all eat it up, and he's no exception. Do you honestly think I'm going to expose him to your dirty minds so he'll end up being dirtier than other people have already made him?" Implicit here, of course, was the threat this mother felt from every quarter when it came to her son's sexual knowledge and attitudes.

Such parents saw consequences for themselves as well as for their children in what the children might learn from the interview. Many spoke of the relationship they had with their children which they did not want to disturb. Some of these parents had a rational concern about their children's reactions to a questionnaire which they (the parents) were not permitted to see in advance. Other parents prefer to function not only as a helping hand but also as a helping censor to the child, delaying his reactions to the reality of his self or, more particularly, to those realities of self that the parent feels will alter the viewpoint of the child and thus the parent-child relationship. The harm they saw was not so much in the information the younger adolescent might acquire by filling out the questionnaire, but instead in *what the younger child might learn about himself or herself.* No parent who expressed such concern was pressed to sign the authorization.

1.4.1.2 Techniques for obtaining parental consent

Regular procedures were used to obtain written parental consent for the participation of each adolescent respondent. A parent was always asked to read and sign the interview authorization form before an interview was conducted or a questionnaire filled out. Interviewers carefully explained the study according to their instructions. The consent form and letter stated the nature of the study, its importancc to all parents, the name of the author, the assurance of absolute confidentiality to the respondent, and the fact that the parents would not be permitted to sit in on any interviewing or examine the questionnaire. The parent indicated his or her understanding of these conditions in authorizing the child's participation.

It was also stated that we needed everyone's cooperation because loss of data from members of the master sample could compromise the value of the findings. Households were being selected on a national sample basis, it was pointed out, and it would be impossible to seek the cooperation of someone outside the sample.

For those households where a parent would not sign a consent form, the interviewer recorded the reasons. A follow-up letter was written by the author to some parents requesting their cooperation when the problem seemed to be only a misunderstanding. Some additional parental consents were obtained with this follow-up letter.

1.4.2 Obtaining adolescent respondent cooperation

1.4.2.1 Nature of adolescent concerns

The problems of learning directly from young people their sexual beliefs and activities are considerable.

1. Young people, like everyone else, want privacy. They do not want their personal lives intruded upon by people whom they do not know, owe nothing to, and never expect to see again.
2. Young people are not always likely to see how they can benefit from cooperating in a study of their sexuality. They know they are the subject of much concern and may believe they are overresearched. They question the validity of much that is written about them, and they do not like someone to make headlines or profits from opening up their minds.
3. Young people—again, like others—are not always sure whether they want to participate in a study in which they are expected to tell the truth about their personal lives. Sex, with all its ubiquity in mass media and public discussion, is often confined to humorous talk between adolescents and adults. Serious discussion of sex with parents, we found, is often minimal or nonexistent. The possibility of parental curiosity or even punishment disturbs some young people. Most studies have not sufficiently assured absolute confidentiality. Indeed, there is probably no area of activity about which young people feel more insecure and private than their sexual attitudes and behavior.

We encountered relatively little expression of adolescent concern about this study, largely because of the pains taken to explain it in detail. At the time interviewers were seeking the parents' authorization, a few adolescents indicated to their parents that they were not interested. Whether these young persons' rejections were influenced by their parents' attitudes is not known, although a few interviewers suggest this is the case. Some young people were presumably consulted by parents who had expressed a "let's wait and ask my child" attitude and were subsequently reported by the parents to have said no.

The major concern of adolescents was undoubtedly confidentiality, and many worried about this despite the assurances we offered. There must have been some adolescents who did not want to deal with anything sexual for personal psychological reasons. And some people, young and old alike, are against surveys of any kind and consider them to be an invasion of privacy or simply an annoyance.

The reasons why some young people did not fill out the questionnaire despite their parents' authorization were, for the most part, the usual ones: some made and broke appointments; some were away or could not be located; some were ill. A certain number of adolescents, however, agreed to fill out the questionnaire and were then unwilling to answer questions concerning their sexual attitudes and behavior.

1.4.2.2 Techniques for obtaining cooperation

The nationwide sample of adolescents was contacted within a few weeks after their parents had granted permission for their participation. They were given a letter from the author to read and also a combination letter/consent-form from the author which they were asked to sign before the interview began.

At the outset adolescent respondents were told that the purpose of the study was to learn about young people's attitudes and behavior on social and sexual subjects. Our scientific interest in their personal values was emphasized. Interviewers were prepared to state that the resulting information would be put to very good use in studying existing laws and social institutions. The world lacks knowledge about what young people really think and do, we pointed out, and this would be an opportunity for young people to express their opinions and beliefs directly.

The need for reassuring the respondents about the confidentiality of the study was as important as actually providing this anonymity. In order to emphasize that parents were in no way involved in the study, respondents were told why an authorization form had been submitted to parents in advance. Children of parents who had deferred signing the consent form until speaking with their children were sent a separate letter by the author. Most important of all, the security procedures were thoroughly explained.

1.4.3 Learning the truth from adolescents

Young people have no more trouble telling the truth than anyone else. But telling the truth about sex can be a substantial problem for the adolescent, and we still know very little about how to assure we are learning the truth from him.

The adolescent is not always sure about himself or herself in matters of sex. Inner conflicts are many; pleasures and pains are diverse. Moreover, adolescent sexuality is a very private form of self-communication involving self-esteem and guilt feelings, hopes and fears, and acceptance and rejection by others.

In this study the adolescent was not merely asked to talk about events outside himself; he was questioned about what preoccupation he might have with himself and his body. This study requested the adolescent to answer personal questions honestly. But adolescents sometimes answer in ways that perhaps reflect boredom or resistance to the establishment or to intrusion into their lives. Upon occasion adolescents may also say what they think the interviewer wants to hear.

It is not easy to regulate the behavior of those inclined to falsify because they feel ashamed or guilty of what they think or do, or because they feel the need to boast. But we did our best to prevent such falsification. Interviewers were trained to maintain a neutrality toward the respondents and the subject matter of the study. Interviewers understood that they had to guard not only against influencing respondent answers by what they said or how they expressed themselves, but they also had to exercise these precautions in the same way so that all respondents would be equally uninfluenced.

Because both the interview and the questionnaire were long, the interviewer was trained to be sufficiently flexible to maintain the interview relationships until the interview or questionnaire was completed. Friendly persuasion or cajolery was used when a respondent became restless. In the personal interview it was important for the interviewer to probe for further details surrounding each answer in order to learn insofar as possible why the respondent answered as he did.

These precautions and training techniques, summarized only briefly here, represent the best professional efforts we could make to assure truthfulness in the interviews and questionnaires. Our tests for internal consistency within the questionnaire satisfy us that most of the adolescents were generally consistent in their responses to questions.

1.5 American adolescents: who they are

1.5.1 A description of our sample of American adolescents and its comparison with the U.S. 1970 Census of Population

At the time of the 1970 Census of Population, there were in the continental United States approximately 27.1 million adolescents between the ages of thirteen and nineteen: 13.7 million boys and 13.4 million girls. 45% of them were between the ages of thirteen and fifteen, while 55% were sixteen to nineteen years of age. 86% were classified by the Bureau of the Census as "white," while 14% were classified as "nonwhite."

The statistical findings of this study are based upon a national probability sample that conforms quite closely in its composition to the entire adolescent population of the country as reflected by the 1970 census data.

Composition of total U.S. adolescent population aged 13–19 and sample of adolescents aged 13–19 interviewed

	U.S. census	National sample interviewed in this study
Boys		
Boys 13–15	22.8%	22.7%
Boys 16–19	27.8	27.8
Subtotal	50.6%	50.5%
Girls		
Girls 13–15	22.0	22.0
Girls 16–19	27.4	27.5
Subtotal	49.4%	49.5%
TOTAL	100.0%	100.0%
White	85.8	86.1
Nonwhite	14.2	13.9
TOTAL	100.0%	100.0%

Geographically, the adolescent population of America is distributed across the country in very much the same way as the adult population. Our national sample adequately reflects this distribution.

Geographic distribution of total U.S. adolescent population and adolescents interviewed

Regions of United States	U.S. census: Adult population	U.S. census: Adolescent population	National sample interviewed in this study
Northeast	5.9%	5.6%	2.8%
Middle Atlantic	18.8	17.2	19.9
East North-Central	19.5	20.3	21.2
West North-Central	8.0	8.3	9.7
South Atlantic	15.2	15.3	17.8
East South-Central	6.2	6.7	5.8
West South-Central	9.3	9.9	7.2
Mountain	3.9	4.4	5.5
Pacific	13.2	12.3	10.1
TOTAL	100%	100%	100%

The following tables summarize the characteristics of our national sample with respect to locality size, household income, number of people in household, religious feeling, claimed presence in school, claimed school grades, and sexual intercourse experience.

Locality size	National sample interviewed in this study
Large metropolitan areas	35%
Small metropolitan areas	34
Nonmetropolitan and rural areas	31
TOTAL	100%
Household income	
Under $5,000	19%
$5,000 to $9,999	27
$10,000 to $14,999	25
$15,000 and over	29
TOTAL	100%
Number of people in household	
3 or less	19%
4	21
5	28
6	15
7 or more	17
TOTAL	100%
Religious feeling	
Very religious	12%
Somewhat religious	49
Not very religious	28
Not at all religious	11
TOTAL	100%
Claimed presence in school	
In school	81%
Not in school	19
TOTAL	100%
Claimed school grades	
Superior	15%
Good	28
Average	52
Poor	5
TOTAL	100%
Sexual intercourse experience	
Virgins	48%
Nonvirgins	52
TOTAL	100%

II. Personal Values and Sexual Attitudes: Building Blocks for Sexual Behavior

The next several chapters are concerned with what adolescents believe about sex: as it involves themselves, their generation, their parents, and society. These attitudes and personal values have much to do with why a person remains sexually inexperienced or, if he decides to participate, what happens in the process of having sex.

A major purpose of this study was not only to inventory adolescent sexual activity but also to learn the answers to questions such as:

How important is sex to young people, compared with other aspects of their lives?

How do young people assess their own maturity?

Are young people confident about their own sexuality and satisfied with their sex lives?

To what extent do adolescents identify themselves with young people, as compared to their community, their race, their religion, their own sex?

In what ways, if any, do adolescents consider themselves superior to older people?

Do adolescents have any conceptions of sexual morality and normality?

What kind of sexual relationships do young people want with each other?

How well do young people and their parents communicate with each other in matters of sex?

Are young people as sexually permissive with themselves as they are with others?

How do young people feel about sex education?

How important is love to the adolescent, and what connection do young people make between love and sex? Do they want sex without love?

Do adolescents want to use sex to combat their parents or the establishment?

Most adolescent sexual activities are not accidental. Although adolescents often tend more to believe in what they do rather than do what they believe, sexual inexperience or experience happens by conscious choice. Adolescent sexuality starts as a form of self-communication in which boys and girls begin asking themselves who they are and what they want to do with themselves. Their changing bodies and their pleasurable responses to many sources of sexual stimulation both contribute to the judgments that each young person makes about himself.

Why is it that sex is so frequently a point of controversy between young people and their parents? Do both parents and children see adolescent sexuality as the great watershed in their relationship, where children gradually abandon their parents as people to love and obey in favor of contemporaries? It is true that children who are developing their own sexual maturity can no longer have childish adoration for their parents nor continue to be the same love objects of their parents. This requires a mutual understanding and love to which both parent and child are immensely sensitive.

Adolescents report their parents' reactions either with bewilderment or as something they have grown to expect. They speak little of parents' possessiveness or unwillingness to let them grow up. They often take the initiative in putting their parents to the test in sexual matters, and their parents take greatest concern of all in young people's permissiveness and tolerance toward youthful sexual behavior.

The major conflict in contemporary America between adolescents and elders lies with the child's sudden needs for self-identity and personal freedom upon reaching adolescence. Parents are reluctant to let go. As with so many others, parents often feel isolated and alone; they intuitively know that life has increasingly become a phenomenon of every person for himself. Even a child too big to hug and smother with kisses is still someone the parent wants to closely identify with and at least verbally embrace.

Many parents feel powerless to stop what they believe is a declaration of war against them by their children, and many of their children are quick to say they have given up and go their separate ways without hope of finding any real meeting of the minds. Mass communication, the bomb, the pill, the desire for instant gratification are all stock explanations for the reasons adolescents demand a new role for themselves and are tuning out their parents in favor of their own peer groups.

But perhaps the reasons lie elsewhere. The explanation emerging in the next several chapters is threefold: the rising use of the situational ethic in place of dogmas of morality; new forms of sexual relationships; and a generational consciousness and chauvinism among today's adolescents. Adolescents intuitively feel that these factors are deepening the separation between society and themselves.

2. Sex and Love: Adolescent Self-Perception

I like myself sexually, because it makes me want to do and feel things. But how can I tell this to my folks?

A sixteen-year-old girl

Sex is my Magna Charta. There are lots of things I don't mind doing because my parents want me to or think it's good for me. But I know what's good for me as far as sex is concerned, and I'll use it as I see fit. Sex comes from my insides, and I'm the only one there. Tell me to believe that's not true? No way! Unless I'm only somebody's slave.

A seventeen-year-old boy

If whoever invented us, you know, didn't want us to have intercourse, why did he make us fit together so perfectly?

A fifteen-year-old girl

2.1 Self-definition of adolescence and its problems

Young people's reaction to society's definition of adolescents

Self-perceived maturity level

2.2 Generational identification and differentiation

Generational consciousness

Generational chauvinism

Incidence and meaning of generational chauvinism

Marijuana as a generational issue

Sex as a potential generational issue

2.3 Role of sex and love in the adolescent self-image

Self-realization

Overall self-realization

Sexual self-realization

Love and self-realization

Relative importance of sex among adolescent concerns

2.4 Uses of sex

Sex for the sake of physical pleasure

Sex as a means of communication

Sex as a search for new experience

Sex as an index of maturity

Sex in the service of peer group conformity

Sex as a challenge to parents

Sex as a challenge to society

Sex as reward and punishment

Sex as an escape from loneliness

Sex as an escape from other pressures

2.5 Mysteries of sex and love

2.6 Salient findings

2.1 Self-definition of adolescence and its problems

Self-awareness, always present, burgeons with adolescence. Sexuality is a major medium for the self-communication that converts raw instincts into motives and motives into ideals. The sequence of physiological change is carefully noted by children as they see their bodies changing. Growing up in accordance with predetermined biological and neurological imprints requires that the adolescent always be straining to catch up with new desires and emotions.

Young people sometimes seem more dogmatic about themselves than they really are. It is not that they always want to do whatever they please or that they never have any concern about what others think. Instead, they want to originate their own ideas and values; they want to put their personal imprint on what they think and do; some want to influence their surroundings by their ideals.

The adolescent searches for his or her self-identity in many mirrors. When adolescents cannot make things happen consistent with the ways they see themselves, they reshape ideas and events inside their minds in accordance with their personal values. Thus, as the adolescent seeks to justify himself, things are interpreted and events are experienced mentally, often without reference to the real world.

Thomas J. Cottle describes this aspect of youthful introspection very well:

> It is the inside of their heads they want to get to know, just as we used to want to get inside some girl's clothes. More and more younger adolescents are feeling for the interior of experiences and for the ways in which these experiences spray their insides, and then speak to them from their trapped states. What [they] cannot make happen on the outside [they] often will play over and over again on the inside until it comes out "right"; until it makes, as it were, a new kind of sense or nonsense.*

Adolescents complain they are pressured to adopt the conventions of their society with respect to many things, not the least of which is sex. They report that it is not always easy for a young person

* Thomas J. Cottle, "The Connections of Adolescents," *Daedalus* 100 (1971): 1201.

to determine which sexual feelings and ideals are his own and which derive from peer pressures for conformity, parental advice, pornography, or mass media.

2.1.1 Young people's reaction to society's definition of adolescents

Many young people object to the proposition that they must be "adolescents." They know they are young, have limitations, and need family support. But they bridle at a formally defined "adolescence" which carries with it obligations to engage in specific types of work and play—obligations that society imposes on adolescents. Despite reservations many have about whether they are prepared to be adults, young people resent being labeled collectively: each seeks his own identity as a human being rather than as a member of a group whose life-style and image he often feels society arbitrarily defines.

35% of the boys and 31% of the girls in our sample of adolescents agree with the statement, "I believe that most young people can go directly from childhood to adulthood without being forced to go through a period of years that society defines as adolescence" (Table 217). Older respondents reacted less negatively to their inclusion in "adolescence" than younger respondents, but of this group, those with intercourse experience reacted more negatively than the virgins did.

The objection to adolescence as a period through which one must pass is confirmed by young people's distaste for labels being imposed on them by older people. 76% of all adolescents object "when older people think of me as an adolescent" (Table 79), and 83% of all adolescents object "when older people think of me as a child" (Table 131). The fact that older people apply these labels is a sore point; 63% of adolescents who objected to older people seeing them as children nonetheless conceded, "In some ways, I still think and act somewhat like a child."

2.1.2 Self-perceived maturity level

Adolescents are divided about whether or not they see themselves as children or as adults. Even those who deny being either children or adults do not call themselves adolescents but instead describe themselves as combining qualities of both. Their definitions of maturity vary widely and include how they think and act, their degree of dependence on their parents, their ability or willingness to have sex, and their feelings about whether or not they could make a living on their own.

There is a certain maturity reflected in young people's admission that they do not always think and act as adults do. But most adolescents are ambivalent in defining their own maturity. 73% of all adolescents agree, "I'm not a child any more, but I'm not an adult yet, either" (Table 254). A majority still cling to childhood; 61% of all boys and 65% of all girls confirm, "In some ways, I still think and act somewhat like a child" (Table 212). 54% of all adolescents agree with the statement, "I think like an adult, but I feel a lot younger" (Table 12).

A majority of younger adolescents and nearly half of all adolescents (45% of all boys and 48% of all girls) agree, "If I had to go out into the world on my own right now, I think I'd have a pretty hard time of it" (Table 52). Adolescents in substantial numbers acknowledge dependency and their tendencies to either think or feel in ways that children do, but fewer are willing to concede that they view themselves as children. For example, only 37% of all adolescents affirm, "I still tend to think of myself as a child because there are a lot of things I can't do on my own" (Table 63). Fewer older adolescents agree with this statement than younger adolescents.

Although there may be many reasons why a young person does not have sexual relations, readiness for sex is one measure of self-perceived maturity. 20% of all boys and 25% of all girls have had no sexual activity with another person. 41% of all boys and 55% of all girls have not had sexual intercourse; of those adolescents without intercourse experience, 56% agree they have never had sex because they "are not ready for it" (Table 304). The great majority of those who say they are not ready are in the younger age-group. Lack of readiness for sex, we found, included feelings of several kinds: preoccupation with other things despite an awareness and interest in sex; belief that at the present one is not capable of enjoying sexual relations fully; concern about how best to communicate with members of the opposite sex; and fear that the emotional requirements of sexual relations are too great.

2.2 Generational identification and differentiation

Not surprisingly, most adolescents strongly identify themselves with members of their own generation rather than with older people or special interest groups.

In the main, young people (68%) believe that their own personal values are shared by most American adolescents (Table 94), while 52% believe their personal values are not shared by most of the older people in this country (Table 90).

A feeling of superiority over older people exists among some

Adolescents agreeing with statements contrasting young people with older people

	All adolescents	Boys			Girls		
		All	13–15	16–19	All	13–15	16–19
"Young people these days tend to be more idealistic than most older people in their forties or fifties" (Table 213).	78%	76%	68%	83%	80%	79%	81%
"Young people these days understand more about sex than most older people in their forties or fifties" (Table 218).	67	65	59	70	69	64	73
"Young people these days tend to be less materialistic than most older people in their forties or fifties" (Table 226).	60	61	54	66	59	53	63
"Young people these days understand more about friendship than most older people in their forties or fifties" (Table 246).	57	58	53	62	56	54	57
"Young people these days understand more about what is really important in life than most older people in their forties or fifties" (Table 230).	56	59	47	68	54	49	58
"Young people these days understand more about love than most older people in their forties or fifties" (Table 248).	51	54	60	50	47	49	46
"Twenty years from now, most of the people in my generation are going to be living happier lives than most older people in their forties or fifties live now" (Table 252).	49	48	51	46	50	47	53
"Young people these days tend to be less considerate of others than most older people in their forties or fifties" (Table 228).	46	46	60	34	47	51	43
"Young people these days understand more about honesty than most older people in their forties or fifties" (Table 206).	45	43	37	48	46	39	52

American adolescents. 53% of the adolescents believe, "My generation is going to do a better job of running things than the last generation has done" (Table 222). Boys (55%) feel this more strongly than girls (50%), and neither group feels less confident of this as it grows older. Although interviews did not reveal a widespread counterculture devoted to discrediting older generations, young people feel that society's future rests not only with young people but also, and even more importantly, with contemporary adolescent values. The facing table shows the percentage of adolescents who believe their values are superior to those of older people. Note that with few exceptions older adolescents feel stronger than younger adolescents about the superiority of adolescent values.

2.2.1 Generational consciousness

We asked our national sample this question: "Most people *identify* (feel they have a great deal in common with) a lot of different groups. But they identify with some groups more strongly than with others. Which *one* of the groups listed below do you identify with *most* strongly?" (Tables 402 and 403). The groups we asked them to consider were:

Young people of my own generation, wherever they may live, whatever their race or religion, and regardless of whether they are boys or girls.

People who live in my community, whatever their race or religion, and regardless of whether they are male or female, young or old.

People of my own religion, wherever they may live, whatever their race, and regardless of whether they are male or female, young or old.

People of my own race, wherever they may live, whatever their religion, and regardless of whether they are male or female, young or old.

Males/females, wherever they may live, whatever their race or religion, and regardless of whether they are young or old.

We found that young people are characterized by a high degree of *generational consciousness.* 58% of all adolescents identify with others of their own age rather than with others of their own race, religion, community, or sex (Table 402). They think of themselves primarily as being members of their own generation and look upon their youth as the main factor that differentiates them from other segments of the American population.

Among boys this tendency toward generational identification increases with age: 67% of the older boys as compared to 49% of the younger boys identify primarily with their own generation. Among girls the generational identification level does not vary significantly with age.

The emergent phenomenon of black consciousness has received much publicity in recent years, but only a minority of nonwhite adolescents indicate identification with "people of my own race" (18%) rather than with "young people of my own generation" (55%). Racial consciousness among young whites is even lower; only 10% identify with "people of my own race," while 57% identify with "young people of my own generation."

Members of all religious denominations were far more likely to identify with "young people of my own generation" than with "people of my own religion"; residents of small communities as well as large ones were far more likely to identify with other adolescents rather than with other residents of their own community.

2.2.2 Generational chauvinism

As stated earlier, the generational consciousness of most young people today goes beyond mere generational identification; it contains a substantial component of outright *generational chauvinism*. Adolescents not only believe that their values are different from those of their elders but maintain in large measure that their values are superior to those of the older generation.

Does this mean that adolescents consider themselves superior to their elders? What implications do these findings have for adolescents' willingness to work within the system? Will sexual behavior, as is already true about marijuana, become a generational issue leading to confrontation between adolescents and society? In what ways might sex and love be used by adolescents to challenge the existing political system and new technology?

2.2.2.1 Incidence and meaning of generational chauvinism

More than half of our national sample of adolescents agree with six out of nine value statements we offered to measure the existence of generational chauvinism. The average number of items assented to was 5.7 for the sample as a whole. The *value statements* are worded dogmatically, asserting the superiority of both the values and the behavior of "young people these days" compared to "most older people in their forties and fifties." They involve fundamental values on which older people pride themselves, such as honesty (about which young people are least chauvinistic), idealism (about which young people are the most chauvinistic), friendship, what is important in life, consideration for others, and love.

Inherent in adolescent chauvinism is not only rejection of older people's values in favor of their own, but also a strong feeling of superiority on the part of young people. Should this be interpreted as a growing confrontation with society, or have young people always felt this way?

2.2.2.2 Marijuana as a generational issue

The use of marijuana has come close to causing direct confrontation between adolescents and older generations. Stiff sentences have been meted out in many states to adolescents using or possessing marijuana. In part, this can be attributed to ignorance of marijuana and confusion about whether or not it is a hard drug; society naturally opposes the addiction and destruction that hard drugs have caused among young people. But opposition to marijuana has undoubtedly been in considerable part because it is an element of adolescent counterculture and is representative of youth's challenge to society's more traditional ways of behavior.

One of the factors most strongly related to generational chauvinism is usage of marijuana, with users being significantly more likely than nonusers to agree with almost all of the items in our generational chauvinism scale. Only 30% of the adolescents in our national sample responded positively to the statement: "I like to smoke marijuana sometimes"; but 48% of the older boys agreed with this statement (Table 126). Our findings about the incidence of marijuana use are generally consistent with the best and most current estimates from other sources.

Only 10% of our total sample (rising to 22% among the older boys) were willing to go so far as to agree that "smoking marijuana is an important thing in my life" (Table 30). But the true importance of marijuana as a generational issue is indicated by the fact that 73% of all adolescents—including 82% of the older boys and 78% of the older girls—agree that "whether or not to use marijuana should be up to each person to decide for himself, like with alcohol and tobacco" (Table 130). This almost universal permissiveness about marijuana use is in very strong contradiction to the attitudes held by most segments of the adult population, and it would probably be difficult to find any other simply defined issue about which adolescents disagree so markedly with their elders.

Marijuana use is significantly related to sexual behavior. Users are twice as likely (80% as against 40%) to have had intercourse experience, a difference which cannot be entirely accounted for by the fact that the incidence of both intercourse experience and marijuana usage tend to increase with age. Among those who have had intercourse experience, moreover, marijuana users are significantly more likely than nonusers to be "adventurers"; among those who are still virgins, the marijuana users are more likely than the nonusers to have had at least some beginning sexual experience.

The use of marijuana, of course, is related not only to generational chauvinism and to sexual behavior, but also to a wide variety of other attitudinal variables. Half of the marijuana users, for instance, as compared to just over a third of the nonusers, decline to identify themselves with either of the two major political parties.

2.2.2.3 Sex as a potential generational issue

As for youthful sexuality, many adolescents tell us they only want to practice what their parents preach—a quiet, sometimes nonconformist, but usually routine way of life that for some heavily features sexual activity and for others includes it without particular emphasis. Or they will differ strongly with their parents. The majority of adolescents are not troubled by society's disapproval of adolescent sexual behavior. But most adolescents have no desire to break the law or combat society, even though they consider both as somewhat irrelevant to their own living patterns and personal values. They have a tolerance for most sexual activity short of forced and incestuous sex, but fewer adolescents are as permissive in sexual behavior they choose for themselves. Thus we cannot pin down sex as a generational issue; we can neither prove nor disprove that it is in the name of sex or free love or sexual adventurism or any other sex-related issue that today's adolescents are insisting to be heard or asking to be judged. Perhaps sex will become a generational issue only if society makes it so.

2.3 Role of sex and love in the adolescent self-image

Sexuality is clearly a personal resource for many adolescents. It is a lever that young people use in comparing themselves with parents and society. Adolescents describe sex as a personal resource in many ways: sex is "natural" and is fulfilling; sexual activity is one's own doing and stems from one's own decision-making process; for some, it makes a relationship with another seem more important than simply a passing or tentative friendship; it can also serve as a positive way to compensate for the aspects of life that seem irrational and unnecessary to young people—quarreling parents, poverty, the killing in Vietnam, racial injustice.

2.3.1 Self-realization

2.3.1.1 *Overall self-realization*

Most young people believe they have values; fewer express satisfaction with how they are putting them to use. 86% of all adolescents do feel they have personal values of their own (Table 192), and 61% of all adolescents agree, "In general, I think that so far I've been able to achieve most of the things that I've set out to achieve" (Table 273). These measures of overall self-realization differ significantly with the age and gender of the respondent. 95% of the older girls, compared with 75% of the younger girls, feel they have their own personal values; 89% of the older boys, compared with 81% of the younger boys, feel this way. Older boys are more pessimistic, however, than all other adolescents about their achievements.

Many do not view themselves as accomplishing their full potential: 36% of the boys and 27% of the girls agree with the extreme statement, "The way I'm living right now, most of my abilities are going to waste" (Table 263). Again, the percentage increases sharply for older boys. In personal interviews young people seldom discussed their abilities in terms of their goals and ambitions. In part this can be attributed to their disdain for the educational system, which they feel fails to develop their personal resources to accomplish relevant things. This is also because of the genuine uncertainty that many adolescents have about the future. They distrust what the adult establishment will permit them to accomplish, and many wonder what form America will take in the event of uprising by minority groups, the impoverished, or people who want no more war.

Young people have been trained to view their self-realization in terms of what they *do*. Grades, graduation, jobs, careers are strongly stressed to many who are nonetheless increasingly tending to define themselves in terms of the kind of persons they want to *be*. Substantial dissonance exists in the minds of many adolescents between being and doing, with young people drifting without decision about what they want to do in order to be sure of being what they want to be. Because their own sexuality offers a way of being through doing, self-realization in sex and love assumes strong importance for many adolescents.

2.3.1.2 *Sexual self-realization*

Our interviews indicated that young people view the realization of their own sexuality in terms of physical pleasure, the extent of their self-confidence about sex and their relationships with others, their attractiveness, and the good or harm they are doing themselves.

Sex offers young people the opportunity to play at being themselves, while in a perfectly serious way satisfying several other commonplace goals: getting along with members of the opposite sex, being nice to others and not hurting them, increasing self-confidence and self-esteem, and being wanted by others.

A person's sex life is what he identifies as the feelings and implementation of his sexuality. One may conceivably crowd virtually every waking minute of the day and night with sexual activities, or one may do little more than fantasize about future sexual activities; in either case we are discussing one's sex life. A majority of adolescents (60%) believe they get a lot of satisfaction out of their sex lives (Table 18).

Younger girls are less often satisfied sexually than older girls and all boys. Those without intercourse experience report a lot of satisfaction from their sex lives half as frequently as those with intercourse experience.

Adolescents agreeing, "I get a lot of satisfaction out of my sex life."

Boys		Girls		All	
13–15	16–19	13–15	16–19	Virgins	Nonvirgins
62%	63%	49%	62%	38%	80%

Why are those who are older and more sexually experienced expressing so much more satisfaction with their sex lives? After all, sexual involvement brings with it greater complexity of emotional pleasures and pains. There are more opportunities for rebuff, frustration, and broken-off relationships; and the excitement of sex begins to pall for those who find that their sex lives do not evolve to expected levels of physical delight or emotional satisfaction. The explanation probably lies in the belief of young people that their sex lives become more satisfying with the accomplishment of sexual intercourse and that the difficulties mentioned above are not necessarily sexual. On the other hand, some younger adolescents also may wonder what sexual satisfaction they should have. One sixteen-year-old girl sums up her concern as follows:

> I know other chicks who have really fantastic sex and I don't know what they do to have fantastic sex—whether it's other positions. But I don't know. I guess we could think them up ourselves. But it's like having fantastic champagne and not being able to enjoy it because you don't even know it's champagne. You know it's a drink but you don't know what to look for that makes it really great.

> I know what I'm missing and I don't know how to go about finding it. But I will someday and I just hope that it's with my boyfriend because he's a fantastic person.

Whether adolescents are satisfied or dissatisfied with their sex lives, they are usually confident about their sexual feelings and attainments. They feel they compare favorably with their contemporaries. Thus, 85% of all adolescents believe, "In general . . . my sex life is pretty normal for a person my age" (Table 26); and 87% of all adolescents agree, "All in all, I think my head is pretty well together these days so far as sex is concerned" (Table 36). However, self-confidence in sex is indeed a corollary of sexual satisfaction, with 77% of those expressing satisfaction from their sex lives also asserting their self-confidence about sex (Table 358).

30% of the boys and 22% of the girls believe, "Some of my sexual activities are probably harmful to me" (Table 195). From our interviews we learned that the kind of "harms" some adolescents feel they are doing themselves in sexual activities include damage to their relationship with parents, contraction of VD, and undue preoccupation with sex to the detriment of other activities.

2.3.1.3 Love and self-realization

Adolescents who say they love or are loved by someone with whom they are currently having sexual intercourse score a higher rating on belief of their own achievement than others; they also score higher in their assertion that they do have personal values of their own.

Love is not worshiped by most young people, but it is a goal that young people seek. To love or be loved is clearly ego-satisfying. Almost no adolescents look for the love of their lives in their early years, but some girls insist that they want love with someone to be part of their everyday activities. They seek peer relationships that bolster their self-confidence and self-esteem rather than formal "loves" —relationships that provide a feeling of belonging to someone who "understands" them and with whom they can talk.

2.3.2 Relative importance of sex among adolescent concerns

Although most adolescents do a lot of thinking about sex, a majority do not give sex the highest priority in their lives. 34% of all who have engaged in intercourse agree, "Sometimes I think I am addicted to sex" (Table 328). 66% of all adolescents disagree with the statement, "It isn't healthy for someone my age to go for a long time without having sex" (Table 98). Yet 77% of all respondents say, "Some people I know are so much involved in sex that it's the most important thing in their lives" (Table 176).

The concern of adolescents for their nervousness or health without sex varies. 57% of all nonvirgin older boys and 29% of all nonvirgin older girls believe, "If I go for a long time without having sex, I get to feeling uptight" (Table 300). Adolescents also express concern about young people their age going without sex. Girls are clearly much less concerned than boys, especially at the younger age, and those without intercourse experience are less frequently worried about the question of going without sex than those who have had sexual intercourse. The boys and girls expressing the most concern are those who are having intercourse during the current month.

Adolescents agreeing, "It isn't healthy for someone my age to go for a long time without having sex" (Table 98).

	Boys	Girls
All	39%	20%
Age 13–15	35	16
Age 16–19	44	23
Virgins	21	13
Nonvirgins	52	28
Current intercourse experience	57	30
No current intercourse experience	47	24

In breaking down the sexual behavior groups, we see that concern increases with sexual experience. Sexual adventurers express the greatest concern of all, with 56% agreeing, "It isn't healthy for someone my age to go for a long time without having sex" (Table 98). In contrast, only 14% of the sexually inexperienced agreed with this statement.

Respondents were asked to rank twenty-one activities in their order of importance. Included were such sexual activities as "making out," having a good relationship with one particular girl or boy, and having sex with a number of different girls or boys. The results showed that "having fun" and "learning about myself" ranked very high in comparison to other activities for all girls and boys; for adolescents in the thirteen- to fifteen-year-old group, getting along with parents was one of the most important activities. All girls and the younger boys affirm the importance of preparing to earn a good living when they are older, while older boys give more stress to their self-preparation for being rather than for doing. Boys consistently give one of the very lowest ratings to "trying to change the system."

Ranked as least important by all groups of boys and girls (absolute least important for girls and second least important for boys) is "having sex with a number of different girls/boys." "Making out with boys" was also in the least important category for the older girls and all girls. Having a good relationship with one particular girl or boy ranked high, but not highest, depending on age.

Sex, at least in the terms expressed in our questions, does not command the highest importance for adolescents when they compare it with other activities. It is clear that the adventurer philosophy of having many different sex partners lacks primary importance for a majority of adolescents. "Making out" is considered juvenile by older girls. The following table indicates the activities considered most and least important by adolescents.

Activities considered most and least important by adolescents

	Three items most often picked as very important	Three items most often picked as least important
All boys	Having fun Becoming independent so that I can make it on my own Learning about myself	Getting loaded and hanging out Having sex with a number of different girls Trying to change the system
Boys 13–15	Preparing myself to earn a good living when I get older Having fun Getting along with my parents	Getting loaded and hanging out Having sex with a number of different girls Trying to change the system/ Doing creative or artistic things
Boys 16–19	Learning about myself Becoming independent so that I can make it on my own Preparing myself to accomplish meaningful things	Getting loaded and hanging out Having sex with a number of different girls Trying to change the system
All girls	Learning about myself Having fun Preparing myself to earn a good living when I get older	Having sex with a number of different boys Getting loaded and hanging out Making out with boys
Girls 13–15	Learning about myself Preparing myself to earn a good living when I get older Getting along with my parents	Having sex with a number of different boys Getting loaded and hanging out Trying to change the system
Girls 16–19	Learning about myself Becoming independent so that I can make it on my own Preparing myself to accomplish meaningful things	Having sex with a number of different boys Getting loaded and hanging out Making out with boys

2.4 Uses of sex

Young people generally do not want to use other people sexually by exploiting them or taking unfair advantage of their feelings. We found little evidence of the deliberate use of sex by adolescents to manipulate people, except in some instances of one refusing to have intercourse until the other person would comply with some wish. Prostitution is a very infrequent activity among young people, and we found virtually no girls or boys who identified themselves as prostitutes.

But sex does have many uses because sexuality is present in so many aspects of the adolescent's daily life. Because so many Americans believe that physical pleasure is the main purpose of adolescent sexual behavior, we deal with it first among the uses of sex. But the many other uses of sex are not dominated by physical pleasure, any more than eating is dominated by its physical gratifications.

2.4.1 Sex for the sake of physical pleasure

69% of all adolescents disagree with the statement, "The most important thing in a sexual relationship is just the sheer physical pleasure of having sex" (Table 266). Older girls express their disagreement very strongly, with 86% disagreeing, compared with 62% of the older boys. Except in the case of sexual adventurers, proportionally more adolescents disagree in the older age-groups than in the younger. In considering the factor of sexual experience or inexperience, those whom we call serial monogamists (having a serious sexual relationship) disagree at a higher rate (81%) than all other sexually experienced or inexperienced adolescents.

It is interesting to compare these findings with the responses to the statement, "The only reason young people these days have sex is for physical enjoyment" (Table 121). As boys and girls grow older, their rate of disagreement with this statement also increases. Again, more monogamists (75%) disagree with this sole explanation for sex than do any other category of sexually experienced or inexperienced adolescents.

Presumably, more adolescents agree with this "only-reason" statement than with the "most-important-thing" statement because young people are more sensitive to the concept of a "relationship" with another and the uses they make of sex than they are about whether or not they should have sex.

Virgins also show their strong value orientation, however, with precisely the same small percentage of virgins as monogamists agreeing that the most important thing in a sexual relationship is just the sheer pleasure of having sex. Those adolescents with no current active intercourse experience more often assume the importance of the physi-

Adolescents agreeing with statements about importance of physical pleasure in sex

	All adoles-cents	Boys 13–15	Boys 16–19	Girls 13–15	Girls 16–19	Virgins	Non-virgins
"The only reason young people have sex these days is physical enjoyment" (Table 121).	36%	43%	29%	42%	31%	40%	31%
"The most important thing in a sex relationship is just the sheer physical pleasure of having sex" (Table 266).	26%	39%	34%	21%	12%	19%	33%

cal element in sexual relations than those who are currently having sexual relations. Can it be that the former are more cynical, or do they simply miss sex, or are they less inclined to be currently active sexually for reasons in part reflected by their agreement with this statement?

2.4.2 Sex as a means of communication

Communication with their peers is not easy for many adolescents. Clique membership is by no means common for young people, despite their identification with their own generation. Some adolescents find it very difficult to make friends and tend to be loners. They find meeting people difficult and the development of a friendship even more so. They lack the ability to put their reactions into words, and they do not always know how to extract opinions and ideas from other young people. Small talk comes hard for many young people who need to know others well before they have anything much to say; but they do not know how to know others well.

For some, having sex with another is the ideal means to introduce meaningful communication. A sexual relationship frees some of their inhibitions, and in the happiness of their emotional and physical reactions ideas come and words flow.

"It's like getting inside a girl's head," one fifteen-year-old boy observes.

> It isn't that you just know a girl better after you've had sex with her. It's that you open up with each other, and you trust each other, and you find yourself saying things that maybe you never even thought out for yourself before. I get to know a girl a lot better after we've balled, better than I used to think I had a right to know anybody.

And a sixteen-year-old girl points out that, "Maybe you should ball first, then talk, and then ball again. Because I find that I've got a whole new basis for having sex with somebody, you know, after balling gets us to talking together."

"It's the best way to talk with somebody—sex is. That doesn't mean you have to say anything, but it sure is good communication," a seventeen-year-old girl told us. "I can understand a lot better why boys act like they do, and I can talk better with lots of boys just because I've had sex with one boy."

34% of all adolescents agree with the statement, "Having sex together is a good way for two people to become acquainted" (Table 279). More young people with intercourse experience agree with this than those who have not had intercourse, and substantially more boys (50%) agree than do girls (17%).

2.4.3 Sex as a search for new experience

Adolescence is traditionally a period of experimentation. The search for sexual experience is sometimes nothing more than a desire to experiment with one's body and one's emotions. But new sexual experiences for young people involve other dimensions: conquest, surrender, diversion, status, accomplishment, information. The sexual experience also holds many compensations for the adolescent as an escape from routine or loneliness.

63% of the respondents agree that sex is "one of the few human activities where there is always something new to be discovered" (Table 237), with 68% of the nonvirgins also agreeing. Its forbidden quality is attractive to many. 40% of the boys and 36% of the girls agree with the statement, "A lot of the pleasure in sex would be lost if it did not seem to be such a forbidden activity" (Table 257).

Young people do not have sex because it is forbidden or because they are trying to break any rules or violate any laws; the challenge lies in the suggestion that something strongly frowned upon or forbidden could be unusually pleasurable. What is forbidden must be worth trying, if only to discover why it is forbidden—regardless of whether it will be harmful or not. If sexual activity seemed forbidden by one's peer group, rather than by parents or society, the new-experience attraction would probably be minimal.

The new experience is not confined to having sex as compared with not having sex. Once enjoying sex, a whole new world of experimentation is opened to many adolescents. Experimentation and new experience in sex takes many forms: new techniques, new people, new occasions, new ways to satisfy or to show one's affection, new uses to be served.

The relationship between a boy and girl will determine the extent to which each is willing to pursue a habitual pattern of sexual activities or seek new experiences together. 50% of the boys and 39% of the girls agree with the statement, "There isn't anything in sex that I wouldn't want to try, at least once" (Table 134). Some young people spoke of sexual intercourse as a unique experience each time it occurs no matter how frequently one has had sex in the past.

For a few, the use of sex as a new experience is also indicated by the belief of 52% of the boys and 27% of the girls that "over a period of time, I think it's better to have sexual relationships with several different people, rather than just one person" (Table 238). But 76% of the older girls disagree with this statement as compared with 44% of the older boys. The personal benefits felt in multiple relationships and sexual adventurism are described in later chapters dealing with sexual relationships.

2.4.4 Sex as an index of maturity

Just as a certain number of sexually inexperienced young people believe they are not yet ready for sex, 62% of the boys and 51% of the girls agree with the statement, "About the time I became able to have sex, I started to feel more grown up" (Table 118).

2.4.5 Sex in the service of peer group conformity

Findings described in later chapters emphasize the tolerance that some adolescents have for the sexual activities of other young people, while at the same time they are far more stringent in defining their own personal sexual morality. Many young people also feel that the sexual activities of others are useful to cite to their parents in explaining their own sexual attitudes and behavior.

One would expect that many young people use sex in order to demonstrate to their peers that they are "with it" or in order to gain acceptance in the eyes of others. Indeed, 62% of all adolescents and 58% of the intercourse-experienced adolescents agree, "When it comes to sex, a lot of young people these days do the things they do just because everyone else is doing it" (Table 249). Younger adolescents believe this more often than older ones; almost half as many more younger boys agreed than did older boys.

As for themselves, fewer young people feel that their sexual behavior is influenced by others. 72% of the boys and 79% of the girls agree, "So far as sex is concerned, what other young people do doesn't have any influence on what I myself do" (Table 47). Only 26% of the boys and 14% of the girls concede, "On one or more occasions I've done sexual things mostly because the people I was hanging out with at the time expected me to" (Table 70).

Difference in age among boys makes a very significant difference in the tendency to conform. Younger boys have a far greater tendency to conform to their peers in sexual matters than older boys and almost all girls. 39% of the younger boys—as compared with 16% of the older boys and 14% of girls in all categories—say they did some sexual things because others they were hanging around with expected them to (Table 70). And 34% of the younger boys—as compared with 18% of the older boys and 20% of the girls in all categories—conceded that they were influenced by what other young people do as far as their own sexual activities are concerned (Table 47). 32% of the younger boys (proportionally 2½ times more than the older boys) and 22% of the younger girls (proportionally 4 times more than the older girls) also agreed with the statement, "On one or more occasions, I've had sex with a girl/boy mostly because people would have put me down if I hadn't" (Table 323).

One sixteen-year-old girl told us:

> I was really timid and so they would usually force—I mean they wouldn't force it, but they would use words with force in them. Like if it was my boyfriend he'd say, "I'm going to leave you if you don't" and "This is what I really want. You've got to make me feel good." So I'd usually end up losing the guy.

Conformity also can be a counterpressure.

> You just couldn't be labeled with the words kids would call chicks they knew were making it with all different guys. That was really prejudice too. It's just like adults. Kids were exactly the way their parents were. They'd label things. If you wanted to go to bed with somebody, right away the guys would be so immature that they'd go to school and tell everybody. Mostly you don't want other chicks to know because they would be really cruel. They'd start calling you a whore. They'd stop talking to you and it was really stupid. So you usually didn't go all the way with somebody because the guys would tell and you didn't want your friends to know, because all of a sudden they'd stop talking to you.

In any case, the pressure to conform is usually exercised by the boy attempting to persuade the girl to have sex. Otherwise, the influence of conformity is generally exerted only by example rather than by argument or enticement (with the exception of a few special situations such as where one is being asked to join an orgy or is a member of a group whose participants decide to pair off and have sex).

2.4.6 Sex as a challenge to parents

There is little tendency for young people to behave sexually in ways calculated to hurt, challenge, or spite their parents. 6% of all boys and 6% of all girls did concede that "On one or more occasions, I've done sexual things mostly to spite my parents" (Table 66). Only 1% of the older boys agreed. Young people will sometimes exaggerate statements of their attitudes in order to test their parents' reactions. But unconscious efforts at pregnancy or promiscuity or marriage in order to challenge one's parents are untested in this study because few signs of such feelings emerged in our personal interviews. However, 53% of all adolescents disagreed with the statement, "When it comes to sex, some young people do the things they do mostly to spite their parents" (Table 215). Girls may acknowledge their greater ability to do damage to their parents in this regard, for only 42% of the older girls disagreed as compared with 62% of the older boys.

2.4.7 Sex as a challenge to society

One reason adolescence is such a conflict-filled period is that young people begin to feel they are better qualified than others to decide what is right and what is wrong for themselves. At the same time, their freedoms are being regulated not only by parents but also by schoolteachers, social workers, and police and probation officers; these representatives of society are traditionally conservative and bent upon preserving the mores of society, which they have usually accepted as their own. Adolescents sometimes feel caught in the crunch between growing sexual desires and social requirements that these desires be inhibited.

Young people disagree with society in many ways, including their sexual attitudes and behavior; but they seldom consciously and deliberately use sexual intercourse as a means for challenging society. 13% of the boys and 10% of the girls said that on one or more occasions they have done sexual things mostly to show that they "don't care what society thinks" (Table 9). Only a slightly larger percentage of the nonvirgins agree. Expressing one's independence from society, however, is not a direct challenge to society but an assertion of one's adversary relationship to those who symbolize repression or opposition to any change in society. Adolescents have not organized along power structure lines to implement their sexual attitudes. The only exceptions are sexual minorities such as homosexuals (Gay Liberation), but such activities are very largely confined to older postadolescents.

As individuals, adolescents behave independently so far as sex is concerned. Thus, 62% of all adolescents (69% of all boys and 55% of all girls) affirm, "So far as sex is concerned, I do what I want to do, regardless of what society thinks" (Table 183). Indeed, 38% of all adolescents acknowledge, "My sexual behavior would not be acceptable to society" (Table 270). 61% of all young people agreed with the statement that emerged in several of our personal interviews: "Showing that young people have sexual freedom is one way of making the older generation realize that things are really changing in the world" (Table 244).

2.4.8 Sex as reward and punishment

Marriage counselors report that sex is frequently used as a reward or punishment. In a marriage situation an angry unwillingness to communicate with one's spouse in the wake of a quarrel is often typified by refusal to have sex. It may be argued that the reason is one of petulance or that one partner feels that he or she is not in the mood for intercourse, but the punishment motive is clearly present. People also grant or seek sexual rewards for something they have said or done.

A majority of older boys and girls agree that sex is used by some adolescents in this way.

Adolescents agreeing with statements about the use of sex for reward or punishment

	All adolescents	Boys 16–19	Girls 16–19	Non-virgins
"Some boys use sex to reward or punish their girl friends" (Table 204).	59%	52%	74%	65%
"Some girls use sex to reward or punish their boyfriends" (Table 221).	69%	71%	74%	74%

Are older girls more objective about this phenomenon than older boys? An equal majority of older girls agree that sex is used for reward and punishment by both boys and girls, while many more older boys see themselves as being rewarded or punished than rewarding or punishing.

Young people translate sex for reward and punishment into their own personal sexual experiences. Younger adolescents are particularly affected. 44% of all the younger nonvirgin boys and 27% of all the younger nonvirgin girls affirm, "On one or more occasions, I've refused to ball a girl/boy unless she/he would do something that I wanted her/him to do" (Table 320). Monogamists report doing this the least often (18%); twice as many adventurers as monogamists report doing this one or more times.

The same thing frequently happens in reverse, particularly with respect to boys and girls when they are younger. 47% of the younger boys and 15% of the younger girls agree, "On one or more occasions, a girl/boy refused to ball me unless I would do something that I didn't want to" (Table 331). No one feels this more than younger boys; younger boys report this three times more often than younger girls, while older boys feel this way only half as frequently as younger boys.

2.4.9 Sex as an escape from loneliness

Almost no young person said that he or she had sex with another person in order to stave off loneliness. This is a traditional reason that girls have given in the past when they felt "giving" sex was necessary to keep the interest or affection of a boy they would otherwise lose. Contemporary youthful sexuality has caused fewer girls to object to having sex. Boys feel less desperate about having to have sex with a particular girl, because it is so easy for them to find another. It is true that this works against the girl who insists on maintaining her virginity, but it is also true that a boy will tolerate her sexual refusal in a non-exclusive relationship from which she is willing to let him stray sexually.

2.4.10 Sex as an escape from other pressures

For many young people sex is a diversion from the tensions and pressures they encounter in growing up. 51% of all adolescents and 46% of those with sex experience agree, "Young people these days sometimes have sex mostly to take their minds off other things that are going down" (Table 73).

Our findings indicate that the feelings resulting from the sexual act often transport the sex partner from immediate reality to at least a short-lived euphoria. Preoccupation with one's body and one's physical reactions tend to shut out the problems of the world. The adolescent is probably better able than the adult to separate his sexual experience from life's daily problems. During sexual acts the defeating and the distasteful aspects of reality may become almost irrelevant and therefore more tolerable. The young person who feels dominated by circumstances out of his control is nevertheless able to exert control over his sexual pleasures and those of his sex partner. The youthful mind that can put problems aside in sexual relations returns to those problems with a feeling that they are less formidable and can be deferred again by similar means. This appears to be why 46% of all nonvirgins agree, "Having sex helps take my mind off some of the bad things that happen to me" (Table 301). Proportionally twice as many boys feel this way than girls.

2.5 Mysteries of sex and love

Adolescents, like most of us, often do not want to analyze their motives thoroughly, even though they may pretend to themselves and others that they know exactly why they do what they do. Their own sexuality is a mystery to them.

Sex, for all of its articulation in our society, holds new opportunities for feeling and experiencing so far as adolescents are concerned. Sexual experience only whets the appetites of many for more sexual experience. As previously mentioned, 63% of all adolescents agree that sex is one of the few human activities where there is always something new to be discovered (Table 237). Some girls report their belief they are making progress in feeling physical pleasure and using new emotions with new sexual experiences and new sexual partners. Boys learn more from girls than they concede, despite their general lack of desire to seek special satisfaction for their girl sex partners.

Young people are even more mystified by love than they are by sex. They often argue about the semantics of love: loving someone, being in love, falling in or out of love, making love. They willingly define love, as we shall see; but love essentially represents the fulfillment of what they want to feel in their relationships with other people. A few moments of love is as authentic to them as a lifetime of love.

Sex and love are not formulas for young people. Adolescents both work and play at sex, and many are interested in what rules they can follow to make sex more exciting and rewarding. Their own sexuality is an extension of their own images in the sense that they seek to convey to their sex partners what they see in themselves. Sexual expression offers infinite means by which the adolescent can explore himself; sexual activities permit two people to share that experience of exploration and self-definition. To view one's self through one's physical drives and reactions in the process of sexually relating to another person is never dull to the adolescent. The mysteries of sex and love are not necessarily lost in frequent sexual relations.

2.6 Salient findings

1. Despite the personal reservations many adolescents have about whether or not they are prepared to be adults, 35% of the boys and 31% of the girls agree, "Most young people can go directly from childhood to adulthood without being forced to go through a period of years that society defines as adolescence." 76% of all adolescents object "when older people think of me as an adolescent" and 83% of all adolescents demur "when older people think of me as a child."

2. Yet 61% of all boys and 65% of all girls agree they "still

think and act somewhat like a child," while 73% of all adolescents agree, "I'm not a child any more, but I'm not an adult yet, either." Older girls, more often than boys, identify their thinking and actions as childlike despite the common assumption that older girls are more mature than older boys.

3. Mention of dependency causes more adolescents to accept the label of childhood; 45% of all boys and 48% of all girls agree, "If I had to go out into the world on my own right now, I think I'd have a pretty hard time of it."

4. Generational chauvinism is strong among many adolescents. 58% of all adolescents identify themselves more with young people of their own generation than with people living in their own community or those of their own race, religion, or sex. 44% believe their personal values are not shared by most of the older people in this country. Except for the values of honesty and what is really important in life, a majority of adolescents consider their personal values to be superior to those of older people in their forties and fifties.

5. 86% of all adolescents feel they have personal values of their own, and 61% of all adolescents agree, "In general, I think that so far I've been able to achieve most of the things that I've set out to achieve." However, 36% of the boys and 27% of the girls agree with the extreme statement, "The way I'm living right now, most of my abilities are going to waste."

6. The great majority of adolescents believe they get a lot of satisfaction out of their sex lives. Younger girls are less often satisfied than boys and older adolescents. Those without intercourse experience report dissatisfaction with their sex lives more than twice as often as those with intercourse experience. However, 85% of all adolescents believe, "In general . . . my sex life is pretty normal for a person of my age."

7. 77% of all respondents say, "Some people I know are so much involved in sex that it's the most important thing in their lives." 57% of older boys and 29% of older girls believe they "get to feeling uptight" when they don't have sex.

8. In rating the relative importance of twenty-one activities in their lives, "having fun" and "learning about myself" rank very high for all boys and all girls. "Getting along with my parents" is one of the three most important activities for younger boys and girls. Sex does not have a high priority for adolescents when they compare it with other activities. Having sex with a lot of different people is least important or second least important to boys and girls in all age groups.

9. Three-quarters of all adolescents agree that what other young people do has no influence on their sexual behavior.

10. 69% of all boys and 55% of all girls affirm, "So far as sex is

concerned, I do what I want to do, regardless of what society thinks."

11. 46% of all nonvirgins agree, "Having sex helps take my mind off some of the bad things that happen to me." Almost twice as many boys feel this way than girls.

12. A large majority of adolescents disagree that the most important thing in a sexual relationship is the sheer physical pleasure of having sex, with even a larger majority disagreeing that the only reason young people have sex is for physical enjoyment.

13. 52% of the older boys and 74% of the older girls agree that some boys use sex to reward or punish their girl friends; 71% of the older boys and 74% of the older girls agree that some girls use sex to reward or punish their boyfriends. Older nonvirgins are more stringent about themselves. Only 24% of the older boys and 11% of the older girls say they have refused to have intercourse with someone unless he or she would do something they wanted done, while younger boys and girls report twice as often that they have refused to have intercourse to reward or punish someone.

14. 50% of the boys and 39% of the girls agree, "There isn't anything in sex that I wouldn't want to try, at least once." And 63% of all adolescents agree that sex is one of the few human activities where there is always something new to be discovered.

3.
Sex and Parents

I'm not going to pretend that I don't know what's happening. If my daughter comes in at five in the morning, her skirt backwards and wearing some guy's sweater, I'm not going to ask her, "Did you have a nice time at the movies?" . . . I don't plan to fail!

A sixteen-year-old girl

My parents are liberal, but if I ask them [*about sex*] *they'll want to know why I want to know.*

A fifteen-year-old girl

Parents are very poor people for raising kids. 'Cause they have too much emotions involved in the kid . . . they cannot really sit down and judge what's really best for the child.

A seventeen-year-old boy

Of all adolescents, 39% subscribe to the statement, "I have never really gotten to know my father" (Table 64); and 25% subscribe to the statement, "I have never really gotten to know my mother" (Table 141).*

Are so many adolescents and their parents really strangers to each other? Children begin to want to break out of the parent-child relationship as they move into adolescence. Each adolescent moves toward independence at his or her own speed, sometimes prudently and sometimes not. Their attitudes toward parents are often interpreted by parents and society as being antisocial, but this is not necessarily the case. A large number of adolescents (38% of the boys and 49% of the girls) agree with the statement, "Young people don't really want independence from society; they only want independence from their parents" (Table 277).

The adolescent's developing sexual attitudes and behavior tend to strain his relationship with his parents. The adolescent is testing his own reactions to what his parents expect from him; he increasingly challenges what he has been taught to believe and accept as he learns to think for himself. In adolescence comes the question: "What things defined as wrong for children are really all right for me?"

3.1 How young people relate to their parents

3.1.1 Respect, affection, and alienation

The majority of adolescents in this study like and respect their parents. The so-called generation gap is nevertheless a factor in adolescent-parent relationships. However, it is not based as much on the conflicting interests of different age-groups as it is on the belief of many young people that their parents do not always deal honestly and forthrightly with them.

* In small part these figures reflect the death of a parent or the separation or divorce of parents. But whatever the reason, the fact that so many adolescents feel they have never really gotten to know their parents has an important bearing on how young people view their own sexuality.

Adolescents who believe their parents do not really like them suffer from more than a generation gap, but their number is relatively few (Table 14).

Adolescents agreeing, "My parents don't really like me."

All adolescents	Boys 13–15	Boys 16–19	Girls 13–15	Girls 16–19
6%	3%	7%	6%	7%

More young people, but still a minority, express weak affection for their parents (Table 46).

Adolescents agreeing, "I don't feel any strong affection for my parents."

All adolescents	Boys 13–15	Boys 16–19	Girls 13–15	Girls 16–19
21%	20%	30%	16%	18%

As young people (especially boys) grow older, fewer care for their parents or feel liked by them. One stumbling block clearly has to do with how well respondents feel they know their parents. Older boys and girls feel they know their mothers better than they do their fathers (Tables 64 and 141).

Adolescents agreeing, "I've never really gotten to know my father."

All adolescents	Boys 13–15	Boys 16–19	Girls 13–15	Girls 16–19
39%	23%	44%	49%	40%

Adolescents agreeing, "I've never really gotten to know my mother."

All adolescents	Boys 13–15	Boys 16–19	Girls 13–15	Girls 16–19
25%	23%	30%	24%	22%

Affection for one's parents and respect for them are two different things. More adolescents have strong respect for their parents than have strong affection for them. 88% "have a lot of respect" for their parents as people (Table 148).

Adolescents agreeing, "I have a lot of respect for my parents as people."

All adolescents	Boys 13–15	Boys 16–19	Girls 13–15	Girls 16–19
88%	84%	89%	89%	89%

As boys and girls grow older, respect for parents' opinions decreases slightly among both boys and girls (Table 19).

Adolescents agreeing, "I have a lot of respect for my parents' ideas and opinions."

All adolescents	Boys		Girls	
	13–15	16–19	13–15	16–19
80%	79%	71%	89%	81%

Adolescent alienation from parents tends to take two forms: young people give up believing they can get along with their parents, or they have as little to do with them as possible. Only a few who cannot get along with their parents actually despise them. However, most adolescents also realize that "getting along" is a joint effort requiring the abilities and desires of all concerned. In saying this, adolescents concede their patience is sometimes short. 19% of all adolescents agree, "I've pretty much given up on ever being able to get along with my parents" (Table 83). Regardless of whom they deem responsible, 26% of all young people agree with the statement, "Most of the time I can't stand to be around my parents, and I have as little to do with them as possible" (Table 21). Older boys feel this even more strongly, with 33% agreeing.

Adolescents' hostility toward their parents often centers on some event or problem in which they feel one or both parents totally failed them. Some young people blame their confusion about sexual matters on their alienation from their parents. A sixteen year old who says, "I blame my father that I'm fucked up sexually," describes what she feels ignited her growing anger toward him:

> I resent him because when I was in the seventh grade I didn't get along with my teachers in school. They'd continually call my parents and say, "She's being nasty to us. And she's telling us to shut up. And she's telling us that we're wrong." No one else was doing that then. No one else was into rebellion but myself. I didn't have any friends at that school. People there really disliked me. They called me a hippie behind my back. And I was political and I was just by myself and I stopped doing my schoolwork. And my father, from the time I was in seventh grade until I did, would say, "You're going to drop out." Every time something happened he'd say, "Why don't you just drop out now?"—which was not legal. It wasn't legal to drop out when I did, but they finally stopped harassing me about it because they knew that I wasn't going to go back to school.
>
> My father showed no understanding. At that time he had no conception of a teacher being bad. To my parents, the teacher was always right. No matter what it was that I had done. The first reason I got into a fight with one of my teachers—it was like a history teacher in the eighth grade. She said Columbus discovered America. And I said but

> Columbus discovered Indians in America. And I got suspended from school for arguing with my teacher. I don't know why they never threw me out of school, because they called my parents all the time. I got suspended for lighting incense in school and they thought it was to cover up the smell of dope and it wasn't. My parents took all my good clothes away from me and said you're only to wear these clothes. At that time when they did that to me—I don't know how it happened—but it changed my whole sexual life. I became very resentful about everything. I became very, very bitter. I'm really fucked up sexually.

3.1.2 Seeking agreement and disagreement

Many adolescents look for a common ground in conversations with their parents. They listen, ask questions, make comments; they test and probe. But 14% of all adolescents agree they sometimes express "invented" opinions to their parents just to make them "uptight" (Table 8).

A sixteen-year-old boy says:

> You pick out your own ideas after listening to your parents. I have to decide on the basis of my own experience. Basically, I wish they would let me have my own opinions. They see my opinions, but they won't understand them. I wish they could see my points of view, but they can't.

More than agreement, or even consensus, young people want to establish a *modus vivendi* with their parents. Most adolescents want to get along with their parents. They want to feel comfortable about expressing opinions and revealing at least a little bit of themselves. Conversational subjects that are emotionally safe for all concerned represent a start toward seeking agreement or disagreement. Most adolescents (68%) wish that they and their parents could agree more about things in general (Table 89); fewer (48%) wish the same for social and political issues (Table 17). 50% of all adolescents think that their parents' ideas about most things are wrong but that their parents have a right to their own opinions (Table 42).

It is not surprising that young people value parental opinions about sex in relation to how they view their parents' attitude toward them. One sixteen-year-old boy dismissed his father's opinions because of what he believes is his father's total disregard for what is important about his life:

> He keeps talking with me, not wanting me to do the idiotic things I do. That's what he calls them. Idiotic. Such as forgetting to take out the trash. You know, he never really gets to discussing anything that matters. It's just shit—well, in my opinion. I've really come to doubt myself, you know. Being my age, as he so constantly reminded me. I

> came to doubt myself about what is valid. Does forgetting about the trash mean I'll forget to lock my car in later life? You know, just because I do some things he doesn't like—is it that important? I don't know. I don't know.
>
> That's why you develop your own ideas about what sex is before you have it. I came to put sex on a pretty low level as far as relationships are concerned. It's much more important to have mental harmony with other people and then you go on to sex. The sex won't work if you don't see each other's good points, understand each other, be able to live together.

But some young people strongly believe in bringing out disagreement with their parents when it exists. They relish identifying and talking about the point at issue, often to the anguish of their parents. "If I can't be frank about what I think when I'm talking with my folks, what good are they?" typifies the attitudes of many. This is not hostility, nor even emotionalism; but it is a rationality that is disturbing or tiresome to parents who cannot tolerate disagreement with their children. Adolescents frequently recognize and take advantage of these traits.

3.1.2.1 *Sexual values and attitudes*

Many young people disagree with their parents about sex. Only a few adolescents (36%) agree that they share common attitudes with their parents about sex (Table 62). Fewer than half as many older boys as older girls feel that their attitudes concerning sex are "pretty much the same" as those of their parents.

A slight majority of adolescents, especially the younger ones, believe that one of the most important tasks of growing up is "to learn to live with parents' ideas and opinions about sex" (Table 199). When talking to their parents about sex, 34% of the boys and 30% of the girls try to persuade them to their way of thinking (Table 181).

Adolescents have less respect for their parents' opinions about sex (65%) than about their opinions in general (80%). 56% of the boys and 75% of the girls agreed that they have a lot of respect for their parents' ideas and opinions about sex (Table 115), but this agreement lessens as adolescents grow older.

Adolescents agreeing, "I have a lot of respect for my parents' ideas and opinions about sex."

All adolescents	Boys		Girls	
	13–15	16–19	13–15	16–19
65%	66%	47%	80%	70%

Still, as with the case of parental ideas and opinions in general, many adolescents (58%) believe that although they think their parents' ideas about sex are wrong, their parents have a right to their own opinions (Table 10). However, 65% of the boys and 56% of the girls resolve the threat of continued disagreement by not talking with their parents about their sex lives—"because I consider it a personal subject and nobody's business but my own" (Table 53).

3.1.3 Effect of young people's sexual behavior on parent-child relations

Disagreements about sexual attitudes and behavior influence how well parents and adolescents in some families get along. The family is a testing ground for conflict; young people not only learn to live with their parents' opinions but also to live with whatever conflicts result. Conflicts need not always be avoided, as we reported earlier, but most young people have little understanding of how to manage conflicts with their parents. In turn, parents do not seek to show their children the benefits of conflicting opinions about their behavior, especially when the adolescent behavior in question carries a heavy emotional load for the parents as well as the child.

Speaking from their own point of view, 43% of the boys and 32% of the girls believe that some of their sexual activities are probably harmful to their relationships with their parents (Table 190), although older boys (36%) thought this to be the case less frequently than younger boys (51%).

As close-mouthed as young people are about their sexual behavior, the pressures generated between parent and child about sex have varying effects on parent-child relationships. Most young people prefer to be open and candid; they prefer to project their chosen image by what they say or do not say, rather than by concealment and falsehoods. 37% of all adolescents agree, "The fact that I have to conceal my sexual activities from my parents makes it hard for me to be close to them" (Table 132). On the other hand, 18% of adolescents agree, "In my family we're all very open with each other, so it's difficult or impossible to have any secrets about sex" (Table 80).

Adolescents clearly do not like to be questioned about their sexual behavior, although few (13% of the boys and 12% of the girls) complained, "My parents are always bugging me with questions about my sexual behavior" (Table 93). The constant questioning or flow of comments irritates young people as an intrusion upon their personal affairs and their ability to gauge what is right for themselves. Parental comments may be inoffensive or at worst tasteless, but their irritation potential is high. A seventeen-year-old girl complained about what she felt she could discuss with her parents in this vein:

> Lately they [her parents] have gotten into a thing with any guy who asks me out: "Oh, I think he really likes you." It's just garbage I don't feel I need. If he likes me, I can tell. I don't need my parents to say "I think he really likes you." "Oh, good, he wants to take you out." I've gone out with people who are in the theater, and I guess my parents don't consider me going and watching a play a date, even though it really is—so they feel I haven't dated at all. I don't feel it's any of their business whether I date or not. I don't feel they should push me one way or another.

Yet adolescents like to have their sexuality somehow acknowledged so they need not feel guilty about concealment; many do not like their parents to instruct them about sexual behavior and then pretend they are unaware that their rules are being violated. Young people benefit more from disagreement as a form of acknowledgment than they do from the pretense that they have no sexual behavior at all. 65% of the nonvirgins believe their parents assume that they have had sex (Table 167); 26% of the sexual beginners who have not had intercourse believe their parents assume that they have had it. Respondents have told of many incidents, even of parental discovery of a member of the opposite sex in their bedrooms, where the parent acted as though nothing untoward had occurred. Young people puzzle over this absence of acknowledgment and sometimes become angry when they can secure no parental reaction, even as their sexual conduct becomes more blatant.

Mutual acknowledgment between children and parents concerning children's sexual attitudes and behavior can take place in many ways without any explicit reference to what a child is doing or what a child wants to know. One eighteen-year-old adventurer reports that his mother and he had a good understanding during his young adolescence:

> If you probed my father deep down, he'd tell you that he disapproved of sex and talking about it. But he's always left it up to my mother and me to discuss. Of course we don't really discuss it, but we understand each other. I don't go to my mother and say, "Hey, mother, guess what! I just laid a chick." But she more or less knows what I'm doing and even tries to help in her way. For example, I can bring a girl home and she doesn't mind. If the girl and I are at home, or before I bring her over, when she goes away, she says: "Now, I'll be back at six. I'll be back at six, now." She understands.

One girl describes how a boy lived in her bedroom for several months.

> My mother never asked me anything about it. I don't tell her anything anyway. I don't know what she assumed, but I know that all this boy and I did was stay up all night and watch television and then watch the sun rise. But my mother acted as though it was none of her business.

3.1.4 Why children leave home

The young person who does not believe he can get along with his parents is ripe for departure from home. Adolescents need to feel that some measure of compatibility exists between themselves and their parents. Food, clothing, and shelter mean little to some adolescents if this ingredient in their lives is missing. A strong clue to the number of adolescent runaways exists in the fact that 25% of all boys and 13% of all girls agree with the statement, "I've pretty much given up being able to get along with my parents" (Table 83). An adolescent's sexual behavior would be only one factor in his decision to leave home; and unless a particular sexual partner were involved, it is usually not reason enough by itself. In fact, the majority of boys (61%) and girls (64%) agree that living at home does not interfere with their sex lives (Table 122), although fewer boys agree with this as they grow older.

Concerning those who have left home, 58% of all adolescents agree, "A lot of people are leaving home these days because they are seeking sexual freedom" (Table 241). Those with intercourse experience do not agree with this any more frequently than do virgins. The fact that so many adolescents think this is true about those who have left home is significant for what it tells us about those adolescents who remain domiciled with their parents.

Young people usually need their parents more than they are willing to say. It is when their need is great and they feel rejected that the chances increase that they may leave home. This is certainly different than leaving home because they do not need their parents.

One fourteen-year-old girl who had left home told us:

> I really think that at a young age you need both your parents. If you don't know one isn't your real parent, then that's cool; but if you're old enough and you know one isn't your real parent, it's sort of shocking to somebody that's really dependent on your mother and father. Like I was really dependent. You can get so dependent on your parents and they leave you for one second, you really feel scared. I think both parents should be there, at the beginning.

The folklore of the wicked stepmother is reality for some adolescents. A sixteen-year-old girl who has left home describes the problem she had getting any information about sex from her stepmother:

Like the moment my father and her got married. I mean, after the week after they got married, she came up to us and she said, "I really dislike you two girls. The only reason I'm taking care of you is because I'm your father's wife and I have to take care of you." And I was, like ten, and my sister was twelve. The moment she was married to our father, like she didn't even know us. I don't think she had talked to us for an hour apiece. She only said "I don't like you," even though she was to be a part of our lives. What could you do? What could you say? You couldn't go to your father and tell him, "That's what your old lady said." That would completely blow his mind.

3.2 Parent-child communication—and the lack of it

3.2.1 Desire for communication

Young people want to be able to talk with their parents about sex. 50% of the boys and 63% of the girls agreed to this, and their agreement increases as they grow older and acquire sexual experience (Table 144).

Adolescents agreeing, "I would like to be able to talk with my parents about sex."

Boys		Girls			
13–15	16–19	13–15	16–19	Virgins	Non-virgins
47%	52%	57%	69%	54%	59%

3.2.1.1 What parents want their children to know about sex

Most adolescents are unaware of what their parents want them to know about sex. Many do not care; but other young people generate their own assumptions, which generally reflect upon the intelligence or personal integrity of parents in dealing with children. What they feel their parents would like them to know include:

"Nothing they don't know."
"Anything, so long as they don't know I know."
"What I am old enough to know, but they want to decide."
"Nothing really important before I get married."
"The horrors of VD."
"How babies come."
"A lot about love and a little about sex."
"How to keep from getting pregnant."
"How miserable it is to have a baby."
"How to keep from getting VD."
"How people have sexual intercourse."

"Why one should wait for sex until he or she gets married."
"Bad girls."
"Bad boys."

Most adolescents believe that they must ask the questions before they receive information from parents about sex topics they consider important and that therefore they will receive helpful sex information only about whatever they ask. Seldom volunteered—and thus indicating to adolescents that these are taboo subjects parents do not want them to know about—are the following:

"Techniques of sexual intercourse."
"How to get more physical satisfaction out of sex."
"How to choose a sexual partner."
"Advantages and disadvantages of living with someone."

A few adolescents say their parents discuss the advantages and disadvantages of living with someone if they are engaging in this kind of sexual behavior. Otherwise, not many adolescents believe that their parents want them to have a well-balanced knowledge and insight about their own sexuality. It is likely, some young people concede, that parents want their children to know more about sex and even different things about sex than parents volunteer to tell them.

A great many, if not most, adolescents assume their parents prefer them to learn about sex from their friends or "off the street." One seventeen-year-old girl reports that her mother told her: "I had to learn about sex myself, and you are going to have to learn all about it in the same way. I had to; now you've got to. I am not going to talk about it with you."

3.2.1.2 What children want their parents to know about sex

One girl told us: "I wish my parents could overcome their own early training, so they could realize that sex is natural and beautiful." We found that 51% of the boys and 44% of the girls agreed with this statement (Table 128).

Young people do not believe their parents are ignorant about the physical aspects of "just plain sex." But many feel that their parents may not know as much as they (their children) would like them to know about how to really enjoy sex. Some believe their parents are too old or too incompatible or too set in their ways to comprehend the humanity and excitement of sex as young people perceive it.

49% of the boys and 55% of the girls affirmed the statement, "When I talk with my parents about sex, I try to tell them what is going on with young people today, even though they don't approve of it" (Table 49). This is consistent with the wish to which a large majority (74%) of all adolescents subscribe: "I wish my parents understood that what I do sexually is pretty tame compared to some of the sexual things that go on today" (Table 25).

3.2.2 Communication process

When there is adequate communication between parent and adolescent about sex, it is usually either quite generalized or quite specific. Young people will sometimes disguise their problems in general or vague questions; the wise parent will usually not suggest that the problem under discussion in fact is the child's problem, even though he knows he may be giving an answer that is very important to the child. Some young people understand this; they keep to an unspoken agreement with their parents *not* to concede they are talking about themselves.

Thus a small minority of young people (16%) often ask their parents for advice about sexual matters (Table 6), but 46% of the boys and 39% of the girls affirm, "I am comfortable talking with my parents about sex in general, but I avoid telling them what I myself do" (Table 194).

What young people perceive as their parents' attitude toward sex will influence their ability to communicate effectively with their parents. 28% of the adolescents agree with this statement: "My parents believe that it's all right for young people to have sex before getting married, if they are in love with each other" (Table 186). On the other hand, 51% of the adolescents (some of whom may be included in the above) agree with this statement: "My parents try to seem broad-minded about sex, but actually they're pretty uptight when it comes down to what I myself want to do" (Table 178).

3.2.2.1 Perceived adequacy of communication

Do most parents ask their adolescents to deny or ignore their sexual feelings? As mentioned earlier, many adolescents feel they are left to fend for themselves—to grow up with their sexual needs without any real supervision or explicit assistance. When the parent decides that it is wrong for the child to be left alone in matters of sex, it may be too late for the adolescent to change the attitudes he has already developed.

The adolescent knows that in the communication process the parent frequently is protecting himself from open recognition of what the child faces or how the child has solved a given sexual situation.

As a seventeen-year-old honor student told us: "My parents have got to know that I sometimes sleep with a girl. But we have an agreement in my family. I won't talk about it and neither will they. I won't advocate it, and they won't forbid me to do it. I won't say it is right, and they won't say it is wrong."

Many young people believe that their parents do not know what to say or do in communicating to them about sex. The following points summarize their observations about parental effectiveness in communication to them about sex:

1. Parents are unwilling or unable to find out what the problems of their children really are.
2. Parents offer advice based on the recollections of their own adolescent sexuality, but they are largely ignorant of what sexuality is like for adolescents today. Such parents, however, often believe that they have good rapport with their children.
3. Some parents who are totally out of touch with the values of young people impute their own values and goals to their children.
4. Parents tend to overlook the fact that adolescents are very sensitive to parental sexual attitudes and behavior.
5. Parents are untruthful to themselves about young people and their sexual behavior. They often use youthful sexual behavior to discredit other aspects of adolescent life.

Because most adolescents do not believe they and their parents find it easy to talk with each other about sex (Table 125), it is not surprising that 72% of the boys and 70% of the girls say that they and their parents do *not* talk freely about sex (Table 69).

3.2.2.2 Barriers to communication

A critical barrier, whatever its cause, is the adolescent's assumption that one or both of his parents are unwilling to discuss sex with him. Once a young person feels that his parents do not want to discuss sex, it is difficult for either parent or child to remove the causes for this reaction. The young person often believes that his parent is just pretending a willingness to talk, or the young person feels that he must guard against "making concessions" or "becoming a hypocrite" by pretending to listen or to agree with what a parent says. These inferences about parental willingness to communicate on sexual matters take many forms. 23% of all adolescents affirm, "My parents and I sometimes talk about sex, but it makes them very uncomfortable" (Table 11). Even more adolescents (30%) say that talking about sex with their parents "makes me very uncomfortable" (Table

76). 42% of all boys and all girls thirteen to fifteen years old do not talk about sex with their parents because "their attitude is that I'm too young to know anything" (Table 40).

Another barrier to full communication is the young person's judgment about how firmly set his parents' opinions are. Adolescents generally do not like to volunteer information which they feel their parents will not understand, cannot accept, or will worry about. A majority of adolescents tell their parents only what they think the parents will accept (see Section 3.2.3.2).

Earlier we referred to another barrier: 60% of all adolescents say they do not talk with their parents about their own sex activities "because I consider it a personal subject and nobody's business but my own" (Table 53). Boys report this more frequently than girls; nonvirgins more often than virgins. But age makes no difference in this reaction. We have already discussed the reactions of young people who feel their parents are pestering or bugging them about their sexual behavior (Table 93)—boys and girls who are developing a strong personal privacy barrier against communication about sex as a result of the way they feel their parents communicate with them.

Few young people refer to the sex lives of their parents as a barrier or an aid to communication. But many young people were unable to differentiate between disobeying bad advice and disobeying good advice because it was based on their suspicions of parental hypocrisy concerning extramarital sex activities. As one seventeen-year-old boy told us: "What could my dad say to me, considering what he had been doing? Oh, I think he's right, but who is he to say it?"

3.2.2.3 *Parent surrogates*

In the absence of adequate communication with parents, some young people learn to lean on another person who functions as a parental counselor in sex matters. A young person who lacks real parents because of death or divorce sometimes seeks a parent substitute or parent surrogate. But most young people who feel abandoned by one or both of their parents in sexual matters do not readily assign the role of counselor to another adult.

When traumatic problems occur with parents, young people will sometimes go elsewhere. One sixteen-year-old girl told us:

> We had a neighbor lady who was really groovy. Her children were grown up and she seemed to know everything, so we'd go to her. She did seem to know everything too. I'd go to her and say about my period, for instance, "Uh, look at this." "Oh," she'd say, "that's all right." And she'd tell me how the same thing happened to her and she did this and she did that. So I just got a Kotex and put it on.

What does frequently happen, however, is that young people become their own parent surrogates. They ask themselves questions about how they would deal with the children they will have someday —fantasy children of tomorrow who symbolically represent the real problems of today. Girls sometimes translate their problems into problems that might face their future sons, thus extending their role playing to include their sex partners as well.

Although we did not ask young people what they would do if they were parents, they frequently volunteered such information in the course of describing their communication problems with their parents. A sixteen-year-old girl put it this way when she compared her mother with the parent she hoped to be:

> Parents should acknowledge that people do fuck, which was hard for me to realize because my mother didn't acknowledge this. And just because you have to be home by one doesn't mean you can't fuck from eleven to one. . . . Well, I really hope I'll be a lot closer to my daughter than my mother and I were.

3.2.3 Communication content

Someday a very thorough study will be done comparing what children and parents actually say to each other about sex with what each hears the other saying. In this study we have only investigated what children believe their parents are telling them and what they say they are communicating to their parents. Whether or not parents agree with what their children report hearing from them was not investigated. The important fact is that—quite naturally—what a young person thinks he is hearing from his parents about sex has much to do with that child's judgment of his parents' attitudes toward him. There are few other subjects of discussion as powerful in forming the young person's perception of how his parents view him.

3.2.3.1 What children hear their parents telling them

People tend to look back on their childhood in terms of how they view their lives today. Thus, the way a person perceives the past tells us something about how he perceives the present. Many young people feel they were not given a healthy start in their attitudes toward sex. 44% of all adolescents say that they were taught sex was wrong when they were children (Table 187); younger boys (57%) report this more frequently than older boys (35%). 57% of the boys and 53% of the girls deny that when they were children, they were taught that sex was natural and healthy (Table 124).

58% of all young people conclude that their parents "think that the only reason young people have sex is for physical enjoyment" (Table 143). 33% of the boys and 49% of the girls say their parents tell them that they are too young to have sex (Table 159); younger boys (39%) and younger girls (61%) are more likely to be told this than older adolescents.

A large majority of young people report that their parents have not discussed masturbation, birth control, or venereal disease with them. Only 18% of all boys and 16% of all girls have been told about masturbation by their parents (Table 57). This is a small proportion of adolescents even in light of the low incidence of full and free discussion of sex. Masturbation is a subject that is perhaps as unpleasant for most parents to discuss as we found it is for many adolescents, or perhaps the adolescent in his or her distaste for the topic prefers to say no to any suggestion that such discussion take place.

31% of all girls and 18% of all boys say their parents have told them about birth control (Table 38). 33% of all girls and 24% of all boys say their parents have told them the facts about VD (Table 127).

Adolescents whose parents have told them about masturbation, birth control, and VD

	Boys			Girls		
	All	13–15	16–19	All	13–15	16–19
Masturbation	18%	10%	20%	16%	19%	14%
Birth control	18	16	20	31	29	32
VD	24	27	22	33	35	32

Why are so few adolescents informed about these topics by their parents? And why are fewer boys informed about birth control and VD than girls? In what ways does lack of communication with parents influence adolescent behavior with respect to birth control and VD? In our interviews a few young people suggested that these topics were so important to their parents that they (the parents) did not know how to discuss them. But do the children who cannot perceive how their parents feel really understand this? It is possible that in some families the more important the parents consider a sexual topic to be, the greater is the chance that the adolescent children will assume the topic is unimportant because there is no communication about it from the parents.

A large majority of young people (81%) believe that their parents frown on homosexuality (Table 51). Some girls (27%) and boys (28%) agree that their parents are anxious about whether or not they are going to get married (Table 91). A majority of adolescents (72%) feel that their parents believe sex is immoral unless it is between two people who are married to each other (Table 37), and not surprisingly most young people believe their parents do not want them to have intercourse before marriage.

Young people differ widely in their reactions to their parents' views on intercourse before marriage. A Catholic girl, for instance, recalls how her Catholic parents are reacting to her monogamous relationship. She has been living with someone for a year and a half, and she believes her parents at least understand her point of view, despite the fact that she knows they want her to marry.

> My parents would really dig us to get married. Our religious differences are a problem. He's Jewish and I'm Catholic. Jewish is a completely different race to them. They really dig him though. They don't really mind too much that we're not married, but they'd like us to get married legally. My father says you love each other and you're happy. That's all you need. But at the same time he wishes we would. They say this time right now, you know, young kids aren't getting married so often, they're living together. So they say, "Go ahead and live together." I don't know whether they think it will be just a short time we'll be together or not. This is okay too. We don't want to get married. We're making them realize that it isn't just going to be for a couple of years or, you know, a short time. It's really a lasting thing.

But parental views opposing sexual intercourse before marriage also provoke unusual inferences by some young people about what their parents want them to believe. 22% of the boys and 6% of the girls feel that their parents would be happier if sex outside of marriage were reserved for loveless or nonaffectionate relationships, thus agreeing with the statement: "My parents think that if I have to have sex before getting married, they would rather I do it with a girl/boy that I don't love" (Table 171).

One young person sees this viewpoint as proof that his parents are "hypocrites": "They don't want their little boy to have loving sex, only dirty sex. They think if I have dirty sex that somehow it's less dirty than if I have loving sex. Yet they go around talking as though sex were dirty. What do they want anyway?"

Most young people do not give their parents high marks for liberality as far as sexual behavior among adolescents is concerned. Yet 29% of all adolescents (30% of the boys and 29% of the girls) agree with the statement, "My parents believe that anything two people want to do sexually is moral, so long as they both want to do it and it doesn't hurt either one of them" (Table 39).

3.2.3.2 What children tell their parents

The majority of young people do not communicate fully with their parents. Some of them adopt the same hypocritical attitude about communication that they accuse their parents of having about sex. They do not seek disagreement or quarrels; they seek détente or actual disengagement from conflict in whatever discussions they have with their parents about sex.

Thus 55% of the boys and 48% of the girls affirm that when talking with their parents about sex, "I try to tell them only what I think they can accept" (Table 44). About the same number of boys (57%) and a few more girls (58%) agree with the statement, "My parents think that I pretty much agree with their ideas about sex, and I don't say anything that would make them think different" (Table 95).

In conversations with their parents, young people tend not to volunteer their opinions on the specifics of sexual techniques or deviations, choosing a sex partner, masturbation, or one's physical enjoyment of sex. The great proportion of adolescents discuss sex with their parents on a somewhat abstract basis, as though it were a public issue or a matter for popular discussion about adolescents in general —little is voiced about *themselves*.

In this vein, 52% of all adolescents (fewer boys than girls) affirm that they tell their parents what young people are generally saying and doing about sex (Table 49), even though their parents do not approve of it. Most young people think that their own attitudes and behavior are similar to those of other young people, even though they may believe they are more experienced or sophisticated than others.

Sometimes adolescents do seek to explain their sexual attitudes to their parents. The younger person is generally less experienced and still has more to learn from his parents; the older adolescent, generally with more experience, is less willing to discuss what he or she does and is also less inclined to believe that further discussion with one's parents will result in more agreement with them. "I have told my parents that I disagree with the way they think about sex," assert 26% of the older adolescents, versus a lower percentage of the younger adolescents (Table 33). The statement, "When talking to my parents about sex, I try to persuade them to my way of thinking," is true for 34% of the boys and 30% of the girls responding (Table 181). Only 22% of the boys and 6% of the girls try to make their parents think that they have had more sexual experience than they have actually had (Table 139).

3.3 Parental influence on adolescent attitudes and behavior

It is impossible to establish a cause-and-effect relationship between parental controls and adolescent sexual attitudes and behavior. Most adolescents (75%) believe that their parents trust them to use their "own best judgment when it comes to sex" (Table 119), and almost as many (63%) believe their parents think, "My sexual activities are pretty much my own personal business" (Table 136). We do not know whether parents would confirm this or not. Not surprisingly, the majority (77%) of the sexually inexperienced boys and girls assume their "sexual behavior is pretty much the way my parents would want it to be" (Table 96), while a nearly equal majority of nonvirgin boys and girls (66%) express disagreement with this statement. These reactions tell us that young people do not think that their sexual behavior is very strongly influenced by parents once it is under way.

Young people do not consider that their sexual behavior is formally controlled by *any* element in society—least of all by their parents. Even when they view their sexual attitudes and behavior as being consistent with those advocated by their parents, young people view themselves as thinking and acting in harmony with, rather than in obedience to, their parents' wishes. They view their sexuality as very much a part of their personal selves and not as an area of thinking or activity which is subject to obedience to outside forces.

3.3.1 Unanticipated effects of attempts at parental control

If sex is forbidden or frowned upon by parents, does sex become more attractive to young people as a result? Is it just a coincidence that the majority of young people having sexual experience also have parents who dislike adolescent sexual behavior? We have no direct answer to these questions. However, we know that 19% of the nonvirgins agree with the statement, "I started experimenting with sex partly because it was such a forbidden topic around my house" (Table 74).

A substantial number of younger girls and younger boys have questions they say they do not ask their parents because they feel it would lead to direct confrontation about their own sexual activity—whether they are having sexual relations or not. In the younger age group, 39% of the boys and 26% of the girls say they would like to ask their parents for information about birth control (Table 166). And 47% of the younger boys and 36% of the younger girls say they would like to ask their parents for information about VD, but they are afraid that their parents might ask whether they're having sex (Table 158). 57% of all girls agree with the statement, "One of the reasons why many young girls these days don't use birth control pills is that they're afraid their parents will find them" (Table 242).

The young girl who does not ask her parents about birth control runs greater risks of pregnancy as a result. We do not know whether girls are discouraged from having sexual intercourse because they are not encouraged by their parents to ask questions about contraception or to concede its use. Yet, 58% of the sexually experienced younger girls agree, "I don't use birth control pills or other contraceptives because my parents might find them" (Table 303). Does the parent whose girl fears discovery of her birth control pills or other contraceptives consciously instill this fear in the belief that she will therefore not have sexual intercourse?

36% of the boys and 34% of the girls believe that their parents "are anxious that before I get too old I should find the right girl/boy to marry" (Table 157). Proportionally twice as many of the inexperienced adolescents (40%) feel this pressure as do sexual beginners (21%); 47% of the adventurers agree with this statement. In view of adolescents' strong opposition to early marriage, it is dubious that very many are marrying any earlier as a result of their belief about such parental concern. But parents' worries about marriage can encourage children to move into sexual relationships—particularly if accompanied by earlier parental encouragement to go out on dates, which 26% of the boys, 13% of the girls, and 36% of the adventurers report was the case ever since they were twelve or thirteen years old (Table 129). 34% of the nonvirgins, compared with 20% of the virgins, believe their parents are anxious about whether or not they are going to get married (Table 91).

Considerably fewer virgins credit their parents with these anxieties. Young people who believe their parents are encouraging them to date early and marry early are more deeply involved in sexual activities than those young people who do not believe this. Parents exerting pressure may be inadvertently causing sexual behavior they do not anticipate. Children's behavior can also cause parental pressures. In any case we see in the table on the following page that a higher percentage of nonvirgins and adventurers than of virgins believe their parents have tried to influence their behavior.

Parental influence on young people's sexual attitudes and behavior is perhaps most strongly determined by parental example. In the personal interviews, adolescents often refer to parental infidelities, quarreling, separation, and divorce—many young people feel that their childhood lives had been damaged as a result. Young people also refer to the impact of parental example on their own attitudes toward sex, love, and marriage.

Adolescents agreeing with statements about parents' encouragement and anxieties

	All adolescents	Virgins	Non-virgins	Adven-turers
"Ever since I was 12 or 13 years old my parents have encouraged me to go out on dates" (Table 129).	19%	15%	23%	36%
"My parents are anxious about whether or not I'm going to get married" (Table 91).	28	20	34	42
"My parents are anxious that before I get too old I should find the right girl/boy to marry" (Table 157).	35	30	39	47

Younger adolescents are about evenly divided on the statement, "My parents practice what they preach about love and sex," while more older children agree (Table 55).

In personal interviews young people also raise the question of the relationship between their parents and whether their parents can understand a sex or love relationship. Until adolescents start dating and relating to members of the opposite sex, most of them see their parents only in terms of their mother and father roles, existing only as parents and not as people who have a relationship of their own.

How do adolescents feel about their parents' relationship with each other? The majority of the younger adolescents (74% of the boys and 68% of the girls) believe that their parents are still very much in love (Table 27), while the older group less frequently agrees. 31% of all adolescents believe that their "parents don't get along with each other very well" (Table 184), and 36% of all adolescents agree with the statement, "So far as I know, my parents have never really gotten sexually passionate about each other" (Table 150). Younger boys are particularly pessimistic about their parents' passions; nearly twice as many younger boys (50%) as younger girls (29%) agree about their parents' lack of passion for each other.

We sought a correlation between intercourse experience and the response to the two statements about parental relationships ("So far as I know, my parents have never really gotten passionate about each other" and "My parents don't get along with each other very well"). There was little difference in sexual activity between those agreeing and those disagreeing with the statement on parental passions. But proportionately more sexual adventurers than any other group agreed with the statement on parental discord.

Adolescents agreeing with statements about parents' relationship with each other

	All adolescents	Virgins	Non-virgins	Adventurers
"So far as I know, my parents have never really gotten passionate about each other" (Table 150).	36%	35%	37%	40%
"My parents don't get along with each other very well" (Table 184).	31%	27%	34%	48%

3.4 Salient findings

1. Almost half of all adolescents agree that young people do not really want independence from society; they only want independence from their parents.

2. Many adolescents feel their parents are strangers to them. 39% of all adolescents believe they have never really gotten to know their fathers; 25% believe they have not gotten to know their mothers.

3. 60% of all adolescents believe their parents do not know what their young people want out of life.

4. While very few adolescents feel they are not liked by their parents, 21% say they don't feel any strong affection for their parents. However, 88% of all adolescents have a lot of respect for their parents as people.

5. Most adolescents want to get along with their parents; 68% wish that they and their parents could agree more about things in general. 50% believe their parents' ideas about most things are wrong, but that their parents have a right to their own opinions. 14% agree that they invent opinions just to put their parents uptight.

6. Fewer than half as many older boys as older girls feel that their attitudes concerning sex are pretty much the same as those of their parents. Only one-third of all adolescents believe that they share common attitudes with their parents about sex.

7. Adolescents have less respect for their parents' opinions about sex (65%) than about their opinions in general (80%). As adolescents grow older, agreement with their parents' opinions on matters of sex diminishes.

8. 43% of the boys and 32% of the girls believe that some of their sexual activities are probably harmful to their relationship with their parents, although older boys believe this less frequently than younger boys.

9. 65% of the nonvirgins believe their parents assume that they have had sex; 26% of the sexual beginners who have not had intercourse also believe their parents assume this.

10. Perhaps the most annoying factor for the adolescent in parent/adolescent communication about sex is the parents' unwillingness to acknowledge their children's sex problems or sexual behavior. Many young people feel their parents lie to themselves about their children's sexual behavior.

11. 72% of the boys and 70% of the girls say that they and their parents do not freely talk about sex. In fact, most adolescents are at a loss to know what their parents want them to know about sex. They feel a great need to learn specific facts about techniques and problem situations rather than hear abstract discussions and morality lectures.

12. Only 18% of all boys and 16% of all girls have been told about masturbation by their parents.

13. In the younger group 47% of the boys and 36% of the girls would like to ask their parents for information about VD, but they are afraid their parents would ask them whether they are having sexual intercourse.

14. A majority of adolescents only tell their parents what they think their parents will accept in matters of sex. 57% of the boys and 58% of the girls agree with the statement, "My parents think that I pretty much agree with their ideas about sex, and I don't say anything that would make them think different."

15. 74% of all adolescents wish their parents would understand that "what I do sexually is pretty tame compared to some of the sexual things that go on today."

16. A strong clue to the number of adolescent runaways exists in the fact that 25% of all boys and 13% of all girls agree, "I've pretty much given up being able to get along with my parents." And 58% of all adolescents agree, "A lot of people are leaving home these days because they are seeking sexual freedom."

17. 51% of the boys and 44% of the girls agree, "I wish my parents could overcome their own early training, so that they could realize that sex is natural and beautiful."

18. Some young people select parent surrogates or substitutes for discussions about sex.

19. The majority of the younger adolescents (74% of the boys and 68% of the girls) believe that their parents are still very much in love. Almost two-fifths of all adolescents believe their parents have never really become sexually passionate with each other.

20. Parental concerns about dating and marriage may be crowding many adolescents into sexual activities earlier than would otherwise be the case.

4.
Love, Friendship, and Sexual Behavior: New Personal Values and Relationships

I wouldn't mind if he had sex with somebody else if it was a one-nighter or something like that. I know he loves me.

A sixteen-year-old girl describing her feelings for her lover

Girls are people. They enjoy things and love and hate like everyone else. It's sickening to see a male using a woman. . . .

A nineteen-year-old male

I would not go to bed with a guy unless I were willing to marry him. That's a way of showing a guy you love him. Otherwise it's immoral.

A sixteen-year-old girl who has had intercourse with several men

I think it's nice to be able to have sex with a friend.

A sixteen-year-old sexual adventurer

4.1 Self-communication and conscience

4.2 Sexual rights and wrongs: judging sexual behavior of oneself and of others

- **Sex and institutional values**
  - *Sex and society*
  - *Sex and the law*
  - *Sex and the church*
- **Sex and personal values**
  - *Girls' virginity before marriage*
  - *Sex before marriage*
  - *Sex outside marriage*
  - *Homosexuality*
  - *Sex for money*
  - *Hurt and force*
  - *Sexual irresponsibility*
  - *Concepts of morality and immorality*
  - *Concepts of normality and abnormality*
- **Limits of tolerance**

4.3 Acceptable and desired contexts of sexual behavior

- **Concepts of love**
  - *Durable love*
  - *Transient love*
- **Concepts of "relationship"**
- **Competition and accommodation in sex roles**

4.4 Salient findings

According to one fourteen-year-old girl: "It's sort of a cop-out to have sex just for sex." Sexual behavior among adolescents is seldom purely physical. 60% of all adolescents do not believe that the only reason young people have sex is for physical enjoyment (Table 121). Of course young people enjoy sex for its physical effects, but their sexuality is filled with human values. At the same time, most adolescents have little interest in other people's sexual behavior; they see sex as a highly personal thing. They do not view sex as a social problem, and so they are not very interested in what society has to say about it. Yet they know that society does have concern; parents, teachers, and mass media "never stop talking about sex," in the opinion of many young people.

Virtually every adolescent has his or her own criteria for evaluating sexual behavior. Few adolescents acknowledge parental controls of sexual conduct, even though they may not reject parental guidance. Sex is not seen as a series of dos and don'ts. Personal autonomy and the situation ethic are the order of the day; young people prefer to decide for themselves what is right and wrong sexually. They perceive what they do sexually largely in terms of the purpose for which it is intended and the manner in which it is done.

One's sexuality develops in the process of interacting with others. Explicit genitality (concern and preoccupation with one's own sex organs) becomes less disturbing as the youthful adolescent learns that other adolescents are also preoccupied with their own bodily sexual developments. Seeing others in shower and swimming pool and indulging in locker room conversation and humor, dirty stories and tales of exploit, questions and answers, and preadolescent sex games (which satisfy one's curiosity of what another person looks like without clothing): all of these activities and many more are described by adolescents as means by which they discovered the development of other young people's sex organs and the stimulation that one's sex organs can provide. Although adolescents have solitary worries about themselves, each person begins to realize that he or she is not alone with these physical desires and sources of pleasure.

Adolescents gradually begin to realize the extent to which sex flows through the various aspects of society in which other adolescents participate: the novels and short stories they are assigned to read at school, the movies their friends recommend they see, the product choices that advertising asks them to make, the sex crimes featured in the headlines, the accessibility of pornography, the sexual behavior of other young people which they see and hear about.

Sometimes slowly, sometimes rapidly, the adolescent perceives that his own values, which are emerging from new information and insights, influence the ways in which sex will affect his conception of himself and his relationships with other young people. The adolescent realizes that sooner or later he will be having sexual experiences with others.

4.1 Self-communication and conscience

With respect to sexual behavior, conscience is not passé among adolescents. In exploring the existence and application of conscience, we define *conscience* as self-interrogation in which one's central concern is whether or not he or she is behaving in accordance with his personal values. It is a series of questions and answers—very clearly articulated by some young people and almost subconsciously expressed by others—by which one evaluates his or her own personal behavior. Personal values are those "ought" judgments or statements that label certain behavior as right or wrong, such as "I ought to see her again" or "I ought not to have intercourse with him."

86% of all young people believe they have personal values of their own (Table 192), with 90% also agreeing, "It's important that I try to develop my own set of personal values" (Table 288). Older adolescents felt more strongly about this, with 93% of the boys and 97% of the girls agreeing. One important characteristic of adolescence is the child's desire to consciously formulate his own personal set of wants. Although he may balk at conforming to society's norms, the adolescent understands the need for a personal moral code. 86% of all adolescents agree that it is right for people to make their own moral code, deciding for themselves what is moral and what is immoral (Table 28).

As far as sex is concerned, most young people (84%) believe that they have come to definite conclusions about what they think is right and wrong for themselves (Table 56). Relatively fewer boys (70%) than girls (82%) believe "There are some things that I wouldn't do because my conscience would bother me" (Table 77). Only a relatively few adolescents (27%) agree that they sometimes take part in sexual activities that are not consistent with their religious beliefs (Table 81), perhaps largely because so few of them have what they would consider very strong religious feelings or affiliations. However, proportionally more than twice as many nonvirgins (37%) than virgins (16%) had this concern, and the difference of degree of religious belief between virgins and nonvirgins is small.

An adolescent seldom tries to separate emotion from physical reaction except when the two diverge so that one brings pleasure and the other brings pain. This happens, for example, when one finds himself doing something sexual that he physically enjoys but is ashamed of doing, or when a girl is emotionally gratified about the satisfaction she is giving a boy even though she suffers pain in the act.

Many young people see emotional calm and stability resulting from their sexual experiences. In feeling very much at peace with themselves and self-contented, many young people believe they are satisfying their consciences. In describing how he came to love a girl for the first time, a sixteen-year-old boy tells how he believes sex and love combine to give him peace of mind:

> When I first saw her, I had a feeling. There was something in her eyes. I could tell she was very definitely a warm person, and then I got to know her after a month. She was warm and passionate and good looking, and she gave me the respect that she didn't try to run my life and I didn't try to run hers. A lot of the time we were very possessive about each other, but still we weren't trying to run each other's lives totally. It was just a thing that came about. It grew on me. It's like wine—it aged for the better. If it's really true love, it will last for a long time.
>
> Mainly what a person's ideas of sex are comes from the first one they fall in love with.
>
> When I have love and sex, I'm definitely a happier person. You see those little posters about sex relieves tension. I really believe that sex and love cut down a lot of your hassles because you know that there is someone who cares for you very much. After I get married, I'll come home from work and walk in my house and see my wife and there will be love. It's like taking a vacation—it's beautiful.

Young people generally refrain from judging the behavior of others as immoral or abnormal. However, a majority of young people avoid sexual acts or sexual situations that they consider immoral (Table 152) or abnormal (Table 85).

The fact that young people are willing to apply these concepts of morality and normality to themselves suggests that they are putting them to use either in deciding what to do or in judging what they have done.

Young people do not feel guilty or upset about their permissiveness with respect to sexual behavior. This is clearly shown in the

Adolescents agreeing with statements on avoidance of sexual acts they consider immoral or abnormal

	All adoles-cents	Boys	Girls	Virgins	Non-virgins
No personal participation in sex act considered immoral	75%	66%	85%	81%	69%
No personal participation in sex act considered abnormal	74%	70%	78%	82%	67%

dialogue one of our interviewers had with two boys, sixteen and seventeen, who spoke of sexual behavior they disapproved of. One boy spoke of his own behavior and the other described an act that he had witnessed.

The sixteen-year-old boy described a sexual relationship with his sister, which he considered to be abnormal. He was about twelve or thirteen at the time, and his sister was a year older. They had been talking together about sex, and the event just "suddenly began to happen."

> How did I feel? Oh, wow. I was kind of jumpy, you know. She was—I don't know—in a way I felt bad about it after I did it, but while I was doing it I thought it was OK.
>
> INTERVIEWER: How did you feel later?
>
> Like I didn't know what was going to happen so I worried some about a year or two. You know, I just had it on my conscience. . . . I knew I did it and it was my sister. . . . It gives you a funny feeling. . . . I was worrying that she might say something to someone and then they'd tell my parents.

The seventeen-year-old boy thought sex with animals was abnormal but was unwilling to condemn someone he had witnessed in the act:

> I ran into this dude in the woods, and he was doing it to this pony. And it was really far out. I didn't say anything. . . . It didn't bother me. It was him, you know. It's his thing; it's not me. It was him, you know. Not me.
>
> INTERVIEWER: Did you want to know him?
>
> Well, I want to know everyone. I was shocked. It was something different—unusual. But I didn't say nothing to him, I didn't even let him know I was aware that he was there.
>
> INTERVIEWER: How come?
>
> I just happened to see him, and I watched him for a while. It didn't bother me really. If he wanted to ball a pony, let him ball it. When I first saw him I thought he was kind of goofy; but now I guess if that's his thing, let him do it.

Personal guilt feelings come and go. 37% of those with intercourse experience and 28% of the virgins said that sometimes they feel guilty about their sexual behavior (Table 99). 47% of all younger boys expressed this concern. But for most young people guilt is not simply a question of doing something right or doing something wrong. As one fourteen-year-old girl put it: "There is no right thing. There are just opinions. Like being pure."

Neither the fact that they indulge in sexual activities nor their choice of partners tends to make young people feel guilty. Rather, those who feel guilty often do so because they believe they are deceiving parents or friends who have different expectations about their sexual behavior. We do not know whether these guilt feelings lessen self-esteem; we only know that those who feel guilty are reacting to the conflict between their behavior and the expectations of others whose respect they want.

Many young people include what they have learned from their parents and community in evaluating their own behavior, even though they seldom apply such criteria to others. But situation ethics and self-interest are more crucial. Personal convenience and physical desire inevitably become more important in guiding self-appraisal of sexual behavior. Above all, most adolescents do not think of sex as inherently right or wrong. This is a key difference young people see between themselves and adult society with respect to evaluating adolescent sexual behavior.

Adolescents do not consider sex as their exclusive property, but they clearly utilize sex as a medium of communication among themselves. Nor do they view sex as a separate part of their lives. Sexual behavior—or the lack of it—is well integrated into their pattern of daily thoughts and activities. This is one more reason why most young people do not feel influenced by a sexual morality separate from larger ethical questions.

4.2 Sexual rights and wrongs: judging sexual behavior of oneself and of others

Adolescents often have clearly defined standards of sexual behavior for themselves: they have criteria of acceptance and rejection; they suffer inner doubts in that they are aware of when they are doing something in which they do not believe. On the other hand, throughout this chapter we see many instances where adolescents extend tolerance toward attitudes or behavior that they would definitely reject for themselves.

59% of all young people have not come to any definite conclusions about what they think is sexually right and wrong for other people (Table 43). Their definitions of right and wrong are highly personalized, and they show little interest in judging other people's behavior in matters of sex. Because they view sexual behavior as personal behavior, they do not see its importance to society. As one fifteen-year-old girl put it:

> I wouldn't label any sex acts immoral. Nothing I can think of. Take rape. Obviously somebody likes rape. But not even rape is immoral, you know. It's bad, of course. I have a derogatory opinion of the word immoral. Anti-God. It's meaningless, the whole word. The more widespread something becomes, the less badly it's accepted. Prostitution isn't immoral any more.

Her sexual morality is also geared to the specific situation:

> It is not right for people to do anything unless there is mutual consent. There has got to be some discretion. Balling in the street would be offensive to me because I just respect people's opinions. If a father and his kid mutually agreed to sex, I suppose I would condemn it. But each specific case for the individual is important. . . . I don't think statutory rape is wrong, because it is mutual consent. If two people happen to love each other and the girl is under sixteen, the man shouldn't be arrested.

The same girl suggested that perhaps immorality is a "sex act that is all right or acceptable to me that is not moral for someone else. But maybe that's just 'unwise,' like going to bed with someone the first time you meet him."

Traditional double standards about what is morally right for males and morally wrong for females are rejected by the majority of all adolescents except younger girls (Table 61). Older boys are in agreement with older girls concerning this point and younger boys agree far more often than younger girls. Agreement also increases with age and sexual experience.

"So far as sex is concerned, I think that what is morally right for boys is morally right for girls too."

All adolescents	Boys		Girls		Virgins	Non-virgins
	13–15	16–19	13–15	16–19		
62%	65%	69%	41%	71%	51%	73%

4.2.1 Sex and institutional values

4.2.1.1 Sex and society

The majority of young people believe that society's rules about sex are for society's own benefit rather than their own. Young people do not deny their membership in society, but their generational chauvinism often causes them to speak of society as though it were an organization or force apart from themselves. Many believe that their own values are ignored by society for two reasons: (1) because society expects young people to subscribe to its customs regardless of what they think; and (2) because most adults define young people's sexual behavior as based almost completely on physical enjoyment. Some adolescents assume that society views sex as a kind of physical goody which young people do not deserve or are not old enough to experience before marriage.

It is interesting that, despite these beliefs, plus the general alienation that many young people feel from an older society, a majority of all young people (57%) agree, "Our society's values concerning sex come from many generations of accumulated wisdom" (Table 197). At the same time, 77% of all adolescents—with virgins and nonvirgins being in close agreement—believe, "The sexual behavior of most young people today would not be acceptable to society as a whole" (Table 233).

Adolescents are more stringent about their own personal sexual behavior: 38% of all young people affirm they would *not* personally, "so far as sex is concerned, do anything that society would disapprove of" (Table 50). But it is the sexually inexperienced adolescents who are really demanding of themselves in this regard, 67% of whom agree with the above statement. At the same time, most adolescents do not seek to satisfy society before they satisfy themselves: 62% of all adolescents affirm, "So far as sex is concerned, I do what I want to do, regardless of what society thinks" (Table 183). Not surprisingly, virgins (44%) much less frequently side with this position of sexual independence from society's opinions than do nonvirgins (79%).

4.2.1.2 *Sex and the law*

Young people are largely oblivious to the law as it pertains to their sexual behavior. Many would be surprised or astonished to know that much of their sexual behavior (including intercourse between unmarried persons) is a violation of the law in most states. Young people do not deliberately violate the law in matters of sex; they simply consider laws about sex irrelevant to their personal behavior.

Even more so than in the case of folkways, adolescents are unconcerned with what the law permits or proscribes concerning their own personal sexual behavior. Despite their support of laws for regulating other people's behavior, over half of the adolescents and 69% of all nonvirgins agree with the statement, "When deciding for myself what to do or not to do so far as sex is concerned, I don't pay any attention to what the laws say" (Table 92). However, fewer adolescents (42%) and nonvirgins (56%) are willing to have anything to do with any sex acts that are against the law (Table 120).

There is a difference between lack of desire to break the law on sexual matters and flouting social convention. The much-publicized sex play at large public gatherings of young people, for example, is a kind of conspicuous action inspired by the desire to do something different which will shock some elements of the community and offend the sensibilities of policemen, whom they see as adult or parental representatives. Although adolescents are generally permissive about other people's sexual behavior, they support, in greater numbers than one might anticipate, laws prohibiting or restricting many types of sexual activities. Opinions about whether laws should govern certain forms of behavior vary according to the respondents' age, gender, and sexual experience. The main features of adolescents' opinions about laws governing sexual behavior are as follows:

1. A great majority of all adolescents, regardless of personal characteristics and sexual experience, support laws against rape.
2. The prohibition of homosexuality attracts the next highest amount of support for laws. Support is fairly even among all concerned, except that it is significantly higher among younger boys.
3. Catchall legislation—or general laws against unnamed sex acts—arouses the widest variance in support from adolescents. Opinions depend on the age and sexual experience of the respondent: younger boys and girls and virgins are the strongest supporters of such laws.
4. Proportionally twice as many virgins support laws against fornication as do nonvirgins, while two-thirds as many nonvirgins support statutory rape legislation as do virgins. Of unusual note is the fact that older girls give 20% greater support to laws against intercourse with a girl under sixteen as do girls under sixteen.
5. Younger boys support film censorship laws twice as frequently as do older boys, while girls of both age-groups give virtually equal support in proportions about halfway between the two male age-groups.
6. Except for rape and homosexuality, there is significantly less support among nonvirgins than virgins for laws prohibiting certain types of sexual behavior.

Adolescents supporting laws prohibiting types of sexual behavior

	All adolescents	Boys			Girls			Virgins	Nonvirgins
		All	13–15	16–19	All	13–15	16–19		
Against rape (Table 72)	95%	92%	88%	96%	98%	98%	99%	95%	96%
Against homosexuality (Table 20)	59	63	72	55	55	58	52	62	56
Against prostitution (having sex for money) (Table 239)	58	49	61	40	67	74	60	69	48
Against some kinds of sex acts (Table 67)	57	55	69	44	59	67	52	70	45
Against having sex with a girl under sixteen years (Table 59)	49	40	39	40	59	52	64	61	38
For government censorship of magazines or books no matter how extreme about sexual matters (Table 232)	44	43	39	47	45	47	43	49	40
For trying to keep people from seeing any kind of sex movies* (Table 250)	31	31	42	22	32	30	33	39	25

* ". . . even if they're so dirty I wouldn't want to see them myself."

4.2.1.3 Sex and the church

A seventeen-year-old boy who thinks about his religion in connection with his sexual behavior sometimes feels that his religion helps him to avoid guilt feelings—in part because he believes he provides affection to girls who need it:

> I don't have any written book on right and wrong, but I do believe that Jesus Christ died as my savior. There are no moral punishments to what I have done because usually when I do have sex with a person I do care about them in one way or another. There are times when you do feel very guilty because there is something about the person like they're childish, and it kind of turns you off even though

> you agree to have sex and it does go on and happen. And later on when I think about it, I feel guilty and it doesn't happen again with that girl. I always think that there are some people who need love and there are some people who really don't. Sometimes a girl is desperate for love like she has just lost someone she really cares about and she feels this loss and she doesn't feel like a whole person—like someone who got back from Vietnam and lost both of his arms. People who do need love have an empty feeling inside and get really desperate, and so you're able to grab on to anything that will give you love even though you find out that it can't be a thorough experience.

Most adolescent respondents describe the church's attitude toward sex as being negative and ineffectual. Despite the increasingly publicized attitudes of some theologians and churchmen toward sex as a humane and liberating force, a substantial number of all respondents—regardless of their religious preference or the lack of it—look upon the values of organized religion as being irrelevant to their sexuality.

Thus, 49% of all adolescents (including 55% of the nonvirgins) believe churches teach that enjoyment of sex is sinful (Table 229). 37% of all respondents agree, "One of the reasons why young people stop going to church is because churches teach that enjoyment of sex is sinful" (Table 245). 31% of all virgins believe this, compared with 43% of all nonvirgins. 28% of those saying they are very religious and 38% of those saying they are somewhat religious also agree (Table 350).

"A person who truly loves God doesn't have sexual relations outside of marriage" was agreed to by 43% of all adolescents (Table 227). Proportionally nearly twice as many of the sexually inexperienced (53%) agreed to this as did serial monogamists (28%) who share close but nonetheless unmarried sexual relationships.

To inquire into possible optimism on the part of young people about the church, we asked them to react to the statement, "Churches are really doing their best to understand young people's ideas about sex" (Table 253). 45% of all adolescents agreed with this statement, but agreement and disagreement vary considerably by age, gender, and intercourse experience. Barely one-half of those who are very religious or somewhat religious agree, while 75% of those who are not religious at all disagree (Table 353).

A comparison of the reactions of adolescents to the three statements in the immediately following table offers several striking findings. Prejudices against organized religion die hard, or else the church offends the sensibilities of nearly half of all adolescents with respect to sin and sex. Proportionally about 25% more boys and nonvirgins than girls and virgins believe churches teach that enjoyment of sex is sinful. Fewer girls and older boys than younger boys believe that churches are doing their best to understand young people's ideas about sex.

Adolescents agreeing with statements about role of the church

	All adolescents	Boys			Girls			Virgins	Nonvirgins
		All	13–15	16–19	All	13–15	16–19		
"Churches teach enjoyment of sex is sinful" (Table 229).	49%	53%	55%	51%	45%	42%	47%	42%	55%
"Churches are really doing their best to understand young people's ideas about sex" (Table 253).	45	50	61	40	41	43	39	51	41
"One of the reasons why young people stop going to church is because churches teach that enjoyment of sex is sinful" (Table 245).	37	37	39	35	37	39	36	31	43

Exactly one-half of all adolescents rarely, if ever, go to religious services but still think of themselves as being fairly religious (Table 112). 20% of all boys and 10% of all girls replied true to the statement, "One of the reasons I stopped going to church is because churches teach that sex is sinful" (Table 189).

Of those who say they are very religious (Table 351), 40% concede that they sometimes take part in sexual activities that are not consistent with their religious beliefs, as compared with 27% of all adolescents (Table 81). When they go to church, 20% of all adolescents sometimes feel guilty about their sexual behavior (Table 65). Only 22% of those who feel that churches teach that enjoyment of sex is sinful and 29% of those going to religious services fairly often have these guilt feelings sometimes at church (Table 355).

34% of all adolescents either view God as a somewhat impersonal force or assume their sex life is of little relevance to God. 41% of all young people with intercourse experience and 27% of those with no intercourse experience do not think that "God has any interest in my sex life" (Table 58). But those who are religious feel very strongly otherwise. Only 8% of the very religious and 21% of the somewhat religious agree that God does not have any interest in their sex lives (Table 352).

Of those with intercourse experience, 50% said they sometimes worry about whether God would approve of their sexual behavior (Table 182), with a few more nonvirgins expressing concern than virgins. No significant differences in opinions were reflected by differences in gender or age of the respondents.

One seventeen-year-old girl monogamist discusses how she perceives herself in relation to God and marriage. A staunch Catholic, she strives to protect her love and sexual relationship "from" the Church.

> Marriage is always a handsome man and a white beautiful gown. But that's about it. The rest of it is responsibilities, which I don't really think I need any more of right now. To me, whenever I want to speak to God it's just me and God. I don't have to go through like a priest or a church or anything like that, you know. It's the same with marriage. I really don't feel I have to go to somebody and hear them say like now, you're really married. I feel that I'm living with somebody and I love him very much and I feel that, you know, like if I tell the person I'm living with that I'm married to you—like spiritually—and he tells me the same thing, then we're automatically married as far as I'm concerned. Not because we go to a priest and he tells us we're married and he gives us a piece of paper. We're married because we want to. And I think that's more lasting than a piece of paper.
>
> To me there's—to me my marriage would be a big thing only because I would be telling society we could live together now. That's marriage. I have this piece of paper. Now I can live with him. Now I can go to bed with him. Now I have the right. But I think we have the right anyway. Anybody has that right to live together if they love each other. I mean, I don't think other people should butt into what you're doing. Like it's none of their business at all.

The fact that so many adolescents think of God in connection with their sexual behavior does not contradict the concern that many have about the compatibility of their religious beliefs with their sexual activity. These findings, plus our other data on society, law, and conscience, suggest that organized religion could find new potentials for influencing the adolescent were it able to change its reputation for equating enjoyment of sex with sinful behavior.

4.2.2 Sex and personal values

The unwillingness of young people to condemn the sexual behavior of others asserts itself most strongly in the area of personal values. We learn that a majority of adolescents are not willing to label others as wrongdoers, even for things they do not want to do themselves.

There are two important exceptions to adolescent permissiveness about others in addition to rape and, to a certain extent, homosexuality. Young people strongly *oppose* the use of sex to hurt or use someone. They also oppose any relationship that is forced.

The next subsections describe the values and attitudes that adolescents apply to various issues of sexual behavior. Adolescents' reactions differ from issue to issue, yet adolescents sometimes reflect far greater differences among themselves about any one issue, depending upon their age, gender, and intercourse experience. Beyond our summaries presented here, further detailed analysis is required to determine precisely how the changes in values are related to and influenced by aging and sexual experience.

4.2.2.1 Girls' virginity before marriage

Boys and girls alike do not demand that a girl be a virgin when she marries or even when she meets the boy she is going to marry. 65% of all boys disagree with the statement, "I wouldn't want to marry a girl who isn't a virgin at marriage" (Table 103). Even more boys—71%—disagree with the statement, "A girl who goes to bed with a boy before marriage will lose his respect" (Table 200). And 65% of all boys disagree, "A girl should stay a virgin until she finds the boy she wants to marry" (Table 208), although only 47% of the girls disagree with the same statement.

A minority of boys assert they would not want to marry a nonvirgin, and this percentage decreases as age and sexual experience increase. Nonvirgin boys report twice as frequently as virgin boys that they would not be unwilling to marry a girl with intercourse experience.

Percentage of boys who would not want to marry a nonvirgin

All boys	Boys 13–15	Boys 16–19	Virgins	Nonvirgins
30%	38%	23%	42%	21%

As boys and girls grow older and become sexually experienced, they are less likely to condemn a girl who has sex with a boy before marriage. More younger adolescents than older ones believe that a girl should remain a virgin until she finds the boy she wants to marry. Older adolescents and nonvirgins more frequently agree with the *value* of remaining a virgin than they agree with the idea that a girl is going to lose a boy's respect by sleeping with him. This is consistent with other findings about adolescent tendencies not to condemn or label other young people for their sexual behavior.

Adolescents agreeing with statements about girl's virginity before marriage

	All adolescents	Boys		Girls		Virgins	Nonvirgins
		13–15	16–19	13–15	16–19		
"A girl who goes to bed with a boy before marriage will lose his respect" (Table 200).	34%	45%	13%	52%	33%	55%	15%
"A girl should stay a virgin until she finds the boy she wants to marry" (Table 208).	42%	44%	26%	58%	43%	58%	27%

4.2.2.2 Sex before marriage

Boys and girls assume that there is nothing wrong with sex without marriage. Yet most respondents (68%) were unwilling to criticize as foolish those young people who get married without having had sex together (Table 203).

Sexual relations without marriage are not condemned by a majority, even when the participants are not intending marriage. 76% of all boys and 67% of all girls agree that two people should not have to get married just because they want to live together (Table 201). And almost as many boys and girls (73% and 60%, respectively) believe that marriage is just a legal technicality for two people who love each other and are living together (Table 291). The greatest support from all adolescents (80% of all boys and 72% of all girls) is offered for the statement, "It's all right for young people to have sex before getting married if they are in love with each other" (Table 196).

Thus, our findings indicate that a majority of young people do not oppose sexual relations between people who do not plan to marry one another, and an even greater number of people support sexual relations between people who do intend to marry one another. Adolescents with intercourse experience are substantially more lenient in this regard than those without.

4.2.2.3 Sex outside marriage

Young people are considerably less tolerant of extramarital sex than they are of sex without marriage. 54% of the boys and 70% of the girls disagree with the statement, "It's all right for married people to have sexual relations with other people once in a while for the sake of variety" (Table 281). 26% of the girls and 24% of the virgins agreed with the statement; boys and nonvirgins showed a greater liberality in this respect by responding 42% and 43%, respectively, in agreement. With 60% agreeing with the statement, sexual adventurers proved to be the most tolerant of such behavior. However, of all adolescents agreeing, 32% nonetheless also affirm, "If I were married and my wife/husband had sexual relations with someone else, I would divorce her/him."

4.2.2.4 Homosexuality

75% of all adolescents (boys, 78%; girls, 72%) assert that the idea of two men having sex together is disgusting (Table 29). Fewer adolescents (54%), although still a majority, disagree with the statement, "If two boys want to have sex together, it's all right so long as they both want to do it" (Table 255). About the same number of adolescents opposed the statement, "If two girls want to have sex together, it's all right so long as they both want to do it" (Table 259). Almost no difference exists between boys and girls concerning each of these statements.

Attitudes toward homosexuality are discussed in detail in Chapter 11, but it is important to note here that personal values concerning the role of sex in friendship and loving relationships play an important part in some young people's unwillingness to condemn homosexuality among men. Men are thought by some boys and girls to need to give or receive love which cannot always be reciprocated by women. As for homosexuality among women, some folklore exists to the effect that boys are titillated by the thought and accordingly lend their approval, but no such thought predominates here. And except for those girls who spoke of their own bisexual activities in our depth interviews, few girls spoke in favor of female homosexuality.

Although there is widespread criticism of homosexuality, it is also obvious that it is viewed with tolerance by many young people, especially those with sexual experience. Examining the positions taken by virgins, nonvirgins, and sexual adventurers (who represent one category of nonvirgins), we find the following percentages of each group expressing tolerance for various forms of homosexuality:

Adolescents' response to statements about homosexuality

	Virgins	Nonvirgins	Adventurers
Disagree that idea of two men having sex together is disgusting (Table 29)	17%	29%	29%
Believe if two boys want to have sex together, it's all right if both want to do it (Table 255)	32	50	54
Believe if two girls want to have sex together, it's all right if both want to do it (Table 259)	31	50	58

44% of the boys and 39% of the girls express a willingness to tolerate bisexual behavior: "It's all right for a person to have sexual relations with both males and females, if that's what the person wants to do" (Table 282). 53% of nonvirgins and 29% of virgins agree. The greatest contrast is between adventurers and inexperienced, where 63% and 30% agree, respectively.

4.2.2.5 *Sex for money*

For many of the older adolescents, sex for money and prostitution are not the same thing. Prostitution is an occupation—full time or part time—while sex for money is an avocation that some adolescents could not clearly contrast with prostitution even though they did not consider it prostitution. Sex for money can be sex as a reward or thanks for "an expensive night on the town." Boys are more permissive than girls concerning girls having sex for money: 60% of the older boys and 40% of the older girls agree with the statement, "It's not wrong for a girl to have sex with someone for money, if that's what she wants to do" (Table 247). Younger girls were more permissive (48%), and 62% of those with intercourse experience, compared with 37% of all virgins, did not object to a girl taking money for sex.

The reactions of boys and girls to statements implying a double standard about sex for money reveal little contrast. A majority of all boys (54%) and all girls (68%) would lose respect for a girl if they found out she had had sex for money (Table 209), and approximately the same percentages of boys and girls disagreed with the statement, "There's nothing wrong with paying a girl for sex, if a boy can't get sex in any other way" (Table 214). Younger boys, however, are far less tolerant of the concept of sex for money.

Again, large majorities of those expressing the permissiveness described here do not extend this permissiveness to themselves. Of the boys who agreed, "It's not wrong for a girl to have sex with someone for money, if that's what she wants to do," 68% also say, "I would never pay a girl money to have sex with me." Of the girls who agree with the former statement, 82% say, "I would never have sex with a boy for money." 58% of the boys who agree, "There's nothing wrong with paying a girl for sex, if a boy can't get sex in any other way," nonetheless agree, "I would never pay a girl money to have sex with me." 79% of the girls who agreed with the former statement say, "I would never have sex with a boy for money."

4.2.2.6 *Hurt and force*

Despite the strong permissiveness expressed by adolescents toward most sexual behavior, any behavior in which things were done to a person that he or she doesn't like are strongly frowned on. The vast majority of adolescents (91%) agree, "Hurting another person is wrong" (Table 243), while 65% of all respondents agree, "Where sex is concerned, anything people want to do is all right so long as they want to do it and it doesn't hurt them" (Table 240). The emphasis on not hurting and mutual want may be offered by some respondents to justify their permissiveness.

Although boys are a little more tolerant than girls, 76% of all respondents agree with the statement, "It would be wrong to take advantage of a girl who was stoned or drunk by having sex with her" (Table 271).

One boy told us, "If a girl has led a boy on, it's all right for the boy to force her to have sex." A majority of the boys and girls (69% and 71%, respectively) disagreed with this statement, although younger girls (33%) were more tolerant than even the nonvirgin and adventurer groups (Table 251). Perhaps some younger girls are inclined to feel they would never do such a thing and, accordingly, believe a girl who would do such a thing only gets what she deserves.

4.2.2.7 *Sexual irresponsibility*

Few young people are willing to label specific examples of the sexual behavior of their contemporaries as irresponsible. However, young people are not very generous to their adolescent contemporaries as a whole. 74% of all adolescents agree with the statement, "Too many young people these days are irresponsible where sex is concerned" (Table 289). Nonvirgins (74%) are hardly less critical, with 76% of the adventurers agreeing; younger boys (64%) are the most lenient.

4.2.2.8 Concepts of morality and immorality

Despite the protestations of many young people that they do not know what is meant by "immoral," more adolescents than not are willing to label some kinds of sexual behavior as immoral. However, a 57% majority are unwilling to agree, "Sexual activities that society is opposed to are immoral" (Table 211).

A difference in the interpretation of loving someone and liking someone influences respondents' definitions of moral and immoral sex. 52% of all adolescents believe, "Sex is immoral, unless it's between two people who love each other" (Table 207). This contrasts with a lesser 39% of all adolescents who affirm, "Sex is immoral, unless it's between two people who like each other and have something in common" (Table 220). These statements are not easy to reconcile. One might have anticipated that considerably more adolescents would have said that sex is immoral if you do not like each other, while being willing to reserve judgment about its morality if two people did not love each other.

Adolescents agreeing with statements on what makes sex immoral

	All adolescents	Girls 13–15	Virgins	Non-virgins
"Sex is immoral, unless it's between two people who like each other and have something in common" (Table 220).	39%	35%	40%	38%
"Sex is immoral, unless it's between two people who love each other" (Table 207).	52%	60%	61%	44%

It would seem that many adolescents respond strongly to the word "love," while caring less about whether people like each other or have something in common when they have intercourse. Perhaps love is intimately tied to the concept of sexual morality in the minds of younger girls and virgins. Those with intercourse experience react similarly to both questions, while virgins affirm almost 50% more often than nonvirgins that sex is immoral without love. In fact much higher proportions of younger girls and virgins believe sex is immoral without love than believe sex is immoral in the absence of affection and having something in common.

One other factor needs to be considered. Later in this chapter, in discussing the concepts of love and like, we learn that 71% of all adolescents agree, "I wouldn't want to have sex with a girl/boy unless

I liked her/him as a person" (Table 164), and that 61% of all adolescents affirm, "I wouldn't want to have sex with a girl/boy unless I loved her/him" (Table 174). Again, the younger girls in their responses to the two statements emphasize their greater concern for loving a person than liking a person in a sexual act. We also find that 50% more older boys, 31% more nonvirgins, and two times as many adventurers say they do not want to have sex with someone they do not like as a person than say they do not want to have sex with someone they do not love. Perhaps boys in particular have a very great desire to like their sex partner regardless of whether they love her, do not want to commit themselves to expressing love for a sex partner, and—unlike girls—tend much less to idealize the concept of love or give love a morality connotation.

The adolescent definition of immorality is unclear, and only a minority of young people are willing to concur with society's more conservative approach to acceptable sexual activities. Young people, however, largely agree with two key tenets of sexual morality: (1)

Adolescents believing certain sexual acts are immoral

	All adolescents	Boys			Girls		
		All	13–15	16–19	All	13–15	16–19
A boy forcing a girl to have sex, no matter what the circumstances (Table 216)	88%	85%	82%	87%	92%	88%	94%
Between people too young to understand what they are getting out of it (Table 225)	69	63	73	55	75	79	73
Two people of same sex to have sex with each other (Table 198)	62	62	70	56	61	61	61
A young person having sex only for physical enjoyment and nothing else (Table 260)	52	49	56	44	55	61	51
A white boy and black girl having sex together, even if both wanted it (Table 32)	33	33	46	23	33	40	28
A white girl and black boy having sex together, even if both wanted it (Table 22)	30	29	34	25	31	37	27
Unless it's between two people who are married to each other (Table 231)	25	21	38	7	30	38	23

69% of all adolescents agree, "Anything two people want to do sexually is moral, as long as they both want to do it and it doesn't hurt either one of them" (Table 223). (2) 72% of all adolescents concur, "When it comes to morality in sex, the important thing is the way people treat each other, not the particular things that they do together" (Table 258).

Other specific attitudes toward morality with respect to sexual behavior were explored. Force in sex, sex for people too young to understand what they are getting out of it, homosexuality, and sex for physical enjoyment only—in decreasing order—are the kinds of sexual behavior most frequently labeled immoral by our adolescent respondents. The majority of respondents are unwilling to term other types of sexual behavior as immoral.

4.2.2.9 Concepts of normality and abnormality

Adolescents do not easily define normal and abnormal sexual behavior. When asked about forms of normal and abnormal behavior, our interviewers were often greeted by, "Please repeat that again," or "What's that?" or "I never heard of it." Adolescents lack society's conception of what is normal or abnormal. The terms mean little to them personally and are not terms found in the common sexual vocabulary of the average adolescent.

Nonetheless, at least one clear-cut result did emerge concerning adolescents' concepts of normality and abnormality. Young people tend to decide that sexual behavior is abnormal not so much on the basis of what is done, but rather on the basis of who is doing it.

This result perhaps emerges most strikingly in the responses given by sexual adventurers to our questions probing attitudes toward sexual abnormality or unnaturalness. 71% of the adventurers, compared with 46% of all adolescents, agree with the statement, "There is no kind of sex act that I would think of as being abnormal, so long as the people involved want to do it" (Table 261). So for this group, presumably, no sex acts are inherently abnormal. Similarly, 61% of the adventurers do not consider oral sex to be abnormal (Table 147). But unspecified sex acts between brother and sister, parent and child, and members of the same sex are variously considered to be abnormal by 63% to 76% of the sexual adventurers. This relative tolerance for a wide variety of sex *acts* versus proportionally strong labeling as "abnormal" of unspecified acts defined in terms of certain types of participants is a pattern that is repeated by all age, demographic, and sexual behavior groups. Yet it is this ambivalence by some adolescents (not always adventurers) that encourages them to believe that some

Adolescents believing certain sex acts are abnormal or unnatural

	All adoles-cents	Boys			Girls			Virgins	Non-virgins	Adven-turers
		All	13–15	16–19	All	13–15	16–19			
A brother and sister having sex together, even if both wanted it (Table 45)	82%	78%	69%	86%	85%	84%	85%	89%	74%	69%
Two boys having sex together (Table 34)	80	81	83	79	80	83	77	84	76	65
A parent and child having sex together, even if both wanted it (Table 140)	78	71	71	72	85	84	85	83	74	63
Two girls having sex together (Table 87)	76	74	75	73	77	81	74	84	67	76
No kind of sex act abnormal as long as people involved want to do it (those disagreeing) (Table 261)	48	45	48	42	50	46	54	55	40	26
Oral sex (Table 147)	38	37	49	27	38	50	28	48	28	30

types of human behavior such as youthful homosexuality are "abnormal or unnatural" but "all right so long as they both want to do it."

4.2.3 Limits of tolerance

As they grow older and accumulate sexual experience, adolescents become increasingly tolerant of the sexual activities of others.

But their tolerance for the sexual behavior of others is not infinite. This very substantial tolerance converts to intolerance for the following kinds of behavior:

1. Sexual relations that are incestuous or in which one partner is forced to participate.
2. Sexual exploitation of others. The difference between exploitation and persuasion is thin but significant. Sexual exploitation occurs in their minds when someone demands sexual compliance in the name of a love or friendship which does

not exist, which causes the sexual partner to make sacrifices of time, money, or self-esteem which he or she would not otherwise do.

3. Pretense and hypocrisy in sexual relations. Young people do not want to pretend to a permanence in their sexual relationships that neither party anticipates.

4.3 Acceptable and desired contexts of sexual behavior

4.3.1 Concepts of love

It is argued in many quarters that increasing sexual permissiveness and the prevalence of sex in our mass media are dehumanizing the emotions of our youth and depriving many adolescents of any meaningful perception of love. Sex in this form is seen as being purely physical behavior that downgrades mature love and discourages young people's respect for each other as human beings.

But the attitudes and behavior of many young people force us to reject this view. A new kind of love is being worked out by American adolescents in a strongly sexual context. Mutuality and belonging are emphasized by many young people in describing what love means to them. Young people are resisting the subject-object expression of love by speaking in terms of "we," "us," and "our love for each other."

One result of this greater emphasis on mutuality in love has been a lessening need to require sex as a fundamental condition of a love relationship. 82% of all adolescents denied that the most important thing in a love relationship is sex (Table 236), with the intercourse-experienced (82%) no less firm in their conviction about this than the virgins (81%).

One eighteen-year-old girl's comments are typical of many: "You don't necessarily have to have sex with people you love. . . . I think love is when you care about somebody and you want to do things for them, and you have concern for what that other person does."

A seventeen-year-old girl expresses similar reactions in describing how she feels love and sex strengthen each other:

> To just have someone who can take what I'm giving. That's what *we* need, not what I need. It's got to be *we*. If it's not a we, then we haven't got anything. It's got to be me and my mate together. . . . It's when two people get together and they find this thing together. It's like one person getting into another, like you want to hold someone so much that you want to go right through him. You want to go inside. That's what's happening in sex. That's what you can do.

Love that emphasizes feelings of mutuality is said by many adolescents to be a dependable assurance of immense sexual satisfaction. Mutuality is seen as being intellectual, physical, or both. Sometimes adolescents are not sure where mutuality leading to sexual relations actually begins. One eighteen-year-old boy puts it this way:

> I think when you're with a person you love, you can enjoy taking your time. When you're with a person you don't love, it's just waiting for the body to get to specific stages. When you are with a person you love, it's waiting for your body, your mind, and your emotions to reach each stage, and it takes a longer time. If it's someone you're just having sex with, you see them and you're just going to have sex. You're not going to see them today and kiss them one way and see them tomorrow and kiss them another way and drag it out for days and weeks. If you're just going to have sex with someone, you're just going to have sex as fast as it takes.
>
> But a friend of mine thinks differently. I really do think that the relationship should start on an intellectual basis and not on a physical one. But my friend thinks that he has lots of good reasons why it should start on a physical basis. He says that the first thing you see about someone is their body, so the first thing you should react to is their body. Then if you get to know their mind, great. If the emotions are good together, great. But he does it in that order for those reasons.
>
> But I still think that if you're with someone that you love, you don't even have to have intercourse. You can get satisfaction out of just doing other things. I can get satisfaction out of just sleeping with someone. I really like waking up and finding them there in the morning. To me that's so great!

Another finding about the relationship between love and sex which young people are working out is seen in the agreement of 45% of all young people to the statement, "Physical attractiveness of the other person is more important in love than it is in sex" (Table 256). 44% of those with intercourse experience believe that physical attractiveness is more important in love than in sex. Thus we see that love is not judged solely in nonphysical terms by many young people.

Many young people do not want to have sex with someone unless they feel some kind of love. This includes a desire not to deceive the other person by expressing a nonexistent love. Many boys have traditionally said, "I love you," in order to pave the way for intercourse. Yet, 73% of all boys do not agree with the statement, "There's nothing wrong with telling a girl that you love her—even if you don't—if that's what it takes so she will have sex with you" (Table 108).

One test for the expression of love as a rationale for sex lies in people's tendencies to declare love for another person, whether they feel it or not. To say I love you in these times is easy enough, considering the pop poetry, pop music, and pop philosophy that stress the importance of love in young people's lives. But 83% of all boys and 93% of all girls declare, "I don't tell a girl/boy that I love her/him unless I really do" (Table 156). It might be expected that this percentage would fall drastically as age and sexual experience increase, but this is not the case.

Without defining love, nearly half of the boys and three-fourths of the girls agreed they wouldn't want to have sex with someone "unless I loved her/him" (Table 174). Boys and girls, in the same proportions, would not want to have sex with someone "unless she/he loved me" (Table 168). More girls feel this way than do boys; many more younger than older boys feel this way. However, sexual adventurers are very much the exception, with over three-fifths disagreeing.

Tolerance for others should not be confused with the codes young people establish for themselves. Young people are quite stringent concerning their own requirements. Thus, 75% of all young people with intercourse experience agree with the statement, "I wouldn't want to have sex with a boy/girl unless I liked him/her as a person" (Table 164). Fewer adolescents—but still a majority—say they would not want to have sex with someone "unless I loved him/her" (Table 174). This coincides with the opinion of 57% of all adolescents that "I wouldn't want to have sex with a boy/girl only for the physical enjoyment of doing it, and nothing else" (Table 161). Proportionally more older girls support this statement than younger girls; so do very many more older girls than older boys.

Adolescents do not always feel they must love before they have sex. Sometimes they do not feel they can love another until they know whether they are sexually compatible. Others feel that sex is a medium of communication in which they may or may not find love for each other. Still others see love as naturally flowing from the sexual intimacy. But most adolescents feel that the expression of love is a commitment to another that having intercourse is not. Especially among boys, having intercourse with a girl is more of a discrete, individual event which he can cope with, while expressing and feeling love demands a continuity of emotions that take the form of an emotional commitment he may be unwilling to make. In other words, intercourse is viewed as an act that he can put behind him rather than an act that involves him on a continuing basis.

Traditionally girls have been thought to merge sex and love into the same experience. They have been said to be able to feel love without sex, but not sex without love. But increasing numbers of girls feel that they can separate sex and love, enjoying sex by itself under certain circumstances, and are perhaps even encouraged to experience more love without sex as a result. These girls speak of the sheer gratification they receive from relationships that are explicitly sexual. They are not impressed with the need to express or feign love in order to justify sex; they feel no guilt in not doing so.

Perhaps the belief of many adolescents—that sex partners need not necessarily know each other for a long time before sexual intercourse—is pertinent here. 58% of all boys and 19% of all girls think it is all right for someone to have sex with a person he has known only a few hours (Table 111); 46% of all boys and 16% of all girls would not think it wrong if they had "sex with a girl/boy I'd just met and hadn't gotten to know" (Table 165).

The kinds of love which adolescents describe to us in our interviews can best be classified as durable love and transient love.

4.3.1.1 Durable love

Few adolescents see marriage in their immediate future. Their feelings about marriage range from ambivalence and a desire not to think about it to outright hostility to marriage as an institution. But young people do associate a particular kind of love with marriage: a love that is supposed to last for life and that is rewarding to family life. We call this kind of love *durable love.*

Young people are not surprised that people in love may want to get married, and 68% of all adolescents believe it is natural for lovers to react in this way (Table 262). This suggests that the idea of marriage moves through their minds, despite the fact that they may not intend to act on it.

70% of all young people believe in a love that lasts for life, "if two people are really in love" (Table 224). But durable love is a kind of love that very few adolescents believe they have experienced, and it is a kind of love that most young people do not want to deal with during adolescence. But they comprehend the existence of such love and are able to talk about it. On the other hand, young people see no inconsistency in a profound love that lasts for a relatively short period. 58% of the girls and 60% of the boys agree that it is possible for love to be real and strong but still not last for more than a few years (Table 280). 48% of all adolescents believe that a love can be real and strong but still not last more than a few weeks (Table 235). However, 59% of these adolescents believing that a love may not last more than a few weeks also agree, "If two people are really in love, that love should last for life"—an interesting differentiation between the possible and the desirable.

4.3.1.2 Transient love

Two types of transient love that adolescents express for each other are monoaffectional love and multiaffectional love. As is evident from their names, monoaffectional love is an attachment to one person and multiaffectional love is a simultaneous attachment to several people. Each type calls for a specific kind of sexual behavior and set of sexual attitudes.

1. Young people experiencing monoaffectional love do not view their love objectively, and such love is often intense and dramatic. They have standards by which they almost instantly gauge their affection; they do not await the passage of time so that they can view either themselves or their love in perspective. Once their standards are met, sexual relations may be acceptable because of their desire for sexual gratification, for belonging sexually to someone for the time being.

The shortness of "the time being" is irrelevant to the intensity of their feeling of love and their desire for sex. They view love itself as existing for the time being, and they know that time can bring changes in their relationship that will eliminate both the feeling of love and the desire for sex. Girls who feel this kind of love want to belong to someone; boys combine an aggressive desire for physical experience with a wish for the self-confidence that successful sexual experience brings.

These casual short-term monoaffectional relationships frequently exist without sex and often begin as friendships. Friendship is generally, but not always, considered nonsexual; its chances for duration are thought to be less once a sexual relationship begins. As one boy put it: "I have girl friends, and I have friends who are girls. I don't ball friends who are girls if I want us to stay friends. They feel the same way, you know, and we spend more time sharing other things."

A fourteen-year-old girl agrees: "When you start having sex with a friend, it's different. Then you're looking at each other in other ways and you lose some of your common interests to sex. I am not against having sex with friends, but I know what I'm giving up."

"A friendship is always going to last longer than a sexship," said one sixteen-year-old boy.

> It's kind of understood that we aren't bound to each other for marriage or anything like that when we are having sex. But in a friendship you don't think about ways you don't want to get tied up with each other—you're just loyal and interested in each other for other things that keep on going, no matter what.

Friendship can offer the long-term qualities that a sexual relationship short of marriage does not. The way in which adolescents describe friendship is a clue to the dilemma they see in married love. The difficulty of merging the affection of friendship with the affection of the casual sex relationship—even though both of them may be called love—may be an important clue to the concern many adolescents have about the effects of marriage on love. (See Chapter 14.)

2. Multiaffectional love differs little from monoaffectional love, except that those practicing the former feel they can love several people during the same period of their lives, even stopping and restarting a sexual relationship with the same person. One or more of such loves can last for a few weeks or a few years. The person having these loves feels perfectly secure and honest about loving more than one person sexually during the same time period. Adolescents engaging in multiaffectional love are usually the sexual adventurers described in Chapter 10.

Many adolescents feel they have the ability to have simultaneous, loving sexual friendships with more than one person. Thus, 42% of all boys and 39% of all girls disagreed with the statement, "I don't think it would be possible for a boy/girl to be really in love with more than one girl/boy at the same time" (Table 155). And 52% of the nonvirgins agreed with the statement, "Over a period of time, I think it's better to have sexual relationships with several people, rather than just one person" (Table 238).

Young people are aware that those with whom they are having sexual relationships are often having sex with others. The multiaffectional lover frequently has sex with a person who has only one sexual relationship; so the question arises as to how a partner feels about sharing his or her lover with others. Boys feel a possessiveness that girls do not. Few boys believe their girl friends would have a sexual liaison with anyone else. Many girls, on the other hand, tell of their monoaffectional sexual liaisons with boys whom they know are sometimes having sex with others.

4.3.2 Concepts of "relationship"

The word *relationship* is frequently mentioned by adolescents in describing how they function affectionately and sexually with other young people. This term connotes a process in which two people (usually a boy and a girl) jointly participate in fulfilling one another's desires. This usually entails sexual activities and other modes of communication that suit the personalities and circumstances of the two partners (telephoning, doing homework together, attending parties together, traveling together).

A relationship has no formality or ritual about it and carries no connotations of "going steady," engagement, or marriage. The couple does not necessarily feel bound or obligated by their ties. Relationships can be converted into marriage, but they are not necessarily preludes to marriage, and they do not require sexual fidelity. One partner may drop the relationship in order to have sex with another person.

To some in our respondent group, a relationship does not demand love any more than it demands marriage. Love entails obligations that have temporal meanings and feelings which disturb the typical older adolescent. A relationship can dissolve overnight, and even if one rather than both partners decides to "split," the dissolution is mutually understood in advance and therefore mutually accepted. To be in love, on the other hand, means a mutual preoccupation that for some compromises their independence. Because of the psychological commitment involved in "being in love," young people know "falling out of love" to be a difficult emotional experience.

Having a relationship represents a more feasible basis for sexual experience as can be seen in the words of one eighteen-year-old girl:

> I think sex should definitely be saved for a relationship. I think it's something very special and I don't think it should be thrown around thoughtlessly with anyone. It should be with someone you have something with. You don't have to be madly in love with them or go with them for years and years and years, but just this idea of casual dates I don't believe in. . . . Really the only way you can have a sexual relationship with somebody is to live with them. Not like this going out with your boyfriend and you have to wait until your mother's not home or his mother's not home. Or borrowing someone's apartment is for the birds, you know. It's kind of a silly little game when you're running around hiding from everybody. Ridiculous!

The sexual relationship is abandoned by two young people when the desired results of the relationship are not produced, not merely when the sexual activity itself is considered unsatisfactory. In most relationships, however, sex is a very important means to the ends of belonging, security, and self-esteem—with adolescents willing to tolerate a variety of dissatisfactions with themselves and hang-ups in the other person for the compensation of such meaningful sexual activities.

4.3.3 Competition and accommodation in sex roles

Adolescents seldom express ambivalence or concern about their sex roles. Despite the commercialized efforts of certain authors and clothing manufacturers to promote "unisex," boys and girls respect their unique qualities and their differences.

Many boys become upset with accusations of making girls sex objects, although they feel that to a considerable extent this has been the girl's choice rather than a condition forced upon her. As one adolescent told us: "Girls are people. They enjoy things and love and hate like anyone else. It's sickening to see a male using a woman . . .

talking about 'She's a really good lay' or 'I really like her cunt.' I think women really feel shitty about it. . . . No, many really feel good about it or they wouldn't have let it go on this long." In referring to his own current girl friend: "I've been sort of warned, 'You'd better not use me,' when I had no intention of doing so. She was looking for a pattern, but she didn't have enough intake of experience with me to know."

In many adolescent relationships, the partners make accommodations to one another to the degree that neither the boy nor the girl has absolute requirements in his or her sexual activities, nor does either have specified duties in their relationship. One hint of adolescent opposition to assuming traditional roles lies in the informality of the nonsex roles: cooking, cleaning, bringing in money are often spontaneous acts on the part of young people sharing the same household, and these are activities which they say they do not want to see frozen as responsibilities assigned to one person or the other.

4.4 Salient findings

1. A majority of adolescents oppose having sex for physical pleasure alone. At the same time many feel that adults assume physical pleasure is the main or only reason adolescents engage in sexual intercourse before marriage. Emotions and physical reactions are usually combined in the adolescent's perception of a sexual experience.

2. Genitality gradually converts to sexuality as adolescents begin perceiving the widespread consciousness of sex on the part of other adolescents and the ubiquitous presence of sex in many dimensions of living.

3. 90% of all adolescents believe it is important that they develop their own personal values, and 84% of all young people believe they have come to definite conclusions about what is right and wrong for them as far as sex is concerned.

4. Three-fourths of all adolescents believe they have not personally participated in sex acts they would consider immoral or abnormal; most adolescents, however, want to define for themselves what is meant by immorality or abnormality in matters of sex.

5. Adolescents are far more permissive about the sexual behavior of others than they are about their own sexual behavior.

6. 28% of all virgins and 37% of all those with intercourse experience sometimes feel guilty about their sexual activities. Guilt results more from deceiving others who trust them rather than from sexual behavior itself.

7. Most adolescents do not think of sex as being inherently right

or wrong, but instead judge sex in terms of the purpose for which it is used and the reactions of both partners to a sexual experience. They believe that society would disapprove of their sexual behavior, although they are not deliberately seeking to flout society or break the law by their sex acts. They are oblivious to the law as it pertains to their sexual behavior.

8. Traditional double standards about what is morally right for males and morally wrong for females are rejected by the majority of adolescents except younger girls; fewer adolescents profess these double standards as their age and sexual experience increase.

9. 76% of all boys and 66% of all girls agree that two people should not have to get married just because they want to live together.

10. Most adolescents believe that the church's attitudes toward sex are negative and ineffectual; 49% of all adolescents believe churches teach that enjoyment of sex is sinful. Yet 43% believe that churches are doing their best to understand young people's ideas about sex.

11. 41% of all nonvirgin adolescents believe God has no interest in their sex life, although 50% of all nonvirgins say they sometimes worry whether God would approve of their sexual behavior.

12. Adolescents are about evenly divided on whether or not it is all right for boys to have sex with each other and girls to have sex with each other. However, nearly three-fourths of all adolescents who agree that homosexual and bisexual activities are all right for consenting young people also affirm they have never personally engaged in them and would never want to.

13. Older adolescents and those with intercourse experience more often than not agree, "It's not wrong for a girl to have sex with someone for money, if that's what she wants to do." Yet a majority of adolescents agree they could lose respect for a girl if they found out she had sex for money. Again, young people are more stringent about their own conduct; a majority of those accepting this behavior from others say they would never give or take money for sex themselves.

14. 74% of all adolescents agree with the statement, "Too many young people these days are irresponsible where sex is concerned."

15. Over two-thirds of all adolescents agree that anything two people want to do sexually is moral, as long as they both want to do it and it does not hurt either one of them. A majority of all adolescents are unwilling to agree that sexual activities are immoral because society is opposed to them.

16. Younger adolescents and those without sexual experience are far more likely than older and sexually experienced adolescents to consider sexual relations immoral between two people who do not

love each other. Many who do not consider unloving sex immoral for others say that they would want to love their sex partners.

17. The sexual act considered immoral by the greatest number of adolescents (88%) is a boy forcing a girl to have sex.

18. The sexual acts considered immoral by the fewest number of adolescents are those occurring between unmarried people (25%) and interracial sex with both sex partners wanting it (30% and 33%).

19. Homosexual and incestuous sex acts are those which are considered abnormal or unnatural by the greatest number of adolescents; oral sex is considered abnormal or unnatural by the least number of adolescents. Approximately a quarter of all older boys and girls consider oral sex to be abnormal or unnatural.

20. Nearly three-fifths of all boys and nearly a fifth of all girls with intercourse experience believe it is all right for someone to have sex with another person he has known only a few hours.

21. Love is being emphasized by many adolescents as stressing *we* and *our* in an expression of "I love *us*" rather than a subject-object relationship of "I love you" or "she loves me." A love that emphasizes mutuality is considered to be an excellent assurance of sexual satisfaction.

22. Many adolescents do not feel they must love their sex partner; more nonvirgins reject sex with someone they dislike (75%) than sex with someone they do not love (57%). The expression of love is a commitment to another person that many boys and some girls do not want to make; they sometimes see it as a stronger commitment to someone than is sexual intercourse.

23. Two kinds of love most frequently described are durable love and transient love; transient love is either monoaffectional or multiaffectional. Durable love generally exists between two adolescents strongly committed to one another and planning to marry; transient love involves short-term although perhaps very intensive affection.

24. Some girls, particularly those in a transient love situation, extend permission to their partners for occasional sexual infidelity for reasons they believe actually strengthen their love relationship.

25. The majority of adolescents have some affection for their sex partners, and most guard against using a person or being used sexually.

26. Except in the case of obvious personality disorders, most young people are fairly honest with their sex partners. They are candid about whether they want to continue sexual relations and willingly express doubts to each other about the satisfaction they achieve from their sexual relationship.

III.
Sexual Behavior

Although every adolescent has ideas and attitudes about sex, 22% of all adolescents have neither engaged in beginning sexual activities nor have had sexual intercourse. Perhaps sex is not foremost in the minds of the inexperienced, but we count sexual inexperience as a form of sexual behavior that is also important to learn about and understand.

We found that 48% of American adolescents are virgins, and 52% of American adolescents (59% of the boys and 45% of the girls) have had sexual intercourse one or more times.

The sexual behavior of all adolescents is outlined in the table on the next page. Full definitions of the sexual behavior groups employed in this book will be found in the Technical Appendix.

We learned from our personal interviews with adolescents, that two kinds of sexual behavior predominate among those adolescents who are no longer virgins and who continue to have sexual intercourse. Each of these two major types of sexual behavior is often accompanied by distinctive personal values and sexual attitudes. When we obtained our data from the national sample of adolescents, we once again found these two forms of sexual behavior and values emerging as predominant; we defined these as *serial monogamy without marriage* and *sexual adventurism*. The serial monogamist is an adolescent who feels that he or she has a relationship with a sex partner of some lasting quality, regardless of length of time the relationship lasts. The monogamist generally does not have intercourse with another during that relationship. We say "serial" because one such relationship is often succeeded by another. Serial monogamy without marriage was found to be the most frequent type of active sexual behavior. More monogamists are girls than boys.

The sexual adventurer, on the other hand, moves freely from one sex partner to the next and feels no obligation to be faithful to any sex partner. Less concerned with love for the other sex partner than self-love, the sexual adventurer needs affection and idolatry in quantities that are usually never satisfied. More boys are adventurers than girls.

American adolescents—sexual behavior groups*

	Total	Boys	Girls	13–15	16–19	White	Non-white
Virgins (All adolescents who have not had sexual intercourse)	48%	41%	55%	63%	36%	55%	49%
Sexually inexperienced (Virgins with no beginning sexual activities)	22	20	25	39	9	25	23
Sexual beginners (Virgins who have actively or passively experienced sexual petting)	17	14	19	12	21	20	9
Unclassified virgins (Virgins who for whatever reason could not be classified in the above groups)	9	7	11	12	6	9	17
Nonvirgins (All adolescents who have had sexual intercourse one or more times)	52	59	45	37	64	45	51
Serial monogamists (Nonvirgins having a sexual relationship with one person)	21	15	28	9	31	19	14
Sexual adventurers (Nonvirgins freely moving from one sexual intercourse partner to another)	15	24	6	10	18	11	18
Inactive nonvirgins (Nonvirgins who have not had sexual intercourse for more than one year)	12	13	10	15	10	11	14
Unclassified nonvirgins (Nonvirgins who for whatever reasons could not be classified in the above groups)	4	7	1	3	5	4	5
Current intercourse-experienced (Nonvirgins who have had sexual intercourse during the preceding month)	31	30	33	15	45	24	31
Non–current intercourse-experienced (Nonvirgins who have *not* had sexual intercourse during the preceding month)	21	29	12	22	19	21	20

* The numbers of adolescents with masturbation and homosexual experience are described in Chapters 5 and 11, respectively.

The following points should be kept in mind when studying the incidence of sexual behavior and the tables in the next seven chapters:

1. Unless otherwise specified, all totals refer to the sexual behavior of all adolescents as of one specific point in time: March 1972.

2. In discussing sexual activities of various kinds "during the preceding month," we refer to answers given to specific questions about sexual activities during the thirty days immediately prior to the day the questionnaire was filled out.

3. For the following reasons, we believe that these totals of sexual behavior accurately reflect sexual behavior in which all adolescents in the United States are engaging.

   a. The national probability sample was accurate with respect to its representative quality. Chapter 1 shows the extent to which the national sample of adolescent respondents corresponds to the 1970 census of the U.S. population with respect to age, gender, and geographic distribution. The Technical Appendix describes in detail the manner in which the national sample was taken.

   b. The methods used to obtain parental and adolescent permission for participation in this survey worked sufficiently well so that the households of those adolescents who were interviewed do not differ significantly from the households in which adolescents were not interviewed.

   c. The techniques used to assure confidentiality for the participating adolescent not only helped obtain this wide adolescent participation but also most surely encouraged truth-telling on the part of those adolescents who did have sexual experience.

   d. The seriousness of the entire undertaking and our measures of internal consistency satisfy us that there was no tendency among adolescents to report sexual experiences they did not have.

Members of different categories of adolescents naturally differ in their number of sexual intercourse partners. The number of sexual intercourse partners both during one's lifetime and during the past month, as well as the frequency of sexual intercourse during the past month, reveal much about the differences between the serial monogamist and the sexual adventurer.

Average cumulative number of sexual intercourse partners of adolescents	
All nonvirgins	7.1
Serial monogamists	4.2
Sexual adventurers	16.3
Boys	9.8
13–15	4.3
16–19	12.4
Girls	3.5
13–15	1.8
16–19	4.1

Average cumulative number of sexual intercourse partners during preceding month	
All nonvirgins	1.5
Serial monogamists	1.1
Sexual adventurers	2.3

Average frequency of sexual intercourse during preceding month	
All nonvirgins	8.0
Serial monogamists	9.6
Sexual adventurers	5.1

The following table shows the composition of each sexual behavior group. These characteristics are repeated and discussed in more detail in each one of the chapters dealing with them.

Composition of adolescent sexual behavior groups

	All	Virgins	Inexperi-enced	Begin-ners	Non-virgins	Monog-amists	Adven-turers
Sex							
Male	52%	43%	45%	43%	57%	36%	80%
Female	48	57	55	57	43	64	20
Age							
13–15	42	58	78	32	32	20	31
16–19	58	42	22	68	68	80	69
Race							
White	86	87	87	94	85	89	80
Nonwhite	14	13	13	6	15	11	20
Religious feeling							
Very religious	12	16	19	14	10	11	15
Somewhat religious	49	55	57	55	45	50	40
Not very religious	28	21	17	26	32	23	31
Not at all religious	11	8	7	5	13	16	14
Claimed presence in school							
In school	81	97	97	96	71	61	65
Not in school	19	3	3	4	29	39	35
Claimed school grades							
Superior	15	15	18	17	15	21	5
Good	28	28	30	23	29	31	27
Average	52	53	47	58	51	46	62
Poor	5	4	5	2	5	2	6
Regions of United States							
Northeast	22	26	21	27	20	21	11
North Central	31	32	30	36	30	26	31
South	32	23	29	17	38	38	47
West	15	19	20	20	12	15	11
Locality size							
Large metropolitan areas	35	41	34	51	32	34	27
Small metropolitan areas	34	32	37	24	35	34	34
Nonmetropolitan and rural areas	31	27	29	25	33	32	39

5. Masturbation

I think masturbation can be good training for sex.

A sixteen-year-old sexually inexperienced girl

I masturbate three or four times a week even when I am having intercourse.

A seventeen-year-old male sexual adventurer

I've tried masturbating to some thoughts I didn't dig.

A fifteen-year-old girl

5.1 Definition and nature of masturbation

5.2 Incidence of masturbation
- **Age at first experience**
- **Masturbation among virgins**
- **Masturbation among nonvirgins**

5.3 Adolescents currently masturbating
- **Incidence**
  - *Relationship between intercourse and masturbation*
- **Frequency of act and of orgasm**

5.4 Pleasures and pains of masturbation
- **Enjoyment and fantasy thinking**
  - *Role of marijuana*
- **Guilt feelings**
- **Substitute for intercourse or orgasm**
- **Personal privacy and disgust: implications of findings**

5.5 Salient findings

5.1 Definition and nature of masturbation

We define masturbation as the act of manipulating one's sex organs in order to induce sexual pleasure without the participation of another person. Although young people sometimes masturbate in the company of others and can therefore be said to be sexually stimulated by the presence and example of others, physical stimulus during masturbation is applied to the sex organ only by the person himself. We did not include in our definition those forms of masturbation involving physical contact with another person.

In our questionnaire we defined masturbation as follows. For girls: "Most girls sometimes play with their sex organ while they are growing up. If a girl does this in order to experience a pleasant sensation, it is called masturbation"; for boys: "Most boys sometimes play with themselves sexually while they are growing up. If a boy does this and has an erection, it is called masturbation."

49% of all adolescents say they have masturbated; 58% of all boys and 39% of all girls have masturbated at least once (Tables 407 and 408). The incidence and frequency of masturbation vary among the diverse sexual behavior groups studied here.

There are no respondents with whom we spoke who are not aware of masturbation as a form of sexual behavior. However, only 18% of the boys and 16% of the girls acknowledge that their parents have talked to them about masturbation (Table 57).

5.2 Incidence of masturbation

5.2.1 Age at first experience

Although in some cases masturbation first occurs after the individual has begun having sexual intercourse, most masturbation begins before the first sexual intercourse, sometimes years before. More girls masturbate at an earlier age than do boys. Most girls who masturbate have masturbated before the age of thirteen; the majority of boys who masturbate have had their first masturbation experience before the age of fourteen.

One fifteen-year-old virgin decribes her first masturbation experience:

> When I was a child I had this toy rabbit, and I used to masturbate with this rabbit and put it between my legs and squeeze real hard. I didn't know that this was masturbation, because the only kinds I'd read about were using your fingers or rubbing something between your legs and I never really knew that this was. So I read a book—I read a couple of books that talked about sex and talked with a couple of friends of mine who were doctors.

Younger boys and girls in our sample report a much earlier age of first masturbation than do their older counterparts. We do not know why this is true, but we must assume that the explanation lies within one or more of these assumptions:

1. Children are masturbating at an earlier age than in the past.
2. Younger adolescents recall with greater accuracy the date of prepubescent first masturbation.
3. Younger adolescents are more candid about masturbation even though they have guilt feelings, particularly if masturbation is habitual. Their candor may result from the fact that they are not expected to engage in intercourse rather than masturbation.

Age at which boys and girls with masturbation experience first masturbated (Table 409)

	All	Boys	Girls
10 or under	20%	12%	33%
11	11	12	8
12	14	15	13
13	29	36	18
14	18	17	19
15–19	8	8	9
TOTAL	100%	100%	100%

5.2.2 Masturbation among virgins

Masturbation is less common among virgins (34%) than among nonvirgins (62%); and among virgins 49% of the beginners, compared with 32% of the inexperienced, have masturbated (Table 411).

When we view the incidence of masturbation by male and female virgins, we have a different perspective of the sexually inexperienced and the sexual beginners. Proportionally twice as many boy beginners masturbate as do inexperienced boys; but about the same proportion of girl beginners masturbate as do inexperienced girls. Among boys without intercourse experience, there may be a relationship between masturbation and sexual experience in the form of petting. Perhaps some boys are introduced to orgasm through the manipulation of their genitals by girls in the sexual petting experience. This does not seem to be a significant factor with beginner girls, despite the fact that some do experience orgasm through sexual petting.

Incidence of masturbation among virgins

Virgin boys			Virgin girls		
All	Inexperienced	Beginners	All	Inexperienced	Beginners
41%	32%	69%	28%	32%	34%

5.2.3 Masturbation among nonvirgins

Sexual intercourse stimulates some young people to masturbate for the first time. We can conjecture that some boys and girls want to experience through masturbation the same pleasure they receive in sexual intercourse. Unfortunately, our survey did not tell us whether or not adolescents whose masturbation begins after the first sexual intercourse had previously engaged in sexual petting. In any case, we see a substantial rise in the incidence of masturbation among those who have had sexual intercourse.

62% of all nonvirgins masturbate, as compared to 34% of all virgins. There is no real difference between the nonvirgin sexual behavior groups; 64% of the monogamists masturbate, as do 66% of the adventurers.

Masturbation jumps nearly 50% from male virgins to male nonvirgins (Table 407) and, again, virtually 50% from female virgins to female nonvirgins (Table 408).

Incidence of masturbation among virgins and nonvirgins

All boys		All girls	
Virgins	Nonvirgins	Virgins	Nonvirgins
41%	69%	28%	53%

5.3 Adolescents currently masturbating

5.3.1 Incidence

28% of all adolescents report they are currently masturbating (Table 411). By "currently masturbating," we mean masturbation once or more during the preceding month. Proportionally more older than younger adolescents, more boys than girls, and more nonvirgins than virgins are currently masturbating. However, the number of people currently masturbating is obviously less than the 49% of all adolescents who have masturbated at least once or more during their lives.

Adolescents currently masturbating (Table 410)

Boys			Girls		
All	13–15	16–19	All	13–15	16–19
36%	33%	39%	21%	15%	26%

A substantial percentage of adolescents not currently masturbating have nonetheless had masturbatory experience (Tables 407, 408, 412, and 413).

	All boys		All girls	
	Virgins	Non-virgins	Virgins	Non-virgins
Percentage who have masturbated	41%	69%	28%	53%
Percentage who are currently masturbating	30%	40%	10%	34%

Proportionally three times as many sexual beginners and nonvirgins masturbated during the preceding month as did the sexually inexperienced.

Virgins and nonvirgins currently masturbating (Table 411)

Virgins			Nonvirgins		
All	Inexperienced	Beginners	All	Monogamists	Adventurers
19%	13%	35%	37%	38%	37%

The percentage of nonvirgins currently masturbating is nearly twice as great as that of virgins, but this is accounted for by the large difference in incidence of current masturbation between female and male virgins noted in Section 5.2.2. Female nonvirgins masturbate in almost the same proportions as male nonvirgins. However, 67% of the female adventurers are currently masturbating compared with 30% of the male adventurers (Tables 412 and 413).

5.3.1.1 Relationship between intercourse and masturbation

Are adolescents who experienced sexual intercourse during the preceding month more likely or less likely to have also masturbated during the preceding month?

37% of all nonvirgin adolescents who had current intercourse experience—sexual intercourse during the past month—masturbated within the past month. 37% (by coincidence the same percentage) of nonvirgins who did not have intercourse during the preceding month *did* masturbate (Table 359).

36% of the nonvirgin boys who had intercourse during the preceding month also masturbated during that period, but 44% of those who did *not* have intercourse during the preceding month also masturbated during the month (Table 360). In other words, a higher percentage of boys without current intercourse, compared to those currently having intercourse, do currently masturbate. One can conclude from this figure that there is some tendency for males to forego masturbation if they have intercourse.

The story is different for girls. 39% of the nonvirgin girls who had intercourse during the preceding month also masturbated; 20% of the nonvirgin girls who did not have intercourse during the preceding month masturbated during the past month (Table 361). This means that girls currently having intercourse report current masturbation twice as often as girls who do not have current intercourse.

In comparing these data, we believe that there may be a significant connection between intercourse and masturbation—current sexual intercourse seems to decrease masturbation among boys, while it appears to increase masturbation among girls. In other words, males may be satisfied sexually from intercourse and are less likely to masturbate. Females, however, may be aroused but frustrated by their current intercourse; therefore they may be more likely to masturbate as well. The sources of these satisfactions and dissatisfactions must include the presence or absence of orgasm, personal relations between sex partners, and the frequency of both current intercourse and current masturbation.

5.3.2 Frequency of act and of orgasm

30% of all currently masturbating adolescents have masturbated only once or twice during the preceding month. 18% of all currently masturbating adolescents have masturbated at least eleven times, and 7% have masturbated twenty or more times during the past month (Table 362).

Boys masturbate more frequently than do girls. As for those with current masturbatory experience, 43% of all girls masturbated once or twice during the preceding month compared with 21% of the boys. 10% of all currently masturbating boys, versus 3% of all currently masturbating girls, masturbated twenty or more times in the preceding month.

Adolescents masturbating during preceding month

	All	Boys	Girls
Once or twice	30%	21%	43%
Three or four times	29	36	18
Five to ten times	23	21	27
Eleven to nineteen times	11	12	9
Twenty or more times	7	10	3
TOTAL	100%	100%	100%

14% of all adolescents currently masturbating *never* masturbated to orgasm during the preceding month.* This was true for 6% of the boys and 29% of the girls. 61% of all adolescents reached an orgasm *every time* they masturbated during the current month; this was the case for 79% of the boys and 26% of the girls who were currently masturbating.

Frequency of orgasm in masturbation (Tables 363 and 364)

	Adolescents masturbating during preceding month		
	All	Boys	Girls
Every time during preceding month	61%	79%	26%
Sometimes during preceding month	25	15	45
At no time during preceding month	14	6	29
TOTAL	100%	100%	100%

5.4 Pleasures and pains of masturbation

Young people consider masturbation pleasurable and useful not only for sexual release but also for psychic and sexual stimulation. Things they would not ordinarily think about or would not feel comfortable thinking about are somehow licensed in the masturbation experience.

5.4.1 Enjoyment and fantasy thinking

59% of all adolescents who have current masturbatory experience agree that they usually enjoy masturbating a great deal or somewhat. 6% say they do not enjoy their masturbation at all.

Proportionally more boys claim to enjoy masturbating than do girls. 65% of the boys enjoy masturbating a great deal or somewhat, compared to 49% of the girls (Table 418).

* Orgasm was explained on the questionnaire as follows: "Sometimes masturbation results in a climax, or orgasm—what most young people refer to as 'coming.' "

Enjoyment of masturbation (comparison of boys and girls)

	Boys currently masturbating			Girls currently masturbating		
	All	13–15	16–19	All	13–15	16–19
Enjoy a great deal	19%	16%	20%	12%	6%	14%
Enjoy somewhat	46	53	41	37	35	38
Enjoy a little	27	24	30	48	52	46
Enjoy not at all	8	7	9	3	7	2
TOTAL	100%	100%	100%	100%	100%	100%

Nonvirgins report enjoying masturbation a little more frequently than do virgins, although proportionally more of the sexually inexperienced (26%) get a great deal of enjoyment out of masturbation than do members of any other sexual behavior group (Table 419).

Enjoyment of masturbation (comparison of virgins and nonvirgins)

	Virgins currently masturbating		Nonvirgins currently masturbating	
	Inexperienced	Beginners	Monogamists	Adventurers
Enjoy a great deal	26%	12%	15%	17%
Enjoy somewhat	36	36	43	47
Enjoy a little	31	50	40	27
Enjoy not at all	7	2	2	9
TOTAL	100%	100%	100%	100%

Masturbation and fantasy thinking go well together for many young people: each is a solitary activity that meets an otherwise unmeetable need. From what adolescent respondents tell us about their experiences in masturbation, it seems clear that fantasy thinking substantially enhances the psychic pleasure of the experience. Moreover, for the sexually inexperienced fantasy thinking is clearly a substitute for real experience. Only 11% of the boys and 7% of the girls who are currently masturbating say they never daydream or fantasize during masturbation (Table 414).

Age makes a difference in the amount of daydreaming and fantasy during masturbation. Not as many older as younger girls daydream most of the time during masturbation; older girls report more often than younger girls that they daydream some of the time. Older boys are virtually the same as younger boys in the frequency and intensity of their daydreaming during masturbation (Table 414).

While differences are not large, the inexperienced are more likely to daydream most of the time or never than any of the other sexual behavior groups (Table 415). Although a majority of the inexperienced (80%) daydream most or some of the time during masturbation, only 71% of the virgins, compared to 89% of the nonvirgins, daydream most or some of the time when they masturbate. Adventurers (90%) and monogamists (91%) daydream most or some of the time.

Fewer girls than boys say they daydream most of the time during masturbation, but girls are almost twice as likely as boys to say they daydream some of the time (Table 414).

Frequency of fantasizing during masturbation

	Boys currently masturbating	Girls currently masturbating
Most of the time	57%	46%
Some of the time	23	44
Rarely or never	20	10
TOTAL	100%	100%

Pornography—most often in the form of pictures—is available to so many young people that it seemed wise to learn the extent of its use in masturbation. Although pictures need not necessarily be pornography, many boys and some girls at least occasionally make use of pictures during masturbation.

5% of all currently masturbating adolescents look at pictures most of the time when they masturbate. None of the older girls say they do, but 18% of the younger girls say they look at pictures most of the time when they masturbate. In fact, 50% of the younger girls say they look at pictures most or some of the time when they masturbate, compared to 10% of the older girls and 25% of the younger boys (Table 416).

57% of the girls, compared to 32% of the boys, say they never look at pictures while masturbating. 64% of the older girls, compared to 29% of the older boys, say they never look at pictures while masturbating (Table 416). Fewer older boys than younger boys say never, while proportionally half again as many older girls than younger girls say never.

Frequency of use of pictures during masturbation
(comparison of boys and girls)

	All adolescents currently masturbating	Boys currently masturbating		Girls currently masturbating	
		13–15	16–19	13–15	16–19
Most of the time	5%	5%	5%	18%	0%
Some of the time	25	20	35	32	10
Rarely	29	38	31	10	26
Never	41	37	29	40	64
TOTAL	100%	100%	100%	100%	100%

When we view daydreaming behavior of the various sexual behavior groups during masturbation, we can better understand the differences in masturbatory fantasy with respect to gender and age. As groups, virgins and nonvirgins do not differ greatly in the frequency of their picture viewing during masturbation, but individual sexual behavior groups within these large categories reveal significant differences (Table 417).

No monogamists say they look at pictures most of the time, and 41% of the monogamists say they never do. 54% of the beginners say never, as compared with 40% of the inexperienced. The adventurers are a little more permissive about their own picture viewing during masturbation than are all other currently masturbating adolescents.

Frequency of use of pictures during masturbation
(comparison of virgins and nonvirgins)

	Virgins currently masturbating		Nonvirgins currently masturbating	
	Inexperienced	Beginners	Monogamists	Adventurers
Most of the time	13%	6%	0%	10%
Some of the time	37	12	23	31
Rarely	10	28	36	27
Never	40	54	41	32
TOTAL	100%	100%	100%	100%

It was decided not to include alternative forms of fantasy thinking during masturbation in the questionnaire, but personal interviews with other respondents have revealed some interesting data. The basic categories of fantasy thinking differ between boys and girls among the sexually inexperienced. Our depth interviews reveal that they include the following:

For boys

- Sex with someone who is forced to submit
- Sex with more than one female
- Group sex
- Sex when one is forced to submit
- Varying degrees of violence to the other person
- Oral and anal sex

For girls

- Sex with a male who is much admired
- Sex with one or more males when one is forced to submit
- Inflicting mild violence on the other person
- Oral sex (passive)

No significant frequency of homosexual fantasy thinking was discovered among boys or girls.

Many needs are satisfied through these varieties of fantasy thinking. The orgasm, or climax, comes faster and, with girls, is better assured by fantasies. Hostilities toward others can be satisfied sexually through masturbation, as can desires for experiences people do not want to have in reality. Some young people feel that masturbation is good training for sexual intercourse; some girls learn not only what an orgasm is like but also the best manual techniques to produce one.

Some young people relieve their doubts and insecurities through the medium of masturbation. One fifteen-year-old girl reported that she thought not only of "things my boyfriend does to me and good-looking men I've seen someplace before or that I've talked to," but also of other "more useful" things as well:

> And I could find out a lot of my fears that way because I've tried masturbating to some thoughts that I didn't dig. Such as oral sex, you know. That was a long time ago, and I've finally come to that thought. Anal sex I tried masturbating to, but I couldn't come to that. I'm not really free about that. I have had that [anal sex] with my boyfriend before, but I didn't really dig it, you know.

Another seventeen year old feared that she might be a lesbian because of her lack of interest in men. So she masturbated while picturing naked women and girls in her mind to see whether or not she could have a climax. "I couldn't ever come while I thought about them," she told us, "so I was sure that that wasn't my hang-up. I was glad for that!"

5.4.1.1 Role of marijuana

Marijuana users enjoy masturbation in substantially greater proportions than nonusers. 27% of the marijuana users, compared with 8% of the nonusers, get a great deal of enjoyment from masturbation; 48% of the users, compared with 38% of the nonusers, enjoy masturbation somewhat (Table 367).

Enjoyment of masturbation (comparison of marijuana users and nonusers)

	All adolescents currently masturbating	Users currently masturbating	Nonusers currently masturbating
Enjoy a great deal	16%	27%	8%
Enjoy somewhat	43	48	38
Enjoy a little	35	24	43
Do not enjoy at all	6	1	11
TOTAL	100%	100%	100%

The association between marijuana usage and enjoyment of masturbation is reasonably uniform among boys and girls who are currently masturbating. Although boys as a whole enjoy masturbation more than all girls, the girl marijuana users enjoy masturbation at the same levels as do all boys. Thus, for example, 20% of the girl marijuana users enjoy masturbation a great deal, compared with 19% of all boys and 4% of the girl nonusers; 44% of the girl users enjoy masturbation somewhat, compared to 51% of the boy users (Table 426).

Marijuana users, more often than nonusers, tend to fantasize during masturbation. 58% of the users, compared to 48% of the nonusers, fantasize most of the time during masturbation. 37% of the users, compared to 26% of the nonusers, fantasize some of the time during masturbation. However, 15% of the nonusers, compared to 3% of the users, never fantasize while masturbating (Table 365).

Marijuana usage and daydreaming are associated significantly for boys who currently masturbate but not for girls (Table 424). 95% of all boy marijuana users daydream and fantasize most or some of the time during masturbation, compared with only 68% of the boy nonusers. Among girls the difference is less marked. 95% of girl marijuana users fantasize most or some of the time during masturbation, compared with 85% of girl nonusers.

A relationship also exists between marijuana use and picture viewing during masturbation (Table 366). Marijuana users are less likely to *never* use pictures during masturbation than nonusers. And 37% of marijuana users view pictures at least rarely while masturbating, compared with 22% of the nonusers. Girl marijuana users almost never view pictures most of the time during masturbation, compared with 10% of the girl nonusers. In fact, three times the percentage of girl nonusers than girl users view pictures most or some of the times they masturbate.

On the other hand, picture usage by boy marijuana users during masturbation is very frequent as compared with that by boy nonusers. 44% of all boy marijuana users view pictures most or some of the time they masturbate, compared with 28% of boy nonusers. And 44% of the boy nonusers, compared to 16% of boy marijuana users, say they never view pictures during masturbation (Table 425).

Why is there a clear relationship between marijuana use and enjoyment and fantasy thinking during masturbation, especially among boys? This is not a study of drugs, and we are not competent to judge what effects, if any, marijuana might have on responses to the masturbation experience. Perhaps the boy or girl who uses marijuana is more likely to be a person with more pronounced sexuality, particularly the kind of sexuality that affords a richer fantasy life. The marijuana user may be freer in both the acknowledgment and enjoyment of masturbation and the fantasy pleasures that he or she finds can go with it.

5.4.2 Guilt feelings

Guilt feelings and anxieties about masturbation are mostly of another era. American culture acknowledges masturbation in its books and movies; the medical profession and most churches generally no longer frown upon it; parents are usually thought to accept its existence, although only 17% of all adolescents say their parents have "talked with me about masturbation" (Table 57).

The strong enjoyment of masturbation by many is one indication that young people may not feel guilty about it. But because one can feel guilty about what one enjoys, we asked all those who masturbated during the preceding month: "How about feelings of guilt, anxiety, or concern about masturbation? Do you have such feelings often, sometimes, rarely, or never?" 51% of all adolescents responded that they rarely or never have such feelings (Table 420).

Frequency of guilt, anxiety, or concern about masturbation
(comparison of boys and girls)

	All adolescents currently masturbating	Boys currently masturbating	Girls currently masturbating
Never	19%	17%	22%
Rarely	32	38	21
Sometimes	32	26	44
Often	17	19	13
TOTAL	100%	100%	100%

A smaller proportion of girls than boys feel guilty about masturbation either often or never, but substantially more girls feel guilty about masturbation sometimes. Older girls and boys report proportionally twice as often as their younger contemporaries that they never feel guilty about their masturbation. The older girls (29%) most frequently express no guilt feelings about their masturbation; 19% of all boys assert that they often have guilt feelings about their masturbation (Table 420).

Monogamists are the least guilt-ridden group among the nonvirgins: 30% of them never have guilt feelings, compared with 22% of the adventurers; and 13% often feel guilty, compared with 29% of the adventurers. Among virgins the differences between the sexually inexperienced and the sexual beginners are great. 25% of the inexperienced say they never feel guilty or concerned about masturbation. On the other hand, only 4% of the sexual beginners say they never have guilt feelings, while 22% have them often (Table 421).

Frequency of guilt, anxiety, or concern about masturbation (comparison of virgins and nonvirgins)

	Virgins currently masturbating		Nonvirgins currently masturbating	
	Inexperienced	Beginners	Monogamists	Adventurers
Never	25%	4%	30%	22%
Rarely	21	50	20	16
Sometimes	54	24	37	33
Often	0	22	13	29
TOTAL	100%	100%	100%	100%

From what we learned earlier about daydreaming and fantasizing on the part of marijuana users, it is not surprising that marijuana users have less anxiety and guilt feelings about their masturbation than nonusers (Table 368). 9% of all marijuana users often feel guilty about masturbation, compared with 23% of all nonusers. Twice the percentage of marijuana users (27%) as nonusers (13%) never feel guilty or anxious about their masturbation.

One inevitable factor of personal guilt is the extent to which young people believe their own personal behavior is unique. Of the adolescents currently masturbating, 60% believe they masturbate about the same or less often than other boys or girls their own age (Table 422). Older boys and younger boys react in similar proportions to each other and to all adolescents. Girls are slightly above the average of current masturbators in their belief they masturbate more often than other girls their age. But younger girls are exceedingly high—more than twice the rate of older girls and three times the rate of younger boys—in their belief that they masturbate less often than girls their age.

The level of guilt of young girls who masturbate is very high; this may explain their willingness to believe they masturbate less than others. 76% of the younger girls have guilt feelings about their masturbation often or sometimes, compared with 48% of the older girls and 45% of all boys.

Among the sexual behavior groups, there are no significant differences from the national average of currently masturbating adolescents, except for 27% of the beginners who say they masturbate more often than others their age (Table 423).

Marijuana usage makes a considerable difference in how boys and girls respond to the question of how frequently they masturbate compared with others their age (Table 428), although the differences seem relatively small when we consider marijuana users and nonusers as a whole (Table 369). This is because the use of marijuana works in one direction for boys and in another direction for girls in their reactions and responses.

A larger proportion of boy marijuana users (22%) than boy nonusers (16%) believe they masturbate more often than other boys their age; a very much smaller percentage of girl marijuana users (17%) than girl nonusers (30%) believe they masturbate more often than other girls their age. Twice the percentage of girl nonusers (38%) as girl users (15%) say they masturbate less often than girls their age. Younger girls' guilt feelings and their low incidence of marijuana use is one explanation for this finding.

5.4.3 Substitute for intercourse or orgasm

One other major source of potential guilt feelings occurs in the person who masturbates deliberately in place of having sex or obtaining desired sexual satisfaction with another person. This happens when:

- The adolescent is frustrated in not being able to have intercourse or petting with his or her sex partner.
- The adolescent fails to have an orgasm in petting or intercourse.
- The adolescent wants to avoid having intercourse with another (including one who may have homosexual feelings).
- The adolescent deliberately uses drugs to depress or enhance desires for sexual intercourse and masturbates as a consequence of induced fantasy or lessened inhibitions.

We can reach no firm conclusion about these matters, but the data reveal considerable possibilities for further study. As we reported earlier, the data show that there is more masturbation among those who are currently sexually active than among those who are not. It can only be assumed that having a sex partner sometimes encourages the desire for intercourse when that partner is not available, with one's emotions and physical desire building up to the point where masturbation seems to be a very necessary physical release.

The young person who reacts defensively to his or her masturbation may also see it as a lessening of status and self-esteem. Young people view sexual intercourse and orgasm as being increasingly accepted; some feel that it is expected by society. The person who does not seek intercourse will probably not have this reaction, but those who want intercourse or orgasm will not be satisfied with a substitute experience. Masturbation for this person is an admission of desire to have sexual recognition by another.

A sixteen-year-old girl adventurer wanted masturbation for the orgasms she never had, but "masturbation never did anything for me":

> I figured if I did it, I did it. There's nothing wrong with it. If I felt like it would feel good, I would just do it all the time probably. But it never did anything for me because I hated stuff like that when you're alone. My whole trip on anything sexual was that I wasn't by myself. That's probably why I'm not interested in that. The only time anything really like an orgasm would happen was when I read this pornographic book.

She describes how she first masturbated and her concerns about it:

> I was reading it and I got turned on, and I was so shocked because I didn't know what was happening. I was so tired and I was reading and reading. And here I am reading and I realized I was turned on by this book and that was the only other time I felt sexual stimulation.
>
> You know what happened—I never told anyone about this, but I guess it doesn't matter. I was lying down and I had both hands on my book and all of a sudden I had this sensation that I knew what it was because it had happened before but I was so shocked with myself for having it with the book that it really freaked me out. I kind of classified that as a fantasy. I stopped and thought, My God, this is very strange, and I felt like a pervert and then I thought, These books are written for a reason. I was trying to rationalize it and all these things. I couldn't figure out whether it was right or wrong. I still don't know if it was right or wrong. I just know that it happened. And things happen the way they happen so I decided not to bother myself with it.

Young people must experience some physical release in masturbation; the number of adolescents who masturbate and their frequency testify to this. But the adventure, the feeling of conquest or being possessed, and, above all, the love relationship are absent.

5.4.4 Personal privacy and disgust: implications of findings

Anyone can lack guilt feelings about something he does and still be reticent or defensive in talking about it. Almost no one feels guilty about going to the bathroom, but in American culture there is a wide spectrum of anxieties and insistence on privacy surrounding the process of elimination. The humor and obscenities on the subject only mask people's unwillingness to discuss the facts of their own toilet training and bathroom behavior.

Among the sex practices we discussed, there seems to be none about which young people feel more defensive or private than their masturbation. A few young people felt that questions dealing with masturbation in the personal interviews were an intrusion.

We uncovered no superstitions about masturbation dealing with impotency, the spoiling of later sexual experiences, or mental illness. What we did uncover were some suggestions of adolescent personal distaste for the fact that they handled their own bodies in order to achieve sexual relief. Handling one's own body and the various ways of manipulating one's sex organs seem to be offensive to some people. Unlike sexual intercourse or even more deviant forms of sexual behavior, the word *masturbate* grates for many when mentioned out loud. Masturbation, though a private matter, is considered socially unacceptable by many, and some may feel that their self-esteem or even sexuality is compromised by admission of masturbation.

Masturbation is even the one form of sexual activity that some young people classify as abnormal for themselves—solitary, contrived, and devoid of all affection except for one's self, which is being treated as an object. "To play with oneself" is a derogatory term often used in other contexts as an unrewarding or useless form of activity.

Because of the problems anticipated in obtaining a candid response from some adolescents about their masturbation, we deliberately worded our initial question on the subject to foster openness. Although we gave respondents the printed instruction at the top of the page, "If you have *never* masturbated, please skip to the next yellow page," we asked this leading question: "How old were you the very first time that you masturbated?" We did this, knowing that the problem was not one of encouraging adolescents to say they masturbated when they did not, but that the problem was to be sure they would deal honestly and candidly with the question if in fact they have ever masturbated. We are confident that the results on masturbation do not suffer from overreporting. If anything, masturbation is underreported, despite our efforts.

5.5 Salient findings

1. There seems to be no sex practice discussed in this study about which young people feel more defensive or private about than masturbation. Superstition is seldom a factor. Self-esteem, embarrassment, and personal disgust seem to be the major inhibiting factors.

2. 58% of the boys and 39% of the girls of all ages say they have masturbated one or more times.

3. Most girls who masturbate have done so before or while they were twelve years old; 33% of all girls with masturbation experience had done so before they were eleven years old. Most boys who masturbate have had their first masturbation experience before or while they were thirteen.

4. Younger boys and girls masturbated at a much earlier average age than did older adolescents.

5. Masturbation at least once is less common among virgins (34%) than among nonvirgins (62%).

6. 37% of all nonvirgin adolescents who have current intercourse experience also masturbated within the past month.

7. 14% of all adolescents currently masturbating *never* masturbated to orgasm during the past month.

8. Boys masturbate more frequently than girls. Of those currently masturbating, 43% of the girls and 21% of the boys masturbated once or twice during the past month; 12% of the girls and 22% of the boys masturbated eleven or more times during the past month.

9. Of those currently masturbating, 65% of the boys, compared to 49% of the girls, enjoy their masturbation a great deal or somewhat. The sexually inexperienced more frequently report a great deal of enjoyment from masturbation than members of any other sexual behavior group.

10. Only 11% of the boys and 7% of the girls who are currently masturbating say they never daydream or fantasize while they are masturbating.

11. Some adolescents masturbate in order to test their ability to have an orgasm and to gain pleasure from it.

12. Marijuana users enjoy masturbation in substantially greater proportions than nonusers. Of those currently masturbating, 27% of the marijuana users, compared to 8% of the nonusers, report a great deal of enjoyment. More marijuana users fantasize during masturbation than nonusers.

13. 51% of all masturbating adolescents rarely or never express feelings of anxiety or guilt about their masturbation. Sexual adventurers most frequently report often having guilt or anxiety feelings about masturbation.

14. Of those adolescents currently masturbating, 80% believe they masturbate about as much as other boys or girls their own age.

6.
The Sexually Inexperienced

When I want to start balling, I'll know it. Every kid has to decide for himself. If I want to stop, I'll know that too.

A fifteen-year-old virgin boy's declaration of sexual independence

I want to wait until I'm older and more knowledgeable. When you're so young, you don't know hardly anything about life. I'm glad I waited so far.

A seventeen year old boy

Any guy who tried to touch me should have gotten the impression of my not being interested in sexy men. I slapped 'em hard and told them to go to hell. One guy got it on both cheeks.

An eighteen-year-old married respondent who was a virgin before marriage

I know a lot of girls who are messing around, but I don't think they really know what they are getting into. I know they think I'm a square. But they don't think that much about it—like what it's doing to them—kinda lowering them.

A seventeen-year-old virgin

6.1 Definition and incidence of sexual inexperience

6.2 Characteristics of the sexually inexperienced
- **Personal characteristics**
  - *Sex*
  - *Race*
  - *Age*
  - *Region and locality size*
  - *Religious feeling*
  - *School and school grades*
- **Differentiating social attitudes**
  - *Self-definition of adolescence and maturity*
  - *Generational chauvinism*
  - *Relationship with parents*
  - *Importance and use of marijuana*

6.3 Inexperienced adolescents' perceptions of themselves

6.4 Pressures for sexual experience from peers

6.5 Differentiating sexual attitudes
- **Readiness for sex and need for sexual activity**
- **Identification with parents**
- **Identification with society and laws**
- **Moral and immoral sex**
- **Normal and abnormal sex**
- **Other areas**

6.6 Sex education and knowledge of sex

6.7 Reactions to sexually experienced adolescents

6.8 Salient findings

22% of American adolescents have had no sexual experience. 20% of all boys and 25% of all girls either do not want sexual activity as a matter of principle or have not found the person with whom there is a mutual desire to have sexual relations.

6.1 Definition and incidence of sexual inexperience

By "sexual inexperience" we mean the total absence of any sexual contact with another person, other than kissing, that either aimed at or resulted in pleasurable physical reactions. By this definition a person who masturbates is still regarded as sexually inexperienced in the absence of intimate physical relations with another person.*

Broken down by age-groups, sexual inexperience declines as the adolescent grows older. The significant break-off is at sixteen years of age for all adolescents, the percentage of people having sexual experience rising from 68% at fifteen years of age to approximately 90% at sixteen years of age. At age nineteen approximately 5% of all adolescents remain sexually inexperienced.

Our personal interviews found that young people lacked sexual experience (including intercourse) for three major reasons. Almost no one said he or she had refrained from any sexual activity because he or she did not believe in having any kind of sex. These reasons were incorporated into our national sample questionnaire and reported in the order of the frequency of response from the inexperienced:

1. 75% of the inexperienced reported, "I've never had sex with a girl/boy, because I'm not really ready for it" (Table 304).
2. 58% of the inexperienced reported, "I've never had sex with

* Because we did not question respondents in the mass sample about participation in oral or anal sex, it is possible for an adolescent to have had either and still qualify as sexually inexperienced in this survey. But the likelihood is small that one would have had either type of sexual experience and not have indulged in any beginning sexual or intercourse activity.

a girl/boy because I haven't met a girl/boy who I would want to have sex with" (Table 302).

3. 39% of the inexperienced reported, "I've never had sex with a girl/boy, because I haven't met a girl/boy who wants to have sex with me" (Table 305).

All respondents had the opportunity to indicate true or false to each of these statements. Girls most often said they were not ready for sex (56%) and knew no boy they wanted to have sex with (56%). Similarly, 56% of the boys felt they were not ready, and 55% knew no girl they wanted to have sex with. Fewer boys and girls replied true to the statement that they didn't have sex because they had met no one who wanted it with them, although proportionally twice as many boys gave this reason as did girls.

Age seems to make an important difference in the reasons that young people give for their lack of sexual experience. A substantial majority of the younger virgin boys and girls said they were not ready for sex, while a small majority of younger and older virgins explain they have not yet found the person they want. The fact that fewer older adolescents (especially boys) find readiness for sex a problem suggests their interest and willingness once the appropriate sex partner is discovered.

Percentage of virgins who report that they have not had sex because they have not met anyone they would want to have sex with (Table 302)

Virgin boys			Virgin girls			Inexperi-
All	13–15	16–19	All	13–15	16–19	enced
55%	56%	52%	56%	60%	51%	58%

As boys and girls grow older, they also feel less concern about being wanted by someone else for sex. Older girls (10%) feel this is much less a problem than do older boys (25%).

Percentage of virgins who report that they have not met anyone wanting sex activities with them (Table 305)

Virgin boys			Virgin girls			Inexperi-
All	13–15	16–19	All	13–15	16–19	enced
36%	42%	25%	18%	25%	10%	39%

6.2 Characteristics of the sexually inexperienced

6.2.1 Personal characteristics

6.2.1.1 Sex

45% of all sexually inexperienced adolescents are male and 55% are female.

6.2.1.2 Race

87% of all sexually inexperienced adolescents are white and 13% are nonwhite, representing only a very slight variation from the proportion of whites (86%) and nonwhites (14%) in the national adolescent population.

6.2.1.3 Age

The age distribution shows that the great majority of the sexually inexperienced (78%) are between thirteen and fifteen years of age. In contrast, 42% of all adolescents are thirteen to fifteen years old.

The average age of the sexually inexperienced adolescent in the entire adolescent population is 14.7. For inexperienced boys it is 14.6; for inexperienced girls it is 14.7.

6.2.1.4 Region and locality size

The geographic distribution of sexually inexperienced adolescents corresponds fairly closely to the geographic distribution of the national sample of adolescents. The West, however, has a higher proportion of sexually inexperienced adolescents.

Geographic location of all adolescents surveyed and of sexually inexperienced adolescents

	National sample of adolescents	Sexually inexperienced adolescents
Northeast	22%	21%
North Central	31	30
South	32	29
West	15	20
TOTAL	100%	100%

The distribution of the sexually inexperienced in terms of locality size fairly closely matches that of the entire population of adolescents.

Comparison of all adolescents surveyed and sexually inexperienced adolescents by locality size

	National sample of adolescents	Sexually inexperienced adolescents
Large metropolitan areas	35%	34%
Small metropolitan areas	34	37
Nonmetropolitan and rural areas	31	29
TOTAL	100%	100%

6.2.1.5 *Religious feeling*

The sexually inexperienced adolescents describe their religious feeling as follows:

- 19% claim to be very religious (a higher percentage than any other sexual behavior group).
- 57% claim to be somewhat religious (also a higher percentage than any other sexual behavior group).
- 17% claim to be not very religious.
- 7% claim to be not at all religious.

Thus, 76% of the sexually inexperienced are either very or somewhat religious, in contrast with 55% of the nonvirgins and 61% of the total adolescent population.

6.2.1.6 *School and school grades*

Of the sexually inexperienced, 97% report they are currently in school. The school grades of this group of sexually inexperienced adolescents are reported as follows:

- 18% report superior grades.
- 30% report good grades.
- 47% report average grades.
- 5% report poor grades.

20% more of the inexperienced receive superior school grades than the average adolescent.

6.2.2 Differentiating social attitudes

The sexually inexperienced differ from other sexual behavior groups in four major ways:

1. Self-definition of adolescence and maturity
2. Generational chauvinism

3. Relationships with parents
4. Importance and use of marijuana

6.2.2.1 Self-definition of adolescence and maturity

Of the sexual behavior groups studied, the sexually inexperienced are the least confident that they can get along well on their own. Indeed, 64% of the sexually inexperienced affirm, "If I had to go out into the world on my own right now, I think I'd have a pretty hard time of it" (Table 52).

More than any other group, the sexually inexperienced are ambivalent about whether they function as children or adults. Proportionally, two and a quarter times as many inexperienced as beginners say, "I still tend to think of myself as a child because there are a lot of things I can't do on my own" (Table 63); and 90% of the inexperienced affirm, "I'm not a child anymore, but I'm not an adult yet, either" (Table 254).

6.2.2.2 Generational chauvinism

In most cases in which we measured whether or not adolescents considered themselves superior to older people in their forties and fifties, the sexually inexperienced were the least frequently willing to agree with statements arbitrarily asserting adolescent superiority.

67% of the inexperienced, versus 93% of the beginners and 81% of the nonvirgins, saw adolescents as more idealistic (Table 213).

36% of the inexperienced, versus 57% of the beginners, believe "my generation is going to do a better job of running things than the last generation has done" (Table 222).

57% of the inexperienced, versus 40% of the beginners and 43% of the nonvirgins, believe young people tend to be less considerate of others (Table 228).

Proportionally, almost twice as many nonvirgins as inexperienced adolescents (36%) believe young people understand more about what is really important in life than most older people (Table 230).

The sexually inexperienced are less frequently willing than the other behavior groups to assume their superiority over their elders and to be chauvinistic about youth. Consistent with the above results,

29% of the inexperienced, compared with 46% of the beginners, gave higher points to adolescents rather than older people on honesty (Table 206).

6.2.2.3 Relationship with parents

The sexually inexperienced differ strongly from other behavior groups in how they respond to their parents. This is later reflected in the section on sexually differentiating values and attitudes; the inexperienced differ much less with their parents than do members of other behavior groups concerning matters of sex.

While the sexually inexperienced share many reactions to their parents with sexual beginners, there is a difference between the two groups with respect to affection for parents. Thus, only 12% of the inexperienced feel they do not have any strong affection for their parents, as compared with 20% of the beginners and 45% of the adventurers (Table 46). (Actually, fewer monogamists [16%] lack this feeling of affection than do beginners, but monogamists are a special case because of the guilt feelings some have for openly flouting their parents' beliefs by maintaining a continuing and often open sexual relationship.)

43% of the inexperienced agree, "My parents don't understand what I want out of life" (Table 78), compared with 61% of the beginners and 64% of the monogamists.

6.2.2.4 Importance and use of marijuana

Of the inexperienced and beginners, 5% feel that smoking marijuana is an important thing in their lives (Table 30), compared with proportionally more than twice as many monogamists and four times as many adventurers.

13% of the inexperienced and beginners agree they like to smoke marijuana "sometimes," compared with 44% of the monogamists and 58% of the adventurers (Table 126).

6.3 Inexperienced adolescents' perceptions of themselves

Most of the sexually inexperienced feel satisfied about their status, especially those among the younger adolescents. They regard their inexperience as their choice, their decision. They are, in the main, neither defensive nor ashamed of themselves, nor are they frustrated or preoccupied with the fact they do not have sex.

Most young people who want sex have sex. As is shown at the beginning of this chapter, people who have not had sexual intercourse generally do not feel they are unwanted by anyone; they simply do not feel they are ready for it and/or they have not found the person they desire to have sexual relations with. They know their friends have found sexual relations easy enough to have, and they have no fear that they can have sex when they desire it.

Conformity is relatively unimportant to both boys' and girls' decision making concerning sexual relations. Undoubtedly some inexperienced adolescents react to a need to view themselves as potentially successful sex partners and even in some cases to boast to others about exploits they have fantasized rather than experienced. But this is a pressure of conformity that influences how they define their sexual selves to themselves and others, not a conformity that requires them to have sexual relations.

Nor do they feel that their decision is forced: none of the inexperienced spoke as though they were compelled *not* to have sex; no interviewee referred to his parents as preventing sex, despite the fact that some felt their parents prohibited it. The possibility of upsetting or disappointing parents or others was present in the minds of some. But this was a factor to be weighed, not an outright prohibition they felt was imposed upon them. Some younger boys (22%) and girls (9%) even agreed, "I started experimenting with sex partly because it was such a forbidden topic around my house" (Table 74).

Young people who did not feel ready for sex do not seem to suffer any lack of self-esteem or any lack of confidence in their ability to have or enjoy sexual relations.

The inexperienced did not perceive themselves as being abnormal, although 43% of the inexperienced believed it would be "abnormal or unnatural" if a boy did not have sex some time before marriage (Table 41) and 24% of the inexperienced believed the same thing about girls (Table 114).

Some inexperienced adolescents felt they do not know enough about themselves or about human nature. One fifteen-year-old girl said, "I want to wait until I am older and more knowledgeable. When you're so young, you don't know hardly anything about life. If the guy doesn't understand that's how I feel, it's so stupid. It'll be his tough luck." This girl had thought through her position carefully, even to the point where she wanted to maintain a relationship with one boy so much that she was willing to permit his having sex with another: "If he really loves me but doesn't want to wait for the experience [sexual intercourse], he can go out and ball anybody he wants. Just so long as he still really loves me, you know?"

6.4 Pressures for sexual experience from peers

Among adolescents, pressure from would-be sex partners is immediate and direct. Most girls are amused and complimented by the efforts and do not feel threatened. As one inexperienced nineteen-year-old girl said about one boyfriend:

> It was just juvenile, sitting in the back seat and making out. It was such a drag. It's hot in this car and it's cramped—and this duke just wants to get laid and I really, really don't want to go through with all this and so I wouldn't. I just didn't dig it because they were really clumsy in their attempts.

The four main reasons given to girls by boys wanting sexual pleasure are: it's a lovely experience; the boy's love for the girl needs to be satisfied; other people are doing it; and the girl will feel better as a result. None of these reasons are persuasive to the girl who does not care for the boy or is not interested in petting or having sex. On the other hand, they are equally unnecessary for the girl who knows she wants sexual relations with a particular boy.

A seventeen-year-old boy expresses surprise at the ease with which he can persuade girls to have sexual relations.

> Well, many times I was shocked at the results of just telling a girl that I loved her and how that changed her views. Like when I'm first talking to a person I can never have sex or something like that. But when it really comes down to it and you both have a warm, passionate feeling toward each other, I think the idea changes quite a bit no matter how you've been raised, because experience is still the best teacher. And the best thing to do is to grab the experience while you can and gain all the knowledge that you can. I think that's the way a lot of girls think.
>
> It's also important to convince her that there's nothing wrong with it if you do sincerely love each other. And I am telling her that I don't want to force her into my ideas, but if she really loves me there is nothing wrong with it. I say that's what sex was based upon in the beginning. Sometimes a girl will be a little standoffish and you have to let her think about it. But mainly when she thinks about it and her emotions aren't mixed up with it, her mind changes quite a bit. When a girl's emotionally involved in the idea, she is not able to think about it as clearly as a person who is not.

A seventeen-year-old girl discusses what she calls "emotional blackmail."

> Well, there's the emotional blackmail thing . . . I mean if you love me you would, and if you don't love me I guess you won't. That's one way.
>
> Another way which some boys do a lot but which was tried with me only once is when a boy says that if you won't have intercourse, he'll say you did. That is really blackmail. When it happened to me, the next day a lot of people came up to me and asked me for some body, which I did not quite expect to hear. They were asking me for

myself. Some body not being a person . . . some body being my body. But a lot of boys have some ways of trying to talk you into doing something you really don't want to do. They say you really want to do it anyway, so why not? They say your body wants to do it physically even though you don't want to do it emotionally, and they ask you to consider your body more than your mind.

This is not to say that various gambits initiated by boys do not succeed. They do succeed daily, as demonstrated in detail in Chapter 8 concerning one's first experience of sexual intercourse. Few gambits are used by sexual beginners as we learn in Chapter 7, because two people who spend any time together and are at all sexually inclined tend to find themselves engaged in at least occasional sexual petting activities without formal suggestions or informal gambits. Boys tend to give considerable thought to what they should say to persuade girls about sexual intercourse and how they should say it, while girls do not generally plan any gambits or games but express themselves spontaneously when they feel the occasion requires it.

6.5 Differentiating sexual attitudes

The inexperienced are second only to adventurers in the number of ways their sexual values and attitudes are unique from those of other behavior groups. The major differences lie in their attitudes toward:

1. Readiness for sex and need for sexual activity
2. Identification with parents
3. Identification with society and laws
4. Moral and immoral sex
5. Normal and abnormal sex
6. Other areas

6.5.1 Readiness for sex and need for sexual activity

Proportionally twice as many inexperienced (75%) as beginners (37%) agree, "I've never had sex with a girl/boy, because I'm not ready for it" (Table 304). 39% of the inexperienced, compared with 14% of the beginners, are willing to concede they have never had "sex because I haven't yet met a girl/boy who wants to have sex with me" (Table 305). Both of these statements reflect a greater lack of self-confidence on the part of the inexperienced. This conclusion is further buttressed by the fact that 33% of the inexperienced think of themselves as being sexually attractive, versus 60% of the nonvirgins (Table 162). On the other hand, when it comes to the question of not having sex "because I haven't yet met a boy/girl who I would want to have sex with" (Table 302), inexperienced (58%) and beginners (51%) nearly agree.

Readiness for sex may in part be reflected by knowledge of what actions need to be taken in connection with sexual activity. Proportionally three times more inexperienced females (57%) than nonvirgin females affirm, "There isn't any place where I could go to get birth control pills or contraceptives" (Table 105).

60% of all adolescents, with no variation between older boys and girls, claim they "get a lot of satisfaction" out of their sex lives (Table 18). Only half as many inexperienced claimed satisfaction (33%), versus 47% of the beginners and 80% of the nonvirgins. A question that must go unanswered in this study is whether or not dissatisfaction with one's sex life is a function of one's personality, age, emotional factors, or in fact the degree of one's sexual experience. Whatever the combination of factors, the inexperienced group distinguishes itself by the relatively large number of its members who are not satisfied with their sex lives.

6.5.2 Identification with parents

The stronger relationship with parents mentioned earlier is borne out by the attitudes of the sexually inexperienced toward their parents in matters of sex; these attitudes contrast strongly with the attitudes of other sexual behavior groups toward their parents. A major consideration is that the sexually inexperienced not only feel younger than other groups—which, indeed, they are—but they feel less confident in discussing sex with their parents because of their youth. Among virgins, proportionally more than twice as many inexperienced (44%) as beginners (19%) agree they do not talk about sex with their parents "because their attitude is that I'm too young to know anything" (Table 40).

The sexually inexperienced are far less critical of their parents' sexual ideas than are members of other sexual behavior groups. The percentage of virgins believing their parents' ideas about sex are wrong is much smaller than the corresponding percentage of nonvirgins (Table 10). Moreover, virgins, to a lesser degree than nonvirgins, express the wish that they could agree more with their parents (Table 13).

Of the inexperienced, 77% believe that their sexual behavior is "pretty much" the way their parents would want it to be, versus 28% of the nonvirgins (Table 96). This confidence is reinforced by the belief on the part of 81% of the inexperienced that their parents do *not* assume they are having sex (Table 167).

Thus, most of the inexperienced feel that their relationships with their parents are not hurt by disagreements about sexual behavior. (No doubt a very large factor in this result is the fact that their sexual behavior by our definition is confined to masturbation or insignificant activities not reported by respondents.)

Adolescents agreeing, "Hassles about my sexual behavior cause a lot of bad vibes between myself and my parents" (Table 75).

All adolescents	Virgins		Nonvirgins	
	Inexperienced	Beginners	Monogamists	Adventurers
19%	5%	13%	27%	38%

In considerable part, this evidence of concern on the part of so few must be due to thc fact that only 18% of the inexperienced feel the effect of any concealment of sexual activity on their closeness to their parents (Table 132).

6.5.3 Identification with society and laws

The sexually inexperienced express a strong desire for society's approval of their sexual conduct. Again, of course, the fact that their sexual behavior is minimal argues against any conflicts in their own minds between their sexual behavior and society's expectations. Nonetheless, their pattern of responses suggests strong ideals on the part of many against violating laws or social mores.

Thus, 67% of the inexperienced agree, "So far as sex is concerned, I wouldn't do anything that society would disapprove of" (Table 50), while proportionally less than half as many beginners and a third as many nonvirgins agreed.

Moreover, it is in accordance with society's expectations that a majority of the inexperienced identify what is moral and immoral.

Adolescents agreeing, "Sexual activities that society is opposed to are immoral" (Table 211).

All adolescents	Virgins		Nonvirgins
	Inexperienced	Beginners	
38%	60%	33%	27%

The sexually inexperienced are also committed to the law to a far greater degree than other behavior groups, at least with respect to their sexual values and attitudes. Not only do they tend to support existing laws to a greater degree than others, but they support laws which control sexual behavior. However, it cannot always be clear, without further analysis beyond the scope of this report, to what extent we are describing support for laws because they are laws or support for laws as means for enforcing what respondents believe in.

30% of the inexperienced are somewhat in the minority when they agree that there should not be any laws against having sex with a girl under the age of sixteen (Table 59). Relatively half again as many beginners and twice as many nonvirgins oppose such laws. Even 44% of younger girls—the very girls in whose interest such laws are written—oppose these "statutory rape" laws.

In fact, the inexperienced are in several ways uniquely differentiated from other sexual behavior groups with respect to their attitudes toward laws about sex. Other than statutory rape, the stand taken by the inexperienced in favor of legislation is particularly marked with respect to prostitution, fornication (sexual intercourse among the unmarried), and movie censorship.

Adolescents supporting various sex laws

	All adolescents	Virgins: Inexperienced	Virgins: Beginners	Nonvirgins
Against prostitution (Table 239)	58%	78%	54%	48%
Against statutory rape (Table 59)	49	68	53	38
Against fornication (Table 219)	37	58	40	25
For movie censorship (Table 250)	31	49	22	25

The inexperienced are also unique in the high proportion that favor unnamed laws that would restrict sexual behavior. 65% of the inexperienced, compared to 47% of the beginners and 27% of the nonvirgins, term *false* the statement: "When deciding for myself what to do or not to do so far as sex is concerned, I don't pay any attention to what the laws say" (Table 92).

6.5.4 Moral and immoral sex

Values stressing morality in sexual behavior were usually highly favored by the sexually inexperienced. The fact that fewer inexperienced adolescents than any other group favor the idea that people should decide for themselves what is moral or immoral (Table 28) is confirmed by the uniquely strong moral stands the inexperienced take on interracial sex, sexual intercourse before or outside of marriage, and sex for physical pleasure only.

This attitude toward the sexually experienced is one of several examples where the differentiating sexual values and attitudes make the inexperienced unique, even with respect to beginners, who judge sexual intercourse more liberally despite the fact that they too are still virgins. This disagreement is also shown, for example, by the number of inexperienced who believe, "A girl who goes to bed with a boy before marriage will lose his respect" (Table 200).

All adolescents	Virgins		Nonvirgins
	Inexperienced	Beginners	
34%	66%	42%	15%

Undoubtedly it is in part the lack of sexual experience as well as their greater adherence to religious beliefs that causes only 13% of the inexperienced (versus 23% of the beginners and 37% of the nonvirgins) to believe that they have sometimes taken part in sexual activities that are not consistent with their religious beliefs (Table 81).

6.5.5 Normal and abnormal sex

Few of the inexperienced are concerned about the normality of going without sex or its effects on their health. 14% of the inexperienced agree, "It isn't healthy for someone my age to go for a long time without sex," compared with 30% of all adolescents, 42% of all nonvirgins, and 56% of all sexual adventurers (Table 98). Although a majority of the inexperienced tend to believe that many girls are losing their virginity while unmarried, proportionally twice as many inexperienced (38%) as beginners, and three times as many inexperienced as nonvirgins, *deny,* "Most girls these days have sexual intercourse before they are married" (Table 275). Confirming this is the unwillingness of inexperienced adolescents to agree that young people who get married without ever having sex together are foolish (Table 203); 13% of the inexperienced agree, compared with 24% of the beginners and 39% of the nonvirgins.

Oral sex is considered abnormal or unnatural by 57% of the inexperienced, compared with 38% of the beginners and 28% of the nonvirgins (Table 147).

The inexperienced group tends to be strongly opposed to interracial sex. Almost twice the proportion of inexperienced as beginners or nonvirgins feel that sex between a white boy and a black girl is immoral even if both of them want to do it (Table 32). Not so many inexperienced, however, believe that sex between a white girl and black boy is immoral under the same circumstances (Table 22). Interracial sexual relations become acceptable to more adolescents once they have experienced sexual intercourse and view intercourse as a more commonplace activity.

Adolescents believing that interracial sex is immoral, even if both partners want it

	All adoles-cents	Virgins		Non-virgins
		Inexperi-enced	Begin-ners	
White boy/black girl	33%	50%	29%	27%
Black boy/white girl	30%	41%	27%	26%

73% of the inexperienced feel that sex for physical enjoyment and nothing else is an immoral act (Table 260). Proportionally almost three times as many inexperienced as beginners and eight times as many inexperienced as nonvirgins disagree that it is all right for young people to have sex before getting married if they are in love with each other (Table 196). In fact, 53% of the sexually inexperienced commit themselves to the statement, "Sex is immoral, unless it's between two people who are married to each other" (Table 231), compared to 21% of the beginners and 14% of those with intercourse experience.

The inexperienced are consistent between how they judge others' sexual behavior and what they want for themselves. Proportionally, more than twice as many of the inexperienced boys than either beginner or nonvirgin males assert they would not want to marry a girl who is not a virgin at marriage (Table 103).

Virgins		Nonvirgins
Inexperienced	Beginners	
54%	22%	21%

To the inexperienced, what is and is not abnormal in sexual relations is not frequently considered a matter for individual choice. Adolescents responded in terms of their degree and liberality of sexual experience to the statement, "There is no kind of sex act that I would think of as being abnormal, so long as the people involved want to do it" (Table 261).

Virgins		Nonvirgins	
Inexperienced	Beginners	Monogamists	Adventurers
30%	45%	52%	71%

6.5.6 Other areas

The inexperienced definitely do not feel that having sex together is a good way for two people to become acquainted (Table 279). Again, the rate of agreement moves upward depending on the degree and liberality of one's sexual experience.

Virgins		Nonvirgins	
Inexperienced	Beginners	Monogamists	Adventurers
14%	25%	38%	60%

Paying a girl for sex is considered wrong by 81% of the sexually inexperienced, even "if a boy cannot get sex in any other way," as compared with 69% of the beginners and 49% of the nonvirgins (Table 214).

Guilt—sometimes influenced by parental relationships, religious feelings, or other factors—often discourages adolescents' willingness for sexual experimentation. A girl describes how she felt as a sexually inexperienced thirteen year old:

> In the beginning when I started going out with guys I felt they couldn't touch me at all. And if they tried, I felt that they were really dirty guys because of my religion—going to church and the priest was saying sex is a sin, adultery. Like you'll be sent to hell, you'll burn in hell. And I believed them—I thought if I let them touch me I'll be dirty for the rest of my life. It's really funny that that's what I believed; I really believed it. So I thought the only good way is to wait until I am married and I can have sex with my husband. Then it will be perfect and everybody will love me and nobody will be mad at me. I really wanted to but at the same time I thought, Wow, if I ever got pregnant, man—like my dad, I mean he's brought us up and he doesn't want to see us ruined. He wants us to get a good education. He had so many hopes for us that I felt if I ever got pregnant it would ruin everything because I never thought of abortion, or even taking the pill, and that's what kept me from ever making it with anybody when I first started going out.
>
> The parties we used to go to, everybody would be making it with each other—just kissing and touching each other. I could see it, you know? And I wanted to do that, too. So I did. And someone put his hand on my breast or something like that and I felt really good. I felt really guilty. I would want him to go on and at the same time I'd say, "No, no." He'd say "Aw, come on, you'd really like to," and I'd say, "No I don't. No I don't." And of course, I'd usually have my way.

6.6 Sex education and knowledge of sex

Sexual inexperience does not necessarily dictate lack of knowledge about sex, or lack of interest in what is being said about sex. Although they are not involved in sexual activities, 78% of the inexperienced agree with the statement, "Sex education courses in school are valuable for young people" (Table 285). Not surprisingly, only a small percent of the inexperienced young people (12%), compared to 22% of the nonvirgins, agreed with the statement, "Sex education courses in school can't teach me anything" (Table 3).

But the criticisms are strong. A fifteen-year-old boy describes his sex education in school.

> It was boring. Everyone knew ahead of time what they were going to talk about. Big words. Very technical. They never once mentioned sexual intercourse. All about how fast the sperms travel. Blah, blah, blah. It never changed my opinion about anything. If you're a virgin—I learned at school—there must be something wrong with you. If you have not had intercourse by eighth grade, then you're probably a fag. That's what everybody said, you know. I heard it in sex education class not from the teacher but from the kids.

The inexperienced learn about sex mostly from the inexperienced. Exceptions occur in instances such as that described by an older girl recalling her days as one of the sexually inexperienced.

> One night I went over to see a woman I know and her husband. I walked in, and her and her husband were like kissing on the couch and she didn't have any clothes on and stuff like that. And I coughed and stepped out and she said, "Come in, come in." And then she just got up and put her robe on and her and her husband, like they were really cool about it. Like I was really shocked. But I tried to act mature, you know, and start talking to them and everything and what I came for. The next day she said, "You know like I'm sorry you got embarrassed, but to us it's like really natural and our children see us. There's nothing really bad about it." Then she started telling me it's good for people to see other people nude, and she started telling me about sex. And every time after that when I had my boyfriend, I always went to her—to us she was more natural than she was to her own kids.

Whether or not there is a dearth of useful or serious material about sex in mass media, more sexually inexperienced than experienced agreed with the statements, "I have never read a serious magazine article about sex" (Table 149) and "I have never read a serious educational book about sex" (Table 48). Indeed, as sexual experience increases, the number of adolescents to whom these statements pertain decreases.

Adolescents agreeing with statements about sexual information

	Virgins			
	All	Inexperienced	Beginners	Nonvirgins
Never read a serious magazine article about sex	39%	42%	31%	27%
Never read a serious educational book about sex	52%	65%	38%	37%

The sexually inexperienced score similarly to all younger boys in what they have *not* read of a serious nature on sex, but a much higher percent of the inexperienced are "sexually illiterate" than all younger girls. Fewer inexperienced adolescents than all younger boys indicate a cynicism for sex education courses, which is not explained by the fact that there are a few more girls than boys among the ranks of the sexually inexperienced. However, sexually inexperienced or not, the younger girls clearly demonstrate more interest in obtaining reading materials or are better served by sex education courses.

Why are the sexually inexperienced so lacking in reading materials about sex? And why have few of them read a serious magazine article or book about sex? The answer would seem to be that they lack access to these materials in the proportions reported here, particularly in view of their unwillingness to dismiss sex education classes as unuseful.

One source of information and insight for the sexually inexperienced involves those young people who have had one or a few bad sexual experiences and who desire virtually no sexual contact as a result. None of these people seemed permanently scarred by such encounters, but they frequently wanted to resume their sexually inexperienced life as though it had never been otherwise. Thus they often assume some of the protective coloration of the sexually inexperienced. One girl in her early teens whose father had tampered with her sexually wanted nothing of sex until she found the person she was going to marry. Another sixteen-year-old girl described how she used a first intercourse experience that she did not enjoy to support her natural reticence for any sexual relations.

> When I went out with people and if they wanted to ball me or something, I used to really use that experience as an excuse and blame everything on that. I would say, "Well, I'm not gonna, you know, ball anybody until I feel right about it because I had a bad experience which taught me a lot," and all this kind of crap. All it was was just using that as an excuse. It was an easy way of out-talking somebody. And it worked.

A bad experience that motivates people to become "inexperienced" once again introduces considerable introspection and self-analysis. "It taught me a lot and made me feel my own worth. It can strengthen your morals and teach you a lot. Or it can make you reactionary about boys and make you frigid and stuff like that."

6.7 Reactions to sexually experienced adolescents

The sexually inexperienced have no hostility or intolerance toward their experienced contemporaries. They do not label their behavior as immoral and they seem to consider it as normal—simply a choice that differs from their own. They feel sorry for the girl who has become pregnant or decided upon an abortion, but they do not condemn her by saying that she was wrong to have sex. Sexually inexperienced girls talk about the experiences of their girl friends more than sexually inexperienced boys talk about the sexual activities of boys they know. This is consistent with so many boys' greater desire not to seem sexually inexperienced.

Despite the fact that sex is so common and "so easy to have," most of the sexually inexperienced are not jealous of others nor do they suffer any loss of self-confidence or self-esteem when comparing themselves with their experienced contemporaries. Instead, the prevalence of sex seems to help the inexperienced believe that they can have sexual activities any time they desire, and therefore the reasons they have for not petting and not having intercourse make them unique among their friends.

6.8 Salient findings

1. 20% of all boys and 25% of all girls have had no sexual experience. All other adolescents have had sexual intercourse and/or beginning sexual activities.

2. Three major reasons given for never having any sexual experiences, in the order agreed to by all virgin adolescents, are:

Because I'm not ready for it;
Because I haven't met a girl/boy who I would want to have sex with;
Because I haven't met a girl/boy who wants to have sex with me.

10% of the older virgin girls and 25% of the older virgin boys agree they have not met anyone who wants to have sex with them.

3. 45% of all sexually inexperienced adolescents are male and 55% are female. 87% are white and 13% are nonwhite. 78% are between thirteen and fifteen years of age.

4. In most cases, the inexperienced exhibit less generational chauvinism than members of any other sexual behavior group. 40% of the sexually inexperienced compared with 78% of the serial monogamists and 79% of the sexual adventurers believe they could get along on their own. 60%, or twice the proportion of any other sexual behavior group, agree that they still think of themselves as children because there are many things they cannot do on their own.

5. The incidence of marijuana use and belief in its importance is far less among the sexually inexperienced than among any other sexual behavior group.

6. The great majority of the sexually inexperienced do not feel that their lack of sexual activities is forced by parents, society, or

other young people. They consider their sexual status as their choice, their decision. Most of them do not frown on the sexual behavior of others.

7. 33% of the inexperienced claim satisfaction with their sex lives compared with 80% of all nonvirgins.

8. 44% of the inexperienced, compared with 19% of the sexual beginners, agree that they do not talk about sex with their parents "because their attitude is that I'm too young to know anything." They are far less critical of their parents' attitudes about sex than members of other sexual behavior groups, the great majority believing that their sexual behavior is "pretty much" the way their parents would want it to be.

9. 60% of the inexperienced believe sexual activities society is opposed to are immoral; much larger proportions of the inexperienced than other behavior groups believe in laws restricting sexual behavior.

10. Oral sex is considered abnormal or unnatural by 57% of the inexperienced compared with 38% of the sexual beginners and 28% of the nonvirgins. The inexperienced are far more often inclined to label sex acts as abnormal or unnatural regardless of what the sex partners themselves think.

11. Proportionately almost three times as many inexperienced as beginners and eight times as many inexperienced as nonvirgins do not believe that it is all right for young people to have sexual intercourse before getting married even if they are in love with each other.

12. A higher proportion of the sexually inexperienced than any other group believe they have never read any serious books or magazine articles about sex. But 78% of the inexperienced believe sex education courses are valuable for young people.

7. The Sexual Beginner

I forced myself not to feel badly when they touched me, because I feared I was frigid or weird or something like that. So I gritted my teeth. I didn't dislike what they were doing, but it was the way they made me feel while they were doing it. Like that's what made me stop. You know, I'd start thinking this is really disgusting. So I'd stop right there.

A fourteen-year-old girl
beginner

But a lot of people have some ways of trying to talk you into doing something you really don't want to do. And a lot of people say you really want to do it anyway, so why not? And realizing your body may want to do it, physically you may want to do it but mentally you can't—it will really mess you up if you do.

A fifteen-year-old girl
beginner

I know what was extremely important to me and to most of the girls I know and that was the first time . . . and I really desperately wanted to say [to a girl who is still a virgin] . . . 'Make it good!' It's taken so lightly now. That's bad, because I didn't give it serious thought and I should have.

A seventeen-year-old girl
who recently lost her
virginity

In our survey 17% of all adolescents—14% of all boys and 19% of all girls—are sexual beginners. In other words, they are virgins who have participated in beginning sexual activities but who have not had sexual intercourse. Most young people begin sexual activities by "making out," "necking," "feeling up," and "petting" or "heavy petting." Beginning sexual activities can start among young people who may be together for reasons having nothing to do with sexual activities. Even if they have not developed strong desires, most young adolescents have a strong awareness of sex, and so there are curiosities to satisfy by sex play. There is a desire to discover how their bodies react to other people's bodies. But there is relatively little evidence of sustained beginning sexual activity among American adolescents; this suggests a combination of infrequent sexual beginning activity and a beginning period of relatively short duration for a large number of adolescents.

7.1 Definition and incidence of beginning sexual activities

Beginning sexual activities involve various levels of kissing and touching another's body and exposing one's own body to another for sexual pleasure without having sexual intercourse. The action is often, but not always, mutual. Touching and feeling may involve a multitude of contacts. The boy may feel the girl's breasts and pubic area, and the girl may touch the boy's penis and testicles. Breasts may be caressed and kissed; sex organs may be caressed, rubbed, and manipulated—sometimes to orgasm. Of all sexual beginners:

98% of all adolescent girls have had their breasts felt by boys (Table 513).

46% of all adolescent girls have had their sex organ felt by boys (Table 519).

45% of all adolescent girls have felt the sex organs of boys (Table 525).

32% of all adolescent boys have had their sex organ felt by girls (Table 524).

56% of all adolescent boys have felt the sex organs of girls (Table 518).

95% of all adolescent boys have felt girls' breasts (Table 512).

7.2 Characteristics of sexual beginners

7.2.1 Personal characteristics

7.2.1.1 Sex

43% of all sexual beginners are male and 57% are female.

7.2.1.2 Race

In our national sample 86% of the adolescents were white and 14% were nonwhite. We found, however, that 94% of all sexual beginners are white and 6% are nonwhite. This finding suggests that nonwhites may remain sexual beginners for a shorter period of time than whites.

7.2.1.3 Age

The average age of all sexual beginners in the adolescent population is 16.1 years. For boy beginners it is 16.1 years; for girl beginners 16.0 years.

Percentage of inexperienced adolescents and beginners by age

Age	All adolescents	Inexperienced	Beginners
13–15	42%	78%	32%
16–19	58%	22%	68%

7.2.1.4 Region and locality size

Geographically, sexual beginners are not distributed in the same proportions throughout the United States as the total adolescent population. About 20% more beginners than the proportion of all adolescents are located in the Northeast, 33% more in the West, and 80% fewer in the South.

Geographic location of adolescents surveyed and of sexual beginners

Region	National sample of adolescents	Sexual beginners
Northeast	22%	27%
North Central	31	36
South	32	17
West	15	20
TOTAL	100%	100%

The distribution of beginners by locality size varies even more from the proportions of the total adolescent population. Sexual beginners are distributed at a rate 46% greater than total adolescents in large metropolitan areas and at a rate lower than adolescent distribution in the smaller areas.

Comparison of all adolescents surveyed and sexual beginners by locality size

	National sample of adolescents	Sexual beginners
Large metropolitan areas	35%	51%
Small metropolitan areas	34	24
Nonmetropolitan and rural areas	31	25
TOTAL	100%	100%

7.2.1.5 Religious feeling

Sexual beginners tend to be more religious than the average adolescent.

14% say they are very religious.
55% say they are somewhat religious.
26% say they are not very religious.
5% say they are not at all religious.

7.2.1.6 School and school grades

96% of all sexual beginners are in school, their grades average less than those of each sexual behavior group except those of the adventurers.

17% report superior grades.
23% report good grades.
58% report average grades.
2% report poor grades.

7.2.2 Differentiating social attitudes

The major social attitudes of sexual beginners are discussed in Section 6.2.2 of Chapter 6. Some values of the beginners, however, need special mention.

This group is more strongly affirmative about personal planning than any other sexual behavior group. Only 19% of the beginners agree, "I don't much believe in planning for the future; life right now is the most important thing" (Table 68). Yet proportionally twice as many inexperienced and nonvirgins agree with this negative statement about planning for the future.

This tendency is confirmed in the desire of the beginners not to have a large number of children. 63% of the beginners, compared with 43% of the inexperienced, affirm, "Because of the problem of overpopulation, I would not want to have more than two children" (Table 177).

Beginners also demonstrate a strong unwillingness to identify themselves as revolutionaries (Table 142). 13% of the beginners tend to think of themselves as being political revolutionaries, compared with 23% of the inexperienced, 30% of the monogamists, and 45% of the adventurers. Consistent with this conservative view of themselves, only 16% of the beginners, compared with proportionally more than twice as many inexperienced and nonvirgins, are willing to agree, "LSD and other psychedelic drugs have had a beneficial effect on the spiritual development of many persons" (Table 82). Sexual beginners do not agree any more frequently than the nonvirgin behavior groups with the statement, "I think like an adult, I feel a lot younger" (Table 12); 56% say true to this statement, compared to 53% of the nonvirgins.

7.3 How sexual beginners begin

For adolescents, sexual curiosity often precedes desire, and curiosity can be provoked by many things. 13% of all adolescents agree that they started experimenting with sex partly because "it was such a forbidden topic around my house" (Table 74). 18% of the boys agree to this versus 7% of the girls.

Most young people seldom tarry for long with a partner in this stage. Either they move to sexual intercourse in a relatively short time, or one or both partners resume beginning-sex with another partner. The boy is the more likely to move on to another sex partner for intercourse, although very possibly continuing to maintain beginning sexual activities with the girl who will not engage in intercourse. In some instances, the beginning sexual activity is a prelude to intercourse activity on the same occasion. But the initial beginning sexual experience is usually confined to nonintercourse activity, and this is often male contact with a girl's breasts and/or female contact with a boy's penis.

A seventeen-year-old monogamist describes her feelings about petting.

> I guess I started petting when I first started going out. I really liked it, so I thought why not? And also, this next door neighbor I had told me once, "If you believe something is right—if you really believe it's right and everybody else thinks it's wrong—if it's right for you, then it's right. And if it's wrong, then it's wrong." And I thought that was really smart. I felt that what wasn't harmful was right. And what really actually bodily hurt was wrong. And it wasn't hurting me at all and I liked it; so I said, Why not? And I did it.
>
> Heavy petting, I guess, is touching everything above the waist. I mean he wouldn't be removing clothing or anything like that. That was really strange. I never thought of that—touching the guy. I think that's something chicks think of as pretty far along. . . . I suppose if I had known and I really dug the guy, I suppose I would have—and I knew that he liked it. The guy never brought it up and actually showed me. I mean, he never actually took my hand and put it inside his clothes.

She describes the petting techniques:

> Boys would use lines. Like I said, most of the guys would get together and start talking about who they had made it with and how they'd come on or something like that, and where. Mostly, I suppose, it was at the drive-in. You'd go to the drive-in and park in the back. You'd sit close to the person and all of a sudden he'd put his arms around you and he'd be reaching down inside your blouse. You'd push his hand away. He wouldn't actually say anything, but he'd think he was really cool, you know.
>
> They'd put their arms around you and they'd slowly drop it to your shoulder and slowly into your blouse. You'd jerk his hand away, and you'd smile or something like that and you'd turn back to the movie and he'd start doing it again. And you'd say, "no," "come on," "stop," or something like that. And he'd say, "What's wrong? There's nothing wrong with it." And he knew you dug it, and you knew he really wanted to.
>
> So it would just get around to it again. This time he'd go further, and he'd undo your bra and that would start it. You'd start kissing and he'd start feeling you. Not that many words, except if you were really a prude. I thought I was pretty much of a prude actually, but I thought I dug it. I felt a lot about the guys and saying all they want to do is go out with me for sex or something like that, but at the same

time I dug it and thought it wasn't bad for me. And so I did it. But after a while I wanted to go further and further. And then I started getting really paranoid and feeling guilty. I'd start thinking of my father and if he was watching us—like I'd actually feel him watching us even if he wasn't anywhere around. That would make me feel so guilty that I would immediately stop. And the guy would say, "Okay, if you don't want to, I won't make you." They were always cool about it. They would always say, "If you don't want to—I only will if you want to." And then I'd say, "I don't want to." I was usually pretty nasty, I guess. Usually I would just make out. It was usually rarely that I ever talked to the person. I mean we'd talk and we'd be friends but not really being intellectual or anything like that. . . . We'd go to a show or something like that, that's all.

Males do not always take the initiative. One adventuress of fifteen describes her first beginning sexual activities with an older boy.

Right before I was ten, my mother told me the whole trip because she had the feeling that I was going to get my period soon; and sure enough, right before I was ten I started getting my period. That's pretty young. But I knew what was happening now, and I didn't care because I had no reason to. But I asked him to go to bed with me when I was eleven, and he said no.

I let him go through a whole trip with him molesting me—at any time. I was home alone until about six o'clock every day because I think my father worked then. My mother worked then, for sure. But I remember leading him on. I'd meet him in the alley so nobody could see. I used to ride my bike. It was really sick. It was really a bad thing. He ended up getting another job and moving away. One day I just realized it was not right. When I started realizing what was happening. He didn't turn me on in the sense that a man should turn a woman on.

I was letting him do whatever he wanted. There's only two parts of your body you can be stimulated with. It was a very bad thing. I'd let him get me so stimulated, and I didn't know what was happening, because I was never fulfilled.

7.3.1 Starting ages and current incidence of beginning sexual activities

Boy and girl sexual beginners differ considerably with respect to the age at which they commence beginning sexual activities. 57% of all boy beginners had touched a girl's breast by the time they were fourteen years old (Table 514); 40% of all beginning girls report their breasts had been touched by the time they were fourteen (Table 515).

Boys have felt the sex organs of girls at an earlier age than their sex organs have been felt by girls. And girls have had their sex organs touched by boys at a younger average age than that of boys whose sex organs have been touched by girls. Two conclusions can be drawn from these facts: the boy seeks earlier contact with the girl's body, and the average male beginner is older than his sex partner.

Although more beginners are girls than boys, boy beginners are proportionally more active sexually than are girl beginners. Thus, a smaller percentage of girls than boys were involved in breast contact during the preceding month. 53% of the boys say they felt a girl's breast during the preceding month (Table 516), while only 40% of the girls report that this happened to them within the preceding month (Table 517).

This phenomenon of proportionally greater male than female activity is also repeated in other beginning activities. 36% of all boy beginners report they touched a girl's sex organ by the time they were fourteen years old (Table 520). 25% of the girl beginners say this happened to them by the time they were fourteen years old (Table 521), but it did not happen to a majority of the beginning girls until they had reached the age of sixteen. 43% of the beginner boys report they touched a girl's sex organ within the past month (Table 522), while 29% of the girls report this happening to them during the past month (Table 523).

31% of all girl beginners say that by the time they are fourteen years old they have touched a boy's penis (Table 527), although 56% of the boy beginners say they experienced penis contact by fourteen years of age (Table 526). Yet, within the past month only 9% of the beginning boys say a girl had touched their sex organs (Table 528), although 33% of the girl beginners say they had touched a boy's penis within the past month (Table 529). In penis-contact activity, this reverse differential in incidence can probably be explained by assuming that a high percentage of girls must be experimenting with males over nineteen years of age who are not represented in our sample.

The starting age of beginning sexual activities differs considerably for virgin beginners and nonvirgins. The following tables contrast the starting ages for all beginners and all nonvirgins.

Age of first breast contact (comparison of beginners and nonvirgins)

	Boys		Girls	
	Beginners	Nonvirgins	Beginners	Nonvirgins
12 or under	8%	42%	9%	14%
13	30	16	7	23
14	19	27	24	18
15	15	3	28	22
16	8	7	25	7
17 or over	20	5	7	16
TOTAL	100%	100%	100%	100%

Age of first vagina contact (comparison of beginners and nonvirgins)

	Boys		Girls	
	Beginners	Nonvirgins	Beginners	Nonvirgins
13 or under	14%	48%	14%	13%
14	22	21	11	20
15	44	10	12	26
16	6	11	26	18
17 or older	14	10	37	23
TOTAL	100%	100%	100%	100%

Age of first penis contact (comparison of beginners and nonvirgins)

	Boys		Girls	
	Beginners	Nonvirgins	Beginners	Nonvirgins
12 or under	22%	13%	7%	4%
13	13	16	13	1
14	21	12	11	18
15	9	15	0	24
16	0	28	27	21
17 or older	35	16	42	32
TOTAL	100%	100%	100%	100%

7.4 Differentiating sexual attitudes

Sexual beginners reveal something of their ambivalence toward sex in their sexual attitudes. Three areas are of special interest:

1. Self-confidence
2. Relationship with parents and society
3. Marriage and children

Beginners (88%) are as satisfied as nonvirgins (86%) that their sex life "is pretty normal for a person my age" (Table 26). Indeed, 94% of all beginners say, "All in all, I think my head is pretty well together these days so far as sex is concerned"; 93% of the monogamists and 81% of the adventurers agree (Table 36).

7.4.1 Self-confidence

47% of the beginners, compared with 33% of the inexperienced, assert that they get a lot of satisfaction out of their sex lives (Table 18), but this is much lower than the percentages of adventurers (81%) and monogamists (88%) who assert this. Their indecision is reflected in their unwillingness to judge what is right and wrong for others: 41% of the beginners, compared with 58% of the inexperienced and 58% of the adventurers, affirm, "So far as sex is concerned, I have pretty much come to definite conclusions about what I think is right and wrong for other people" (Table 23).

Only 16% of the beginners believe that some of their sexual activities are harmful to them, compared with proportionally twice as many inexperienced and a little more than twice as many adventurers (Table 195).

7.4.2 Relationship with parents and society

As do the inexperienced, virtually all of the beginners indicate little fear of parental hostility. They wish, however, that they could have more agreement with their parents about right and wrong with respect to sex. However, 75% of all beginners, versus 47% of the inexperienced and 55% of the nonvirgins, believe, "My parents practice what they preach about love and sex" (Table 55).

While a small minority of adolescents agree, "I started experimenting with sex partly because it was such a forbidden topic around my house" (Table 74), only 4% of the beginners agree with it, compared to 10% of the inexperienced and 19% of the nonvirgins. Beginners distinguish themselves for lack of felt pressure from parents in yet another way: 15% of the beginners, compared with 22% of the inexperienced and proportionally over twice as many nonvirgins, believe that their parents are anxious about whether or not they are going to get married (Table 91).

Again, beginners' self-confidence with parents reflects itself in their willingness to discuss sex without fearing their parents might make assumptions about their sexual activities. 15% of the beginners agree with the statement, "I'd like to ask my parents for information about birth control, but I'm afraid to because they would ask whether I'm having sex with girls/boys" (Table 166), compared with 25% of the inexperienced and 34% of those with sexual experience.

Beginners also transfer the self-confidence they feel with their parents to their perception of society's acceptance of their sexual behavior: 17% of the beginners believe their sexual behavior would not be acceptable to society, versus 24% of the inexperienced and 54% of the nonvirgins (Table 270).

Moral constraints, however, operate in the minds of a majority of beginners, although they are less pronounced than is the case with the inexperienced. 53% of the beginners, versus 68% of the inexperienced, agree, "Sex is immoral, unless it's between two people who love each other" (Table 207). Only 36% of the beginners agree that sex is immoral "unless it's between two people who like each other and have something in common" (Table 220).

7.4.3 Marriage and children

The beginners' relationship with their parents is undoubtedly a factor in the fact that only 17% of the beginners support married people having sexual relations with other people "once in a while for the sake of variety" (Table 281). 26% of the inexperienced think this is all right, as do 33% of the monogamists and 60% of the adventurers.

Beginners are the least adventurous about having children without marriage. 8% agree that "Someday, I will probably want to have children—but it won't matter whether or not I get married first" (Table 180). 15% of the inexperienced are willing to entertain this idea, along with 39% of the monogamists and 56% of the adventurers.

Beginners are less in support of abortion than is any other sexual behavior group.

Adolescents agreeing, "If two people are going to have a baby that neither person really wants, it is all right for the girl to have an abortion" (Table 278).

All adolescents	Virgins		Nonvirgins	
	Inexperienced	Beginners	Monogamists	Adventurers
51%	48%	37%	60%	70%

Beginners see marriage as being advantageous to the sexual relationship. 88% of all beginners agree, "Marriage would make sex even more enjoyable, because both people would know that they really belong to each other" (Table 265); 70% of the inexperienced and 60% of the nonvirgins also agree.

But beginners do not condemn sex without marriage. Only 21% of the beginners agree, "Sex is immoral, unless it's between two people who are married to each other," as compared to 53% of the sexually inexperienced (Table 231).

7.5 Use of marijuana

Sexual beginners sample marijuana at the same rate as do the sexually inexperienced. 13% of all beginners agree that they "like to smoke marijuana sometimes," as compared to 46% of the nonvirgins (Table 126). 5% of all beginners also agree, "Smoking marijuana is an important thing in my life," as compared to 5% of the sexually inexperienced and 16% of the nonvirgins (Table 30). Beginners (75%) are nearly as permissive as nonvirgins in their agreement that the use of marijuana "should be up to each person to decide for himself, like with alcohol and tobacco" (Table 130). 79% of all beginners believe that drugs are much more harmful than alcohol (Table 138).

26% of the beginners agree, "Marijuana increases sexual pleasure," compared to 37% of the inexperienced and 42% of the nonvirgins (Table 286).

7.6 Sex education and knowledge of sex

Being younger, on the average, than nonvirgins and often anticipating sexual intercourse for themselves in the future, most sexual beginners have many questions which they believe sex education, books, and magazines can answer. They have more interest and more respect for what they can learn from sex education courses than the nonvirgins have; however, relatively few beginners or inexperienced agree with statements condemning sex education courses. Beginners are also more likely to feel that they have encountered serious magazine articles and books about sex than the inexperienced virgins.

Adolescents agreeing with statements about sexual information

	Non-virgins	Virgins		
		All	Inexperienced	Beginners
"I have never read a serious educational book about sex" (Table 48).	37%	52%	65%	38%
"I have never read a serious magazine article about sex" (Table 149).	27	39	42	31
"Sex education courses in school can't teach me anything" (Table 3).	22	12	12	10
"Sex education courses in school are not valuable for young people" (Table 285).	14	17	16	15

In our personal interviews several beginners said that they wished they had been told more about "how kids get into sex." "It's not that I want to be told what is wrong for me to do," one seventeen-year-old boy observed, "but why can't they tell us how you get into these situations and how you can get out of them?"

Maybe they're afraid they'll teach us how to seduce somebody. But anyone who wants sex can find somebody else who wants sex if that's all they want. We all want sex in some way or other. But I think fewer people would want it if they weren't so curious. They've got to satisfy our curiosity. If they don't, more guys and chicks will go all the way to find out for themselves. And if all they say is that it's bad for us, a lot of kids will do it to find out if it's really as bad as they say. Just tell us, that's all, and let us decide. Maybe more kids will decide like what their parents want. But if they have the facts, maybe kids will more often decide what's right for them. And maybe that isn't so bad either.

7.7 Reasons for refraining from intercourse

The major reason the sexual beginner does not have sexual intercourse is that he or she considers it unnecessary rather than unwanted. Many adolescents do not require sexual intercourse to obtain sexual satisfaction. Intimacy, passion, and affection characterize many beginning relationships, and orgasm occurs for some adolescents in beginning sexual activities.

But even with these satisfactions, why do beginners who have never had intercourse continue not wanting to have intercourse? How do their reasons compare with the sexually inexperienced who have yet to engage in any beginning sexual activities?

A bare majority (51%) of the beginners agree they have never had sex with a boy or a girl because they have not found a person they want to have sex with. A small percentage (14%) say there is no one who wants to have sex with them. Only half the percentage of beginners as inexperienced say they are not really ready for sex.

Reasons for refraining from intercourse (comparison of inexperienced adolescents and beginners)

	All virgins	Inexperienced	Beginners
"I haven't yet met a girl/boy who I would want to have sex with" (Table 302).	56%	58%	51%
"I'm not really ready for it" (Table 304).	56	75	37
"I haven't yet met a girl/boy who wants to have sex with me" (Table 305).	26	39	14

Some girls avoid intercourse because they do not want to use birth control or resort to abortion. One fifteen-year-old girl said: "I never thought of abortion, or even taking the pill, and that's what kept me from ever making it with anybody when I first started going out."

The pressures increase on sexual beginners to have intercourse once they are involved in petting activities. Even though, as one sixteen-year-old girl told us, "Usually the farthest my boyfriends expect is kissing and necking," girls know that more is sometimes expected. But sexual beginners often do not know what to expect of themselves.

Some adolescents who are currently engaging only in beginning activities have had intercourse in the past. (In this study they are categorized as unclassified nonvirgins and not as beginners.) The members of this group are satisfied to maintain their sexual behavior on a beginning basis. They may not want to have intercourse with anyone in the foreseeable future; they may not want to have intercourse with a current partner with whom they are willing to go only so far; or they are working to a point in their feelings where they will want to have sexual intercourse once again.

7.8 The advanced sexual beginner

Advanced sexual beginners have developed their sexual activities to a point of sophistication and imagination exceeding that of many partners in sexual intercourse. We do not have an accurate count of their numbers, but they are classified as sexual beginners only because they have not had sexual intercourse. As advanced sexual beginners, their sexual relationships are often monogamous without intercourse and without marriage, because they do not habitually move serially from one sex partner to another.

Our depth interviews with some adolescents reveal that the desire for sexual intercourse is sometimes lessened by low expectations for its success compared to the satisfaction and enjoyment the advanced beginner secures by various forms of sex and love play without intercourse. Adolescents, usually older ones, who obtain this degree of satisfaction from what we call beginning sexual activities, defer having intercourse for all of the traditional reasons. Yet, some adolescents also understand that they are more confident of the sexual and emotional satisfaction they can receive without having sexual intercourse.

A sixteen-year-old advanced beginner spoke in complete candor.

> I don't want my girl friend to want anything else. We concentrate on each other's needs, and you can't possibly concentrate like this when you're having sexual intercourse, from what I've heard. I know just how to satisfy her and she knows just how to satisfy me. I might climax, all right, if I went into her, but I wouldn't have the

> lead-up she gives me and I couldn't arouse her as I do now with my hands and my body and by what I say. I've read enough about sex to know that.

Asked if he thought his girl friend believed this too, he said that he thought she did.

> She once told me that I was too mature and too sophisticated just to want to come into her so we could say that we had had intercourse. We both have our orgasms. She doesn't want to be a virgin because we're not married. She wants to be a virgin because she's having too much pleasure at this stage. I'm not going to urge it any different.

One eighteen-year-old girl probably has the makings of a sexual adventurer, but for now she is content to pet to orgasm with a few boys she knows. For two years she was a sexual beginner with one boy in whose sexual companionship she developed into an advanced sexual beginner. She said,

> When we sometimes pretend we're different people and he spends a lot of time with my passions, a boy isn't using you in the same way that he is when he's just possessing you for intercourse. Of course he's enjoying himself too, but we feel very close to each other this way when he does things to me and I do things to him. We challenge each other to do our best for each other.

Three conclusions emerge for consideration in understanding adolescent sexuality in these advanced sexual beginner relationships.

First, sexual intercourse is not a goal that is anticipated as much by advanced sexual beginners as it is by the beginners themselves. They feel neither the physical longing nor the psychological frustration that many of the sexually inexperienced and ordinary beginners experience. However, for whatever reason—a particular kind of passion, a desire to achieve this particular milestone, a need for the commitment that intercourse is felt to offer—most beginners clearly move to intercourse without experiencing the advanced beginner phase.

Second, the advanced sexual beginner will sometimes have greater physical and emotional satisfaction from his and her sexual activities than will the person for whom intercourse is a fairly routine physical and emotional satisfaction. The female advanced beginner does not complain of the absence of orgasm or the inability of her partner to satisfy her. The variety of activities with one's mouth, hands, and body, the degree of fantasizing, and the efforts to satisfy each other will often characterize the advanced beginner experience but be missing from the foreplay and intercourse activity of many nonvirgins.

Third, advanced beginning activity often becomes an important form of communication and mutuality between a boy and girl; sexual intercourse in the absence of imagination and sophisticated technique may not serve this function. While the element of physical satisfaction is very much involved in the advanced sexual beginning activity, clearly the sex partners do not depend on this satisfaction alone. The willingness to accomplish more than one's own orgasm and the degree of concern each sex partner expresses for the other are significant ingredients of the advanced beginning sexual experience that undoubtedly generate more emotional and sexual satisfaction for the advanced beginner sex partners than many sex partners find in the sexual intercourse they describe.

Some parents and young people criticize the advanced sexual beginning activities leading to orgasm as differing little from sexual intercourse, and accordingly label the advanced sexual beginner with the pejorative term of "technical virgin." The assumption implicit in this reasoning is that the technical virgin is no more moral than the nonvirgin and in fact is being a hypocrite about his or her virginal status. If, however, we consider the morality of virginity in terms of how young people view the issue—as a question of how and to what purpose sex is used rather than simply whether or not people engage in sex—it is clear that whatever one's reason for postponing the physical and symbolic act of intercourse, the postponement is deliberate, rational, and moral in the mind of the advanced beginner who awaits the occasion, the sex partner, or the marital status considered appropriate for sexual intercourse.

7.9 Salient findings

1. 17% of all adolescents are sexual beginners. Their average age is 16.1 years. They seek and often find sexual satisfaction without sexual intercourse.

2. Most adolescents apparently spend a relatively short period of time in the sexual beginning stage.

3. Sexual beginners tend to be more religious than the average adolescent. 14% consider themselves very religious; 55% say they are somewhat religious.

4. 96% of all sexual beginners are in school. Their grades average less than those of each of the other sexual behavior groups except the adventurers.

5. The most politically conservative of the sexual behavior groups, 13% of sexual beginners think of themselves as being revolutionaries, compared to 45% of the sexual adventurers who consider themselves revolutionaries.

6. Only half as many beginners as inexperienced and nonvirgin

adolescents believe that LSD and other psychedelic drugs have a beneficial effect on the spiritual development of many persons.

7. Boys are younger when they first have felt the sex organs of girls than when their sex organs have been first felt by girls.

8. 57% of all boy beginners have touched a girl's breasts by the time they are fourteen years old; 40% of all beginning girls report their breasts have been touched by the time they were fourteen. 98% of all beginning girls say their breasts have been touched by boys.

9. Although 33% of the girl beginners report they had touched a boy's penis within the past month, only 9% of the boys report this current experience. This difference in incidence can probably be explained by the fact that a higher percentage of girls must be experimenting with males over nineteen years of age not represented in our sample.

10. 75% of all beginners, compared with 47% of the inexperienced and 55% of the nonvirgins, believe, "My parents practice what they preach about love and sex."

11. A higher percentage of sexual beginners than any other behavior group have a stable and happy relationship with their parents in such matters as parental pressure, agreement and disagreement about sex, and willingness to seek information about sex. 17% of the beginners support marital infidelity "once in a while for the sake of variety," compared to 26% of the inexperienced, 33% of the monogamists, and 60% of the adventurers.

12. Beginners are supportive of the concepts of out-of-wedlock children and abortion to a lesser extent than any other behavior group. Only 37% of the beginners, compared with 70% of the adventurers, would agree to abortion rather than have an unwanted child.

13. Beginners in the great majority disagree with statements that sex education courses cannot teach them anything.

14. 53% of the beginners agree that sex is immoral unless it is between two people who love each other, while only 21% of the beginners believe sex is immoral unless it's between two people who are married to each other. Obviously love has far more significance to this behavior group than marriage, although 88% of all beginners believe that marriage would make sex even more enjoyable because both people would know that they really belong to each other.

15. An important type of beginner is the advanced sexual beginner, one who pets to orgasm, usually but not always with the same person. From advanced sexual beginning activities, the boy or girl often generates and receives more sexual and emotional satisfaction than is the case with many partners in sexual intercourse.

8.
The First Sexual Intercourse

I felt really guilty. Like, I thought, I wondered if my mother really knew. Like when I came in from the drive-in, I felt I had guilt, just guilt, written all over my face.

An eighteen-year-old girl describing her first sexual intercourse at sixteen

Once you've had sex, you know, you're really like trying to justify it in your own mind. I mean, so you change your views really drastically.

A seventeen-year-old girl

Well, I had never done it before. It was a kind of a new experience. Like a child playing with a dog or a cat, you know. The parent brings home the pet and you wonder about it. Pretty soon you get kind of attached to it. And it becomes your plaything. Pretty soon you take the dog out for a walk and you get pretty attached to it.

A nineteen-year-old married man discussing his first sexual intercourse

I was fifteen and he was twenty-six or twenty-seven. I was a virgin, and I was horny and curious and all of that. So I balled him and I didn't like it and I didn't dislike it. But he didn't try to make it nice for me.

A seventeen-year-old girl describing her first sexual intercourse

52% of all adolescents have had sexual intercourse (Table 404). In other words, 59% of the boys and 45% of the girls are nonvirgins. How does the first intercourse happen? How does the experience of first sexual intercourse differ for boys and girls? What do girls and boys feel they gain and lose when they lose their virginity?

8.1 Significance of first sexual intercourse

Girls often give the first act of sexual intercourse lesser significance than do boys. We used the following measures of significance in assessing adolescents' retrospective reactions to their first intercourse:

1. Belief that first intercourse represented some kind of milestone in one's personal life
2. Personal impressions after first intercourse, with respect to such labels as "afraid," "thrilled," "raped," "sorry," "guilty," "joyful," "mature," "disappointed"
3. Feelings ascribed to one's sex partner after first intercourse
4. Effects on relations between the two sex partners
5. Belief one would do it again—at that same age and with the same sex partner

For most boys first sexual intercourse assumes its greatest significance before it happens. Boys have strong anticipations of physical pleasure; many boys anticipate that their status and self-esteem will be increased by their first sex act.

The physical reaction, while not always satisfactory or living up to anticipations, is greatest in most boys immediately after their first intercourse. But intercourse has psychological rewards as well. Many feel that a milestone has been reached and that they are closer to being adults after the first intercourse encounter. Boys report twice as frequently as girls that they experienced feelings of maturity, joy, and thrill after their first intercourse (Table 510).

Not much time elapses, however, before the experience becomes either one of many successive incidents of intercourse or gets swallowed up in the stream of many different experiences a boy has in growing up. After first intercourse most boys do not feel they have lost something or sacrificed their integrity or a quality of their personalities. Some boys feel their virginity is something to rid themselves of. Boys rarely complain that they were forced into their first intercourse experience by their sex partners, although many feel the event was unplanned or accidental.

The usual adolescent girl does not anticipate her first sexual intercourse as an isolated experience. Few girls doubt they will have it; but they seem to fantasize about it in advance less often than boys, except when their immediate sexual needs are great. Because many adolescents view sexual behavior as a personal moral question, they tend to have certain criteria about the circumstances under which they will have sexual intercourse. Most nonvirgin girls say they follow the criteria they set for themselves.

Once she has had her first sexual intercourse, a girl often feels different about herself—not deprived or bereft of her virginity, but different *within* herself. She seldom feels raped or violated by the experience, although she may feel her first sex partner was insensitive. She does feel more mature and experienced—but in a mildly defensive sense. She sometimes feels the need to rationalize what she has done and to feel more sympathetic with girls who have also had their first sexual experience. This reaction is not diminished even when she continues to have intercourse with the same or other boys. She is, as one girl told us, "now on the other side of the fence," or, as another girl put it, "You're like trying to justify it in your mind . . . so you change your views really drastically." Many girls characterize their first intercourse as a "learning experience"; girls many times more frequently than boys report reactions of guilt, sorrow, and disappointment (Table 510).

This changing self-perspective—not just the sexual intercourse itself—makes the first intercourse so significant to many girls. An event in itself can be dismissed, but its effects on oneself cannot.

Some girls wonder at the "magnitude of giving one's self" to another: "After that experience," a fifteen-year-old girl told us in describing her first sexual intercourse of a few months ago, "it really screwed me up. I didn't get uptight because I still like boys. But I decided I'd be very careful and I haven't balled since." By "screwed up," she means that she "couldn't understand myself . . . couldn't be sure why I would think one thing and do another . . . couldn't trust myself so much anymore."

A girl, now fourteen, describes how she lost her virginity at twelve: "I was—aaah—I remember it was the most horrible thing that ever happened to me. I guess it was because I was too young."

Still another girl, who lost her virginity at thirteen with someone she loved, recalls the occasion differently.

> I knew what was going to happen to me, and I wasn't scared, because I trusted him. I knew that he wouldn't hurt me. But I just kind of was in shock, you know. I remember he was asking me: "Are you okay?" I just lay there. It doesn't make me feel bad or anything even though I was pretty young, so I guess it isn't going to leave me with a complex. And I can talk about it.

The psychic effects of first intercourse may be harder to accept for the girl who has it with someone she feels little affection for than for the girl who feels she loves her first sex partner. A girl may feel that the physical experience was extremely unusual, and that it is a far more natural experience with someone she loves.

8.2 Circumstances of first sexual intercourse

Boys rehearse the first sexual intercourse over and over again in their fantasies, but girls seldom plan the first intercourse. One form of evidence showing the lack of advance planning concerns the use of contraceptive devices: the majority of boys and girls used nothing.

8.2.1 Use of birth control

A majority of all nonvirgin adolescents answer no to the question: "The first time that you had sex with a girl/boy, did either you or the girl/boy make use of any birth control method, or do anything else to cut down on the risk of the girl/you becoming pregnant?" (Table 429). Thus, neither sex partner used any birth control method in 55% of the cases of first intercourse; another 13% are not sure if the other sex partner (girls) used a contraceptive device.

Use of birth control in first intercourse (boys and girls)

	All	Boys	Girls
Yes—used birth control method or did something	32%	28%	37%
Boy did not—didn't know if girl did	13	23	—
No—did nothing	55	49	63
TOTAL	100%	100%	100%

The older the boy sex partner at the time of first intercourse, the more frequently the girl made some effort to avoid pregnancy. Almost twice as many girls whose sex partner was seventeen to nineteen years old used some method of birth control during their first intercourse compared to girls whose sex partner was sixteen years old or less.

Use of birth control in first intercourse (girls)

	Age of first boy sex partner	
	13–16	17–19
Girl did use some birth control method	26%	45%
Girl did not use some birth control method	74	55
TOTAL	100%	100%

More details about the use of birth control methods are found in Chapter 13.

8.2.2 Place

Girls and boys most frequently had their first intercourse in their own home or in their first sex partner's home. For boys the single most frequent place of first intercourse was outdoors. This does not vary significantly by age for either boys or girls, except that younger boys had their first intercourse outdoors almost 50% more frequently than older boys (Table 530).

Girls and boys differ somewhat in naming certain locations as the site of their first intercourse. This is not unexpected, because we know that girls more frequently had their first intercourse with an older boy (nonadolescents, in many cases), while boys more often had first sex partners their own age or younger. Hotels or motels attracted virtually no boys or younger girls, although 8% of the older girls name a hotel or motel as the place they had their first intercourse. All girls (24%) report the automobile as their first intercourse location 50% more often than all boys (16%), three times more frequently than young boys (7%), who, of course, were not likely to be driving their own cars (although they could have had intercourse in the girl's automobile). Because of the more frequent use of the outdoors for first intercourse by younger boys (34%), all boys report twice as frequently as all girls that they had their first intercourse outdoors.

In the past the automobile would have ranked much higher as a location for first intercourse; currently, the automobile may offer mobility to a continuing sexual relationship but is less frequently the locus for one's first sexual intercourse. The use of a hotel or motel more frequent than 2% for all adolescents might also have been ex-

Reported places of first intercourse

	All	Boys	Girls
Outdoors	20%	26%	13%
In the sex partner's home	20	19	21
In an automobile	20	16	24
In my home	19	21	18
In a friend's home	10	9	10
Somewhere else	9	9	9
In a hotel or motel	2	0	5
TOTAL	100%	100%	100%

pected, but clearly the locale has moved from automobile and hotel to home. One possible explanation for this lies in the number of younger adolescents who are having their first intercourse. As the average age of first intercourse becomes lower, the adolescent is less likely to have a license to drive or to be able to afford a hotel or motel room.

The locus of first intercourse also suggests increased parental permissiveness and greater adolescent daring. We learned from our interviews that many parents are not blind to situations at home in which their adolescent children are sexually involved with friends and boarders. In Chapter 3 we quote young people whose parents would leave the house with a friendly warning about when they would return, fail to question a girl who came in very late or stayed out all night, or ignore the presence of an obvious sexual partner of their son or daughter.

But parental "permission" is only one dimension; many adolescents feel a sense of bravado about their use of their home for sexual activities. As a result of more mothers working and of increased family mobility, the mother's authority in many homes has lessened. An empty home after school offers more convenience and security for youthful sexual activities than might have been true for many families in past years. A young person resenting a mother's frequent absence from the home may sometimes retaliate through sexual behavior he or she knows the mother would disapprove.

8.2.3 How it happens

There is no set length of friendship or acquaintance before the first intercourse. Some people have had their first intercourse within minutes or hours after meeting, and others have had their first intercourse months or years after they have met each other.

A girl describes her first intercourse which she had when she was about sixteen and a half years old.

> We went with each other for a couple of years before we did anything except necking. I'll never forget that evening. We were at a friend of a friend's house—they were real rich, twelve bedrooms and all that bit. We were just sitting in one of their many bedrooms during the party. And we were talking about an hour. And then we just kind of got into things. I don't know—it was the way we felt about each other and everything. I didn't even need any lessons or anything. It just came natural. We talked about it before, but we never made any specific time or anything like that. I was a scared one all along, and I was the one who balked. It wasn't that we didn't have a place. But I kind of sat down and thought everything over a lot, and it didn't seem terribly wrong if two people really loved each other. I just can't go with any guy, you know. Like I really have a feeling for him.
>
> Yes, it was his idea but we both agreed. I had to agree, because I wasn't scared anymore.

A boy tells of his first intercourse at age fourteen with a girl he had met the same evening.

> When I was fourteen I began to worry. I had sex in my mind and I was completely accepting the idea. It must have been three months or four months after my birthday when I met this girl—at school. It was my first date. That's when it happened. Actually she was going out with a friend of mine—he and I were double-dating. We all had dinner at his apartment at first. My friend was going with her when it happened. We were all at his apartment and sat down at the table and he got out a bottle and began to spin it. The way it was spun—I can't remember all of the exact details—my blind date and my friend stayed and I went with this other girl who was his date down to the park. We were sitting in the park and we both knew what we wanted to do, although we never expected to go quite that far.
>
> I had never kissed a girl before, but I just kissed her, you know, the only way I knew how.
>
> And that's what happened. I just kept right on going. One thing followed the other and the other and the other. I remember being very nervous but the more I got into it . . . I took her clothes off and I felt her and I felt my body against hers and I realized that this isn't really that complicated or that unusual. It relieved my tensions. It was like a big question I had that was finally answered. The question was how, where, and when. Like I say, as it progressed I became less and less nervous and more able to enjoy what was happening. In the beginning I must have been pretty numb, I guess, because I was too self-conscious, and I suppose it might have been a small letdown in the beginning. This had been built up to be a very great thing. In a way, I was expecting the world to tumble down. I just knew it was going to be something great, but I didn't know how.

First intercourse sometimes comes as more of a surprise to the boy than to the girl. Sometimes boy and girl meet who do not know each other, and the girl is more anxious for intercourse than the boy. A sixteen-year-old boy describes his first intercourse when he was fifteen.

> I got aware of sex when I was thirteen or fourteen from *Playboy* and magazines like that. But when it actually happened to me in bed, I was more or less raped. My mom had a friend over and she brought her daughter. Her daughter was an insane type. I don't even remember what her face looked like. Her hair was real frizzy and everything. And she came in real late one night and she used to sleep in the dining room. The night before, she stayed home with some fellow or something, and her mother yelled at her when she came home early the second night. And she got mad and went out in the garden and took a bottle of vodka and drank the whole thing. I remember because I was watching her from my room. She drank the whole bottle, and it was funny, really, really funny. And then she came up to my room and she started doing this whole number on me—*on me.* I was really scared. I was petrified. I almost wanted to cry. She just started talking to me and all those other things, and we just had sex. It was always something I wanted to do, but I wanted to back out at the last moment with her. It had no basis. It had no Christianity basis or anything like that. It was just on the sphere of something I wanted to happen. It should happen. And so it had to happen.
>
> It was pretty incredible. I don't know for sure how I felt. It was quite like not knowing what to do. That was the whole overtone of the thing. It wasn't a beautiful or relaxing thing, but I told everybody it was great and I had to tell everybody.

The first sexual intercourse happens not only because one person wants it, but also because the prospective sex partner wants it as well. Usually one person wants it more than the other before it actually happens, despite the fact that certain respondents felt that their first intercourse resulted from strong mutual desires. A sixteen-year-old boy describes his efforts to persuade a girl to have her first intercourse.

> This girl is a very nice girl. She will only go so far, and that is it. There is no way I can make her see reason. I tell her there's a million ways not to get pregnant, but she won't listen to logic. I have stuffed books and articles and things in her. I mean, trying to give her literature to read on the subject itself. *The Humanist Manifesto,* articles on psychology, and so forth.

Techniques vary in approaching a person for first intercourse or in trying to convince a person to have it. One sixteen-year-old adventurer describes his method this way: "I'm enough of an extrovert that I can go up and say, 'My name is Bill. How do you do. What's your phone number?' It works with some girls; it doesn't work with other girls. But it works often enough for me."

Another eighteen-year-old adventurer tells us, "I'm just not that outgoing. But I'll talk to them; I'll get to know them a little bit; and

I'll ask them out. And then everything follows step. I'll kiss them first, and maybe I'll get on top of them, and then I'll take her blouse off. It all follows step."

When girls use techniques to persuade boys to have intercourse with them, they are usually more aggressive. At least they feel that they are. However, in many cases their attitude is ambivalent. On the one hand, most girls who are willing to have intercourse with a boy do not believe that the boy is unwilling, except in cases where they have not known each other for long or where the girl feels a developing, tender love for a boy whose feelings she cannot predict and whose friendship she does not want to lose. On the other hand, she is not sure whether or not she is violating the role of a girl as she understands it. Once, however, she has convinced the boy, whether he was willing or not, there are usually no regrets.

A sixteen-year-old monogamist describes one episode in her life when she was still a sexual adventurer: she convinced a schoolmate he should have his first intercourse with her.

> I told someone one time that he was going to stay over with me. I was living in a school dorm. I just said, "Some night you're going to stay all night."
>
> He just looked at me and said, "What?"
>
> And then one night he was over, and I had already planned on the fact that he was staying. There was no way that he was going to leave. I was tired—very sleepy.
>
> He said, "Why don't you go to sleep?"
>
> I said, "Okay, I guess we can go to sleep." He didn't realize anything.
>
> He said, "Well, I guess I'm going to go back."
>
> I said, "You're not going to go back. You're staying."
>
> "I'm staying?"
>
> "Yes, you're staying."
>
> "But I didn't tell anyone I was going to stay."
>
> And I listened and it was pouring outside. I said, "The gods are on my side—you're staying."
>
> And then he said, "I'm staying—what can I say?"
>
> I guess he hadn't expected to stay. He didn't have his toothbrush or anything. But he stayed.

Techniques for introducing the idea of intercourse mean nothing unless they are reciprocated. Young people look for signals from each other that may escape anyone else's perception. They are nonetheless significant for the two people involved because they indicate whether or not the two want to have sexual relations. An eighteen-year-old adventurer who had exchanged such signals with many girls younger than he describes the signs he looks for in virgins.

> I guess it's in the voice. Something very provocative. Of course if I were describing this to a Martian, the Martian wouldn't know

what provocative is. But it's a difference in mood. Not even the words that anybody says. You can say words in ways that will change their meaning completely. Maybe you speak lower. A lowered voice. Where the other person can hardly hear you. When a girl talks to me that way, I know what she is thinking.

A smile makes a difference. Talking like that, going back and forth with each other takes different lengths of time. It depends how open-minded a girl is. It depends if she can look at things objectively. It also depends on her feelings to you. Some people are obviously going to like me and others are obviously not. And they might like me a great deal or maybe just a little bit. This accounts for how long it takes.

8.3 Age at first sexual intercourse

Of all adolescents with intercourse experience, 13% (17% of the boys and 7% of the girls) had their first sexual intercourse at the age of twelve or under (Table 405).

As shown in the following table, among nonvirgin adolescents 71% of the boys and 56% of the girls had sexual intercourse by age fifteen. Only 5% of the nonvirgin boys and 17% of the nonvirgin girls waited until they were eighteen or nineteen to have their first sexual intercourse.

Age of first intercourse of nonvirgin adolescents

	All nonvirgins	Nonvirgin boys	Nonvirgin girls
12 or under	13%	17%	7%
13	15	18	12
14	15	18	11
15	22	18	26
16	15	12	21
17	9	12	6
18 or 19	11	5	17
TOTAL	100%	100%	100%

The adventurer has his first intercourse at a much earlier age than the monogamist and all other nonvirgins. By the time they are fourteen years old, 60% of all adventurers have had their first intercourse, compared to 43% of all nonvirgins, including the sexual adventurers themselves (Table 340). The age of first intercourse may be a predictor of subsequent sexual behavior. In Chapters 9 and 10 we discuss in detail the age of first intercourse for the serial monogamist and the adventurer.

8.4 First intercourse partner

8.4.1 Age of first sex partner

26% of all nonvirgins had their first sexual intercourse with partners their own age. 14% of all nonvirgins had their first sexual intercourse with partners younger than themselves, and the remaining 60% with partners who were older. Almost a third of all nonvirgins had their first intercourse with someone a year or two older than they were (Table 400).

A close examination of the data shows that more boys than girls have their first sexual intercourse with partners their own age or younger; girls more often than boys have their first sexual intercourse with sex partners older than they are. Although some boys had their first intercourse with girls older than they, a larger percentage of girls than boys chose first intercourse partners several years their senior.

8.4.2 Relationship with first sex partner prior to intercourse

Of all nonvirgin girls, 57% say their first intercourse partner was someone they were going steady with, compared to 25% of the nonvirgin boys making the same claim. Although many girls have ambivalent feelings toward marriage and often want to postpone it (see Chapter 14), 36% of the girls view their first intercourse partner as a boy they were going steady with and planned to marry. This contrasts strongly with 7% of the boys whose first intercourse was with girls they intended to marry.

44% of all nonvirgin boys said their first sex partner was a girl they knew slightly or had met only a little while before they first had

Relationship with first sex partner prior to intercourse

	Boys	Girls
My wife/husband after we were married	0%	2%
A girl/boy I was going steady with and planned to marry	7	36
A girl/boy I was going steady with but had no definite plans to marry	18	21
A girl/boy I knew well and liked a lot, even though we weren't going together	31	25
A girl/boy I knew slightly and was more or less friendly with	19	5
A girl/boy I had met only a little while before the time we had sex together	25	10
Someone who raped me	—	1
TOTAL	100%	100%

sex together (Tables 508 and 509). Only 15% of the girls said their first sex partner was a boy they knew slightly or had met only a short time before. Virtually none of the boys report having their first sexual intercourse with a prostitute.

In assessing what adolescents recall about relationships with their first partners prior to sexual intercourse, the following is clear.

1. Many more boys than girls prefer and acknowledge a shorter and less intense relationship with their first intercourse partners prior to intercourse.
2. The majority of girls offer rationalizations for their first intercourse in terms of the strength of their affection for the boy and the possibility of marriage they saw at the time. But when they view the experience in retrospect, they say that they were not determined to marry their partners. Similarly, girls who continue to have sexual intercourse with their first sexual partner sometimes tend to downgrade the seriousness of the relationship at the time of first intercourse. The girl who says that her partner in her first sexual intercourse was someone she planned to marry is often no longer very interested in marrying that person. Many girls who planned to marry the boy with whom they first had intercourse now say they are presently not interested in marrying anyone.

   Girls who subsequently have intercourse with other boys do not as frequently label the new sex partners as boys they intend to marry. There are strong exceptions to this trend, however, such as the eighteen-year-old serial monogamist who had already been successively engaged to marry six boys with whom she had gone to bed. As she put it, "I would never go to bed with a boy unless I was going to marry him."
3. In our interviews older and younger boys demonstrated the same lack of intention to marry their first sex partner. Unlike girls who often believe that their first intercourse is with partners they may marry, boys tend to avoid any consideration of marriage. For some boys, if they had felt at the time that their first intercourse represented a commitment to marry, they would have considered refraining from having intercourse with that girl.
4. Girls generally feel less secure than do boys in the relationship with first sex partners prior to intercourse. They feel they would have been less likely to be the ones terminating the relationship than their boyfriends, and many feel that an important purpose accomplished by the first intercourse was not only to satisfy the boy but to strengthen their relationship.
5. In a few instances the relationship is formally defined by girl

and boy alike prior to the first intercourse, but in most cases it is the response of each sex partner to the first intercourse that helps the boy and girl decide how much a sense of belonging each feels with the other. Girls often assume that they are not the first nor necessarily the exclusive person with whom the boy is having sexual intercourse. Boys tend to assume that the girl's intercourse experience is her first and that they have a greater control over the relationship than does the girl.

8.4.3 Assumed prior experience of first sex partner

There is a consistency between the amount of experience boys and girls prefer on the part of their first intercourse partner and the amount of experience they assume the partner has actually had. 61% of the girls know for sure or believe that their first intercourse partners "had sex with one or more girls before me," while 41% of the boys are certain or believe they were not the first boy their partners had sex with (Table 433). Some boys and girls who have had no sexual intercourse assume that intercourse experience is desirable on the part of their first intercourse partner.

Adolescents agreeing, "When a boy has sex for the first time, it should be with a girl who is sexually experienced" (Table 276).

Boys	Girls	Virgins	Nonvirgins
34%	23%	19%	38%

Adolescents agreeing, "When a girl has sex for the first time it should be with a boy who is sexually experienced" (Table 293).

Boys	Girls	Virgins	Nonvirgins
40%	35%	24%	50%

Boys generally do not want to have their first intercourse with girls who are experienced in sexual intercourse. They do not want to be "successors" who are going to be compared with others, nor do they like to ask themselves questions about how well they are doing compared with someone else their first sex partner may have had. While they might be too egotistical to feel that first intercourse is a learning experience for them, many boys would like to function as sex and love teachers for their partners.

There are exceptions. For example, a fourteen-year-old boy told us he was grateful that his first intercourse was with an experienced sixteen-year-old girl: "It was a completely new experience and hard to relate to anything. She was very understanding and let me take my time. It couldn't have been better that she be so experienced."

Girls, on the other hand, often welcome an experienced sex partner for their first intercourse—not the kind of experience that typifies the sexual adventurism and wanderlust we describe in a later chapter but the kind that imparts a knowledge of what sexual intercourse is and a sensitivity to what a girl desires. Unlike the boy, she seldom desires to instruct or conquer.

There are various reasons why boys and girls have these attitudes. Some girls assume that inexperienced boys may not understand their expectations from the first intercourse. A fourteen-year-old girl told us: "A girl should ball the first time with a guy who isn't a virgin. Because, I guess, well you know, girls doing it for the first time can go through a lot of pain and maybe they're scared and they're not certain exactly what's going on. So the boy should have experience." And an eighteen-year-old girl describing her first intercourse said, "It seemed like he was an awful child about it. He didn't really care, and he tried everything he could to talk me out of it. He didn't seem very worried about what he meant to me. He was just kinda like a little boy, you know."

If they learn from the experience, girls do not necessarily feel resentful toward their first intercourse partners who they realize did not care much for them. Girls are casual about their first sexual intercourse as a learning experience, perhaps more to protect their own emotions and to avoid exhibiting too much possessiveness toward the first intercourse partner than for any other reason.

Girls report 50% more frequently than boys their sureness or belief that their first sex partner had previous intercourse experience. This is partially explained by the fact that a higher percentage of boys *have* had their first sexual intercourse at an early age than have girls (see Section 8.3 of this chapter). In addition, more girls are having their first intercourse with boys older than themselves; older boys have an even greater probability of having had previous intercourse experience. A second reason why more girls believe their first sex partners have had intercourse experience stems from the impression of prior experience that some boys try to leave with girls during first intercourse. A third reason is that some girls may try to convince their partners that they have not had intercourse previously, even though they have.

8.5 Reactions to first sexual intercourse

A sixteen-year-old monogamist goes into detail about how her first sexual intercourse came about, observing that it was a lot different "from saying 'let's go and play tennis.' " She feels that boy and girl must know each other well.

Two people have got to really know each other. You build up your feelings and talk about it lots. I don't know. Then it just comes natural so that nobody asks a dumb question.

He did it with me like I guess boys usually do it. Usually the guy does something first. First he starts making out. To him it's like kissing and all. Then he goes down the neck. Then he goes down a little farther. And then the next thing you know, off comes the blouse. And then the next thing you know, off comes his pants. And then you're at it. After we get our clothes off, for him all he had to do was to feel my naked body lying against him and he was ready. For me, all he had to do was make out a little. That's all he had to do to get me ready, and also to look at me with a certain look. . . . He would give me tender touches to get me into a mood and then look at me as though to ask if we were ready and I'd look back saying I was. And then I thought it would happen if it was going to happen. Otherwise, I thought we'd fool around a little longer. Kissing and feeling each other.

What were my feelings? I don't know how to explain them except that they were warm feelings. Physically close feelings. There's just something about him that is just shining out bright. Don't ask me to explain it. I just feel attracted to something inside of him. It's not looks. It's the way he acts or something.

The only thing I could think of is the wanting each other, sharing each other. When he began to touch me, that first time I just got chills and quivers and all that stuff through my body. It still happens. Sometimes warmth too. But it just tingled all over—feet, spine, head. Like when we got started into intercourse, I never wanted to be quitting. Just go on forever. We don't talk to each other; we just look at each other. We don't have to talk.

A seventeen-year-old adventuress recalls her first intercourse at age fourteen:

We slept on the floor because there weren't any couches or anything. We only did it so that we could make love. So it was like unplanned, and I hadn't used any kind of contraceptive. So we were on the floor and we smoked a joint and as gross as it sounds we just fucked. And it was just as I thought it would be. And he also didn't know I was a virgin, and he never knew. And that was it. It was over. I had known him about four weeks, which was longer than I have known anybody else.

It was the first time that I had made love, but it wasn't the first time that anybody had touched me. I knew what it was going to feel like. I always know things like that. I always know how things are going to be. Something like that that I've waited for. And I really enjoyed it. It was fun. It was something new to do. I didn't think about getting pregnant, because my period—since I got it so young—had stopped. I didn't get it for about a year, and then the next year I got it about five times, and it's always been super mixed up since then. So I didn't care. I wasn't thinking about it and he wasn't thinking about it, which made me resent him later. I went into the kitchen and I took a clean towel and I cleaned myself with it and put it in the hamper. And that's all I remember. I saw him after that for a few months. And it was very natural, you know. We used to make love in my room after school all the time. And we used to park and get it on all the time. I never slept any place with him after that. That was the only time. I slept at his house once, but my mother knew. She didn't tell me that she knew, but she knew I wasn't where I said I was going to be. It was obvious I wasn't where I said I was going to be.

8.5.1 Immediate reactions

Young people have a wide variety of reactions to their first sexual intercourse. Their perception of self undergoes change. They view their bodies differently. They react to their sexual partners, to their families, and to society in a different way because they perceive themselves differently and because they know something about themselves which they assume few others would guess or understand.

The following table shows how boys and girls recall their emotional reactions to their first intercourse when they respond to the question, "Which of the words below accurately describe how you felt the first time that you had sex with a girl/boy?"

Adolescents' immediate reactions to their first intercourse* (Table 510)

	All	Boys	Girls
Excited	37%	46%	26%
Afraid	37	17	63
Happy	35	42	26
Satisfied	33	43	20
Thrilled	30	43	13
Curious	26	23	30
Joyful	23	31	12
Mature	23	29	14
Fulfilled	20	29	8
Worried	20	9	35
Guilty	17	3	36
Embarrassed	17	7	31
Tired	15	15	14
Relieved	14	19	8
Sorry	12	1	25
Hurt	11	0	25
Powerful	9	15	1
Foolish	8	7	9
Used	7	0	16
Disappointed	6	3	10
Raped	3	0	6

* Percentages add to more than 100% because most respondents reported more than one reaction.

Boys and girls show great differences in their reactions to their first sexual intercourse. Of the most frequently mentioned reactions by all adolescents, we see that there is a very frequent mention by either boys or girls but not both.

Most frequently mentioned immediate reactions to first intercourse

	All	Boys	Girls
Excited	37%	46%	26%
Afraid	37	17	63
Happy	35	42	26
Satisfied	33	43	20
Thrilled	30	43	13

Boys expressed reactions to first intercourse such as "excited," "happy," "satisfied," "thrilled" two to three times as frequently as girls; girls three times as often as boys mention being "afraid" at the time of their first sexual intercourse. Perhaps because each individual experiences a large number of reactions, all but one received less than 50% mention by either boys or girls; in any case it is not easy to evaluate immediate reactions to first intercourse.

We chose twenty-one items by which we sought to measure relative emotional reactions in two basic categories: (1) Positive, optimistic, generally affirmative, self-confident feelings; (2) Negative, pessimistic, anxious, self-doubting feelings.

The emotional reactions and their frequency of mention by boys and girls are classified in this table and in the table on page 205.

Percentage of adolescents reporting positive, optimistic, generally affirmative, self-confident feelings about first intercourse

	Boys	Girls
Excited	46%	26%
Happy	42	26
Satisfied	43	20
Thrilled	43	13
Joyful	31	12
Mature	29	14
Fulfilled	29	8
Relieved	19	8
Powerful	15	1

There are some vital differences by age at the time of intercourse in adolescents' own reactions to their first intercourse. Fear, fatigue, curiosity, relief, and happiness at first intercourse are in considerably

Percentage of adolescents reporting negative, pessimistic, anxious, self-doubting feelings about first intercourse

	Boys	Girls
Afraid	17%	63%
Guilty	3	36
Worried	9	35
Embarrassed	7	31
Sorry	1	25
Hurt	0	25
Used	0	16
Disappointed	3	10
Foolish	7	9
Raped	0	6

greater evidence among the boys fifteen and above compared to the thirteen- and fourteen-year-old boys. Boys report negative reactions other than fear with approximately the same frequency regardless of age.

Older and younger girls at the time of first intercourse share the same reported frequency of fear. Older girls were more frequently satisfied than younger girls. But girls fifteen and younger report twice as frequently as girls sixteen and older that they were excited, and four times more frequently that they were joyful. Younger girls report only half as frequently as older girls that they felt hurt, foolish, or disappointed.

Why did the girls who were younger at the time of their first intercourse more frequently feel positive and affirmative reactions and less frequently react with negative emotions that the older girls? Was the sex act more spontaneous for them? Did they expect more and therefore experience more? Were they less mindful of any negative consequences for themselves? Why were the older boys more affirmative in their reactions than the younger ones? The data from the interviews and the questionnaires is mixed; we cannot provide a definitive answer to why these differences exist.

Three basic questions need to be asked about our findings:

1. Did these reactions and the differences between boys and girls actually occur, or are their recollections influenced by what has since happened to these adolescents?
2. Why do girls respond to their intercourse so much less optimistically and more negatively than boys do?
3. Do boys and girls with intercourse experience feel differently about their current sexual activities than they do about their first intercourse?

Probably most adolescents reacted to their first sexual intercourse as they say they did. It is a memorable experience we are asking them to relive, and it is doubtful that its memories are dissolved or blurred to the point of inaccuracy. But the data should not be misread. The fact, for example, that a girl respondent did not select certain optimistic terms such as "excited," "happy," or "fulfilled" does not mean that she responded in the opposite way to her first intercourse. No girl was asked to indicate whether she was unexcited, unhappy, or unfulfilled.

There is no doubt that adolescents reporting today on their first intercourse are influenced by what has happened to them between then and now. But we would speculate that to a considerable (albeit unmeasurable) degree, respondents' attitudes today reflect their attitudes at the time of the event. People behave in terms of what they anticipate they will be thinking and doing in months and years to come—sometimes unconsciously and other times very consciously indeed. Even a thoughtless act invites some anticipation on the part of the actor concerning how he will view himself and the event in which he participates.

The majority of nonvirgin girls do not view sex as negatively now as they report they did after first intercourse. In fact, it may be that girls respond so much less optimistically to the initial event because they have found that sex is a richer and more pleasurable experience than it was the first time. In many cases, girls report they consented to participate under more pressures than they realized at the time. Their own lack of knowledge, whatever pain they feared or endured, concern with discovery, and guilt—were all parts of the first intercourse experience; but many girls have felt them less frequently with increasing intercourse experience. Section 8.6.1 later in this chapter indicates that a majority of girls believe their relationship with their first intercourse partner was maintained at an even level or strengthened, sometimes including a very high frequency of sexual intercourse. This strengthening of the relationship may contribute much to lessening girls' fears and other anxieties.

Boys respond more positively than girls because they clearly felt less anxiety-ridden at the time of first intercourse. They knew what they wanted in the sense of the physical act; they did not particularly anticipate how they would feel about it later. Most boys certainly did not view it as an experience that would remain a part of them. They saw their virginity as more of a liability than an asset.

Girls were more often serious about their sex partners than boys prior to first intercourse. More girls than boys knew their first intercourse partners longer, and more girls than boys felt they had a deeper involvement with their first sex partners. It may be that girls had considerably more fears of the effects of intercourse upon their relationship, thinking these thoughts while the sex act was actually taking place. Might their enjoyment and optimism have been sometimes compromised as a result? Did they often fail to receive signals from their partners that the intercourse experience was in fact bringing them closer together? How many of them worried about whether they would not be abandoned in favor of some other girl?

If proportionally more boys than girls considered their pre- and postintercourse relationships as relatively unimportant, were many of these boys able to be more optimistic, affirmative, and free-spirited because they cared less about what happened to the relationship in the aftermath of first intercourse?

8.5.2 Perceived reactions of first intercourse partner

Adolescents recall the reactions of their first partner in sexual intercourse in many ways. To ask this question a week or several years after first intercourse will not necessarily tell us how that first partner actually did react. Any interpretation about the partner's reactions is filtered through the respondent's own reactions to this first experience. More important, in any event, is how the adolescent's beliefs about the first partner's reactions reflect his own mentality and possibly influence his own subsequent history of sexual activity.

To learn what adolescents believe were the reactions of their first sex partners to this same intercourse occasion—whether it was the partners' first intercourse or not—we asked all nonvirgins the following question: "Of course, you weren't inside this girl's/boy's head at the time, and you can't know for sure how she/he felt then. But if you had to *guess,* which of the words below do you think might accurately describe how she/he felt when you had sex with her/him for the very first time?" The reactions are summarized in the following table.

Immediate reactions ascribed to first intercourse partner by adolescent nonvirgins* (Table 511)

	All	Boys	Girls
Excited	48%	43%	55%
Afraid	22	23	22
Happy	42	39	46
Satisfied	41	35	50
Thrilled	36	39	31
Curious	20	22	16
Joyful	25	30	19
Mature	19	17	22

	All	Boys	Girls
Fulfilled	30%	30%	30%
Worried	14	12	15
Guilty	9	8	10
Embarrassed	8	8	9
Tired	17	20	13
Relieved	12	16	8
Sorry	6	3	9
Hurt	3	3	3
Powerful	18	7	31
Foolish	5	7	2
Used	4	5	2
Disappointed	9	6	13
Raped	2	4	0

* Percentages add to more than 100% because most respondents reported more than one reaction.

The most significant finding is the extent to which boys' impressions of girls' reactions differ from the reactions that girls say they actually had to their first intercourse. Boys did not report negative reactions on the part of the girls nearly as often as the girls reported their own negative reactions.

Girls' reactions to first intercourse compared with those ascribed to them by boys

	Frequency of reaction reported by girls	Frequency of reaction attributed to girls by boys
Afraid	63%	23%
Worried	35	12
Guilty	36	8
Embarrassed	31	8
Sorry	25	3
Hurt	25	3
Used	16	5

Boys differ by age in how they ascribe some reactions to girls. Boys sixteen and older err considerably more than younger boys with respect to girls' reactions of excitement, satisfaction, joyfulness, and fulfillment.

Proportionally almost twice as many older girls than younger girls feel the boy was satisfied and felt mature, although only half as many saw them as being thrilled. What girls describe as the reactions of boys to first intercourse far more closely corresponds to what boys report were their reactions than the reverse situation just discussed. Consider the optimistic and affirmative reactions of boys, for example.

Boys' reactions to first intercourse compared with those ascribed to them by girls

	Frequency of reactions reported by boys	Frequency of reactions attributed to boys by girls
Excited	46%	55%
Afraid	17	22
Happy	42	46
Satisfied	43	50
Thrilled	43	31
Joyful	31	19
Mature	29	22

8.6 Effects of intercourse on relationship with first partner

8.6.1 First intercourse

Whatever the prior relationship between a boy and a girl, it is inevitably influenced by their first experience of sexual intercourse. New nonvirgins react both to the fact one or both are having a milestone experience, how each feels he or she is being treated by the other, and whether they want to have intercourse together again.

We asked all respondents with intercourse experience this question: "Did the relationship become stronger or weaker as a result of having had sex together?" (Table 432). Respondents differ by both age and gender in their estimate of the effects of first intercourse on their prior relationship with their first intercourse partner. Almost half of all adolescents believed the relationships they had with their sex partner became stronger as a result of their first intercourse. 56% of the girls believe the relationship was strengthened, compared to 41% of the boys. Almost a quarter of the boys and girls felt that their relationship stayed about the same. Only a few boys and girls—but more girls than boys—felt the relationship had been weakened as a consequence of the respondent's first intercourse.

Adolescents who had affirmative feelings about first intercourse such as mature, powerful, thrilled, and joyful tended to feel their relationship had been strengthened. Those who had negative feelings about first intercourse such as hurt, disappointed, used, and foolish often believed that their relationship was about the same or had been weakened.

Effect of first intercourse upon adolescents' relationship with first intercourse partner

	All	Boys	Girls
Became stronger	48%	41%	56%
Stayed about the same	23	22	24
There wasn't any to begin with	19	25	11
Became weaker	10	12	9
TOTAL	100%	100%	100%

The effects of first intercourse on relationships are probably determined as much by prior expectations and the condition of the prior relationship as by the circumstances of the intercourse. Sometimes subsequent events threaten to deflate the ego and can introduce all kinds of rationalizations in a sex partner after first intercourse.

An eighteen-year-old male recalls his first intercourse experience, which, he says, he hoped would cement the relationship between himself and his partner. But relationships prior to first intercourse are often flimsy because of age, personality, and exposure to new sexual opportunities. Such relationships are not usually influenced one way or another by the first intercourse of both partners.

> I was thirteen and she was ten. We were trying out having sex for the first time. She was my very best friend's sister. It happens, believe me. I know a lot of ten- or eleven-year-old girls who are pregnant now. Anyway, ours lasted for one or two years. But we really didn't mean much to each other. We had nothing.

For example, the young man who had intercourse with another boy's date in the park hardly saw that girl again.

> We had sex just that one time. After that she avoided me. She wouldn't say hello to me. Maybe if I had been a little less self-confident, it would have disturbed me. Why was she doing this? She must have had her reasons. But I have always been—for some reasons, I don't know why—but I have been so self-assured of myself that it never bothered me. I guess it's my background. It isn't something we discuss very much in my family, but it's somehow been inculcated in me that I am better. I know it isn't true now; but I guess you still have this feeling in your subconscious, and it will probably always be there until I die. It's not something that you can logically eliminate. But it sure helps when it comes to reacting to a girl who ignores you after your first experience with her.
>
> Of course, our maid had given me a very romantic idea of it all. And being a woman's point of view, I suppose everything was built up to be much more involved and less superficial about first sex. Because I certainly didn't have any love for that girl. So it couldn't have been anything more than a physical thing.

8.6.2 Subsequent intercourse

Another test of the adolescent's subsequent relationship with his or her first intercourse partner is whether or not the two partners had sexual intercourse again with each other. 61% of all nonvirgins (53% of the boys and 70% of the girls) did have intercourse again one or more times with their first intercourse partners (Table 435). This confirms the findings that more girls than boys believed their prior relationship maintained an even level or grew stronger after first intercourse.

It should be remembered, however, that sex partners might elect to defer further intercourse for reasons that would not necessarily indicate a leveling off or weakening of their relationship. "Do you really love me?" might receive a satisfying response with a single act of intercourse. If one or both partners' curiosity were the main motivating factor of first intercourse, it might be satisfied as well. Guilt feelings, illness, lack of proximity, and a desire to wait (for whatever reason) might all be factors which singly or in combination defer subsequent intercourse. A relationship might also be terminated for reasons having nothing to do with the impact of first intercourse.

The strength of these subsequent sexual relationships is also demonstrated by the frequency of sexual intercourse adolescents had with their first intercourse partners after the first intercourse occasion. 46% of the nonvirgin girls had intercourse with their first sex partners seven or more times, compared to 35% of the boys. 54% of the boys had intercourse four times or less with their original sex partner after the first time, compared to 35% of the girls (Table 436).

Girls have had subsequent intercourse with their first sex partners at a considerably greater rate of frequency than boys. The fact that many girls developed monogamous relationships whose participants have intercourse much more often than other nonvirgins is largely responsible for this.

All respondents reporting subsequent intercourse with first intercourse partner

Number of intercourse times	All	Boys	Girls
1 or 2	22%	32%	12%
3 or 4	23	22	23
5 or 6	15	11	19
7 to 20	16	19	12
21 to 99	11	9	16
100 or more	13	7	18
TOTAL	100%	100%	100%

8.6.3 Retrospective reactions

All reactions reported are of course retrospective; they were not immediately recorded at the time they occurred. The retrospective reactions we are discussing are a person's feelings about whether he or she is happy or unhappy that first intercourse occurred when it did and whether or not the choice of a first intercourse partner is considered to have been a good one. Adolescent respondents were asked: "Looking back at it now, are you glad that this particular girl/boy was the first one you ever had sex with? Or if you had it to do over again, would you rather have had sex for the first time with a different girl/boy?" (Table 434). We also asked adolescents: "If you had it to do all over again, do you wish that you had waited until you were older before having sex with a girl/boy for the first time, are you glad you did it when you did, or do you wish that you had done it when you were younger?" (Table 431).

In retrospect, boys are more often happier than girls about their choice of first intercourse partner and their age at the time they had their first intercourse. Boys and girls do not differ with respect to whether they picked the appropriate sex partner for first intercourse; two-thirds of both boys and girls believe they did.

The key finding is that 54% of the girls and 67% of the boys agree with the statement, "I'm glad I did it when I did," concerning their first intercourse. However, girls report nearly three times as often as boys that "I wish I had waited until I was older before having sex with a girl/boy for the first time"; 40% of the girls feel this way compared to 14% of the boys (Table 431). And 19% of the boys, compared to 6% of the girls, agree with the statement, "I wish I had done it when I was younger."

Retrospective reactions of adolescent nonvirgins to first intercourse*

	All	Boys	Girls
I'm glad it was this particular girl/boy	69%	70%	67%
I wish it had been a different girl/boy	31	30	33
I wish I had waited until I was older	26	14	40
I'm glad I did it when I did	61	67	54
I wish I had done it when I was younger	13	19	6

* Two tables combined cause these figures to add up to 200%.

A much larger sample would have been necessary to cross-tabulate accurately many of the immediate and retrospective reactions to first sexual intercourse by adolescents' age at the time it happened. But this much is clear:

1. The negative immediate reactions that so many girls report having to their first intercourse would seem in many cases to correlate with their wish in retrospect that they had waited until they were older. Their fears must have been an important factor in their reactions at the time. The fact that many of their sex partners were older than they undoubtedly is a factor in the reaction of some girls, although two-thirds of the girls express satisfaction with the boy who was their first intercourse partner. And to the extent that a girl's subsequent relations with her sex partner were important to her, 80% of the girls believe that their relationship with the first intercourse partner was stronger or stayed about the same; 56% saw it stronger and 24% saw it remaining about the same. The girls' heavy frequency of intercourse with their first intercourse partners also confirms this.
2. Boys generally remain considerably more optimistic than girls about the outcome of their first intercourse. In mood and self-esteem, in choice of partner, and in the time in their lives that first intercourse occurred, boys tended to score themselves high. It is true that fewer boys saw a strengthened relationship; 63% of the boys believe that their relationship with their first intercourse partner was stronger or stayed about the same, 41% believe it was stronger, and 22% think it remained about the same after first intercourse. However, 25% report their belief that they had no such relationship in the first place.

In comparing boys with girls, however, we should not overlook the fact that 14% of the boys as compared to 40% of the girls wish they had waited until they were older and that 19% of the boys compared to 6% of the girls wish they had had their first intercourse when they were younger. The number of boys and girls who express these dissatisfactions with the timing of first intercourse, while a minority, should not be overlooked.

8.7 Salient findings

1. 52% of all American adolescents have had sexual intercourse. 59% of the boys and 45% of the girls are nonvirgins.

2. 25% of the boys had their first intercourse with a girl they met only shortly before, while 36% of the girls had first intercourse with a boy they planned to marry.

3. 55% of all nonvirgin adolescents report that neither sex partner used birth control in their first intercourse; another 13% are not

sure. 74% of the girls whose sex partners were thirteen to sixteen years old did not use birth control; however, the older the boy sex partner at the time of first intercourse, the more frequently the girl made an effort to avoid pregnancy.

4. 40% of all adolescents had their first intercourse experience in their own or their sex partner's home; only 2% had it in a hotel or motel. Parental permissiveness and absence from home may play an important role in causing the home to be so frequently used as the location for first intercourse.

5. 13% of all adolescents with intercourse experience (17% of the boys and 7% of the girls) had their first sexual intercourse at the age of twelve or under. By age fifteen, 71% of the nonvirgin boys and 56% of the nonvirgin girls had had sexual intercourse.

6. 60% of the nonvirgins had their first sexual intercourse with partners who were older than they; 14% had first intercourse with those who were younger; and 26% of the nonvirgins' first intercourse partners were the same age.

7. 25% of the boys and 57% of the girls reporting on their first intercourse say they were going steady with their first sex partners; 36% of the girls and 7% of the boys had their first intercourse with someone they planned to marry at the time. 44% of the boys reporting on their first intercourse say their first sex partner was a girl they knew slightly or had met only a little while before.

8. While 41% of the boys knew for sure or believed their first sex partners were not virgins, 61% of the girls knew for sure or thought this about their first sex partners.

9. Girls believe 50% more often than boys that their first sex partner had previous intercourse experience.

10. Fear is the reaction that girls most frequently report after their first intercourse (63%). However, only 23% of the boys ascribe fear to girls with whom they had their first intercourse.

11. 46% of the boys say they were excited after their first intercourse. Excitement is the immediate reaction to first intercourse most frequently reported by boys.

12. A much higher proportion of boys than girls were positive, optimistic, and generally affirmative in their immediate reactions to first intercourse; a much higher proportion of girls than boys were generally negative, pessimistic, and fearful in their immediate reactions to first intercourse.

13. 41% of the boys and 56% of the girls thought their relationship with their sex partners was strengthened as a result of their first intercourse.

14. 61% of all adolescents reporting on their first intercourse

(53% of the boys and 70% of the girls) had intercourse again one or more times with their first intercourse partners.

15. 69% of all nonvirgins (70% of the boys and 67% of the girls) are glad they had their first intercourse experience with their respective partners. 67% of the boys and 54% of the girls are glad they did it when they did, while 14% of the boys and 40% of the girls wish they had waited until they were older.

9. The New Sexual Relationship: Serial Monogamy Without Marriage

When I get horny, I really, really want to have sex, and we don't. But when he wants to have sex, I feel into it but I don't really feel horny.

A seventeen-year-old girl monogamist, complaining about her inability to have an orgasm

When I have love and sex, I'm definitely a happier person . . . I really believe that sex and love cut down a lot of your hassles because you know that there is someone who cares for you very much.

Mainly, what a person's ideas of sex are comes from the first one they fall in love with.

A sixteen-year-old nonvirgin boy

9.1 Definition and incidence of serial monogamy

Serial monogamy without marriage—an increasingly frequent sexual relationship between adolescent boys and girls—is a relationship between two people of uncertain duration and to which both partners generally intend to be true. Either partner, however, may depart when he or she desires, often to participate in another such relationship. A serial monogamist is an unmarried nonvirgin who is having a close sexual relationship with a sex partner and who rarely or never has sex with another person during the life of the relationship. Many serial monogamists enter into a series of such relationships over a period of years. Usually the boy and girl do not live together—in fact, each is usually living with parents at home. In some cases, however, the two may share the same household. They do many things together and as a couple comply with many of the living patterns of married life, without marriage.

21% of all adolescents can be defined as serial monogamists.*

Total number of intercourse partners (monogamists and all nonvirgins)

	Monogamists	All nonvirgins
1	47%	35%
2–3	15	22
4–6	16	19
7–15	22	15
16 or more	0	9
TOTAL	100%	100%

* Adolescents assigned to the monogamist behavioral group are:

1. Nonvirgins who have not had intercourse during the preceding month but who have engaged in one or more preintercourse activities during the preceding month and affirm that they have sex mostly or only with just one person.
2. Nonvirgins who have had intercourse during the preceding month, say that they have sex with only one person, and say that they never have sex with anyone else.
3. Nonvirgins who have had intercourse during the preceding month, say that they have sex mostly or only with just one person, do *not* say that they never have sex with anyone else, but who have *not* during the preceding month engaged either in intercourse or any preintercourse activity with *more than two* different people.

28% of all girls and 15% of all boys are monogamists. Among those who have had sexual intercourse, 40% qualify as monogamists.

Throughout his or her intercourse experience the adolescent serial monogamist has had an average of 4.2 sex partners. But nearly half of all monogamists have not had more than one sex partner (Table 341).

9.2 Essential ingredients

Many young people consider serial monogamy a convenient and ethical means of having sex without marriage. It offers the opportunity for regular sexual contact with one another at whatever frequency they desire. No ritual attends entering or departing from the serial monogamous relationship. No one has a title, and neither participant feels that the relationship is legally binding.

Both partners see their relationship as meaningful and lasting, without commitment to any specified duration. While it is not usual for monogamous partners to make an oath of sexual fidelity to the other, it is usually understood they will not have sexual relations outside of their relationship. 56% of the adolescent monogamists, compared with 51% of the sexually adventuring adolescents, agree, "I don't think it would be possible for a boy/girl to have a real relationship with more than one girl/boy at the same time" (Table 170).

9.2.1 How monogamists choose their partners and view their relationship

Many monogamists feel that the circumstances of their first sexual intercourse had much to do with their decision to enter into a monogamous relationship rather than just have sex with their partner a few times and then move on to other sex partners. A seventeen-year-old girl describes in detail how her first intercourse initiated her monogamous liaison.

> We were just friends at first. It was really strange, because I was on a thing where I liked him but I didn't show it to him because I didn't think he liked me, as a girl friend, anyway. I was so lonely at the time; I thought, "I'm so horny, if I do find a boyfriend, I want to go to bed with him." So we had dinner at my house and we got drunk. Not really drunk, because I knew what I was doing. But I wanted to go to bed with him and he wanted to go to bed with me, so we did. And it was really strange, because I was still on a guilty trip. It was my sister's house and I didn't really know him—he was my boss—and it was a really strange thing for me. Like it completely blew my mind. Like I can't really explain it. It was just really weird, but I really didn't think he liked me that well, at all.

And like, after I went to bed with him, well, like I wanted to go to bed with him, and he wanted to go to bed with me. But I didn't think he really *liked* me beyond that, and I really didn't like him beyond that either. I just didn't want him to just feel nothing for me. So the next day I felt really guilty. We both had to work that day together, and so we both drove to work and that day we really didn't look at each other at all. But it was really strange, because he really wanted to go out with me again and so we did. And we found out that we really did dig each other. I mean we were both lonely, and the first opportunity that came we went out together and we found out that we were really, really compatible and that the situation came up at such a really good time. I learned to overcome my guiltiness. Of course he helped me a lot, because I found out that he really loved me. Because most of the time I found out for me that guys were just out to go to bed with you. That's the way I thought of them. And when I found out that he had gone to bed with me and actually really liked me, that blew my mind too. But it was a strange situation, because we had to work together too. But we overcame that. Most people tell me it's hard to work with someone you arc going out with and you really dig. Also we had to put on this farce for everybody. So during work, we'd sneak a minute out and go to the bathroom and kiss. But the rest of the time we were okay because we had gotten over that frustration of not being able to touch each other. After work we'd just laugh and go out to dinner and all our frustrations of the day would be gone. So it was really nice.

When asked whose idea it was when she first had sex with her partner, this monogamist replied:

I think it was very mutual. I really do, because we were really having a good time, the first time. Because we had a nice dinner—we had a barbecue and we were laughing and we were really getting to know each other. And we were purposely getting drunk so we would lose all our inhibitions. Because we had to, the first time. We just couldn't come out and say, "I want to go to bed with you." And we went inside, and he sat down and I sat down too. I guess I started it because I went into the bathroom and took off my bra and I came out and told him. I said, "Look, I took off my bra," and then he knew it was okay, and I suppose that's the way I wanted it. And I made him know that I did—that it was cool to go ahead.

At the beginning of our relationship when we went to bed, after that we knew that we wanted to go to bed together again. And we also knew that we liked each other. So, yes, the next time we went out we did go to bed together. But the thing was that I didn't want my parents to know that I was seeing somebody and going to bed with them, so it had to be really secretive, you know. We had a hard time finding a place to go and talk to each other and be able to make love. So we'd take trips to the beach and stuff like that or visit friends that were cool. Or just go to his house. His parents were really cool, too, about it. Like they didn't disturb us. I suppose they knew what we were really doing but they didn't make any hassle about it. Because I know when they first met me they were sort of shocked. Because I'm Mexican

> and he's Jewish. I suppose they were not really that shocked, because they didn't believe it was going to last for long.

The choice of partner in serial monogamy is usually a prudent one. It is not always done with deliberation, but most young people have criteria about who their sexual partners in monogamy should be. They see their emotions as well as their time and energy being spent in such a relationship, and so they look forward to a generous psychic profit from it.

A common requirement of each party is that the other will not expect or press for marriage. It is true that some serial monogamists enter into their relationship in anticipation of marriage; perhaps one or both partners seek to learn what it is like to live together. But the code of serial monogamy requires that neither party enter into the relationship with the unspoken assumption of marriage.

Expectations concerning the future relationship are often optimistic. With marriage definitely not a consideration except for those who have made specific commitments to one another, there is no specified period of time the serial monogamous relationship is expected to last. Tomorrow is considered vague and holds no promise of how long the relationship will continue. However, 55% of all monogamists answer "yes" or "probably" to this question about themselves and the other person in their relationship: "Do you plan to get married to your partner?" 25% say "no" or "probably not" (Table 376).

The monogamist seeks a sexual partner who is compatible in conversation and mutual understanding. An eighteen-year-old girl describes this.

> Really the main thing in a good relationship is if you can talk about things, because if you can't talk about things it's not really worthwhile. And you have to be able to enjoy the same things, but especially be able to talk, because that means, you know, if a person can really understand you and your feelings. And if you're willing to listen to the other person and things like that.

Another important criterion, especially for girls, is that the relationship be reciprocal enough to justify sex in their own minds. Reciprocation takes many forms, but an important requirement for many —in addition to "love," which is discussed below—is that the other person express strong feelings in return. Said one sixteen-year-old girl:

> It's like a total giving of yourself and likewise. I don't think I have to be in love to have sex with somebody, but it's sure got to be more than just liking somebody. A pretty solid foundation and a pretty solid relationship. And you have to feel right about it. You have to know that you really love a person and that's what you have to do. And you have to know they feel that way too.

The desire for dependence, even when it is denied, is often asserted as a form of possessiveness by girls. According to a seventeen-year-old monogamist:

> I know that when I'm involved with somebody I always expect a lot of their time. And I don't want to get out there and say, "Look, you have to do it," because I know I really can't tie one person down unless they want that—unless they want to go that far. I'm very possessive when I'm with somebody. That's a certain application of being with somebody a certain amount of time—not just being with them for two days and then split. Being able to depend on seeing them regularly like every day. I'd want to see them as much as I could without getting too uptight. I don't want to become completely dependent on somebody.

9.2.2 Prerogatives each person assumes for self and partner

Adolescents who are serial monogamists consume a great deal of time talking about what they mean to each other. They tell each other. They show each other. And they sometimes discuss with others the seriousness of their own relationships.

Boys and girls involved in monogamous relationships do not ask each other how long their relationship will last or whether one is considering a "split." They do talk about what they are doing, the sexual satisfaction they are giving each other, and ways in which they can satisfy each other more. A girl in an initial or early monogamous relationship often sees herself as a student of her sexual partner. In her learning and in his willingness to teach her, she judges the strength of their relationship.

If serial monogamists do not probe intensely into the sensitivities of their partners, they do assume certain prerogatives for themselves and conclude that their partners in turn have done the same for themselves. Generosity with sexual favors is expected to the extent of one's emotional capabilities. Opportunities for new experiences—not necessarily sexual—are both assumed and freely permitted. The willingness to talk things out, to listen, to help one's partner to self-understanding is often stressed.

Sexual fidelity is usually demanded more often by the boy than by the girl. The boy is more often confident than the girl that he is "the one" for the other sex partner. The boy probably considers the girl as something of a possession during their relationship, even though he will freely admit her right to depart from it. He will see less reason and less excuse for his partner to have sex with another.

The girl, on the other hand, generally does feel more dependence on the boy than he does on her. She feels more concern about the justification for their close intimacy, and one important justification which she can control is how she feels and behaves with respect to her partner. More girls than boys give a higher priority to their monogamous relationship than to sexual experimentation outside the relationship. (Section 9.6 of this chapter discusses the question of sexual fidelity and infidelity in detail.)

9.3 Active monogamous relationships

9.3.1 History and duration

The great majority of monogamists feel they have a close relationship with their sex partner. The number saying otherwise is so low that we are unable to test their behavior or attitudes to see what we can learn about them.

"Would you say that you have a close relationship with this girl/boy, a casual relationship, or no real relationship at all?" (Table 371).

Close relationship	86%
Casual relationship	13
No real relationship	1
TOTAL	100%

52% of all monogamists have had their relationship with one partner for one year or more. The length of this relationship accounts for the substantially fewer number of sex partners that the monogamist has had over his or her lifetime compared with those of the adventurer. But many such relationships are short-lived; 21% of all monogamous relationships reported by respondents have been in existence for three months or less.

Duration of existing serial monogamous relationships (Table 372)

Length of time	Monogamists
2 years or more	23%
13–24 months	29
4–12 months	27
3 months or less	21
TOTAL	100%

But sexual relations do not necessarily begin when two people meet, or even when their relationship begins. Many adolescents report they had a relationship with their partner before they began having sex together. Although 23% of all monogamists report their relationship has lasted more than two years, only 12% of all monogamists report having sex with the same partner for the same period of time.

"And for how long have you been having sex with this girl/boy?" (Table 373).

Length of sexual relationship	Monogamists
2 years or more	12%
13–24 months	12
4–12 months	46
3 months or less	30
TOTAL	100%

9.3.2 Current level of sexual activity

Monogamists engage in more current sexual behavior (occasions of sexual intercourse during the preceding month) than do any other group of sexually active adolescents. 93% of all monogamists have had sex one or more times during the past month, compared with 81% of the adventurers (Table 344). The currently active monogamist had sex an average of 9.6 times during the past month, compared with the currently active adventurer's average of 5.1 times.

Frequency of intercourse during preceding month of nonvirgins with current intercourse experience (Table 348)

Number of intercourse times	All	Nonvirgins with current intercourse experience: Monogamists	Adventurers
1 time	14%	9%	22%
2 times	15	11	21
3 times	13	11	17
4 times	13	13	12
5–8 times	12	15	8
9–12 times	12	15	6
13–19 times	11	10	14
20 or more times	10	16	0
TOTAL	100%	100%	100%

The high incidence of sexual activity is of course not explained by the number of different sex partners available to the monogamist during the past month. The average number of people with whom currently active nonvirgins have had intercourse during the past month are as follows:

All nonvirgins	1.5%
Monogamists	1.1
Adventurers	2.3

92% of all currently active monogamists had intercourse with but one sex partner during the past month, while only 47% of all currently active adventurers made the same claim.

Number of different intercourse partners during the preceding month (Table 346)

	Nonvirgins with current intercourse experience		
	All	Monogamists	Adventurers
1	76%	92%	47%
2	11	8	18
3	7	0	20
4	4	0	11
5 or more	2	0	4
TOTAL	100%	100%	100%

The difference in sexual activity between monogamists and adventurers is highlighted by the fact that adventurers not only have intercourse less frequently, but they also divide their sexual activity among more individuals. These differences undoubtedly can be explained not only by the nature of monogamist and adventurer personalities, but also by the consequences each type of behavior creates. Thus:

1. Monogamists have greater physical access to one another than do adventurers and their sex partners.
2. One can assume that social distance is less and psychological access is greater for the monogamist and his partner than for the adventurer and his partner. Mutual expectations and willingness to facilitate intercourse are undoubtedly greater in the case of the monogamist than the adventurer. The adventurer will meet and court several more people for sexual purposes than will the monogamist over the same time period.
3. Contraceptive devices are more frequently used by the sexual monogamist group. During the preceding month 66% of the monogamists, compared with 46% of the adventurers, *always* used a contraceptive or birth control device (Table 383).
4. Frequency of female orgasm in sexual intercourse correlates strongly with enjoyment of sex and therefore presumably with interest in having sex. Girl monogamists can therefore be expected to have sexual relations more often than adventurers because they have orgasms more frequently than adventurers do. 51% of all female monogamists report that they have

orgasms usually or almost always, as compared to 29% of all other female nonvirgins (Table 339).

The fact that many people do live together does not automatically assure sexual satisfaction, especially to the girl monogamist. One sixteen-year-old monogamist who is very much in love with her boyfriend describes in detail how much she enjoys the sex act because of the satisfaction he gets; but she fails to get the physical satisfaction she badly needs.

> I really dig him to look at me. We just lie side by side with our hands across each other's stomachs and we touch each other and we look at each other and smile and we kiss each other and it's really nice. I like to do it when the house is clean, like I don't want to have anything else on my mind—I really dig everything to be in perfect shape. I can be free to think about F—— and he can think about me. I like to spend a lot of time before, touching each other—just lying in bed and talking and at the same time touching each other. And then we slowly get into it—just faster and faster. But I really dig it when it's just slow and comfortable, like in the morning or in the afternoon when we've worked really hard. Then going to the river and wash ourselves, then lying down and just talking, then just take off our clothes—really comfortable and cool. It's just a gradual thing that I really dig. A lot of times F—— likes to get it over with really fast, and I don't really dig that at all. He has to go do this or go do that and it's like he's not really into it, it's just a thing where he has to let out a . . . not hostility . . . I mean he just wants to have sex. And that's all it is to me, just having sex. I can't really enjoy it that much because he's going so fast—he reaches his climax so fast that to me I'm not taking any part of it. What I dig is when we're really going slow and touching each other and really getting into each other's bodies and massages and things like that. A lot of times it's not like that at all. We have so many things to do on the place that for both of us sex isn't that important. I mean it's important, but I can't get him to slow down to my pace.

In response to the question, Have you talked to him about it, she replied,

> I try to show him more than talk to him. He knows when I dig it, and he knows when I don't. He knows when we're going slow I enjoy it more and he does too. If it's right before we get up, he wants breakfast, so we go through it really fast. If it's the way I like it, it's very slow.
>
> Everytime we have sex he reaches an orgasm, but not me. He says, "Tell me what you want, tell me what you want." And we've already started, you know, and I have to be aroused slowly. If we've already started intercourse, then I can get into it, but it's sort of shot.
>
> I haven't reached an orgasm. I used to feel it was very, very important. And there was something wrong with me. But now I feel that there's nothing wrong. It's just that I'm not into it—I don't know—maybe I do feel that there's something wrong and I'd like to learn,

because I feel that F—— doesn't know that much about sex and I'd like to experiment. Both of us would. It's just that everytime we have sex it's not a thing we experiment with. We never really experiment. Like I said, I have different positions that I like and I really get aroused. But then halfway in it I start losing my pleasure in it. It seems sort of monotonous. Like him coming in and out, in and out. Like it doesn't please—I mean I don't feel anything. And I don't know why. Like everytime we've had sex he's reached an orgasm.

I feel I want to experiment and I have to be taught sex because we're both very immature about it. He's happy reaching an orgasm and I'm not. I don't mind that much, I want him to be fulfilled, because I feel an orgasm is fulfillment. I really don't mind that much if I don't, because I feel that I'm getting pleasure anyway because I'm giving him pleasure and it feels sort of good to me, too, except that I don't reach the orgasm.

Sometimes it feels real good to me. I feel I'm getting higher and higher, but all of a sudden it's just cut off. And that's really frustrating.

I suppose it's because he is furiously reaching a point where it's really good and then he moves. I guess that's why. And I say will you stay there and we're kissing and stuff like that, and he stays put where I tell him to and like I don't know where to go from there. Like what do I do next? It's really weird because I haven't learned at all—still —what's going on.

Both of us have talked about different ways of learning more about sex and we both know we need to change, like him getting on top of me. But I think that any way we do it, I still wouldn't reach an orgasm. And I don't know why. It's really frustrating, because I feel I'm cut off just when I'm really feeling good. And all of a sudden it's not feeling good anymore.

When he's in a hurry, he's not really in a hurry; he doesn't think of himself as in a hurry but I do. He asks me which way I want it. But when he's in a hurry . . . well, I guess I'm really stupid myself. But I think of him as in a hurry, so I say, "It's okay," instead of, "No, get in back of me," or another way I like it. Because he's in a hurry I feel that he can do it any way and I still don't feel anything. That's my attitude. My attitude's really bad towards it. Unless I know that I'm really going to enjoy it because it's a matter of how he comes in . . . it's really bad. I have to change my attitude, too. But I don't know why I feel that way. I just do. And I really wish I could know why. Sex is really puzzling to me.

9.4 Characteristics of serial monogamists

9.4.1 Personal characteristics

9.4.1.1 Sex

64% of the serial monogamists are female, and 36% are male. This is a disproportionate number of females, considering the fact that

43% of the nonvirgins are female. The explanation probably lies with one or both of the following assumptions: many female monogamists have sexual relationships with male adolescents who do not consider themselves monogamists or many female monogamists have sexual relationships with men who are older than nineteen.

9.4.1.2 Race

89% of all serial monogamists are white; 11% are nonwhite.

9.4.1.3 Age

The average age of the serial monogamist is 17.1 years.

80% of all monogamists are in the older age-group. This compares with 68% of the nonvirgins and 58% of the total adolescent population who are also in the older age-group. Thus, monogamists are clearly the oldest in composition compared with any other sexual behavior group.

Age composition of sexual behavior groups

Age	All adolescents	Nonvirgins	Sexual adventurers	Monogamists
13–15	42%	32%	31%	20%
16–19	58%	68%	69%	80%

9.4.1.4 Region and locality size

Sexual monogamists are unevenly distributed in the north central and southern regions of the United States compared with the adolescent population as a whole. The distribution is as follows:

Geographic location of adolescents surveyed and of serial monogamists

	National sample of adolescents	Monogamists
Northeast	22%	21%
North Central	31	26
South	32	38
West	15	15
TOTAL	100%	100%

As to locality size, monogamists are distributed quite evenly and in almost identical proportions to adolescents as a whole.

Large metropolitan areas	34%
Small metropolitan areas	34
Nonmetropolitan and rural areas	32
TOTAL	100%

9.4.1.5 Religious feeling

The pattern of monogamists' religious feeling closely follows that of the national population of adolescents and varies little from that of nonvirgins. More monogamists are nonreligious than are members of any other group.

11% say they are very religious.
50% say they are somewhat religious.
23% say they are not very religious.
16% say they are not at all religious.

9.4.1.6 School and school grades

Monogamists being the oldest group, it is not unexpected that fewer monogamists than members of any other group are in school. However, the figure—61%—is unusually low. It may be that there is a direct connection between the high number of females who are monogamists and the demands of the monogamous relationship that accounts for some not being in school. Moreover, some older monogamists have graduated from high school and have not gone to college.

However, those monogamists who are in school obtain higher school grades than members of any other sexual behavior group. 52% of all monogamists receive grades of superior or good, compared, for example, with 43% of all adolescents, 48% of the sexually inexperienced, 44% of all nonvirgins, and 32% of all sexual adventurers.

9.4.2 Differentiating sociopolitical attitudes

Serial monogamists do not differ strikingly from the other sexual behavior groups in their social and political viewpoints. As we found in our personal depth interviews, monogamists certainly have opinions on all of the major issues. They are not without viewpoints and ideals; it is only that they are not uniquely different from other groups.

9.5 Role of love

9.5.1 Incidence of love

A very large majority of serial monogamists believe they love their sex partners and believe that they are loved by their sex partners (Tables 374 and 375).

Monogamists who love person with whom they have sexual relationship	
Yes	86%
I'm not really sure	11
No	3
TOTAL	100%

Monogamists who believe they are loved by person with whom they have sexual relationship	
Yes	81%
I'm not really sure	11
She/he says so	8
No	0
TOTAL	100%

9.5.2 Perceived importance of love

Love for one person at a time attracts greater support from the serial monogamists than from the adventurers. 49% of all monogamists agree, "I don't think it would be possible for a boy/girl to be really in love with more than one girl/boy at the same time" (Table 155).

Girls more often than boys express the importance of love in the serial monogamy relationship. The reasons for their attitudes have been reported earlier. The expression of their attitudes sometimes takes a very intense and moralistic form. Physical pleasure by itself generates moral ambivalence in some girls, although they accept physical pleasure with enthusiasm when it is accompanied by their feeling of loving and being loved. A fourteen-year-old girl monogamist, who would not now have a sexual relationship without love, describes how she came to feel this way:

> I guess I learned a lot from him. I only balled him once . . . and I didn't want to, but it wasn't that I was afraid to say no and it wasn't that I would be embarrassed to say no. But I didn't really love him, and I didn't think he really loved me. . . . He only was the type who

> really made you enjoy it. And that is the only reason I'm not sorry that I did ball him . . . because I didn't agree with him. For him it was only pleasure, but he made it so open and good that it was really beautiful, even though you weren't madly in love with each other, you know. He would ball with anyone. Everyone was special to him. I balled with him then, but I would never do it again because now I really know.

Some girls emphasize love so strongly in their relationship that they believe they must sometimes deny sex to themselves and their partners in order to affirm love. One fourteen-year-old girl tells of her boyfriend who "always wants to ball and that's all there is to it":

> Sometimes it gets into my head that it's something I don't want to do or it's against my better judgment, and I try to explain to him that something just tells me "don't." I know he tries to understand and he says he won't get mad . . . but then he'll just get up and start playing his guitar and it makes me feel very bad because I know he's trying to take his mind off it. But still, well, I guess for a boy there's no in-between because once they get excited or something you just can't say no. . . . I want to make him happy. But I don't want him to think that every time he wants it he'll get it.

Strong desires for a love relationship complicate the serial monogamous relationship and cause inner turmoil within some girls. Some girls want strong demonstrations of love, while others are satisfied with its mere affirmation. The demonstration of love, especially when the girl is not always sure what form it should take, sometimes creates the fear of being bound to someone. This fear may cause many young people to avoid marriage, which is seen as a pressure to conform in an obligatory fashion to another person's concept of how two people should live together. Some girls such as this mature nineteen year old recognize this.

> In my experience I wouldn't want somebody to go drastically out of their way and change their life-style just to make me feel more comfortable, because I don't want that at all. I don't want anyone to make concessions to me in the way they think or live just because we happen to be loving, because I would want the same freedom myself.

But then this same girl defines love differently from most adolescent girls, as indeed do many girl serial monogamists.

> Love is a groove—getting off on another person and being able to function independently and still have something between you. I think the independent thing has a great deal to do with it. . . . You can't make this person sign a contract that will say, "I will love you forever," or for whatever amount of time, and you can't have them say, "I will show my love for you in these ways," because it's just something you're both doing, and the minute you start demanding of

> the other person, it's pain. That's when things start to fall apart and you get headaches. That's not love when you demand.

Then, too, the girl monogamist must feel that she loves her partner; she is more demanding of herself in terms of whether she loves him. One sixteen-year-old girl tells how she believes she must feel toward her monogamist partner:

> I think [love is] giving yourself to somebody—really giving—and caring for that person more than yourself. It's a kind of a loss of all self-concern at one point. It's like I feel I have to give myself in all ways, and you don't become attached at all to what you might feel. You just give whatever you can to them—you think of them before anything else—before yourself. . . . At first when you get it you become a little frightened, because you don't know how far you're getting into it.

Involvement in emotional depth is frightening to some girls, who sometimes depart from relationships because they cannot cope with their own emotions. Some girls realize that the love they demand of themselves for others will frighten some male partners and may provoke other males to use them in some fashion.

> I never realize that until things get really bad. When I get involved with somebody I do have to give myself completely, and I do that too soon a lot of times and it's taken advantage of. . . . And it hurts very badly. Very badly. I think I'll never get over it. And of course I do, but at that time you think you'll never live without that person.

Some girl monogamists who give greatly of themselves frequently burn up their relationships. In starting and stopping them every few weeks or months they would seem to qualify as sexual adventurers, except that they are wholly faithful to their partners during the life of the relationship. Their feeling of loving another rises steeply if they believe their feelings are reciprocated, and the relationship suddenly intensifies for them. "I think you have to be involved for a couple of weeks or at least a month before you can realize what you've got. I don't think you can say within a couple of days that you've got love there."

Finally, the girl monogamist wants to be sure that she is not confusing love for her partner with emotional or intellectual reactions.

> I believe you can love someone for their head and really get into their mind in a very, very beautiful intellectual relationship where the emotional and the physical, if they exist, aren't of such priority. . . . But I want to be sure of what I have so I don't try to have sex with the wrong kind of person. We wouldn't make it and I might never know why.

Many adolescents believe, "Over a period of time, I think it's better to have sexual relationships with several different people, rather than just one person" (Table 238). Fewer serial monogamists believe this than any other category of intercourse-active adolescents: 37% of all monogamists, as compared to 68% of all adventurers.

Serial monogamy is open to infidelity in two ways: by having sex occasionally with another and by the mutual understanding that one can terminate the relationship in favor of another sex partner. Despite the emphasis that monogamists give to love, serial monogamous relationships generally dissolve because one partner "falls out of love" with another.

9.6.1 Incidence

We do not know for certain with whom each serial monogamist shared all of his and her sexual experiences during the preceding month. However, we previously mentioned that 8% of the currently active monogamists had sex with more than one person during the preceding month, as compared with 53% of the active sexual adventurers (Table 346).

Monogamists do not frequently have sexual relations with others outside their relationship. In their history of sexual activity monogamists have had an average of 1.1 sex partners. 80% of all monogamists replied never in response to the question: "Do you have sex with other girls/boys?" (Table 377).

Monogamists having sex with others than partner in current relationship

	Monogamists
Frequently	3%
Occasionally	7
Very rarely	10
Never	80
TOTAL	100%

Moreover, 70% of all monogamists declare that their sex partners never have sex with others (Table 378). (See table on page 235.)

9.6.2 Attitudes and their consistency with behavior

How do serial monogamists feel about their partners having sexual intercourse with others? The fact that fidelity is not usually a condition of the sexually monogamous relationship has already been mentioned; but the sensitivities and attitudes of the monogamous re-

Monogamists' opinion of how often their partners have sex with others

	Monogamists
Frequently	1%
Occasionally	10
Very rarely	5
I think so, but I'm not sure	1
Never	70
I don't think so, but I'm not sure	13
TOTAL	100%

veal even deeper-seated reasons why they are tolerant to some degree of random infidelity for themselves.

How monogamists feel and behave about fidelity to their sex partners is of crucial importance in understanding the impact of serial monogamy on the institution of marriage. For marriage as we know it today is subject to change if young people between the ages of thirteen and nineteen maintain their present philosophies about sex without marriage and about the extent to which they will tolerate infidelity on the part of their sex partners.

How consistent are adolescents in their reasoning on infidelity? Does the fact that people love and know they are loved influence their sexual loyalties to their partners? Do they tolerate infidelity by their partners if they choose to wander sexually themselves? Do they perceive that their partners want the freedom to have sex with another from time to time? Do they respond with their own infidelity to partners they believe are not "uptight" at the prospect? How many are nonpermissive about their own behavior and that of their partners and desire only partners who feel the same way?

We do not presently know the extent to which love for a sex partner or feeling of being loved by a sex partner influences an adolescent monogamist's tendencies to infidelity or willingness to tolerate it on the part of another. As we described earlier in Section 9.5, the great majority of monogamists love their sex partners and feel loved by them—so many, in fact, that one must assume at least monogamists who commit infidelity include those monogamists who love and are loved. Adolescents, like adults, will sometimes have intercourse with people they do not profess to love and will sometimes have intercourse with another in addition to the person they love. Moreover, 50% of all monogamists assert they do *not* agree with the statement, "I don't think it would be possible for a boy/girl to be really in love with more than one girl/boy at the same time" (Table 155).

Unless the outside sexual excursion is flaunted, the offending boy or girl will usually not be dropped by his or her monogamist partner. This infidelity in some respects is welcomed, because it helps emphasize the fact that neither party is considering marriage and neither party wants the other person to assume otherwise. What we have been calling sexual infidelity is only one of a pattern of infidelities or irregularities that sexual monogamists deliberately maintain at a low level of magnitude so that each knows that the other is willing to cooperate in maintaining his personal freedom. Other irregularities can include not knowing the other person's whereabouts, tardiness, and casual association with others.

To test the reactions of all nonvirgin adolescents to the idea of one's having sex with someone other than one's current sex partner, we asked all nonvirgins to reply true or false to the following statements:

1. "If I were to have sex with another girl/boy, just occasionally, it wouldn't really put my girl friend/boyfriend uptight." 31% of the monogamists agreed, as compared to 54% of the adventurers (Table 316).
2. "If my girl friend/boyfriend were to have sex with another boy/girl, just occasionally, it wouldn't really put me uptight." 38% of all monogamists agreed, as compared to 44% of all adventurers (Table 325).

We used "uptight" as a term of concern that we thought was expressive and meaningful to the adolescent but which would not connote anger, hostility, or hate. Thus, we could be sure to register any perceived negative reactions rather than miss them because we inquired about them in language so strong they would be rejected by the respondent.

24% of all monogamists who say they could have sex with another person without getting their girl or boy friend uptight have in fact had sex with another person frequently or occasionally, while only 4% who disagree with this statement, "If I were to have sex with another girl/boy, just occasionally, it wouldn't really put my girl friend/boyfriend uptight," have committed infidelity to that partner frequently or occasionally (Table 379).

18% of all monogamists who say they wouldn't really be uptight if their partner occasionally had sex with another have themselves had sex with another, while only 6% of those who say any infidelity on the part of their partner would put them uptight have themselves engaged in this behavior (Table 380).

This rationalization becomes even clearer and more consistent when we view these attitudes and behavior from another direction. We find that 73% of the monogamists who have intercourse with persons other than their partners believe that it does not put their partners uptight and that 66% of those who are unfaithful to their partners in monogamy say they would not be uptight if their partners were to occasionally have intercourse with another.

We find a consistency between those monogamists who rationalize their own infidelity and those who rationalize the infidelity of their partners. 28% of those who believe that if they were to have sex with another their partner would not really be put uptight believe that their partner does have sex with another frequently or occasionally (Table 381). On the other hand, those believing their partner committed sexual infidelity occasionally (none believed frequently) amounted to only 4% of those who believe their sex partner would be uptight if they were to commit infidelity. Thus, it is evident that considerably more monogamists who assume their behavior would not disturb their partners attribute infidelity to their partners than those who feel their own behavior would disturb their partners.

Does this work in reverse? We find that 24% of those who say they would not be uptight if their partners occasionally had sex with another attribute frequent or occasional infidelity to their partner, as compared to 4% of those who said they would be uptight at such behavior by their partner (Table 382).

In summary, the following propositions can be stated about monogamists' tolerance of sexual infidelity—on their part and on the part of their partners in the monogamous relationship:

26% of the monogamists are permissive themselves and perceive their partners as being permissive.

15% are permissive themselves but feel that their partners would *not* be.

16% are *not* permissive themselves but feel that their partners would be.

43% are not permissive and do not perceive their partners as being permissive.

It is also very important to view infidelity in the words of several monogamists. A nineteen-year-old girl described her first reaction to infidelity on the part of her monogamist partner:

> He was at work and didn't come home for that night. It was the beginning of our relationship, because I was sixteen and he was twenty-five. I moved in to live with him because of outside circumstances, not because I was in love with him and wanted to live with him. He was just there. And it got to be I was more attached to him;

> and when he didn't come home, I freaked out, but when he did come home and we talked about it, I felt very good about it and then progressively every time it happened, I felt better and better to where I didn't freak out anymore. And when I did it, he didn't freak out, and it got to be a good understanding. I think [it was] mostly because we don't want to get married. I don't want to be married in any respect and neither does he. So perhaps we create these circumstances so we won't be married in any respect whether on a piece of paper or whether we just won't see anyone else or whatever.

Infidelity is not supported for its own sake, despite the assertions of many girl monogamists that they do not blame the male for seeking experience or occasional variation. Concern and jealousy are by no means absent. What makes itself felt is the belief that personal freedom of the whole human being is expected—the very quality we mentioned above which so many adolescents feel is threatened by marriage. But the desire to serve the whole human being goes beyond that. Young people so want to be wanted for their own sakes that they do not want to stifle sexual competition for fear that they will seem less desirable in contrast with the unobtainable. They also fear their partner's love for them will not be as great as it would be if it survived the test of alternative sexual options.

This means that they do not view either the physical pleasure of sex or the love they seek to give and receive as requiring sexual exclusivity. In fact, many feel sexual exclusivity can cause emotional needs to suffer and the relationship to pall as a result.

Some adolescents express these sentiments in terms of fairness.

> You can't put ties on someone, because that's really not fair. It depends really on how much you are involved, in terms of sleeping with [someone]. Just saying, asking, telling somebody not to sleep with anybody else when you're not married is really a lot to put on somebody. . . . I don't think that anyone has the right to tell someone with whom they can and cannot sleep.

Serial monogamists feel this way about their partners' rights in considerable part because they feel so strongly about their own freedom from the demands or possessiveness of others.

> I don't feel anyone has the right to ask me not to sleep with someone else. I really don't. I believe that. But I think that if I were involved with somebody and we had something very beautiful, it would sort of be an unsaid thing. It would be there. It's hard to say it when it's really happening: "It's all right, do what you want." Because it can hurt. It really can hurt. But I think it can mess up a lot of things when you become too possessive about that.

One's assumption might be that this philosophy would be more appropriate for the sexual adventurer. As we shall see, however, the sexual adventurer makes more demands and suffers from greater ambivalence about the fidelity of his sexual partners even though, by definition, adventurism offers no fidelity. A great strength of the monogamous relationship for many young people is that fidelity is assumed to prevail in part because infidelity is understood and permitted.

The same serial monogamist continues:

> If my boyfriend had sex with someone else, I think I would be very hurt in a way. There's always that in everyone, I guess. But I would strive to put it out of my mind. It's all unnecessary to me to make a big thing out of that. It's not going to do anything good for the relationship. . . . I wouldn't let it affect me that much—not enough to jeopardize the relationship. . . . What's the point of that?

A seventeen-year-old girl adventurer felt similarly: "I'm not going to go berserk over whether he's seeing someone else or what he's doing with the other person or whether the other person is nicer than me or anything. Because you worry yourself to death like that."

Boy serial monogamists view the fidelity question the same way that girls do, but for different reasons. As do girls, they know they can be possessive, demanding, and sufficiently unsure of themselves to intrude upon the personal freedom of their sexual partners. They also feel strongly about the need for their partners to be whole human beings, although they are less apt to feel this way than are girl monogamists. Because more serial monogamy relationships are assumed at the girl's initiative, a special kind of girl—perhaps more perceptive or sensitive—is more often attracted to this initiative-taking relationship.

From our depth interviews it seems that although boys may have less patience than girls, they can feign patience more easily and so wait out with more casualness the girl who momentarily strays from the relationship.

9.7 Differentiating sexual attitudes

Serial monogamists are of course a considerably less inhibited group than virgins when it comes to their sexual values. They are seldom dogmatic about what is moral or normal. At the same time they are also by far the more sensitive to their sexual partners, very much committed to the morality of sex without marriage and little concerned about what society thinks about their sexual behavior except that they feel sensitive about their relationship with their parents.

The differentiating sexual viewpoints that uniquely distinguish the serial monogamists occur with respect to:

1. Sexual satisfaction
2. Relationship with parents
3. Identification with society
4. Sensitivity toward sex partners

9.7.1 Sexual satisfaction

88% of all monogamists assert they get a lot of satisfaction out of their sex lives, compared with 81% of the adventurers and 38% of those without intercourse experience (Table 18). All that we have learned about the monogamist indicates that he and she find serial monogamy—with particular emphasis on the sexual relationship of the moment—the most ideal means of combining physical desires and emotional satisfactions. This same feeling of self-contentment undoubtedly contributes to their unwillingness to condemn other people or even to make up their minds about what the sexual behavior of other adolescents should be. Only 37% of the monogamists, compared with 58% of the adventurers and 58% of the inexperienced believe, "So far as sex is concerned, I have pretty much come to definite conclusions about what I think is right and wrong for other people" (Table 23).

Consistent with this is their disbelief in a double standard for boys and girls, a viewpoint that is undoubtedly a result of the closer relationship they enjoy with their sex partners. 83% of the monogamists believe "So far as sex is concerned, I think that what is morally right for boys is morally right for girls too" (Table 61). Only 16% of the monogamists disagree (1% are not sure), as compared with twice as many adventurers and almost three times as many virgins.

9.7.2 Relationship with parents

The relationship between parents and monogamists in many instances undergoes more strain than adolescent-parent relationships for any other sexual behavior group. The monogamist's sexual behavior is usually (though not always) the most open, the most acknowledged, and the least confidential because of the regularity of contact between the same sex partners. Parents of adventurers, for example, can more easily ignore the question of whether their children have sexual intercourse because the adventurer is seeing a greater number of young people.

Thus, more monogamists than those belonging to any other group acknowledge the discomfort of their parents concerning their sexual values and activities; 32% of the monogamists, compared with 24% of the adventurers and 17% of the virgins, agree with the statement, "My parents and I sometimes talk about sex, but it makes them very uncomfortable" (Table 11). And 74% of the monogamists express the wish that they and their parents could agree more about what they think is "right and wrong where sex is concerned," as compared with 64% of the adventurers and 45% of the virgins (Table 13).

9.7.3 Identification with society

The monogamous relationship, being an open and acknowledged relationship, inevitably represents the greatest challenge to a society that outlaws fornication in most states and still speaks of the wrongs of premarital sex. But monogamists feel society's disapproval less than adventurers; only 17% of the monogamists were willing to agree "So far as sex is concerned, I wouldn't do anything that society would disapprove of" (Table 50).

At the same time, monogamists are not titillated about society's viewpoint toward their sexual relationships. Many clearly find their regular relationships satisfactory and almost an institutionalized part of their lives. 22% of the monogamists, compared with 35% of all nonvirgins and 41% of the virgins, think, "A lot of the pleasure in sex would be lost if it did not seem to be such a forbidden activity" (Table 257).

One seventeen-year-old monogamist describes the concessions she and her mate are willing to make to society.

> A lot of times we tell people that we're married, just for convenience. Because it is really convenient to be married. Because if you meet people and they can't like you right off and they have to talk with you a long time before you get acquainted, you have to tell them you're married or they'll be prejudiced against you. A lot of times, when we go into a real estate office or motel, we say we're married. It isn't just us they're prejudiced against, it's me—someone will ask himself, "What's this girl anyway? She's going to bed with fifty million people and stuff like that."

Sex outside of marriage is quite naturally of minimal concern to monogamists, even less so than to adventurers and far less than to the inexperienced.

Adolescents agreeing, "Sex is immoral, unless it's between two people who are married to each other" (Table 231).

Nonvirgins		Virgins	
Monogamists	Adventurers	Beginners	Inexperienced
11%	17%	21%	53%

Monogamists, it will be recalled, are similar to all adolescents in religious feeling, except that a few more monogamists say they are not religious at all. This, plus the fact that they are engaged in the most serious of all sexual relationships outside of marriage, causes fewer monogamists (28%) than other groups to support the statement: "A person who truly loves God doesn't have sexual relationships outside of marriage" (Table 227). Considerably more adventurers and virgins—41% and 50%, respectively—agree with this statement.

Self-confidence and interest in their own behavior is undoubtedly why so many monogamists know of magazine articles and books on sex they regard as serious. Monogamists are the most literate group with respect to reading serious materials about sex. Adolescents saying they have never read serious materials about sex tend to respond according to the seriousness of their sexual relationships and whether or not they have had sexual intercourse. Based on the responses of all behavior groups, we can infer that adolescents have considerably less respect for or contact with serious books than with magazines concerning sexual matters.

	Nonvirgins		Virgins	
I have never read:	Monogamists	Adventurers	Beginners	Inexperienced
A serious educational book about sex (Table 48)	25%	48%	38%	65%
A serious magazine article about sex (Table 149)	17%	32%	31%	42%

A majority of all adolescents deny that VD is a serious problem, but monogamists probably feel less exposure and therefore less concern about getting VD or suffering its consequences. 30% of the monogamists agree, "Getting VD or venereal disease isn't really a very serious problem because one can always go to a doctor and get it cured," compared with 17% of the adventurers and 14% of the virgins (Table 24).

9.7.4 Sensitivity toward sex partners

Members of no sexual behavior group are strongly distinguished by a unique sensitivity toward their sex partners. But monogamists do show such sensitivity in a few respects.

Knowing the obligations of love and wanting to avoid binding ties with one another, the male monogamist is less likely to use the word "love" with abandon or for reasons of persuasion. Thus, 93% of all boy monogamists believe it is wrong to tell a girl "you love her—even if you don't—if that's what it takes so she will have sex with you" (Table 108). Again, this uniqueness may also result from the fact that the male monogamist is generally not actively seeking other sexual partners and therefore has no problems of persuasion other than with the girl with whom he has a going sexual relationship. 40% of the male adventurers, on the other hand, as compared with 7% of the male monogamists and 16% of the male virgins, see nothing wrong in a boy telling a girl he loves her in order to persuade her to have sex with him.

Again, along with the great majority of adolescents, 92% of the monogamists *deny* that the most important thing in a love relationship is sex (Table 236). 7% of the monogamists believe sex is the most important thing in a love relationship, versus 18% of the inexperienced and 25% of the adventurers.

73% of the monogamists, compared with 53% of the adventurers and 49% of the inexperienced, believe, "Some boys use sex to reward or punish their girl friends" (Table 204). With so many girls being monogamists, this result is not unexpected, because 74% of all older girls believe this as compared with 52% of all older boys.

Monogamists differ strikingly from adventurers in their interracial sexual experience. 82% of the monogamists and 48% of the adventurers say, "I've never had sex with a person of another race" (Table 318). This is explained both by the more conservative temperament of the monogamists and the fact that the average thirteen- to nineteen-year-old monogamist has had 4.2 sex partners, compared with the average thirteen- to nineteen-year-old adventurer's 16.3 sex partners.

9.8 Use of marijuana

Proportionally fewer serial monogamists make use of marijuana than do sexual adventurers but monogamists report three times more often than virgins that they use marijuana (Table 126).

44% of the serial monogamists agree they like to smoke marijuana sometimes (Table 126), and 12% agree with the statement, "Smoking marijuana is an important thing in my life" (Table 30). Nearly twice as many adventurers (22%) believe marijuana is important to them.

9.8.1 Effects of marijuana and alcohol on sex experience

Almost the same number of monogamists (40%) as sexual adventurers (42%) agree that marijuana increases sexual pleasure (Table 286).

The fact that the statement does not speak of "*my* sexual pleasure" makes it impossible to assume how many monogamists are speaking of their own sexual pleasure as a result of pot smoking. However, we have found that, among monogamists, 55% of the marijuana smokers, as compared to 27% of the nonsmokers, agree, "Marijuana increases sexual pleasure." 59% of those who say that marijuana increases sexual pleasure are in fact marijuana smokers.

24% of the monogamists, compared with 42% of the adventurers, agree with the statement, "On one or more occasions, under the influence of alcohol, I've had sex with someone that I wouldn't have had sex with otherwise" (Table 299).

34% of the monogamists believe that alcohol increases sexual pleasure, with adventurers agreeing in similar proportions (Table 269). Monogamists find increased sexual pleasure from alcohol less frequently than do virgins, particularly less than the younger boys (45%) and all girls (50%). In this connection, it is significant that only 25% of the sixteen- to nineteen-year-old boys agree that alcohol gives them sexual pleasure.

Personal interviews indicate that monogamists who have taken marijuana and other drugs do not take them to enhance the sexual experience. The effects of specific drugs on the sexual experience are known to their users and are exploited accordingly. Some drugs magnify the sensual qualities of the sexual experience; others strongly depress physical enjoyment by inhibiting both sensitivity and feeling. For this reason, some young people who fear the communication and outwardness they feel are required in the sexual relation will use a drug either as a quasi-substitute for the orgasm obtained in the intercourse or to banish sexual desires from the mind entirely. The addict to most drugs has virtually no interest in sex, partly because of his sense of priorities and partly because of his poor physical and emotional condition.

9.9 Reactions to other types of sexual behavior

Sexual monogamists view other adolescent sexual behavior tolerantly and with an air of slight superiority. They usually have little dissatisfaction with their own sex lives, and they know it. They usually feel no envy toward the adventurers. They feel no missionary zeal about their relationships, because they are not inviting other adolescents to join them. Their combination of personal freedom and sexual satisfaction are such that they do not believe other young people's sexual behavior interferes with their own or offers any attractions that are not available to them.

9.10 Salient findings

1. Serial monogamy without marriage is a close sexual relationship of uncertain duration between two unmarried adolescents from which either party may depart when he or she desires, often to participate in another such relationship.

2. 21% of all American adolescents and 40% of all those who have had sexual intercourse are serial monogamists without marriage. 28% of all girls and 15% of all boys are monogamists; 80% of all monogamists are in the older age-group.

3. The code of serial monogamy requires that neither party enter into the relationship with the unspoken assumption of marriage. However, 55% of all monogamists answer "yes" or "probably" to the question: do you plan to marry your partner?

4. The serial monogamist has had an average of 4.2 sex partners. But nearly half of all serial monogamists have had only one sex partner.

5. 52% of all monogamists have had their relationship with one partner for one year or more.

6. 93% of all monogamists have had sex once or more often during the preceding month, compared with 81% of the adventurers. Currently active monogamists had sex an average of 9.6 times, while currently active sexual adventurers averaged 5.1 times during the preceding month.

7. 66% of the monogamists compared with 46% of the adventurers *always* used a contraceptive or birth control device during the preceding month.

8. 51% of all female monogamists report that they have orgasms usually or almost always, as compared to 29% of all other female nonvirgins.

9. A very large majority of serial monogamists (86%) believe they love their sex partners and 81% believe that they are loved by their sex partners.

10. 37% of all monogamists compared to 68% of all adventurers believe, "Over a period of time, I think it's better to have sexual relationships with several different people, rather than just one person."

10. Many monogamists are not opposed to occasional sexual infidelity on the part of their sex partners and do not bind their partners to a promise of absolute fidelity. Yet only 8% of the currently active monogamists had sex with more than one person during the past month, as compared with 53% of the active sexual adventurers. Approximately three-quarters of all monogamists say they have never had intercourse with anyone else during their present relationship, and believe the same of their sex partners.

11. 73% of the monogamists who have intercourse with persons other than their partners believe that it does not put their partners uptight, and 66% of those who are unfaithful to their partners say they would not be uptight if their partners were occasionally to have intercourse with another.

12. 88% of all monogamists assert they get a lot of satisfaction out of their sex lives, compared with 81% of the adventurers and 38% of those without intercourse experience.

13. 74% of the monogamists express the wish that "my parents and I could agree more about what we think is right and wrong where sex is concerned," compared with 64% of the adventurers and 45% of the virgins.

14. 93% of all boy monogamists believe it is wrong to tell a girl "you love her—even if you don't—if that's what it takes so she will have sex with you."

15. Fewer serial monogamists make use of marijuana than sexual adventurers, but monogamists report three times more often than virgins that they use marijuana.

10.
Sexual Adventuring and Wanderlust

I'm sure my father has a sex life outside of marriage. If he doesn't, he's crazy. I think like when you get married, there's certain expectancies—but that's no reason to shut off your emotions. If you get sexually attracted to someone else, that's no reason to shut them off just because you've got a piece of paper that says you're man and wife.

A sixteen-year-old boy sexual adventurer viewing his future

If you really dig a boy, it's all right to have sex with him even if you've only known him for a few hours.

A fourteen-year-old girl virgin and 19% of all adolescent girls thirteen to nineteen

If you really dig a girl, it's all right to have sex with her even if you've only known her for a few hours.

58% of all adolescent boys thirteen to nineteen

10.1 Definition and incidence of sexual adventurism

The adolescent sexual adventurer is a young man or young woman who seeks many sexual mates. He or she has no interest in a continuous or monogamous relationship with one sexual partner. For many the desire for sexual relations is sometimes more important than sexual satisfaction itself.

15% of all American adolescents are sexual adventurers. 24% of all American boys and 6% of all American girls are sexual adventurers. Among the adolescents who are nonvirgins, 15% are sexual adventurers.*

Currently active sexual adventurers had intercourse with an average of 2.3 people in the past month. The adolescent sexual adventurer has had an average of 16.3 sex partners.

Average number of intercourse partners

	Adventurers	All nonvirgins
1	1%	35%
2–3	20	22
4–6	34	19
7–15	15	15
16 or more	30	9
TOTAL	100%	100%

* Adolescents assigned to the sexual adventurer behavior group are:
1. Nonvirgins who have had intercourse during the past month and deny that they have sex mostly or only with just one person.
2. Nonvirgins who have had intercourse during the past month, say that they have sex mostly with just one person, deny that they never have sex with anyone else, and have engaged either in intercourse or in one or more preintercourse activities with *three or more* different people during the past month.
3. Nonvirgins who have not had intercourse in the past month, deny that they have sex mostly or only with just one person, and have engaged in one or more preintercourse activities with *three or more* different people during the past month.

10.2 Essential ingredients of sexual adventurism

There are two major types of sexual adventurers who emerge from our research. The first will have a number of partners. Each such adventurer may point with pride to his or her sexual partner of the moment and describe the partner with devotion. Moreover, the adventurer believes what he is saying and would be offended if another of his sexual partners accused him of disloyalty or the inability to love her because he had sex with someone else.

Sexual adventurism in its second form may express itself in highly truncated forms of serial monogamy in which the adventurer maintains a single sexual relationship but only for a short time. Such a sexual relationship can flower, be abandoned, and be born again. Such liaisons can even be regularly scheduled, depending on when the two people can see each other.

Most adventurers (56%) believe that it is possible for a boy/girl to "be really in love with more than one girl/boy at the same time" (Table 155). Age and amount of sexual experience seem to make little difference in this reaction.

10.2.1 How sexual adventurers view their adventurism

Many complex psychological theories are suggested by the behavior of the person who moves rapidly from one sex partner to the next. Is the sexually adventuring adolescent trying to prove something to himself? Has the girl who goes to bed with anyone abdicated her self-respect? Does the boy who can love every girl he meets truly love only himself? Do sexually adventuring girls seek a love they idealize but will never find?

We do not pretend to have the answers to these questions. But these are not questions that preoccupy sexual adventurers. They view their adventurism as a way of life: they are students of their own sensuality, looking to others for what they can supply to their own self-indulgence. They like and respect their bodies, and they believe their bodies are meant to provide sexual satisfactions and rewards.

However, sexual adventurers among adolescents cannot generally be called sybarites who are concerned only with physical pleasures. They do not view their adventurism as their sole reason for being, nor is sexual pleasure their only ambition. They do know how to have fun and enjoyment from their sexual activities, and they are seldom desperate people constantly looking for rewards they can never obtain. They see their sexual desires not unlike other adolescents, but they are freer, less inhibited, and more outer-directed in how they relate their sexual desires to others. In sexual matters they concentrate more on the variety of others rather than on developing mature emotions in themselves, and so a deepening sexual relationship with one person does not attract them.

It is doubtful whether sexual adventurers know their sex partners as well as serial monogamists know theirs. Adventurers regard their adventurism as "creaming," or partaking of the best possible moments—the most exciting, loving, and passionate—with one person and then moving on to the next. These best possible moments are moments of feeling rather than moments of knowing or analyzing or understanding. They are moments of intense enjoyment and anticipation of additional enjoyment. They enhance self-image and contribute much to the narcissistic makeup of any person who takes pride in his or her sexual attractiveness.

Adventurers do not regard their sexual adventurism in a wholly selfish way. They want to satisfy their partners as well as be satisfied. They do not adventure in order to hurt others. They regard their gifts of sex as compensation for the physical desires of their sex partners, which they both empathize with and encourage. They see their adventurism as a means of communication, an extension of their physical and loving selves. Sexual adventuring provides the opportunity for what one might call "seed love"—affection that one offers another in small but sufficient quantity from one's own self-love in order to generate as much possible reciprocation from one's partner in order to in turn feed that self-love.

68% of all sexual adventurers agree, "Over a period of time, I think it's better to have sexual relationships with several different people, rather than just one person" (Table 238). They feel that the one partner relationship is a major disadvantage to loving another, to sexual enjoyment, and to personal freedom. An unmarried relationship with one person is not sufficiently less binding than a married relationship. It is the identification with one person that the sexual adventurer strongly resists.

Sexual adventurers also view new and different sexual activities as an essential ingredient of their sexual activities pattern. 75% of all adventurers agree, "Sex is one of the few human activities where there is always something new to be discovered" (Table 237), compared with 59% of the monogamists.

The greatest tolerance of other sexual activities and the least willingness to condemn other people as immoral or abnormal is characteristic of the sexual adventurer. This is quite naturally reflected in how the adventurer views his own activities; 49% of all adventurers agree, "There isn't anything in sex that I wouldn't want to try, at least once" (Table 134).

True to their narcissistic personalities, sexual adventurers like to be praised for their sexual abilities. The ability to give sexual satisfaction is especially wanted by girls.

One seventeen-year-old girl adventuress viewed her adventurism as the only means by which she could satisfy her intense sexual curiosity.

> I'm certainly not a nympho or anything like that. It isn't just the physical thing with me. But I'm not into love either, you know. It's like I have this tremendous curiosity about how to do things and what other people like to do physically—in my mind. It bugs me if I'm not always trying to find out—like I'm never going to be satisfied until I learn what a certain teacher I know likes to feel in bed. What does he know that I don't feel—that may be something I don't know. But I've got to find out.

10.2.2 Prerogatives adventurers assume for selves and sex partners

Because ego satisfaction and subjectivity are crucial elements in the sexual adventurer's personality, he or she is usually far more preoccupied with self than with sex partner.

"As long as she wants me, I'm happy with her," said one sixteen-year-old boy. "Tough shit if she changes her mind, because then I'll not worry about her anymore."

"Don't matter what he thinks about us, because there ain't no us. It's him and me, and if I decide it's not and if he decides it's not then one of us splits and that's that. I don't care for no understanding," a fifteen-year-old girl said. "It's more funner this way, but sure I like him [one of her boyfriends] lots. I like anyone I'm with lots."

Sexual adventurers insist primarily on their freedom to have sex with anyone they choose. They do not mention their freedom *not* to have sex with anyone, which suggests that the thought of not having sex is distant from their minds. But, more important, the decision to have sex with another is their own. We do not know the extent to which the sexual adventurer is having sex with another sexual adventurer, but we believe the girl sexual adventurer is more likely to have sex with a boy sexual adventurer or a boy having his first encounter than with a monogamist who is breaking fidelity for the moment. The male adventurer is more likely to have sex with a girl who does not regard herself as an adventuress.

The sexual adventurer also does not want to be obligated to the sex partner in nonsexual aspects of their lives. The willingness to be obligated in other ways is usually a nonsexual function. Convenience and accessibility with respect to sexual activities may encourage a boy or girl to support another economically, but otherwise the relationship is confined very much to the bed and to the mundane considerations that any sexual liaison involves: the logistics of where and when and the safeguards against pregnancy and discovery.

Sensitivities of partners cannot much concern the sexual adventurer. To worry about whether the other person will react with hurt to breaking off the relationship is inconsistent with wanderlust, for the adventurer knows that every sexual relationship he starts will also terminate. But of their relationship it would be unfair and probably incorrect to say the question of their partners' feelings never arises in their minds, for we know that adventurers can love a few or many people without feeling unfaithful to anyone. Whether this kind of love is one-directional, with the emphasis on giving rather than receiving, is the subject of the next section.

"I always know that I'm not going to finish what I start," said one eighteen-year-old boy. "I'll find out more or less about a girl—maybe I'll even grow to love her—but we're not going into other things very deeply. If she expects me to do that, then we've got something serious going that I don't want to stay with."

But another boy, a nineteen year old, put it differently.

> I'll always—well, at least I'll almost always—tell a girl right from the start that I love her. If she wants to believe it the very first time we fuck—I mean that if she thinks anybody really believes seriously that he loves her even before they've done anything together—then why not say so if she wants to hear it that bad? But I'm counting on her not believing me, you know. And if she don't believe me, that's really what I want her to believe—but meanwhile, I've made her respectable if that's what she wants.

10.3 Role of love

Sexual adventurers speak less of love than other intercourse-experienced adolescents. Some may believe they love their sex partners, but they are not filled with the desire to love their sex partners. This is an important differentiating characteristic of the adventurer.

It is easy for the adventurer to feel love for another person when the parameters of a relationship are confined to sexual pleasure. Other tests the adventurer might subject his sex partner to are usually irrelevant. Except insofar as these matters may bear on the sexual relationship, the qualities that one might want in a long-term partner, such as grace, education, the kind of parent one would make, hopes, fears, ambitions for the future, have little interest to the adventurer in evaluating his or her sex partner.

This ease of love permits the girl adventurer to believe she loves any person she willingly sleeps with, if this is psychologically necessary for her. And she is enabled to move in and out of love quite rapidly without confusion or remorse. A seventeen-year-old adventuress observed: "I've fallen out of love many, many times. And so many people say it's not possible. I've fallen out of love—I mean, I just don't love that person anymore. And it's just as fast as falling in love."

Asked about her feelings toward the many boys with whom she had had sexual relationships, she added, "I think they're all love, so I can't say one isn't and one is. I think they all are. No matter how short they've lasted. If it'd only lasted a couple of minutes, I'd still think it was love."

The sexual adventurer often converts a friendship into a sexual relationship, but sometimes the affection or love that characterized the friendship is damaged. They believe that nonsexual friendships have a greater possibility of long duration.

"Oftentimes with me," a fifteen-year-old adventurer told us, "a lot of the friendships I've had that started with sex have deteriorated into just a sex thing, without discussing and getting into rapping and things like that. But a friendship on a regular level, on the other level, just stays there . . . it doesn't ruin fast."

A seventeen-year-old boy adventurer told us: "My best friend and I got into a sexual thing for a while and after a while that's all it was. And after a while we realized that if we wanted to keep our friendship as a friendship, we'd have to get rid of the sex."

Many sexual adventurers believe sex is a pathway to love. They see sex as a means of communication, and we must evaluate whether they are adventurers in part because they cannot otherwise communicate effectively with members of the opposite sex, or whether the sexual activity becomes their principal form of communication. A sixteen-year-old sexual adventurer said:

> I think a lot of relationships get started because people dig each other sexually and they get to know each other because of the sex and the time they spend on it. It's good to have sex at the beginning of the relationship if they want to. A lot of people can't communicate their feeling of love in any other way but sex, because they're not affectionate people and they can't talk about their feelings—or at least you can communicate a greater sense of love through sex.

If sex is a means to secure love, then it naturally follows for many sexual adventurers that love is unnecessary for sex. "I don't agree that you can only have sex when you're in love or something like that," said the same sixteen year old. " 'Cause I think sex is definitely a human emotion and it's not . . . it goes along the lines of love, but it doesn't always necessarily. You don't always eat because you are hungry. You eat for different reasons."

A few adventurers recognized the fact that strong love for the other person made them less ego-involved in the sex act. "When you're having sex with someone you love," a seventeen-year-old adventuress told us, "it's always a very gentle and I think beautiful thing. I think when you're having sex and it's just a strong sexual thing, you just want to get him to do it all, you don't care how. You're not as sensitive. It's different."

On the other hand, friendships for some adventurers are frequently rich with sexual connotations. One sixteen-year-old girl adventurer told us:

> I've had a lot of friends—very good friends—who I've had sex with. I guess it's sort of an unsaid thing in a friendship. You dig each other—you dig each other as bodies and also have a nice head thing. It's very nice to have sex, but you don't get a very attached feeling. It just stays at that point. It doesn't grow into anything else, and I think that's really nice. I think it's a nice feeling to have sex with a friend.

10.4 Characteristics of sexual adventurers

10.4.1. Personal characteristics

10.4.1.1 Sex

Males dominate the sexual adventurer group: 80% of adventurers are boys and 20% are girls. The contrast with the composition of all adolescents and other sexual behavior groups is striking.

Sex composition of adolescent sexual behavior groups

	All adolescents	Nonvirgins		
		All	Monogamists	Adventurers
Male	52%	57%	36%	80%
Female	48%	43%	64%	20%

10.4.1.2 Race

80% of all sexual adventurers are white and 20% are nonwhite. Nonwhites constitute a slightly larger proportion of sexual adventurers than they do of any other sexual behavior group.

10.4.1.3 Age

The average age of all sexual adventurers is 16.8 years. The majority of adventurers are seventeen to nineteen years of age. However, 52% of all adventurers are seventeen to nineteen compared with 70% of all monogamists.

Age composition of adolescent sexual behavior groups

Age	All adolescents	Nonvirgins		
		All	Monogamists	Adventurers
13–15	42%	32%	20%	31%
16–19	58%	68%	80%	69%

10.4.1.4 *Region and locality size*

Sexual adventurers are concentrated in the South, more so than members of any other sexual behavior group. They are substantially fewer in the northeast part of the United States compared with other adolescent groups.

Geographic location of adolescents surveyed and of sexual adventurers

	National sample of adolescents	Adventurers
Northeast	22%	11%
North Central	31	31
South	32	47
West	15	11
TOTAL	100%	100%

Because so many of the adventurers are located in the South, it is not surprising that more of their numbers are in nonmetropolitan areas compared with other sexual behavior groups.

Comparison of adolescents surveyed and sexual adventurers by locality size

	National sample of adolescents	Adventurers
Large metropolitan areas	35%	27%
Small metropolitan areas	34	34
Nonmetropolitan and rural areas	31	39
TOTAL	100%	100%

10.4.1.5 *Religious feeling*

Sexual adventurers express their religious feelings as follows:

15% believe they are very religious.
40% believe they are somewhat religious.
31% believe they are not very religious.
14% believe they are not at all religious.

10.4.1.6 School and school grades

65% of all adventurers are in school. They have lower grades (as a group) than members of other sexual behavior groups. Only 5% receive superior grades, compared with 21% of the monogamists and 15% of the total adolescent population. The bulk of adventurers (62%) receive average grades in about the same proportions as the sexual beginners (58%).

10.4.2 Differentiating sociopolitical attitudes

Adventurers are an amalgam of radical and chauvinist when we evaluate how they uniquely differentiate themselves from other groups in social and political attitudes. They are at odds with their parents, with the older generation, with society, and—in some respects—with themselves.

Fewer adventurers go often to religious services than do members of any other group. They do not look to organized religion for personal assistance in any great numbers.

Adolescents agreeing, "I go to religious services fairly often" (Table 154).

Nonvirgins		Virgins	
Adventurers	Monogamists	Beginners	Inexperienced
25%	45%	52%	69%

In fact, 28% of the adventurers affirm that "One of the reasons I stopped going to church is because churches teach that sex is sinful" (Table 189). Fewer than half of the other sexual behavior groups agree.

10.4.2.1 Generational chauvinism

Although the sexually inexperienced are least chauvinistic about youth, the other three groups are, with two exceptions, uniformly chauvinistic. More adventurers than members of any other group believe, "Young people these days understand more about what is really important in their lives than most older people in their forties and fifties" (Table 230).

Nonvirgins		Virgins	
Adventurers	Monogamists	Beginners	Inexperienced
75%	64%	52%	36%

Relatively greater support is shown by the adventurer group for the statement, "Young people these days understand more about love than most older people in their forties and fifties" (Table 248).

Nonvirgins		Virgins	
Adventurers	Monogamists	Beginners	Inexperienced
70%	48%	36%	39%

This is particularly interesting in view of the considerably lesser emphasis adventurers give to love in any formal sense; 40% of the male adventurers see nothing wrong in saying they love a girl in order to persuade her to have sex if other means do not succeed.

10.4.2.2 Relationship with parents

Of all the sexual behavior groups, sexual adventurers are most in conflict with their parents. 80% of all adolescents assert they have a lot of respect for their parents' ideas and opinions; but only 61% of the adventurers share this view, compared with 78% of the monogamists and 87% of the virgins (Table 19).

Relatively few adolescents agree with the statement, "I can't stand to be around my parents, and I have as little to do with them as possible" (Table 21). But proportionally twice as many adventurers (46%) subscribe to this viewpoint than do monogamists.

Thus, 35% of the adventurers agree, "I have pretty much given up on ever being able to get along with my parents," as compared with 21% of the monogamists and 9% of the virgins (Table 83).

The quarreling and disagreement suggested above need not necessarily compromise affection for one's parents, but two and a half times as many adventurers (45%) as monogamists and three times as many adventurers as virgins affirm, "I don't feel any strong affection for my parents" (Table 46).

Many sexual adventurers do not feel they have gotten to know either parent; 58% of all adventurers feel they have never gotten to know their fathers and 40% believe they have never gotten to know their mothers (Tables 64 and 141). Evidence that parental relationship is a cause (despite the fact that this belief on the part of the adventurer can of course also be an effect) of the adventurer's sexual values and behavior is seen in the strong belief on the part of many adventurers that they have never really gotten to know either of their parents. This problem is an element in the lives of all adolescents and increases with age and sexual experience.

The fact that adventurers are so different from other groups with respect to attitudes toward both parents is also significant when

Adolescents agreeing with statements about how well they know their parents

	"I've never really gotten to know my father"	"I've never really gotten to know my mother"
All adolescents	39%	25%
Boys 16–19	44	30
Girls 16–19	40	22
Adventurers	58	40
Monogamists	48	32
Beginners	31	18
Inexperienced	35	16

we recall that 80% of the adventurers are boys; they, in fact, most frequently feel they never got to know their mothers. It is true that more adventurers feel they know their mothers better as compared with their fathers, but this condition holds for all of the groups.

62% of all adolescents believe that their parents get along with each other very well (Table 60). Broken down by sexual behavior group, 62% of the virgins and 66% of the monogamists also subscribe to this belief, but only 45% of the adventurers agree.

10.4.2.3 Identification with society

45% of all adventurers think of themselves as being revolutionaries, compared with 30% of the monogamists and 18% of the virgins (Table 142). Adventurers (24%) twice as often as virgins believe, "Violence is the only way to get the kind of changes that I would like to see in our society" (Table 88). Once again, however, we have an example of how more of the inexperienced (despite, or because of, their youth) more clearly resemble the adventurers than do the beginners.

Adolescents agreeing, "Violence is the only way to get the kind of changes that I would like to see in our society."

Nonvirgins		Virgins	
Adventurers	Monogamists	Inexperienced	Beginners
24%	8%	16%	8%

Adventurers have comparatively strong reactions against obeying society's folkways and laws. 82% of all adventurers, compared with 53% of the monogamists and 41% of all virgins, affirm: "I find it hard to accept the idea of conforming to society in matters of clothing and personal grooming" (Table 35). Almost as many adventurers find it hard to "accept the idea of obeying laws that I don't agree with" (Table 7).

Nonvirgins		Virgins	
Adventurers	Monogamists	Inexperienced	Beginners
74%	60%	46%	49%

10.5 Differentiating sexual attitudes

Adventurers are by far the most distinctive of the sexual behavior groups in their sexual attitudes. They fail to follow the norms or variations in so many aspects of sexual behavior that we must conclude we are dealing with a special kind of personality. Much more remains to be said about how the adventurer distinguishes himself or herself; we examine here only the most salient differences between the adventurer and the other behavior groups.

The most pronounced differences occur with respect to the following classes of sexual attitudes:

1. Self-confidence and self-esteem
2. Relationship with parents
3. Identification with society
4. Concern with own sexual health
5. Abdication of personal responsibilities
6. Permissiveness about sexual activities
7. Group sex

46% of the adventurers say the statement, "The way I'm living right now, most of my abilities are going to waste" (Table 263), applies to them, while only a little more than one-quarter of all other sexual behavior groups feel this way. Adventurers do not seem to blame their failures on their sexual activity, but their sexual activity in some cases seems to be detracting seriously from the time and effort they might be giving other things.

10.5.1 Self-confidence and self-esteem

For all of their sexual activity, adventurers as a group see relatively little relationship between sex and life's meaning. In our personal interviews, many adventurers reveal (as we indicate elsewhere in this chapter) that they sometimes feel almost driven in their sexual wanderlust and that they believe they are functioning with little purpose and self-contentment. 43% of the adventurers affirm, "Having sex doesn't make my life any more meaningful," compared with 18% of monogamists (Table 321).

Sexual desires are by no means always fulfilled. 66% of all adventurers say, "There are many times when I get horny but don't have anyone to ball," compared with 44% of monogamists (Table 322). And adventurers (50%), virtually twice as often as monogamists (27%), agree, "Sometimes I think that I am addicted to sex, the way some people are addicted to drugs" (Table 328).

Although adventurers feel free to have sex with as many different sex partners as they desire, many feel that prospective sex partners have used sex as a reward or punishment technique with them (Table 331).

Nonvirgin adolescents agreeing, "On one or more occasions, a girl/boy has refused to ball me unless I would do something that I didn't want to do."

All	Boys	Girls	Adventurers	Monogamists
22%	31%	11%	33%	15%

But adventurers reciprocate in the same proportions. Almost a third as many more adventurers as above affirm, "On one or more occasions, I've refused to ball a girl/boy unless she/he would do something that I wanted her/him to do" (Table 320). In fact, adventurers (36%) feel this way twice as often as monogamists (18%).

Adventurers are the least likely by far to deny that their conscience would prevent them from doing some things. 51% of the adventurers, compared with 82% of the monogamists and 71% of all nonvirgins, agree with the statement: "There are some things that I wouldn't do because my conscience would bother me" (Table 77). 54% of all adventurers also agree with the statement, "So far as sex is concerned, I still haven't really made up my mind about what I think is right and wrong for myself" (Table 133).

Perhaps this ambivalence is reflected by the tendency of so many adventurers (34%) to agree, "On one or more occasions, I've done sexual things mostly because the people I was hanging out with at the time expected me to" (Table 70). This reaction was expressed almost three times as often by adventurers than by virgins.

Adventurers are willing the most often to believe they know more than what sex education courses can teach them. 27% of all adventurers agree that "Sex education courses in school can't teach me anything," while monogamists and virgins agree only half as often (Table 3).

10.5.2 Relationship with parents

As was mentioned previously, the relationship between adventurers and their parents is the most conflict-ridden of all among the four behavior groups. Sex and the adventurer's sexuality are undoubtedly among the most difficult aspects of the relationship between the adolescent adventurer and his or her parents.

15% of the adventurers say, "When it comes to sex, my attitudes and my parents' attitudes are pretty much the same" (Table 62), compared to 39% of the monogamists and 46% of the virgins. Clashes resulting from these conflicting attitudes about sex are undoubtedly partly responsible for the fact that 14% of the adventurers—at a rate twice that of all adolescents—believe the statement, "My parents don't really like me" (Table 14).

Perhaps many adventurers generalize from their current hostilities back to their childhood education about sex; on the other hand, perhaps adventurers are reporting conditions in the home that helped make them what they are. 64% of the adventurers—with another 10% not sure—label as false the statement, "As a child, I was taught that sex was natural and healthy" (Table 124); and adventurers (67%), twice as often as virgins and 50% more often than monogamists, agree with the statement, "When I was a child, I was taught that sex was wrong" (Table 187).

"My parents don't get along with each other very well," is affirmed almost twice as often by adventurers (48%) than by monogamists (26%) (Table 184). Adventurers more frequently than others view their parents as not only "old-fashioned" but also as insensitive to the meaning of sex to young people today. 72% of all adventurers, compared with 58% of the monogamists and 31% of the virgins, affirm their wish that their parents "could overcome their own early training, so they could realize that sex is natural and beautiful." (Table 128).

Adventurers feel more harried by their parents than members of any other behavior group in several matters of sex. Perhaps responding to their parents' reactions to their conduct, nearly half of the adventurers believe, "My parents are anxious about whether or not I'm going to get married" (Table 91).

Twice as often as monogamists and over three times more often than virgins, 26% of the adventurers agree, "My parents think that if I have to have sex before getting married, they would rather I do it with a girl/boy I don't love" (Table 171). We included this statement in our questionnaire because adventuresome sex was necessarily a loveless thing for many parents when they were adolescents: a boy did not respect or intend to marry a girl who would have sex with him and a girl condemned herself for being willing to have sex while unmarried. We wondered whether young people today would believe that their parents wanted the loveless sex situation to prevail for their children as well.

10.5.3 Identification with society

If sexual behavior is for some adolescents a means of challenging society, adventurers are the ones who are most frequently carrying out this philosophy in their sexual attitudes and behavior. 66% of all adventurers, as compared to 21% of all virgins, affirm, "My sexual behavior would not be acceptable to society" (Table 270). At the same time, adventurers do identify with their peers in one way: a third of the adventurers—at twice the frequency of monogamists—agree with the statement, "On one or more occasions, I've done sexual things mostly because the people I was hanging out with expected me to" (Table 70).

Of course the unique personality of the adventurer contributes to his or her attitudes about sex. If the adventurer is not antisociety, there is nonetheless some cynicism and even distrust in the adventurer's attitude toward society. Adventurers even rank highest (41%) among all behavior groups in their agreement that "The cancer scare about cigarette smoking has been exaggerated" (Table 267). Fewer adventurers than monogamists (albeit a majority of adventurers) agree, "There are serious flaws in our society, but the system is flexible enough to solve them" (Table 86).

10.5.4 Concern with own sexual health

55% of all adventurers agree, "If I go for a long time without having sex, I get to feeling uptight" (Table 300). Uniquely preoccupied with the physical benefits of sex, adventurers (44%) agree twice as often as monogamists and virgins, "The most important thing in a sexual relationship is just the sheer physical pleasure of having sex" (Table 266).

Sex and health are important to each other in the rationale of the adventurer. 56% of all adventurers believe, "It isn't healthy for someone my age to go for a long time without having sex" (Table 98). Adventurers feel this way 50% more frequently than monogamists and three times as often as virgins. But they also feel this way about boys and girls in general. 50% of all adventurers, compared to 31% of the monogamists and 28% of the virgins, agree, "I would consider it abnormal or unnatural for a girl not to have sex until she gets married" (Table 114).

10.5.5 Abdication of personal responsibilities

"Abdication" may be too strong a term to describe the attitude of the adventurer toward his or her personal sexual responsibilities. This description is not meant to be pejorative: "abdicate" simply means to yield one viewpoint in favor of alternative viewpoints which sexual adventuring and wanderlust require.

The question of fidelity to one's partner is a moot one for most adventurers. 54% of the adventurers agree, "If I were to have sex with another girl/boy, just occasionally, it wouldn't really put my girl friend/boyfriend uptight" (Table 316). 31% of the monogamists agreed; again, their current sexual relationship is somewhat different than that which the adventurer enjoys with his or her sex partner of the moment.

"Someday, I will probably want to have children—but it won't matter whether or not I get married first," is affirmed by 56% of the adventurers, compared with 39% of the monogamists and 12% of the virgins (Table 180).

At almost double the rate of monogamists (24%), 42% of the adventurers concede that under the influence of alcohol they have had sex with someone that they would not have had sex with otherwise (Table 299).

10.5.6 Permissiveness about sexual activities

Adventurers distinguish themselves most of all in their readiness to accept a wide variety of sexual activities. Adventurers, along with other adolescents, do in the main condemn incest, forced sex, and homosexuality as immoral. But any sexual activity involving voluntarily participating heterosexual boys and girls finds strong tolerance from them.

All adolescents are tolerant of other people's sexual activities in the abstract, and adventurers are the most so; 87% of all adventurers believe, "Where sex is concerned, anything people want to do is all right so long as they want to do it and it doesn't hurt them" (Table 240). At twice the rate of virgins and somewhat more frequently than monogamists, 71% of the adventurers also agree, "There is no kind of sex act that I would think of as being abnormal, so long as the people involved want to do it" (Table 261).

Adventurers do not often consider sex for money as forced sex.

59% of the adventurers do not agree, "The laws against prostitution (having sex for money) should continue to remain in force" (Table 239). Nor do a majority of adventurers feel their respect for a girl would necessarily be compromised if they learned she accepted money for sex; less than one half of the adventurers (43%) affirmed, "If I found out that a girl had had sex for money, even once, I would lose respect for her" (Table 209). 55% of the monogamists and 71% of the virgins thought otherwise.

Sexual experience is highly valued by the adventurer. For this reason many adventurers believe that one's first encounter in sexual intercourse should be with an experienced sex partner. Half of all adventurers believe, "When a boy has sex for the first time, it should be with a girl who is sexually experienced" (Table 276). Not surprisingly, perhaps because so many boys are adventurers, a greater number of adventurers (60%) agree, "When a girl has sex for the first time, it should be with a boy who is sexually experienced" (Table 293).

Having many sex partners rather than one or a few is of course what mainly distinguishes the adventurer from other nonvirgins. Three times more frequently than virgins and twice as often as monogamists, adventurers (68%) believe that it is better to have sexual relationships with several different people rather than just one person (Table 238). Almost twice as often as monogamists, adventurers (60%) agree, "For the sake of variety, it's all right for married people to have sexual relations with other people once in a while" (Table 281). Twice as often as virgins, adventurers (63%) agree it is all right for a person to have sexual relations with both males and females, if that is what the person wants to do (Table 282).

Adventurers are somewhat informal in their attitudes toward meeting, knowing, and relating to another person for purposes of sexual intercourse. Twice as frequently as monogamists and four times as frequently as virgins, 82% of the adventurers agree, "If you really dig a girl/boy, it's all right to have sex with her/him even if you've only known her/him for a few hours" (Table 111). Only 35% of all adventurers believe, "It would be wrong for me to have sex with a girl/boy I'd just met and hadn't gotten to know"; monogamists agreed twice as frequently (70%) (Table 165).

Differences between adventurers and monogamists such as these do not exist only because of the personality and attitudes of the adventurer. The monogamist must also, by definition, have strong leanings toward certain types of sexual behavior. It would be surprising if a majority of monogamists were to feel comfortable about a boy having intercourse with a girl after knowing her for only a few hours.

The average monogamist does not pursue others; may deny this past element in his or her life, if, indeed, it was ever there; and may reject adventurism in favor of a more stable series of monogamous relationships.

Love and adventurism, as we have already learned, may not be opposites, but they are by no means complementary in the sexuality of many adventurers. A third of all adventurers, compared with two-thirds of all monogamists, agree with the statement, "I wouldn't want to have sex with a girl/boy unless she/he loved me" (Table 168).

Because several young people have referred to sex as a medium of communication and as the means by which they learned to know people much better, we asked adolescents to agree or disagree with the statement, "Having sex together is a good way for two people to become acquainted" (Table 279). 60% of the adventurers agreed, compared to 38% of the monogamists and 19% of all virgins.

Generally, double standards as traditionally applied to girls and women do not appeal to adventurers, who differentiate themselves from other sexual behavior groups in this regard. Although male adventurers are less willing than male monogamists to marry a girl who is not a virgin (Table 103), a higher proportion of adventurers than monogamists, who themselves are permissive, disagree with the statement, "A girl should stay a virgin until she finds the boy she wants to marry" (Table 208). Only 20% of all adventurers agreed, compared to 31% of all monogamists and 58% of all virgins.

There is one major exception to adventurers' intolerance of double standards. 55% of the adventurers compared with 31% of the monogamists affirm, "When it comes to deciding how far a boy and girl should go where sex is concerned, it is up to the girl to decide" (Table 274).

Adventurers are more flexible concerning the race of their sex partners; 26% of all adventurers, in contrast to 55% of the monogamists, agreed with the statement, "I don't think that I would want to have sex with a person of another race" (Table 15).

10.5.7 Group sex

Adventurers like to feel they can enjoy sex under a wide variety of conditions. Their greater willingness to indulge in group sex is an example of this. Compared with 67% of the monogamists, 39% of the adventurers (the lowest proportion of agreement of all the sexual behavior groups) agreed with the statement, "I would be embarrassed about having sex with a girl/boy if there were anyone else in the same room" (Table 104).

Group sex attracts very few adolescents, and then mostly only adventurers. One seventeen-year-old adventuress describes the experience.

> Different situations have come up where I have had sex with two other people or three maybe, and I like it. I guess everyone goes through that—well, maybe not everyone—but if I'm not involved with a marriage type of thing with somebody, a very heavy type of relationship, I dig it. I don't know how I'd feel about doing it with someone I was really in love with and having sex with him with somebody else too. I know that I dig it with people I'm sexually attracted to—I like it then—but I feel that if I were really involved with somebody in a really having, loving relationship, I don't know how I would feel about having sex with him and also with somebody else. And even though it's not going to be the heavy thing on me if he has sex with somebody else, I just don't want to be there. I wouldn't want to be part of it.
>
> I've done sex in a group of people quite a lot. I can't remember the number of times, but quite a lot. Sometimes it's been a guy and another girl—three of us. Or two guys and myself. Or there have been other times when there's been a lot of people—six, seven, eight, nine people. But that hasn't happened that much. I'm really not into group sex more than a couple of people. I like it with two other people. I like that—a threesome—that's nice.
>
> The first time I was in a group sex situation, it was kind of interesting. I used to take a lot of drugs—I've been through a lot of drugs, and I used to do a lot of downs. Not so that I would get really messed up—sloppy that's ridiculous, but one or two gets you feeling very nice and all your inhibitions are gone. You just do what you want. And that was really the times when I was really getting into group sex. I was into Seconals and things like that, and that got me feeling—I really wasn't inhibited. So I guess that helped. If you're feeling something for someone and you really want to get into something like that and you're feeling kind of high, it's a lot easier. A lot of times I've done it, it seemed like just a natural thing to have it.
>
> Yes, I felt that way the first time I had group sex. Especially the first time, it seemed natural. The first time I had sex with just two guys. I had had sex with one of them before but with the second guy it was the first time.

One seventeen-year-old boy adventurer looked at group sex as a humorous phenomenon.

> Group sex makes intercourse comical. It's like a bunch of people getting together and clowning around. It's like a big joke. Nobody's serious. I've only done it with some people when I've been stoned, or at least a little stoned, nothing serious.
>
> I remember one time I was having group sex. It was hilarity—the desire to do something different. We all loved each other in a way—kind of a unison of one. You pretty much stick to one person, but there was a little switching around. The people who were going together stayed together. There's less jealousy in that situation than when the other person has sex with somebody. There's got to be a feeling where

I'm going with a girl and that's why group sex doesn't interest me. In a group set, there isn't much jealousy if you haven't gotten to know anyone seriously. I couldn't switch if I were in love with one person there.

A seventeen-year-old girl adventuress did not enjoy group sex.

There's one sexual experience that I did leave out which was having two people doing things to me at the same time but not with each other. Two males—but not having anything to do with each other.

Somebody was like feeling me and talking to me and another person was not even saying anything and was trying to get my underwear off and by the time he got my underwear off the other person was all ready to ball me and I wasn't ready for it and I stopped the whole thing. But I didn't stop it until they both were like—it was like I was just sitting there talking and it was like the most natural thing in the world. I felt removed and I still feel removed sometimes I guess when I'm having sex. I think it flusters me and freaks me out so much. It did then, you know; two people were doing two different things to me at the same time and I wasn't responding to either of them except one of them I was kissing. Then I was kissing the other one and it's just like it blows my mind when I think of it because it bothers me now and it didn't bother me then. I always thought it would be the other way around.

10.6 Behavioral history

The sexual adventurer differs considerably from other adolescents, with girl adventurers being especially unique. To the extent that mind and sexual desire combine to produce adventurism, the data indicate that the sexual adventurer's destiny may sometimes be predictable in early adolescence. One dimension of predictability involves the age of first sexual intercourse and the total number of sex partners. However, we cannot assume that sexual adventurism results from early sexual intercourse, nor can we assume that late first intercourse assures the absence of sexual adventurism.

10.6.1 Age at first sexual intercourse

The age at first intercourse varies for the different groups, with adventurers beginning at the earliest average age of all (Table 340). 43% of all adventurers have their first intercourse experience at thirteen years of age or before, compared with 15% of all monogamists. The rate of conversion from virginity to nonvirginity drops for the adventurer group at age fourteen, while dropping for the monogamist group at age sixteen. The age at first intercourse for all adventurers and monogamists is as follows:

Age at first intercourse	Adventurers	Monogamists
12 or under	21%	6%
13	22	9
14	17	11
15	15	25
16	10	23
17	7	8
18	8	18
TOTAL	100%	100%

10.6.2 Cumulative number of sex partners

All nonvirgin boys have had sexual intercourse with an average of 9.8 girls. All nonvirgin girls have had sexual intercourse with an average of 3.5 boys. All adolescent sexual adventurers have had sex with an average of 16.3 persons.

As compared to monogamists, sexual adventurers accumulate a very large number of different sex partners. 47% of all monogamists have had only one sex partner, while 45% of the adventurers have had a total of seven or more sex partners (Table 341).

Our data do not show us the number of sex partners adventurers and monogamists will have accumulated as of any specific age from thirteen to nineteen. However, Tables 342 and 343 reveal that boys and girls in the younger and older age-groups have accumulated varying totals of different sex partners during their lifetimes.

Number of different intercourse partners	Nonvirgins: Boys 13–15	Nonvirgins: Boys 16–19	Nonvirgins: Girls 13–15	Nonvirgins: Girls 16–19	Adventurers
4–6	15%	27%	13%	14%	34%
7–15	19	18	1	16	15
16 or more	3	19	0	4	30
TOTAL	37%	64%	14%	34%	79%

The percentage of boy and girl nonvirgins who have had a total of four or more sex partners increases substantially with age. 37% of the boys in the younger age-group have had four or more different sex partners, compared to 64% of the boys in the older age-group. 14% of the younger girls have had four or more different sex partners, compared with 34% of the older girls.

10.7 Active adventurism behavior

Sexual adventurers are more active than monogamists with respect to the number of sex partners they have had during the past month and less active than monogamists with respect to the number of occasions on which they have had intercourse during the preceding month.

10.7.1 Number of current sex partners

Adventurers have had sex with an average of 2.3 different sex partners during the past month, compared with the monogamists' 1.1 sex partners. 53% of all adventurers had two or more different sex partners during the preceding month, compared to 8% of the monogamists. 47% of all adventurers, compared to 92% of all monogamists, had one sex partner during the past month.

Number of different sex partners during past month of active nonvirgins (Table 346)

	Adventurers	Monogamists
1	47	92
2	18	8
3	20	0
4	11	0
5 or more	4	0
TOTAL	100%	100%

10.7.2 Frequency of intercourse

We measured the frequency of sexual intercourse in two ways: the *most recent* occasion on which respondents had sex and the number of times they had intercourse during the preceding month.

81% of all adventurers had their most recent intercourse experience during the preceding month, compared to 93% of all monogamists (Table 344). Surely one explanation for more sexual adventurers having had less current intercourse experience than monogamists is that more adventurers are boys and more monogamists are girls. 53% of all nonvirgin boys, compared to 73% of all nonvirgin girls, had sexual intercourse at least once during the preceding month (Table 345). The fact that so many boys are sexual adventurers is of course one explanation for the smaller number of boys having current intercourse; we have already referred to the problems associated with adventurism intercourse as compared with monogamous intercourse.

Number of times active nonvirgins had intercourse during past month (Table 348)

	Adventurers	Monogamists
1 time	22%	9%
2 times	21	11
3 times	17	11
4 times	12	13
5–8 times	8	15
9–12 times	6	15
13–19 times	14	10
20 or more times	0	16
TOTAL	100%	100%

We found no relationship between the number of sex partners an adventurer had during the preceding month and the number of times he or she had intercourse during the preceding month. We did not learn how many times the adventurer had sex with each sex partner during the preceding month, and so we do not know whether or not the typical adventurer tends to distribute the number of intercourse occasions fairly evenly among the sex partners he or she has.

10.8 Techniques and feelings in sexual intercourse

Elsewhere we refer to the relatively unsophisticated techniques and insensitivity to one's sex partner that characterize many adolescents' approach to sexual intercourse. Among those whom we interviewed in depth, male and female adventurers more frequently express interest in sexual fantasy and foreplay than do monogamists and other nonvirgins. Although adventurers are generally more technique-oriented than monogamists, they are less frequently concerned with mutual sharing and relating to their sex partners in other ways that can also influence physical pleasure in the intercourse experience. When adventurers concentrate on technique, it is usually for technique's sake alone in the immediate intercourse situation.

Many adventurers offer observations about their physical feelings before and during sexual intercourse and what is important to them. Of particular interest are their comments on sexual foreplay, fantasy in connection with intercourse, and female orgasm.

One reason the sexual adventurers like their way of life is because they feel that "sex gets better and better as it goes along." The adventurer believes that what he is able to learn from sex he can often apply to his own personality in other aspects of living. Boy and girl adventurers give great emphasis to feeling—"Just like you learn to speak, you learn to feel. In a way I can understand that, because feelings are very important to me. But I think it's something you learn. Just like you learn to love, you learn to speak, you learn to think, so you learn to feel."

10.8.1 Sexual foreplay

The behavior between two people as their minds and emotions close in on each other for sexual intercourse takes place quickly or in many steps, depending upon the immediate emotions and ambitions of the sex partners.

One eighteen-year-old adventurer discusses how his own self-confidence is improved as the girl indicates her willingness to have intercourse: "My voice changes as I become more or less self-confident. My behavior does also, I suppose. Because when I know I am being approved by a girl, it gives me license to be myself totally and I don't have to hide anything. I don't have to change anything. I am really myself."

He goes on to discuss how people who are ready for intercourse signal to each other through their eyes:

> Well, perhaps the way a person looks at you has something to do with it. A wide-eyed look—that's what I look for—a wide-eyed look by the girl, an allured look as opposed to a bored, monotonous look that just stares and stares and stares. This look is different. It's alive. . . . It looks at you as though she wanted something. There is also a lot of irony about how she might look. There's that devilish look—look what I'm going to do or look what I've done. It's on their faces, and so it must be on mine too.
>
> As a general rule it's me that gets them started. Following the voice and the look and all of this crap. Then you move your body up against this person and you very carefully put your lips against hers. That's step number two. You must be alone in case you're not by now. That's step number three. Step number four comes when you remove this person's attire. Then he removes his attire, the person who initiated it all. Then they feel each other's bodies for about five minutes. With me, that probably does it. I find that I can enjoy the sex act a lot more if I build up to it more. Actually, five minutes isn't right. It's more like fifteen minutes.

This same adventurer suggested that he did not vary foreplay with each girl. We sought to clarify the situation. This particular young man had no experience with oral sex or anal sex. His pattern of behavior was very much the same from girl to girl, although he did recognize differences in girls' reactions and tried to meet them to a degree.

When you've known a girl for a long time you begin to notice patterns. I follow a pattern every time I have sex. The other person does too. When you catch on to this, you can cooperate with it rather than fight it and try to do something different. All little things, lots of little things. But when you add them up and put them all together, it spells out total harmony.

Little things—what rouses her very much and I do it. When you're kissing, you get to realize what you each like. For example, with kissing, for one girl it's important to be putting your lower lip between her upper lip and her lower lip. These things are not very significant, but they add up. Maybe she enjoys being held very tightly in her back, so you do this. . . . You notice these things by their breathing, if it's intensified you know it's doing something. Mainly breathing, and I suppose emotion too. But the more aroused a girl is the faster her heart beats and the faster she breathes. Then there are some vocal things too like sighs and big breaths.

One boy adventurer, like many of them, does not vary foreplay in accordance with the particular person that he is with. He does make his own assumptions, however, about how a girl feels.

Usually a girl's breasts will harden. Most girls like to be felt a lot. They like to be massaged. I don't know how to describe this difference in pressure—but it's light pressure as opposed to deep pressure. All over the body. I never touch a girl's sex organs. I always seem to be the one to decide when it's time to go in. Why that moment instead of another? Well, that's when I reach the point I can no longer wait. If I wait too long I might get myself all run down.

I'll tell you something more about foreplay. I make it different because some girls have very nice boobs; others don't. Some have very nice legs; others don't. You feel a sensual pleasure during foreplay in the way of—I'll tell you the symptoms rather than the actual feelings. I find that sometimes my heart begins to beat very fast. The same sensation as when you're out of breath, a shortness of breath. Not that I do have a shortness of breath. I'm perfectly full of breath, but it's still the same feeling. And then again, there's the actual touch. The same kind of thing you feel when you touch a table or a chair instead of a wall. It feels good rather than flat and stoney. And I really can't describe it any better than that. Oh, one thing. What I enjoy most about foreplay is my legs rubbing against hers. And I also like stomachs too. I could never get the same feeling by just touching her legs or touching her boobs that comes from feeling all of her at once with all of me. That's why the sensations are different to me in intercourse than they are in foreplay. It means that all of me, my penis included, is participating. The sensations are different when all of me is up against all of her. It's when your whole body is in contact with another whole body that my big arousal comes.

10.8.2 Fantasy concerning intercourse

This study was not intended to probe the depths of emotional and fantasy life during sexual intercourse. However, some findings have emerged which help us better understand adolescent sexuality and the personality of the adventurer. Many adventurers do little fantasy thinking during sexual intercourse, and they seldom regard it as a technique by which to enhance emotional or physical enjoyment of the intercourse experience itself.

One conclusion we have reached is that most adolescents exercise little imagination and fantasy during sexual intercourse. They are more preoccupied with the fact it is happening, the question of mechanics, and concern for success or failure—however the adolescent may define success and failure. (The attempt to formulate a common definition for perceived success and failure in sexual intercourse was abandoned after the personal depth interviews, because virtually every adolescent had his or her own definition or lacked any definition.)

There is considerably more fantasizing about intercourse—and by no means exclusively with one's own sex partner—at times other than the actual intercourse occasion. Fantasy thinking during masturbation is described in Chapter 5. Some other examples will be given later in this section.

One sixteen-year-old adventuress describes what she enjoys saying and hearing in the way of fantasy during intercourse.

> Sometimes I fantasize a whole scene with them and I tell them about it. Sometimes I will fantasize being with somebody and tell them the whole story, just different things. And I dig telling them because I know it excites them. I do that a lot.
>
> For example, I guess I would imagine a scene in a big beautiful bed—this is one, but it could be so many different things—in a beautiful big bed, king-size, with beautiful satin sheets—just doing everything to each other like absolutely everything that was whatever he wanted, I would do. I would talk about our staying in bed all day and all night, just doing whatever we pleased.

The fantasies of one adventuress outside of intercourse deserve reading for two reasons. One is the manner in which certain books became her sexual bibles. Certain books, ranging from works of great merit to commercialized pornography, often become important to individual adolescents for circumstantial reasons that deserve far more study. Believing that some books are scientific or literary or "mind blowing," those adolescents typified by this girl get caught up in the attitudes and behavior of fictionalized personalities or case histories that have no valid bearing on their sex lives. The consequences are sometimes injurious, because deviation and depravity often are assumed to be norms which the unsophisticated or sexually hungry adolescent believes he or she must follow.

The second reason for quoting this girl at such length is that some female adventurers are addicted to sex—not as nymphomaniacs but as passive victims who have grown to dislike males so violently that they justify their beliefs by meeting and succumbing to vicious types of older boys or men. Fantasies such as those described below often accompany these hostilities, if not the actual experiences themselves. Females engaging in such activities have no sexual satisfaction from their contact with the pimp and the pervert, but they do find satisfaction in their fantasizing about the worst that can happen to them at the hands of men.

An eighteen-year-old girl adventurer who had no orgasm or satisfaction in intercourse with over fifty men describes her fantasies outside of intercourse.

> I used to have incredible fantasies. I used to fantasize about all the people I wanted to be with. I'd fantasize about my prince. I got into it for a really long time. And I lived one of them for a period of time after my first lover. I had dreams and daytime dreams. Sitting down and thinking and closing my eyes and saying there was someone there. But it was out of loneliness. I got into such a heavy analysis trip of it that I couldn't continue it because I became so aware of it that it stopped. They were like. . . . He was okay. He was pretty good to me. I had incredible fantasies of meeting somebody who was physically very abusive. I read a book a long time ago—*The Story of O.* My sister had never read it. I showed it to her, and she just freaked when she read it. She told me to hide it. Everybody has read it. Every adult who is not an ignorant dolt has read that book—including my father. He found it in my room and he threw it out. The guy who was the social worker of my first lover, he found it—his wife found it in my purse one day. She tore it up and threw it out because she read part of it. I was never allowed in the house after that. That was the reason I just thought of that. I had about eight copies of that book. That book was my fantasy for years. That book fucked up my sexual life for a long time. My father told me that book was inhuman—that that book was written by a female who hated men. That book was my fantasy.
>
> Somebody else came out with a book, too. See, there was a trip behind that book. I don't really remember the book; I just remember a few things from it and the idea of it, but I remember reading it about five times. The book didn't turn me on like a pornographic book turns people on, but it turned me on in the sense that it stimulated me—like my adrenalin—but it didn't just stimulate me physically. And I'd read it and I'd sit there; and that book caused one of the heaviest dreams that I have ever had in my entire life. But I had the dream about four years after I had read the book. I got hold of that book when I was about twelve, and that just blew it. I read it when I was thirteen and fourteen, and I haven't seen it since—so that was about three years ago. And I really have fantasies about me being O. And I told my sister about it, and she said, "Don't you realize why O's name is O?—it's because she is nothing." And my concept was the exact opposite: I said she was superwoman.
>
> My girl friend's sister had all these strange books. She had another book about this woman who ran this hotel. A place where she

would tie kids—males and females—together and make them have sex with each other. And that book just freaked me out. That was when I was thirteen, too.

I didn't have any fantasies about that except I had a dream about making love with somebody in a bathtub. I still remember that, because I thought it was very funny. It didn't mean anything—it was just an absurd dream as far as I could see. But *The Story of O* made me have these fantasies . . . these desires. . . . In *The Story of O* she tries to seduce another female, and I always knew inside how I wanted to be seduced by a man, and since it never happened, I kind of transferred it and had a fantasy about seducing a female when I was about thirteen.

No male has ever seduced me. Seduced me in a very feminine way. I can't explain it. I always wanted to be—it's like men give women flowers so that they can have them. So that they can eventually get something together. And women give themselves to men so that they can have a man. And I always worked like that. I never gave a man a chance to seduce me, because I gave myself immediately without any hesitation; and I think I really resented men for that. Even at that time. Even when I was fourteen, I had this one sexual fantasy that I was being seduced by an older woman; instead of me being seduced, I wanted to be the seducer because of *The Story of O*. . . . But O's friend had a little sister who was just dying to have a part of everything, and that's who I guess I identified with because she was distant from everything else. And she was also so young. So I had a fantasy about being seduced by an older woman—but I have absolutely no idea where it came from.

I still don't know what it feels like, because I still have never been seduced by a man. I have no desire to have any physical relationship with a female. But I think the reason that I had any kind of fantasy with a female—I don't know why an older female, I just know that it's there—and I have a feeling that it's still there, but I just block it. But I think it's a female because females are more compassionate than men. Women are definitely more compassionate than men. Women's relationships with each other are always closer than a woman's relationship with a man.

I know one female who is gay, and I work with her. She is not ashamed of it, and she doesn't care if anyone knows; but she won't talk about it. I know she's gay because it's there. It's very strange because most of the gay females that I have ever met are . . . I have a theory as to what it is—that everyone in this whole world is gay. And that people fantasize that they want it and they get into it and they have it. And people that decide that they don't want it have something else. And if they don't have one of those two things then they're miserable.

10.8.3 Female orgasm

Two-thirds of all adventurers agree on the importance of the orgasm for the girl sex partner (Table 327). At least a third of the girl adventurers are satisfied by their orgasm frequency. However, the rate of female orgasm is considerably less among girl adventurers than it is among girl monogamists.

A seventeen-year-old boy sees orgasm in the girl as a challenge with every sex partner.

> Orgasm in the other person is important to me because it's a high form of sexual pleasure and I want to give the other person as much pleasure as possible. It is difficult with some girls. I play with her or then we have oral sex, and I keep doing one or the other until it happens.
>
> Sex is a very growing thing. Like sort of every time you have sex, you experience it more. I don't think there could be one sexual experience just like another, so each thing is a different experience and you learn from each different experience.

A fourteen-year-old boy feels it is selfish if only he has an orgasm.

> If I'm having a relationship with a girl, it's important to me that she have an orgasm. Otherwise I'd feel that I haven't given anything and I'm taking it all.
>
> That doesn't mean though that you can't be yourself. I feel that when you have sex with a person you should be yourself. Be what you are and not have responsibilities and expectations and things like that. Don't try to live up to the other person's expectations.

A nineteen-year-old adventuress describes her first experience with an orgasm.

> It first happened to me when I was sixteen, and it was nice. To tell you the truth, I wasn't really sure that's what it was. It happened a couple of more times and then I knew. But the first time—unless it's only me—I found out that the first time I do anything it's never the best in sex. Once I learned what muscles to use here and how to do this, it gets much better. That's why it doesn't bother me that the first time I had an orgasm I wasn't too sure about it.
>
> I mentioned it to my boyfriend. I said "What do you suppose that was?"
>
> He said, "You had an orgasm."
>
> I said, "Really, was that what it was?" I said, "It was nice, but I'm not too sure that's what it was."
>
> He said, "Yes, that's what it was," and then we did it some more and it got better and better and I knew that that was it.
>
> It's always different and it's always the same, too. Sometimes I have to work harder at it—sometimes I don't have to work at it at all. The nicest is when I'm not concentrating on it and when I'm not working at it.
>
> But I never expect him to obey instructions from me. I never say do this and do that and neither does he, because I think that would detract. It would make it all a conscious effort rather than something that's just occurring and natural.

A sixteen-year-old girl who is a sexual adventuress describes her frequent orgasms.

> They are fantastic. It's like the most beautiful release of everything. It really gets you to that point. It really keeps you in there. How can I describe it? It's just a fantastic release.
>
> When I'm having sex with somebody . . . when I have an orgasm, I know it's coming and from there it just gets really intense. You know you're going to reach that certain point and it grows and grows and grows and finally you have an orgasm and it's just beautiful because you just let it go.
>
> I remember when I was young, very young . . . I have to this day incredible sexual peaks—absolutely unbelievable. But I remember when I was younger—about six or seven—in my sleep I would just be aware that I was experiencing some fantastic feeling. I didn't know what it was then. But in my dream, and I didn't know what I was dreaming of, but it would cause me to have an orgasm in my sleep. And I remember just waking up as I'm having it, and I didn't know what it was that I was feeling. I wanted it to happen again, but I didn't know how it had happened.
>
> I started masturbating when I was very young. I started finding different parts of my body and playing with certain parts, and I felt that feeling again. And so I knew I had it there. I love my body.
>
> There are two or three activities that can make me have an orgasm. I like to be eaten. I like that rather than when I'm actually having intercourse with him—that is, I like to have my orgasm separately. I know I can have an orgasm when I'm being eaten or fingered. I can have orgasm one, two, three—one after another when I'm being eaten or fingered. I feel it all over—my breasts and my nipples get very hard. My feet have muscle contractions—spasms in a way—throughout my whole thighs, my legs, my feet, my whole body.

10.9 Use of marijuana

More sexual adventurers sample marijuana than do other classes of young people, and they have considerably more tolerance about its use than others do. 58% of all adventurers agree that they "like to smoke marijuana sometimes," compared with 46% of all nonvirgins (Table 126). The fact that 13% of all beginners and inexperienced sometimes smoke marijuana demonstrates that the kind of adolescent who tends to be a sexual adventurer also tends to carry his adventuring to activities other than sex.

57% of all adventurers believe that "drugs are more harmful than alcohol," compared to 63% of all monogamists and 84% of all virgins (Table 138).

22% of the sexual adventurers also agree, "Smoking marijuana is an important thing in my life," while only 12% of monogamists and 4% of all virgins agree (Table 30).

Permissiveness toward the use of marijuana is also greater among adventurers, 84% of whom agree, "Whether or not to use marijuana should be up to each person to decide for himself, like with alcohol and tobacco" (Table 130). This form of permissiveness is relatively high among all adolescents; 73% of all adolescents, 65% of the virgins, and 81% of the monogamists maintain this same level of tolerance for marijuana.

42% of adventurers, compared with 40% of monogamists and 33% of virgins, agree, "Marijuana increases sexual pleasure" (Table 286). But only 31% of adventurers, compared to 34% of monogamists and 48% of beginners, believe, "Alcohol increases sexual pleasure" (Table 269).

10.10 Attitudes toward other types of sexual behavior

Sexual adventurers do not evidence significantly more feelings of doubt, guilt, or shame than other young people. They lack the self-righteousness of some of the sexually inexperienced, the satisfaction and self-contentment of many serial monogamists, and the anticipations of the sexual beginner. Most are happy about their sex lives but not always satisfied with themselves as human beings. Perhaps they are a little bit smug about the sex and love they obtain in return for their minimum investment of obligation and responsibility. But some adventurers, such as the girl we cited at length, are lost souls whose adventurism has led them to become passive victims of the more selfish and unscrupulous adventurers.

Adventurers (76%) rank as high as all adolescents in their agreement that "Too many people these days are irresponsible where sex is concerned" (Table 289). They are at the top (95%) of all sexual behavior groups believing, "Hurting another person is wrong" (Table 243).

Most adventurers do not look down upon others. More adventurers than say so probably look forward to settling down to a monogamous relationship in later life. But the majority would not consider sexual monogamy during adolescence. Despite the fact that boy adventurers usually have sex with girls who want to believe they are having a relationship with deepening potential, these boys do not intend to change their pattern of sexual behavior. As long as their sex partners tolerate all that goes with adventurism, boy adventurers will undoubtedly continue to prefer it to other forms of sexual behavior. Many girl adventurers feel similarly.

We do not know whether most adventurers do inevitably convert to a more steady relationship with one sex partner, or how frequently this occurs during adolescence. The fact that the average serial monogamist has had relatively few sex partners suggests not, but further study is required. In fact, we also need to learn whether such conversion, if it takes place, is more frequently directly to serial monogamy without marriage or to marriage itself.

10.11 Salient findings

1. Sexual adventurers view their adventurism as a way of life. They seek many mates without interest in initiating or maintaining a sexual relationship. They insist primarily on their freedom to have sex with anyone.

2. 15% of all American adolescents are sexual adventurers: 24% of all boys and 6% of all girls are adventurers.

3. Currently active sexual adventurers had intercourse with an average of 2.3 people in the preceding month. During adolescence, the sexual adventurer has an average of 16.3 sex partners.

4. New and different sexual activities are important to the adventurer. 75% of all adventurers agree, "Sex is one of the few human activities where there is always something new to be discovered," compared with 59% of the monogamists. 49% of all adventurers agree, "There isn't anything in sex that I wouldn't want to try, at least once."

5. Males dominate the sexual adventurers; 80% of these are boys and 20% are girls.

6. Those adventurers who are in school average lower grades (as a group) than members of other sexual behavior groups. Only 5% receive superior grades, compared with 21% of the monogamists and 15% of the total adolescent population.

7. Adventurers believe more than twice as frequently as members of any other sexual behavior group that the way they are living most of their abilities are going to waste.

8. 28% of the adventurers affirm, "One of the reasons I stopped going to church is because churches teach that sex is sinful." Only half as many adventurers as members of any other group attend church services often.

9. Most adventurers believe that it is possible for a boy or girl to be really in love with more than one girl or boy at the same time. Age and amount of sexual experience seem to make little difference in this reaction.

10. 40% of the male adventurers see nothing wrong in saying they love a girl in order to persuade her to have sex if other means do not succeed.

11. 80% of all adolescents assert they have a lot of respect for

their parents' ideas and opinions, but only 61% of the adventurers share this view.

12. Twice the proportion of adventurers (46%) as monogamists (21%) agree they cannot stand to be around their parents. And adventurers much more frequently than any other group feel they have not gotten to know their fathers (58%) or their mothers (40%).

13. Three-quarters of all adventurers find it hard to accept the idea of obeying laws they do not agree with and twice the percentage of adventurers (82%) as virgins (41%) find it hard to accept the idea of conforming to society in matters of clothing and personal grooming.

14. Over one-half of all adventurers like to smoke marijuana sometimes. Adventurers are also unique in the importance they credit marijuana as being in their lives; 22% of all adventurers affirm this compared with 12% of the monogamists and 4% of all virgins.

15. Almost twice the percentage of adventurers (50%) as monogamists (27%) agree with the statement, "Sometimes I think that I am addicted to sex, the way some people are addicted to drugs."

16. At almost double the rate of monogamists (24%), 42% of the adventurers concede that under the influence of alcohol they have had sex with someone they would not have had sex with otherwise.

17. A third of the adventurers affirm that refusal to have sex is a reward or punishment technique they use and is used against them.

18. 71% of the adventurers agree, "There is no kind of sex act that I would think of as being abnormal, so long as the people involved want to do it." Adventurers are the least likely of all groups to deny that their conscience would prevent them from engaging in certain sexual activities.

19. 82% of the adventurers agree that it is all right to have sex with someone you "really dig" even if you have only known that person for only a few hours.

20. 60% of the adventurers, compared to 38% of the monogamists and 19% of all virgins, agree, "Having sex together is a good way for two people to become acquainted."

21. Adventurers far more frequently than other nonvirgins emphasize the physical benefits of sex and express concern about boys and girls going without sex.

22. 43% of all adventurers, compared with 15% of all monogamists, have their first intercourse experience at thirteen years of age or younger.

23. Adventurers generally respond with little favor to double standards being applied to girls' and boys' sexual behavior.

24. Adventurers (95%) believe that "hurting another person is wrong."

25. Adventurers are usually more technique-oriented than monogamists in connection with sexual intercourse, but they are far less likely to relate to their partners in nonsexual matters. Female adventurers report much less frequently than female monogamists that they have orgasm during intercourse.

11.
Adolescent Homosexuality

If love is so very important, what's more important: two people loving each other or the fact they both happen to be men?

A nineteen-year-old
nonhomosexual male

I don't think I've ever met a lesbian; but if I did, I wouldn't know what to do or say. I'd just keep out of her way.

A nineteen-year-old girl
who had a homosexual
experience when she was
fourteen

I get as much from a chick as I do with a guy. But it's a different kind of thing.

A seventeen-year-old girl
who emphasizes she has
had sex, not homosexual
experiences, with girls

We found relatively little homosexual behavior among adolescents. Despite the great visibility of homosexuality in American society—in certain arts and professions, in the headlines, and on television talk shows, in "gay liberation" demonstrations, in some urban areas—only 9% of all adolescents report ever having one or more homosexual experiences.

Homosexual behavior on a continuous basis and self-acknowledgment of one's own homosexuality are generally an adult rather than an adolescent phenomenon in contemporary American society. Whether or not the seeds of adult homosexuality are born in infancy, adolescence, and/or family relationships, the great majority of adolescents neither engage in homosexual behavior nor anticipate they ever will.

11.1 Definition and incidence of homosexual behavior

Homosexual behavior and tolerance for homosexuality are two different phenomcna. Homosexual behavior occurs when people of the same sex seek sexual stimulation and/or satisfaction with each other. Tolerance for homosexuality involves feelings about and attitudes toward other people's homosexual behavior.

Most young people have heard of homosexuality. Only 9% of all boys and 10% of all girls said they had not (Table 332). Most of those who had not heard of homosexuality were in the younger age group. 9% of all adolescents (11% of the boys and 6% of the girls) have had at least one active homosexual experience (Table 333).

Additional adolescents have had homosexual advances made to them by adolescents and adults, even though they have not had actual homosexual experiences. 25% of all adolescents report that on one or more occasions a member of their sex tried to persuade them to have sexual relations (Table 102).

Current levels of homosexual behavior are minimal: 2% of all boys and virtually no girls reported having one or more homosexual experiences during the preceding month.

As boys grow older, more of them report having had homosexual experiences. For some reason, girls do not—in fact, fewer older girls than younger girls report homosexual advances having been made to them.

Frequency of homosexual advances and experiences

	Boys		Girls	
	13–15	16–19	13–15	16–19
One or more homosexual advances made to them	27%	45%	17%	11%
One or more homosexual experiences	5%	17%	6%	6%

11.2 How adolescents view homosexuality

When homosexuality "makes you feel good" or when one or both homosexual partners believe they love each other, many adolescents not only do not oppose homosexuality but in fact support it for any young people who have these reactions. More important, although less often specifically mentioned, is the desire on the part of many young people to see people shed stereotyped sex roles. They see laws against homosexual behavior as labeling people as perverse only because they are different. They dislike perversity when it goes to extremes (for example, an adult attacking a child); but they realize that "perverse" is a label that society can use to isolate someone without due process of law or humanity.

Most young people are amused by adolescents who "freak out" on something—that is, exaggerate their love for music, history, coffee, or anything else. The same is true in sexual matters. Such persons are usually felt to be playacting a homosexual role to satisfy a basic need. Once most adolescents feel their freedom intruded upon, they may still not criticize another's homosexuality but they ask that person to play-act with someone else. Says a sixteen-year-old girl, "You [a homosexual] can do it without feeling guilty. If you have a clear mind that that's what you have to be because something happened to you, it's all right."

Speaking of a homosexual boy she knows, this same girl says:

> He's nice. We're good friends. But he gets embarrassing—not for me, but I'm sorry for him. When they have to exaggerate like that, then they must have really had some psychological problems. He's always going around asking: "Is my makeup all right?" Big deal. He thinks he's a beautiful woman. He goes into women's bathrooms to

> look at his made-up face. He shouldn't do that. He's embarrassing real women too.

Young people seldom categorize others arbitrarily. Accordingly, they do not generally divide people into arbitrary categories such as heterosexuals and homosexuals. They may think of someone as being "into homosexuality" or say, "That's his bag" about someone's homosexual activities, but they are slow to view that person as automatically and forever destined to have relations with people of his own sex. Nor do most adolescents habitually use such terms as "fag" or "dyke" or "fairy." They neither laugh at homosexuals nor do they mimic any supposed mannerisms or behavior and they do not become emotionally disturbed at the sight of homosexuals. Homosexuality may be neither sacred nor sublime in the typical adolescent's mind, but neither does it rank high among those things that amuse or enrage him.

Young people are sympathetic to homosexual behavior primarily for three other reasons. The first is their belief that love is so accidental that no one can predict when and with whom it will occur. One sixteen-year-old girl asked:

> What if I find a wonderful love with another girl? Should I say no, that I will never let this happen to me under any circumstances? What if there would be no one else? If this is true for me when I am honest about myself, how can I say it hasn't already been true for someone else. Wouldn't that be dishonest?

A second reason is the rejection on the part of many young people of culture-imposed sex roles. They resist the assumption that males must consistently think and behave in one way and females in another. Thus, for example, it is a mistake to assume that "unisex" fashion is a form of homosexual behavior even though it may be one expression of youthful tolerance for homosexuality. An important appeal for some adolescents of commercialized unisex clothing and hair styles is that they can dress independently of their expected sex roles. Adolescents also tend to be tolerant and may even support more radical departures from traditional sex roles.

A seventeen-year-old boy asserted:

> Look, people have to start realizing that just because you're different, you know, that it doesn't mean they're less of a person than you are. I don't like roles. Women's liberation is not only liberating women from their roles but they're definitely eliminating a role for the man too. I see no reason why a man should completely support a wife or, you know, why a wife should completely support a man. It's like Women's Lib is not just for a woman but for a man too.

One seventeen-year-old adventuress speaks of her bisexual activities as offering a different kind of sexual relationship—and therefore different roles with other girls than she experiences when she has sexual intercourse with boys.

> I have had sex with chicks. I have never had sex with chicks for just the sexual thing. I can have sex with a guy and it's just a sexual thing, but when I have sex with a chick it's been the people or chicks I have had sex with, for whom I have felt a beautiful friendship—really beautiful. We really love each other. It's not just a sexual thing. It's really beautiful.
>
> I don't know whether it's kind of like you're in love or not. Yes, kind of. But not in love. We're not in love. It's just that we have a tremendous friendship. But there is a sexual thing between us. We dig each other. It's really beautiful. It's just more of a love thing. It's not just "I want to have sex with her." It's love, and that makes a difference right there if you've got that to begin with.
>
> I have to say that I get as much having sex with a chick as I do with a guy, but in a different way. Because, as I said, I don't have sex with a chick unless there's that love there, so that when I do have it it's beautiful because the love is there. And chicks can satisfy me; but it is different. It's not the same kind of thing as with a guy. I can't say I wouldn't have sex with another chick just for the physical thing—I'd never say that—but I haven't.

Young people are looking for the inner person. This is the third reason why many adolescents not only tolerate but also approve of homosexuality for some people. By viewing the behavior rather than the person as being homosexual, the adolescent sees homosexuality as a way of expressing oneself or of coping with life. They do not fault such behavior "if no one else is being hurt in the process."

Some boys have a curiosity about having sex with boys and have therefore deliberately experimented with it. Others would like to have an occasion to satisfy this curiosity, which is based more on idle fantasizing than on prurience or compulsion. Girls almost never expressed this curiosity, but it is our guess that more than we discovered in our research may have had and satisfied this curiosity.

Although they don't view homosexuality as a disgrace or a compulsion, most adolescents do not want it for themselves. Most young people (79%) agreed with the statement, "I've never had sex with another boy/girl, and I'm sure I'd never want to" (Table 163).

Adolescents agreeing, "I've never had sex with another boy/girl and I'm sure I'd never want to."

All adolescents		Boys			Girls		
Virgins	Nonvirgins	All	13–15	16–19	All	13–15	16–19
84%	75%	78%	78%	78%	80%	81%	78%

73% of the boys and 72% of the girls implicitly reject homosexuality for themselves by agreeing, "If I had children and any of them turned out to be a homosexual, I would be very upset" (Table 146).

Some young people thought they might participate in homosexual activities for money, 11% of the older boys and 14% of the boys with intercourse experience agreed, "It's just possible that sometime, if I really needed the money very badly, that I might have sex with a man who would pay me for it" (Table 106). The great majority of the boys who say this have already had one or more homosexual experiences.

We had a hypothesis that boys are less tolerant of male homosexual behavior than girls are of female homosexual behavior, and that more boys than girls would express antagonism toward such behavior as being abnormal or unnatural. This hypothesis was *not* confirmed.

41% of the boys in speaking of boys and 40% of the girls in speaking of girls agree, "If two boys/girls want to have sex together, it's all right so long as they both want to do it" (Tables 255 and 259). Sexually experienced boys and girls tend to tolerate homosexuality between members of their own sex more often than inexperienced adolescents do.

Adolescents agreeing, "If two boys/girls want to have sex together, it's all right so long as they both want to do it."

Boys (about boys)					Girls (about girls)				
All	13–15	16–19	Virgins	Non-virgins	All	13–15	16–19	Virgins	Non-virgins
41%	40%	42%	32%	50%	40%	40%	40%	31%	50%

However, approximately twice as many boys and girls found homosexuality among members of their own sex abnormal or unnatural than found it "all right if they both want to do it." 81% of all boys agreed, "Two boys having sex together is something that I would consider abnormal or unnatural" (Table 34), and 77% of all girls agreed

Adolescents' agreement with statements about homosexuality

	All adolescents	Boys	Girls
Two boys having sex together is all right if both want it	41%	41%	41%
Two boys having sex together is abnormal and unnatural	80	81	80
Two girls having sex together is all right if both want it	41	41	40
Two girls having sex together is abnormal and unnatural	76	74	77

that two girls having sex together is abnormal or unnatural (Table 87). This is another example of how more adolescents are tolerant of the participants in a particular sex act than they are of the sex act itself.

But permissive as they may be about other young people's homosexual and bisexual behavior, the majority of adolescents do not accept homosexual behavior for themselves. Of boys (41%) who agree, "If two boys want to have sex together, it's all right so long as they both want to do it," 68% also agree, "I've never had sex with another boy, and I'm sure I'd never want to." Of girls (40%) who agree, "If two girls want to have sex together, it's all right so long as they both want to do it" (Table 259), 75% say, "I've never had sex with another girl, and I'm sure I'd never want to." Of the adolescents (42%) who agree, "It's all right for a person to have sexual relations with both males and females, if that's what the person wants to do" (Table 282), 75% say, "I've never had sex with another boy/girl, and I'm sure I'd never want to."

11.3 Homosexual advances

Tolerance of homosexuality is sufficient to minimize both the perception and memory of homosexual advances experienced by boys and girls. Young people do not always know that a homosexual advance is being made to them, especially when it is made by someone their own age or by an older person who is considered a family friend. And unless the incidents are characterized by force or revulsion, they are not likely to be recalled while completing a self-administered questionnaire.

More boys recalled homosexual advances than girls. 37% of the boys and 14% of the girls said, "On one or more occasions, another boy/girl or a grown man/woman has tried to get me to have sex with him/her" (Table 102). There is no reason to believe that young people to whom homosexual advances have been made differ substantially from the rest of the adolescent population.

Not surprisingly when we view the age of first homosexual experiences in the next section, we find that proportionally more older boys (45%) and younger girls (17%) report homosexual advances than do younger boys (27%) and older girls (11%). 38% of all nonvirgins compared to 12% of all virgins have received homosexual advances (Table 102).

11.4 First homosexual experience

The first homosexual experience is not always easy for the adolescent to define. We defined homosexual behavior in the following question: "Have you yourself ever done anything with another boy/girl, or with a grown man/woman, that resulted in sexual stimulation or satisfaction for either or both of you?" We believe that some respondents had experiences in late childhood or in early adolescence which they fail to acknowledge to themselves were homosexual. In fact, these experiences may not have been homosexual but merely a part of the childhood playing or learning process in which children view and touch each other's bodies. Such an experience would not imply a tolerance of homosexuality and could not be interpreted as reflecting attitudes either for or against homosexuality.

11.4.1 Age at first homosexual experience

Of those who report having a homosexual experience, the majority of boys had their first homosexual experience when they were eleven or twelve years old and the majority of girls when they were six to ten years old. By the time they have reached their thirteenth birthday, 78% of all adolescents reporting homosexual experiences have had one or more homosexual experiences (Table 334). Thus, it is clear that those who are to have homosexual experiences in adolescence usually have their first one in preadolescence. The only alternative explanation is that many who have homosexual experiences during adolescence (from thirteen years onward) are not reporting these facts to us.

Age at first homosexual experience

	Adolescents with homosexual experience		
	All	Boys	Girls
6–10	31%	16%	57%
11–12	47	56	32
13–17	22	28	11
TOTAL	100%	100%	100%

In our sample of male adolescents, only 4% of those currently thirteen to fifteen years old have had a homosexual experience prior to reaching the age of thirteen, as compared to 11% of those currently sixteen to nineteen years old. Why should there be such a difference between the ages of first homosexual experience reported by younger and older boys? Younger adolescents tend to regard their preadolescent and early adolescent experiences far more seriously than do older adolescents. Thus younger boys may be more ashamed of their participation in a homosexual experience than older boys are. (Our data show that younger boys have less tolerance for homosexuality than do older boys.) Therefore the younger boy may be substantially underreporting his first homosexual experience.

Another explanation, though more dubious, is that several years ago boys were having their first homosexual experience at an earlier age than they have been during the last few years. But now, owing to society's increasing permissiveness about youthful heterosexual behavior, boys may engage in sexual activities at an early age with girls, rather than turning to other boys for sexual release. However, we have no evidence to confirm or refute this hypothesis.

11.4.2 Age of first homosexual partner

37% of all adolescents reporting their homosexual experience say they had their first homosexual experience with someone older than they. 12% of the boys and virtually none of the girls had it with an adult. Girls (77%), more frequently than boys (56%), had their first experience with someone their own age or younger (Table 335).

Age of first homosexual partner

	Adolescents with homosexual experience		
Relative age	All	Boys	Girls
Younger boy/girl	24%	29%	14%
Boy/girl of about same age	39	27	63
Older boy/girl	29	32	23
Adult	8	12	0
TOTAL	100%	100%	100%

It can be inferred from this data either that there are more adult male than female homosexuals or that more adult male homosexuals than female homosexuals are making advances to adolescents. Still another possibility is that more adult male homosexuals than female homosexuals are successful in completing their intentions with adolescents. Whatever explanation is correct, we assume that there is a greater proclivity toward homosexual experiences on the part of the male in both adolescence and adulthood.

11.5 Significance of adolescent attitudes concerning homosexuality

Obviously there are confirmed homosexuals among adolescents, but the incidence of homosexual behavior among adolescents is considerably lower than one would suppose. Current homosexual behavior is minimal: 2% of all boys and virtually no girls have had a homosexual experience during the preceding month. We do *not* know whether or not other adolescents who reported past homosexual experience have had more than a single first experience.

The visibility of homosexuality, as well as the tolerance that young people have for other people's homosexual experiences, perhaps mistakenly persuades many people that there is far more homosexuality among young people than there really is. It may be that this talk and tolerance encourage some adolescents to try to become committed to homosexual behavior, but it is not the purpose of this study to answer this question.

Homosexual behavior does increase as boys grow older and as they accumulate heterosexual experience. The fact that 17% of the older boys, compared with 5% of the younger boys, have had one or more homosexual experiences strongly confirms this. This may be a clue to our earlier stated proposition that homosexuality is more of a postadolescent or adult phenomenon in American society.

Adolescents are more tolerant of homosexuality among other young people because they feel that only by being so can they best understand themselves. Some know they have dearly loved people of their own sex. Some have felt sexual stimulation only being around or working with members of their own sex. They recognize the ambivalent but suppressed feelings they sometimes have within themselves as being dominant. And the desire of many for new experience discourages their condemnation of another new sexual experience even when it is one they do not want.

We do not learn from this study what happens to trigger commitment to homosexuality in childhood or early adolescence. More studies are clearly called for to investigate this question.

Homosexuality, to the extent that it is one's psychic choice rather than a biological compulsion, may also be fostered by the desire of some adolescents to identify with those they consider an oppressed minority. The fact that 59% of all adolescents (63% of all boys and 55% of all girls) support laws against homosexuality (Table 20) may encourage an adolescent who wants to be different. Of the legislation restricting sexual behavior, only laws against rape drew more support from adolescents than laws against homosexuality.

It is all too easy, when we are dealing with numbers and percentages, to dismiss a percentage as being "low" or "only such and such." However low even a 2% of all boys figure may seem, when projected to the total of all adolescents we are speaking of many thousands of boys. Whatever problems they may have and whatever problems are caused for them as a result of their homosexual behavior will inevitably generate additional personal hurt and dissidence in our society.

11.6 Salient findings

1. Despite the visibility of homosexuality in American society, only 9% of all adolescents (11% of the boys and 6% of the girls) report having one or more homosexual experiences.

2. As boys grow older, they report more frequent homosexual experiences. But girls do not; in fact, fewer older girls report homosexual advances having been made to them than do younger girls.

Of those who report having a homosexual experience, the majority of boys have their first experience when they are eleven to twelve years of age; the majority of girls when they are six to ten years old.

3. Recalling their homosexual experience(s), girls (77%) more frequently than boys (56%) had their first homosexual experience with someone their own age or younger.

4. More boys (37%) than girls (14%) received homosexual advances from young people and adults.

5. Only 9% of all boys and 10% of all girls said they had not heard of homosexuality. Most of those who have not heard of homosexuality are in the younger age-group.

6. Some young people think they could sometimes participate in homosexual activities for money; 11% of all older boys and 14% of nonvirgin boys agree, "It's just possible that sometime, if I really needed the money very badly, that I might have sex with a man who would pay me for it."

7. 41% of the boys in speaking of boys and 40% of the girls in speaking of girls agree, "If two boys/girls want to have sex together, it's all right so long as they both want to do it." Nonvirgin boys and girls more often than virgins tend to tolerate homosexuality between members of their own sex.

8. Reasons for adolescent tolerance of homosexuality are mainly the following:

> The homosexual is playacting a role to satisfy a basic need.
>
> Love is so accidental that no one can predict when and with whom it will occur.
>
> Preassigned sex roles are rejected in favor of "being yourself."
>
> It is the behavior rather than the person that is labeled homosexual; the person underneath is the most important.

9. Over three-fourths of all adolescents find the act of homosexuality among members of their own sex abnormal or unnatural, again evidence that more young people are tolerant of the participants in a particular sex act than they are of the sex act itself.

10. Adolescents are far less tolerant of homosexuality for themselves than for others. Three-fourths of all young people agree, "I've never had sex with another boy/girl and I'm sure I'd never want to."

11. Virtually three-fourths of all boys and girls affirm, "If I had children and any of them turned out to be homosexual, I would be very upset."

12. Only laws against rape are supported by more adolescents than laws against homosexuality.

IV. Adolescent Sexual Behavior and Social Change

The influence of sexuality in every adolescent's life is seen in the words and sexual behavior of the adolescents themselves. They run a wide gamut of emotional reactions and consequences, ranging from the beautiful and the sublime to the bitterly disappointed and badly hurt.

The effects are also widespread for contemporary American society. Adolescents are having sexual intercourse at an earlier age than ever before, and they are bringing less maturity and less rationality to bed with them. Like drivers on the road for the first time without information and experience, they often endanger themselves and their sex partners without knowing why.

Thus, despite the fact that America's birth rate is declining, the rate of pregnancies remains high; abortion has become a popular post-intercourse form of birth control. The incidence of venereal disease continues in what many public health officials label as epidemic proportions.

It is assumed by many that marriage is being deferred by adolescents who feel they need not marry in order to have sexual intercourse. What seems more likely, however, is that many adolescents are finding greater personal and sexual satisfaction in not getting married as early as they might be expected to. It is not that adolescents demand the right to have intercourse before marriage; it is that they want to have intercourse at a younger age and will not be forced to marry in order to have sexual intercourse. The difference, while admittedly subtle, has strong implications for the institution of marriage. Most young people want to be married and have children—eventually. But their concept of marriage turns out to be a stricter and longer-range one than most young people feel has been demonstrated by their parents, many of whom *with* marriage have been serial monogamists in pursuit of the one "ideal marriage" among many that would satisfy them.

The next three chapters deal specifically with pregnancy and birth control (including abortion), venereal disease, and marriage. The final chapter outlines our conclusions from the entire findings and discusses their implications for American society and living patterns.

12.
Pregnancy, Birth Control, and Abortion

I'm afraid of childbirth. The movie I've seen at school shows a girl about to have a baby screaming and cringing in bed, and I'm afraid of its really hurting me.

A fifteen-year-old girl

I believe in birth control. I know how many sperm there are, how tiny they are, and how fast they go.

A sixteen-year-old girl

I would want an abortion right off. I mean, at this age I really don't want one [a baby]. *It would tie you down and you hear stories of sixteen-year-old girls having babies and they can't finish school and they can't get an education. And they usually dump the child somewhere and have to become a prostitute because they have nothing else to be.*

A fifteen-year-old girl

They shouldn't be doing it in the first place. Every girl you interview in the United States you've got to tell not to do it.

A seventeen-year-old boy

12.1 Concern about pregnancy
Attitudes toward adolescent pregnancy

12.2 Anticipated outcomes in event of pregnancy
Relative desirability of alternative outcomes
Male assumptions about responsibility
Actual outcomes of pregnancies

12.3 Attitudes toward abortion

12.4 Incidence of birth control
Methods used
Methods reported by girls
Methods reported by boys

12.5 Girls' reasons for not using contraception
Lack of information
Lack of availability
Opposition in principle
Lack of motivation
Personal carelessness and forgetfulness
Too much trouble
Concern that parents will find birth control devices
Disapproval of birth control by sex partner
Belief that spontaneity of sex act is hurt
Belief that birth control is the boy's responsibility
Abortion as an alternative
Belief that pregnancy is impossible or unreal

12.6 Salient findings

10% of all American female adolescents report that they have been pregnant at least once. 11% of all younger nonvirgin girls and 28% of all older nonvirgin girls report having been pregnant. 28% of all nonvirgin girls with intercourse experience during the preceding month report they have been pregnant, compared with 7% of all nonvirgin girls who did not have intercourse during the preceding month (Table 480).

13% of all nonvirgin boys and 21% of nonvirgin boys who have had intercourse the preceding month report they believe they have made a girl pregnant (Tables 477 and 478). Fewer boys report they made a girl pregnant than girls report having been made pregnant. We do not believe that boys underreported this consequence of their sexual intercourse. Many boys, however, may not have known they made their sex partner pregnant. Some boys may know of their sex partner's pregnancy but believe—or persuade themselves to believe—that another male is the father. And evidence cited in the chapters on first intercourse and serial monogamy demonstrates that many girls have intercourse with men older than nineteen, by whom some may have become pregnant.

A popular belief in contemporary America is that birth control—in particular "the pill"—has increased sexual intercourse among adolescents. Many young people are said to be having sexual intercourse they would not otherwise have, because they have little threat of pregnancy; some parents are even thought to be more permissive as a result. And two-thirds of the nation's nonvirgin adolescents agree with the statement, "The main reason why people are more casual about sex these days is because birth control is easily available to everyone" (Table 295).

But continuing pregnancies are proving otherwise. And 40% of all nonvirgin girls agree, "Sometimes I don't really care whether or not I get pregnant" (Table 310).

12.1 Concern about pregnancy

No unmarried respondent, girl or boy, seriously expressed a hope for pregnancy as an outcome of his or her sexual relationship. Several respondents in personal interviews asserted that they knew many unmarried girls who, for reasons discussed in a later section, wanted to get pregnant.

But some adolescent girls seemed very casual about the idea of their becoming pregnant. In further analyzing the response to the statement, "Sometimes I don't really care whether or not I get pregnant" (Table 310), we learn that 50% of all nonvirgin girls thirteen to fifteen and 36% of those sixteen to nineteen agree.

The young girl who does not care may be reacting to a mood of discouragement or despair—about her sex partner, her home life, her future. A few girls in the sample may have felt at times that being pregnant would attract attention or sympathy, enable her to marry her sex partner, or permit her to have the experience of having a baby and choosing whether to keep it or not. Of course, concern about becoming pregnant and wanting to have a baby are two different things. Whether this attitude accurately reflects a girl's willingness or tendency to use contraception or whether it is a predictor of pregnancy requires further study. However, of the girls who took no precautions against pregnancy when they were having intercourse during the preceding month, 28% agree, "Abortions are so easy to get these days that I don't really worry about getting pregnant."

There are several ways in which adolescents express their concern about pregnancy, and girls and boys generally express different types of concern. Two specific measures were used to evaluate concern for pregnancy among girls and boys who are currently having sexual intercourse.

The first was *worry*. All girls with intercourse experience were asked: "Do you ever worry about the possibility that you might become pregnant?" (Table 451). They responded as follows: never, 16%; hardly ever, 14%; sometimes, 41%; often, 29%.

Girls differed little in whether they worry about pregnancy, regardless of their age and whether or not they had sexual intercourse during the preceding month. Older girls were no more concerned than younger (Table 451); girls who had intercourse during the preceding month were more often concerned about pregnancy than the other nonvirgin girls (Table 452). (See the following table.)

In our interviews no unmarried boy expressed the desire for his sex partner to become pregnant. Boys in the national sample were not asked whether they care if their sex partner becomes pregnant. However, many boy respondents in our interviews expressed few or no feelings of responsibility concerning their sex partner's pregnancy. Abortion, the gradual disappearance in most communities of shotgun

Nonvirgin girls' concern about possible pregnancy

Degree of worry	Nonvirgin girls All	Nonvirgin girls 16–19	Nonvirgin girls with current intercourse experience
Never	16%	15%	17%
Hardly ever	14	13	12
Sometimes	41	42	36
Often	29	30	35
TOTAL	100%	100%	100%

marriages, and the use of the pill and intrauterine devices which a boy need never see or hear about all tend to lessen boys' feelings of responsibility toward the possible pregnancy of their sex partners.

Over one-quarter of all nonvirgin boys often worry about making a girl pregnant; over three-quarters of them worry often or sometimes (Table 450). Older boys worry only a little more frequently than do younger boys (Table 449). But boys who are currently having intercourse responded "sometimes" more frequently than did all nonvirgin boys.

Nonvirgin boys' concern about making girls pregnant

Degree of worry	Nonvirgin boys All	Nonvirgin boys 16–19	Nonvirgin boys with current intercourse experience
Never	18%	16%	9%
Hardly ever	6	6	2
Sometimes	48	49	60
Often	28	29	29
TOTAL	100%	100%	100%

In comparing boys' and girls' concern about pregnancy, some interesting differences emerge. Although among those currently having intercourse a slightly higher percent of girls than boys are often concerned, boys express much more concern than girls at the sometimes level. And girls report nearly three times more frequently than boys that they never or hardly ever worry. Thus, 89% of all boys currently having intercourse are often or sometimes worried about their sex partners becoming pregnant, as compared to 71% of the girls currently having intercourse.

A second measure of concern about pregnancy is the extent to which fear of pregnancy discourages sexual intercourse. 44% of the nonvirgin girls and 33% of the nonvirgin boys responded yes to the question, "Have you ever wanted to have sex with a girl/boy but decided not to do so because you were afraid that the girl/you might become pregnant?" (Tables 475 and 476). Boys and girls who had intercourse during the preceding month express this concern a little less frequently in these same proportions.

12.1.2 Attitudes toward adolescent pregnancy

Young people are often contemptuous of girls who become pregnant. Both boys and girls alike tended to fault the girl—not for wanting a baby, not for having a baby if she wanted it, but for becoming pregnant with a baby she didn't want.

Adolescents who criticize the pregnant girl assume that she knows the facts, can gain access to a birth control device, and is free to use it. They feel that such a girl wants to be pregnant even though she may not really want a baby.

One nineteen-year-old boy is very much against abortion because he feels that many females are so animalistic about sexual intercourse that pregnancy is irrelevant to them. He had only contempt for girls who get pregnant, because, he feels, they start human life without thinking.

> That's a lot of baloney that they don't want to [have a baby]. At the time, they want to so much they don't know what. . . . When they're having their sexual act, nothing is going through their mind except what's on top of them. The whole building could fall down, but they would just have to finish that act. Because at that moment you could walk in on them and say, "You're going to become pregnant right now! You're going to be pregnant! I know it!" And they wouldn't give a damn. They'd have to finish before you could talk with them. So I don't want to hear they don't want a child. They don't want it *after,* of course; they don't want it afterwards. But that's something else.

12.2 Anticipated outcomes in event of pregnancy

12.2.1 Relative desirability of alternative outcomes

We asked all adolescents with any intercourse experience these two questions. To girls: "If you were to become pregnant, which *one* of the things listed below would you *most prefer* to do, if you could have things your way?" (Tables 455 and 456). To boys: "If you were to make a girl pregnant, which *one* of the things listed below would you *most prefer* that she do, if you could have things your way?" (Tables 453 and 454).

Most of the girls said they would have the baby and either get married or bring the baby up themselves. Over a third of all girls would marry immediately for this reason. Compared to younger girls, however, older girls more frequently give strong support to abortion and oppose marriage.

3% of the younger girls, compared to 23% of the older girls, support abortion; older girls much less frequently support marriage or bringing up the baby themselves. Although older girls are in a better position to marry because they are close to finishing high school and can better pick the person they would want to marry, girls in this age-group have a personal independence they lacked a few years earlier which they do not want to yield to marriage.

Older girls do not want to consult their parents and leave a decision up to them as to what should be done; 16% of the younger nonvirgin girls would consult their parents. Girls who are currently active sexually are in the main older girls. The older and more sexually active the girl, the more likely she is to support abortion or depend on the father.

Nonvirgin girls' preferred action in case of own pregnancy

	Nonvirgin girls			Nonvirgin girls with current intercourse experience
	All	13–15	16–19	
Have the baby and get married	38%	45%	36%	37%
Have the baby and bring it up myself	18	29	14	13
Have an abortion	18	3	23	24
Have the baby and count on the father to help me bring it up	15	3	20	20
Have the baby and give it up for adoption	7	4	7	5
Tell my parents and let them decide what to do	4	16	0	1
TOTAL	100%	100%	100%	100%

Regardless of their age, the largest percentage of boys (30%), even more than girls (18%), prefer abortion as a solution for an unwanted pregnancy (Tables 453 and 454). But boys who are currently having intercourse express a slight preference for their girl friends to have the baby and count on them to help bring it up or to have the baby and get married. Parents are depended upon for a decision largely by some of the younger boys.

Less than one-fourth of the adolescents currently having intercourse support abortion, and a majority favor having the baby and raising it with or without marriage. Boys and girls currently having intercourse differ significantly on only two points: a small number of

Nonvirgin boys' preferred action in case of sex partner's pregnancy

	Nonvirgin boys			Nonvirgin boys with current intercourse experience
	All	13–15	16–19	
Have an abortion	30%	27%	31%	22%
Have the baby and get married	24	20	26	23
Have the baby and count on me to help bring it up	23	15	26	28
Tell her parents and let them decide what to do	9	21	5	12
Have the baby and bring it up herself	7	1	10	10
Have the baby and give it up for adoption	7	16	2	5
TOTAL	100%	100%	100%	100%

boys want the girl's parents to make a decision, while almost no girls do; and boys and girls differ as to whether they should marry or whether the girl should raise the baby with the boy's help.

Nonvirgin boys' and girls' preferred actions if girls become pregnant

	Adolescents with current intercourse experience	
	Boys	Girls
Have an abortion	22%	24%
Have the baby and give it up for adoption	5	5
Have the baby and count on boy to help bring it up	28	20
Have the baby and girl bring it up herself	10	13
Have the baby and get married	23	37
Tell girl's parents and let them decide what to do	12	1
TOTAL	100%	100%

61% of the boys and 70% of the girls currently having intercourse believe the girl should have the baby and raise it, either married or unmarried and whether or not the boy helps her. 5% of the boys and girls in this group support having the baby and giving it up for adoption, while 22% of the boys and 24% of the girls would prefer an abortion.

All girls currently having intercourse were asked the question,

"Sometimes people can have things their own way, and sometimes they can't. If you were to become pregnant, which *one* of the things listed below do you think you would *actually* do?" (Tables 457 and 458). This question was asked to find out if there was a difference between what a girl said she would prefer to do and what she would actually do in case of pregnancy. Responses of the female groups as a whole indicate that girls vary little between the actions they would prefer to take and the actions they believe they would have to take in event of pregnancy. The same percentage of all girls believe they would have an abortion; a slightly lower percentage believe they would get married. More girls feel it would be necessary to consult their parents for a decision than would prefer to take that action.

Preferred versus probable actions girls with current intercourse experience would take in case of pregnancy

	All girls with current intercourse experience	
	What girls would prefer to do	What girls believe they would have to do
Have an abortion	24%	23%
Have the baby and give it up for adoption	5	4
Have the baby and count on the father to help me bring it up	20	18
Have the baby and bring it up myself	13	17
Have the baby and get married	37	31
Tell my parents and let them decide what to do	1	7
TOTAL	100%	100%

12.2.2 Male assumptions about responsibility

The action a boy thinks he would take if his sex partner became pregnant is another area we probed. What a boy says he will do in the event of pregnancy does not predict with certainty what he would actually do. We nonetheless sought to learn the boy's attitude toward himself and his sex partner in view of the risk he assumes in having intercourse.

We asked each boy with intercourse experience, "If you were to make a girl pregnant, do you think you would or would not do each of the things listed below?" Respondents were asked to indicate yes, maybe, or no alongside each alternative (Tables 459 through 474). The responses of boys who are having current intercourse and those of all nonvirgin boys do not differ significantly.

Most of the nonvirgin boys rank first among eight possible actions their desire to help the girl do "whatever she decided to do," although 74% of the older boys checked yes as compared to 50% of the younger boys (Table 469). Second choice among both age groups was the response, "I would help her bring up the child"; 61% of the older and 38% of the younger boys responded yes to this alternative (Table 467). Older boys (33%) responded yes twice as frequently as younger boys (15%) to the idea of marrying the girl (Table 471).

Younger boys differ from older boys in whether they would employ deception were their sex partners to become pregnant (Table 459). 52% of the younger boys responded yes or maybe to the alternative in which they would say that it was someone else who made their sex partner pregnant; only 32% of the older boys responded likewise.

Abortion ranks fifth among the alternatives given a yes response by both older and younger boys; 24% of the older boys and 22% of the younger boys would help arrange and pay for an abortion (Table 465). Another quarter of the boys replied maybe and half of the boys responded no to abortion. This is consistent with our findings that abortion is approved by little more than a quarter of the boys when they are personally involved.

Actions nonvirgin boys would take if sex partner became pregnant (percentage responding yes)

	Nonvirgin boys		
	All	13–15	16–19
Help her do whatever she decided to do (Table 469)	66%	50%	74%
Help her bring up the child (Table 467)	54	38	61
Discuss it with my parents to see what they think (Table 473)	29	23	32
Marry her (Table 471)	27	15	33
Help arrange and pay for an abortion (Table 465)	23	22	24
Talk to her about it and help her decide what to do, but that's all (Table 463)	20	38	11
Say that it was someone else who had made her pregnant (Table 459)	7	12	5
Say that it was the girl's problem, and none of my business (Table 461)	5	2	6

12.2.3 Actual outcomes of pregnancies

Girls who became pregnant generally took one of three actions: they chose to bring up the child themselves, they had an abortion, or they married the father.

12.3 Attitudes toward abortion

Young people in the majority favor abortion under certain circumstances, at least for others. 51% of all adolescents, including 55% of all boys and 46% of all girls, agree, "If two people are going to have a baby that neither person really wants, it is all right for the girl to have an abortion" (Table 278). 59% of all nonvirgins support abortion under these circumstances.

In response to the same question, 56% of all Catholics also favor abortion. Girls whose personal religious preference is Catholic, however, are less inclined to favor abortion; only 31% of all Catholic girls agree with the statement. There is little difference in support between older and younger adolescents. The highest rate of support comes from sexual adventurers (70%).

Regardless of religious preference, 49% of the boys and 42% of the girls who consider themselves as very or somewhat religious agree, "If two people are going to have a baby that neither person wants, it is all right for the girl to have an abortion."

Almost half of all young people consider the world's overpopulation a factor in their feelings about abortion. 49% of all boys and 49% of all girls agree with the statement, "It's immoral to bring an unwanted child into this overpopulated world, especially now that abortions are so easy to get" (Table 296). 49% of the adventurers agree with this statement, as compared with 70% of those who favored an abortion to prevent an unwanted child from being born.

37% of all boys would not feel guilty about it if they were to make a girl pregnant and she had an abortion; and 37% of all girls would not feel guilty about having an abortion themselves. 31% of all virgin adolescents also agreed with this statement (Table 97).

Nonvirgin adolescents do not always accept abortion for themselves when they accept it for others. Exactly one-half of all boy nonvirgins agree with the statement, "If I were to make a girl pregnant, I wouldn't want her to have an abortion, because taking the life of an unborn child is wrong" (Table 317). 60% of the nonvirgin girls also agree, "I would never want to have an abortion, because taking the life of an unborn child is wrong" (Table 317). A higher proportion of younger nonvirgin girls (76%) believe this than do older nonvirgin girls (54%).

The reasons for this opposition expressed by nonvirgins to abortions for themselves or their sex partners are not always religious. Taking the life of an unborn child is disturbing to over one-half of those with intercourse experience, but religion is a major factor in the reasoning of only some who express this viewpoint. Only 43% of those who say they oppose abortion because taking an unborn child's life is wrong also affirm that abortion is against their religion. Indeed, only 28% of all nonvirgin girls and 27% of all nonvirgin boys (with no difference between the responses of older and younger adolescents) agree with the statements, "If I were to get a girl pregnant, I wouldn't want her to have an abortion, because it is against my religion" and "I would never want to have an abortion, because it is against my religion" (Table 324).

Moreover, only a minority of boys and girls view abortion as the action they most prefer or are most likely to take if their sexual intercourse results in pregnancy. It was previously reported that 18% of the girls with intercourse experience and 24% of the girls currently having intercourse would choose abortion as the action they would prefer to take if they became pregnant; 22% of the boys currently having intercourse would choose abortion as the action they would most prefer their girl friends to take if they made their girl friends pregnant. And 23% of the nonvirgin girls and boys believe that abortion would be their first choice if they did what they had to do (as opposed to what they would prefer to do) in the event of pregnancy.

Some young women express outright hostility to marriage and dependence on the male for economic support; they assert their ability to maintain a household by themselves if need be. But, as the chapter on marriage indicates, very few girls believe they want the responsibility of bringing up children without a man. Nor do many girls believe that the absence of a father is anything but unhealthy for a child unless there is a substantial absence of love between father and mother in the home. Most girls feel the emotional toll of having a baby and yielding it for adoption as being too great. These girls see abortion as their only solution.

Although many girls feel free to have abortions, they realize the possible emotional consequences an abortion entails. A sixteen-year-old girl describes the effects of an abortion on her best girl friend as follows:

> She knew she wasn't taking the pill and was fucking anyway, you know. She was able to get an abortion quickly and quietly. But it really blew her out. 'Cause like she got into a free clinic and they were very quick and efficient while her parents were away. They never

knew. She did it all in one week—in and out of the hospital—no infections—one, two, three.

But no one took care of her head, and it really screwed her up. "Guess what," she later came and told me, "I almost had twins."

The few girls with whom we spoke who had had abortions were almost sickened by their memories of the event; they did not want to discuss it in any detail. It was something they believe they had to do, but they preferred to view the abortion as a surgical necessity rather than the taking of life from within them.

12.4 Incidence of birth control

Most girls and boys who have intercourse make use of some kind of birth control method. More girls report the use of contraceptives or birth control pills in connection with intercourse than boys. Some boys, if they are not using a condom, pay little heed to what, if any, method is used, and so their rate of reporting is less.

At the time of first sexual intercourse, 55% of all nonvirgin adolescents report that neither they nor their partners used any birth control method or did anything to cut down on the risk of the girl becoming pregnant (Table 384). There is a sharp difference between the sexual behavior groups in the use of contraceptives and other ways of cutting down pregnancy risk during the first intercourse. 48% of the monogamists, compared to 17% of the adventurers, report that something was used or tried; 32% of all nonvirgins said that a birth control effort was made by themselves or their sex partners (Table 384).

Those who did and did not have intercourse during the preceding month also reported differing efforts at birth control during their first intercourse experience. 36% of those with active intercourse experience report definite birth control efforts in their first intercourse, compared with 25% of those without current intercourse experience (Table 385).

What one does—or shares—in the way of birth control efforts during the first intercourse is a useful predictor of birth control efforts during current intercourse activities. Among those adolescents who took some kind of precaution against pregnancy the first time they had intercourse, 78% say they *always* took such precautious during the preceding month. Among those who took no precautions during their first intercourse, only 49% assert they *always* took such precautions during the preceding month.

Two additional measures were used to establish the incidence of use for methods of birth control. One was the question, "The very last time that you had sex with a girl/boy, did either of you use any kind of contraceptive or birth control method, or do anything else to cut down the risk of the girl/your becoming pregnant?" (Tables 506 and 507). 47% of the boys reported they or the girl did; 60% of the girls said they or the boy did. 45% of all boys and 40% of all girls who had sexual intercourse during the preceding month responded, "No, neither of us did." 8% of all boys did not and were not sure whether or not their partners did.

Among the adolescents describing their most recent intercourse during the preceding month, the absence of any form of contraception differs greatly by age-group.

Adolescents replying that neither used contraception during most recent intercourse

Nonvirgins			
Boys		Girls	
13–15	16–19	13–15	16–19
23%	50%	45%	38%

One would normally assume that the use of contraception would increase with the age of the adolescent participating in sexual intercourse. But for all boys, *nonuse* doubled from the younger to older group. For all girls, use increased very little. The reason for this surprising decrease in birth control use among older boys is not clear except that older boys are more frequently sexual adventurers than younger boys, and sexual adventurers consistently practice less birth control.

The younger boys tend to practice some form of birth control in the majority of intercourse situations in which they report participating. 66% of the younger boys, compared to 22% of the older boys, say they used a contraceptive device or a birth control method (Table 506).

The second additional measure utilized in this study was to inquire into the frequency of contraceptive use on the part of those having sexual intercourse during the preceding month. 14% of the nonvirgins (12% of the monogamists and 18% of the adventurers) report that neither a contraceptive device nor a birth control pill of any kind was used during any of their intercourse occasions in the preceding month.

59% of all nonvirgins report that some kind of a birth control method was *always* used during their intercourse occasions in the preceding month; among these nonvirgins are 66% of the monogamists and 46% of the adventurers (Table 383).

Considerably more use of birth control efforts was made during the preceding month in sexual intercourse in which one or both of the sex partners were monogamists. Four reasons explain this constantly higher usage. First, more girls than boys are monogamists and more boys than girls are adventurers; girls make slightly more constant use of birth control methods than boys (Table 481). Second, monogamists are more experienced with each other, both as sexual types and sex partners. They also tend to be more demanding of each other and more sensitive toward each other in the intercourse situation; greater use of birth control is the result. Third, any intercourse occasion involving one monogamist is obviously more likely to involve another monogamist rather than an adventurer, who would be less demanding of birth control. Four, greater sexual activity presumably encourages greater consciousness of the risk of pregnancy; monogamists, it will be recalled, have sexual intercourse much more frequently than adventurers. We learn, for example, that of the girls who had intercourse one to five times in the preceding month, 59% report that they *always* took some kind of pregnancy precaution, while 75% of those having intercourse six or more times in the preceding month always took some kind of precaution against pregnancy.

12.4.1 Methods used

12.4.1.1 Methods reported by girls

The following table indicates the frequency with which various birth control methods were used. Each girl was asked to check the frequency she used each of the methods listed in the questionnaire.

The birth control method that girls most frequently report using when they are having intercourse is birth control pills (33%); the second method that girls most frequently report always being used was withdrawal of the boy's penis before ejaculation (17%).

19% of the girls indicated, "I just trusted to luck that I wouldn't become pregnant," as a birth control method always used; 8% cited as a method always used, "I didn't think about whether or not I might become pregnant." Methods most frequently reported as never being used were the diaphragm, contraceptive jelly, contraceptive douche, and the intrauterine device.

The birth control methods authorities generally consider most reliable are the condom, birth control pills, the intrauterine device, and the diaphragm. The smallest percentage of girls that always use one or more of these devices is 33% and the largest percentage of girls who always use these devices is 44%. Undoubtedly the correct percentage is close to 33%, so about a third of the girls having intercourse always use a method of contraception considered reliable.

Birth control methods: girls' reported frequency of use during past month's intercourse

	Always	Sometimes, once, or twice	Never	TOTAL
"I used birth control pills" (Table 487).	33%	2%	65%	100%
"The boy withdrew before ejaculating (coming)" (Table 485).	17	17	66	100
"The boy used a condom (rubber)" (Table 483).	9	15	76	100
"I used a contraceptive foam" (Table 493).	8	0	92	100
"I used the rhythm method" (Table 499).	5	9	86	100
"I used an intrauterine device (coil, IUD)" (Table 489).	2	0	98	100
"I used a contraceptive douche" (Table 497).	0	1	99	100
"I used a diaphragm" (Table 491).	0	0	100	100
"I used a contraceptive jelly" (Table 495).	0	0	100	100
"I just trusted to luck that I wouldn't become pregnant" (Table 503).	19	18	63	100
"I didn't think about whether or not I might become pregnant" (Table 505).	8	10	82	100

Birth control pills are used more frequently than one might anticipate in view of the concern that many girls express about them. However, birth control pills are the best-known birth control method and believed to be the most reliable by girls with current intercourse experience. Considering the number of girls who do not use birth control pills, it is significant that virtually 100% of the girls never use a diaphragm and that only 2% report using an intrauterine device. Only 66% of the girls report that they never depend upon the boy's withdrawal before ejaculation (these respondents may have used some other birth control method, however).

12.4.1.2 Methods reported by boys

At first glance, there are inconsistencies between the birth control methods reported by girls and boys. This certainly seems to be the case when comparing the table listing girls' reported methods in the preceding section with that listing the methods reported by boys. But boys do not always know when a girl is using some birth control methods. Unless they ask, they could not know, because there is usually little they will see for themselves. Also, some girls are having current intercourse with males older than nineteen; such males are of course not represented in this sample. Older males are presumably more experienced sex partners; they would be expected to be more sophisticated in their use of birth control methods and more concerned with the techniques of birth control their adolescent girl sex partners are using.

Birth control methods: boys' reported frequency of use during past month's intercourse

	Always	Sometimes, once, or twice	Never	TOTAL
"I used a condom (rubber)" (Table 482).	25%	15%	60%	100%
"I withdrew before ejaculating (coming)" (Table 484).	20	36	44	100
"The girl used birth control pills" (Table 486).	17	21	62	100
"The girl used the rhythm method" (Table 498).	9	22	69	100
"The girl used a contraceptive foam" (Table 492).	6	21	73	100
"The girl used an intrauterine device (coil, IUD)" (Table 488).	5	21	74	100
"The girl used a contraceptive douche" (Table 496).	5	15	80	100
"The girl used a diaphragm" (Table 490).	3	17	80	100
"I just assumed that the girl was using something, but I don't know what it was" (Table 501).	3	36	61	100
"I made sure that the girl was using something, but I don't know what it was" (Table 500).	2	27	71	100
"I just trusted to luck that the girl wouldn't become pregnant" (Table 502).	18	28	54	100
"I didn't think about whether or not the girl might become pregnant" (Table 504).	16	33	51	100

Thus, we find a major difference in the reported use of the condom; 25% of the boys say they always use a condom, while only 9% of the girls say that the boy always used a condom. 17% of the boys say their girl sex partners always used birth control pills, while 33% of the girls say they always used birth control pills. Boys and girls report with the same frequency that they always use withdrawal before ejaculation as a birth control method, but boys report twice as frequently as girls that they have practiced withdrawal at least "sometimes" or "once or twice." Again, however, this may be attributable to a greater degree of experience on the part of some girls' male sex partners than is reflected among the adolescent boys reporting to us in the national sample of adolescents.

It is clear that only a small minority of boys currently engaging in intercourse always know what kind of birth control method is being used. Far more frequently than girl adolescents, however, they report that some sort of a birth control method was used at least "sometimes" or "once or twice." A higher percentage of girls than boys consistently reported "never."

12.5 Girls' reasons for not using contraception

In view of the fact that so many young people always or occasionally ignore birth control methods for themselves, their reasons for not using them assume considerable importance. These reasons demonstrate not only a lack of information, motivation, and—for some—availability, but they show that the continued risk of pregnancy does not interfere with a great deal of intercourse.

12.5.1 Lack of information

Not many young people have either full or accurate information about the various means of birth control or how they are used. If the responsibility for adequate information begins with one's parents, we find that 68% of all girls and 80% of all boys deny that their parents have told them the facts about birth control (Table 38). Nonvirgins (23%) report receiving information from their parents only a little less frequently than do virgins (27%), while 31% of adventurers have been informed by their parents about birth control.

Young people want birth control information from their parents if they feel they can obtain it without arguments or seeming to reveal their own sexual interests. 29% of all boys and 25% of all girls agree, "I'd like to ask my parents for information about birth control, but I'm afraid to because they would ask whether I'm having sex with girls/boys" (Table 166). Older boys (21%) feel this need for information and the risk of expressing it to their parents only about half as often as younger boys do (39%).

The lack of information concerning various methods of birth control is strongly reflected among girls who have had sexual intercourse and even among those who are currently active sexually. The table below shows the percentages of intercourse-experienced girls who say they have never heard of each of the following birth control methods.

Birth control methods nonvirgin girls have never heard of

	Girls who have had intercourse at least once	Girls who have had intercourse during past month
Birth control pills (Tables 386 and 387)	Virtually none	Virtually none
Intrauterine device (Tables 388 and 389)	24%	14%
Rhythm method (Tables 398 and 399)	21	19
Diaphragm (Tables 390 and 391)	11	8
Contraceptive douche (Tables 396 and 397)	11	8
Contraceptive foam (Tables 392 and 393)	7	2
Contraceptive jelly (Tables 394 and 395)	5	2

Considerable doubts, confusion, and even misinformation characterize adolescent attitudes toward birth control pills. Weight gains, cancer, headaches, and malfunctioning of one's sexual organs are among the worries expressed by girls who do not take birth control pills despite their convenience. Some boys do not want their girls to take birth control pills because of what they have heard about them. 56% of all boys and 70% of all girls, as well as 63% of all nonvirgins, believe the statement, "Birth control pills can be physically harmful to a girl" (Table 191).

12.5.2 Lack of availability

The availability of birth control information is a function of knowing where to go to obtain necessary information and assistance, devices, or ingredients. 30% of all girls (46% of younger girls; 18% of older girls) say that there is not any place where they could go to get birth control pills or contraceptives (Table 105). 32% of all younger nonvirgin girls and 89% of the girls with current intercourse experience who did not always take pregnancy precautions when having intercourse during the preceding month agreed with the statement, "I don't know where to get birth control pills or any other kind of reliable contraceptive" (Table 311).

Although doctors and clinics dispense birth control information more freely than ever, 11% of the girls who have had sexual intercourse at least once confirm they were put very "uptight" by the attitude of a doctor whom they asked for birth control pills or other contraceptives (Table 309). More significantly, 24% of the girls who did not always use birth control during current intercourse also agreed with this statement. Some girls in the personal interviews feel that doctors or clinics have been patronizing or almost abusive to them.

Many girls speak of the cost of contraception, still not knowing about the assistance offered at cost or free by Planned Parenthood and other organizations. 15% of all girls who had sexual intercourse during the preceding month without always using birth control agree that they cannot "afford to buy birth control pills or any other reliable kind of contraceptive."

Age makes a difference in perceived availability of birth control; many more younger girls with intercourse experience than older girls do not know where to obtain reliable birth control devices, or cannot afford to purchase them.

	Nonvirgin girls	
	13–15	16–19
Don't know where to get birth control (Table 311)	32%	9%
Can't afford to purchase birth control (Table 314)	25%	13%

Sex education courses do not seem to be making the impact they might concerning birth control information. Many girls complain that they learn about the speed sperm swim and the pains of childbirth, but feel that these are "scare tactics" and that they have learned little about how to prevent birth control from interfering with the spontaneity and ease of sexual relations.

12.5.3 Opposition in principle

Few girls are opposed in principle to birth control. 17% of the younger girls and 10% of the older girls, virgin and nonvirgin, reply true to the statement, "I wouldn't use birth control or contraception because it's against my religion" (Table 4). Clearly, religion is seldom a reason for not using birth control. Only 11% of the girls who did not always utilize some method of birth control during the past month offered religion as a reason. And children from Catholic families (16%) are no different from all adolescents (16%) in their declaration that they would not use birth control for religious reasons.

One other question of principle arises, a farfetched one perhaps, but difficult to classify elsewhere. Some girls hint that they feel a need to be pregnant. Some call it principle; other girls call it womanhood. Whatever their role, statements such as these deserve consideration in evaluating the disregard that so many girls have for pregnancy and their willingness to resort to abortion if necessary.

> Maybe it's the experience of being pregnant I need—a motherhood kick. I think that has a lot to do with it. You're not a womanly person in society until you know you can have children. Sometimes in the back of my head it would be nice to know I'm a normal person and can have a baby.

12.5.4 Lack of motivation

There are several basic reasons why adolescent girls are not motivated to use birth control, even when they understand it and have access to it. One reason is opposition to birth control in principle, which is discussed above. However, many girls who are opposed to birth control in principle are not opposed to it in practice. Other reasons why adolescent girls are not motivated to practice birth control include the following:

12.5.4.1 Personal carelessness and forgetfulness

Personal carelessness is admitted by many. 45% of all adolescent girls who had intercourse during the preceding month without always using birth control methods agree with the statement, "Sometimes when I have sex, I just get careless and forget to do anything to cut down the risk of my becoming pregnant." 15% of these same girls also agreed with the statement, "Sometimes I just get careless and forget to take my birth control pills."

There is no stock explanation for this forgetfulness beyond the fact that taking the pill is an easily deferred daily action which is sometimes forgotten as one twenty-four-hour period dissolves into another.

12.5.4.2 Too much trouble

Of those girls who did not always use any contraceptive device during the preceding month when they had intercourse, 38% agree with the statement, "Except for birth control pills, most other birth control methods are just too much trouble for me." 49% of all older nonvirgin girls also confirm this (Table 308).

12.5.4.3 Concern that parents will find birth control devices

Many girls speak of their inability to keep pills or other devices in their purses or around the house because of the threat of discovery by parents or other members of the family. They speak of "family closeness," "lack of privacy for personal possessions," and "how my sisters and brothers are into everything."

57% of all girls and 67% of the girls currently having intercourse but not using birth control pills agree, "One of the reasons why many young girls these days don't use birth control pills is that they're afraid their parents will find them" (Table 242). 52% of all girls who didn't always use birth control methods when having intercourse during the past month also agree with this statement.

58% of all younger nonvirgin girls and 31% of all girls having sexual intercourse during the preceding month without always using birth control confirmed a more explicit statement, "I don't use birth control pills or other contraceptives, because my parents might find them" (Table 303).

12.5.4.4 Disapproval of birth control by sex partner

8% of all nonvirgin girls say they have boyfriends who disapprove of birth control pills or other contraceptives (Table 312). This is reported more frequently by younger girls (15%) and girl adventurers (13%).

12.5.4.5 Belief that spontaneity of sex act is hurt

Much has been said in the popular literature to the effect that many girls do not use birth control because it would interfere with the spontaneity of their lovemaking. The assumption is that girls would prefer to risk pregnancy than to make advance provisions or momentarily interrupt their sex play to utilize a contraceptive. 71% of all nonvirgin adolescents agree with the statement, "If a girl uses birth control pills or other methods of contraception, it makes it seem as if she were *planning* to have sex" (Table 185). And 74% of the girls who did not always use birth control methods when having intercourse last month also agree with this statement.

12.5.4.6 Belief that birth control is the boy's responsibility

Only 14% of all girls (virgins and nonvirgins) answer true to the statement, "If I have sex with a boy, making sure that I don't get pregnant is *his* responsibility" (Table 107). Whatever responsibility for birth control the typical girl might think her male sex partner should have, she is unwilling to trust him with it. As one fourteen-year-old girl expressed it: "The girl should be responsible for birth control. I wouldn't trust a man for birth control as far as I can throw him. They're not the ones who have the babies; they don't have to worry."

12.5.4.7 Abortion as an alternative

For many girls, abortion is becoming a form of insurance against pregnancy because it is a postintercourse method of birth control. In our interviews many girls mention that they are not motivated to use birth control because they can always depend on abortion to terminate an unwanted pregnancy. 21% of all younger nonvirgin girls in the thirteen-to-fifteen age-group and 28% of the girls having sex during the preceding month without always using birth control replied true to the statement, "Abortions are so easy to get these days that I don't really worry about getting pregnant" (Table 330).

12.5.4.8 Belief that pregnancy is impossible or unreal

Some girls believe they cannot become pregnant, or convince themselves that they are not really having intercourse. We asked all girls to agree or disagree with this statement, "If a girl truly doesn't want to have a baby, she won't get pregnant even though she may have sex without taking any birth control precautions" (Table 287).

Girls believing pregnancy impossible for girl not using birth control but not wanting baby

All girls	Girls having intercourse during preceding month without always using birth control
30%	46%

Some girls believe pregnancy cannot happen to them or they are unwilling to use birth control because they would be acknowledging to themselves that they are actually having sexual intercourse. Those girls who feel pregnancy cannot happen to them offer no solid reasons for their thinking. An interview with a fourteen-year-old girl who does not use birth control went like this:

Q. Why don't you take precautions about getting pregnant?

A. Because I'm not worried about getting pregnant. I'm not worried about any guy getting me pregnant.

Q. Who is it up to to keep from getting pregnant?
A. It's up to both of us. After all, both of us can reproduce.
Q. Well, do you do anything at all to keep from getting pregnant?
A. No.
Q. Well, what would you do if you did become pregnant? [This question was asked to determine whether she would acknowledge under any circumstances that she could become pregnant.]
A. Oh, I have no idea. I would go crazy. I wouldn't know what to do.

She would say nothing else on the subject. Like other respondents who answered in this vein, this girl did not want to think about the many consequences of becoming pregnant, and to avoid such thoughts, she avoids the idea that she can become pregnant.

An eighteen-year-old girl who does not believe in abortion and sees no alternative to having a baby if she were to become pregnant, expressed her disbelief in the possibility of her pregnancy in this way:

> Like when I'm having sex, I don't really connect it with getting pregnant 'cause I've never been pregnant, you know, and a lot of my friends have but I just can't picture it happening to me. And like you really don't connect it, you know, until once you've been pregnant. Because when it's never happened you say, "Why should it happen?" or, "It's never happened yet," you know. You always look at the other person and say, "It happened to them, but it'll never happen to me." And I . . . I don't really kinda put it together. I don't . . . you just don't worry about it. You don't believe it can happen to you. I've been thinking about it, but it's not upmost in my mind.

The girls who do not want to admit to themselves that they are having sexual experiences will also sometimes refrain from using birth control. When this happens, it is usually in one's early sexual experiences.

> Pills? That's what I should have taken. But I didn't want them. I didn't want them because that's like coming right out and admitting, "*I AM FUCKING,*" you know. I didn't want to admit that to myself. . . . I was trying so hard to think I wasn't fucking that the thought I might get pregnant never entered my mind.

12.6 Salient findings

1. 10% of all American female adolescents and 23% of all nonvirgin girls report that they have been pregnant at least once.

2. 40% of all nonvirgin girls (50% of the younger girls and 36% of the older girls) agree, "Sometimes I don't really care whether or not I become pregnant."

3. Of the girls who took no precautions against pregnancy when

they were having intercourse during the preceding month, 28% agree, "Abortions are so easy to get these days that I don't really worry about getting pregnant."

4. 89% of all boys currently having intercourse are often or sometimes worried about their sex partners becoming pregnant, compared with 71% of the girls currently having intercourse.

5. Nearly half of the nonvirgin girls, a third more than nonvirgin boys, have sometimes avoided intercourse because they were afraid of a resulting pregnancy. Boys and girls who had intercourse during the preceding month express this concern a little less frequently.

6. Responding to the question of what they would most prefer to do if they became pregnant, most nonvirgin girls would have the baby and either get married or bring the baby up themselves. Girls differ very little between what they say they would prefer to do and what they believe they would actually do if they became pregnant. This challenges the assumption that most girls favor abortion for themselves as a last resort even though they may depend on it in preference to birth control methods.

7. 30% of all nonvirgin boys say they would prefer abortion for their girl friends if the latter become pregnant. But boys who are currently having intercourse more frequently say that if they actually made a girl pregnant, they could be counted on to help bring up the baby and/or get married if the girl wanted the baby.

8. Young people by a small majority are not opposed to abortion for others under certain circumstances. 51% of all adolescents agree, "If two people are going to have a baby that neither person really wants, it is all right for the girl to have an abortion." 56% of all Catholics agreed with this statement, with Catholic girls agreeing to a lesser extent. The highest rate of support comes from sexual adventurers (70%).

9. Almost half of all young people consider that "It's immoral to bring an unwanted child into this overpopulated world, especially now that abortions are so easy to get."

10. One-half of all boy nonvirgins agree, "If I were to make a girl pregnant, I wouldn't want her to have an abortion, because taking the life of an unborn child is wrong." 60% of the nonvirgin girls also agree, "I would never want to have an abortion, because taking the life of an unborn child is wrong."

11. At the time of first sexual intercourse 55% of all nonvirgins report that no effort was made to cut down on the risk of the girl becoming pregnant. Those who took precautions against pregnancy during their first intercourse are more likely to have taken them *always* during the preceding month.

12. In answer to the question, "This very last time that you had sex with a girl/boy, did either of you use any kind of contraceptive or birth control method?" 47% of the boys reported they or the girl did; 60% of the girls say they or the boy did.

13. The more frequently a girl is currently having intercourse, the more frequently she reports that some kind of birth control effort was always made during the past month. Of the girls who had intercourse one to five times in the preceding month, 59% report that they always took some kind of pregnancy precaution; 75% of those having intercourse six times or more in the preceding month always took some kind of precaution against pregnancy.

14. The birth control method that girls report most frequently always being used is birth control pills (33%); the second method girls most frequently report always being used is the boy's withdrawal of his penis before ejaculation (17%). Virtually none of the girls report using a diaphragm and only 2% report using an intrauterine device.

15. 25% of the nonvirgin boys say they always use a condom, while only 9% of the girls say that the boy always uses a condom.

16. 68% of all girls and 80% of all boys deny that their parents have told them the facts about birth control. Nonvirgins report receiving birth control information from their parents only a little less frequently than virgins, and adventurers have been informed by their parents most often of all the sexual behavior groups.

17. 56% of all boys and 70% of all girls believe that birth control pills can be physically harmful to a girl.

18. 89% of the girls who did not always take any pregnancy precautions when having intercourse during the preceding month say they do not know where to get birth control pills or any other kind of reliable contraceptive.

19. Nearly one-half of the girls having intercourse during the preceding month without always using a birth control method believe that a girl who truly does not want a baby will not have one, even in the absence of birth control.

20. 71% of all nonvirgin adolescents agree, "If a girl uses birth control pills or other methods of contraception, it makes it seem as if she were planning to have sex." 74% of the girls who did not always use birth control methods when having intercourse the past month also agree.

21. 46% of younger girls say there is no place where they could go to get birth control pills or other contraceptives.

22. 58% of all younger nonvirgin girls say they do not use birth control pills or other contraceptives because their parents might find them.

23. 13% of all nonvirgins compared with 16% of all adolescents and 16% of the children from Catholic families say they would not use birth control or contraception "because it is against my religion."

13. Venereal Disease: An Ancient Hazard in Modern Life Style

Fact: If you are going to go to bed with somebody, you've got to face anything these days.

A nineteen-year-old sexual adventuress

QUESTION: *What is the best way of avoiding VD?*
ANSWER: *Not having sex. That is the best way and the way I used.*

A seventeen-year-old married girl

I was scared to have sex for a while because all I heard from my father about sex was VD, VD, VD—you can get VD from anybody—you can die from it. He never told me anything good about sex.

A sixteen-year-old boy

Most young people are aware of the near epidemic prevalence of venereal disease in the United States. Most of them know VD is transmitted through sexual contact and that anyone can have it. A minority of young people say their parents have told them the facts about VD (Table 127); sex education classes and television are mentioned as sources of information by some.

More older than younger adolescents and more boys than girls claim they did not hear the facts of VD from their parents. Nearly 50% more older girls than older boys confirmed discussing VD with their parents.

Adolescents who were told about VD by parents

Boys			Girls		
All	13–15	16–19	All	13–15	16–19
24%	27%	22%	33%	35%	32%

Only 25% of boys and girls with intercourse experience and 32% without intercourse experience have been told the facts of VD by their parents. 29% of all adolescents (47% of the younger boys and 36% of the younger girls) agree, "I'd like to ask my parents for information about VD, but I'm afraid to because they would ask whether I'm having sex with girls/boys" (Table 158). Most of those expressing this concern are younger adolescents.

13.1 How adolescents view giving and getting VD

Most young people do not think of themselves in terms of either giving or receiving VD. It is something distasteful they can "get" or "catch" only by chance. They feel they have only themselves to blame "if it happens"; but they assume responsibility only after they have contracted VD, not before.

But the casual way in which young people view themselves as

givers and receivers is only half the story of their viewpoint toward VD. Their attitude toward VD itself is not so casual. 78% of all young people disagree with the statement, "Getting venereal disease isn't really a very serious problem, because one can always go to a doctor and get it cured" (Table 24). Younger girls and sexual beginners yet to have intercourse disagree with this statement in the greatest numbers of all. On the other hand, the groups most in agreement with this statement are monogamists and younger boys. We do not know the reasons for this, especially in the case of the monogamists. Monogamists would have the most to lose from VD, in transmitting it to someone with whom they have a sexual relationship and to whom they would presumably prefer not to have to reveal they had contracted from another partner. Monogamists are more frequently casual about catching VD than the adventurers, whose level of concern matches that of all virgins and all girls.

Adolescents responding false to the statement, "Getting VD or venereal disease isn't really a very serious problem because one can always go to a doctor and get it cured."

All adolescents	78%
Boys	75
13–15	73
16–19	76
Girls	82
13–15	86
16–19	79
Virgins	84
Inexperienced	81
Beginners	88
Nonvirgins	73
Monogamists	70
Adventurers	83

13.1.1 Expression of personal responsibility

84% of the boys and 93% of the girls agree with the statement, "If a boy finds out that he had VD, he should immediately tell any girl he has recently had sex with" (Table 284). We assume the response would have been almost the same if a girl had been the one to find out she had VD. The high percentage of agreement with this statement is important, considering that educational campaigns and parental advice about VD almost never ask the adolescent to perceive himself as a VD carrier.* Yet, surely the boys answering a question worded in this way could perceive themselves as potential carriers.

As is discussed in the next section, young people are willing to assume the risks of catching VD, largely because of their considerable distaste for asking their sex partners whether they might have it and partly because they cannot tolerate the idea that they would have sex with a person who would have a venereal disease. But there is a third factor, perhaps even more important than the other two, which also bears upon personal responsibility. Education and propaganda have focused on how not to get VD—sufficiently so, that the young person exposed to these campaigns may strongly feel the social disrepute of having VD. These reactions suggest the value of telling adolescents that VD is a common occurrence to which anyone having intercourse could be exposed. This would reduce the shame associated with VD and lessen any unwillingness adolescents might have to seek treatment for it.

Two other gauges of personal responsibility with respect to VD are a desire to defer sex because of fear of VD and the avoidance of someone who is thought to have had VD and is now cured.

Nonvirgins agreeing, "Have you ever wanted to have sex with a girl/boy but decided not to do so because you were afraid of catching VD, or venereal disease?" (Table 297).

All	Boys	Girls	Monogamists	Adventurers
29%	34%	23%	28%	37%

Again, despite the fact that a majority of adolescents feel that getting VD is a serious problem, the majority express their willingness to take a risk, despite conscious fears of contracting VD. Girls consider boys a lesser VD risk than boys consider girls. Perhaps girls are less willing to consider the question carefully when the occasion for intercourse arises. Some girls also report feeling confident that they could see evidence of VD on their male partner's sex organ, an advantage the boy does not have should his female partner be infected.

Once again, fewer monogamists say they have denied themselves sex because of the threat of VD. Can it be that they do not feel the question applies to their sex partners, with whom they feel they have

* In some personal interviews with parents, we learned that parents do not feel squeamish about mentioning VD if they talk with their children about sexual matters in much detail. However, their reasoning parallels that of their children: they discuss VD only in terms of the dangers of catching it rather than in terms of passing it on to others. Parents feel that children must be saved from being innocent victims of VD rather than be directly told of the disgrace of victimizing others. VD educational campaigns still give greater emphasis to how to avoid getting the disease rather than to how to avoid giving the disease to others.

a more stable relationship than the adventurers have with theirs? Yet, monogamists permit occasional infidelity.

Adventurers of both sexes, not surprisingly, express the strongest willingness to forgo sex out of fear of catching VD, although it could be argued that they have so many chances for sex that they can deny themselves a sex partner with greater ease than others—certainly greater ease than the monogamist who would find it more difficult to challenge a partner of longer standing and deny that partner intercourse. 49% of all adolescents and 59% of all those having intercourse during the preceding month would avoid having sex with a person who has had VD but is known to be completely cured. As sexual experience increases, so does the corresponding unwillingness to abandon intercourse. Younger boys and girls feel the strongest about this, with the rate of agreement falling more sharply below a majority on the part of older boys than older girls (Table 100).

Adolescents agreeing, "If I heard that a girl/boy had had VD, I would avoid having sex with her/him even after she/he was completely cured."

All adolescents	49%
Boys	46
13–15	59
16–19	36
Girls	52
13–15	58
16–19	47
Virgins	58
Inexperienced	64
Beginners	54
Nonvirgins	41
Monogamists	43
Adventurers	42

13.1.2 Concern and willingness to assume risks

Risking VD is an inevitability for those who are experienced in sexual relations. Despite the assertions that they choose their partners carefully, they know they cannot detect whether or not their partners have VD. This encourages their casualness of attitude that likens VD to an avocational hazard. It is an undesirable consequence of a desirable activity.

A seventeen-year-old single female adventurer hates the idea of getting VD but acknowledges that intercourse is so prevalent in her social set that once a person introduces VD, many others are likely to come down with it. The moral question of promiscuity or intercourse outside of marriage never arises. She describes the advent of VD among her friends as follows:

> Jeanne has a girl friend named Mary, and Jeanne's husband's name is Ted. Ted has a brother named Bill. Jeanne had a lover named Dick. Dick had a girl named Sally. Sally had a boyfriend named I don't know what. Well it started out with Frank, a nice kid. He's got everything he wants. It just happens that he's Ted's brother, and that's how he happened to get mixed up in this. Frank got it I don't know where. He gave it to Sally. Sally went to bed with Dick and gave it to Dick. He went to bed with Jeanne and gave it to Jeanne. Jeanne went to bed with her husband, Ted, and gave it to Ted. Then Teddy went to bed with Mary and gave it to Mary. Mary went to bed with Bill [the respondent's fiancé] and gave it to Bill. It's stupid.

Partly to learn reactions to the church in a practical matter involving sexuality and partly to measure concern about VD, the respondents were asked to agree or disagree with the statement, "Churches could do things that would be a big help in keeping down VD among young people who have sex" (Table 205). 52% of all boys and 64% of all girls agreed with this statement. It was interesting to note that this statement was agreed with by 63% of boys and girls who have had sexual intercourse, while 52% of the sexually inexperienced people believed it.

13.1.2.1 Reasons expressed for concern and lack of concern

Reasons for concern about getting VD are straightforward and explicit. They seldom involve mention of VD's possible consequences to one's body despite the fact that a majority of people believe the disease is serious. Essentially, the areas of concern are:

1. The inconvenience of seeking and accepting medical treatment
2. The desire, particularly on the part of younger respondents, that their parents not know
3. The ugliness of the symptoms and the "dirtiness" of VD

It would not be a fair observation to say that there was general unconcern, for no one expressed a desire to contract VD. However, the avocational risk factor mentioned earlier looms high as a form of unconcern: young people are generally willing to take the risks involved in preference to not having intercourse and in preference to carefully inquiring into possible risks with their sex partners.

One form of unconcern already mentioned is the confidence that "it won't happen to me." Another form of unconcern is the belief that one's sex partner is simply not the kind of person to have VD. As one eighteen-year-old girl put it: "I know for a fact they [the boys with whom she has had intercourse] couldn't give it to me, because they weren't hanging around with anybody who could give it to them."

Young people generally have sexual intercourse with someone for whom they feel affection; thus, they identify with the character of their sex partner. The strongly publicized connotations of disgrace and dirtiness associated with VD do not permit them to believe they would be having sex with the kind of person who would have VD. An eighteen-year-old girl's remarks typify this attitude.

> I guess it's hard to picture the person that you're having relations with as ever having VD. VD is kinda . . . it kinda seems dirty, you know. It's like a disease you get from doing something lousy or something like that. You can't picture yourself deserving it.

A sixteen-year-old girl is reminded of what she learned about VD from friends and high school sex education.

> I just knew vaguely it was a disease you got from fucking. For a long time I called it vereneal disease. . . . It just never dawned on me that anyone I went to bed with would have VD. It's such a seedy thing. . . . Maybe that's the trouble. The films in school always typified these people as being the seedy type, so you don't look for it.

Those who have had VD are often prepared to rationalize the episode as a kind of learning experience. It is another variation of the avocational hazard factor. If a person wants intercourse, it is not easy to decide against the experience on the basis of the VD risk or to take the prospective sex partner into one's confidence and assess the possible consequences. If drugs or alcohol figure in the first encounter, concern is still further lessened by loss of ordinary inhibitions. One girl who was "stoned" the night she lost her virginity expressed her lack of concern as follows:

> And then when I found out I had the clap, I couldn't tell my father that. . . . I told myself this was a learning experience and everything happens for the best and I should be happy about it. . . . So I went to a friend's doctor, and she paid the bill. And it came to something like sixty dollars. For a fourteen-year-old kid, how could you get sixty dollars when you get a two-dollar-a-week allowance. So I paid her back in a month, and I mowed lawns and baked cookies for the money.

13.2 Adolescent experience with venereal disease

We asked each nonvirgin respondent to reply true or false to the following statement: "I have never had VD, or venereal disease." This statement was worded negatively so that younger and more sensitive persons would not be shocked and because we wanted to assure our respondents that we were not assuming they had had VD.

11% of all nonvirgin boys and 10% of all nonvirgin girls have had VD (Table 298). 4% of all nonvirgin boys and 2% of all nonvirgin girls are unsure whether or not they have had VD. Virtually every boy and girl over fifteen years of age who was interviewed has one or more friends who had once had VD.

13.2.1 Characteristics of adolescents contracting VD

Older adolescents have a 50% higher incidence of VD than that of younger adolescents, with boys and girls having nearly the same incidence. This can be accounted for by the fact that older adolescents have intercourse with more sex partners and more frequent intercourse with their sex partners.

Nonvirgin adolescents indicating they have had venereal disease

All nonvirgins	10%
Boys	11
13–15	8
16–19	12
Girls	10
13–15	7
16–19	11
Monogamists	12
Adventurers	11

13.3 Salient findings

1. 11% of all nonvirgin boys and 10% of all nonvirgin girls have had VD. Older adolescents have a 50% higher incidence of VD than that of younger adolescents.

2. Most nonvirgins cannot believe they would have sexual intercourse with anyone infected with VD. They consider such a possibility a personal reflection on themselves and virtually an impossible question to discuss with their prospective sex partner.

3. Only 25% of boys and girls with intercourse experience and

32% without intercourse experience believe they have been told the facts of VD by their parents.

4. 29% of all adolescents (47% of the younger boys and 36% of the younger girls) agree, "I'd like to ask my parents for information about VD, but I'm afraid to because they would ask whether I'm having sex with girls/boys."

5. 78% of all young people disagree with the statement, "Getting venereal disease isn't really a very serious problem because one can always go to a doctor and get it cured."

6. 84% of the boys and 93% of the girls agree with the statement, "If a boy finds out that he has VD, he should immediately tell any girl he has recently had sex with."

7. 34% of the nonvirgin boys and 23% of the nonvirgin girls agree they sometimes have wanted to have sex with a girl/boy but decided not to do so because they feared catching VD as a result.

8. Large numbers of adolescents will avoid partners they know to have had VD. 49% of all adolescents and 59% of all those having intercourse during the preceding month agree with the statement, "If I heard that a girl/boy had had VD, I would avoid having sex with her/him even after she/he was completely cured."

9. 52% of all boys and 64% of all girls agree, "Churches could do things that would be a big help in keeping down VD among young people who have sex."

14. Sex and the Marriage/Family Question

I hate marriage. I think that when you sign a thing that says you're devoted to each other, it's just a commitment. It doesn't make you love each other. I don't believe in marriage.

A thirteen-year-old virgin girl

I look back on my own life and I wish so much that my parents had gotten a divorce. The hell we went through, the arguments, the lack of love. . . . A kid may turn around and say to himself: "Why should I get married? My parents didn't love each other and they got married."

A nineteen-year-old boy sexual adventurer

QUESTION: *Are there any reasons why you might want to get married other than to give your children a name?*
ANSWER: *No.*

Interview with a seventeen-year-old girl who is very much in love

If two people love each other and are living together, getting married is just a legal technicality.

Statement with which two-thirds of the young people in our national sample expressed agreement

14.1 Disappearing concept of "premarital sex"

The term *premarital sex* has traditionally been a label applied to whatever sexual relations adolescents were having before marriage. It is a concept that is becoming increasingly outmoded, because young people are not scheduling marriage on their life agenda simply to gratify their sexual needs or in order to legalize their sexual relationships. To discuss sex before marriage with many young people is to invite the response: "What marriage? I'm not planning to get married."

Many adolescents feel no obligation to marry. In fact, they often feel obligated *not* to marry early in life. Most young people are not searching for mates; they are not saving for rings, weddings, and their household furnishings; in short, they are not planning futures in terms of marriage.

Social pressures against premarital sex and in favor of marriage have little influence on most adolescents. In fact, they do not seem conscious of such pressures. In Chapter 4 it was shown that the sex before marriage question is very much on the minds of many parents and that adolescents are well aware of their parents' attitudes. Thus, a majority of young people (72%) believe their parents think sex before marriage is immoral (Table 37); only 12% of the young people in our national sample (17% of the boys and 6% of the girls) believe that their parents would want them to live with their prospective marriage partner before marriage (Table 172).

Despite what they believe their parents think, however, 72% of all adolescents agree, "Two people shouldn't have to get married just because they want to live together" (Table 201). Younger girls are as strong in their support of this statement as are older girls, although younger boys are less likely than older boys to express agreement. As might be expected, a somewhat larger proportion of boys than girls support the statement, as do a larger proportion of those with intercourse experience versus those without such experience. But the most significant fact is that agreement with this statement is expressed by more than half of the adolescents at *every* age and experience level.

Adolescents agreeing, "Two people shouldn't have to get married just because they want to live together."

Boys	76%
13–15	63
16–19	87
Girls	67
13–15	66
16–19	67
Virgins	64
Inexperienced	55
Beginners	71
Nonvirgins	78
Monogamists	80
Adventurers	78

Conversely, only 25% of all adolescents—primarily the young and the sexually inexperienced—believe, "Sex is immoral, unless it is between two people who are married to each other" (Table 231).

Clearly, then, the idea of marriage as an event that should take place before having sex is an ineffective argument for parents to use in attempting to persuade their children to refrain from sexual relations. Moreover, the fact that most adolescents fail to perceive marriage as a milestone because so many regard it as a millstone is not the only reason why the concept of premarital sex has so little relevance to adolescents. Many believe that it is abnormal or unnatural for young people not to have sexual intercourse during adolescence.

55% of all boys and 54% of all girls think it "abnormal or unnatural for a boy not to have sex until he gets married" (Table 41). 42% of all boys and 27% of all girls think it "abnormal or unnatural for a girl not to have sex until she gets married" (Table 114). There is no significant difference between younger and older adolescents with respect to acceptance of these statements.

However, this does not automatically mean that adolescents believe they must have unmarried sex only with the person they intend to marry, nor does it mean that they believe they must have sex with their prospective marriage partner before marriage. Only 29% of all adolescents (36% of the older boys and 28% of the older girls) agreed with the statement, "I wouldn't want to marry a girl/boy until I'd lived with her/him first" (Table 169).

Demise of the traditional male-female double standard with respect to virginity at marriage is further substantiated by another finding of our study: although 54% of all boys refuse to condemn female virginity at marriage as "abnormal or unnatural," only 30% of all boys (23% of the older boys) say that they "wouldn't want to marry a girl who isn't a virgin at marriage" (Table 103).

14.1.1 How significant is the widespread availability of birth control?

Conventional wisdom asserts that widespread access to the birth control pill and other contraceptive devices has encouraged not only more sexual intercourse among young people than existed in the past but also a considerably higher incidence of sexual intercourse than would otherwise be the case.

One challenge to this assumption lies in the findings reported in Chapter 12; many young people having intercourse dislike or have no ready access to the birth control pill, are *not* using contraceptive devices, and consider abortion an acceptable alternative. Of course, it may well be that the great publicity surrounding the existence and availability of birth control does in fact stimulate greater willingness to have sexual relations even though those having intercourse are not taking advantage of these new methods.

But other perhaps greater reasons for increasing sexual relations may be that many young people no longer feel that they should have to wait to have sex with each other until they are married, and that they no longer anticipate marriage in the foreseeable future as many adolescents did in previous generations. Moreover, many adolescents do not believe they are compelled to marry even if they become pregnant—keeping one's baby without marriage is far more acceptable than it once was.

For all of these reasons the widespread availability of birth control has not been the major factor in the change in premarital sex behavior; marriage is simply no longer the condition many young people feel they have to meet before they can freely have sexual relations together.

One might argue that people are unwilling to marry in order to bed down with each other because they do not intend to marry each other anyway. That argument is not wholly valid, however, because 39% of those having a serious sexual relationship (20% of the boys and 52% of the girls) plan to marry their partner (Table 401).

14.2 Desire and lack of desire for marriage

We measured the respondents' desire or lack of desire for marriage in two ways: young people's plans to marry those with whom they are currently having a concentrated sexual relationship and young people's expectations with respect to eventual marriage, regardless of whether or not they presently have any particular partner in mind.

Among those adolescents who are currently involved in sexual relationships, 25% of the older boys and 50% of the older girls say that they plan to marry their current sex partners (Table 401); and an overwhelming majority of *all* young people, whether or not they are involved in relationships and irrespective of their opinions about marriage, do expect that they will eventually want to marry.

85% of all boys and 92% of all girls agree with the statement, "Someday, I will probably want to get married and have children" (Table 2). There is no significant difference either between boys and girls or between older and younger adolescents concerning the expectation to marry. It is equally clear that the intention of 89% of all respondents to marry—eventually—does not influence sexual activity during adolescence. Expectation of eventual marriage is equally high among those with and without intercourse experience, and among those who are and are not currently sexually active. Even among the sexual adventurers, 73% expect that they will "someday" want to marry and have children. Nor, as we shall see in the next section, does intention to marry have any significant bearing upon the reasons young people express in favor of or in opposition to marriage. The main unanswered question that emerges is what effect young people's attitudes toward marriage will have upon the success of their eventual marriages.

14.3 How adolescents view marriage

14.3.1 Reasons for favoring and opposing marriage

Marriage, as the saying goes, is the tie that binds. It is the legally binding and obligatory dimension of marriage that is the largest source of both adolescent favor and opposition to marriage. Few see marriage as anything more than a definition of a relationship which society sanctions and enforces between two people. What is more important to the majority of respondents are the feelings that two people have for each other and the way they treat each other.

Although a few young people believe that marriage will disappear in its present form in the next few decades, most of them accept marriage as a continuing institution. They are much taken by the speculation of social commentators about the various forms marriage might take, but they have few suggestions about what alternative forms of marriage they would favor. Anyone who is satisfied by marriage, they feel, should be privileged to benefit from it.

Adolescent perceptions of marriage turn on whether or not their immediate goals will be satisfied or harmed by assuming its obligations. Even when their own personal goals coincide with those they traditionally associate with marriage, they see marriage as a high price to pay for attaining those goals. Even more crucially, they do not seek lifelong companionship and financial security in their immediate postadolescent life. They are moving away from their own family ties, and few seek to replace them with new ones. This is the context in which the great majority of respondents argue for or against marriage—even those who assume that they will undoubtedly eventually marry and have children.

What must not be underestimated is the unwillingness of a significant number of young people to make hard plans for the future. For some, this reflects a disbelief in any meaningful future, but for most it is a simple preoccupation with the present. Commitment to the future is not to their liking; and when most adolescents think of marriage, they think of commitment—not commitment to ideas or principles, but to relationships that may inhibit their personal freedom.

Supporting this is the fact that 35% of the boys and 30% of the girls "don't much believe in planning for the future; life right now is the most important thing" (Table 68).

Essentially, six reasons in favor of marriage are put forth by adolescents.

1. Marriage is a natural state for people in love.
2. Sex is more enjoyable because of the sense of belonging to one's partner.
3. Personal security is assured, in that there is far less likelihood of one person walking out on another.
4. A sexual relationship is legalized and sanctioned by society.
5. There may be many good business reasons for two people to have a legal relationship.
6. The girl is pregnant.

In more detail:

1. Many adolescents think of marriage as a natural state for lovers. 61% of all boys and 75% of all girls agree that "If two people are in love, it's only natural for them to want to get married" (Table 262). Young people believe that love is vital for a successful

marriage, and most girls believe very strongly in a marriage that will be filled with love for them.

2. 68% of all respondents affirm a feeling of belonging: "Marriage would make sex even more enjoyable, because both people would know that they really belong to each other" (Table 265). Serial monogamists, who emphasize their sexual relationships with each other, are clearly not as enthusiastic as sexual beginners about the contribution marriage makes to sexual enjoyment; 38% of the monogamists disagreed with the above statement, as did 32% of the adventurers. In fact, the bad effect of marriage on the sexual relationship is discussed below as one of the arguments against marriage emerging most frequently in our interviews with nonvirgins.

3. The proposition that feelings of insecurity about one's mate can be minimized by marriage was often offered as a reason to favor marriage. However, respondents seldom saw this argument as benefiting their own self-confidence or sense of well-being, and it was rather offered in behalf of others whom respondents felt needed this type of security.

> My girl friend can't feel safe about anyone unless she has a way of tying her boyfriend down. How else can she do it except by marriage? He's liable to leave her anyway when he feels like it, but at least she won't be worrying about the possibility all the time.

> Jim is going to have to get married before he feels sure that Nan belongs to him. Otherwise, you know, he'll always wonder. It wouldn't even matter if she balled someone else once in a while, and he probably would too. But he'd know who belonged to who.

4. The idea that marriage is a legal technicality is offered both to favor and oppose marriage. "Why not?" asked one girl who favored marriage. "A legal technicality can't hurt them if they are living together anyway." "If you're having children, you should get married for their sake," is typical of how most young people feel about others who are having children and want to keep them. "It legalizes sex"; "The neighbors won't look down on us"; and "If our parents will be happy, what difference does it make?"—arguments like these, while offered in favor of marriage, are more negative reasons rather than indicating wholehearted support for it.

5. The same spirit prevailed in the almost cynical mention of the business benefits of marriage. Marriage was variously described as "a convenience for people who want to buy land," or "good for acquiring a joint bank account when you're marrying money," or "a good business relationship."

The negative quality of the arguments offered in favor of marriage is particularly pronounced when contrasted with the idealism and love that characterize the relationships young people seek to establish with one another (see Chapter 4). Positive reasons were not offered except in connection with love (item 1 above).

6. There is considerable disagreement about whether or not pregnancy is a valid reason for marriage. Those who regularly use birth control and feel no threat of pregnancy cannot understand such an emergency. Abortion, as our data indicate in Chapter 12, is acceptable to many—undoubtedly more than ever before. Having the baby and giving it up for adoption is approved by some.

The arguments that are offered against marriage gather essentially around three main points.

1. Young people enjoy informally relating to each other sexually and feel no need or desire for a socially sanctioned means to accomplish this.
2. Their love and sexual relationship would be harmed by the binding relationship of marriage.
3. Marriage is undesirable until they are absolutely sure they find the person they will want to live and have children with, without threat of divorce or separation.

In more detail:

1. The elements of social compulsion in getting married bother many. According to a fifteen-year-old virgin who is waiting to have sexual intercourse until she finds the right person: "The court says you *have* to get married and you can't live with another person unless you're married. . . . I think it's stupid! Why should you have to get married in order to live with someone you love?"

A fourteen-year old girl says, "The only difference between living together and being married is that you sign a paper. I think," she adds, "when you sign a thing that says you're devoted to each other, it's just a commitment. It doesn't make you love each other."

A fourteen-year-old girl who is very much in love with her boyfriend feels marriage is an invention of adults who cannot comprehend young love.

> They say it's a disgrace if you're going to go to bed with a boy before you marry—if you have sexual acts. They won't face that, because before you marry you may be in love with a boy and you know that boy's going to marry you and you're going to marry that boy. They just don't understand, I guess.

2. The second major reason offered against marriage is the harm many young people feel it will do to their sexual relationship. One phase of this thinking is well put by a seventeeen year old who has not had sexual intercourse.

> Because we are not automatically getting married earlier, we need not automatically say we are in love; and if we are not able to say we are in love, how can we be expected to marry and have sex and have children together? This would be the most immoral of all.

For many adolescents marriage implies an unloving relationship, one that not only does not depend for its existence on love but also perpetuates living together long after love has left. If people need not marry each other in order to love each other, and if they need not marry each other any longer to "make love" to each other, it is thought to be an insult to a love relationship to demand its consummation in marriage. Somehow, they feel, marriage drives away love by forcing each party's profession of love for the other.

Although the advantages of personal security are expressed by some respondents as a reason why others might want to marry, they are not described as a virtue. If you can't be sure that the other person won't walk out on you, their reasoning goes, then perhaps you should get married. But it is almost always added that it is precisely *that* insecurity which should discourage marriage in the first place. "You should get married only to the person you don't worry about, and you should not get married to the person you do worry about."

Above all, young people fear their feelings for each other will be hurt by marriage. A sixteen-year-old girl compares the effect of marriage on love with Christmastime. "If you give somebody a present, you shouldn't really give it with the idea of getting something back, you know. . . . You give out of love because you want to see them smile or something."

Another sixteen-year-old girl does not think "you must grow up and have just one relationship and fall in love and get married for your whole life. For me, I think I'm probably going to have a lot of relationships before I get married."

Boys are even more adamant on the subject. The double standard that minimized affection during old-time "premarital" sex has disappeared, because a boy will marry his "old lady" if he is really satisfied she is the one he wants to commit himself to. Experimentation is important, not just for the sake of sexual adventuring and wanderlust, but to try out relationships. Not just trying out girls, but trying out relationships by testing one's self and the girl.

3. The third and perhaps most sensitive objection to marriage for many young people is seen in their lack of sympathy for divorce. They do not oppose divorce; quite the contrary, they affirm its necessity over and over again in special cases. But they are mindful of the consequences of divorce for children, and they want a marriage that offers the least probability of divorce. They view traditional marriage

as a kind of serial monogamy on the part of people who marry over and over again in search of a happy relationship.

A few more sophisticated young people recognize such a search as being doomed to failure because it is an effort to find a marriage —not a relationship—that will live up to the searcher's concept of ideal marriage. Perhaps this is the main underpinning for the agreement of 78% of all adolescents with the statement, "I can't see myself getting married until I know it will last for the rest of my life" (Table 193). Even sexual adventurers agree; 76% look for a very long-lasting marriage. Unexpectedly, however, as boys grow older they are more likely to agree with the above statement, while as girls grow older they tend more to disagree. Unless girls have a greater desire to marry as they grow older, the explanation for this is not clear.

14.3.1.1 Responsibilities and marriage

Are many young people opposed to marriage because they do not want the responsibilities of marriage? What do they consider the responsibilities of marriage to be? Do they feel they can meet these responsibilities outside of marriage? All three questions need to be answered before we can judge the extent to which opposition to marriage is based on evasion of responsibilities.

Young people do not concede that having children invites responsibilities they do not want. Only 13% of all adolescents agree, "I don't think I will want to have children, because I don't like the idea of having all that responsibility" (Table 188). Children are seen as a substantial burden to shoulder in one's early life, but it is a responsibility that most young people anticipate they will eventually assume. The nonvirgins expressed more resistance to the responsibility of having children, and 20% of the adventurers indicated agreement with the statement.

Most young people do not give careful thought or anticipation to their future lives five, ten, or fifteen years away; they neither assume nor shirk responsibilities they might have in the future. For the time being, however, most of them do not want to assume any more responsibilities than they absolutely have to: personal convenience, learning interests, and sometimes career concerns are far more important. An eighteen-year-old male artist unfavorably contrasts sexual security with the new responsibilities he would have if he were to marry.

> One time I could really dig marriage if I knew I could come home and get laid anytime. I could come home anytime I desired to

> have sex and it would be there. But I would have to get a job. I would have to be secure because I'd have another person I'd be responsible for. Keeping clothed, buying Christmas presents and birthday presents and anniversary presents. They're all part of being married. I'd really have to do the whole thing and it would be a lot of financial things that would come in. I think it would . . . hamper my artistic freedom and abilities.

Marriage is seen as a joint effort between man and woman. But the responsibilities of marriage except the eventual long-time marriage with children have not been carefully thought through by most young people other than those who are seriously contemplating marriage. They do not think of marriage as a formal relationship or even as an institution which calls for attitudes, techniques, and ways of living. They do not think of homes, estates, saving money for the future. The major responsibility most young people see in the marriage is that of staying together with their spouse.

Finally, most young people believe that their most significant responsibilities as human beings are those of personal relationships which they can meet outside of marriage. Responsibilities to each other and personal freedom of choice and mobility are the main responsibilities that young people want to think about or assume, if they want any at all, and they do not feel they are evading any such responsibilities by refraining from marriage. In fact, some young people clearly believe they are behaving in a more responsible way toward their sex partners by not pressing marriage upon them.

A fifteen-year-old girl put it this way as she described the relationship she would have with her husband, from whom she expressed the hope she would have five or six children, a big house, and lots of money:

> I don't know. I can't explain it, you know. But a good marriage relationship where we'd be happy and we wouldn't always have to spend our time together. Go our separate ways if we wanted to. Like my mother, when she first got married, she was married to my father for twelve years. They were always unhappy but they felt they had to stay together because of me and my brother. But if me and my husband get upset, then we'll just separate, you know. I don't feel you just have to stay with somebody if you don't want to. So if you don't have a good relationship, you know, then it's just like a spark in your life, you know, and it goes away. Then I just think—I can't explain, but that's how I feel. . . . You always think you'll have a happy life, but I don't know. Nothing happens until it does.

14.3.2 Attitudes toward companionate marriages

Many versions of companionate marriage have been proposed in the twentieth century, with sexual relations being their mainspring.* We discussed this kind of marriage in some respondents' depth interviews. Young people do not generally favor it. The fact that a companionate type marriage would be legalized disturbed them, not because they prefer their sexual relations to be illegal but because they want to avoid a specific relationship with a specific person to be acknowledged by a legal ceremony, written up in legal records, and having formalized status that would require formal action to dissolve. It is the binding quality imposed from the outside that they do not want, no matter what its informality or minimal legal obligations. For those opposed to marriage, the same objections to traditional marriage apply for any version of a companionate marriage as well.

Another version of the companionate marriage often takes place in the commune. In those communes where social organization is loose and flexible, sexual freedom is often considerable. People in these communes live together without legal marriage ceremonies and sometimes share sexual favors along with other personal resources. Adolescents are sympathetic to communes, although most know little about them. 66% of all adolescents believe that many people who live in communes are finding meaning and brotherhood in their way of life (Table 179).

But many young people also express doubt about the value of the commune because of their self-segregation and isolation from the world at large. Some have expressed doubts about the freedom of thought and independence of action that communes permit their participants. They wonder to what extent the participants really want to share their personal belongings. A willingness to be poor is not the same as constantly yielding a portion of what one owns to others. One sixteen-year-old girl wondered if "it would make some people even more introverted, just clutching everything they have more to themselves instead of just sharing with everybody."

An eighteen-year-old boy saw communes, as did several, being poor training for a way to live.

> It's no place to be if you really want to learn to live with others. It's true that you're close to people and have to depend on each other. But that's just it, you know. Depending on each other means you get

* Judge Ben Lindsay proposed in the early 1900s that young people be authorized to participate in a probationary marriage relationship that would test their ability to live together. More recently, Margaret Mead has proposed that society recognize a second kind of marriage: a first or temporary marriage in which man and woman would not take the sacrament of marriage under God or assume certain legal obligations but would obtain legal permission to live together for the practice, for the pleasure, and for the mutual understanding they now seek in relationships outside of marriage. The partners in this type of marriage relationship take no lifetime vows. In the later traditional and lasting marriage, unlike the first, children would be a natural goal. People would enter into this relationship with very strongly defined legal obligations to remain together once they had children.

to be like each other or you can't make out. The more you're like each other, the harder it's going to be to get along with all the different types outside when the time comes.

Shared sex may be provocative fantasy material, but young people discussing sexual behavior in communes saw it as a price of living together rather than a benefit. A seventeen-year-old girl wondered about "some communes [that] are gung ho for quick sex and everything like that which I don't agree with. It just becomes—it just turns into a physical action like going to the bathroom. Something that feels good that you have to do."

An eighteen-year-old girl adventurer was more explicit.

> I'm a privacy freak. I don't believe in . . . what do they call some of those communes? Gang bang? That's a bunch of bullshit. They don't have any respect. If somebody loves you, they respect you. If they respect you, they kinda want to keep you respectable . . . sheltered, . . . not hidden in the corner, but so you're a lady.

14.3.3 Sexual prerogatives adolescents assume for selves and partners in marriage

Over one-half of all adolescents do not believe that it is possible for a boy or a girl to be really in love with more than one person at the same time (Table 155). But as boys grow older, they tend to change their minds. Girls remain about the same regardless of their age. As people move from virginity to intercourse experience, they also shift strongly in the direction of believing that people (of their own sex) can love more than one person at the same time.

	Boys		
	All	13–15	16–19
Do not believe a boy can love more than one girl at the same time	55%	69%	43%

	Girls		
	All	13–15	16–19
Do not believe a girl can love more than one boy at the same time	58%	55%	61%

Adolescents were fairly consistent with the following table when they were asked about their spouses' possible infidelity in their own future marriages. 54% of all adolescents and 62% of all sexual adventurers agreed with a milder statement: "If I were married and my wife/husband had sexual relations with someone else, I would be angry about it, but it would not in itself be enough reason to get divorced" (Table 101). Boys and girls are virtually tied in their agreement.

Adolescents agreeing, "It's all right for married people to have sexual relations with other people once in a while for the sake of variety" (Table 281).

All adolescents	34%
All boys	42
All girls	26
All virgins	24
All nonvirgins	43
Monogamists	33
Adventurers	60

Still fewer adolescents (41%) and adventurers (44%) agreed that "If I were married and my wife/husband had sexual relations with someone else, I would divorce her/him" (Table 160). Girls were just a little bit more permissive; 34% of the older girls, compared to 40% of the older boys, say they would divorce their spouse under these circumstances. Nonvirgins (38%) agree with this statement almost as frequently as virgins (45%).

Questions about divorcing someone to whom an adolescent is not yet married are very hypothetical indeed and can only be taken as indicative of their current feelings. But it is a significant commentary on how strongly many young people feel about infidelity in marriage despite the willingness of many to tolerate it among themselves as unmarried monogamists and adventurers.

The fact that adolescent toleration of infidelity is by no means wholly extended to the prerogatives of marriage suggests that many adolescents are intolerant about marital infidelity in their changing views toward marriage. This appears to be a major explanation for their active sexual behavior before marriage, the desire to defer marriage, and the importance of duration and children in marriage. If the youthful revolution in premarital sex represents a social trade-off with promiscuity outside of marriage, the assumption that adolescent sexual activity will encourage later adultery may be highly questionable.

14.4 Marriage and children

To young people marriage means children. Marriage is considered undesirable until they are sure they are marrying the person they can continue living with after they have children. The presence of both a father and mother in the household is considered vital.

Yet, children and marriage are not perceived as absolutely going together. Only one girl in our survey suggested that were she to become pregnant she would feel obliged to marry, and then she was not sure that she would necessarily want to marry the baby's father. Raising one's child alone is not anticipated with pleasure, but the responsibility is acknowledged and thought to be perfectly feasible. Above all, a marriage should not be maintained only for the children's sake. Divorce, while considered exceedingly undesirable, is much preferred to a household without love.

14.4.1 Traditional two-parent family

Young people strongly believe in a two-parent family. Despite their antagonism toward playing highly structured roles in American society, they believe in the institutions of fatherhood and motherhood. Opinions of what being a mother or father means differ almost from person to person. Young people see parents sharing a good many of the more routine chores of raising a family. But there is a parenthood mystique they cannot deny, and which the children of divorced or separated parents particularly embrace; these children often feel they were deprived of a dimension in childhood that neither parent could wholly compensate for in the absence of the other.

Most important to many adolescents, however, is the relationship that a child enjoys with each parent. They perceive this as being more important than everyone living at home together. Thus, 63% of all adolescents agree that "It's not so important that a child live in a home with both of his parents, so long as he has a good relationship with each of his parents individually" (Table 264).

But adolescents express concern for children who are deprived of both parents in the household. 72% of all boys and girls agree, "It is really a tragedy if a couple that has children breaks up" (Table 283). Adolescents of all varieties of sexual experience agree in just about these same proportions. They are very explicit on this score. An eighteen-year-old girl says:

> If there is nothing between the two of you—if it's like being at a bus station with other people and nothing more—then you can break up. But if there is something there, you should stay together with your children. You're the one who brought them here, and you're the one who's going to fuck them up if you leave.

At the same time, 68% of all adolescents believe, "If parents no longer love each other, it's better for their children that the parents break up rather than continue to live together unhappily" (Table 294). Older girls (78%) tend to feel this way more often than others. One seventeen-year-old girl put it this way:

> I know that in a lot of cases a child needs both parents, but you have to take into consideration what is better; a child who is going

to live in a household where there is no love at all, with pressures and tension and everything which will ruin his psychological views on marriage and the future.

14.4.2 Children without marriage

Many girls in our personal interviews indicate their willingness to consider having children without marriage, particularly in the case of accidental pregnancy. Their reasons are blurred, but apparently are based on a greater unwillingness to experience an abortion than deliberately to have and raise children without a husband. Even these girls, however, do not dismiss the idea that a man—perhaps the father of the child—would be a member of the household.

Boys indicate a greater willingness than girls to have children without first getting married. 29% of all adolescents agree, "Someday, I will probably want to have children—but it won't matter whether or not I get married first" (Table 180). 43% of the older boys, compared with 27% of the older girls, subscribed to this view. A majority of the adventurers (56%) and a near majority of all nonvirgins (45%) also agreed.

Willingness to consider having children out of wedlock increases substantially with age among both girls and boys, but boys are considerably more willing to entertain the idea than girls. Girls presumably have a greater concern than boys both for the responsibility of bringing children into the world under these circumstances and the potential problems of raising children without a spouse.

14.4.3 Marriage without children

Most girls indeed want children, whether they want to be married or not. They have the responsibilities of raising children in mind and they have the population crisis in mind—but this seldom deters them, despite their seeming ambivalence. One sixteen-year-old adventuress put it this way:

> Well, I feel if I really want a baby, I'm going to have it even as much as I know about the population crisis. I know myself I want to have babies very much. But then I do think, my God this world has so many problems already. It has so many people that it's not fair to bring another human—to put that on someone—like to bring another human life here—to put that on somebody. It's a big load and I really don't know my head. . . . I know though that I want to have babies. It's not fair in a lot of ways, but I know that's what I want.

Most boys want children too. However, as we pointed out earlier, they think of marriage and children as an eventuality rather than as a near-future reality that will interfere with their sexual freedom.

In fact, boys are less likely than girls to cite overpopulation as a reason for not having children. 42% of all boys and 33% of all girls would not agree with the proposition, "Because of the problem of overpopulation, I would not want to have more than two children" (Table 177). It can be argued that younger adolescents tend to want more children than do older adolescents.

Adolescents disagreeing with desire to limit one's children to two because of overpopulation

13–15		16–19	
Boys	Girls	Boys	Girls
53%	43%	33%	26%

The question of population becomes an issue for young people only as they grow older and seems to be more important to girls than to boys.

Only a few more than a quarter of all adolescents "would not want to have children in the kind of world we live in today" (Table 151). More boys feel this than girls, perhaps because of the greater involvement young men feel in America's military activities. Adventurers feel this very strongly, indeed, perhaps because of their greater antisocietal tendencies.

Adolescents agreeing about not wanting to have children in the kind of world we live in today

All adolescents	Boys 16–19	Girls 16–19	Adventurers
30%	33%	24%	52%

We learned earlier that few older boys (13%), and even fewer older girls (10%), agreed that they might not want children because they did not "like the idea of having all that responsibility" (Table 188). This was considered still another measure that indicates most adolescents believe in having children and want them despite the current importance to them of their childless sexuality without marriage.

14.5 Assumptions about own anticipated marriage

We have already reported on various comments that adolescents make about their own marriages, particularly with respect to the sexual expectations and prerogatives they foresee. Boys and girls are in sufficient agreement so that if they inquire into each other's sexual attitudes and talk them out before marriage, they should not be mismated because of misunderstanding or disagreement about the sexual lives they want to lead together.

A major criticism of early marriage cited early in this chapter dealt with marriages characterized by quarreling, separation, and divorce. Duration of the life of the marriage is clearly one of the concerns of adolescents, and this is borne out by the fact that 78% of all adolescents affirm, "I can't see myself getting married until I know it will last for the rest of my life" (Table 193). Younger boys (70%) express this less frequently than do younger girls (85%), while older boys and older girls score at about the same level, along with the adventurers and other nonvirgins. Recalling that 41% of all adolescents were unwilling to say they would not divorce their spouse in the event of infidelity (Table 160), it is clear that duration has very high priority in the criteria by which most adolescents will evaluate their prospective marriages.

14.6 Adolescent sexuality and the significance of marriage

Most young people expect eventually to be married and have children. Many see marriage as both a grown-up relationship and a lifelong responsibility which gets in the way of enjoying their youth. As adolescence nears its end, even the older adolescents do not seem any more interested in considering marriage at this time in their lives.

It is the binding quality of marriage that disturbs young people more than anything else. For some, the fact that marriage is legally binding is not so disturbing as it is disgusting—that people feel so insecure or distrustful with one another that they must marry regardless of what "being forced to stay together" will do to their sexual relations and their love for each other.

The quality of love is lifelike but not lifelong for most adolescents, and so they do not want to blend the concepts of love and obligation with each other until they know they possess compatible elements of both. These are considered the only guarantee of a sexually happy marriage. They want to know that their marriage is made to last sexually for reasons having nothing to do with being legally required and religiously expected to live with each other for the rest of their lives.

Premarital sex among American adolescents will only increase, with greater numbers of people than ever before involved in monogamous sexual relationships. Serial monogamy will be a marriage substitute for many, despite society's traditional association of monogamy with marriage rather than without marriage. But marriage will be less and less a reason for waiting to have sexual intercourse because marriage, to adolescents, is less the sexual institution that it is to their elders. What many adolescents are saying is that marriage is neither the time nor the place in one's life for one to be striving for sexual satisfaction or for self-fulfillment on a sexual plane. A person should know his sexual self by the time he is married, and know both what he wants and expects to achieve sexually in his marriage relationship. Boys and girls believe that this calls not only for knowing intimately one's prospective marriage partner as a sex partner, but knowing one's self as well.

Adolescents have no radical view about the form that marriage will take in the coming years. They are perfectly satisfied to leave marriage alone and let those who will have it enjoy it when they feel they want it. But adolescent sexuality will undoubtedly never be a captive of the marriage institution again, and adolescents would strongly resist any society that ever sought a return to premarital chastity and early marriage.

14.7 Salient findings

1. Two-thirds of all adolescents agree that if two people love each other and are living together, getting married is just a legal technicality which they should not be required to comply with.

2. However, 85% of all boys and 92% of all girls, and equally high majorities of those with and without intercourse experience, expect someday to marry and have children. A majority of adolescents believe that if two people are in love it is perfectly natural for them to want to get married.

3. The availability of birth control may be a less important explanation of intercourse among unmarried adolescents than such reasons as an unwillingness to await marriage, a belief they may not marry, and a willingness to raise a child without the presence of a father in the household.

4. The legally binding and obligatory dimension of marriage is the largest source of both adolescent favor and opposition to marriage. Many adolescents believe their love for each other and sexual compatibility are damaged by the suggestion of marriage.

5. 72% of all young people believe their parents think that sexual intercourse before marriage is immoral; 12% think their parents would want them to live with their prospective marriage partner before marriage.

6. Over half of all boys and girls think it is abnormal or unnatural for a boy not to have sexual intercourse until he gets married;

27% of all girls and 42% of all boys think the same conclusion holds for girls.

7. 54% of all boys refuse to condemn female virginity at marriage as abnormal or unnatural; even fewer (30%) say they would not want to marry a girl who was not a virgin at marriage.

8. Three-fourths of all adolescents do not want to marry until they are satisfied that their marriage will last for the rest of their lives. Sexual adventurers are equally strong in these beliefs.

9. Young people generally do not favor companionate marriage for some of the same reasons they oppose ordinary marriage.

10. 34% of all adolescents agree that for the sake of variety it is all right for married people to have sexual relations with other people once in a while.

11. 45% of all boys and 37% of all girls would divorce their spouse if they found the spouse was having sexual relations with someone else.

12. A strong factor in adolescents' desire for a lifelong marriage is their belief that children need two parents in the household. Although most adolescents agree that divorce is sometimes necessary, nearly three-fourths of them agree, "It is really a tragedy if a couple that has children breaks up."

13. 29% of all adolescents "probably want to have children, but it won't matter whether or not I get married first."

14. As adolescents grow older, they become more concerned about the number of children they would have in view of the world's overpopulation. And 30% of all adolescents say they would not want to bring children into the kind of world we have today.

15. Adolescent Sexuality: An Overview

15.1 Forerunner sexual behavior groups
- **Nature of love**
- **Fidelity and infidelity**

15.2 Social control
- **Parent-adolescent relationships**
- **Religion and the church**
- **Marriage and the family**
- **Neglect of birth control**
- **Venereal disease**

15.3 Sexuality and self-satisfaction
- **Intimacy and fun**
- **Potential of beginning sexual activities**

15.4 A final word

Adolescent sexuality is a natural phenomenon; it is not immoral in the eyes of most young people. They do not believe that sexual behavior in itself has anything to do with being a good or bad person; for them, sexual activities have no relevance to morality except in the way they are used. This, plus the test of what freely consenting people find they can enjoy, is the basis for their toleration of the sexual behavior of others, regardless of whether or not they are more stringent about themselves.

Many young people feel a responsibility to assess a potential sexual relationship in terms of what it can do for or to the people involved. Previously, they believe, there was little or no real personal responsibility being exercised in sexual matters; it was as if society was your body's caretaker and you had little choice in the matter.

The results of our study show that young people today frequently apply the situational ethic to sexual activity. Adolescents need personal values ("ought" judgments of what is right and what is wrong) to apply to these situations. The situational ethic says *not* that people will do what they please but that they will do what they believe is best to meet the requirements of a given situation.

The basic question for adolescents is the purpose served by sex, not whether or not they are disobeying the law or flouting religious tradition. They see most sexual situations as personal ones that defy cataloging, and so the adolescent does not accept laws or religious dogma as relevant to the problems sex partners must work out for themselves. They have only their personal values and physical desires to depend upon.

Perhaps adolescent sexuality and its justification by the situational ethic will rouse American society to new efforts to encourage the adolescent to identify his and her personal values and to learn how to put conscience to use. Conscience is a personal resource that can be neglected in favor of obeying the dictates of society's spokesmen: parents, clergymen, public officials, doctors, and teachers. In spite of adolescents' need for the initiative to compare what they think and do to their personal values, school and church give little attention to the task of using self-interrogation to mobilize personal values. Young people want to know whom they should choose for sex partners. They wonder about technique and gratification, the uses of sex, the roles of male and female, the meaning of love—but education for values is often left to the street, to the film, to pornography, and to pop poetry and records.

Some parents, clergymen, and educators realize that an adolescent's sexuality in part depends on how well he or she knows how to put his personal values to work. We know from our findings in Chapters 2 and 4 that young people have these values. We also know that they frequently consider them alien to their parents' and to those of other major agencies of social control. Whether or not these adolescent personal values will be of major interest to society will have much to do with how adolescent sexuality continues to express itself. Meanwhile, since they are not schooled to convert values into behavior, it should not be surprising that adolescents will not always behave in accordance with their own personal values.

15.1 Forerunner sexual behavior groups

As more adolescents become sexually experienced at earlier ages, new relationships are evolving for those who want to have sex without marriage. The trend in adolescent sexual behavior is not toward promiscuity. Although we have documented sexual adventurism, there seems a greater tendency for adolescents to pursue a monogamous sexual relationship without marriage. Even for those who intend to marry, living together will more frequently be the proving ground for a couple who want to learn more about how well they relate to each other before they make a decision to marry.

Young people want to relate to each other in ways other than marriage. They look to their sex partners not for what the years ahead hold for each other but for what life has to offer today. Even a single intimate interlude offers comfort and solace to many adolescents; their commitment involves what each can mean to the other at the moment. The values to be realized by such a relationship may not be as enduring or deeply felt as those enjoyed by many married couples, but some self-realization is accomplished in sharing a sexual relationship with another.

The commune appears to interest relatively few adolescents. Much talked about, the commune draws commentaries from those who see a substitute for marriage evolving. But the commune's sexual sharing has little interest for most adolescents; the personal relationship most adolescents (particularly girls) desire is nullified. Group sex is a lark for those who find their marriage obligations dull or routine, but it is not often sought by young people.

Adolescents eschew forms of self-segregation that freeze their mobility and opportunity to meet all kinds of people. While "families" and "colonies" and "cooperatives" continue to attract those adolescents who pursue an ideal of how people can live together, the adolescent's loner instinct more often prevails.

What other kinds of sexual behavior can we expect besides serial monogamy and sexual adventurism? One form that may emerge might be called "advanced sexual contacts," in which one's sexual behavior is confined to sexual beginning activities. (This is discussed in detail in Section 15.3.2.)

15.1.1 Nature of love

Society has traditionally differentiated between love and sex, and this has affected adolescents in several ways. Many feel they must believe or profess to believe they love their sex partners. Love is not easy for adolescents to define, but mutuality receives strong emphasis —mutual affection, mutual understanding, mutual concern for each other's problems. Love is seen as participation in a self-fulfilling relationship; it embraces both parties, while each maintains his and her own individuality.

The major development with respect to adolescent love is the willing admission that love is neither submission to another nor an obligation to love forever. The types of love discussed in Chapter 4 show that the intensity of love is more important to adolescents than duration and that possession of one another neither demonstrates love nor assures it. The ability to relate to each other is the key ingredient: one does not love another because she is intelligent or he is handsome, but because of what the two mean to each other. If people mean much to each other, they will not feel compelled to test each other by demanding commitments or promises to marry.

What does this mean for the future of love as it is commonly defined in America today? Responsibility to one another will *not* constitute an essential element in the kind of love that more adolescents will prefer to have. The trend is not in the direction of irresponsibility, either, but toward requiring adolescents to care for themselves while they nurture their common relationship. Dependency (not to be confused with trust) and submissiveness will become increasingly less attractive to adolescents in a love relationship.

Sexual satisfaction will become a more important requirement of love when the relationship is a sexual one. Friendships will more frequently involve love, even though the explicitly sexual element will be missing; sex and friendship will therefore continue to mix less well than sex and love. There may be an increasing tendency for adolescents to believe they can love more than one person at a time. This tendency will not be confined to sexual adventurers. Multiaffectional love will increase because of the growing requirements for sexual satisfaction and because of the entry of sex into more aspects of adolescents' daily lives. There may be more adolescents for whom even specialized relationships (for example, a common bond limited to books or music) will not be complete without the sexual act.

15.1.2 Fidelity and infidelity

The strength of serial monogamy for many of its participants lies in the infidelity that it permits—not promises, not encourages, but only permits. The important thing, of course, is that "infidelity" is a term that society uses to describe the breaking of a vow to a relationship; it is the content of the vow, however, that determines whether or not intercourse outside of the relationship has a connotation of infidelity for many adolescents.

Some young people do not want to pledge sexual fidelity in return for being able to enjoy a sexual relationship or as a sign of their love. And many young people also state they would not seek divorce from a spouse they discovered has had sexual relations with another.

This reassessment of fidelity may presage widespread disregard of some aspects of both the Judeo-Christian tradition and the law. Adultery is a violation of the commandments of American common law and religions; it goes unpunished because so many married people commit adultery at least once and because so few are willing to press charges. But under no circumstances do traditional marriages begin with an understanding that sexual infidelity is permitted; serial monogamy does.

A major argument offered against marriage by many adolescents is the legal requirement of sexual fidelity; it is also a motive ascribed by many adolescents to those people who do marry early in life: to find a partner who will not have sex with another. It is very likely that we shall see more marriages on the part of young people either formally or informally renouncing the provision of sexual faithfulness. Whether they will attach more value to their love for each other remains to be seen.

15.2 Social control

Man's sexuality has always been a central concern of law and society. Even when the church ruled, there is good reason to believe that the need for social and political order were as much the source of its moral code as were God or His self-appointed spokesmen. In the absence of birth control, passion had too many disorderly consequences for both the political and economic definitions of the family and the need for people to be legally accountable and belong, without dispute of paternity, to whoever was god, king, parent, or slaveholder.

Concern for sexuality is seen in the definition and operation of social institutions today. Some of these institutions are changing, sometimes radically, in an effort to be relevant; others are still locked in combat with changing sexual mores. The social controls of law, customs, and traditional values exercise certain restraints on adolescent sexuality; but they are becoming less effective.

15.2.1 Parent-adolescent relationships

Most adolescents have little communication with their parents about sex. They believe that their parents refuse to acknowledge their sexual behavior or that their parents find their sexual attitudes so disagreeable that they refuse to discuss them. Most young people believe they have been given little or no information about sex from their parents, despite their feeling that sex is an issue of conflict between them. Many adolescents feel they have never gotten to know their mothers and fathers; they often feel unloved.

With this felt absence of effective communication about sexual matters, parents run a risk of being ineffective in fostering their adolescent children's personal well-being and ethical development. Can the parent demonstrate that he wants to guide and counsel his children while at the same time showing a willingness to let go? Or will the importance of the parent's role in the adolescent's emotional world dwindle to one of combat and intrusion?

There are no established rules to follow in fathering or mothering an adolescent. And this study is not intended to be a parents' manual or a critique of present-day parenthood. But some of our findings offer hope for a more effective parental function and for the freer expression of love within the home. Perhaps the best suggestions come from today's adolescents, who will be tomorrow's parents. Perhaps today's parents can benefit from what adolescents say they would do as parents.

Adolescents will probably be more stringent about their children's sexual behavior than they found their parents to be. But they will be more likely to acknowledge their children's sexuality—treating it sometimes seriously and sometimes humorously in open communication about youthful values and sexual behavior.

Adolescents will probably assess their children's actions more in terms of altruistic values (love, compassion, willingness to share) than in terms of conventional achievement (high grades, popularity). Tomorrow's parents will probably agree with their children no more than parents now agree with adolescents. Their main goal, however, will not be agreement but a mutual airing of views.

Adolescents do not want their marriages to be threatened every time a quarrel occurs, nor do they want to constantly raise in their children's minds the question of whether or not they will remain together. As is true of many families today, quarrels and disagreements will be accepted as part of a wholesome long-term relationship rather than as a reason for the marriage to flounder.

15.2.2 Religion and the church

It is fashionable to assume that young people in general are alienated from religion. But many young people go to church, even if more do not because they consider church irrelevant. The clergy has been forced to appeal to several generations simultaneously; it is a difficult task to maintain tradition for older people while responding to adolescents' need for relevance and social gospel. But many adolescents agree that the church can work in behalf of youth's ideas.

Pioneering efforts among adolescents have already been made by some denominations as well as individual churches and temples. Religious and social agencies have gone in search of the adolescent in urban neighborhoods where runaways congregate or where bars predominate; counseling services have been set up for the pregnant, the addicted, and the emotionally disturbed; clergymen are sometimes assuming local missionary and ombudsman tasks among youth, which stretch their talents beyond their preaching and church administration duties. There has been a fundamentalist revival of Jesus as the ultimate folk hero; the thousands of youngsters who have become "Jesus freaks" have chosen Jesus in this new light as their salvation.

The most difficult task for some churches will be to welcome those adolescents who are full of sexuality and empty of any recognized religious persuasion. Most churches have firm doctrinal rules for membership; yet they have attracted many adolescents to their dances, gymnasiums, theater groups, and counseling services. Perhaps some churches over the next decade will sponsor "seeker societies" in which adolescents can discuss their personal values, test them against others, and learn how to conduct their own search for meaning.

For most adolescents, religion is the search for meaning. They will accept help in asking the right questions, but they want the conclusions to be their own. Their sexuality raises many questions about the meaning of life: What is pleasure? What purposes in life are served by sex? Whom should one marry? How can one better relate to others? For some adolescents, newly discovered passions are not without moments of thankfulness and even reverence. But above all, the ultimate question for almost all adolescents remains: Who am I?

15.2.3 Marriage and the family

Not a few boys and girls heap scorn on marriage as an outmoded, obsolete institution they doubt they will participate in; they express revulsion for what they believe are legal ties and moral obligations that smack of entrapment rather than a love relationship. Many of these adolescents are already having sexual intercourse without marriage; many others intend to. The large majority of adolescents, however, intend to marry and have children. But they intend to love and be loved several times before they marry.

It is doubtful that trial or companionate marriage will become law. Adolescents wanting to marry can marry in the usual way now; adolescents who want to live with each other for sexual and other reasons reject any effort to bind or obligate them to one another. Some call this rejection a lack of responsibility on the part of adolescents—an unwillingness to assume the burdens of building and sharing a life and household. But adolescents themselves ask what responsibilities they are shirking if these are responsibilities they do not want. They are not satisfied they can easily find the right person to live a lifetime with. Some view society as owing them a living or at least a handout, but most believe they owe themselves and society the benefits of lives lived with the largest possible number of options. Their career planning and decision making are leisurely, and so they have no set life-style or earnings level. It is irresponsible, they contend, to want to marry under these circumstances.

It would be a serious error to assume, however, that adolescent reluctance to marry is confined to objections concerning legal bonds and lifetime commitments. Few adolescents explicitly challenged the institution of the family in their discussion of marriage, but those who did discuss the family reveal what may well be in the minds of others. One nineteen-year-old boy, for example, tells of his belief that the family is often against the best interests of both the individual and society.

> I think the family has always encouraged selfishness and clannishness. After all, before there were any corporations the family has been the device that accumulates money and power and titles and then hands them down from generation to generation. The family kept the woman in the household, kept children at work in the fields and in the mines and at the sewing machines. The family kept slaves. In fact, I'll bet the family

> was the last to give up all of these uses of people as property. What is the divine right of kings if it is not the preservation of the power to rule in the hands of the same family? Why should a king or a queen, or for that matter the town's laundryman or restaurateur, have to always come from the same family?

Some young people believe that the institution of the family has lent itself to sexual exploitation. Fidelity, they suggest, is often not so much faithfulness to love as allegiance to family power and coercion. These young people also see the family as encouraging sex to be only a genital pleasure used to secure personal self-gratification and control over others and to be used to procreate rather than to enjoy and love.

The implications of this thinking for America's living patterns are provocative. The family has traditionally frozen male and female into what are often highly stereotyped father and mother roles, discouraging many adults from loving and sharing relationships with one another and usually discouraging any personal friendships outside the family with members of the opposite sex. Many children believe they are watching their parents fail to achieve an intimate marriage. It is easier for father and mother to fill specific roles of breadwinner-father and housekeeper-mother and depend on each other's traditional roles than on each other. But in the new relationship that many adolescents envisage, husband and wife must share, must be intimate, must want a direct one-to-one relationship.

If the present patterns of adolescent sexuality continue, one can suppose that divorce rates will lessen in about ten years. Many people who should never marry may no longer feel the necessity of doing so; they will live together without marriage. Others may be less apt to divorce because of the variety of sexual experience they enjoy before their marriage; mate selection processes may become more discriminating in the process of working at the relationship of living and loving together before marriage under conditions permitting lengthy self-observation.

Marrying later and without pressure to consummate sexual desire, men and women will give more attention to the nonsexual characteristics of married life. Whether to have children and how many, the prerogatives of each spouse in the household, whether the wife should work outside the home and in what capacity: all will be more carefully reviewed by two people considering marriage.

With the more emotional and subjective factors already laid at rest, young people will be more likely to seek professional counsel before marriage. Many adolescents will defer marriage indefinitely or will even be counseled to decide against marriage. This would be consistent with a trend that has already developed in marriage counseling: the belief that sometimes the husband and wife need to be saved from their marriage more than the marriage needs to be saved. As a result of sexual freedom before marriage, some adolescents who would otherwise marry will learn that they do not respond well to living with someone.

Although the church marriage ceremony may become increasingly less important, it is possible that a new form of ethical fealty will develop in which people make a pledge to each other not in God's name but in the name of a set of ethical principles that will have the sanction of many religious denominations.

15.2.4 Neglect of birth control

Almost no adolescent suggests that he or she has intercourse for pregnancy. The purpose is pleasure, not having children. In the past the prohibition of birth control was intended to minimize sexual intercourse for pleasure. Yet, intercourse for pleasure abounds while birth control methods are often rejected, ignored, or neglected.

There seem to be five major reasons for neglect of contraception.

1. Elements of casualness, spontaneity, and misinformation seem to characterize the sexual experiences of many adolescents. Protection from pregnancy has a relatively low priority for many adolescents. But awareness is often stifled by the sex partners themselves. The boy often avoids raising the question because he does not want to assume responsibility or cause the girl to change her mind. In many cases the girl does not want to acknowledge the possible consequences of sexual intercourse.
2. Some girls use their bodies to satisfy their emotional needs. For a certain type of girl, the fact that she can become pregnant and can have an abortion becomes a plank in her platform of personal freedom.
3. Pregnancy is no longer the proof or outcome of what society considers an immoral act.
4. Considerable ignorance and misinformation exist about the efficacy and use of birth control pills, diaphragm, and IUD.
5. Abortion is becoming a widespread form of postintercourse birth control. As pregnancy becomes increasingly less feared because of social acceptance of adolescent sexual intercourse, so abortion may become increasingly commonplace because of social acceptance of pregnancy outside marriage.

The following suggestions are offered to parents, schools, churches, and birth control organizations who want to discourage pregnancies among adolescents:

1. Address all information and arguments to boys as well as girls. Girls must know that boys know.
2. Describe in sex education classes and planned parenthood clinics the many techniques of sexual love and gratification that can occur *without* sexual intercourse.
3. Reduce emphasis on the drawbacks of not having a husband when pregnant and give more attention to deprivations in mobility and personal freedom.
4. Make birth control information and devices available; but, more importantly, work to motivate their use.
5. Emphasize the ineffectiveness of some contraceptives. The number of pregnancies should be reduced because of a shift to more effective methods.
6. Wage a substantial campaign against depending upon abortion as a form of birth control. Abortion should be offered as a last resort to prevent unwanted births. Emphasize the possibility of sterility from repeated abortions.
7. Glamorize contraception. Its importance should be stressed as a part of the love ritual of the sex act. Just as with pleasure giving, both boy and girl should be encouraged to discuss very frankly with each other what is being done to prevent pregnancy.

15.2.5 Venereal disease

It is evident that the incidence of VD has not been lessened by publicizing its evils and emphasizing that it is transmitted through sexual intercourse. Nor has it been helpful to condemn what society calls promiscuity, because adolescents do not tend to condemn those who enjoy sex with more than one partner. To control VD, adolescents should be impressed with the following points:

1. VD is widespread among people having sexual contact. The implications of immorality or promiscuity must be removed from VD.
2. Sexual partners must be candid with each other about the possibility of their having been exposed to VD.
3. It is disgraceful to be a VD carrier and to infect others. To give VD to someone you like or love, to someone who trusts

you—this is a social disgrace which everyone should guard against committing.

4. According to our findings, most girls believe that the final responsibility for contraception rests with them. One contraception device, however, that boys are usually expected to furnish is the condom. The condom has an important prophylactic function—it can substantially cut down the transmission of VD. Where there is doubt or ambivalence about VD, girls and boys alike should be encouraged to utilize a condom if they are unwilling to forego intercourse. This means that girls as well as boys should have ready access to condoms, and that condom manufacturers should be encouraged to be explicit about the protective function of their product.

15.3 Sexuality and self-satisfaction

Sexual activity—adventurous or monogamous—is a way for an adolescent to generate his or her own subculture while ducking some traditions of society and government. American adolescents have struck out into the world of generating their own self-satisfactions in place of those traditionally expected of them. Thus is created the desire to find new companions or friends with whom adolescents can share their acquisitions and have tangible relationships.

15.3.1 Intimacy and fun

Modern adolescent sexuality is definitely not a cop-out from love or the responsibilities of living. In fact, it opposes what many adolescents feel is a prevailing cop-out of anonymity and alienation, the rigid traditionalism of the Protestant ethic, and an unaesthetic, anti-intellectual, and antihumanistic society.

To many adolescents, the most highly valued aspect of sexual activity is the personal intimacy and sharing it permits between two people. In contemporary American life the desire for intimacy with another is sometimes greater among young people than it is among adults. Many adults concede they cannot tolerate friends, lovers, or spouses "getting into their heads" or asking to share their inner thoughts. Adolescents have many questions they need to ask and answer about themselves, and they need to talk with each other about these questions and answers. They are not usually dogmatically committed to principles which discourage intimacy with those with whom they would communicate. Being as situationally oriented as they are and often being willing to view themselves as people apart from their parents, they have no psychological equity in the absolutes of family traditions and feel no need to "correct" another person's behavior or to equip another person to live a better life than he or she has lived.

Contemporary America has escalated depersonalized sex almost as though it were resisting sexual intimacy for those who could benefit from it. Commercialized vice and hard-core pornography have been permitted to expand. Many adolescents feel their parents object to adolescent sexual activities, even those performed in the name of love and affection and humanity. A father is often seen as one who will very likely reject a sexual experience for his daughter but will not reject his daughter's exposure to a movie replete with sexual sadism or his son's military indoctrination to kill.

In this context, sex has become a social issue with many adolescents who indulge in sex not to combat parents or society but to seek intimate personal relationships. Sex is the means by which such young people can not only assert their independence and freedom but—even more important—be themselves in what they feel is a sea of impersonality and inhumanity. Undoubtedly the rules of a community or of a family that demand the promise of marriage before sexual intercourse or expressly forbid sex regardless of how two people feel about each other cause the sex act to become more intimate for many.

One final note on adolescent involvement and initiative. For many adolescents sexual behavior—despite the pains that often go with it—is simply a lot of fun. Physical pleasure, love, beauty—with an earthiness and humanity to go with them—are fun. In addition, "fun" in the expression of adolescent sexuality is not antisocial. It might be seen in the sense of the French idiom "épater les bourgeois," which means "to astonish the bourgeois." Part of the fun of contemporary sexual behavior may be eliciting astonishment or even outrage from older people.

15.3.2 Potential of beginning sexual activities

Our data show that some boys and girls are seeking to generate a society that values love and affectionate relationships and that treats men and women as whole people rather than as sexual beings. It is true that adolescents are making some mistakes; they may opt for intercourse before they are ready; they may mistake genital sex for sexual love; they may often ignore love in favor of genital satisfaction. But in general they are trying to become whole and feeling people.

Our study has shown what we consider an unfortunate tendency toward premature intercourse among adolescents. Most adolescents are giving themselves little time for beginning sexual activities and move directly to sexual intercourse. One reason for this may be that in our society sexual intercourse is widely considered the only valid expression of sexual love. Another reason may be the unwillingness of many parents to consider advanced sexual beginning activities as morally different from sexual intercourse.

We feel strongly that beginning sexual activities should be encouraged. These activities enable a person to learn much about his and her values in sexual matters. "Do I want to relate to the other person, or do I want an orgasm that is simply urged on by the other person's cooperation?" "Does he or she exist only for my need?" "Do I feel I love this person only to satisfy my needs?" "Is my own orgasm the sole or dominant reason for having sex or is the sexual good of the other person also my major goal?"

These are questions that a person learns to ask and answer about himself and his sexual relations with others during beginning sexual activities. They are not questions that can be asked and answered by one who is still sexually inexperienced. And if the petting stage is quickly sidetracked it may be much more difficult for one to perceive and ask these questions during first or later intercourse.

Beginning sexual activity also permits one to realize the extent to which one's own sexual satisfaction can be obtained. In the petting process, all manner of experimentation is both permitted and possible in contrast to early adolescent sexual intercourse when momentum, thrust, and male orgasm seem to be the dominant elements of the process. Unfortunately we lack national sample data about whether or not beginning sexual activities enhance first intercourse; interviews with young people convince me that these activities do.

The advantages of beginning sexual activities include the following:

1. Adolescents would learn how to communicate better with one another about sexual matters. Of particular concern is discussion of contraception and VD.
2. Adolescents would be more likely to realize the humanizing and loving aspects of sexual activity.
3. Marriage, as a social institution, may have a greater chance of survival in a society that encourages the early possibilities for sexual love and mutuality rather than early sexual

intercourse in accordance with arbitrarily defined sexual roles.

The following actions are recommended to parents and educators who want to help adolescents achieve their full sexuality:

1. Call a halt to denigration of beginning sexual activities and "technical virgins."
2. Avoid emphasizing stereotyped male and female roles in sexual relations. Encourage boys and girls to realize there is much that male and female share in common as individuals.
3. In sex education emphasize the techniques that heighten one's own physical pleasure and encourage sensitivity toward the sex partner.

15.4 A final word

Our findings indicate general patterns of adolescent sexuality. However, it must be remembered that each young boy and girl is a unique person. To understand any adolescent, it is necessary to recognize his own personal values and experiences. This study is meant to enable parents to help adolescents ask themselves important questions about their sexuality and responsibilities.

In viewing today's adolescent sexuality, it is natural to speculate if there has been a change from adolescent sexuality of the past. Has there been a sexual revolution? Will there be one? There are many opinions on this, ranging from the assertion that young people are no different than they ever were to the belief that there will be sex in the streets by 1975.

There is nothing in our findings that tell us that young people are the same or different than they were five or twenty-five years ago, because this study was designed only to learn what adolescents are thinking and doing at the present time. Nor can we claim that our predictions of future trends of adolescent sexuality and its impact upon American society are more than extrapolations from what we have learned about what is happening today. But we feel that our inquiry is an important first step in obtaining the kinds of information and perspectives that, with additional studies and comparative data from other times and cultures, can lead to greater insight into the complex amalgam of values and behavior that constitute adolescent sexuality, and thereby to a greater understanding of human sexuality in general.

Tables of Information

Table 1

"If I had to go out into the world on my own right now, I think I could get along pretty well."

	True	Not Sure	False	TOTAL
All adolescents	60%	1%	39%	100%
Boys	64	0	36	100
Boys 13–15	43	0	57	100
Boys 16–19	81	0	19	100
Girls	57	1	42	100
Girls 13–15	41	0	59	100
Girls 16–19	70	2	28	100
Virgins	47	1	52	100
Inexperienced	40	0	60	100
Beginners	55	3	42	100
Nonvirgins	73	0	27	100
Monogamists	78	0	22	100
Adventurers	79	1	20	100

Table 2

"Someday I will probably want to get married and have children."

	True	Not Sure	False	TOTAL
All adolescents	89%	2%	9%	100%
Boys	85	3	12	100
Boys 13–15	85	0	15	100
Boys 16–19	85	5	10	100
Girls	92	1	7	100
Girls 13–15	94	0	6	100
Girls 16–19	91	2	7	100
Virgins	92	1	7	100
Inexperienced	90	0	10	100
Beginners	92	3	5	100
Nonvirgins	85	3	12	100
Monogamists	92	0	8	100
Adventurers	73	6	21	100

Table 3

"Sex education courses in school can't teach me anything."

	True	Not Sure	False	TOTAL
All adolescents	17%	2%	81%	100%
Boys	20	1	79	100
Boys 13–15	28	2	70	100
Boys 16–19	13	1	86	100
Girls	15	3	82	100
Girls 13–15	16	3	81	100
Girls 16–19	15	2	83	100
Virgins	12	3	85	100
Inexperienced	12	3	85	100
Beginners	10	3	87	100
Nonvirgins	22	1	77	100
Monogamists	14	0	86	100
Adventurers	27	1	72	100

Table 4

"I wouldn't use birth control or contraception because it's against my religion."

	True	Not Sure	False	TOTAL
All adolescents	16%	5%	79%	100%
Boys	19	8	73	100
Boys 13–15	28	12	60	100
Boys 16–19	13	4	83	100
Girls	13	2	85	100
Girls 13–15	17	2	81	100
Girls 16–19	10	2	88	100
Virgins	20	7	73	100
Inexperienced	19	7	74	100
Beginners	16	4	80	100
Nonvirgins	13	3	84	100
Monogamists	9	2	89	100
Adventurers	16	4	80	100

Table 5

"Sometimes I get sexually aroused from the music that I hear."

	True	Not Sure	False	TOTAL
All adolescents	30%	2%	68%	100%
Boys	33	2	65	100
Boys 13–15	29	1	70	100
Boys 16–19	37	2	61	100
Girls	28	2	70	100
Girls 13–15	27	1	72	100
Girls 16–19	29	2	69	100
Virgins	18	2	80	100
Inexperienced	17	1	82	100
Beginners	23	3	74	100
Nonvirgins	42	1	57	100
Monogamists	39	2	59	100
Adventurers	47	1	52	100

Table 6

"I often ask my parents for advice about sexual matters."

	True	Not Sure	False	TOTAL
All adolescents	16%	0%	84%	100%
Boys	12	0	88	100
Boys 13–15	11	0	89	100
Boys 16–19	12	0	88	100
Girls	21	1	78	100
Girls 13–15	22	1	77	100
Girls 16–19	20	0	80	100
Virgins	18	1	81	100
Inexperienced	15	2	83	100
Beginners	23	0	77	100
Nonvirgins	14	0	86	100
Monogamists	17	0	83	100
Adventurers	12	0	88	100

Table 7

"I find it hard to accept the idea of obeying laws that I don't agree with."

	True	Not Sure	False	TOTAL
All adolescents	59%	0%	41%	100%
Boys	66	0	34	100
Boys 13–15	62	0	38	100
Boys 16–19	70	0	30	100
Girls	52	1	47	100
Girls 13–15	54	1	45	100
Girls 16–19	51	0	49	100
Virgins	49	1	50	100
Inexperienced	46	1	53	100
Beginners	49	0	51	100
Nonvirgins	68	0	32	100
Monogamists	60	0	40	100
Adventurers	74	0	26	100

Table 8

"Some of the opinions that I express to my parents are opinions that I invent just to put them uptight."

	True	Not Sure	False	TOTAL
All adolescents	14%	1%	85%	100%
Boys	20	1	79	100
Boys 13–15	23	0	77	100
Boys 16–19	17	2	81	100
Girls	8	1	91	100
Girls 13–15	11	3	86	100
Girls 16–19	6	0	94	100
Virgins	14	2	84	100
Inexperienced	19	1	80	100
Beginners	9	1	90	100
Nonvirgins	14	1	85	100
Monogamists	9	0	91	100
Adventurers	15	2	83	100

Table 9

"On one or more occasions, I've done sexual things mostly to show that I don't care what society thinks."

	True	Not Sure	False	TOTAL
All adolescents	11%	1%	88%	100%
Boys	13	1	86	100
Boys 13–15	17	1	82	100
Boys 16–19	10	1	89	100
Girls	10	2	88	100
Girls 13–15	8	4	88	100
Girls 16–19	11	0	89	100
Virgins	6	2	92	100
Inexperienced	1	2	97	100
Beginners	12	0	88	100
Nonvirgins	17	0	83	100
Monogamists	14	0	86	100
Adventurers	15	0	85	100

Table 10

"I think my parents' ideas about sex are wrong, but they have a right to their own opinions."

	True	Not Sure	False	TOTAL
All adolescents	58%	2%	40%	100%
Boys	64	4	32	100
Boys 13–15	61	1	38	100
Boys 16–19	67	6	27	100
Girls	53	1	46	100
Girls 13–15	51	2	47	100
Girls 16–19	54	0	46	100
Virgins	42	3	55	100
Inexperienced	37	2	61	100
Beginners	44	4	52	100
Nonvirgins	74	2	24	100
Monogamists	73	0	27	100
Adventurers	66	5	29	100

Table 11

"My parents and I sometimes talk about sex, but it makes them very uncomfortable."

	True	Not Sure	False	TOTAL
All adolescents	23%	3%	74%	100%
Boys	19	3	78	100
Boys 13–15	20	2	78	100
Boys 16–19	19	4	77	100
Girls	27	2	71	100
Girls 13–15	22	2	76	100
Girls 16–19	31	2	67	100
Virgins	17	3	80	100
Inexperienced	16	2	82	100
Beginners	16	3	81	100
Nonvirgins	29	2	69	100
Monogamists	32	2	66	100
Adventurers	24	4	72	100

Table 12

"I think like an adult, but I feel a lot younger."

	True	Not Sure	False	TOTAL
All adolescents	54%	1%	45%	100%
Boys	60	1	39	100
Boys 13–15	53	0	47	100
Boys 16–19	67	0	33	100
Girls	47	1	52	100
Girls 13–15	44	1	55	100
Girls 16–19	50	1	49	100
Virgins	55	1	44	100
Inexperienced	57	2	41	100
Beginners	56	1	43	100
Nonvirgins	53	0	47	100
Monogamists	52	0	48	100
Adventurers	55	0	45	100

Table 13

"I wish my parents and I could agree more about what we think is right and wrong where sex is concerned."

	True	Not Sure	False	TOTAL
All adolescents	57%	3%	40%	100%
Boys	54	4	42	100
Boys 13–15	52	4	44	100
Boys 16–19	55	5	40	100
Girls	61	1	38	100
Girls 13–15	58	2	40	100
Girls 16–19	64	0	36	100
Virgins	45	2	53	100
Inexperienced	44	3	53	100
Beginners	46	0	54	100
Nonvirgins	68	4	28	100
Monogamists	74	0	26	100
Adventurers	64	3	33	100

Table 14

"My parents don't really like me."

	True	Not Sure	False	TOTAL
All adolescents	6%	1%	93%	100%
Boys	6	1	93	100
Boys 13–15	3	0	97	100
Boys 16–19	7	2	91	100
Girls	6	1	93	100
Girls 13–15	6	1	93	100
Girls 16–19	7	0	93	100
Virgins	3	1	96	100
Inexperienced	4	1	95	100
Beginners	4	0	96	100
Nonvirgins	9	1	90	100
Monogamists	5	0	95	100
Adventurers	14	4	82	100

Table 15

"I don't think that I would want to have sex with a person of another race."

	True	Not Sure	False	TOTAL
All adolescents	50%	2%	48%	100%
Boys	44	3	53	100
Boys 13–15	64	2	34	100
Boys 16–19	28	3	69	100
Girls	57	1	42	100
Girls 13–15	60	3	37	100
Girls 16–19	53	0	47	100
Virgins	54	3	43	100
Inexperienced	62	2	36	100
Beginners	47	1	52	100
Nonvirgins	47	1	52	100
Monogamists	55	0	45	100
Adventurers	26	0	74	100

Table 16

"My parents and I talk pretty freely about sex in general, but we don't really say what's on our minds when it comes down to really personal things."

	True	Not Sure	False	TOTAL
All adolescents	48%	2%	50%	100%
Boys	48	3	49	100
Boys 13–15	57	2	41	100
Boys 16–19	40	4	56	100
Girls	49	1	50	100
Girls 13–15	52	3	45	100
Girls 16–19	47	0	53	100
Virgins	42	2	56	100
Inexperienced	46	2	52	100
Beginners	41	0	59	100
Nonvirgins	54	2	44	100
Monogamists	57	0	43	100
Adventurers	41	7	52	100

Table 17

"I wish my parents and I could agree more about social and political issues."

	True	Not Sure	False	TOTAL
All adolescents	48%	4%	48%	100%
Boys	48	5	47	100
Boys 13–15	39	4	57	100
Boys 16–19	55	6	39	100
Girls	47	3	50	100
Girls 13–15	43	4	53	100
Girls 16–19	50	2	48	100
Virgins	39	4	57	100
Inexperienced	39	3	58	100
Beginners	38	4	58	100
Nonvirgins	55	5	40	100
Monogamists	60	0	40	100
Adventurers	56	10	34	100

Table 18

"I get a lot of satisfaction out of my sex life."

	True	Not Sure	False	TOTAL
All adolescents	60%	4%	36%	100%
Boys	63	4	33	100
Boys 13–15	62	5	33	100
Boys 16–19	63	3	34	100
Girls	57	3	40	100
Girls 13–15	49	4	47	100
Girls 16–19	62	3	35	100
Virgins	38	6	56	100
Inexperienced	33	6	61	100
Beginners	47	3	50	100
Nonvirgins	80	1	19	100
Monogamists	88	0	12	100
Adventurers	81	0	19	100

Table 19

"I have a lot of respect for my parents' ideas and opinions."

	True	Not Sure	False	TOTAL
All adolescents	80%	1%	19%	100%
Boys	75	1	24	100
Boys 13–15	79	0	21	100
Boys 16–19	71	2	27	100
Girls	85	1	14	100
Girls 13–15	89	2	9	100
Girls 16–19	81	0	19	100
Virgins	87	1	12	100
Inexperienced	87	2	11	100
Beginners	86	1	13	100
Nonvirgins	72	1	27	100
Monogamists	78	0	22	100
Adventurers	61	3	36	100

Table 20

"It's right that we have laws against homosexuality."

	True	Not Sure	False	TOTAL
All adolescents	59%	1%	40%	100%
Boys	63	0	37	100
Boys 13–15	72	1	27	100
Boys 16–19	55	0	45	100
Girls	55	2	43	100
Girls 13–15	58	4	38	100
Girls 16–19	52	0	48	100
Virgins	62	2	36	100
Inexperienced	62	3	35	100
Beginners	57	1	42	100
Nonvirgins	56	0	44	100
Monogamists	53	0	47	100
Adventurers	50	0	50	100

Table 21

"Most of the time I can't stand to be around my parents, and I have as little to do with them as possible."

	True	Not Sure	False	TOTAL
All adolescents	26%	1%	73%	100%
Boys	31	1	68	100
Boys 13–15	29	0	71	100
Boys 16–19	33	2	65	100
Girls	21	1	78	100
Girls 13–15	20	2	78	100
Girls 16–19	23	0	77	100
Virgins	18	2	80	100
Inexperienced	16	2	82	100
Beginners	23	0	77	100
Nonvirgins	34	1	65	100
Monogamists	21	2	77	100
Adventurers	46	0	54	100

Table 22

"A white girl and a black boy having sex together is something that I would consider immoral, even if both of them wanted to do it."

	True	Not Sure	False	TOTAL
All adolescents	30%	2%	68%	100%
Boys	29	2	69	100
Boys 13–15	34	0	66	100
Boys 16–19	25	3	72	100
Girls	31	1	68	100
Girls 13–15	37	2	61	100
Girls 16–19	27	0	73	100
Virgins	35	2	63	100
Inexperienced	41	1	58	100
Beginners	27	0	73	100
Nonvirgins	26	1	73	100
Monogamists	24	0	76	100
Adventurers	22	0	78	100

Table 23

"So far as sex is concerned, I have pretty much come to definite conclusions about what I think is right and wrong for other people."

	True	Not Sure	False	TOTAL
All adolescents	49%	1%	50%	100%
Boys	49	1	50	100
Boys 13–15	56	1	43	100
Boys 16–19	43	1	56	100
Girls	49	2	49	100
Girls 13–15	58	4	38	100
Girls 16–19	42	0	58	100
Virgins	52	3	45	100
Inexperienced	58	3	39	100
Beginners	41	2	57	100
Nonvirgins	46	0	54	100
Monogamists	37	0	63	100
Adventurers	58	0	42	100

Table 24

"Getting VD or venereal disease isn't really a very serious problem because one can always go to a doctor and get it cured."

	True	Not Sure	False	TOTAL
All adolescents	21%	1%	78%	100%
Boys	25	0	75	100
Boys 13–15	27	0	73	100
Boys 16–19	24	0	76	100
Girls	16	2	82	100
Girls 13–15	10	4	86	100
Girls 16–19	21	0	79	100
Virgins	14	2	84	100
Inexperienced	17	2	81	100
Beginners	12	0	88	100
Nonvirgins	27	0	73	100
Monogamists	30	0	70	100
Adventurers	17	0	83	100

Table 25

"I wish my parents understood that what I do sexually is pretty tame compared to some of the sexual things that go on today."

	True	Not Sure	False	TOTAL
All adolescents	74%	3%	23%	100%
Boys	74	4	22	100
Boys 13–15	75	2	23	100
Boys 16–19	72	6	22	100
Girls	74	3	23	100
Girls 13–15	73	3	24	100
Girls 16–19	74	2	24	100
Virgins	68	4	28	100
Inexperienced	62	3	35	100
Beginners	77	2	21	100
Nonvirgins	78	4	18	100
Monogamists	76	0	24	100
Adventurers	72	8	20	100

Table 26

"In general, I think that my sex life is pretty normal for a person my age."

	True	Not Sure	False	TOTAL
All adolescents	85%	1%	14%	100%
Boys	85	1	14	100
Boys 13–15	89	1	10	100
Boys 16–19	82	2	16	100
Girls	85	1	14	100
Girls 13–15	82	1	17	100
Girls 16–19	87	1	12	100
Virgins	84	2	14	100
Inexperienced	83	2	15	100
Beginners	88	1	11	100
Nonvirgins	86	0	14	100
Monogamists	91	0	9	100
Adventurers	89	0	11	100

Table 27

"I believe that my parents are still very much in love with each other."

	True	Not Sure	False	TOTAL
All adolescents	66%	5%	29%	100%
Boys	68	7	25	100
Boys 13–15	74	3	23	100
Boys 16–19	64	10	26	100
Girls	64	4	32	100
Girls 13–15	68	5	27	100
Girls 16–19	61	3	36	100
Virgins	70	6	24	100
Inexperienced	73	8	19	100
Beginners	70	6	24	100
Nonvirgins	63	4	33	100
Monogamists	61	4	35	100
Adventurers	58	4	38	100

Table 28

"I think it's right that people should make their own moral code, deciding for themselves what's moral and what's immoral."

	True	Not Sure	False	TOTAL
All adolescents	86%	1%	13%	100%
Boys	84	1	15	100
Boys 13–15	77	1	22	100
Boys 16–19	89	1	10	100
Girls	88	1	11	100
Girls 13–15	87	1	12	100
Girls 16–19	89	0	11	100
Virgins	81	1	18	100
Inexperienced	74	0	26	100
Beginners	92	1	7	100
Nonvirgins	91	0	9	100
Monogamists	94	0	6	100
Adventurers	91	0	9	100

Table 29

"The idea of two men having sex together is disgusting."

	True	Not Sure	False	TOTAL
All adolescents	75%	2%	23%	100%
Boys	78	2	20	100
Boys 13–15	88	1	11	100
Boys 16–19	70	3	27	100
Girls	72	1	27	100
Girls 13–15	80	2	18	100
Girls 16–19	66	0	34	100
Virgins	82	1	17	100
Inexperienced	80	3	17	100
Beginners	75	0	25	100
Nonvirgins	70	1	29	100
Monogamists	63	0	37	100
Adventurers	66	5	29	100

Table 30

"Smoking marijuana is an important thing in my life."

	True	Not Sure	False	TOTAL
All adolescents	10%	1%	89%	100%
Boys	15	2	83	100
Boys 13–15	8	3	89	100
Boys 16–19	22	0	78	100
Girls	5	1	94	100
Girls 13–15	5	1	94	100
Girls 16–19	6	0	94	100
Virgins	4	1	95	100
Inexperienced	5	0	95	100
Beginners	5	0	95	100
Nonvirgins	16	1	83	100
Monogamists	12	0	88	100
Adventurers	22	2	76	100

Table 31

"When I'm listening to the radio and they start talking about the news, I usually switch to another station."

	True	Not Sure	False	TOTAL
All adolescents	44%	1%	55%	100%
Boys	45	1	54	100
Boys 13–15	52	0	48	100
Boys 16–19	39	3	58	100
Girls	44	0	56	100
Girls 13–15	49	0	51	100
Girls 16–19	40	0	60	100
Virgins	47	0	53	100
Inexperienced	47	0	53	100
Beginners	50	0	50	100
Nonvirgins	42	1	57	100
Monogamists	33	0	67	100
Adventurers	42	5	53	100

Table 32

"A white boy and a black girl having sex together is something that I would consider immoral, even if both of them wanted to do it."

	True	Not Sure	False	TOTAL
All adolescents	33%	1%	66%	100%
Boys	33	1	66	100
Boys 13–15	46	0	54	100
Boys 16–19	23	1	76	100
Girls	33	1	66	100
Girls 13–15	40	2	58	100
Girls 16–19	28	0	72	100
Virgins	40	1	59	100
Inexperienced	50	0	50	100
Beginners	29	0	71	100
Nonvirgins	27	0	73	100
Monogamists	21	0	79	100
Adventurers	27	0	73	100

Table 33

"I have told my parents that I disagree with the way they think about sex."

	True	Not Sure	False	TOTAL
All adolescents	24%	2%	74%	100%
Boys	23	3	74	100
Boys 13–15	20	1	79	100
Boys 16–19	26	5	69	100
Girls	25	0	75	100
Girls 13–15	23	1	76	100
Girls 16–19	26	0	74	100
Virgins	14	1	85	100
Inexperienced	16	1	83	100
Beginners	14	0	86	100
Nonvirgins	33	2	65	100
Monogamists	40	0	60	100
Adventurers	32	4	64	100

Table 34

"Two boys having sex together is something that I would consider abnormal or unnatural."

	True	Not Sure	False	TOTAL
All adolescents	80%	3%	17%	100%
Boys	81	4	15	100
Boys 13–15	83	2	15	100
Boys 16–19	79	5	16	100
Girls	80	2	18	100
Girls 13–15	83	3	14	100
Girls 16–19	77	1	22	100
Virgins	84	2	14	100
Inexperienced	82	0	18	100
Beginners	84	1	15	100
Nonvirgins	76	4	20	100
Monogamists	76	3	21	100
Adventurers	65	7	28	100

Table 35

"I find it hard to accept the idea of conforming to society in matters of clothing and personal grooming."

	True	Not Sure	False	TOTAL
All adolescents	53%	3%	44%	100%
Boys	61	3	36	100
Boys 13–15	52	6	42	100
Boys 16–19	69	1	30	100
Girls	45	3	52	100
Girls 13–15	40	6	54	100
Girls 16–19	49	1	50	100
Virgins	41	5	54	100
Inexperienced	38	3	59	100
Beginners	41	5	54	100
Nonvirgins	64	2	34	100
Monogamists	53	3	44	100
Adventurers	82	0	18	100

Table 36

"All in all, I think my head is pretty well together these days so far as sex is concerned."

	True	Not Sure	False	TOTAL
All adolescents	87%	1%	12%	100%
Boys	86	1	13	100
Boys 13–15	83	1	16	100
Boys 16–19	88	1	11	100
Girls	88	1	11	100
Girls 13–15	84	2	14	100
Girls 16–19	90	1	9	100
Virgins	87	1	12	100
Inexperienced	87	1	12	100
Beginners	94	0	6	100
Nonvirgins	87	0	13	100
Monogamists	93	1	6	100
Adventurers	81	0	19	100

Table 37

"My parents believe that sex is immoral unless it's between two people who are married to each other."

	True	Not Sure	False	TOTAL
All adolescents	72%	3%	25%	100%
Boys	64	5	31	100
Boys 13–15	69	3	28	100
Boys 16–19	61	6	33	100
Girls	79	2	19	100
Girls 13–15	82	4	14	100
Girls 16–19	77	0	23	100
Virgins	72	4	24	100
Inexperienced	77	4	19	100
Beginners	68	1	31	100
Nonvirgins	71	3	26	100
Monogamists	73	1	26	100
Adventurers	64	7	29	100

Table 38

"My parents have told me the facts about birth control."

	True	Not Sure	False	TOTAL
All adolescents	25%	1%	74%	100%
Boys	18	2	80	100
Boys 13–15	16	1	83	100
Boys 16–19	20	3	77	100
Girls	31	1	68	100
Girls 13–15	29	2	69	100
Girls 16–19	32	0	68	100
Virgins	27	1	72	100
Inexperienced	23	1	76	100
Beginners	28	0	72	100
Nonvirgins	23	1	76	100
Monogamists	19	0	81	100
Adventurers	31	4	65	100

Table 39

"My parents believe that anything two people want to do sexually is moral, so long as they both want to do it and it doesn't hurt either one of them."

	True	Not Sure	False	TOTAL
All adolescents	29%	5%	66%	100%
Boys	30	7	63	100
Boys 13–15	35	2	63	100
Boys 16–19	26	11	63	100
Girls	29	3	68	100
Girls 13–15	37	6	57	100
Girls 16–19	22	0	78	100
Virgins	29	5	66	100
Inexperienced	31	6	63	100
Beginners	23	1	76	100
Nonvirgins	29	6	65	100
Monogamists	31	4	65	100
Adventurers	33	13	54	100

Table 40

"I don't talk about sex with my parents because their attitude is that I'm too young to know anything."

	True	Not Sure	False	TOTAL
All adolescents	31%	3%	66%	100%
Boys	30	6	64	100
Boys 13–15	42	2	56	100
Boys 16–19	21	8	71	100
Girls	31	1	68	100
Girls 13–15	42	2	56	100
Girls 16–19	22	0	78	100
Virgins	33	2	65	100
Inexperienced	44	1	55	100
Beginners	19	0	81	100
Nonvirgins	29	4	67	100
Monogamists	31	0	69	100
Adventurers	28	13	59	100

Table 41

"I would consider it abnormal or unnatural for a boy not to have sex until he gets married."

	True	Not Sure	False	TOTAL
All adolescents	55%	2%	43%	100%
Boys	55	2	43	100
Boys 13–15	57	1	42	100
Boys 16–19	54	3	43	100
Girls	54	2	44	100
Girls 13–15	50	4	46	100
Girls 16–19	58	0	42	100
Virgins	47	3	50	100
Inexperienced	43	3	54	100
Beginners	54	3	43	100
Nonvirgins	62	1	37	100
Monogamists	63	0	37	100
Adventurers	59	1	40	100

Table 42

"I think my parents' ideas about most things are wrong, but they have a right to their own opinions."

	True	Not Sure	False	TOTAL
All adolescents	50%	3%	47%	100%
Boys	53	4	43	100
Boys 13–15	61	2	37	100
Boys 16–19	46	7	47	100
Girls	48	0	52	100
Girls 13–15	49	1	50	100
Girls 16–19	47	0	53	100
Virgins	43	1	56	100
Inexperienced	42	1	57	100
Beginners	40	1	59	100
Nonvirgins	57	4	39	100
Monogamists	45	2	53	100
Adventurers	66	8	26	100

Table 43

"So far as sex is concerned, I still haven't really made up my mind what I think is right and wrong for other people."

	True	Not Sure	False	TOTAL
All adolescents	59%	3%	38%	100%
Boys	59	5	36	100
Boys 13–15	53	2	45	100
Boys 16–19	63	8	29	100
Girls	59	1	40	100
Girls 13–15	63	2	35	100
Girls 16–19	56	0	44	100
Virgins	55	2	43	100
Inexperienced	54	2	44	100
Beginners	61	0	39	100
Nonvirgins	62	4	34	100
Monogamists	62	0	38	100
Adventurers	60	8	32	100

Table 44

"When talking with my parents about sex, I try to tell them only what I think they can accept."

	True	Not Sure	False	TOTAL
All adolescents	52%	5%	43%	100%
Boys	55	8	37	100
Boys 13–15	60	4	36	100
Boys 16–19	52	10	38	100
Girls	48	2	50	100
Girls 13–15	47	3	50	100
Girls 16–19	49	2	49	100
Virgins	44	4	52	100
Inexperienced	43	3	54	100
Beginners	54	1	45	100
Nonvirgins	59	6	35	100
Monogamists	58	0	42	100
Adventurers	52	11	37	100

Table 45

"A brother and sister having sex together is something that I would consider abnormal or unnatural, even if both of them wanted to do it."

	True	Not Sure	False	TOTAL
All adolescents	82%	0%	18%	100%
Boys	78	0	22	100
Boys 13–15	69	1	30	100
Boys 16–19	86	0	14	100
Girls	85	1	14	100
Girls 13–15	84	1	15	100
Girls 16–19	85	1	14	100
Virgins	89	1	10	100
Inexperienced	90	1	9	100
Beginners	88	0	12	100
Nonvirgins	74	0	26	100
Monogamists	76	0	24	100
Adventurers	69	0	31	100

Table 46

"I don't feel any strong affection for my parents."

	True	Not Sure	False	TOTAL
All adolescents	21%	1%	78%	100%
Boys	25	1	74	100
Boys 13–15	20	0	80	100
Boys 16–19	30	1	69	100
Girls	17	1	82	100
Girls 13–15	16	1	83	100
Girls 16–19	18	1	81	100
Virgins	14	1	85	100
Inexperienced	12	2	86	100
Beginners	20	0	80	100
Nonvirgins	28	0	72	100
Monogamists	16	0	84	100
Adventurers	45	1	54	100

Table 47

"So far as sex is concerned, what other young people do doesn't have any influence on what I myself do."

	True	Not Sure	False	TOTAL
All adolescents	75%	2%	23%	100%
Boys	72	3	25	100
Boys 13–15	66	0	34	100
Boys 16–19	77	5	18	100
Girls	70	1	20	100
Girls 13–15	78	3	19	100
Girls 16–19	80	0	20	100
Virgins	79	2	19	100
Inexperienced	81	0	19	100
Beginners	75	1	24	100
Nonvirgins	72	2	26	100
Monogamists	76	0	24	100
Adventurers	74	6	20	100

Table 48

"I have never read a serious educational book about sex."

	True	Not Sure	False	TOTAL
All adolescents	44%	1%	55%	100%
Boys	48	1	51	100
Boys 13–15	62	2	36	100
Boys 16–19	36	1	63	100
Girls	40	1	59	100
Girls 13–15	50	2	48	100
Girls 16–19	32	0	68	100
Virgins	52	2	46	100
Inexperienced	65	0	35	100
Beginners	38	0	62	100
Nonvirgins	37	0	63	100
Monogamists	25	0	75	100
Adventurers	48	0	52	100

Table 49

"When I talk with my parents about sex I try to tell them what is going on with young people today, even though they don't approve of it."

	True	Not Sure	False	TOTAL
All adolescents	52%	4%	44%	100%
Boys	49	6	45	100
Boys 13–15	41	4	55	100
Boys 16–19	55	8	37	100
Girls	55	2	43	100
Girls 13–15	58	2	40	100
Girls 16–19	53	1	46	100
Virgins	46	3	51	100
Inexperienced	40	4	56	100
Beginners	55	1	44	100
Nonvirgins	57	4	39	100
Monogamists	57	1	42	100
Adventurers	66	10	24	100

Table 50

"So far as sex is concerned, I wouldn't do anything that society would disapprove of."

	True	Not Sure	False	TOTAL
All adolescents	38%	1%	61%	100%
Boys	36	1	63	100
Boys 13–15	55	1	44	100
Boys 16–19	20	1	79	100
Girls	39	2	59	100
Girls 13–15	52	4	44	100
Girls 16–19	29	1	70	100
Virgins	54	3	43	100
Inexperienced	67	2	31	100
Beginners	31	1	68	100
Nonvirgins	22	0	78	100
Monogamists	17	0	83	100
Adventurers	22	0	78	100

Table 51

"My parents believe that it's immoral for two persons of the same sex to have sexual relations with each other."

	True	Not Sure	False	TOTAL
All adolescents	81%	6%	13%	100%
Boys	80	9	11	100
Boys 13–15	78	5	17	100
Boys 16–19	81	12	7	100
Girls	83	3	14	100
Girls 13–15	78	5	17	100
Girls 16–19	86	2	12	100
Virgins	83	5	12	100
Inexperienced	82	4	14	100
Beginners	88	4	8	100
Nonvirgins	80	7	13	100
Monogamists	81	5	14	100
Adventurers	71	14	15	100

Table 52

"If I had to go out into the world on my own right now, I think I'd have a pretty hard time of it."

	True	Not Sure	False	TOTAL
All adolescents	47%	1%	52%	100%
Boys	45	1	54	100
Boys 13–15	63	0	37	100
Boys 16–19	31	0	69	100
Girls	48	1	51	100
Girls 13–15	64	1	35	100
Girls 16–19	36	1	63	100
Virgins	58	1	41	100
Inexperienced	64	1	35	100
Beginners	51	1	48	100
Nonvirgins	37	0	63	100
Monogamists	35	0	65	100
Adventurers	35	0	65	100

Table 53

"I don't talk with my parents about my sex life because I consider it a personal subject and nobody's business but my own."

	True	Not Sure	False	TOTAL
All adolescents	60%	3%	37%	100%
Boys	65	3	32	100
Boys 13–15	66	0	34	100
Boys 16–19	64	5	31	100
Girls	56	2	42	100
Girls 13–15	57	4	39	100
Girls 16–19	56	0	44	100
Virgins	50	4	46	100
Inexperienced	49	1	50	100
Beginners	56	4	40	100
Nonvirgins	70	1	29	100
Monogamists	68	0	32	100
Adventurers	63	4	33	100

Table 54

"I believe that this society is hell-bent on destroying the planet."

	True	Not Sure	False	TOTAL
All adolescents	53%	2%	45%	100%
Boys	52	1	47	100
Boys 13–15	50	0	50	100
Boys 16–19	53	2	45	100
Girls	54	2	44	100
Girls 13–15	55	3	42	100
Girls 16–19	53	2	45	100
Virgins	50	3	47	100
Inexperienced	54	1	45	100
Beginners	50	1	49	100
Nonvirgins	56	1	43	100
Monogamists	47	0	53	100
Adventurers	67	0	33	100

Table 55

"My parents practice what they preach about love and sex."

	True	Not Sure	False	TOTAL
All adolescents	56%	5%	39%	100%
Boys	56	8	36	100
Boys 13–15	54	4	42	100
Boys 16–19	58	10	32	100
Girls	55	3	42	100
Girls 13–15	47	4	49	100
Girls 16–19	62	1	37	100
Virgins	56	6	38	100
Inexperienced	47	5	48	100
Beginners	75	3	22	100
Nonvirgins	55	4	41	100
Monogamists	56	0	44	100
Adventurers	43	14	43	100

Table 56

"So far as sex is concerned, I have pretty much come to definite conclusions about what I think is right or wrong for myself."

	True	Not Sure	False	TOTAL
All adolescents	84%	2%	14%	100%
Boys	82	2	16	100
Boys 13–15	86	1	13	100
Boys 16–19	78	0	10	100
Girls	87	1	12	100
Girls 13–15	86	2	12	100
Girls 16–19	88	0	12	100
Virgins	83	2	15	100
Inexperienced	87	2	11	100
Beginners	82	1	17	100
Nonvirgins	86	1	13	100
Monogamists	85	2	13	100
Adventurers	91	0	9	100

Table 57

"My parents have talked to me about masturbation."

	True	Not Sure	False	TOTAL
All adolescents	17%	4%	79%	100%
Boys	18	3	79	100
Boys 13–15	16	2	82	100
Boys 16–19	20	3	77	100
Girls	16	5	79	100
Girls 13–15	19	5	76	100
Girls 16–19	14	5	81	100
Virgins	18	6	76	100
Inexperienced	13	4	83	100
Beginners	24	6	70	100
Nonvirgins	17	3	80	100
Monogamists	12	0	88	100
Adventurers	20	4	76	100

Table 58

"I don't think that God has any interest in my sex life."

	True	Not Sure	False	TOTAL
All adolescents	34%	3%	63%	100%
Boys	41	2	57	100
Boys 13–15	46	1	53	100
Boys 16–19	36	2	62	100
Girls	28	3	69	100
Girls 13–15	26	2	72	100
Girls 16–19	29	4	67	100
Virgins	27	3	70	100
Inexperienced	30	0	70	100
Beginners	25	1	74	100
Nonvirgins	41	2	57	100
Monogamists	34	1	65	100
Adventurers	41	6	53	100

Table 59

"I don't believe that there should be any laws against having sex with a girl under the age of 16."

	True	Not Sure	False	TOTAL
All adolescents	49%	2%	49%	100%
Boys	57	3	40	100
Boys 13–15	59	2	39	100
Boys 16–19	56	4	40	100
Girls	39	2	59	100
Girls 13–15	44	4	52	100
Girls 16–19	35	1	64	100
Virgins	36	3	61	100
Inexperienced	30	2	68	100
Beginners	46	1	53	100
Nonvirgins	60	2	38	100
Monogamists	49	0	51	100
Adventurers	60	6	34	100

Table 60

"My parents get along with each other very well."

	True	Not Sure	False	TOTAL
All adolescents	62%	6%	32%	100%
Boys	63	5	32	100
Boys 13–15	73	1	26	100
Boys 16–19	54	9	37	100
Girls	61	7	32	100
Girls 13–15	60	10	30	100
Girls 16–19	62	5	33	100
Virgins	62	6	32	100
Inexperienced	65	7	28	100
Beginners	64	6	30	100
Nonvirgins	62	6	32	100
Monogamists	66	9	25	100
Adventurers	45	9	46	100

Table 61

"So far as sex is concerned, I think that what is morally right for boys is morally right for girls too."

	True	Not Sure	False	TOTAL
All adolescents	62%	3%	35%	100%
Boys	67	3	30	100
Boys 13–15	65	3	32	100
Boys 16–19	69	3	28	100
Girls	57	3	40	100
Girls 13–15	41	4	55	100
Girls 16–19	71	1	28	100
Virgins	51	4	45	100
Inexperienced	48	2	50	100
Beginners	70	0	30	100
Nonvirgins	73	1	26	100
Monogamists	83	1	16	100
Adventurers	64	1	35	100

Table 62

"When it comes to sex, my attitudes and my parents' attitudes are pretty much the same."

	True	Not Sure	False	TOTAL
All adolescents	36%	4%	60%	100%
Boys	28	6	66	100
Boys 13–15	38	3	59	100
Boys 16–19	20	7	73	100
Girls	44	2	54	100
Girls 13–15	38	4	58	100
Girls 16–19	50	0	50	100
Virgins	46	3	51	100
Inexperienced	49	3	48	100
Beginners	44	2	54	100
Nonvirgins	27	5	68	100
Monogamists	39	1	60	100
Adventurers	15	13	72	100

Table 63

"I still tend to think of myself as a child because there are a lot of things I can't do on my own."

	True	Not Sure	False	TOTAL
All adolescents	37%	1%	62%	100%
Boys	35	1	64	100
Boys 13–15	51	1	48	100
Boys 16–19	22	0	78	100
Girls	39	2	59	100
Girls 13–15	45	3	52	100
Girls 16–19	34	1	65	100
Virgins	44	1	55	100
Inexperienced	60	0	40	100
Beginners	26	1	73	100
Nonvirgins	31	1	68	100
Monogamists	30	2	68	100
Adventurers	25	2	73	100

Table 64

"I've never really gotten to know my father."

	True	Not Sure	False	TOTAL
All adolescents	39%	1%	60%	100%
Boys	35	1	64	100
Boys 13–15	23	1	76	100
Boys 16–19	44	1	55	100
Girls	44	2	54	100
Girls 13–15	49	2	49	100
Girls 16–19	40	1	59	100
Virgins	34	2	64	100
Inexperienced	35	0	65	100
Beginners	31	2	67	100
Nonvirgins	44	1	55	100
Monogamists	48	0	52	100
Adventurers	58	3	39	100

Table 65

"Sometimes when I go to church I get to feeling guilty about my sexual behavior."

	True	Not Sure	False	TOTAL
All adolescents	20%	5%	75%	100%
Boys	20	7	73	100
Boys 13–15	29	4	67	100
Boys 16–19	13	9	78	100
Girls	20	3	77	100
Girls 13–15	18	2	80	100
Girls 16–19	22	3	75	100
Virgins	19	4	77	100
Inexperienced	17	4	79	100
Beginners	25	2	73	100
Nonvirgins	22	5	73	100
Monogamists	24	1	75	100
Adventurers	16	16	68	100

Table 66

"On one or more occasions, I've done sexual things mostly to spite my parents."

	True	Not Sure	False	TOTAL
All adolescents	6%	2%	92%	100%
Boys	6	2	92	100
Boys 13–15	11	3	86	100
Boys 16–19	1	1	98	100
Girls	6	3	91	100
Girls 13–15	10	3	87	100
Girls 16–19	4	2	94	100
Virgins	4	3	93	100
Inexperienced	4	1	95	100
Beginners	3	2	95	100
Nonvirgins	9	1	90	100
Monogamists	5	1	94	100
Adventurers	9	2	89	100

Table 67

"I think there are some kinds of sex acts that should be against the law."

	True	Not Sure	False	TOTAL
All adolescents	57%	2%	41%	100%
Boys	55	1	44	100
Boys 13–15	69	2	29	100
Boys 16–19	44	0	56	100
Girls	59	4	37	100
Girls 13–15	67	6	27	100
Girls 16–19	52	3	45	100
Virgins	70	3	27	100
Inexperienced	75	2	23	100
Beginners	64	1	35	100
Nonvirgins	45	2	53	100
Monogamists	40	3	57	100
Adventurers	39	2	59	100

Table 68

"I don't much believe in planning for the future; life right now is the most important thing."

	True	Not Sure	False	TOTAL
All adolescents	33%	2%	65%	100%
Boys	35	2	63	100
Boys 13–15	37	3	60	100
Boys 16–19	34	0	66	100
Girls	30	3	67	100
Girls 13–15	32	5	63	100
Girls 16–19	28	1	71	100
Virgins	27	3	70	100
Inexperienced	38	3	59	100
Beginners	19	1	80	100
Nonvirgins	38	2	60	100
Monogamists	34	1	65	100
Adventurers	44	3	53	100

Table 69

"My parents and I talk pretty freely about sex."

	True	Not Sure	False	TOTAL
All adolescents	26%	3%	71%	100%
Boys	24	4	72	100
Boys 13–15	23	5	72	100
Boys 16–19	25	3	72	100
Girls	28	2	70	100
Girls 13–15	31	2	67	100
Girls 16–19	27	2	71	100
Virgins	26	3	71	100
Inexperienced	25	0	75	100
Beginners	25	1	74	100
Nonvirgins	26	4	70	100
Monogamists	29	1	70	100
Adventurers	24	5	71	100

Table 70

"On one or more occasions, I've done sexual things mostly because the people I was hanging out with at the time expected me to."

	True	Not Sure	False	TOTAL
All adolescents	20%	2%	78%	100%
Boys	26	3	71	100
Boys 13–15	39	3	58	100
Boys 16–19	16	3	81	100
Girls	14	2	84	100
Girls 13–15	14	2	84	100
Girls 16–19	14	1	85	100
Virgins	12	3	85	100
Inexperienced	14	1	85	100
Beginners	10	2	88	100
Nonvirgins	28	2	70	100
Monogamists	22	1	77	100
Adventurers	34	6	60	100

Table 71

"I believe that modern technology is a constructive force."

	True	Not Sure	False	TOTAL
All adolescents	63%	7%	30%	100%
Boys	61	3	36	100
Boys 13–15	56	6	38	100
Boys 16–19	65	1	34	100
Girls	65	12	23	100
Girls 13–15	55	16	29	100
Girls 16–19	72	9	19	100
Virgins	61	11	28	100
Inexperienced	53	12	35	100
Beginners	69	9	22	100
Nonvirgins	64	5	31	100
Monogamists	71	5	24	100
Adventurers	60	4	36	100

Table 72

"I agree that there should be laws against rape."

	True	Not Sure	False	TOTAL
All adolescents	95%	1%	4%	100%
Boys	92	1	7	100
Boys 13–15	88	2	10	100
Boys 16–19	96	0	4	100
Girls	98	1	1	100
Girls 13–15	98	1	1	100
Girls 16–19	99	1	0	100
Virgins	95	1	4	100
Inexperienced	94	1	5	100
Beginners	93	1	6	100
Nonvirgins	96	1	3	100
Monogamists	98	2	0	100
Adventurers	96	2	2	100

Table 73

"Young people these days sometimes have sex mostly to take their minds off other things that are going down."

	True	Not Sure	False	TOTAL
All adolescents	51%	2%	47%	100%
Boys	45	2	53	100
Boys 13–15	54	2	44	100
Boys 16–19	38	3	59	100
Girls	56	2	42	100
Girls 13–15	61	2	37	100
Girls 16–19	52	3	45	100
Virgins	56	3	41	100
Inexperienced	57	3	40	100
Beginners	57	1	42	100
Nonvirgins	46	2	52	100
Monogamists	52	1	47	100
Adventurers	36	2	62	100

Table 74

"I started experimenting with sex partly because it was such a forbidden topic around my house."

	True	Not Sure	False	TOTAL
All adolescents	13%	2%	85%	100%
Boys	18	2	80	100
Boys 13–15	22	3	75	100
Boys 16–19	15	1	84	100
Girls	7	3	90	100
Girls 13–15	9	3	88	100
Girls 16–19	6	3	91	100
Virgins	7	4	89	100
Inexperienced	10	3	87	100
Beginners	4	2	94	100
Nonvirgins	19	1	80	100
Monogamists	14	1	85	100
Adventurers	13	2	85	100

Table 75

"Hassles about my sexual behavior cause a lot of bad vibes between myself and my parents."

	True	Not Sure	False	TOTAL
All adolescents	19%	5%	76%	100%
Boys	18	6	76	100
Boys 13–15	15	8	77	100
Boys 16–19	20	4	76	100
Girls	21	5	74	100
Girls 13–15	19	7	74	100
Girls 16–19	22	4	74	100
Virgins	8	8	84	100
Inexperienced	5	11	84	100
Beginners	13	2	85	100
Nonvirgins	30	3	67	100
Monogamists	27	2	71	100
Adventurers	38	2	60	100

Table 76

"My parents and I sometimes talk about sex, but it makes me very uncomfortable."

	True	Not Sure	False	TOTAL
All adolescents	30%	4%	66%	100%
Boys	34	3	63	100
Boys 13–15	38	3	59	100
Boys 16–19	30	5	65	100
Girls	27	4	69	100
Girls 13–15	29	7	64	100
Girls 16–19	24	2	74	100
Virgins	31	6	63	100
Inexperienced	29	5	66	100
Beginners	40	5	55	100
Nonvirgins	29	2	69	100
Monogamists	28	3	69	100
Adventurers	28	3	69	100

Table 77

"There are some things that I wouldn't do because my conscience would bother me."

	True	Not Sure	False	TOTAL
All adolescents	75%	3%	22%	100%
Boys	70	2	28	100
Boys 13–15	69	2	29	100
Boys 16–19	71	2	27	100
Girls	82	3	15	100
Girls 13–15	79	4	17	100
Girls 16–19	83	2	15	100
Virgins	80	4	16	100
Inexperienced	83	2	15	100
Beginners	85	2	13	100
Nonvirgins	71	2	27	100
Monogamists	82	2	16	100
Adventurers	51	5	44	100

Table 78

"My parents don't understand what I want out of life."

	True	Not Sure	False	TOTAL
All adolescents	60%	2%	38%	100%
Boys	62	2	36	100
Boys 13–15	50	1	49	100
Boys 16–19	71	4	25	100
Girls	58	2	40	100
Girls 13–15	58	2	40	100
Girls 16–19	57	3	40	100
Virgins	50	2	48	100
Inexperienced	43	2	55	100
Beginners	61	0	39	100
Nonvirgins	69	3	28	100
Monogamists	64	1	35	100
Adventurers	77	6	17	100

Table 79

"I don't like it when older people think of me as an adolescent."

	True	Not Sure	False	TOTAL
All adolescents	76%	5%	19%	100%
Boys	77	5	18	100
Boys 13–15	81	3	16	100
Boys 16–19	74	7	19	100
Girls	75	4	21	100
Girls 13–15	70	6	24	100
Girls 16–19	79	3	18	100
Virgins	76	4	20	100
Inexperienced	73	3	24	100
Beginners	80	3	17	100
Nonvirgins	76	6	18	100
Monogamists	79	2	19	100
Adventurers	68	14	18	100

Table 80

"In my family we're all very open with each other, so it's difficult or impossible to have any secrets about sex."

	True	Not Sure	False	TOTAL
All adolescents	18%	2%	80%	100%
Boys	17	2	81	100
Boys 13–15	14	3	83	100
Boys 16–19	19	1	80	100
Girls	19	2	79	100
Girls 13–15	22	2	76	100
Girls 16–19	16	2	82	100
Virgins	17	3	80	100
Inexperienced	20	1	79	100
Beginners	13	0	87	100
Nonvirgins	18	2	80	100
Monogamists	20	1	79	100
Adventurers	25	3	72	100

Table 81

"Sometimes I take part in sexual activities that are not consistent with my religious beliefs."

	True	Not Sure	False	TOTAL
All adolescents	27%	4%	69%	100%
Boys	33	6	61	100
Boys 13–15	36	4	60	100
Boys 16–19	30	7	63	100
Girls	21	3	76	100
Girls 13–15	18	3	79	100
Girls 16–19	23	3	74	100
Virgins	16	4	80	100
Inexperienced	13	3	84	100
Beginners	23	1	76	100
Nonvirgins	37	4	59	100
Monogamists	33	1	66	100
Adventurers	40	8	52	100

Table 82

"I believe that LSD and other psychedelic drugs have had a beneficial effect on the spiritual development of many persons."

	True	Not Sure	False	TOTAL
All adolescents	35%	3%	62%	100%
Boys	37	2	61	100
Boys 13–15	32	4	64	100
Boys 16–19	41	1	58	100
Girls	33	3	64	100
Girls 13–15	42	4	54	100
Girls 16–19	26	3	71	100
Virgins	30	3	67	100
Inexperienced	37	2	61	100
Beginners	16	1	83	100
Nonvirgins	40	2	58	100
Monogamists	41	2	57	100
Adventurers	45	2	53	100

Table 83

"I've pretty much given up on ever being able to get along with my parents."

	True	Not Sure	False	TOTAL
All adolescents	19%	3%	78%	100%
Boys	25	3	72	100
Boys 13–15	19	4	77	100
Boys 16–19	[illegible]	2	68	100
Girls	13	2	85	100
Girls 13–15	14	2	84	100
Girls 16–19	12	3	85	100
Virgins	9	3	88	100
Inexperienced	11	3	86	100
Beginners	9	1	90	100
Nonvirgins	28	3	69	100
Monogamists	21	1	78	100
Adventurers	35	6	59	100

Table 84

"The American Indians had a life-style that I deeply admire."

	True	Not Sure	False	TOTAL
All adolescents	61%	5%	34%	100%
Boys	67	4	29	100
Boys 13–15	56	5	39	100
Boys 16–19	76	3	21	100
Girls	55	7	38	100
Girls 13–15	45	11	44	100
Girls 16–19	63	3	34	100
Virgins	51	7	42	100
Inexperienced	42	8	50	100
Beginners	57	3	40	100
Nonvirgins	70	4	26	100
Monogamists	64	3	33	100
Adventurers	72	4	24	100

Table 85

"I've never taken part in any sex act, or been involved in any kind of sexual situation, that I myself would think of as being abnormal."

	True	Not Sure	False	TOTAL
All adolescents	74%	2%	24%	100%
Boys	70	2	28	100
Boys 13–15	72	3	25	100
Boys 16–19	69	1	30	100
Girls	78	2	20	100
Girls 13–15	72	2	26	100
Girls 16–19	84	2	14	100
Virgins	82	3	15	100
Inexperienced	88	2	10	100
Beginners	87	1	12	100
Nonvirgins	67	1	32	100
Monogamists	72	1	27	100
Adventurers	55	2	43	100

Table 86

"There are serious flaws in our society, but the system is flexible enough to solve them."

	True	Not Sure	False	TOTAL
All adolescents	59%	5%	36%	100%
Boys	58	5	37	100
Boys 13–15	53	7	40	100
Boys 16–19	62	4	34	100
Girls	59	6	35	100
Girls 13–15	56	6	38	100
Girls 16–19	62	5	33	100
Virgins	53	5	42	100
Inexperienced	46	4	50	100
Beginners	66	3	31	100
Nonvirgins	64	6	30	100
Monogamists	67	4	29	100
Adventurers	56	9	35	100

Table 87

"Two girls having sex together is something that I would consider abnormal or unnatural."

	True	Not Sure	False	TOTAL
All adolescents	76%	2%	22%	100%
Boys	74	2	24	100
Boys 13–15	75	1	24	100
Boys 16–19	73	3	24	100
Girls	77	3	20	100
Girls 13–15	81	2	17	100
Girls 16–19	74	3	23	100
Virgins	84	2	14	100
Inexperienced	88	1	11	100
Beginners	78	2	20	100
Nonvirgins	67	3	30	100
Monogamists	70	2	28	100
Adventurers	57	8	35	100

Table 88

"Violence is the only way to get the kind of changes that I would like to see in our society."

	True	Not Sure	False	TOTAL
All adolescents	15%	4%	81%	100%
Boys	19	4	77	100
Boys 13–15	25	6	69	100
Boys 16–19	14	3	83	100
Girls	11	3	86	100
Girls 13–15	15	2	83	100
Girls 16–19	9	3	88	100
Virgins	12	3	85	100
Inexperienced	16	1	83	100
Beginners	8	1	91	100
Nonvirgins	18	4	78	100
Monogamists	8	5	87	100
Adventurers	24	4	72	100

Table 89

"I wish my parents and I could agree more about things in general."

	True	Not Sure	False	TOTAL
All adolescents	68%	4%	28%	100%
Boys	70	5	25	100
Boys 13–15	65	3	32	100
Boys 16–19	73	7	20	100
Girls	67	2	31	100
Girls 13–15	70	1	29	100
Girls 16–19	64	3	33	100
Virgins	62	3	35	100
Inexperienced	59	2	39	100
Beginners	69	1	30	100
Nonvirgins	74	4	22	100
Monogamists	74	2	24	100
Adventurers	72	11	17	100

Table 90

"In general, I think that my basic personal values are shared by most of the older people in this country."

	True	Not Sure	False	TOTAL
All adolescents	44%	4%	52%	100%
Boys	41	4	55	100
Boys 13–15	53	3	44	100
Boys 16–19	32	5	63	100
Girls	47	4	49	100
Girls 13–15	48	5	47	100
Girls 16–19	46	3	51	100
Virgins	48	4	48	100
Inexperienced	57	1	42	100
Beginners	36	4	60	100
Nonvirgins	40	5	55	100
Monogamists	41	1	58	100
Adventurers	40	10	50	100

Table 91

"My parents are anxious about whether or not I'm going to get married."

	True	Not Sure	False	TOTAL
All adolescents	28%	3%	69%	100%
Boys	28	4	68	100
Boys 13–15	23	2	75	100
Boys 16–19	32	5	63	100
Girls	27	3	70	100
Girls 13–15	27	3	70	100
Girls 16–19	28	2	70	100
Virgins	20	3	77	100
Inexperienced	22	2	76	100
Beginners	15	3	82	100
Nonvirgins	34	4	62	100
Monogamists	33	5	62	100
Adventurers	42	6	52	100

Table 92

"When deciding for myself what to do or not to do so far as sex is concerned, I don't pay any attention to what the laws say."

	True	Not Sure	False	TOTAL
All adolescents	54%	4%	42%	100%
Boys	58	4	38	100
Boys 13–15	45	4	51	100
Boys 16–19	68	4	28	100
Girls	49	5	46	100
Girls 13–15	39	5	56	100
Girls 16–19	57	5	38	100
Virgins	36	5	59	100
Inexperienced	32	3	65	100
Beginners	50	3	47	100
Nonvirgins	69	4	27	100
Monogamists	70	1	29	100
Adventurers	69	7	24	100

Table 93

"My parents are always bugging me with questions about my sexual behavior."

	True	Not Sure	False	TOTAL
All adolescents	12%	2%	86%	100%
Boys	13	3	84	100
Boys 13–15	16	2	82	100
Boys 16–19	10	4	86	100
Girls	12	2	86	100
Girls 13–15	16	1	83	100
Girls 16–19	8	3	89	100
Virgins	9	2	89	100
Inexperienced	11	1	88	100
Beginners	9	1	90	100
Nonvirgins	15	3	82	100
Monogamists	11	1	88	100
Adventurers	17	7	76	100

Table 94

"In general, I think that my basic personal values are shared by most of the younger people in this country."

	True	Not Sure	False	TOTAL
All adolescents	68%	2%	30%	100%
Boys	70	2	28	100
Boys 13–15	75	4	21	100
Boys 16–19	66	1	33	100
Girls	67	2	31	100
Girls 13–15	68	2	30	100
Girls 16–19	65	3	32	100
Virgins	65	2	33	100
Inexperienced	65	1	34	100
Beginners	69	2	29	100
Nonvirgins	71	3	26	100
Monogamists	68	1	31	100
Adventurers	73	2	25	100

Table 95

"My parents think that I pretty much agree with their ideas about sex, and I don't say anything that would make them think different."

	True	Not Sure	False	TOTAL
All adolescents	57%	5%	38%	100%
Boys	57	6	37	100
Boys 13–15	61	3	36	100
Boys 16–19	53	8	39	100
Girls	58	4	38	100
Girls 13–15	58	6	36	100
Girls 16–19	57	3	40	100
Virgins	59	5	36	100
Inexperienced	61	2	37	100
Beginners	58	2	40	100
Nonvirgins	55	6	39	100
Monogamists	59	1	40	100
Adventurers	42	16	42	100

Table 96

"My sexual behavior is pretty much the way my parents would want it to be."

	True	Not Sure	False	TOTAL
All adolescents	47%	5%	48%	100%
Boys	40	7	53	100
Boys 13–15	53	3	44	100
Boys 16–19	30	10	60	100
Girls	54	3	43	100
Girls 13–15	62	1	37	100
Girls 16–19	48	5	47	100
Virgins	67	5	28	100
Inexperienced	77	2	21	100
Beginners	62	4	34	100
Nonvirgins	28	6	66	100
Monogamists	25	3	72	100
Adventurers	26	13	61	100

Table 97

Male: "If I were to make a girl pregnant and she had an abortion, I wouldn't feel guilty about it."

Female: "If I had an abortion, I wouldn't feel guilty about it."

	True	Not Sure	False	TOTAL
All adolescents	37%	3%	60%	100%
Boys	37	3	60	100
Boys 13–15	31	5	64	100
Boys 16–19	42	1	57	100
Girls	37	4	59	100
Girls 13–15	33	7	60	100
Girls 16–19	40	2	58	100
Virgins	31	6	63	100
Inexperienced	35	5	60	100
Beginners	28	5	67	100
Nonvirgins	42	2	56	100
Monogamists	47	1	52	100
Adventurers	38	0	62	100

Table 98

"It isn't healthy for someone my age to go for a long time without having sex."

	True	Not Sure	False	TOTAL
All adolescents	30%	4%	66%	100%
Boys	39	3	58	100
Boys 13–15	35	4	61	100
Boys 16–19	44	2	54	100
Girls	20	5	75	100
Girls 13–15	16	8	76	100
Girls 16–19	23	4	73	100
Virgins	16	8	76	100
Inexperienced	14	5	81	100
Beginners	22	4	74	100
Nonvirgins	42	1	57	100
Monogamists	37	2	61	100
Adventurers	56	0	44	100

Table 99

"Sometimes I feel guilty about my sexual behavior."

	True	Not Sure	False	TOTAL
All adolescents	33%	5%	62%	100%
Boys	37	5	58	100
Boys 13–15	47	5	48	100
Boys 16–19	29	4	67	100
Girls	28	6	66	100
Girls 13–15	26	7	67	100
Girls 16–19	29	5	66	100
Virgins	28	9	63	100
Inexperienced	32	6	62	100
Beginners	27	5	68	100
Nonvirgins	37	2	61	100
Monogamists	32	1	67	100
Adventurers	37	3	60	100

Table 100

Male: "If I heard that a girl had had VD, I would avoid having sex with her even after she was completely cured."

Female: "If I heard that a boy had had VD, I would avoid having sex with him even after he was completely cured."

	True	Not Sure	False	TOTAL
All adolescents	49%	4%	47%	100%
Boys	46	3	51	100
Boys 13–15	59	4	37	100
Boys 16–19	36	2	62	100
Girls	52	5	43	100
Girls 13–15	58	8	34	100
Girls 16–19	47	3	50	100
Virgins	58	8	34	100
Inexperienced	64	4	32	100
Beginners	54	6	40	100
Nonvirgins	41	0	59	100
Monogamists	43	1	56	100
Adventurers	42	0	58	100

Table 101

Male: "If I were married and my wife had sexual relations with someone else, I would be angry about it but it would not in itself be enough reason to get divorced."

Female: "If I were married and my husband had sexual relations with someone else, I would be angry about it but it would not in itself be enough reason to get divorced."

	True	Not Sure	False	TOTAL
All adolescents	54%	5%	41%	100%
Boys	54	5	41	100
Boys 13–15	51	10	39	100
Boys 16–19	56	2	42	100
Girls	53	5	42	100
Girls 13–15	53	9	38	100
Girls 16–19	53	2	45	100
Virgins	47	8	45	100
Inexperienced	51	8	41	100
Beginners	44	5	51	100
Nonvirgins	60	2	38	100
Monogamists	57	3	40	100
Adventurers	62	3	35	100

Table 102

Male: "On one or more occasions, another boy or a grown man has tried to get me to have sex with him."

Female: "On one or more occasions, another girl or a grown woman has tried to get me to have sex with her."

	True	Not Sure	False	TOTAL
All adolescents	25%	4%	71%	100%
Boys	37	4	59	100
Boys 13–15	27	6	67	100
Boys 16–19	45	2	53	100
Girls	14	4	82	100
Girls 13–15	17	6	77	100
Girls 16–19	11	2	87	100
Virgins	12	6	82	100
Inexperienced	18	2	80	100
Beginners	6	5	89	100
Nonvirgins	38	1	61	100
Monogamists	41	1	58	100
Adventurers	45	0	55	100

Table 103

Male: "I wouldn't want to marry a girl who isn't a virgin at marriage."

	True	Not Sure	False	TOTAL
All adolescents	30%	5%	65%	100%
Boys	30	5	65	100
Boys 13–15	38	9	53	100
Boys 16–19	23	2	75	100
Girls	NA	NA	NA	NA
Girls 13–15	NA	NA	NA	NA
Girls 16–19	NA	NA	NA	NA
Virgins	42	7	51	100
Inexperienced	54	6	40	100
Beginners	22	9	69	100
Nonvirgins	21	3	76	100
Monogamists	19	0	81	100
Adventurers	27	1	72	100

Table 104

Male: "I would be embarrassed about having sex with a girl if there were anyone else in the same room."

Female: "I would be embarrassed about having sex with a boy if there were anyone else in the same room."

	True	Not Sure	False	TOTAL
All adolescents	65%	5%	30%	100%
Boys	55	5	40	100
Boys 13–15	65	5	30	100
Boys 16–19	46	4	50	100
Girls	76	5	19	100
Girls 13–15	70	8	22	100
Girls 16–19	81	3	16	100
Virgins	76	9	15	100
Inexperienced	76	5	19	100
Beginners	82	5	13	100
Nonvirgins	55	2	43	100
Monogamists	67	3	30	100
Adventurers	39	0	61	100

Table 105

Female: "There isn't any place where I could go to get birth control pills or contraceptives."

	True	Not Sure	False	TOTAL
All adolescents	30%	6%	64%	100%
Boys	NA	NA	NA	NA
Boys 13–15	NA	NA	NA	NA
Boys 16–19	NA	NA	NA	NA
Girls	30	6	64	100
Girls 13–15	46	7	47	100
Girls 16–19	18	5	77	100
Virgins	42	9	49	100
Inexperienced	57	3	40	100
Beginners	27	5	68	100
Nonvirgins	16	2	82	100
Monogamists	15	3	82	100
Adventurers	7	0	93	100

Table 106

Male: "It's just possible that sometime, if I really needed the money very badly, that I might have sex with a man who would pay me to do it."

	True	Not Sure	False	TOTAL
All adolescents	12%	5%	83%	100%
Boys	12	5	83	100
Boys 13–15	13	6	81	100
Boys 16–19	11	4	85	100
Girls	NA	NA	NA	NA
Girls 13–15	NA	NA	NA	NA
Girls 16–19	NA	NA	NA	NA
Virgins	9	8	83	100
Inexperienced	12	3	85	100
Beginners	8	9	83	100
Nonvirgins	14	3	83	100
Monogamists	13	6	81	100
Adventurers	12	3	85	100

Table 107

Female: "If I have sex with a boy, making sure that I don't get pregnant is *his* responsibility."

	True	Not Sure	False	TOTAL
All adolescents	14%	5%	81%	100%
Boys	NA	NA	NA	NA
Boys 13–15	NA	NA	NA	NA
Boys 16–19	NA	NA	NA	NA
Girls	14	5	81	100
Girls 13–15	20	9	71	100
Girls 16–19	9	2	89	100
Virgins	11	9	80	100
Inexperienced	15	5	80	100
Beginners	9	4	87	100
Nonvirgins	17	1	82	100
Monogamists	11	1	88	100
Adventurers	10	0	90	100

Table 108

Male: "There's nothing wrong with telling a girl that you love her—even if you don't—if that's what it takes so she will have sex with you."

	True	Not Sure	False	TOTAL
All adolescents	24%	3%	73%	100%
Boys	24	3	73	100
Boys 13–15	29	4	67	100
Boys 16–19	20	2	78	100
Girls	NA	NA	NA	NA
Girls 13–15	NA	NA	NA	NA
Girls 16–19	NA	NA	NA	NA
Virgins	16	8	76	100
Inexperienced	19	6	75	100
Beginners	12	9	79	100
Nonvirgins	30	0	70	100
Monogamists	7	0	93	100
Adventurers	40	0	60	100

Table 109

Male: "I would never pay a girl money to have sex with me."

Female: "I would never have sex with a boy for money."

	True	Not Sure	False	TOTAL
All adolescents	81%	3%	16%	100%
Boys	72	4	24	100
Boys 13–15	71	7	22	100
Boys 16–19	73	2	25	100
Girls	89	3	8	100
Girls 13–15	89	6	5	100
Girls 16–19	89	1	10	100
Virgins	85	5	10	100
Inexperienced	86	3	11	100
Beginners	84	4	12	100
Nonvirgins	77	2	21	100
Monogamists	84	1	15	100
Adventurers	63	4	33	100

Table 110

Male: "I've never had sex with another boy, but it's possible that sometime in the future I might want to."

Female: "I've never had sex with another girl, but it's possible that sometime in the future I might want to."

	True	Not Sure	False	TOTAL
All adolescents	17%	7%	76%	100%
Boys	18	7	75	100
Boys 13–15	15	10	75	100
Boys 16–19	21	5	74	100
Girls	16	6	78	100
Girls 13–15	15	10	75	100
Girls 16–19	17	3	80	100
Virgins	9	11	80	100
Inexperienced	10	4	86	100
Beginners	8	12	80	100
Nonvirgins	24	3	73	100
Monogamists	27	1	72	100
Adventurers	24	2	74	100

Table 111

Male: "If you really dig a girl, it's all right to have sex with her even if you've only known her for a few hours."

Female: "If you really dig a boy, it's all right to have sex with him even if you've only known him for a few hours."

	True	Not Sure	False	TOTAL
All adolescents	39%	4%	57%	100%
Boys	58	3	39	100
Boys 13–15	44	4	52	100
Boys 16–19	70	2	28	100
Girls	19	5	76	100
Girls 13–15	19	7	74	100
Girls 16–19	20	2	78	100
Virgins	17	7	76	100
Inexperienced	18	2	80	100
Beginners	19	6	75	100
Nonvirgins	59	1	40	100
Monogamists	41	1	58	100
Adventurers	82	0	18	100

Table 112

"I rarely, if ever, go to religious services, but I still think of myself as being a fairly religious person."

	True	Not Sure	False	TOTAL
All adolescents	50%	4%	46%	100%
Boys	54	5	41	100
Boys 13–15	55	8	37	100
Boys 16–19	54	2	44	100
Girls	45	3	52	100
Girls 13–15	52	4	44	100
Girls 16–19	39	3	58	100
Virgins	46	5	49	100
Inexperienced	48	3	49	100
Beginners	47	3	50	100
Nonvirgins	53	3	44	100
Monogamists	43	1	56	100
Adventurers	66	1	33	100

Table 113

"Politically, I tend to think of myself as being a Republican."

	True	Not Sure	False	TOTAL
All adolescents	30%	8%	62%	100%
Boys	32	10	58	100
Boys 13–15	44	11	45	100
Boys 16–19	23	9	68	100
Girls	27	7	66	100
Girls 13–15	33	11	56	100
Girls 16–19	22	3	75	100
Virgins	31	10	59	100
Inexperienced	31	12	57	100
Beginners	29	5	66	100
Nonvirgins	29	6	65	100
Monogamists	26	1	73	100
Adventurers	19	11	70	100

Table 114

"I would consider it abnormal or unnatural for a girl not to have sex until she gets married."

	True	Not Sure	False	TOTAL
All adolescents	35%	4%	61%	100%
Boys	42	4	54	100
Boys 13–15	43	6	51	100
Boys 16–19	42	2	56	100
Girls	27	4	69	100
Girls 13–15	26	4	70	100
Girls 16–19	28	4	68	100
Virgins	28	5	67	100
Inexperienced	24	1	75	100
Beginners	31	4	65	100
Nonvirgins	41	3	56	100
Monogamists	31	3	66	100
Adventurers	50	1	49	100

Table 115

"I have a lot of respect for my parents' ideas and opinions about sex."

	True	Not Sure	False	TOTAL
All adolescents	65%	6%	29%	100%
Boys	56	8	36	100
Boys 13–15	66	7	27	100
Boys 16–19	47	9	44	100
Girls	75	3	22	100
Girls 13–15	80	3	17	100
Girls 16–19	70	3	27	100
Virgins	74	6	20	100
Inexperienced	80	4	16	100
Beginners	72	5	23	100
Nonvirgins	56	6	38	100
Monogamists	70	2	28	100
Adventurers	38	12	50	100

Table 116

"I think that young people and many American business firms could work together to make things better."

	True	Not Sure	False	TOTAL
All adolescents	85%	4%	11%	100%
Boys	82	3	15	100
Boys 13–15	81	6	13	100
Boys 16–19	82	2	16	100
Girls	88	5	7	100
Girls 13–15	89	6	5	100
Girls 16–19	87	5	8	100
Virgins	83	6	11	100
Inexperienced	84	2	14	100
Beginners	85	7	8	100
Nonvirgins	86	3	11	100
Monogamists	90	3	7	100
Adventurers	83	0	17	100

Table 117

"Making money is more important to me than being creative."

	True	Not Sure	False	TOTAL
All adolescents	32%	2%	66%	100%
Boys	36	3	61	100
Boys 13–15	52	4	44	100
Boys 16–19	23	1	76	100
Girls	27	2	71	100
Girls 13–15	35	3	62	100
Girls 16–19	21	1	78	100
Virgins	35	3	62	100
Inexperienced	34	1	65	100
Beginners	36	3	61	100
Nonvirgins	28	2	70	100
Monogamists	21	1	78	100
Adventurers	27	0	73	100

Table 118

"About the time I became able to have sex, I started to feel more grown up."

	True	Not Sure	False	TOTAL
All adolescents	56%	5%	39%	100%
Boys	62	4	34	100
Boys 13–15	58	8	34	100
Boys 16–19	66	1	33	100
Girls	51	5	44	100
Girls 13–15	47	8	45	100
Girls 16–19	54	3	43	100
Virgins	47	7	46	100
Inexperienced	49	4	47	100
Beginners	58	4	38	100
Nonvirgins	65	3	32	100
Monogamists	69	3	28	100
Adventurers	70	0	30	100

Table 119

"My parents trust me to use my own best judgment when it comes to sex."

	True	Not Sure	False	TOTAL
All adolescents	75%	5%	20%	100%
Boys	77	7	16	100
Boys 13–15	78	7	15	100
Boys 16–19	76	7	17	100
Girls	73	3	24	100
Girls 13–15	68	3	29	100
Girls 16–19	77	2	21	100
Virgins	83	5	12	100
Inexperienced	84	3	13	100
Beginners	89	3	8	100
Nonvirgins	68	5	27	100
Monogamists	72	1	27	100
Adventurers	65	10	25	100

Table 120

"I wouldn't want to have anything to do with any sex acts that are against the law."

	True	Not Sure	False	TOTAL
All adolescents	54%	4%	42%	100%
Boys	45	5	50	100
Boys 13–15	62	5	33	100
Boys 16–19	32	5	63	100
Girls	63	3	34	100
Girls 13–15	68	2	30	100
Girls 16–19	59	4	37	100
Virgins	69	4	27	100
Inexperienced	73	2	25	100
Beginners	60	3	37	100
Nonvirgins	40	4	56	100
Monogamists	42	4	54	100
Adventurers	31	5	64	100

Table 121

"The only reason young people these days have sex is for physical enjoyment."

	True	Not Sure	False	TOTAL
All adolescents	36%	4%	60%	100%
Boys	35	5	60	100
Boys 13–15	43	5	52	100
Boys 16–19	29	5	66	100
Girls	36	3	61	100
Girls 13–15	42	5	53	100
Girls 16–19	31	2	67	100
Virgins	40	6	54	100
Inexperienced	49	3	48	100
Beginners	33	7	60	100
Nonvirgins	31	3	66	100
Monogamists	22	3	75	100
Adventurers	34	1	65	100

Table 122

"Living at home with my parents doesn't interfere with my sex life."

	True	Not Sure	False	TOTAL
All adolescents	63%	5%	32%	100%
Boys	61	4	35	100
Boys 13–15	70	6	24	100
Boys 16–19	54	3	43	100
Girls	64	7	29	100
Girls 13–15	67	10	23	100
Girls 16–19	62	4	34	100
Virgins	69	7	24	100
Inexperienced	70	5	25	100
Beginners	67	4	29	100
Nonvirgins	57	4	39	100
Monogamists	58	7	35	100
Adventurers	52	0	48	100

Table 123

"I wish that churches would talk more about the really important things that we need to get done in this country."

	True	Not Sure	False	TOTAL
All adolescents	68%	6%	26%	100%
Boys	69	6	25	100
Boys 13–15	64	6	30	100
Boys 16–19	73	6	21	100
Girls	67	6	27	100
Girls 13–15	61	7	32	100
Girls 16–19	73	5	22	100
Virgins	59	7	34	100
Inexperienced	48	2	50	100
Beginners	63	9	28	100
Nonvirgins	77	5	18	100
Monogamists	81	1	18	100
Adventurers	77	9	14	100

Table 124

"When I was a child, I was taught that sex was natural and healthy."

	True	Not Sure	False	TOTAL
All adolescents	38%	6%	56%	100%
Boys	34	9	57	100
Boys 13–15	35	9	56	100
Boys 16–19	33	8	59	100
Girls	43	4	53	100
Girls 13–15	39	5	56	100
Girls 16–19	46	3	51	100
Virgins	41	7	52	100
Inexperienced	37	4	59	100
Beginners	51	7	42	100
Nonvirgins	36	5	59	100
Monogamists	40	1	59	100
Adventurers	26	10	64	100

Table 125

"My parents and I find it easy to talk with each other about sex."

	True	Not Sure	False	TOTAL
All adolescents	36%	5%	59%	100%
Boys	28	7	65	100
Boys 13–15	29	8	63	100
Boys 16–19	28	6	66	100
Girls	44	3	53	100
Girls 13–15	50	3	47	100
Girls 16–19	39	3	58	100
Virgins	37	7	56	100
Inexperienced	41	3	56	100
Beginners	33	9	58	100
Nonvirgins	35	3	62	100
Monogamists	38	3	59	100
Adventurers	34	1	65	100

Table 126

"I like to smoke marijuana sometimes."

	True	Not Sure	False	TOTAL
All adolescents	30%	3%	67%	100%
Boys	37	4	59	100
Boys 13–15	24	7	69	100
Boys 16–19	48	2	50	100
Girls	22	2	76	100
Girls 13–15	16	2	82	100
Girls 16–19	28	1	71	100
Virgins	12	4	84	100
Inexperienced	13	3	84	100
Beginners	13	3	84	100
Nonvirgins	46	2	52	100
Monogamists	44	1	55	100
Adventurers	58	3	39	100

Table 127

"My parents have told me the facts about VD."

	True	Not Sure	False	TOTAL
All adolescents	29%	3%	68%	100%
Boys	24	3	73	100
Boys 13–15	27	5	68	100
Boys 16–19	22	1	77	100
Girls	33	3	64	100
Girls 13–15	35	4	61	100
Girls 16–19	32	2	66	100
Virgins	32	4	64	100
Inexperienced	29	2	69	100
Beginners	34	3	63	100
Nonvirgins	25	2	73	100
Monogamists	27	1	72	100
Adventurers	25	1	74	100

Table 128

"I wish my parents could overcome their own early training, so they could realize that sex is natural and beautiful."

	True	Not Sure	False	TOTAL
All adolescents	48%	5%	47%	100%
Boys	51	6	43	100
Boys 13–15	44	8	48	100
Boys 16–19	56	5	39	100
Girls	44	5	51	100
Girls 13–15	44	5	51	100
Girls 16–19	44	5	51	100
Virgins	31	7	62	100
Inexperienced	29	3	68	100
Beginners	35	7	58	100
Nonvirgins	62	4	34	100
Monogamists	58	3	39	100
Adventurers	72	2	26	100

Table 129

"Ever since I was twelve or thirteen years old, my parents have encouraged me to go out on dates."

	True	Not Sure	False	TOTAL
All adolescents	19%	4%	77%	100%
Boys	26	3	71	100
Boys 13–15	21	5	74	100
Boys 16–19	29	2	69	100
Girls	13	3	84	100
Girls 13–15	14	4	82	100
Girls 16–19	12	3	85	100
Virgins	15	6	79	100
Inexperienced	14	2	84	100
Beginners	15	4	81	100
Nonvirgins	23	1	76	100
Monogamists	18	1	81	100
Adventurers	36	0	64	100

Table 130

"Whether or not to use marijuana should be up to each person to decide for himself, like with alcohol and tobacco."

	True	Not Sure	False	TOTAL
All adolescents	73%	3%	24%	100%
Boys	72	4	24	100
Boys 13–15	59	8	33	100
Boys 16–19	82	1	17	100
Girls	74	3	23	100
Girls 13–15	68	3	29	100
Girls 16–19	78	3	19	100
Virgins	65	5	30	100
Inexperienced	65	1	34	100
Beginners	75	4	21	100
Nonvirgins	80	2	18	100
Monogamists	81	1	18	100
Adventurers	84	0	16	100

Table 131

"I don't like it when older people think of me as a child."

	True	Not Sure	False	TOTAL
All adolescents	83%	3%	14%	100%
Boys	81	4	15	100
Boys 13–15	79	8	13	100
Boys 16–19	83	0	17	100
Girls	84	2	14	100
Girls 13–15	81	1	18	100
Girls 16–19	87	3	10	100
Virgins	83	3	14	100
Inexperienced	81	1	18	100
Beginners	87	5	8	100
Nonvirgins	83	2	15	100
Monogamists	89	1	10	100
Adventurers	75	0	25	100

Table 132

"The fact that I have to conceal my sexual activities from my parents makes it hard for me to be close to them."

	True	Not Sure	False	TOTAL
All adolescents	37%	6%	57%	100%
Boys	38	7	55	100
Boys 13–15	29	9	62	100
Boys 16–19	45	6	49	100
Girls	36	5	59	100
Girls 13–15	38	7	55	100
Girls 16–19	35	3	62	100
Virgins	21	8	71	100
Inexperienced	18	6	76	100
Beginners	27	5	68	100
Nonvirgins	52	4	44	100
Monogamists	48	3	49	100
Adventurers	57	4	39	100

Table 133

"So far as sex is concerned, I still haven't really made up my mind about what I think is right and wrong for myself."

	True	Not Sure	False	TOTAL
All adolescents	39%	4%	57%	100%
Boys	45	5	50	100
Boys 13–15	46	9	45	100
Boys 16–19	44	2	54	100
Girls	32	3	65	100
Girls 13–15	40	3	57	100
Girls 16–19	26	3	71	100
Virgins	37	6	57	100
Inexperienced	38	3	59	100
Beginners	33	4	63	100
Nonvirgins	40	2	58	100
Monogamists	31	1	68	100
Adventurers	54	0	46	100

Table 134

"There isn't anything in sex that I wouldn't want to try, at least once."

	True	Not Sure	False	TOTAL
All adolescents	44%	4%	52%	100%
Boys	50	5	45	100
Boys 13–15	42	3	55	100
Boys 16–19	56	6	38	100
Girls	39	3	58	100
Girls 13–15	35	3	62	100
Girls 16–19	42	3	55	100
Virgins	34	5	61	100
Inexperienced	29	2	69	100
Beginners	45	4	51	100
Nonvirgins	54	3	43	100
Monogamists	56	1	43	100
Adventurers	49	10	41	100

Table 135

"My parents and I have heavy disagreements about what is right and wrong in regard to sex, but this doesn't bother me."

	True	Not Sure	False	TOTAL
All adolescents	31%	6%	63%	100%
Boys	34	9	57	100
Boys 13–15	29	8	63	100
Boys 16–19	38	10	52	100
Girls	29	4	67	100
Girls 13–15	32	5	63	100
Girls 16–19	26	3	71	100
Virgins	20	7	73	100
Inexperienced	21	4	75	100
Beginners	23	4	73	100
Nonvirgins	41	6	53	100
Monogamists	33	4	63	100
Adventurers	45	10	45	100

Table 136

"My parents think that my sexual activities are pretty much my own personal business."

	True	Not Sure	False	TOTAL
All adolescents	63%	5%	32%	100%
Boys	75	4	21	100
Boys 13–15	73	4	23	100
Boys 16–19	77	5	18	100
Girls	50	5	45	100
Girls 13–15	44	6	50	100
Girls 16–19	55	4	41	100
Virgins	56	7	37	100
Inexperienced	56	3	41	100
Beginners	65	8	27	100
Nonvirgins	69	2	29	100
Monogamists	67	1	32	100
Adventurers	75	1	24	100

Table 137

"Politically, I tend to think of myself as being a Democrat."

	True	Not Sure	False	TOTAL
All adolescents	34%	8%	58%	100%
Boys	33	9	58	100
Boys 13–15	32	7	61	100
Boys 16–19	34	11	55	100
Girls	36	7	57	100
Girls 13–15	36	11	53	100
Girls 16–19	36	4	60	100
Virgins	33	10	57	100
Inexperienced	34	10	56	100
Beginners	31	7	62	100
Nonvirgins	35	7	58	100
Monogamists	45	3	52	100
Adventurers	29	11	60	100

Table 138

"I believe that drugs are much more harmful than alcohol."

	True	Not Sure	False	TOTAL
All adolescents	72%	4%	24%	100%
Boys	72	4	24	100
Boys 13–15	82	5	13	100
Boys 16–19	64	3	33	100
Girls	73	4	23	100
Girls 13–15	75	6	19	100
Girls 16–19	71	4	25	100
Virgins	84	6	10	100
Inexperienced	91	2	7	100
Beginners	79	6	15	100
Nonvirgins	61	3	36	100
Monogamists	63	1	36	100
Adventurers	57	6	37	100

Table 139

"When I talk with my parents about sex I try to make them think I've had more sexual experience than I've actually had."

	True	Not Sure	False	TOTAL
All adolescents	14%	7%	79%	100%
Boys	22	11	67	100
Boys 13–15	28	13	59	100
Boys 16–19	17	9	74	100
Girls	6	4	90	100
Girls 13–15	9	4	87	100
Girls 16–19	4	3	93	100
Virgins	8	8	84	100
Inexperienced	12	8	80	100
Beginners	5	5	90	100
Nonvirgins	20	6	74	100
Monogamists	16	1	83	100
Adventurers	27	15	58	100

Table 140

"A parent and child having sex with each other is something that I would consider abnormal or unnatural, even if both of them wanted to do it."

	True	Not Sure	False	TOTAL
All adolescents	78%	3%	19%	100%
Boys	71	4	25	100
Boys 13–15	71	7	22	100
Boys 16–19	72	1	27	100
Girls	85	2	13	100
Girls 13–15	84	3	13	100
Girls 16–19	85	2	13	100
Virgins	83	4	13	100
Inexperienced	86	2	12	100
Beginners	80	5	15	100
Nonvirgins	74	2	24	100
Monogamists	77	1	22	100
Adventurers	63	3	34	100

Table 141

"I've never really gotten to know my mother."

	True	Not Sure	False	TOTAL
All adolescents	25%	3%	72%	100%
Boys	27	3	70	100
Boys 13–15	23	4	73	100
Boys 16–19	30	2	68	100
Girls	23	2	75	100
Girls 13–15	24	2	74	100
Girls 16–19	22	2	76	100
Virgins	17	4	79	100
Inexperienced	16	3	81	100
Beginners	18	4	78	100
Nonvirgins	32	1	67	100
Monogamists	32	1	67	100
Adventurers	40	3	57	100

Table 142

"Politically, I tend to think of myself as being a revolutionary."

	True	Not Sure	False	TOTAL
All adolescents	26%	7%	67%	100%
Boys	35	7	58	100
Boys 13–15	29	10	61	100
Boys 16–19	40	5	55	100
Girls	17	8	75	100
Girls 13–15	20	12	68	100
Girls 16–19	14	5	81	100
Virgins	18	10	72	100
Inexperienced	23	10	67	100
Beginners	13	7	80	100
Nonvirgins	34	5	61	100
Monogamists	30	1	69	100
Adventurers	45	7	48	100

Table 143

"My parents think that the only reason young people have sex is for physical enjoyment."

	True	Not Sure	False	TOTAL
All adolescents	58%	6%	36%	100%
Boys	60	7	33	100
Boys 13–15	60	9	31	100
Boys 16–19	60	5	35	100
Girls	55	6	39	100
Girls 13–15	52	8	40	100
Girls 16–19	57	5	38	100
Virgins	51	10	39	100
Inexperienced	52	5	43	100
Beginners	51	12	37	100
Nonvirgins	63	3	34	100
Monogamists	59	1	40	100
Adventurers	70	2	28	100

Table 144

"I would like to be able to talk with my parents about sex."

	True	Not Sure	False	TOTAL
All adolescents	57%	5%	38%	100%
Boys	50	5	45	100
Boys 13–15	47	4	49	100
Boys 16–19	52	6	42	100
Girls	63	5	32	100
Girls 13–15	57	7	36	100
Girls 16–19	69	3	28	100
Virgins	54	7	39	100
Inexperienced	51	6	43	100
Beginners	64	3	33	100
Nonvirgins	59	3	38	100
Monogamists	64	1	35	100
Adventurers	60	6	34	100

Table 145

"In general, I feel pretty self-confident about sex."

	True	Not Sure	False	TOTAL
All adolescents	67%	3%	30%	100%
Boys	71	3	26	100
Boys 13–15	70	4	26	100
Boys 16–19	71	2	27	100
Girls	64	3	33	100
Girls 13–15	64	3	33	100
Girls 16–19	64	4	32	100
Virgins	60	5	35	100
Inexperienced	63	3	34	100
Beginners	61	3	36	100
Nonvirgins	74	1	25	100
Monogamists	74	1	25	100
Adventurers	73	2	25	100

Table 146

"If I had children and any of them turned out to be homosexual, I would be very upset."

	True	Not Sure	False	TOTAL
All adolescents	73%	3%	24%	100%
Boys	73	3	24	100
Boys 13–15	79	5	16	100
Boys 16–19	68	2	30	100
Girls	72	3	25	100
Girls 13–15	79	4	17	100
Girls 16–19	66	3	31	100
Virgins	72	5	23	100
Inexperienced	81	1	18	100
Beginners	66	3	31	100
Nonvirgins	73	1	26	100
Monogamists	75	1	24	100
Adventurers	67	2	31	100

Table 147

"Oral sex is something that I would consider abnormal or unnatural."

	True	Not Sure	False	TOTAL
All adolescents	38%	8%	54%	100%
Boys	37	8	55	100
Boys 13–15	49	11	40	100
Boys 16–19	27	5	68	100
Girls	38	8	54	100
Girls 13–15	50	9	41	100
Girls 16–19	28	8	64	100
Virgins	48	10	42	100
Inexperienced	57	8	35	100
Beginners	38	7	55	100
Nonvirgins	28	6	66	100
Monogamists	26	2	72	100
Adventurers	30	9	61	100

Table 148

"I have a lot of respect for my parents as people."

	True	Not Sure	False	TOTAL
All adolescents	88%	3%	9%	100%
Boys	87	2	11	100
Boys 13–15	84	3	13	100
Boys 16–19	89	1	10	100
Girls	89	3	8	100
Girls 13–15	89	4	7	100
Girls 16–19	89	3	8	100
Virgins	89	4	7	100
Inexperienced	88	1	11	100
Beginners	92	4	4	100
Nonvirgins	86	2	12	100
Monogamists	94	1	5	100
Adventurers	79	3	18	100

Table 149

"I have never read a serious magazine article about sex."

	True	Not Sure	False	TOTAL
All adolescents	33%	3%	64%	100%
Boys	36	3	61	100
Boys 13–15	48	5	47	100
Boys 16–19	26	1	73	100
Girls	30	3	67	100
Girls 13–15	37	2	61	100
Girls 16–19	24	3	73	100
Virgins	39	3	58	100
Inexperienced	42	1	57	100
Beginners	31	4	65	100
Nonvirgins	27	3	70	100
Monogamists	17	1	82	100
Adventurers	32	2	66	100

Table 150

"So far as I know, my parents have never really gotten sexually passionate about each other."

	True	Not Sure	False	TOTAL
All adolescents	36%	8%	56%	100%
Boys	42	8	50	100
Boys 13–15	50	8	42	100
Boys 16–19	34	9	57	100
Girls	31	7	62	100
Girls 13–15	29	11	60	100
Girls 16–19	32	5	63	100
Virgins	35	10	55	100
Inexperienced	41	6	53	100
Beginners	28	9	63	100
Nonvirgins	37	6	57	100
Monogamists	32	4	64	100
Adventurers	40	7	53	100

Table 151

"I would not want to have children in the kind of world we live in today."

	True	Not Sure	False	TOTAL
All adolescents	30%	5%	65%	100%
Boys	34	4	62	100
Boys 13–15	34	4	62	100
Boys 16–19	33	5	62	100
Girls	28	5	67	100
Girls 13–15	32	6	62	100
Girls 16–19	24	5	71	100
Virgins	28	6	66	100
Inexperienced	28	1	71	100
Beginners	23	9	68	100
Nonvirgins	33	3	64	100
Monogamists	24	4	72	100
Adventurers	52	2	46	100

Table 152

"I've never taken part in any sex act, or been involved in any kind of sexual situation, that I myself would think of as being immoral."

	True	Not Sure	False	TOTAL
All adolescents	75%	5%	20%	100%
Boys	66	6	28	100
Boys 13–15	66	7	27	100
Boys 16–19	66	6	28	100
Girls	85	3	12	100
Girls 13–15	84	5	11	100
Girls 16–19	85	1	14	100
Virgins	81	5	14	100
Inexperienced	91	2	7	100
Beginners	78	4	18	100
Nonvirgins	69	5	26	100
Monogamists	79	2	19	100
Adventurers	67	7	26	100

Table 153

"The only reason I would get legally married would be to satisfy my parents."

	True	Not Sure	False	TOTAL
All adolescents	20%	4%	76%	100%
Boys	22	6	72	100
Boys 13–15	28	7	65	100
Boys 16–19	17	5	78	100
Girls	17	3	80	100
Girls 13–15	22	3	75	100
Girls 16–19	13	3	84	100
Virgins	22	5	73	100
Inexperienced	25	1	74	100
Beginners	18	5	77	100
Nonvirgins	17	4	79	100
Monogamists	16	1	83	100
Adventurers	22	7	71	100

Table 154

"I go to religious services fairly often."

	True	Not Sure	False	TOTAL
All adolescents	48%	4%	48%	100%
Boys	43	5	52	100
Boys 13–15	56	5	39	100
Boys 16–19	32	4	64	100
Girls	52	4	44	100
Girls 13–15	57	5	38	100
Girls 16–19	48	2	50	100
Virgins	60	5	35	100
Inexperienced	69	1	30	100
Beginners	52	4	44	100
Nonvirgins	36	4	60	100
Monogamists	45	1	54	100
Adventurers	25	7	68	100

Table 155

Male: "I don't think it would be possible for a boy to be really in love with more than one girl at the same time."

Female: "I don't think it would be possible for a girl to be really in love with more than one boy at the same time."

	True	Not Sure	False	TOTAL
All adolescents	57%	3%	40%	100%
Boys	55	3	42	100
Boys 13–15	69	6	25	100
Boys 16–19	43	2	55	100
Girls	58	3	39	100
Girls 13–15	55	4	41	100
Girls 16–19	61	3	36	100
Virgins	63	5	32	100
Inexperienced	68	2	30	100
Beginners	63	5	32	100
Nonvirgins	50	2	48	100
Monogamists	49	1	50	100
Adventurers	43	1	56	100

Table 156

Male: "I won't tell a girl that I love her unless I really do."

Female: "I won't tell a boy that I love him unless I really do."

	True	Not Sure	False	TOTAL
All adolescents	88%	3%	9%	100%
Boys	83	2	15	100
Boys 13–15	86	3	11	100
Boys 16–19	80	2	18	100
Girls	93	3	4	100
Girls 13–15	90	4	6	100
Girls 16–19	96	2	2	100
Virgins	90	4	6	100
Inexperienced	91	2	7	100
Beginners	90	5	5	100
Nonvirgins	87	1	12	100
Monogamists	93	1	6	100
Adventurers	76	2	22	100

Table 157

Male: "My parents are anxious that before I get too old I should find the right girl to marry."

Female: "My parents are anxious that before I get too old I should find the right boy to marry."

	True	Not Sure	False	TOTAL
All adolescents	35%	5%	60%	100%
Boys	36	6	58	100
Boys 13–15	39	6	55	100
Boys 16–19	34	6	60	100
Girls	34	4	62	100
Girls 13–15	29	6	65	100
Girls 16–19	37	3	60	100
Virgins	30	6	64	100
Inexperienced	40	2	58	100
Beginners	21	6	73	100
Nonvirgins	39	5	56	100
Monogamists	40	2	58	100
Adventurers	47	10	43	100

Table 158

Male: "I'd like to ask my parents for information about VD, but I'm afraid to because they would ask whether I'm having sex with girls."

Female: "I'd like to ask my parents for information about VD, but I'm afraid to because they would ask whether I'm having sex with boys."

	True	Not Sure	False	TOTAL
All adolescents	29%	4%	67%	100%
Boys	32	3	65	100
Boys 13–15	47	3	50	100
Boys 16–19	19	4	77	100
Girls	26	4	70	100
Girls 13–15	36	5	59	100
Girls 16–19	18	3	79	100
Virgins	25	6	69	100
Inexperienced	31	2	67	100
Beginners	18	6	76	100
Nonvirgins	32	2	66	100
Monogamists	26	1	73	100
Adventurers	30	5	65	100

Table 159

Male: "My parents tell me that I'm too young to have sex with girls."

Female: "My parents tell me that I'm too young to have sex with boys."

	True	Not Sure	False	TOTAL
All adolescents	41%	5%	54%	100%
Boys	33	6	61	100
Boys 13–15	39	4	57	100
Boys 16–19	28	7	65	100
Girls	49	5	46	100
Girls 13–15	61	6	33	100
Girls 16–19	39	4	57	100
Virgins	40	8	52	100
Inexperienced	48	6	46	100
Beginners	32	9	59	100
Nonvirgins	41	3	56	100
Monogamists	36	1	63	100
Adventurers	44	6	50	100

Table 160

Male: "If I were married and my wife had sexual relations with someone else, I would divorce her."

Female: "If I were married and my husband had sexual relations with someone else, I would divorce him."

	True	Not Sure	False	TOTAL
All adolescents	41%	4%	55%	100%
Boys	45	2	53	100
Boys 13–15	52	3	45	100
Boys 16–19	40	1	59	100
Girls	37	6	57	100
Girls 13–15	40	7	53	100
Girls 16–19	34	5	61	100
Virgins	45	7	48	100
Inexperienced	53	2	45	100
Beginners	45	6	49	100
Nonvirgins	38	1	61	100
Monogamists	34	1	65	100
Adventurers	44	2	54	100

Table 161

Male: "I wouldn't want to have sex with a girl only for the physical enjoyment of doing it, and nothing else."

Female: "I wouldn't want to have sex with a boy only for the physical enjoyment of doing it, and nothing else."

	True	Not Sure	False	TOTAL
All adolescents	57%	4%	39%	100%
Boys	49	4	47	100
Boys 13–15	52	6	42	100
Boys 16–19	46	2	52	100
Girls	65	5	30	100
Girls 13–15	60	6	34	100
Girls 16–19	71	3	26	100
Virgins	60	6	34	100
Inexperienced	60	2	38	100
Beginners	62	6	32	100
Nonvirgins	54	3	43	100
Monogamists	62	3	35	100
Adventurers	56	2	42	100

Table 162

Male: "I usually think of myself as being sexually attractive to girls."

Female: "I usually think of myself as being sexually attractive to boys."

	True	Not Sure	False	TOTAL
All adolescents	48%	6%	46%	100%
Boys	47	6	47	100
Boys 13–15	42	5	53	100
Boys 16–19	52	6	42	100
Girls	49	7	44	100
Girls 13–15	45	8	47	100
Girls 16–19	51	6	43	100
Virgins	35	7	58	100
Inexperienced	33	5	62	100
Beginners	43	7	50	100
Nonvirgins	60	5	35	100
Monogamists	67	2	31	100
Adventurers	56	12	32	100

Table 163

Male: "I've never had sex with another boy, and I'm sure I'd never want to."

Female: "I've never had sex with another girl, and I'm sure I'd never want to."

	True	Not Sure	False	TOTAL
All adolescents	79%	3%	18%	100%
Boys	78	2	20	100
Boys 13–15	78	4	18	100
Boys 16–19	78	1	21	100
Girls	80	4	16	100
Girls 13–15	81	4	15	100
Girls 16–19	78	5	17	100
Virgins	84	4	12	100
Inexperienced	88	2	10	100
Beginners	84	5	11	100
Nonvirgins	75	2	23	100
Monogamists	77	3	20	100
Adventurers	73	3	24	100

Table 164

Male: "I wouldn't want to have sex with a girl unless I liked her as a person."

Female: "I wouldn't want to have sex with a boy unless I liked him as a person."

	True	Not Sure	False	TOTAL
All adolescents	71%	4%	25%	100%
Boys	69	4	27	100
Boys 13–15	68	7	25	100
Boys 16–19	69	2	29	100
Girls	73	5	22	100
Girls 13–15	64	7	29	100
Girls 16–19	79	3	18	100
Virgins	66	6	28	100
Inexperienced	71	3	26	100
Beginners	62	8	30	100
Nonvirgins	75	3	22	100
Monogamists	81	1	18	100
Adventurers	79	2	19	100

Table 165

Male: "I think it would be wrong for me to have sex with a girl I'd just met and hadn't gotten to know."

Female: "I think it would be wrong for me to have sex with a boy I'd just met and hadn't gotten to know."

	True	Not Sure	False	TOTAL
All adolescents	65%	4%	31%	100%
Boys	51	3	46	100
Boys 13–15	61	5	34	100
Boys 16–19	42	2	56	100
Girls	79	5	16	100
Girls 13–15	82	7	11	100
Girls 16–19	77	3	20	100
Virgins	76	6	18	100
Inexperienced	80	2	18	100
Beginners	70	5	25	100
Nonvirgins	55	2	43	100
Monogamists	70	1	29	100
Adventurers	35	3	62	100

Table 166

Male: "I'd like to ask my parents for information about birth control, but I'm afraid to because they would ask whether I'm having sex with girls."

Female: "I'd like to ask my parents for information about birth control, but I'm afraid to because they would ask whether I'm having sex with boys."

	True	Not Sure	False	TOTAL
All adolescents	27%	6%	67%	100%
Boys	29	8	63	100
Boys 13–15	39	6	55	100
Boys 16–19	21	9	70	100
Girls	25	5	70	100
Girls 13–15	26	8	66	100
Girls 16–19	24	3	73	100
Virgins	20	7	73	100
Inexperienced	25	4	71	100
Beginners	15	8	77	100
Nonvirgins	34	5	61	100
Monogamists	32	1	67	100
Adventurers	24	10	66	100

Table 167

Male: "My parents assume that I have had sex with girls."

Female: "My parents assume that I have had sex with boys."

	True	Not Sure	False	TOTAL
All adolescents	42%	5%	53%	100%
Boys	53	6	41	100
Boys 13–15	33	8	59	100
Boys 16–19	70	4	26	100
Girls	30	5	65	100
Girls 13–15	23	8	69	100
Girls 16–19	35	4	61	100
Virgins	16	7	77	100
Inexperienced	15	4	81	100
Beginners	26	5	69	100
Nonvirgins	65	4	31	100
Monogamists	67	2	31	100
Adventurers	79	3	18	100

Table 168

Male: "I wouldn't want to have sex with a girl unless she loved me."

Female: "I wouldn't want to have sex with a boy unless he loved me."

	True	Not Sure	False	TOTAL
All adolescents	59%	4%	37%	100%
Boys	44	4	52	100
Boys 13–15	54	7	39	100
Boys 16–19	35	2	63	100
Girls	75	4	21	100
Girls 13–15	75	5	20	100
Girls 16–19	75	4	21	100
Virgins	66	8	26	100
Inexperienced	71	4	25	100
Beginners	68	6	26	100
Nonvirgins	53	1	46	100
Monogamists	66	1	33	100
Adventurers	36	2	62	100

Table 169

Male: "I wouldn't want to marry a girl unless I'd lived with her first."

Female: "I wouldn't want to marry a boy unless I'd lived with him first."

	True	Not Sure	False	TOTAL
All adolescents	29%	3%	68%	100%
Boys	36	2	62	100
Boys 13–15	36	3	61	100
Boys 16–19	36	2	62	100
Girls	21	5	74	100
Girls 13–15	13	6	81	100
Girls 16–19	28	4	68	100
Virgins	18	6	76	100
Inexperienced	18	2	80	100
Beginners	20	6	74	100
Nonvirgins	39	1	60	100
Monogamists	35	1	64	100
Adventurers	49	2	49	100

Table 170

Male: "I don't think it would be possible for a boy to have a real relationship with more than one girl at the same time."

Female: "I don't think it would be possible for a girl to have a real relationship with more than one boy at the same time."

	True	Not Sure	False	TOTAL
All adolescents	57%	4%	39%	100%
Boys	55	4	41	100
Boys 13–15	60	6	34	100
Boys 16–19	52	3	45	100
Girls	58	5	37	100
Girls 13–15	52	6	42	100
Girls 16–19	63	3	34	100
Virgins	57	7	36	100
Inexperienced	61	3	36	100
Beginners	57	6	37	100
Nonvirgins	56	3	41	100
Monogamists	56	1	43	100
Adventurers	51	2	47	100

Table 171

Male: "My parents think that if I have to have sex before getting married, they would rather I do it with a girl I don't love."

Female: "My parents think that if I have to have sex before getting married, they would rather I do it with a boy I don't love."

	True	Not Sure	False	TOTAL
All adolescents	14%	8%	78%	100%
Boys	22	10	68	100
Boys 13–15	22	10	68	100
Boys 16–19	23	9	68	100
Girls	6	6	88	100
Girls 13–15	10	8	82	100
Girls 16–19	4	4	92	100
Virgins	7	11	82	100
Inexperienced	11	8	81	100
Beginners	5	10	85	100
Nonvirgins	21	6	73	100
Monogamists	13	1	86	100
Adventurers	26	10	64	100

Table 172

Male: "My parents wouldn't want me to marry a girl unless I'd lived with her first."

Female: "My parents wouldn't want me to marry a boy unless I'd lived with him first."

	True	Not Sure	False	TOTAL
All adolescents	12%	4%	84%	100%
Boys	17	4	79	100
Boys 13–15	26	4	70	100
Boys 16–19	10	4	86	100
Girls	6	4	90	100
Girls 13–15	7	5	88	100
Girls 16–19	6	3	91	100
Virgins	10	7	83	100
Inexperienced	15	5	80	100
Beginners	5	5	90	100
Nonvirgins	13	2	85	100
Monogamists	14	1	85	100
Adventurers	12	2	86	100

Table 173

Male: "My parents assume that I haven't had sex with girls."

Female: "My parents assume that I haven't had sex with boys."

	True	Not Sure	False	TOTAL
All adolescents	49%	6%	45%	100%
Boys	39	7	54	100
Boys 13–15	55	8	37	100
Boys 16–19	26	5	69	100
Girls	59	6	35	100
Girls 13–15	69	6	25	100
Girls 16–19	52	5	43	100
Virgins	68	7	25	100
Inexperienced	77	3	20	100
Beginners	64	6	30	100
Nonvirgins	31	6	63	100
Monogamists	28	2	70	100
Adventurers	27	8	65	100

Table 174

Male: "I wouldn't want to have sex with a girl unless I loved her."

Female: "I wouldn't want to have sex with a boy unless I loved him."

	True	Not Sure	False	TOTAL
All adolescents	61%	4%	35%	100%
Boys	47	4	49	100
Boys 13–15	55	4	41	100
Boys 16–19	41	4	55	100
Girls	76	4	20	100
Girls 13–15	75	5	20	100
Girls 16–19	76	4	20	100
Virgins	66	7	27	100
Inexperienced	66	4	30	100
Beginners	70	9	21	100
Nonvirgins	57	1	42	100
Monogamists	64	1	35	100
Adventurers	38	2	60	100

Table 175

Male: "I wouldn't want to have sex with a girl unless she liked me as a person."

Female: "I wouldn't want to have sex with a boy unless he liked me as a person."

	True	Not Sure	False	TOTAL
All adolescents	73%	5%	22%	100%
Boys	70	4	26	100
Boys 13–15	70	6	24	100
Boys 16–19	69	4	27	100
Girls	76	5	19	100
Girls 13–15	67	6	27	100
Girls 16–19	84	4	12	100
Virgins	68	8	24	100
Inexperienced	71	4	25	100
Beginners	66	9	25	100
Nonvirgins	78	1	21	100
Monogamists	88	1	11	100
Adventurers	65	2	33	100

Table 176

"Some people I know are so much involved in sex that it's the most important thing in their lives."

	True	Not Sure	False	TOTAL
All adolescents	77%	3%	20%	100%
Boys	78	2	20	100
Boys 13–15	76	2	22	100
Boys 16–19	81	0	18	100
Girls	75	4	21	100
Girls 13–15	70	5	25	100
Girls 16–19	80	3	17	100
Virgins	69	4	27	100
Inexperienced	67	4	29	100
Beginners	71	2	27	100
Nonvirgins	84	1	15	100
Monogamists	87	1	12	100
Adventurers	84	0	16	100

Table 177

"Because of the problem of overpopulation, I would not want to have more than two children."

	True	Not Sure	False	TOTAL
All adolescents	59%	3%	38%	100%
Boys	57	1	42	100
Boys 13–15	46	1	53	100
Boys 16–19	66	1	33	100
Girls	61	6	33	100
Girls 13–15	50	7	43	100
Girls 16–19	70	4	26	100
Virgins	52	5	43	100
Inexperienced	43	4	53	100
Beginners	63	1	36	100
Nonvirgins	65	1	34	100
Monogamists	69	1	30	100
Adventurers	63	2	35	100

Table 178

"My parents try to seem broad-minded about sex, but actually they're pretty uptight when it comes down to what I myself want to do."

	True	Not Sure	False	TOTAL
All adolescents	51%	5%	44%	100%
Boys	52	4	44	100
Boys 13–15	54	3	43	100
Boys 16–19	51	4	45	100
Girls	49	6	45	100
Girls 13–15	49	7	44	100
Girls 16–19	49	5	46	100
Virgins	39	7	54	100
Inexperienced	37	6	57	100
Beginners	46	4	50	100
Nonvirgins	62	3	35	100
Monogamists	66	1	33	100
Adventurers	55	3	42	100

Table 179

"I believe that many people who live in communes are finding meaning and brotherhood in their way of life."

	True	Not Sure	False	TOTAL
All adolescents	66%	5%	29%	100%
Boys	68	5	27	100
Boys 13–15	65	8	27	100
Boys 16–19	71	3	26	100
Girls	63	5	32	100
Girls 13–15	60	6	34	100
Girls 16–19	65	4	31	100
Virgins	56	7	37	100
Inexperienced	55	6	39	100
Beginners	58	6	36	100
Nonvirgins	74	4	22	100
Monogamists	73	1	26	100
Adventurers	77	3	20	100

Table 180

"Someday, I will probably want to have children—but it won't matter whether or not I get married first."

	True	Not Sure	False	TOTAL
All adolescents	29%	3%	68%	100%
Boys	37	3	60	100
Boys 13–15	29	6	65	100
Boys 16–19	43	0	57	100
Girls	22	3	75	100
Girls 13–15	15	4	81	100
Girls 16–19	27	3	70	100
Virgins	12	5	83	100
Inexperienced	15	3	82	100
Beginners	8	6	86	100
Nonvirgins	45	2	53	100
Monogamists	39	1	60	100
Adventurers	56	0	44	100

Table 181

"When talking to my parents about sex, I try to persuade them to my way of thinking."

	True	Not Sure	False	TOTAL
All adolescents	32%	5%	63%	100%
Boys	34	5	61	100
Boys 13–15	43	1	56	100
Boys 16–19	27	7	66	100
Girls	30	5	65	100
Girls 13–15	31	6	63	100
Girls 16–19	28	5	67	100
Virgins	27	7	66	100
Inexperienced	29	6	65	100
Beginners	27	7	66	100
Nonvirgins	37	3	60	100
Monogamists	32	2	66	100
Adventurers	48	5	47	100

Table 182

"I sometimes worry about whether God would approve of my sexual activities."

	True	Not Sure	False	TOTAL
All adolescents	46%	4%	50%	100%
Boys	49	3	48	100
Boys 13–15	52	4	44	100
Boys 16–19	45	3	52	100
Girls	44	5	51	100
Girls 13–15	46	5	49	100
Girls 16–19	42	5	53	100
Virgins	42	7	51	100
Inexperienced	37	4	59	100
Beginners	52	7	41	100
Nonvirgins	50	1	49	100
Monogamists	51	1	48	100
Adventurers	49	0	51	100

Table 183

"So far as sex is concerned, I do what I want to do, regardless of what society thinks."

	True	Not Sure	False	TOTAL
All adolescents	62%	3%	35%	100%
Boys	69	2	29	100
Boys 13–15	61	3	36	100
Boys 16–19	76	1	23	100
Girls	55	4	41	100
Girls 13–15	53	4	43	100
Girls 16–19	58	3	39	100
Virgins	44	4	52	100
Inexperienced	44	3	53	100
Beginners	53	3	44	100
Nonvirgins	79	1	20	100
Monogamists	80	1	19	100
Adventurers	80	0	20	100

Table 184

"My parents don't get along with each other very well."

	True	Not Sure	False	TOTAL
All adolescents	31%	5%	64%	100%
Boys	34	4	62	100
Boys 13–15	32	0	68	100
Boys 16–19	35	8	57	100
Girls	28	6	66	100
Girls 13–15	24	6	70	100
Girls 16–19	31	7	62	100
Virgins	27	6	67	100
Inexperienced	25	6	69	100
Beginners	29	5	66	100
Nonvirgins	34	5	61	100
Monogamists	26	5	69	100
Adventurers	48	5	47	100

Table 185

"If a girl uses birth control pills or other methods of contraception, it makes it seem as if she were *planning* to have sex."

	True	Not Sure	False	TOTAL
All adolescents	68%	5%	27%	100%
Boys	70	4	26	100
Boys 13–15	71	4	25	100
Boys 16–19	69	4	27	100
Girls	67	5	28	100
Girls 13–15	64	7	29	100
Girls 16–19	68	4	28	100
Virgins	65	8	27	100
Inexperienced	67	5	28	100
Beginners	63	5	32	100
Nonvirgins	71	2	27	100
Monogamists	69	1	30	100
Adventurers	79	0	21	100

Table 186

"My parents believe that it's all right for young people to have sex before getting married, if they are in love with each other."

	True	Not Sure	False	TOTAL
All adolescents	28%	7%	65%	100%
Boys	34	7	59	100
Boys 13–15	36	5	59	100
Boys 16–19	32	8	60	100
Girls	22	7	71	100
Girls 13–15	24	10	66	100
Girls 16–19	20	6	74	100
Virgins	21	9	70	100
Inexperienced	21	7	72	100
Beginners	22	5	73	100
Nonvirgins	35	5	60	100
Monogamists	36	1	63	100
Adventurers	33	11	56	100

Table 187

"When I was a child, I was taught that sex was wrong."

	True	Not Sure	False	TOTAL
All adolescents	44%	3%	53%	100%
Boys	45	4	51	100
Boys 13–15	57	3	40	100
Boys 16–19	35	5	60	100
Girls	42	3	55	100
Girls 13–15	44	3	53	100
Girls 16–19	41	3	56	100
Virgins	34	4	62	100
Inexperienced	43	4	53	100
Beginners	27	0	73	100
Nonvirgins	52	3	45	100
Monogamists	42	1	57	100
Adventurers	67	6	27	100

Table 188

"I don't think I will want to have children, because I don't like the idea of having all that responsibility."

	True	Not Sure	False	TOTAL
All adolescents	13%	4%	83%	100%
Boys	18	3	79	100
Boys 13–15	23	3	74	100
Boys 16–19	13	4	83	100
Girls	8	5	87	100
Girls 13–15	6	6	88	100
Girls 16–19	10	3	87	100
Virgins	6	5	89	100
Inexperienced	7	3	90	100
Beginners	7	1	92	100
Nonvirgins	19	3	78	100
Monogamists	16	2	82	100
Adventurers	20	8	72	100

Table 189

"One of the reasons I stopped going to church is because churches teach that sex is sinful."

	True	Not Sure	False	TOTAL
All adolescents	15%	6%	79%	100%
Boys	20	8	72	100
Boys 13–15	23	9	68	100
Boys 16–19	17	7	76	100
Girls	10	5	85	100
Girls 13–15	12	5	83	100
Girls 16–19	9	4	87	100
Virgins	10	8	82	100
Inexperienced	12	8	80	100
Beginners	9	0	91	100
Nonvirgins	20	4	76	100
Monogamists	11	3	86	100
Adventurers	28	0	72	100

Table 190

"Some of my sexual activities are probably harmful to my relationship with my parents."

	True	Not Sure	False	TOTAL
All adolescents	38%	4%	58%	100%
Boys	43	4	53	100
Boys 13–15	51	4	45	100
Boys 16–19	36	4	60	100
Girls	32	5	63	100
Girls 13–15	33	6	61	100
Girls 16–19	32	4	64	100
Virgins	19	7	74	100
Inexperienced	23	5	72	100
Beginners	18	4	78	100
Nonvirgins	54	2	44	100
Monogamists	53	1	46	100
Adventurers	65	0	35	100

Table 191

"Birth control pills can be physically harmful to a girl."

	True	Not Sure	False	TOTAL
All adolescents	63%	7%	30%	100%
Boys	56	10	34	100
Boys 13–15	48	9	43	100
Boys 16–19	63	11	26	100
Girls	70	4	26	100
Girls 13–15	70	5	25	100
Girls 16–19	70	4	26	100
Virgins	63	9	28	100
Inexperienced	63	12	25	100
Beginners	58	5	37	100
Nonvirgins	63	6	31	100
Monogamists	73	2	25	100
Adventurers	65	5	30	100

Table 192

"I have no personal values of my own."

	True	Not Sure	False	TOTAL
All adolescents	10%	4%	86%	100%
Boys	11	4	85	100
Boys 13–15	16	3	81	100
Boys 16–19	7	4	89	100
Girls	9	5	86	100
Girls 13–15	17	8	75	100
Girls 16–19	2	3	95	100
Virgins	10	4	86	100
Inexperienced	16	3	81	100
Beginners	3	1	96	100
Nonvirgins	11	4	85	100
Monogamists	7	3	90	100
Adventurers	16	5	79	100

Table 193

"I can't see myself getting married until I know it will last for the rest of my life."

	True	Not Sure	False	TOTAL
All adolescents	78%	4%	18%	100%
Boys	75	6	19	100
Boys 13–15	70	9	21	100
Boys 16–19	79	3	18	100
Girls	81	3	16	100
Girls 13–15	85	2	13	100
Girls 16–19	77	4	19	100
Virgins	77	6	17	100
Inexperienced	72	8	20	100
Beginners	88	1	11	100
Nonvirgins	78	3	19	100
Monogamists	82	1	17	100
Adventurers	76	5	19	100

Table 194

"I am comfortable talking with my parents about sex in general, but I avoid telling them what I myself do."

	True	Not Sure	False	TOTAL
All adolescents	42%	5%	53%	100%
Boys	46	5	49	100
Boys 13–15	44	6	50	100
Boys 16–19	47	5	48	100
Girls	39	5	56	100
Girls 13–15	35	5	60	100
Girls 16–19	42	4	54	100
Virgins	36	5	59	100
Inexperienced	32	6	62	100
Beginners	46	1	53	100
Nonvirgins	48	5	47	100
Monogamists	48	3	49	100
Adventurers	52	5	43	100

Table 195

"Some of my sexual activities are probably harmful to me."

	True	Not Sure	False	TOTAL
All adolescents	26%	3%	71%	100%
Boys	30	2	68	100
Boys 13–15	43	4	53	100
Boys 16–19	19	1	80	100
Girls	22	5	73	100
Girls 13–15	23	5	72	100
Girls 16–19	22	4	74	100
Virgins	23	5	72	100
Inexperienced	31	5	64	100
Beginners	16	1	83	100
Nonvirgins	28	2	70	100
Monogamists	27	1	72	100
Adventurers	35	1	64	100

Table 196

"It's all right for young people to have sex before getting married, if they are in love with each other."

	Agree	Not Sure	Disagree	TOTAL
All adolescents	76%	1%	23%	100%
Boys	80	2	18	100
Boys 13–15	70	1	29	100
Boys 16–19	88	3	9	100
Girls	72	0	28	100
Girls 13–15	65	0	35	100
Girls 16–19	77	0	23	100
Virgins	58	2	40	100
Inexperienced	44	1	55	100
Beginners	77	3	20	100
Nonvirgins	92	1	7	100
Monogamists	97	0	3	100
Adventurers	92	2	6	100

Table 197

"Our society's values concerning sex come from many generations of accumulated wisdom."

	Agree	Not Sure	Disagree	TOTAL
All adolescents	57%	5%	38%	100%
Boys	56	6	38	100
Boys 13–15	65	6	29	100
Boys 16–19	48	7	45	100
Girls	59	4	37	100
Girls 13–15	63	5	32	100
Girls 16–19	55	3	42	100
Virgins	61	6	33	100
Inexperienced	64	4	32	100
Beginners	54	4	42	100
Nonvirgins	53	5	42	100
Monogamists	55	0	45	100
Adventurers	48	12	40	100

Table 198

"It's immoral for two persons of the same sex to have sex with each other."

	Agree	Not Sure	Disagree	TOTAL
All adolescents	62%	3%	35%	100%
Boys	62	4	34	100
Boys 13–15	70	2	28	100
Boys 16–19	56	6	38	100
Girls	61	2	37	100
Girls 13–15	61	2	37	100
Girls 16–19	61	2	37	100
Virgins	74	2	24	100
Inexperienced	75	1	24	100
Beginners	77	1	22	100
Nonvirgins	50	4	46	100
Monogamists	54	3	43	100
Adventurers	45	8	47	100

Table 199

"One of the most important tasks of growing up is to learn to live with one's parents' ideas and opinions about sex."

	Agree	Not Sure	Disagree	TOTAL
All adolescents	52%	1%	47%	100%
Boys	50	2	48	100
Boys 13–15	60	1	39	100
Boys 16–19	41	3	56	100
Girls	55	0	45	100
Girls 13–15	58	0	42	100
Girls 16–19	53	0	47	100
Virgins	54	2	44	100
Inexperienced	58	1	41	100
Beginners	45	3	52	100
Nonvirgins	51	1	48	100
Monogamists	46	0	54	100
Adventurers	61	3	36	100

Table 200

"A girl who goes to bed with a boy before marriage will lose his respect."

	Agree	Not Sure	Disagree	TOTAL
All adolescents	34%	2%	64%	100%
Boys	27	2	71	100
Boys 13–15	45	4	51	100
Boys 16–19	13	1	86	100
Girls	41	1	58	100
Girls 13–15	52	0	48	100
Girls 16–19	33	1	66	100
Virgins	55	2	43	100
Inexperienced	66	1	33	100
Beginners	42	2	56	100
Nonvirgins	15	1	84	100
Monogamists	10	0	90	100
Adventurers	11	5	84	100

Table 201

"Two people shouldn't have to get married just because they want to live together."

	Agree	Not Sure	Disagree	TOTAL
All adolescents	72%	0%	28%	100%
Boys	76	1	23	100
Boys 13–15	63	2	35	100
Boys 16–19	87	1	12	100
Girls	67	0	33	100
Girls 13–15	66	0	34	100
Girls 16–19	67	0	33	100
Virgins	64	0	36	100
Inexperienced	55	0	45	100
Beginners	71	0	29	100
Nonvirgins	78	1	21	100
Monogamists	80	0	20	100
Adventurers	78	2	20	100

Table 202

"Churches could do things that would help older people understand young people's ideas."

	Agree	Not Sure	Disagree	TOTAL
All adolescents	78%	3%	19%	100%
Boys	73	4	23	100
Boys 13–15	68	6	26	100
Boys 16–19	78	1	21	100
Girls	82	2	16	100
Girls 13–15	80	3	17	100
Girls 16–19	84	1	15	100
Virgins	76	2	22	100
Inexperienced	71	2	27	100
Beginners	80	1	19	100
Nonvirgins	80	3	17	100
Monogamists	92	1	7	100
Adventurers	74	5	21	100

Table 203

"Young people who get married without ever having had sex together are foolish."

	Agree	Not Sure	Disagree	TOTAL
All adolescents	29%	3%	68%	100%
Boys	38	4	58	100
Boys 13–15	37	3	60	100
Boys 16–19	39	6	55	100
Girls	20	1	79	100
Girls 13–15	14	0	86	100
Girls 16–19	26	1	73	100
Virgins	19	1	80	100
Inexperienced	13	0	87	100
Beginners	24	0	76	100
Nonvirgins	39	4	57	100
Monogamists	40	0	60	100
Adventurers	43	10	47	100

Table 204

"Some boys use sex to reward or punish their girl friends."

	Agree	Not Sure	Disagree	TOTAL
All adolescents	59%	3%	38%	100%
Boys	47	2	51	100
Boys 13–15	42	2	56	100
Boys 16–19	52	2	46	100
Girls	71	4	25	100
Girls 13–15	67	5	28	100
Girls 16–19	74	3	23	100
Virgins	53	3	44	100
Inexperienced	49	3	48	100
Beginners	60	0	40	100
Nonvirgins	65	3	32	100
Monogamists	73	2	25	100
Adventurers	53	7	40	100

Table 205

"Churches could do things that would be a big help in keeping down VD among young people who have sex,"

	Agree	Not Sure	Disagree	TOTAL
All adolescents	58%	3%	39%	100%
Boys	52	4	44	100
Boys 13–15	49	6	45	100
Boys 16–19	54	3	43	100
Girls	64	2	34	100
Girls 13–15	60	3	37	100
Girls 16–19	67	1	32	100
Virgins	52	3	45	100
Inexperienced	54	2	44	100
Beginners	57	0	43	100
Nonvirgins	63	4	33	100
Monogamists	74	0	26	100
Adventurers	53	9	38	100

Table 206

"Young people these days understand more about honesty than most older people in their forties or fifties."

	Agree	Not Sure	Disagree	TOTAL
All adolescents	45%	3%	52%	100%
Boys	43	3	54	100
Boys 13–15	37	1	62	100
Boys 16–19	48	5	47	100
Girls	46	3	51	100
Girls 13–15	39	4	57	100
Girls 16–19	52	2	46	100
Virgins	38	3	59	100
Inexperienced	29	1	70	100
Beginners	46	2	52	100
Nonvirgins	51	4	45	100
Monogamists	55	1	44	100
Adventurers	54	8	38	100

Table 207

"Sex is immoral, unless it's between two people who love each other."

	Agree	Not Sure	Disagree	TOTAL
All adolescents	52%	2%	46%	100%
Boys	50	2	48	100
Boys 13–15	60	3	37	100
Boys 16–19	41	2	57	100
Girls	55	2	43	100
Girls 13–15	60	3	37	100
Girls 16–19	51	2	47	100
Virgins	61	4	35	100
Inexperienced	68	2	30	100
Beginners	53	1	46	100
Nonvirgins	44	1	55	100
Monogamists	45	0	55	100
Adventurers	43	3	54	100

Table 208

"A girl should stay a virgin until she finds the boy she wants to marry."

	Agree	Not Sure	Disagree	TOTAL
All adolescents	42%	2%	56%	100%
Boys	34	1	65	100
Boys 13–15	44	1	55	100
Boys 16–19	26	1	73	100
Girls	50	3	47	100
Girls 13–15	58	2	40	100
Girls 16–19	43	5	52	100
Virgins	58	3	39	100
Inexperienced	60	3	37	100
Beginners	59	0	41	100
Nonvirgins	27	2	71	100
Monogamists	31	2	67	100
Adventurers	20	3	77	100

Table 209

"If I found out that a girl had had sex for money, even once, I would lose respect for her."

	Agree	Not Sure	Disagree	TOTAL
All adolescents	61%	3%	36%	100%
Boys	54	5	41	100
Boys 13–15	65	3	32	100
Boys 16–19	46	6	48	100
Girls	68	1	31	100
Girls 13–15	73	1	26	100
Girls 16–19	64	0	36	100
Virgins	71	1	28	100
Inexperienced	71	1	28	100
Beginners	70	0	30	100
Nonvirgins	52	4	44	100
Monogamists	55	0	45	100
Adventurers	43	11	46	100

Table 210

"Organically grown food is much healthier than the food you get in most supermarkets."

	Agree	Not Sure	Disagree	TOTAL
All adolescents	61%	3%	36%	100%
Boys	60	3	37	100
Boys 13–15	59	5	36	100
Boys 16–19	60	1	39	100
Girls	63	2	35	100
Girls 13–15	61	4	35	100
Girls 16–19	65	1	34	100
Virgins	59	2	39	100
Inexperienced	50	2	48	100
Beginners	69	1	30	100
Nonvirgins	64	3	33	100
Monogamists	63	1	36	100
Adventurers	66	3	31	100

Table 211

"Sexual activities that society is opposed to are immoral."

	Agree	Not Sure	Disagree	TOTAL
All adolescents	38%	5%	57%	100%
Boys	37	6	57	100
Boys 13–15	51	6	43	100
Boys 16–19	26	7	67	100
Girls	38	3	59	100
Girls 13–15	44	5	51	100
Girls 16–19	33	2	65	100
Virgins	49	4	47	100
Inexperienced	60	2	38	100
Beginners	33	1	66	100
Nonvirgins	27	6	67	100
Monogamists	26	0	74	100
Adventurers	35	11	54	100

Table 212

"In some ways, I still think and act somewhat like a child."

	Agree	Not Sure	Disagree	TOTAL
All adolescents	63%	2%	35%	100%
Boys	61	3	36	100
Boys 13–15	67	2	31	100
Boys 16–19	55	4	41	100
Girls	65	1	34	100
Girls 13–15	66	2	32	100
Girls 16–19	65	0	35	100
Virgins	65	2	33	100
Inexperienced	66	1	33	100
Beginners	65	0	35	100
Nonvirgins	61	3	36	100
Monogamists	65	0	35	100
Adventurers	58	8	34	100

Table 213

"Young people these days tend to be more idealistic than most older people in their forties or fifties."

	Agree	Not Sure	Disagree	TOTAL
All adolescents	78%	4%	18%	100%
Boys	76	4	20	100
Boys 13–15	68	6	26	100
Boys 16–19	83	3	14	100
Girls	80	3	17	100
Girls 13–15	79	5	16	100
Girls 16–19	81	2	17	100
Virgins	75	5	20	100
Inexperienced	67	4	29	100
Beginners	93	3	4	100
Nonvirgins	81	3	16	100
Monogamists	79	0	21	100
Adventurers	80	5	15	100

Table 214

"There's nothing wrong with paying a girl for sex, if a boy can't get sex in any other way."

	Agree	Not Sure	Disagree	TOTAL
All adolescents	36%	2%	62%	100%
Boys	42	3	55	100
Boys 13–15	38	2	60	100
Boys 16–19	46	4	50	100
Girls	29	1	70	100
Girls 13–15	28	1	71	100
Girls 16–19	31	0	69	100
Virgins	22	1	77	100
Inexperienced	18	1	81	100
Beginners	29	2	69	100
Nonvirgins	49	2	49	100
Monogamists	55	1	44	100
Adventurers	52	5	43	100

Table 215

"When it comes to sex, some young people do the things they do mostly to spite their parents."

	Agree	Not Sure	Disagree	TOTAL
All adolescents	45%	2%	53%	100%
Boys	38	2	60	100
Boys 13–15	42	1	57	100
Boys 16–19	34	4	62	100
Girls	53	2	45	100
Girls 13–15	51	1	48	100
Girls 16–19	55	3	42	100
Virgins	48	3	49	100
Inexperienced	51	1	48	100
Beginners	46	2	52	100
Nonvirgins	42	2	56	100
Monogamists	50	1	49	100
Adventurers	30	5	65	100

Table 216

"It's immoral for a boy to force a girl to have sex, no matter what the circumstances."

	Agree	Not Sure	Disagree	TOTAL
All adolescents	88%	2%	10%	100%
Boys	85	3	12	100
Boys 13–15	82	3	15	100
Boys 16–19	87	3	10	100
Girls	92	1	7	100
Girls 13–15	88	2	10	100
Girls 16–19	94	2	4	100
Virgins	89	2	9	100
Inexperienced	90	1	9	100
Beginners	89	2	9	100
Nonvirgins	87	2	11	100
Monogamists	87	2	11	100
Adventurers	89	3	8	100

Table 217

"I believe that most young people can go directly from childhood to adulthood without being forced to go through a period of years that society defines as adolescence."

	Agree	Not Sure	Disagree	TOTAL
All adolescents	33%	3%	64%	100%
Boys	35	3	62	100
Boys 13–15	45	3	52	100
Boys 16–19	26	4	70	100
Girls	31	3	66	100
Girls 13–15	33	5	62	100
Girls 16–19	29	3	68	100
Virgins	27	4	69	100
Inexperienced	32	3	65	100
Beginners	20	1	79	100
Nonvirgins	38	3	59	100
Monogamists	31	1	68	100
Adventurers	45	5	50	100

Table 218

"Young people these days understand more about sex than most older people in their forties or fifties."

	Agree	Not Sure	Disagree	TOTAL
All adolescents	67%	2%	31%	100%
Boys	65	3	32	100
Boys 13–15	59	1	40	100
Boys 16–19	70	4	26	100
Girls	69	2	29	100
Girls 13–15	64	3	33	100
Girls 16–19	73	1	26	100
Virgins	57	2	41	100
Inexperienced	57	1	42	100
Beginners	57	1	42	100
Nonvirgins	76	2	22	100
Monogamists	78	1	21	100
Adventurers	70	5	25	100

Table 219

"It's right that we have laws saying people have to be married in order to live together."

	Agree	Not Sure	Disagree	TOTAL
All adolescents	37%	2%	61%	100%
Boys	28	1	71	100
Boys 13–15	40	2	58	100
Boys 16–19	18	1	81	100
Girls	47	2	51	100
Girls 13–15	54	2	44	100
Girls 16–19	40	2	58	100
Virgins	51	2	47	100
Inexperienced	58	1	41	100
Beginners	40	2	58	100
Nonvirgins	25	1	74	100
Monogamists	27	1	72	100
Adventurers	22	0	78	100

Table 220

"Sex is immoral, unless it's between two people who like each other and have something in common."

	Agree	Not Sure	Disagree	TOTAL
All adolescents	39%	3%	58%	100%
Boys	40	3	57	100
Boys 13–15	47	2	51	100
Boys 16–19	34	3	63	100
Girls	38	3	59	100
Girls 13–15	35	3	62	100
Girls 16–19	41	2	57	100
Virgins	40	5	55	100
Inexperienced	44	1	55	100
Beginners	36	4	60	100
Nonvirgins	38	1	61	100
Monogamists	38	1	61	100
Adventurers	45	0	55	100

Table 221

"Some girls use sex to reward or punish their boyfriends."

	Agree	Not Sure	Disagree	TOTAL
All adolescents	69%	2%	29%	100%
Boys	69	1	30	100
Boys 13–15	66	2	32	100
Boys 16–19	71	1	28	100
Girls	70	3	27	100
Girls 13–15	64	5	31	100
Girls 16–19	74	2	24	100
Virgins	65	3	32	100
Inexperienced	67	3	30	100
Beginners	65	2	33	100
Nonvirgins	74	1	25	100
Monogamists	75	1	24	100
Adventurers	79	2	19	100

Table 222

"My generation is going to do a better job of running things than the last generation has done."

	Agree	Not Sure	Disagree	TOTAL
All adolescents	53%	6%	41%	100%
Boys	55	7	38	100
Boys 13–15	52	3	45	100
Boys 16–19	58	9	33	100
Girls	50	5	45	100
Girls 13–15	50	4	46	100
Girls 16–19	50	6	44	100
Virgins	45	6	49	100
Inexperienced	36	4	60	100
Beginners	57	5	38	100
Nonvirgins	60	6	34	100
Monogamists	58	2	40	100
Adventurers	63	5	32	100

Table 223

"Anything two people want to do sexually is moral, as long as they both want to do it and it doesn't hurt either one of them."

	Agree	Not Sure	Disagree	TOTAL
All adolescents	69%	3%	28%	100%
Boys	71	2	27	100
Boys 13–15	64	3	33	100
Boys 16–19	77	2	21	100
Girls	66	4	30	100
Girls 13–15	70	5	25	100
Girls 16–19	62	3	35	100
Virgins	56	4	40	100
Inexperienced	53	5	42	100
Beginners	59	2	39	100
Nonvirgins	80	2	18	100
Monogamists	78	1	21	100
Adventurers	84	0	16	100

Table 224

"If two people are really in love, that love should last for life."

	Agree	Not Sure	Disagree	TOTAL
All adolescents	70%	3%	27%	100%
Boys	64	5	31	100
Boys 13–15	61	4	35	100
Boys 16–19	66	7	27	100
Girls	75	1	24	100
Girls 13–15	81	1	18	100
Girls 16–19	71	0	29	100
Virgins	75	3	22	100
Inexperienced	73	4	23	100
Beginners	77	2	21	100
Nonvirgins	65	4	31	100
Monogamists	70	3	27	100
Adventurers	61	9	30	100

Table 225

"Sex is immoral for people who are too young to understand what they are getting out of it."

	Agree	Not Sure	Disagree	TOTAL
All adolescents	69%	3%	28%	100%
Boys	63	3	34	100
Boys 13–15	73	2	25	100
Boys 16–19	55	4	41	100
Girls	75	3	22	100
Girls 13–15	79	4	17	100
Girls 16–19	73	2	25	100
Virgins	74	4	22	100
Inexperienced	84	1	15	100
Beginners	64	3	33	100
Nonvirgins	64	3	33	100
Monogamists	71	1	28	100
Adventurers	53	5	42	100

Table 226

"Young people these days tend to be less materialistic than most older people in their forties or fifties."

	Agree	Not Sure	Disagree	TOTAL
All adolescents	60%	3%	37%	100%
Boys	61	3	36	100
Boys 13–15	54	4	42	100
Boys 16–19	66	2	32	100
Girls	59	4	37	100
Girls 13–15	53	5	42	100
Girls 16–19	63	3	34	100
Virgins	57	5	38	100
Inexperienced	59	2	39	100
Beginners	60	5	35	100
Nonvirgins	62	2	36	100
Monogamists	63	2	35	100
Adventurers	63	0	37	100

Table 227

"A person who truly loves God doesn't have sexual relationships outside of marriage."

	Agree	Not Sure	Disagree	TOTAL
All adolescents	43%	2%	55%	100%
Boys	47	3	50	100
Boys 13–15	52	3	45	100
Boys 16–19	43	2	55	100
Girls	39	2	59	100
Girls 13–15	50	4	46	100
Girls 16–19	31	1	68	100
Virgins	50	2	48	100
Inexperienced	53	1	46	100
Beginners	48	2	50	100
Nonvirgins	37	2	61	100
Monogamists	28	1	71	100
Adventurers	41	1	58	100

Table 228

"Young people these days tend to be less considerate of others than most older people in their forties or fifties."

	Agree	Not Sure	Disagree	TOTAL
All adolescents	46%	4%	50%	100%
Boys	46	3	51	100
Boys 13–15	60	3	37	100
Boys 16–19	34	4	62	100
Girls	47	3	50	100
Girls 13–15	51	3	46	100
Girls 16–19	43	4	53	100
Virgins	50	3	47	100
Inexperienced	57	1	42	100
Beginners	40	3	57	100
Nonvirgins	43	4	53	100
Monogamists	44	3	53	100
Adventurers	44	0	56	100

Table 229

"Churches teach that enjoyment of sex is sinful."

	Agree	Not Sure	Disagree	TOTAL
All adolescents	49%	4%	47%	100%
Boys	53	2	45	100
Boys 13–15	55	2	43	100
Boys 16–19	51	2	47	100
Girls	45	7	48	100
Girls 13–15	42	9	49	100
Girls 16–19	47	5	48	100
Virgins	42	6	52	100
Inexperienced	47	3	50	100
Beginners	37	5	58	100
Nonvirgins	55	3	42	100
Monogamists	50	3	47	100
Adventurers	54	3	43	100

Table 230

"Young people these days understand more about what is really important in life than most older people in their forties or fifties."

	Agree	Not Sure	Disagree	TOTAL
All adolescents	56%	6%	38%	100%
Boys	59	6	35	100
Boys 13–15	47	7	46	100
Boys 16–19	68	6	26	100
Girls	54	4	42	100
Girls 13–15	49	6	45	100
Girls 16–19	58	3	39	100
Virgins	43	7	50	100
Inexperienced	36	7	57	100
Beginners	52	6	42	100
Nonvirgins	68	4	28	100
Monogamists	64	1	35	100
Adventurers	75	8	17	100

Table 231

"Sex is immoral, unless it's between two people who are married to each other."

	Agree	Not Sure	Disagree	TOTAL
All adolescents	25%	3%	72%	100%
Boys	21	3	76	100
Boys 13–15	38	2	60	100
Boys 16–19	7	3	90	100
Girls	30	2	68	100
Girls 13–15	38	3	59	100
Girls 16–19	23	2	75	100
Virgins	37	4	59	100
Inexperienced	53	1	46	100
Beginners	21	5	74	100
Nonvirgins	14	1	85	100
Monogamists	11	1	88	100
Adventurers	17	0	83	100

Table 232

"The government shouldn't be allowed to censor magazines or books, no matter how extreme they may be about sexual matters."

	Agree	Not Sure	Disagree	TOTAL
All adolescents	53%	3%	44%	100%
Boys	54	3	43	100
Boys 13–15	58	3	39	100
Boys 16–19	50	3	47	100
Girls	53	2	45	100
Girls 13–15	49	4	47	100
Girls 16–19	56	1	43	100
Virgins	46	5	49	100
Inexperienced	49	2	49	100
Beginners	44	5	51	100
Nonvirgins	59	1	40	100
Monogamists	55	1	44	100
Adventurers	65	1	34	100

Table 233

"The sexual behavior of most young people today would not be acceptable to society as a whole."

	Agree	Not Sure	Disagree	TOTAL
All adolescents	77%	2%	21%	100%
Boys	76	3	21	100
Boys 13–15	70	4	26	100
Boys 16–19	81	2	17	100
Girls	77	3	20	100
Girls 13–15	77	6	17	100
Girls 16–19	76	1	23	100
Virgins	74	3	23	100
Inexperienced	70	2	28	100
Beginners	80	3	17	100
Nonvirgins	79	2	19	100
Monogamists	76	2	22	100
Adventurers	92	0	8	100

Table 234

"Churches could be a big help to young people who are trying to find themselves."

	Agree	Not Sure	Disagree	TOTAL
All adolescents	78%	4%	18%	100%
Boys	74	4	22	100
Boys 13–15	76	3	21	100
Boys 16–19	73	5	22	100
Girls	82	3	15	100
Girls 13–15	69	7	24	100
Girls 16–19	92	0	8	100
Virgins	77	2	21	100
Inexperienced	79	1	20	100
Beginners	78	3	19	100
Nonvirgins	79	5	16	100
Monogamists	82	4	14	100
Adventurers	79	8	13	100

Table 235

"It's possible for love to be very real and very strong, but still not last for more than a few weeks."

	Agree	Not Sure	Disagree	TOTAL
All adolescents	48%	2%	50%	100%
Boys	52	1	47	100
Boys 13–15	61	2	37	100
Boys 16–19	45	0	55	100
Girls	45	2	53	100
Girls 13–15	48	4	48	100
Girls 16–19	43	0	57	100
Virgins	49	2	49	100
Inexperienced	50	1	49	100
Beginners	38	3	59	100
Nonvirgins	48	1	51	100
Monogamists	43	1	56	100
Adventurers	56	0	44	100

Table 236

"The most important thing in a love relationship is sex."

	Agree	Not Sure	Disagree	TOTAL
All adolescents	17%	1%	82%	100%
Boys	22	1	77	100
Boys 13–15	31	0	69	100
Boys 16–19	16	0	84	100
Girls	11	2	87	100
Girls 13–15	20	3	77	100
Girls 16–19	4	2	94	100
Virgins	16	3	81	100
Inexperienced	18	1	81	100
Beginners	12	3	85	100
Nonvirgins	17	1	82	100
Monogamists	7	1	92	100
Adventurers	25	0	75	100

Table 237

"Sex is one of the few human activities where there is always something new to be discovered."

	Agree	Not Sure	Disagree	TOTAL
All adolescents	63%	5%	32%	100%
Boys	65	4	31	100
Boys 13–15	63	6	31	100
Boys 16–19	67	2	31	100
Girls	61	6	33	100
Girls 13–15	64	7	29	100
Girls 16–19	58	5	37	100
Virgins	57	9	34	100
Inexperienced	54	6	40	100
Beginners	63	7	30	100
Nonvirgins	68	2	30	100
Monogamists	59	1	40	100
Adventurers	75	0	25	100

Table 238

"Over a period of time, I think it's better to have sexual relationships with several different people, rather than just one person."

	Agree	Not Sure	Disagree	TOTAL
All adolescents	40%	2%	58%	100%
Boys	52	2	46	100
Boys 13–15	49	3	48	100
Boys 16–19	55	1	44	100
Girls	27	3	70	100
Girls 13–15	33	5	62	100
Girls 16–19	21	3	76	100
Virgins	27	4	69	100
Inexperienced	24	2	74	100
Beginners	29	3	68	100
Nonvirgins	52	1	47	100
Monogamists	37	1	62	100
Adventurers	68	0	32	100

Table 239

"The laws against prostitution (having sex for money) should continue to remain in force."

	Agree	Not Sure	Disagree	TOTAL
All adolescents	58%	2%	40%	100%
Boys	49	2	49	100
Boys 13–15	61	0	39	100
Boys 16–19	40	4	56	100
Girls	67	2	31	100
Girls 13–15	74	4	22	100
Girls 16–19	60	2	38	100
Virgins	69	3	28	100
Inexperienced	78	1	21	100
Beginners	54	2	44	100
Nonvirgins	48	2	50	100
Monogamists	53	1	46	100
Adventurers	36	5	59	100

Table 240

"Where sex is concerned, anything people want to do is all right so long as they want to do it and it doesn't hurt them."

	Agree	Not Sure	Disagree	TOTAL
All adolescents	65%	2%	33%	100%
Boys	71	1	28	100
Boys 13–15	64	1	35	100
Boys 16–19	77	1	22	100
Girls	59	3	38	100
Girls 13–15	57	3	40	100
Girls 16–19	61	3	36	100
Virgins	52	3	45	100
Inexperienced	50	3	47	100
Beginners	56	3	41	100
Nonvirgins	77	2	21	100
Monogamists	72	1	27	100
Adventurers	87	2	11	100

Table 241

"A lot of young people are leaving home these days because they are seeking sexual freedom."

	Agree	Not Sure	Disagree	TOTAL
All adolescents	58%	4%	38%	100%
Boys	56	5	39	100
Boys 13–15	64	3	33	100
Boys 16–19	49	6	45	100
Girls	60	3	37	100
Girls 13–15	66	4	30	100
Girls 16–19	55	2	43	100
Virgins	58	4	38	100
Inexperienced	69	1	30	100
Beginners	49	6	45	100
Nonvirgins	57	3	40	100
Monogamists	55	2	43	100
Adventurers	63	7	30	100

Table 242

"One of the reasons why many young girls these days don't use birth control pills is that they're afraid their parents will find them."

	Agree	Not Sure	Disagree	TOTAL
All adolescents	58%	4%	38%	100%
Boys	59	4	37	100
Boys 13–15	58	4	38	100
Boys 16–19	60	4	36	100
Girls	57	4	39	100
Girls 13–15	61	4	35	100
Girls 16–19	55	3	42	100
Virgins	49	4	47	100
Inexperienced	42	1	57	100
Beginners	57	4	39	100
Nonvirgins	67	3	30	100
Monogamists	74	2	24	100
Adventurers	61	6	33	100

Table 243

"Hurting another person is wrong."

	Agree	Not Sure	Disagree	TOTAL
All adolescents	91%	1%	8%	100%
Boys	89	1	10	100
Boys 13–15	82	3	15	100
Boys 16–19	94	1	5	100
Girls	92	2	6	100
Girls 13–15	87	3	10	100
Girls 16–19	96	1	3	100
Virgins	89	3	8	100
Inexperienced	83	3	14	100
Beginners	92	2	6	100
Nonvirgins	92	0	8	100
Monogamists	92	1	7	100
Adventurers	95	0	5	100

Table 244

"Showing that young people have sexual freedom is one way of making the older generation realize that things are really changing in the world."

	Agree	Not Sure	Disagree	TOTAL
All adolescents	61%	4%	35%	100%
Boys	67	5	28	100
Boys 13–15	69	5	26	100
Boys 16–19	65	6	29	100
Girls	55	4	41	100
Girls 13–15	52	6	42	100
Girls 16–19	57	2	41	100
Virgins	52	5	43	100
Inexperienced	47	3	50	100
Beginners	62	4	34	100
Nonvirgins	69	4	27	100
Monogamists	66	1	33	100
Adventurers	60	9	31	100

Table 245

"One of the reasons why young people stop going to church is because churches teach that enjoyment of sex is sinful."

	Agree	Not Sure	Disagree	TOTAL
All adolescents	37%	4%	59%	100%
Boys	37	5	58	100
Boys 13–15	39	5	56	100
Boys 16–19	35	4	61	100
Girls	37	4	59	100
Girls 13–15	39	6	55	100
Girls 16–19	36	2	62	100
Virgins	31	6	63	100
Inexperienced	30	3	67	100
Beginners	31	5	64	100
Nonvirgins	43	3	54	100
Monogamists	40	1	59	100
Adventurers	39	4	57	100

Table 246

"Young people these days understand more about friendship than most older people in their forties or fifties."

	Agree	Not Sure	Disagree	TOTAL
All adolescents	57%	5%	38%	100%
Boys	58	4	38	100
Boys 13–15	53	3	44	100
Boys 16–19	62	5	33	100
Girls	56	5	39	100
Girls 13–15	54	5	41	100
Girls 16–19	57	4	39	100
Virgins	48	5	47	100
Inexperienced	49	3	48	100
Beginners	47	4	49	100
Nonvirgins	66	4	30	100
Monogamists	59	3	38	100
Adventurers	70	5	25	100

Table 247

"It's not wrong for a girl to have sex with someone for money, if that's what she wants to do."

	Agree	Not Sure	Disagree	TOTAL
All adolescents	50%	2%	48%	100%
Boys	57	2	41	100
Boys 13–15	54	1	45	100
Boys 16–19	60	3	37	100
Girls	43	2	55	100
Girls 13–15	48	3	49	100
Girls 16–19	40	1	59	100
Virgins	37	4	59	100
Inexperienced	34	1	65	100
Beginners	42	5	53	100
Nonvirgins	62	0	38	100
Monogamists	67	1	32	100
Adventurers	68	0	32	100

Table 248

"Young people these days understand more about love than most older people in their forties or fifties."

	Agree	Not Sure	Disagree	TOTAL
All adolescents	51%	3%	46%	100%
Boys	54	3	43	100
Boys 13–15	60	1	39	100
Boys 16–19	50	4	46	100
Girls	47	4	49	100
Girls 13–15	49	5	46	100
Girls 16–19	46	4	50	100
Virgins	40	4	56	100
Inexperienced	39	1	60	100
Beginners	36	4	60	100
Nonvirgins	60	4	36	100
Monogamists	48	5	47	100
Adventurers	70	0	30	100

Table 249

"When it comes to sex, a lot of young people these days do the things they do just because everyone else is doing it."

	Agree	Not Sure	Disagree	TOTAL
All adolescents	62%	4%	34%	100%
Boys	60	3	37	100
Boys 13–15	73	2	25	100
Boys 16–19	50	3	47	100
Girls	63	5	32	100
Girls 13–15	67	5	28	100
Girls 16–19	61	4	35	100
Virgins	65	5	30	100
Inexperienced	74	2	24	100
Beginners	60	7	33	100
Nonvirgins	58	3	39	100
Monogamists	54	2	44	100
Adventurers	54	5	41	100

Table 250

"The government shouldn't try to keep people from seeing any kind of sex movies that they want to see—even if they're so dirty I wouldn't want to see them myself."

	Agree	Not Sure	Disagree	TOTAL
All adolescents	66%	3%	31%	100%
Boys	67	2	31	100
Boys 13–15	56	2	42	100
Boys 16–19	77	1	22	100
Girls	64	4	32	100
Girls 13–15	65	5	30	100
Girls 16–19	64	3	33	100
Virgins	57	4	39	100
Inexperienced	51	0	49	100
Beginners	75	3	22	100
Nonvirgins	74	1	25	100
Monogamists	63	3	34	100
Adventurers	84	1	15	100

Table 251

"If a girl has led a boy on, it's all right for the boy to force her to have sex."

	Agree	Not Sure	Disagree	TOTAL
All adolescents	26%	4%	70%	100%
Boys	26	5	69	100
Boys 13–15	29	7	64	100
Boys 16–19	24	3	73	100
Girls	25	4	71	100
Girls 13–15	33	6	61	100
Girls 16–19	18	2	80	100
Virgins	24	6	70	100
Inexperienced	28	0	72	100
Beginners	23	2	75	100
Nonvirgins	27	2	71	100
Monogamists	22	0	78	100
Adventurers	31	2	67	100

Table 252

"Twenty years from now, most of the people in my generation are going to be living happier lives than most older people in their forties or fifties live now."

	Agree	Not Sure	Disagree	TOTAL
All adolescents	49%	7%	44%	100%
Boys	48	8	44	100
Boys 13–15	51	11	38	100
Boys 16–19	46	6	48	100
Girls	50	6	44	100
Girls 13–15	47	6	47	100
Girls 16–19	53	6	41	100
Virgins	38	11	51	100
Inexperienced	42	5	53	100
Beginners	34	6	60	100
Nonvirgins	60	3	37	100
Monogamists	60	3	37	100
Adventurers	67	3	30	100

Table 253

"Churches are really doing their best to understand young people's ideas about sex."

	Agree	Not Sure	Disagree	TOTAL
All adolescents	45%	7%	48%	100%
Boys	50	6	44	100
Boys 13–15	61	7	32	100
Boys 16–19	40	5	55	100
Girls	41	8	51	100
Girls 13–15	43	12	45	100
Girls 16–19	39	5	56	100
Virgins	51	10	39	100
Inexperienced	53	3	44	100
Beginners	58	4	38	100
Nonvirgins	41	4	55	100
Monogamists	37	0	63	100
Adventurers	40	8	52	100

Table 254

"I'm not a child anymore, but I'm not an adult yet, either."

	Agree	Not Sure	Disagree	TOTAL
All adolescents	73%	4%	23%	100%
Boys	72	4	24	100
Boys 13–15	83	5	12	100
Boys 16–19	64	3	33	100
Girls	73	5	22	100
Girls 13–15	85	7	8	100
Girls 16–19	64	3	33	100
Virgins	79	6	15	100
Inexperienced	90	1	9	100
Beginners	77	2	21	100
Nonvirgins	67	3	30	100
Monogamists	60	1	39	100
Adventurers	67	3	30	100

Table 255

"If two boys want to have sex together, it's all right so long as they both want to do it."

	Agree	Not Sure	Disagree	TOTAL
All adolescents	41%	5%	54%	100%
Boys	41	5	54	100
Boys 13–15	40	6	54	100
Boys 16–19	42	4	54	100
Girls	41	6	53	100
Girls 13–15	39	10	51	100
Girls 16–19	43	3	54	100
Virgins	32	8	60	100
Inexperienced	35	3	62	100
Beginners	40	2	58	100
Nonvirgins	50	2	48	100
Monogamists	46	0	54	100
Adventurers	54	3	43	100

Table 256

"Physical attractiveness of the other person is more important in love than it is in sex."

	Agree	Not Sure	Disagree	TOTAL
All adolescents	45%	8%	47%	100%
Boys	40	8	52	100
Boys 13–15	41	9	50	100
Boys 16–19	39	8	53	100
Girls	50	7	43	100
Girls 13–15	54	11	35	100
Girls 16–19	47	4	49	100
Virgins	45	10	45	100
Inexperienced	56	3	41	100
Beginners	42	5	53	100
Nonvirgins	44	6	50	100
Monogamists	48	3	49	100
Adventurers	45	6	49	100

Table 257

"A lot of the pleasure in sex would be lost if it did not seem to be such a forbidden activity."

	Agree	Not Sure	Disagree	TOTAL
All adolescents	38%	7%	55%	100%
Boys	40	7	53	100
Boys 13–15	48	10	42	100
Boys 16–19	33	4	63	100
Girls	36	7	57	100
Girls 13–15	45	12	43	100
Girls 16–19	28	4	68	100
Virgins	41	10	49	100
Inexperienced	39	4	57	100
Beginners	44	4	52	100
Nonvirgins	35	4	61	100
Monogamists	22	2	76	100
Adventurers	34	3	63	100

Table 258

"When it comes to morality in sex, the important thing is the way people treat each other, not the particular things that they do together."

	Agree	Not Sure	Disagree	TOTAL
All adolescents	72%	8%	20%	100%
Boys	70	7	23	100
Boys 13–15	65	10	25	100
Boys 16–19	74	4	22	100
Girls	75	9	16	100
Girls 13–15	76	12	12	100
Girls 16–19	75	6	19	100
Virgins	66	11	23	100
Inexperienced	68	4	28	100
Beginners	75	5	20	100
Nonvirgins	78	5	17	100
Monogamists	79	3	18	100
Adventurers	79	3	18	100

Table 259

"If two girls want to have sex together, it's all right so long as they both want to do it."

	Agree	Not Sure	Disagree	TOTAL
All adolescents	41%	6%	53%	100%
Boys	41	5	54	100
Boys 13–15	36	7	57	100
Boys 16–19	45	4	51	100
Girls	40	7	53	100
Girls 13–15	40	11	49	100
Girls 16–19	40	5	55	100
Virgins	31	9	60	100
Inexperienced	32	4	64	100
Beginners	38	3	59	100
Nonvirgins	50	3	47	100
Monogamists	46	0	54	100
Adventurers	58	5	37	100

Table 260

"A young person who has sex only for physical enjoyment and nothing else is doing something immoral."

	Agree	Not Sure	Disagree	TOTAL
All adolescents	52%	6%	42%	100%
Boys	49	6	45	100
Boys 13–15	56	8	36	100
Boys 16–19	44	4	52	100
Girls	55	6	39	100
Girls 13–15	61	9	30	100
Girls 16–19	51	3	46	100
Virgins	62	8	30	100
Inexperienced	73	2	25	100
Beginners	56	3	41	100
Nonvirgins	43	4	53	100
Monogamists	46	0	54	100
Adventurers	50	3	47	100

Table 261

"There is no kind of sex act that I would think of as being abnormal, so long as the people involved want to do it."

	Agree	Not Sure	Disagree	TOTAL
All adolescents	46%	6%	48%	100%
Boys	49	6	45	100
Boys 13–15	42	10	48	100
Boys 16–19	54	4	42	100
Girls	43	7	50	100
Girls 13–15	44	10	46	100
Girls 16–19	43	3	54	100
Virgins	35	10	55	100
Inexperienced	30	4	66	100
Beginners	45	4	51	100
Nonvirgins	56	4	40	100
Monogamists	52	1	47	100
Adventurers	71	3	26	100

Table 262

"If two people are in love, it's only natural for them to want to get married."

	Agree	Not Sure	Disagree	TOTAL
All adolescents	68%	3%	29%	100%
Boys	61	4	35	100
Boys 13–15	68	4	28	100
Boys 16–19	56	4	40	100
Girls	75	3	22	100
Girls 13–15	80	5	15	100
Girls 16–19	71	1	28	100
Virgins	78	4	18	100
Inexperienced	78	2	20	100
Beginners	80	1	19	100
Nonvirgins	59	3	38	100
Monogamists	64	0	36	100
Adventurers	54	3	43	100

Table 263

"The way I'm living right now, most of my abilities are going to waste."

	Agree	Not Sure	Disagree	TOTAL
All adolescents	31%	4%	65%	100%
Boys	36	4	60	100
Boys 13–15	28	5	67	100
Boys 16–19	43	3	54	100
Girls	27	4	69	100
Girls 13–15	29	7	64	100
Girls 16–19	25	1	74	100
Virgins	27	5	68	100
Inexperienced	27	2	71	100
Beginners	25	1	74	100
Nonvirgins	35	3	62	100
Monogamists	29	1	70	100
Adventurers	46	3	51	100

Table 264

"It's not so important that a child live in a home with both of his parents, so long as he has a good relationship with each of his parents individually."

	Agree	Not Sure	Disagree	TOTAL
All adolescents	63%	4%	33%	100%
Boys	61	3	36	100
Boys 13–15	60	4	36	100
Boys 16–19	62	3	35	100
Girls	65	4	31	100
Girls 13–15	55	7	38	100
Girls 16–19	73	1	26	100
Virgins	56	5	39	100
Inexperienced	55	3	42	100
Beginners	65	1	34	100
Nonvirgins	69	2	29	100
Monogamists	71	0	29	100
Adventurers	79	3	18	100

Table 265

"Marriage would make sex even more enjoyable, because both people would know that they really belong to each other."

	Agree	Not Sure	Disagree	TOTAL
All adolescents	68%	5%	27%	100%
Boys	64	5	31	100
Boys 13–15	67	7	26	100
Boys 16–19	62	4	34	100
Girls	72	5	23	100
Girls 13–15	73	8	19	100
Girls 16–19	71	2	27	100
Virgins	76	7	17	100
Inexperienced	70	3	27	100
Beginners	88	2	10	100
Nonvirgins	60	4	36	100
Monogamists	62	0	38	100
Adventurers	62	6	32	100

Table 266

"The most important thing in a sexual relationship is just the sheer physical pleasure of having sex."

	Agree	Not Sure	Disagree	TOTAL
All adolescents	26%	5%	69%	100%
Boys	36	6	58	100
Boys 13–15	39	8	53	100
Boys 16–19	34	4	62	100
Girls	16	5	79	100
Girls 13–15	21	8	71	100
Girls 16–19	12	2	86	100
Virgins	19	7	74	100
Inexperienced	19	4	77	100
Beginners	19	2	79	100
Nonvirgins	33	3	64	100
Monogamists	19	0	81	100
Adventurers	44	3	53	100

Table 267

"The cancer scare about cigarette smoking has been exaggerated."

	Agree	Not Sure	Disagree	TOTAL
All adolescents	29%	5%	66%	100%
Boys	28	6	66	100
Boys 13–15	26	10	64	100
Boys 16–19	30	3	67	100
Girls	31	4	65	100
Girls 13–15	34	9	57	100
Girls 16–19	27	1	72	100
Virgins	25	6	69	100
Inexperienced	22	4	74	100
Beginners	25	1	74	100
Nonvirgins	33	5	62	100
Monogamists	30	0	70	100
Adventurers	41	7	52	100

Table 268

"The women's liberation movement has been a good thing for women."

	Agree	Not Sure	Disagree	TOTAL
All adolescents	45%	4%	51%	100%
Boys	48	5	47	100
Boys 13–15	50	4	46	100
Boys 16–19	47	5	48	100
Girls	41	4	55	100
Girls 13–15	32	8	60	100
Girls 16–19	47	1	52	100
Virgins	37	5	58	100
Inexperienced	42	2	56	100
Beginners	33	1	66	100
Nonvirgins	51	3	46	100
Monogamists	50	0	50	100
Adventurers	58	3	39	100

Table 269

"Alcohol increases sexual pleasure."

	Agree	Not Sure	Disagree	TOTAL
All adolescents	42%	7%	51%	100%
Boys	34	7	59	100
Boys 13–15	45	10	45	100
Boys 16–19	25	5	70	100
Girls	50	6	44	100
Girls 13–15	53	10	37	100
Girls 16–19	48	3	49	100
Virgins	48	9	43	100
Inexperienced	48	9	43	100
Beginners	48	1	51	100
Nonvirgins	36	5	59	100
Monogamists	34	2	64	100
Adventurers	31	8	61	100

Table 270

"My sexual behavior would not be acceptable to society."

	Agree	Not Sure	Disagree	TOTAL
All adolescents	38%	6%	56%	100%
Boys	46	6	48	100
Boys 13–15	44	7	49	100
Boys 16–19	49	5	46	100
Girls	29	6	65	100
Girls 13–15	23	9	68	100
Girls 16–19	34	3	63	100
Virgins	21	7	72	100
Inexperienced	24	4	72	100
Beginners	17	2	81	100
Nonvirgins	54	4	42	100
Monogamists	55	1	44	100
Adventurers	66	3	31	100

Table 271

"It would be wrong to take advantage of a girl who was stoned or drunk by having sex with her."

	Agree	Not Sure	Disagree	TOTAL
All adolescents	76%	4%	20%	100%
Boys	70	4	26	100
Boys 13–15	75	5	20	100
Boys 16–19	65	4	31	100
Girls	82	5	13	100
Girls 13–15	79	9	12	100
Girls 16–19	84	1	15	100
Virgins	81	6	13	100
Inexperienced	87	2	11	100
Beginners	85	2	13	100
Nonvirgins	71	3	26	100
Monogamists	79	2	19	100
Adventurers	70	4	26	100

Table 272

"The only good reason for getting married is if a baby is on the way."

	Agree	Not Sure	Disagree	TOTAL
All adolescents	9%	4%	87%	100%
Boys	14	4	82	100
Boys 13–15	20	5	75	100
Boys 16–19	9	4	87	100
Girls	5	3	92	100
Girls 13–15	6	7	87	100
Girls 16–19	4	0	96	100
Virgins	9	5	86	100
Inexperienced	15	2	83	100
Beginners	2	2	96	100
Nonvirgins	10	2	88	100
Monogamists	6	0	94	100
Adventurers	14	3	83	100

Table 273

"In general, I think that so far I've been able to achieve most of the things that I've set out to achieve."

	Agree	Not Sure	Disagree	TOTAL
All adolescents	61%	5%	34%	100%
Boys	58	5	37	100
Boys 13–15	66	7	27	100
Boys 16–19	52	4	44	100
Girls	63	5	32	100
Girls 13–15	60	10	30	100
Girls 16–19	66	1	33	100
Virgins	61	6	33	100
Inexperienced	66	5	29	100
Beginners	61	2	37	100
Nonvirgins	61	4	35	100
Monogamists	64	0	36	100
Adventurers	64	6	30	100

Table 274

"When it comes to deciding how far a boy and girl should go where sex is concerned, it is up to the girl to decide."

	Agree	Not Sure	Disagree	TOTAL
All adolescents	42%	5%	53%	100%
Boys	42	5	53	100
Boys 13–15	42	6	52	100
Boys 16–19	42	5	53	100
Girls	41	5	54	100
Girls 13–15	51	8	41	100
Girls 16–19	34	2	64	100
Virgins	40	6	54	100
Inexperienced	38	3	59	100
Beginners	41	2	57	100
Nonvirgins	44	3	53	100
Monogamists	31	1	68	100
Adventurers	55	4	41	100

Table 275

"Most girls these days have sexual intercourse before they are married."

	Agree	Not Sure	Disagree	TOTAL
All adolescents	76%	4%	20%	100%
Boys	72	5	23	100
Boys 13–15	68	4	28	100
Boys 16–19	76	5	19	100
Girls	79	5	16	100
Girls 13–15	74	7	19	100
Girls 16–19	85	2	13	100
Virgins	66	6	28	100
Inexperienced	58	4	38	100
Beginners	80	0	20	100
Nonvirgins	84	4	12	100
Monogamists	83	3	14	100
Adventurers	91	3	6	100

Table 276

"When a boy has sex for the first time, it should be with a girl who is sexually experienced."

	Agree	Not Sure	Disagree	TOTAL
All adolescents	29%	6%	65%	100%
Boys	34	7	59	100
Boys 13–15	37	10	53	100
Boys 16–19	32	4	64	100
Girls	23	6	71	100
Girls 13–15	17	10	73	100
Girls 16–19	28	3	69	100
Virgins	19	10	71	100
Inexperienced	17	6	77	100
Beginners	25	3	72	100
Nonvirgins	38	3	59	100
Monogamists	33	0	67	100
Adventurers	50	4	46	100

Table 277

"Young people don't really want independence from society; they only want independence from their parents."

	Agree	Not Sure	Disagree	TOTAL
All adolescents	43%	7%	50%	100%
Boys	38	8	54	100
Boys 13–15	44	14	42	100
Boys 16–19	33	4	63	100
Girls	49	5	46	100
Girls 13–15	56	7	37	100
Girls 16–19	43	2	55	100
Virgins	45	11	44	100
Inexperienced	44	10	46	100
Beginners	53	5	42	100
Nonvirgins	41	3	56	100
Monogamists	44	0	56	100
Adventurers	41	3	56	100

Table 278

"If two people are going to have a baby that neither person really wants, it is all right for the girl to have an abortion."

	Agree	Not Sure	Disagree	TOTAL
All adolescents	51%	4%	45%	100%
Boys	55	5	40	100
Boys 13–15	52	5	43	100
Boys 16–19	57	5	38	100
Girls	46	4	50	100
Girls 13–15	43	5	52	100
Girls 16–19	50	2	48	100
Virgins	42	7	51	100
Inexperienced	48	3	49	100
Beginners	37	7	56	100
Nonvirgins	59	2	39	100
Monogamists	60	0	40	100
Adventurers	70	3	27	100

Table 279

"Having sex together is a good way for two people to become acquainted."

	Agree	Not Sure	Disagree	TOTAL
All adolescents	34%	3%	63%	100%
Boys	50	3	47	100
Boys 13–15	42	4	54	100
Boys 16–19	57	3	40	100
Girls	17	4	79	100
Girls 13–15	14	7	79	100
Girls 16–19	20	0	80	100
Virgins	19	5	76	100
Inexperienced	14	2	84	100
Beginners	25	1	74	100
Nonvirgins	48	2	50	100
Monogamists	38	0	62	100
Adventurers	60	3	37	100

Table 280

"It's possible for love to be very real and very strong, but still not last for more than a few years."

	Agree	Not Sure	Disagree	TOTAL
All adolescents	59%	3%	38%	100%
Boys	60	4	36	100
Boys 13–15	59	4	37	100
Boys 16–19	61	3	36	100
Girls	58	3	39	100
Girls 13–15	61	6	33	100
Girls 16–19	54	1	45	100
Virgins	54	4	42	100
Inexperienced	52	2	46	100
Beginners	51	2	47	100
Nonvirgins	63	3	34	100
Monogamists	58	0	42	100
Adventurers	65	3	32	100

Table 281

"It's all right for married people to have sexual relations with other people once in a while for the sake of variety."

	Agree	Not Sure	Disagree	TOTAL
All adolescents	34%	4%	62%	100%
Boys	42	4	54	100
Boys 13–15	42	3	55	100
Boys 16–19	42	4	54	100
Girls	26	4	70	100
Girls 13–15	27	9	64	100
Girls 16–19	25	1	74	100
Virgins	24	5	71	100
Inexperienced	26	2	72	100
Beginners	17	2	81	100
Nonvirgins	43	3	54	100
Monogamists	33	1	66	100
Adventurers	60	6	34	100

Table 282

"It's all right for a person to have sexual relations with both males and females, if that's what the person wants to do."

	Agree	Not Sure	Disagree	TOTAL
All adolescents	42%	4%	54%	100%
Boys	44	4	52	100
Boys 13–15	40	3	57	100
Boys 16–19	47	4	49	100
Girls	39	5	56	100
Girls 13–15	37	10	53	100
Girls 16–19	41	1	58	100
Virgins	29	7	64	100
Inexperienced	30	4	66	100
Beginners	33	4	63	100
Nonvirgins	53	2	45	100
Monogamists	52	0	48	100
Adventurers	63	3	34	100

Table 283

"It is really a tragedy if a couple that has children breaks up."

	Agree	Not Sure	Disagree	TOTAL
All adolescents	72%	4%	24%	100%
Boys	72	4	24	100
Boys 13–15	76	4	20	100
Boys 16–19	70	3	27	100
Girls	72	3	25	100
Girls 13–15	72	7	21	100
Girls 16–19	72	0	28	100
Virgins	76	4	20	100
Inexperienced	75	2	23	100
Beginners	80	2	18	100
Nonvirgins	69	3	28	100
Monogamists	71	2	27	100
Adventurers	66	3	31	100

Table 284

"If a boy finds out that he has VD, he should immediately tell any girl he has recently had sex with."

	Agree	Not Sure	Disagree	TOTAL
All adolescents	88%	3%	9%	100%
Boys	84	4	12	100
Boys 13–15	79	4	17	100
Boys 16–19	88	3	9	100
Girls	93	2	5	100
Girls 13–15	91	5	4	100
Girls 16–19	94	0	6	100
Virgins	85	4	11	100
Inexperienced	79	2	19	100
Beginners	99	0	1	100
Nonvirgins	91	2	7	100
Monogamists	95	0	5	100
Adventurers	85	3	12	100

Table 285

"Sex education courses in school are valuable for young people."

	Agree	Not Sure	Disagree	TOTAL
All adolescents	80%	4%	16%	100%
Boys	75	6	19	100
Boys 13–15	68	10	22	100
Boys 16–19	82	3	15	100
Girls	85	3	12	100
Girls 13–15	86	6	8	100
Girls 16–19	84	1	15	100
Virgins	76	7	17	100
Inexperienced	78	6	16	100
Beginners	82	3	15	100
Nonvirgins	83	3	14	100
Monogamists	93	0	7	100
Adventurers	82	3	15	100

Table 286

"Marijuana increases sexual pleasure."

	Agree	Not Sure	Disagree	TOTAL
All adolescents	38%	9%	53%	100%
Boys	37	10	53	100
Boys 13–15	36	12	52	100
Boys 16–19	37	8	55	100
Girls	39	8	53	100
Girls 13–15	43	10	47	100
Girls 16–19	36	6	58	100
Virgins	33	10	57	100
Inexperienced	37	6	57	100
Beginners	26	7	67	100
Nonvirgins	42	8	50	100
Monogamists	40	4	56	100
Adventurers	42	10	48	100

Table 287

"If a girl truly doesn't want to have a baby, she won't get pregnant even though she may have sex without taking any birth control precautions."

	Agree	Not Sure	Disagree	TOTAL
All adolescents	32%	5%	63%	100%
Boys	33	6	61	100
Boys 13–15	40	7	53	100
Boys 16–19	28	5	67	100
Girls	30	4	66	100
Girls 13–15	39	8	53	100
Girls 16–19	22	2	76	100
Virgins	28	7	65	100
Inexperienced	34	4	62	100
Beginners	20	1	79	100
Nonvirgins	34	4	62	100
Monogamists	26	0	74	100
Adventurers	43	3	54	100

Table 288

"It's important that I try to develop my own set of personal values."

	Agree	Not Sure	Disagree	TOTAL
All adolescents	90%	4%	6%	100%
Boys	88	4	8	100
Boys 13–15	82	5	13	100
Boys 16–19	93	4	3	100
Girls	92	3	5	100
Girls 13–15	87	7	6	100
Girls 16–19	97	0	3	100
Virgins	88	6	6	100
Inexperienced	88	3	9	100
Beginners	95	1	4	100
Nonvirgins	92	2	6	100
Monogamists	97	0	3	100
Adventurers	93	3	4	100

Table 289

"Too many young people these days are irresponsible where sex is concerned."

	Agree	Not Sure	Disagree	TOTAL
All adolescents	74%	4%	22%	100%
Boys	68	6	26	100
Boys 13–15	64	8	28	100
Boys 16–19	72	3	25	100
Girls	79	3	18	100
Girls 13–15	74	7	19	100
Girls 16–19	84	0	16	100
Virgins	73	5	22	100
Inexperienced	73	2	25	100
Beginners	78	0	22	100
Nonvirgins	74	4	22	100
Monogamists	82	1	17	100
Adventurers	76	3	21	100

Table 290

"If older people would only remember what they were like when they were young, they would understand how young people think today."

	Agree	Not Sure	Disagree	TOTAL
All adolescents	76%	5%	19%	100%
Boys	79	5	16	100
Boys 13–15	79	8	13	100
Boys 16–19	79	4	17	100
Girls	73	5	22	100
Girls 13–15	74	9	17	100
Girls 16–19	71	3	26	100
Virgins	71	8	21	100
Inexperienced	71	6	23	100
Beginners	84	1	15	100
Nonvirgins	80	3	17	100
Monogamists	80	2	18	100
Adventurers	76	3	21	100

Table 291

"If two people love each other and are living together, getting married is just a legal technicality."

	Agree	Not Sure	Disagree	TOTAL
All adolescents	67%	4%	29%	100%
Boys	73	4	23	100
Boys 13–15	67	4	29	100
Boys 16–19	79	4	17	100
Girls	60	4	36	100
Girls 13–15	60	7	33	100
Girls 16–19	61	2	37	100
Virgins	58	6	36	100
Inexperienced	62	2	36	100
Beginners	60	2	38	100
Nonvirgins	75	3	22	100
Monogamists	71	2	27	100
Adventurers	87	3	10	100

Table 292

"Most boys these days have sexual intercourse before they are married."

	Agree	Not Sure	Disagree	TOTAL
All adolescents	81%	5%	14%	100%
Boys	77	6	17	100
Boys 13–15	67	6	27	100
Boys 16–19	85	5	10	100
Girls	85	4	11	100
Girls 13–15	78	8	14	100
Girls 16–19	90	1	9	100
Virgins	72	5	23	100
Inexperienced	67	3	30	100
Beginners	81	2	17	100
Nonvirgins	89	5	6	100
Monogamists	95	0	5	100
Adventurers	86	7	7	100

Table 293

"When a girl has sex for the first time, it should be with a boy who is sexually experienced."

	Agree	Not Sure	Disagree	TOTAL
All adolescents	37%	5%	58%	100%
Boys	40	5	55	100
Boys 13–15	46	4	50	100
Boys 16–19	36	5	59	100
Girls	35	4	61	100
Girls 13–15	33	9	58	100
Girls 16–19	36	1	63	100
Virgins	24	6	70	100
Inexperienced	21	4	75	100
Beginners	26	1	73	100
Nonvirgins	50	3	47	100
Monogamists	47	2	51	100
Adventurers	60	2	38	100

Table 294

"If parents no longer love each other, it's better for their children that the parents break up rather than continue to live together unhappily."

	Agree	Not Sure	Disagree	TOTAL
All adolescents	68%	5%	27%	100%
Boys	59	8	33	100
Boys 13–15	53	8	39	100
Boys 16–19	65	7	28	100
Girls	76	3	21	100
Girls 13–15	73	5	22	100
Girls 16–19	78	1	21	100
Virgins	66	6	28	100
Inexperienced	58	1	41	100
Beginners	77	7	16	100
Nonvirgins	69	4	27	100
Monogamists	71	0	29	100
Adventurers	68	7	25	100

Table 295

"The main reason why people are more casual about sex these days is because birth control is easily available to everyone."

	Agree	Not Sure	Disagree	TOTAL
All adolescents	61%	5%	34%	100%
Boys	63	4	33	100
Boys 13–15	58	5	37	100
Boys 16–19	67	4	29	100
Girls	58	5	37	100
Girls 13–15	60	9	31	100
Girls 16–19	57	2	41	100
Virgins	54	6	40	100
Inexperienced	55	4	41	100
Beginners	56	1	43	100
Nonvirgins	67	3	30	100
Monogamists	68	0	32	100
Adventurers	66	5	29	100

Table 296

"It is immoral to bring an unwanted child into this overpopulated world, especially now that abortions are so easy to get."

	Agree	Not Sure	Disagree	TOTAL
All adolescents	49%	5%	46%	100%
Boys	49	6	45	100
Boys 13–15	54	6	40	100
Boys 16–19	44	6	50	100
Girls	49	4	47	100
Girls 13–15	43	8	49	100
Girls 16–19	54	1	45	100
Virgins	41	5	54	100
Inexperienced	47	1	52	100
Beginners	38	1	61	100
Nonvirgins	56	5	39	100
Monogamists	58	0	42	100
Adventurers	49	10	41	100

Table 297

Male: "Have you ever wanted to have sex with a girl but decided not to do so because you were afraid of catching VD, or venereal disease?"

Female: "Have you ever wanted to have sex with a boy but decided not to do so because you were afraid of catching VD, or venereal disease?"

Nonvirgin adolescents	Yes	No	TOTAL
All	29%	71%	100%
Boys	34	66	100
Boys 13–15	33	67	100
Boys 16–19	34	66	100
Girls	23	77	100
Girls 13–15	27	73	100
Girls 16–19	21	79	100
Monogamists	28	72	100
Adventurers	37	63	100

Table 298

"I have never had VD, or venereal disease."

Nonvirgin adolescents	True	Not Sure	False	TOTAL
All	86%	4%	10%	100%
Boys	85	4	11	100
Boys 13–15	86	6	8	100
Boys 16–19	85	3	12	100
Girls	88	2	10	100
Girls 13–15	89	4	7	100
Girls 16–19	87	2	11	100
Monogamists	87	1	12	100
Adventurers	85	4	11	100

Table 299

"On one or more occasions, under the influence of alcohol, I've had sex with someone that I wouldn't have had sex with otherwise."

Nonvirgin adolescents	True	Not Sure	False	TOTAL
All	29%	0%	71%	100%
Boys	31	1	68	100
Boys 13–15	42	0	58	100
Boys 16–19	25	1	74	100
Girls	26	0	74	100
Girls 13–15	23	0	77	100
Girls 16–19	28	0	72	100
Monogamists	24	0	76	100
Adventurers	42	1	57	100

Table 300

"If I go for a long time without having sex, I get to feeling uptight."

Nonvirgin adolescents	True	Not Sure	False	TOTAL
All	43%	1%	56%	100%
Boys	53	1	46	100
Boys 13–15	45	0	55	100
Boys 16–19	57	1	42	100
Girls	30	0	70	100
Girls 13–15	34	0	66	100
Girls 16–19	29	0	71	100
Monogamists	42	0	58	100
Adventurers	55	0	45	100

Table 301

"Having sex helps me take my mind off some of the bad things that happen to me."

Nonvirgin adolescents	True	Not Sure	False	TOTAL
All	46%	1%	53%	100%
Boys	56	2	42	100
Boys 13–15	60	2	38	100
Boys 16–19	54	2	44	100
Girls	33	0	67	100
Girls 13–15	33	0	67	100
Girls 16–19	33	0	67	100
Monogamists	43	0	57	100
Adventurers	43	2	55	100

Table 302

Male: "I've never had sex with a girl, because I haven't yet met a girl who I would want to have sex with."

Female: "I've never had sex with a boy, because I haven't yet met a boy who I would want to have sex with."

Virgin adolescents	True	Not Sure	False	TOTAL
All	56%	6%	38%	100%
Boys	55	6	39	100
Boys 13–15	56	6	38	100
Boys 16–19	52	7	41	100
Girls	56	7	37	100
Girls 13–15	60	8	32	100
Girls 16–19	51	5	44	100
Inexperienced	58	3	39	100
Beginners	51	5	44	100

Table 303

Female: "I don't use birth control pills or other contraceptives because my parents might find them."

Nonvirgin girls	True	Not Sure	False	TOTAL
All	29%	1%	70%	100%
Girls 13–15	58	1	41	100
Girls 16–19	17	1	82	100
Monogamists	21	1	78	100
Adventurers	33	0	67	100

Table 304

Male: "I've never had sex with a girl, because I'm not really ready for it."

Female: "I've never had sex with a boy, because I'm not really ready for it."

Virgin adolescents	True	Not Sure	False	TOTAL
All	56%	6%	38%	100%
Boys	56	7	37	100
Boys 13–15	68	8	24	100
Boys 16–19	34	7	59	100
Girls	56	6	38	100
Girls 13–15	63	7	30	100
Girls 16–19	48	4	48	100
Inexperienced	75	2	23	100
Beginners	37	5	58	100

Table 305

Male: "I've never had sex with a girl, because I haven't yet met a girl who wants to have sex with me."

Female: "I've never had sex with a boy, because I haven't yet met a boy who wants to have sex with me."

Virgin adolescents	True	Not Sure	False	TOTAL
All	26%	8%	66%	100%
Boys	36	7	57	100
Boys 13–15	42	7	51	100
Boys 16–19	25	7	68	100
Girls	18	10	72	100
Girls 13–15	25	12	63	100
Girls 16–19	10	7	83	100
Inexperienced	39	4	57	100
Beginners	14	7	79	100

Table 306

Female: "Getting pregnant is something that happens to *other* girls; I just can't believe that it could really happen to *me*."

Nonvirgin girls	True	Not Sure	False	TOTAL
All	15%	0%	85%	100%
Girls 13–15	20	0	80	100
Girls 16–19	13	0	87	100
Monogamists	9	0	91	100
Adventurers	19	0	81	100

Table 307

Female: "Sometimes when I have sex, I just get careless and forget to do anything to cut down the risk of my becoming pregnant."

Nonvirgin girls	True	Not Sure	False	TOTAL
All	28%	2%	70%	100%
Girls 13–15	33	7	60	100
Girls 16–19	26	0	74	100
Monogamists	30	0	70	100
Adventurers	33	0	67	100

Table 308

Female: "Except for birth control pills, most other birth control methods are just too much trouble to use."

Nonvirgin girls	True	Not Sure	False	TOTAL
All	45%	2%	53%	100%
Girls 13–15	35	4	61	100
Girls 16–19	49	1	50	100
Monogamists	47	0	53	100
Adventurers	42	0	58	100

Table 309

Female: "Once I asked a doctor for birth control pills or other contraceptives, and his attitude put me very uptight."

Nonvirgin girls	True	Not Sure	False	TOTAL
All	11%	3%	86%	100%
Girls 13–15	20	6	74	100
Girls 16-19	7	1	92	100
Monogamists	11	0	89	100
Adventurers	21	0	79	100

Table 310

Female: "Sometimes I don't really care whether or not I get pregnant."

Nonvirgin girls	True	Not Sure	False	TOTAL
All	40%	2%	58%	100%
Girls 13–15	50	4	46	100
Girls 16–19	36	0	64	100
Monogamists	30	0	70	100
Adventurers	78	0	22	100

Table 311

Female: "I don't know where to get birth control pills or any other kind of reliable contraceptive."

Nonvirgin girls	True	Not Sure	False	TOTAL
All	16%	3%	81%	100%
Girls 13–15	32	10	58	100
Girls 16–19	9	0	91	100
Monogamists	11	2	87	100
Adventurers	2	0	98	100

Table 312

Female: "I have a boyfriend who doesn't approve of birth control pills or other contraceptives."

Nonvirgin girls	True	No Sure	False	TOTAL
All	8%	3%	89%	100%
Girls 13–15	15	8	77	100
Girls 16–19	6	1	93	100
Monogamists	4	0	96	100
Adventurers	13	0	87	100

Table 313

Female: "Sometimes I just get careless and forget to take my birth control pills."

Nonvirgin girls	True	Not Sure	False	TOTAL
All	10%	5%	85%	100%
Girls 13–15	21	10	69	100
Girls 16–19	5	3	92	100
Monogamists	11	2	87	100
Adventurers	15	0	85	100

Table 314

Female: "I can't afford to buy birth control pills or any other reliable kind of contraceptive."

Nonvirgin girls	True	Not Sure	False	TOTAL
All	17%	2%	81%	100%
Girls 13–15	25	7	68	100
Girls 16–19	13	0	87	100
Monogamists	11	0	89	100
Adventurers	34	0	66	100

Table 315

"It bothers me that I can't seem to be satisfied sexually."

Nonvirgin adolescents	True	Not Sure	False	TOTAL
All	26%	5%	69%	100%
Boys	24	7	69	100
Boys 13–15	32	8	60	
Boys 16–19	20	6	74	100
Girls	29	3	68	100
Girls 13–15	17	10	73	100
Girls 16–19	35	0	65	100
Monogamists	21	2	77	100
Adventurers	32	7	61	100

Table 316

Male: "If I were to have sex with another girl just occasionally, it wouldn't really put my girl friend uptight."

Female: "If I were to have sex with another boy just occasionally, it wouldn't really put my boyfriend uptight."

Nonvirgin adolescents	True	Not Sure	False	TOTAL
All	39%	5%	56%	100%
Boys	48	7	45	100
Boys 13–15	56	14	30	100
Boys 16–19	44	3	53	100
Girls	28	2	70	100
Girls 13–15	46	4	50	100
Girls 16–19	21	1	78	100
Monogamists	31	2	67	100
Adventurers	54	4	32	100

Table 317

Male: "If I were to make a girl pregnant, I wouldn't want her to have an abortion, because taking the life of an unborn child is wrong."

Female: "I would never want to have an abortion, because taking the life of an unborn child is wrong."

Nonvirgin adolescents	True	Not Sure	False	TOTAL
All	54%	7%	39%	100%
Boys	50	9	41	100
Boys 13–15	45	16	39	100
Boys 16–19	52	5	43	100
Girls	60	4	36	100
Girls 13–15	76	10	14	100
Girls 16–19	54	1	45	100
Monogamists	51	1	48	100
Adventurers	53	12	35	100

Table 318

"I've never had sex with a person of another race."

Nonvirgin adolescents	True	Not Sure	False	TOTAL
All	71%	4%	25%	100%
Boys	64	4	32	100
Boys 13–15	75	6	19	100
Boys 16–19	58	3	39	100
Girls	80	3	17	100
Girls 13–15	78	5	17	100
Girls 16–19	82	1	17	100
Monogamists	82	1	17	100
Adventurers	48	4	48	100

Table 319

"On one or more occasions, under the influence of marijuana, I've had sex with someone that I wouldn't have had sex with otherwise."

Nonvirgin adolescents	True	Not Sure	False	TOTAL
All	18%	5%	77%	100%
Boys	22	7	71	100
Boys 13–15	16	13	71	100
Boys 16–19	26	3	71	100
Girls	12	2	86	100
Girls 13–15	9	4	87	100
Girls 16–19	13	1	86	100
Monogamists	17	1	82	100
Adventurers	24	4	72	100

Table 320

Male: "On one or more occasions, I've refused to ball a girl unless she would do something that I wanted her to do."

Female: "On one or more occasions, I've refused to ball a boy unless he would do something that I wanted him to do."

Nonvirgin adolescents	True	Not Sure	False	TOTAL
All	24%	4%	72%	100%
Boys	31	4	65	100
Boys 13–15	44	6	50	100
Boys 16–19	24	3	73	100
Girls	16	4	80	100
Girls 13–15	27	5	68	100
Girls 16–19	11	4	85	100
Monogamists	18	2	80	100
Adventurers	36	4	60	100

Table 321

"Having sex doesn't make my life any more meaningful."

Nonvirgin adolescents	True	Not Sure	False	TOTAL
All	32%	5%	63%	100%
Boys	32	6	62	100
Boys 13–15	44	7	49	100
Boys 16–19	26	6	68	100
Girls	31	3	66	100
Girls 13–15	35	4	61	100
Girls 16–19	29	2	69	100
Monogamists	18	1	81	100
Adventurers	43	5	52	100

Table 322

"There are many times when I get horny but don't have anyone to ball."

Nonvirgin adolescents	True	Not Sure	False	TOTAL
All	55%	5%	40%	100%
Boys	66	4	30	100
Boys 13–15	64	6	30	100
Boys 16–19	67	3	30	100
Girls	40	6	54	100
Girls 13–15	44	10	46	100
Girls 16–19	38	4	58	100
Monogamists	44	2	54	100
Adventurers	66	7	27	100

Table 323

Male: "On one or more occasions I've had sex with a girl mostly because people would have put me down if I hadn't."

Female: "On one or more occasions I've had sex with a boy mostly because people would have put me down if I hadn't."

Nonvirgin adolescents	True	Not Sure	False	TOTAL
All	15%	5%	80%	100%
Boys	18	7	75	100
Boys 13–15	32	13	55	100
Boys 16–19	12	3	85	100
Girls	10	2	88	100
Girls 13–15	22	4	74	100
Girls 16–19	5	1	94	100
Monogamists	12	1	87	100
Adventurers	14	4	82	100

Table 324

Male: "If I were to get a girl pregnant, I wouldn't want her to have an abortion, because it's against my religion."

Female: "I would never want to have an abortion, because it is against my religion."

Nonvirgin adolescents	True	Not Sure	False	TOTAL
All	28%	6%	66%	100%
Boys	27	9	64	100
Boys 13–15	27	13	60	100
Boys 16–19	27	7	66	100
Girls	28	3	69	100
Girls 13–15	30	4	66	100
Girls 16–19	28	2	70	100
Monogamists	29	1	70	100
Adventurers	26	5	69	100

Table 325

Male: "If my girl friend were to have sex with another boy just occasionally, it wouldn't really put me uptight."

Female: "If my boyfriend were to have sex with another girl just occasionally, it wouldn't really put me uptight."

Nonvirgin adolescents	True	Not Sure	False	TOTAL
All	39%	5%	56%	100%
Boys	38	7	55	100
Boys 13–15	35	13	52	100
Boys 16–19	40	3	57	100
Girls	40	2	58	100
Girls 13–15	38	4	58	100
Girls 16–19	41	1	58	100
Monogamists	38	1	61	100
Adventurers	44	4	52	100

Table 326

Male: "I don't like to have sex with a girl when she's having her period."

Female: "I usually experience a lot of pain or discomfort when I have my period."

Nonvirgin adolescents	True	Not Sure	False	TOTAL
All	60%	6%	34%	100%
Boys	64	9	27	100
Boys 13–15	75	8	17	100
Boys 16–19	58	9	33	100
Girls	56	2	42	100
Girls 13–15	66	4	30	100
Girls 16–19	52	1	47	100

Table 327

Male: "It really bothers me a lot if I have sex with a girl and she doesn't seem to be completely satisfied."

Female: "When I have sex, it's very important to me that I reach a climax, or orgasm."

Nonvirgin adolescents	True	Not Sure	False	TOTAL
All	65%	4%	31%	100%
Boys	76	4	20	100
Boys 13–15	64	6	30	100
Boys 16–19	83	3	14	100
Girls	50	3	47	100
Girls 13–15	60	7	33	100
Girls 16–19	45	1	54	100
Monogamists	67	1	32	100
Adventurers	66	4	30	100

Table 328

"Sometimes I think that I am addicted to sex, the way some people are addicted to drugs."

Nonvirgin adolescents	True	Not Sure	False	TOTAL
All	34%	5%	61%	100%
Boys	40	6	54	100
Boys 13–15	57	13	30	100
Boys 16–19	31	3	66	100
Girls	27	2	71	100
Girls 13–15	29	4	67	100
Girls 16–19	26	2	72	100
Monogamists	27	1	72	100
Adventurers	50	4	46	100

Table 329

"I don't get as much physical enjoyment out of sex as I think I should be getting."

Nonvirgin adolescents	True	Not Sure	False	TOTAL
All	37%	6%	57%	100%
Boys	38	10	52	100
Boys 13–15	47	15	38	100
Boys 16–19	34	7	59	100
Girls	34	2	64	100
Girls 13–15	20	4	76	100
Girls 16–19	40	2	58	100
Monogamists	32	2	66	100
Adventurers	39	9	52	100

Table 330

Male: "Abortions are so easy to get these days that I don't really worry about getting a girl pregnant."

Female: "Abortions are so easy to get these days that I don't really worry about getting pregnant."

Nonvirgin adolescents	True	Not Sure	False	TOTAL
All	18%	4%	78%	100%
Boys	20	6	74	100
Boys 13–15	20	11	69	100
Boys 16–19	20	3	77	100
Girls	14	2	84	100
Girls 13–15	21	4	75	100
Girls 16–19	11	2	87	100
Monogamists	15	1	84	100
Adventurers	22	4	74	100

Table 331

Male: "On one or more occasions a girl has refused to ball me unless I would do something that I didn't want to do."

Female: "On one or more occasions a boy has refused to ball me unless I would do something that I didn't want to do."

Nonvirgin adolescents	True	Not Sure	False	TOTAL
All	22%	5%	73%	100%
Boys	31	6	63	100
Boys 13–15	47	11	42	100
Boys 16–19	23	3	74	100
Girls	11	4	85	100
Girls 13–15	15	5	80	100
Girls 16–19	9	3	88	100
Monogamists	15	2	83	100
Adventurers	33	4	63	100

Table 332

"Sometimes, people of the same sex do things together that result in sexual stimulation or satisfaction for either or both of them. When this happens, it is called 'homosexuality.' Have you ever heard of homosexuality?"

	Yes	No	TOTAL
All adolescents	90%	10%	100%
Boys	91	9	100
Boys 13–15	87	13	100
Boys 16–19	93	7	100
Girls	90	10	100
Girls 13–15	84	16	100
Girls 16–19	94	6	100
Virgins	88	12	100
Inexperienced	85	15	
Beginners	93	7	100
Nonvirgins	93	7	100
Monogamists	96	4	100
Adventurers	89	11	100

Table 333

Male: "Have you yourself ever done anything with another boy or with a grown man that resulted in sexual stimulation or satisfaction for either or both of you?"

Female: "Have you yourself ever done anything with another girl or with a grown woman that resulted in sexual stimulation or satisfaction for either or both of you?"

	Yes	No	TOTAL
All adolescents	9%	91%	100%
Boys	11	89	100
Boys 13–15	5	95	100
Boys 16–19	17	83	100
Girls	6	94	100
Girls 13–15	6	94	100
Girls 16–19	6	94	100
Virgins	5	95	100
Inexperienced	5	95	100
Beginners	9	91	100
Nonvirgins	12	88	100
Monogamists	13	87	100
Adventurers	12	88	100

Table 334

Age at time of first homosexual experience

	Adolescents with homosexual experience		
Age at first experience	All	Boys	Girls
6–10	31%	16%	57%
11–12	47	56	32
13–17	22	28	11
TOTAL	100%	100%	100%

Table 335

Relative age of first homosexual partner

	Adolescents with homosexual experience		
First homosexual partner	All	Boys	Girls
Younger boy/girl	24%	29%	14%
Boy/girl of about same age	39	27	63
Older boy/girl	29	32	23
Adult	8	12	0
TOTAL	100%	100%	100%

Table 336

"Some girls sometimes reach a climax, or orgasm, when they have sex. Other girls don't, or do so only on rare occasions. Do you yourself ever have a climax, or orgasm, when having sex with a boy?"

	Nonvirgin girls		
Frequency of orgasm in intercourse	All	Marijuana users	Marijuana nonusers
Rarely or never	57%	45%	66%
Usually or almost always	43	55	34
TOTAL	100%	100%	100%

Table 337

"When I have sex, it's very important to me that I reach a climax, or orgasm."

	True	Not Sure	False	TOTAL
All nonvirgin girls	50%	3%	47%	100%
Girls having orgasm in intercourse rarely or never	34	5	61	100
Girls having orgasm in intercourse usually or almost always	69	0	31	100

Table 338

"I don't get as much physical satisfaction out of sex as I think I should be getting."

	True	Not Sure	False	TOTAL
All nonvirgin girls	34%	2%	64%	100%
Girls having orgasm in intercourse rarely or never	49	4	47	100
Girls having orgasm in intercourse frequently or almost always	16	0	84	100

Table 339

"I get a lot of satisfaction out of my sex life."

	True	False	TOTAL
All nonvirgin girls	77%	23%	100%
Girls having orgasm in intercourse rarely or never	60	40	100
Girls having orgasm in intercourse usually or almost always	98	2	100

Table 340

Male: "Thinking back to *the very first time* that you had sex with a girl, how old were you then?"

Female: "Thinking back to *the very first time* that you had sex with a boy, how old were you then?"

	Nonvirgins		
Age at first intercourse	All	Monogamists	Adventurers
12 or under	13%	6%	21%
13	15	9	22
14	15	11	17
15	22	25	15
16	15	23	10
17	9	8	7
18–19	11	18	8
TOTAL	100%	100%	100%

Table 341

Male: "All in all, how many *different* girls (counting the first one) have you ever had sex with?"

Female: "All in all, how many *different* boys (counting the first one) have you ever had sex with?"

	Nonvirgins		
Number of intercourse partners	All	Monogamists	Adventurers
1	35%	47%	1%
2–3	22	15	20
4–6	19	16	34
7–15	15	22	15
16 or more	9	0	30
TOTAL	100%	100%	100%

Table 342

"All in all, how many *different* girls (counting the first one) have you ever had sex with?"

	Nonvirgin boys		
Number of intercourse partners	All	Age 13–15	Age 16–19
1	23%	25%	22%
2–3	22	38	14
4–6	22	15	27
7–15	19	19	18
16 or more	14	3	19
TOTAL	100%	100%	100%

Table 343

"All in all, how many *different* boys (counting the first one) have you ever had sex with?"

	Nonvirgin girls		
Number of intercourse partners	All	Age 13–15	Age 16–19
1	50%	59%	46%
2–3	22	27	20
4–6	14	13	14
7–15	12	1	16
16 or more	2	0	4
TOTAL	100%	100%	100%

Table 344

Male: "When was the most recent occasion on which you had sex with a girl?"

Female: "When was the most recent occasion on which you had sex with a boy?"

	Nonvirgins		
Most recent intercourse experience	All	Monogamists	Adventurers
Within the past month	62%	93%	81%
More than a month ago	38	7	19
TOTAL	100%	100%	100%

Table 345

Male: "When was the most recent occasion on which you had sex with a girl?"

Female: "When was the most recent occasion on which you had sex with a boy?"

	Nonvirgins		
Most recent intercourse experience	All	Boys	Girls
Within the past month	62%	53%	73%
More than a month ago	38	47	27
TOTAL	100%	100%	100%

Table 346

Male: "And how many *different* girls have you had sex with since this time last month?"

Female: "And how many *different* boys have you had sex with since this time last month?"

	Nonvirgins with current intercourse experience		
Number of intercourse partners in past month	All	Monogamists	Adventurers
1	76%	92%	47%
2	11	8	18
3	7	0	20
4	4	0	11
5 or more	2	0	4
TOTAL	100%	100%	100%

Table 347

Male: "And how many *different* girls have you had sex with since this time last month?"

Female: "And how many *different* boys have you had sex with since this time last month?"

	Nonvirgins with current intercourse experience		
Number of intercourse partners in past month	All	Boys	Girls
1	76%	65%	86%
2	11	13	9
3	7	10	5
4	4	8	0
5 or more	2	4	0
TOTAL	100%	100%	100%

Table 348

Male: "Since this time last month, approximately how many occasions have there been on which you have had sex with a girl?"

Female: "Since this time last month, approximately how many occasions have there been on which you have had sex with a boy?"

	Nonvirgins with current intercourse experience		
Frequency of intercourse in past month	All	Monogamists	Adventurers
1 time	14%	9%	22%
2 times	15	11	21
3 times	13	11	17
4 times	13	13	12
5–8 times	12	15	8
9–12 times	12	15	6
13–19 times	11	10	14
20 or more times	10	16	0
TOTAL	100%	100%	100%

Table 349

Male: "Since this time last month, approximately how many occasions have there been on which you have had sex with a girl?"

Female: "Since this time last month, approximately how many occasions have there been on which you have had sex with a boy?"

	Nonvirgins with current intercourse experience		
Frequency of intercourse in past month	All	Boys	Girls
1 time	14%	16%	11%
2 times	15	16	14
3 times	13	15	12
4 times	13	15	10
5–8 times	12	4	21
9–12 times	12	12	11
13–19 times	11	14	9
20 or more times	10	8	12
TOTAL	100%	100%	100%

Table 350

"One of the reasons why young people stop going to church is because churches teach that enjoyment of sex is sinful."

	Agree	Not Sure	Disagree	TOTAL
All adolescents	37%	4%	59%	100%
Adolescents believing they are—				
very religious	28	4	68	100
somewhat religious	38	3	59	100
not very religious	43	4	53	100
not religious at all	30	9	61	100

Table 351

"Sometimes I take part in sexual activities that are not consistent with my religious beliefs."

	True	Not Sure	False	TOTAL
All adolescents	27%	4%	69%	100%
Adolescents believing they are—				
very religious	40	2	58	100
somewhat religious	29	4	67	100
not very religious	22	6	72	100
not religious at all	15	5	80	100

Table 352

"I don't think that God has any interest in my sex life."

	True	Not Sure	False	TOTAL
All adolescents	34%	3%	63%	100%
Adolescents believing they are—				
very religious	8	0	92	100
somewhat religious	21	3	76	100
not very religious	52	2	46	100
not religious at all	83	6	11	100

Table 353

"Churches are really doing their best to understand young people's ideas about sex."

	Agree	Not Sure	Disagree	TOTAL
All adolescents	45%	7%	48%	100%
Adolescents believing they are—				
very religious	53	5	42	100
somewhat religious	51	6	43	100
not very religious	41	10	49	100
not religious at all	20	5	75	100

Table 354

"Sometimes I take part in sexual activities that are not consistent with my religious beliefs."

	True	Not Sure	False	TOTAL
All adolescents	27%	4%	69%	100%
Adolescents responding true to Table 229*	33	5	62	100
Adolescents responding false to Table 229*	22	2	76	100

*Table 229: "Churches teach that enjoyment of sex is sinful."

Table 355

"Sometimes when I go to church I get to feeling guilty about my sexual behavior."

	True	Not Sure	False	TOTAL
All adolescents	20%	5%	75%	100%
Adolescents responding true to Table 229*	22	2	76	100
Adolescents responding false to Table 229	19	6	75	100
Adolescents responding true to Table 154†	29	1	70	100
Adolescents responding false to Table 154	12	5	83	100

*Table 229: "Churches teach that enjoyment of sex is sinful."
†Table 154: "I go to religious services fairly often."

Table 356

"I don't think that God has any interest in my sex life."

	True	Not Sure	False	TOTAL
All adolescents	34%	3%	63%	100%
Adolescents responding true to Table 154*	19	2	79	100
Adolescents responding false to Table 154	48	2	50	100
Adolescents believing they are—				
very religious or somewhat religious	19	2	79	100
not very religious or not religious at all	60	3	36	100

*Table 154: "I go to religious services fairly often."

Table 357

"I wouldn't use birth control or contraception, because it's against my religion."

	True	Not Sure	False	TOTAL
All adolescents	16%	5%	79%	100%
Religious affiliation				
Catholic	23	7	70	100
Non-Catholic	14	4	82	100
Adolescents believing they are—				
very religious or somewhat religious	19	4	77	100
not very religious or not religious at all	12	6	82	100

Table 358

"In general, I feel pretty self-confident about sex."

	True	Not Sure	False	TOTAL
All adolescents	67%	3%	30%	100%
Adolescents responding true to Table 18*	77	3	20	100
Adolescents responding false to Table 18	53	1	46	100

*Table 18: "I get a lot of satisfaction out of my sex life."

Table 359

"When was the most recent occasion on which you masturbated?"

	Nonvirgin adolescents		
When last masturbated	All	Current intercourse experience	No current intercourse experience
Within the past month	37%	37%	37%
More than a month ago	25	28	20
Never	38	35	43
TOTAL	100%	100%	100%

Table 360

"When was the most recent occasion on which you masturbated?"

	Nonvirgin boys		
When last masturbated	All	Current intercourse experience	No current intercourse experience
Within the past month	40%	36%	44%
More than a month ago	29	40	18
Never	31	24	38
TOTAL	100%	100%	100%

Table 361

"When was the most recent occasion on which you masturbated?"

	Nonvirgin girls		
When last masturbated	All	Current intercourse experience	No current intercourse experience
Within the past month	34%	39%	20%
More than a month ago	19	17	23
Never	47	44	57
TOTAL	100%	100%	100%

Table 362

Frequency of masturbation in past month

Frequency of masturbation	Adolescents with current masturbatory experience: All	Boys	Girls
1–2 times	30%	21%	43%
3–4 times	29	36	18
5–10 times	23	21	27
11–19 times	11	12	9
20 or more times	7	10	3
TOTAL	100%	100%	100%

Table 363

Frequency of masturbation with orgasm in the past month

Frequency of masturbation with orgasm	Adolescents with current masturbatory experience: All	Boys	Girls
Did not masturbate to orgasm	14%	6%	29%
1–2 times	21	17	27
3–4 times	30	40	13
5–10 times	21	19	25
11–19 times	9	12	2
20 or more times	5	6	4
TOTAL	100%	100%	100%

Table 364

Frequency of masturbation without orgasm in the past month

Frequency of masturbation without orgasm	Adolescents with current masturbatory experience: All	Boys	Girls
Did not masturbate without reaching orgasm	61%	79%	26%
1–2 times	17	8	36
3–4 times	5	1	13
5–10 times	8	5	13
11–19 times	5	1	12
20 or more times	4	6	0
TOTAL	100%	100%	100%

Table 365

"When you masturbate, do you daydream or think about things most of the time, only some of the time, rarely, or never?"

Frequency of masturbatory fantasy	Adolescents with current masturbatory experience: All	Marijuana users	Marijuana nonusers
Most of the time	53%	58%	48%
Some of the time	30	37	26
Rarely	7	2	11
Never	10	3	15
TOTAL	100%	100%	100%

Table 366

"How often do you look at pictures while you are masturbating—most of the time, only some of the time, rarely, or never?"

Frequency of use of pictures in masturbation	Adolescents with current masturbatory experience: All	Marijuana users	Marijuana nonusers
Most of the time	5%	4%	6%
Some of the time	25	27	23
Rarely	29	37	22
Never	41	32	49
TOTAL	100%	100%	100%

Table 367

"In general, do you usually enjoy masturbating a great deal, somewhat, a little, or not at all?"

Enjoyment of masturbation	Adolescents with current masturbatory experience: All	Marijuana users	Marijuana nonusers
A great deal	16%	27%	8%
Somewhat	43	48	38
A little	35	24	43
Not at all	6	1	11
TOTAL	100%	100%	100%

Table 368

"How about feelings of guilt, anxiety, or concern about masturbation? Do you have such feelings often, sometimes, rarely, or not at all?"

Guilt or anxiety about masturbation	Adolescents with current masturbatory experience: All	Marijuana users	Marijuana nonusers
Often	17%	9%	23%
Sometimes	32	34	30
Rarely	32	30	34
Never	19	27	13
TOTAL	100%	100%	100%

Table 369

Male: "If you had to guess, would you say that you masturbate more often or less often than most other boys of about your own age?"

Female: "If you had to guess would you say that you masturbate more often or less often than most other girls of about your own age?"

Perceived relative frequency of masturbation	Adolescents with current masturbatory experience: All	Marijuana users	Marijuana nonusers
More often	20%	20%	20%
About the same	60	66	55
Less often	20	14	25
TOTAL	100%	100%	100%

Table 370

"So far as sex is concerned, I have pretty much come to definite conclusions about what I think is right and wrong for myself."

	True	Not Sure	False	TOTAL
All adolescents	84%	2%	14%	100%
Adolescents responding true to Table 23*	91	0	9	100
Adolescents responding false to Table 23	80	1	19	100

*Table 23: "So far as sex is concerned, I have pretty much come to definite conclusions about what I think is right and wrong for other people."

Table 371

Male: "Would you say that you have a close relationship with this girl, a casual relationship, or no real relationship at all?"

Female: "Would you say that you have a close relationship with this boy, a casual relationship, or no real relationship at all?"

Perceived nature of current relationship	All monogamists
Close relationship	86%
Casual relationship	13
No real relationship	1
TOTAL	100%

Table 372

Male: "For how long have you had such a relationship with this girl?"

Female: "For how long have you had such a relationship with this boy?"

Length of time since inception of current relationship	All monogamists
More than 2 years	23%
13 months to 2 years	29
4 to 12 months	27
3 months or less	21
TOTAL	100%

Table 373

Male: "And for how long have you been having sex with this girl?"

Female: "And for how long have you been having sex with this boy?"

Length of time since first intercourse in current relationship	All monogamists
More than 2 years	12%
13 months to 2 years	12
4 to 12 months	46
3 months or less	30
TOTAL	100%

Table 374

Male: "Do you love this girl?"

Female: "Do you love this boy?"

Whether or not current partner is loved	All monogamists
Yes	86%
I'm not really sure	11
No	3
TOTAL	100%

Table 375

Male: "Does she love you?"

Female: "Does he love you?"

Perceived reciprocation of love	All monogamists
Yes	81%
I'm not really sure	11
Male: She says she does; *Female*: He says he does	8
No	0
TOTAL	100%

Table 376

"Do you plan to get married?"

Intention to marry current partner	All monogamists
Yes	43%
Probably	12
We haven't decided	17
Probably not	8
No	17
We haven't talked about it	3
TOTAL	100%

Table 377

Male: "Do you have sex with other girls?"

Female: "Do you have sex with other boys?"

Sexual infidelity	All monogamists
Frequently	3%
Occasionally	7
Very rarely	10
Never	80
TOTAL	100%

Table 378

Male: "Does she have sex with other boys?"

Female: "Does he have sex with other girls?"

Partner's sexual infidelity	All monogamists
Frequently	1%
Occasionally	10
Very rarely	5
I think so, but I'm not sure	1
Never	70
I don't think so, but I'm not sure	13
TOTAL	100%

Table 379

Male: "Do you have sex with other girls?"

Female: "Do you have sex with other boys?"

	Monogamists		
	All	Those responding true to Table 316*	Those responding false to Table 316
Frequently	3%	8%	1%
Occasionally	7	16	3
Very rarely	10	7	11
Never	80	69	85
TOTAL	100%	100%	100%

*Table 316: Male: "If I were to have sex with another girl, just occasionally, it wouldn't really put my girl friend uptight"; Female: "If I were to have sex with another boy, just occasionally, it wouldn't really put my boyfriend uptight."

Table 380

Male: "Do you have sex with other girls?"

Female: "Do you have sex with other boys?"

	Monogamists		
	All	Those responding true to Table 325*	Those responding false to Table 325
Frequently	3%	2%	5%
Occasionally	7	16	1
Very rarely	10	9	10
Never	80	73	84
TOTAL	100%	100%	100%

*Table 325: Male: "If my girl friend were to have sex with another boy, just occasionally, it wouldn't really put me uptight"; Female: "If my boyfriend were to have sex with another girl, just occasionally, it wouldn't really put me uptight."

Table 381

Male: "Does she have sex with other boys?"

Female: "Does he have sex with other girls?"

	Monogamists		
	All	Those responding true to Table 316*	Those responding false to Table 316
Frequently	1%	3%	0%
Occasionally	10	25	4
Very rarely	5	12	2
I think so, but I'm not sure	1	1	1
Never	70	45	80
I don't think so, but I'm not sure	13	14	13
TOTAL	100%	100%	100%

*Table 316: Male: "If I were to have sex with another girl, just occasionally, it wouldn't really put my girl friend uptight"; Female: "If I were to have sex with another boy, just occasionally, it wouldn't really put my boyfriend uptight."

Table 382

Male: "Does she have sex with other boys?"

Female: "Does he have sex with other girls?"

	Monogamists		
	All	Those responding true to Table 325*	Those responding false to Table 325
Frequently	1%	3%	0%
Occasionally	10	21	4
Very rarely	5	8	3
I think so, but I'm not sure	1	1	1
Never	70	59	76
I don't think so, but I'm not sure	13	8	16
TOTAL	100%	100%	100%

*Table 325: Male: "If my girl friend were to have sex with another boy, just occasionally, it wouldn't really put me uptight"; Female: "If my boyfriend were to have sex with another girl, just occasionally, it wouldn't really put me uptight."

Table 383

Frequency of contraceptive use in the past month

	Nonvirgins with current intercourse experience		
Frequency of contraceptive use	All	Monogamists	Adventurers
Always	59%	66%	46%
Sometimes, once or twice	27	22	36
Never	14	12	18
TOTAL	100%	100%	100%

Table 384

Male: "This first time that you had sex with a girl, did either you or the girl make use of any birth control method, or do anything else to cut down on the risk of the girl's becoming pregnant?"

Female: "This first time that you had sex with a boy, did either you or the boy make use of any birth control method, or do anything else to cut down on the risk of your becoming pregnant?"

	Nonvirgin adolescents		
Use of contraception at first intercourse	All	Monogamists	Adventurers
Yes	32%	48%	17%
Boy did not; doesn't know if girl did	13	4	20
No	55	48	63
TOTAL	100%	100%	100%

Table 385

Male: "This first time that you had sex with a girl did either you or the girl make use of any birth control method, or do anything else to cut down on the risk of the girl's becoming pregnant?"

Female: "This first time that you had sex with a boy, did either you or the boy make use of any birth control method, or do anything else to cut down on the risk of your becoming pregnant?"

	Nonvirgin adolescents		
Use of contraception at first intercourse	All	Current intercourse experience	No current intercourse experience
Yes	32%	36%	25%
Boy did not; doesn't know if girl did	13	7	22
No	55	57	53
TOTAL	100%	100%	100%

Table 386

Female knowledge about and use of birth control pills

Knowledge about and use of birth control pills	Nonvirgin girls All	Age 13–15	Age 16–19
Heard about and used	31%	10%	39%
Heard about but never used	69	90	61
Never heard about	0	0	0
TOTAL	100%	100%	100%

Table 387

Female knowledge about and use of birth control pills

Knowledge about and use of birth control pills	Nonvirgin girls All	Current intercourse experience	No current intercourse experience
Heard about and used	31%	40%	7%
Heard about but never used	69	60	93
Never heard about	0	0	0
TOTAL	100%	100%	100%

Table 388

Female knowledge about and use of intrauterine devices

Knowledge about and use of intrauterine devices	Nonvirgin girls All	Age 13–15	Age 16–19
Heard about and used	2%	0%	3%
Heard about but never used	74	48	84
Never heard about	24	52	13
TOTAL	100%	100%	100%

Table 389

Female knowledge about and use of intrauterine devices

Knowledge about and use of intrauterine devices	Nonvirgin girls All	Current intercourse experience	No current intercourse experience
Heard about and used	2%	3%	0%
Heard about but never used	74	83	52
Never heard about	24	14	48
TOTAL	100%	100%	100%

Table 390

Female knowledge about and use of diaphragms

Knowledge about and use of diaphragms	Nonvirgin girls All	Age 13–15	Age 16–19
Heard about and used	2%	0%	3%
Heard about but never used	87	78	90
Never heard about	11	22	7
TOTAL	100%	100%	100%

Table 391

Female knowledge about and use of diaphragms

Knowledge about and use of diaphragms	Nonvirgin girls All	Current intercourse experience	No current intercourse experience
Heard about and used	2%	3%	0%
Heard about but never used	87	89	80
Never heard about	11	8	20
TOTAL	100%	100%	100%

Table 392

Female knowledge about and use of contraceptive foams

Knowledge about and use of contraceptive foams	Nonvirgin girls All	Age 13–15	Age 16–19
Heard about and used	14%	1%	19%
Heard about but never used	79	77	80
Never heard about	7	22	1
TOTAL	100%	100%	100%

Table 393

Female knowledge about and use of contraceptive foams

Knowledge about and use of contraceptive foams	Nonvirgin girls All	Current intercourse experience	No current intercourse experience
Heard about and used	14%	19%	0%
Heard about but never used	79	79	79
Never heard about	7	2	21
TOTAL	100%	100%	100%

Table 394

Female knowledge about and use of contraceptive jellies

Knowledge about and use of contraceptive jellies	Nonvirgin girls All	Age 13–15	Age 16–19
Heard about and used	1%	1%	0%
Heard about but never used	94	85	98
Never heard about	5	14	2
TOTAL	100%	100%	100%

Table 395

Female knowledge about and use of contraceptive jellies

Knowledge about and use of contraceptive jellies	Nonvirgin girls: All	Current intercourse experience	No current intercourse experience
Heard about and used	1%	1%	0%
Heard about but never used	94	97	87
Never heard about	5	2	13
TOTAL	100%	100%	100%

Table 396

Female knowledge about and use of contraceptive douches

Knowledge about and use of contraceptive douches	Nonvirgin girls: All	Age 13–15	Age 16–19
Heard about and used	5%	2%	6%
Heard about but never used	84	78	87
Never heard about	11	20	7
TOTAL	100%	100%	100%

Table 397

Female knowledge about and use of contraceptive douches

Knowledge about and use of contraceptive douches	Nonvirgin girls: All	Current intercourse experience	No current intercourse experience
Heard about and used	5%	5%	5%
Heard about but never used	84	87	77
Never heard about	11	8	18
TOTAL	100%	100%	100%

Table 398

Female knowledge about and use of the rhythm method

Knowledge about and use of the rhythm method	Nonvirgin girls: All	Age 13–15	Age 16–19
Heard about and used	30%	12%	37%
Heard about but never used	49	55	46
Never heard about	21	33	17
TOTAL	100%	100%	100%

Table 399

Female knowledge about and use of the rhythm method

Knowledge about and use of the rhythm method	Nonvirgin girls: All	Current intercourse experience	No current intercourse experience
Heard about and used	30%	35%	16%
Heard about but never used	49	46	57
Never heard about	21	19	27
TOTAL	100%	100%	100%

Table 400

Relative age of first intercourse partner

Relative age of first partner	Nonvirgins
2–3 years younger	5%
1 year younger	9
Same age	26
1 year older	14
2 years older	17
3 years older	9
4 years older	6
5–6 years older	8
7 or more years older	6
TOTAL	100%

Table 401

"Do you plan to get married [to your present sex partner]?"

	Adolescents reporting that they have sex mostly (or only) with just one partner	Boys			Girls		
	All	All	Age 13–15	Age 16–19	All	Age 13–15	Age 16–19
Yes	39%	20%	4%	25%	52%	60%	50%
Probably	14	17	32	13	11	5	13
Probably not	7	8	0	10	6	0	7
No	21	29	9	35	16	3	19
We haven't decided	16	20	32	16	14	29	10
We haven't talked about it	3	6	23	1	1	3	1
TOTAL	100%	100%	100%	100%	100%	100%	100%

Table 402

"Most people *identify* (feel that they have a great deal in common with) a lot of different groups. But they identify with some groups more strongly than with others. Which *one* of the groups listed below do you identify with *most* strongly?"

Primary identification	All adolescents	Boys: All	Boys: Age 13–15	Boys: Age 16–19	Girls: All	Girls: Age 13–15	Girls: Age 16–19
People of my own generation	58%	59%	49%	67%	57%	58%	57%
People who live in my community	19	16	20	13	21	18	24
People of my own religion	11	12	13	11	10	10	9
People of my own race	9	11	13	9	9	10	7
People of my own sex	3	2	5	0	3	4	3
TOTAL	100%	100%	100%	100%	100%	100%	100%

Table 403

"Most people *identify* (feel that they have a great deal in common with) a lot of different groups. But they identify with some groups more strongly than with others. Which *one* of the groups listed below do you identify with *most* strongly?"

		Virgins			Nonvirgins		
Primary identification	All adoles-cents	All	Inexpe-rienced	Begin-ners	All	Monog-amists	Adven-turers
People of my own generation	58%	52%	44%	63%	63%	63%	55%
People who live in my community	19	20	21	20	18	19	26
People of my own religion	11	12	16	6	10	10	9
People of my own race	9	11	14	4	8	6	10
People of my own sex	3	5	5	7	1	2	0
TOTAL	100%	100%	100%	100%	100%	100%	100%

Table 404

Male: "Have you ever had sexual intercourse with a girl?"

Female: "Have you ever had sexual intercourse with a boy?"

		Boys			Girls		
Intercourse experience	All adoles-cents	All	Age 13–15	Age 16–19	All	Age 13–15	Age 16–19
Yes	52%	59%	44%	72%	45%	30%	57%
No	48	41	56	28	55	70	43
TOTAL	100%	100%	100%	100%	100%	100%	100%

Table 405

Male: "Thinking back to *the very first time* that you had sex with a girl, how old were you then?"

Female: "Thinking back to *the very first time* that you had sex with a boy, how old were you then?"

	Nonvirgins						
		Boys			Girls		
Age at first intercourse	All	All	Age 13–15	Age 16–19	All	Age 13–15	Age 16–19
12 or under	13%	17%	36%	11%	7%	24%	0%
13	16	18	28	14	12	30	5
14	15	18	19	17	11	12	11
15	22	18	17	18	26	34	24
16	15	12	0	16	21	0	28
17	9	12	0	17	6	0	8
18–19	11	5	0	7	17	0	24
TOTAL	100%	100%	100%	100%	100%	100%	100%

Table 406

Incidence of masturbation among adolescents

		Boys			Girls		
Whether or not ever masturbated	All adoles-cents	All	Age 13–15	Age 16–19	All	Age 13–15	Age 16–19
Yes	49%	58%	43%	70%	39%	36%	42%
No	51	42	57	30	61	64	58
TOTAL	100%	100%	100%	100%	100%	100%	100%

Table 407

Incidence of masturbation among male adolescents

	Male adolescents						
		Virgins			Nonvirgins		
Whether or not ever masturbated	All	All	Inexpe-rienced	Begin-ners	All	Monog-amists	Adven-turers
Yes	58%	41%	32%	69%	69%	86%	64%
No	42	59	68	31	31	14	36
TOTAL	100%	100%	100%	100%	100%	100%	100%

Table 408

Incidence of masturbation among female adolescents

	Female adolescents						
		Virgins			Nonvirgins		
Whether or not ever masturbated	All	All	Inexpe-rienced	Begin-ners	All	Monog-amists	Adven-turers
Yes	39%	28%	32%	34%	53%	53%	78%
No	61	72	68	66	47	47	22
TOTAL	100%	100%	100%	100%	100%	100%	100%

Table 409

"How old were you *the very first time* that you masturbated?"

	Adolescents with masturbation experience						
		Boys			Girls		
Age at first masturbation	All	All	Age 13–15	Age 16–19	All	Age 13–15	Age 16–19
Age 10 or under	20%	12%	23%	7%	33%	30%	35%
11	11	12	0	19	8	19	1
12	14	15	25	10	13	21	8
13	29	36	31	39	18	17	18
14	18	17	19	16	19	13	22
15–19	8	8	2	9	9	0	16
TOTAL	100%	100%	100%	100%	100%	100%	100%

Table 410

"When was the most recent occasion on which you masturbated?"

		Boys			Girls		
When last masturbated	All adoles-cents	All	Age 13–15	Age 16–19	All	Age 13–15	Age 16–19
Within the past month	28%	36%	33%	39%	21%	15%	26%
More than a month ago	21	22	10	31	18	21	16
Never	51	42	57	30	61	64	58
TOTAL	100%	100%	100%	100%	100%	100%	100%

Table 411

"When was the most recent occasion on which you masturbated?"

		Virgins			Nonvirgins		
When last masturbated	All adolescents	All	Inexperienced	Beginners	All	Monogamists	Adventurers
Within the past month	28%	19%	13%	35%	37%	38%	37%
More than a month ago	21	15	19	14	25	26	29
Never	51	66	68	51	38	36	34
TOTAL	100%	100%	100%	100%	100%	100%	100%

Table 412

"When was the most recent occasion on which you masturbated?"

	Male adolescents						
		Virgins			Nonvirgins		
When last masturbated	All	All	Inexperienced	Beginners	All	Monogamists	Adventurers
Within the past month	36%	30%	20%	55%	40%	46%	30%
More than a month ago	21	11	12	14	29	39	33
Never	42	59	68	31	31	15	37
TOTAL	100%	100%	100%	100%	100%	100%	100%

Table 413

"When was the most recent occasion on which you masturbated?"

	Female adolescents						
		Virgins			Nonvirgins		
When last masturbated	All	All	Inexperienced	Beginners	All	Monogamists	Adventurers
Within the past month	21%	10%	8%	20%	34%	34%	67%
More than a month ago	18	18	24	14	19	19	12
Never	61	72	68	66	47	47	21
TOTAL	100%	100%	100%	100%	100%	100%	100%

Table 414

"When you masturbate, do you daydream about things most of the time, only some of the time, rarely, or never?"

	Adolescents with current masturbatory experience						
		Boys			Girls		
Frequency of masturbatory fantasy	All	All	Age 13–15	Age 16–19	All	Age 13–15	Age 16–19
Most of the time	53%	57%	55%	58%	46%	58%	40%
Some of the time	30	23	23	23	44	28	52
Rarely	7	9	11	8	3	10	0
Never	10	11	11	11	7	4	8
TOTAL	100%	100%	100%	100%	100%	100%	100%

Table 415

"When you masturbate, do you daydream or think about things most of the time, only some of the time, rarely, or never?"

	Adolescents with current masturbatory experience						
		Virgins			Nonvirgins		
Frequency of masturbatory fantasy	All	All	Inexperienced	Beginners	All	Monogamists	Adventurers
Most of the time	53%	51%	59%	45%	54%	51%	51%
Some of the time	30	20	21	21	35	40	39
Rarely	7	13	0	20	4	5	4
Never	10	16	20	14	7	4	6
TOTAL	100%	100%	100%	100%	100%	100%	100%

Table 416

"How often do you look at pictures while you are masturbating—most of the time, only some of the time, rarely, or never?"

	Adolescents with current masturbatory experience						
		Boys			Girls		
Use of pictures in masturbation	All	All	Age 13–15	Age 16–19	All	Age 13–15	Age 16–19
Most of the time	5%	5%	5%	5%	6%	18%	0%
Some of the time	25	29	20	35	16	32	10
Rarely	29	34	38	31	21	10	26
Never	41	32	37	29	57	40	64
TOTAL	100%	100%	100%	100%	100%	100%	100%

Table 417

"How often do you look at pictures while you are masturbating—most of the time, only some of the time, rarely, or never?"

	Adolescents with current masturbatory experience						
		Virgins			Nonvirgins		
Use of pictures in masturbation	All	All	Inexperienced	Beginners	All	Monogamists	Adventurers
Most of the time	5%	8%	13%	6%	4%	0%	10%
Some of the time	25	20	37	12	27	23	31
Rarely	29	21	10	28	33	36	27
Never	41	51	40	54	36	41	32
TOTAL	100%	100%	100%	100%	100%	100%	100%

Table 418

"In general, do you enjoy masturbating a great deal, somewhat, a little, or not at all?"

	Adolescents with current masturbatory experience						
		Boys			Girls		
Enjoyment of masturbation	All	All	Age 13–15	Age 16–19	All	Age 13–15	Age 16–19
A great deal	16%	19%	16%	20%	12%	6%	14%
Somewhat	43	46	53	41	37	35	38
A little	35	27	24	30	48	52	46
Not at all	6	8	7	9	3	7	2
TOTAL	100%	100%	100%	100%	100%	100%	100%

Table 419

"In general, do you usually enjoy masturbating a great deal, somewhat, a little, or not at all?"

	Adolescents with current masturbatory experience						
		Virgins			Nonvirgins		
Enjoyment of masturbation	All	All	Inexpe-rienced	Begin-ners	All	Monog-amists	Adven-turers
A great deal	16%	16%	26%	12%	16%	15%	17%
Somewhat	43	35	36	36	47	43	47
A little	35	43	31	50	31	40	27
Not at all	6	6	7	2	6	2	9
TOTAL	100%	100%	100%	100%	100%	100%	100%

Table 420

"How about feelings of guilt, anxiety, or concern about masturbation? Do you have such feelings often, sometimes, rarely, or never?"

	Adolescents with current masturbatory experience						
		Boys			Girls		
Guilt or anxiety about masturbation	All	All	Age 13–15	Age 16–19	All	Age 13–15	Age 16–19
Often	17%	19%	19%	20%	13%	16%	11%
Sometimes	32	26	24	27	44	60	37
Rarely	32	38	46	33	21	16	23
Never	19	17	11	20	22	8	29
TOTAL	100%	100%	100%	100%	100%	100%	100%

Table 421

"How about feelings of guilt, anxiety, or concern about masturbation? Do you have such feelings often, sometimes, rarely, or never?"

	Adolescents with current masturbatory experience						
		Virgins			Nonvirgins		
Guilt or anxiety about masturbation	All	All	Inexpe-rienced	Begin-ners	All	Monog-amists	Adven-turers
Often	17%	17%	0%	22%	17%	13%	29%
Sometimes	32	33	54	24	32	37	33
Rarely	32	39	21	50	28	20	16
Never	19	11	25	4	23	30	22
TOTAL	100%	100%	100%	100%	100%	100%	100%

Table 422

Male: "If you had to guess, would you say that you masturbate more often or less often than most other boys of about your own age?"

Female: "If you had to guess, would you say that you masturbate more often or less often than most other girls of about your own age?"

	Adolescents with current masturbatory experience						
		Boys			Girls		
Perceived relative frequency	All	All	Age 13–15	Age 16–19	All	Age 13–15	Age 16–19
More often	20%	18%	20%	16%	23%	23%	24%
About the same	60	65	67	65	49	32	57
Less often	20	17	13	19	28	45	19
TOTAL	100%	100%	100%	100%	100%	100%	100%

Table 423

Male: "If you had to guess, would you say that you masturbate more often or less often than most other boys of about your own age?"

Female: "If you had to guess, would you say that you masturbate more often or less often than most other girls of about your own age?"

	Adolescents with current masturbatory experience						
		Virgins			Nonvirgins		
Perceived relative frequency	All	All	Inexpe-rienced	Begin-ners	All	Monog-amists	Adven-turers
More often	20%	25%	23%	27%	18%	10%	19%
About the same	60	55	52	58	62	72	57
Less often	20	20	25	15	20	18	24
TOTAL	100%	100%	100%	100%	100%	100%	100%

Table 424

"When you masturbate, do you daydream or think about things most of the time, only some of the time, rarely, or never?"

	Adolescents with current masturbatory experience						
		Boys			Girls		
Frequency of masturbatory fantasy	All	Marijuana users	Marijuana nonusers	All	Marijuana users	Marijuana nonusers
Most of the time	57%	65%	49%	46%	46%	45%
Some of the time	23	30	19	44	49	40
Rarely	9	3	14	3	0	6
Never	11	2	18	7	5	9
TOTAL	100%	100%	100%	100%	100%	100%

Table 425

"How often do you look at pictures while you are masturbating—most of the time, only some of the time, rarely, or never?"

	Adolescents with current masturbatory experience					
		Boys			Girls	
Use of pictures in masturbation	All	Marijuana users	Marijuana nonusers	All	Marijuana users	Marijuana nonusers
Most of the time	5%	7%	4%	6%	0%	10%
Some of the time	29	37	24	16	11	22
Rarely	34	40	28	21	33	11
Never	32	16	44	57	56	57
TOTAL	100%	100%	100%	100%	100%	100%

Table 426

"In general, do you usually enjoy masturbating a great deal, somewhat, a little, or not at all?"

	Adolescents with current masturbatory experience					
		Boys			Girls	
Enjoyment of masturbation	All	Marijuana users	Marijuana nonusers	All	Marijuana users	Marijuana nonusers
A great deal	19%	31%	10%	12%	20%	4%
Somewhat	46	51	42	37	44	32
A little	27	17	35	48	36	58
Not at all	8	1	13	3	0	6
TOTAL	100%	100%	100%	100%	100%	100%

Table 427

"How about feelings of guilt, anxiety, or concern about masturbation? Do you have such feelings often, sometimes, rarely, or never?"

	Adolescents with current masturbatory experience					
	Boys			Girls		
Guilt or anxiety about masturbation	All	Marijuana users	Marijuana nonusers	All	Marijuana users	Marijuana nonusers
Often	19%	14%	23%	13%	1%	23%
Sometimes	26	22	26	44	52	37
Rarely	38	43	36	21	10	30
Never	17	21	15	22	37	10
TOTAL	100%	100%	100%	100%	100%	100%

Table 428

Male: "If you had to guess, would you say that you masturbate more often or less often than most other boys of about your own age?"

Female: "If you had to guess, would you say you masturbate more often or less often than most other girls of about your own age?"

	Adolescents with current masturbatory experience					
	Boys			Girls		
Perceived relative frequency	All	Marijuana users	Marijuana nonusers	All	Marijuana users	Marijuana nonusers
More often	18%	22%	16%	23%	17%	30%
About the same	65	65	67	49	68	32
Less often	17	13	17	28	15	38
TOTAL	100%	100%	100%	100%	100%	100%

Table 429

Male: "This first time that you had sex with a girl, did either you or the girl make use of any birth control method, or do anything else to cut down on the risk of the girl's becoming pregnant?"

Female: "This first time that you had sex with a boy, did either you or the boy make use of any birth control method, or do anything else to cut down on the risk of your becoming pregnant?"

	Nonvirgins						
		Boys			Girls		
Use of contraception at first intercourse	All	All	Age 13–15	Age 16–19	All	Age 13–15	Age 16–19
Yes	32%	28%	34%	25%	37%	31%	40%
Boy did not; doesn't know if girl did	13	23	33	19	NA	NA	NA
No	55	49	33	56	63	69	60
TOTAL	100%	100%	100%	100%	100%	100%	100%

Table 430

Male: "Have you ever wanted to have sex with a girl but decided not to do so because you were afraid that the girl might become pregnant?"

Female: "Have you ever wanted to have sex with a boy but decided not to do so because you were afraid that you might become pregnant?"

	Nonvirgins						
		Boys			Girls		
Refrained from sex due to fear of pregnancy	All	All	Age 13–15	Age 16–19	All	Age 13–15	Age 16–19
Yes	37%	33%	51%	24%	44%	34%	64%
No	63	67	49	76	56	66	36
TOTAL	100%	100%	100%	100%	100%	100%	100%

Table 431

Male: "If you had it to do all over again, do you wish that you had waited until you were older before having sex with a girl for the first time, are you glad you did it when you did, or do you wish that you had done it when you were younger?"

Female: "If you had it to do all over again, do you wish that you had waited until you were older before having sex with a boy for the first time, are you glad you did it when you did, or do you wish you had done it when you were younger?"

	Nonvirgins						
		Boys			Girls		
Retrospective evaluation	All	All	Age 13–15	Age 16–19	All	Age 13–15	Age 16–19
I wish I had waited until I was older before having sex with a girl/boy for the first time	26%	14%	10%	16%	40%	53%	34%
I'm glad I did it when I did	61	67	79	62	54	44	58
I wish I had done it when I was younger	13	19	11	22	6	3	8
TOTAL	100%	100%	100%	100%	100%	100%	100%

Table 432

Male: "Still thinking about this first girl that you ever had sex with, what happened to your relationship with her after the first time you had sex together? Did the relationship become stronger or weaker as a result of having had sex together?"

Female: "Still thinking about this very first boy that you ever had sex with, what happened to your relationship with him after the first time you had sex together? Did the relationship become stronger or weaker as a result of having sex together?"

	Nonvirgins						
		Boys			Girls		
Effect upon relationship	All	All	Age 13–15	Age 16–19	All	Age 13–15	Age 16–19
The relationship became stronger	48%	41%	42%	41%	56%	51%	58%
The relationship stayed about the same	23	22	24	22	24	23	25
The relationship became weaker	10	12	13	10	9	8	9
There wasn't any relationship to begin with	19	25	21	27	11	18	8
TOTAL	100%	100%	100%	100%	100%	100%	100%

Table 433

Male: "So far as you know, were you the first boy that she had ever had sex with, or had she ever had sex before with one or more other boys?"

Female: "So far as you know, were you the first girl that he ever had sex with, or had he ever had sex before with one or more other girls?"

	Nonvirgins						
		Boys			Girls		
First intercourse partner's previous experience	All	All	Age 13–15	Age 16–19	All	Age 13–15	Age 16–19
I know for sure that I was the first boy/girl that she/he had ever had sex with	28%	33%	34%	32%	22%	12%	26%
I think that I was probably the first boy/girl that she/he had ever had sex with	9	11	5	14	7	11	5
I really don't know whether or not she/he had ever had sex before	13	15	19	13	10	21	5
I think that she /he had probably had sex with one or more boys/girls before me	15	12	18	9	19	23	18
I know for sure that she/he had had sex with one or more other boys/girls before me	35	29	24	32	42	33	46
TOTAL	100%	100%	100%	100%	100%	100%	100%

Table 434

Male: "Looking back at it now, are you glad that this particular girl was the first one you ever had sex with? Or if you had it to do over again, would you rather have had sex for the first time with a different girl?"

Female: "Looking back at it now, are you glad that this particular boy was the first one you ever had sex with? Or if you had to do it over again, would you rather have had sex with a different boy?"

	Nonvirgins						
		Boys			Girls		
Retrospective evaluation of first intercourse partner	All	All	Age 13–15	Age 16–19	All	Age 13–15	Age 16–19
I'm glad it was this particular girl/boy	69%	70%	77%	66%	67%	57%	72%
I wish it had been a different girl/boy	31	30	23	34	33	43	28
TOTAL	100%	100%	100%	100%	100%	100%	100%

Table 435

Male: "After the first time, did you ever have sex with this girl again?"

Female: "After the first time, did you ever have sex with this boy again?"

	Nonvirgins						
		Boys			Girls		
Subsequent intercourse with first partner	All	All	Age 13–15	Age 16–19	All	Age 13–15	Age 16–19
Yes	61%	53%	58%	51%	70%	52%	78%
No	39	47	42	49	30	48	22
TOTAL	100%	100%	100%	100%	100%	100%	100%

Table 436

"On about how many more occasions did you have sex together, after the first time?"

	Adolescents reporting subsequent intercourse with first intercourse partner						
		Boys			Girls		
Number of subsequent intercourse occasions with first intercourse partner	All	All	Age 13–15	Age 16–19	All	Age 13–15	Age 16–19
1–2	22%	32%	28%	34%	12%	34%	6%
3–4	23	22	47	10	23	50	15
5–6	15	11	16	8	19	8	22
7–20	16	19	9	24	12	0	16
21–99	11	9	0	13	16	8	18
100 or more	13	7	0	11	18	0	23
TOTAL	100%	100%	100%	100%	100%	100%	100%

Table 437

Male contraceptive practices: "I use a condom (rubber)."

	Nonvirgin boys		
Use a condom (rubber)	All	Age 13–15	Age 16–19
Never	57%	46%	62%
Sometimes	17	23	14
Usually	11	11	11
Always	15	20	13
TOTAL	100%	100%	100%

Table 438

Male contraceptive practices: "I use a condom (rubber)."

	Nonvirgin boys		
Use a condom (rubber)	All	Current intercourse experience	No current intercourse experience
Never	57%	61%	51%
Sometimes	17	12	23
Usually	11	8	15
Always	15	19	11
TOTAL	100%	100%	100%

Table 439

Male contraceptive practices: "I withdraw before ejaculating (coming)."

	Nonvirgin boys		
Withdraw before ejaculating (coming)	All	Age 13–15	Age 16–19
Never	34%	35%	33%
Sometimes	30	11	39
Usually	16	29	11
Always	20	25	17
TOTAL	100%	100%	100%

Table 440

Male contraceptive practices: "I withdraw before ejaculating (coming)."

	Nonvirgin boys		
Withdraw before ejaculating (coming)	All	Current intercourse experience	No current intercourse experience
Never	34%	34%	34%
Sometimes	30	39	19
Usually	16	9	25
Always	20	18	22
TOTAL	100%	100%	100%

Table 441

Male contraceptive practices: "I make sure that the girl is using birth control pills or some other method of contraception."

	Nonvirgin boys		
Make sure girl is using some method of contraception	All	Age 13–15	Age 16–19
Never	48%	57%	44%
Sometimes	26	27	25
Usually	17	3	24
Always	9	13	7
TOTAL	100%	100%	100%

Table 442

Male contraceptive practices: "I make sure that the girl is using birth control pills or some other method of contraception."

Make sure girl is using some method of contraception	Nonvirgin boys: All	Current intercourse experience	No current intercourse experience
Never	48%	38%	60%
Sometimes	26	25	27
Usually	17	26	5
Always	9	11	8
TOTAL	100%	100%	100%

Table 443

Male contraceptive practices: "I just assume that the girl is using birth control pills or some other method of contraception."

Assume girl is using some method of contraception	Nonvirgin boys: All	Age 13–15	Age 16–19
Never	62%	62%	62%
Sometimes	21	23	20
Usually	9	7	10
Always	8	8	8
TOTAL	100%	100%	100%

Table 444

Male contraceptive practices: "I just assume that the girl is using birth control pills or some other method of contraception."

Assume girl is using some method of contraception	Nonvirgin boys: All	Current intercourse experience	No current intercourse experience
Never	62%	56%	71%
Sometimes	21	24	17
Usually	9	11	5
Always	8	9	7
TOTAL	100%	100%	100%

Table 445

Male contraceptive practices: "I just trust to luck that the girl won't become pregnant."

Trust to luck girl won't become pregnant	Nonvirgin boys: All	Age 13–15	Age 16–19
Never	42%	39%	44%
Sometimes	17	17	17
Usually	16	28	9
Always	25	16	30
TOTAL	100%	100%	100%

Table 446

Male contraceptive practices: "I just trust to luck that the girl won't become pregnant."

Trust to luck girl won't become pregnant	Nonvirgin boys: All	Current intercourse experience	No current intercourse experience
Never	42%	47%	36%
Sometimes	17	20	14
Usually	16	11	22
Always	25	22	28
TOTAL	100%	100%	100%

Table 447

Male contraceptive practices: "I don't think about whether or not the girl might become pregnant."

Think about whether or not the girl might become pregnant	Nonvirgin boys: All	Age 13–15	Age 16–19
Never	39%	39%	39%
Sometimes	29	17	34
Usually	15	25	10
Always	17	19	17
TOTAL	100%	100%	100%

Table 448

Male contraceptive practices: "I don't think about whether or not the girl might become pregnant."

Think about whether or not the girl might become pregnant	Nonvirgin boys: All	Current intercourse experience	No current intercourse experience
Never	39%	40%	37%
Sometimes	29	30	27
Usually	15	6	26
Always	17	24	10
TOTAL	100%	100%	100%

Table 449

"Do you ever worry about the possibility that you might cause a girl to become pregnant?"

Worry about causing pregnancy	Nonvirgin boys: All	Age 13–15	Age 16–19
Never	18%	21%	16%
Hardly ever	6	7	6
Sometimes	48	46	49
Often	28	26	29
TOTAL	100%	100%	100%

Table 450

"Do you ever worry about the possibility that you might cause a girl to become pregnant?"

Worry about causing pregnancy	Nonvirgin boys: All	Current intercourse experience	No current intercourse experience
Never	18%	9%	28%
Hardly ever	6	2	11
Sometimes	48	60	34
Often	28	29	27
TOTAL	100%	100%	100%

Table 451

"Do you ever worry about the possibility that you might become pregnant?"

Worry about possible pregnancy	Nonvirgin girls: All	Age 13–15	Age 16–19
Never	16%	21%	15%
Hardly ever	14	18	13
Sometimes	41	37	42
Often	29	24	30
TOTAL	100%	100%	100%

Table 452

"Do you ever worry about the possibility that you might become pregnant?"

Worry about possible pregnancy	Nonvirgin girls: All	Current intercourse experience	No current intercourse experience
Never	16%	17%	13%
Hardly ever	14	12	19
Sometimes	41	36	56
Often	29	35	12
TOTAL	100%	100%	100%

Table 453

"If you were to make a girl pregnant, which *one* of the things listed below would you *most prefer* that she do, *if you could have things your way?*"

Preferred outcome of pregnancy	Nonvirgin boys: All	Age 13–15	Age 16–19
Have an abortion	30%	27%	31%
Have the baby and give it up for adoption	7	16	2
Have the baby and count on me to help bring it up	23	15	26
Have the baby and bring it up herself	7	1	10
Have the baby and get married	24	20	26
Tell her parents and let them decide what to do	9	21	5
TOTAL	100%	100%	100%

Table 454

"If you were to make a girl pregnant, which *one* of the things listed below would you *most prefer* that she do, *if you could have things your way?*"

Preferred outcome of pregnancy	Nonvirgin boys: All	Current intercourse experience	No current intercourse experience
Have an abortion	30%	22%	38%
Have the baby and give it up for adoption	7	5	8
Have the baby and count on me to help bring it up	23	28	18
Have the baby and bring it up herself	7	10	4
Have the baby and get married	24	23	25
Tell her parents and let them decide what to do	9	12	7
TOTAL	100%	100%	100%

Table 455

"If you were to become pregnant, which *one* of the things listed below would you *most prefer* to do, *if you could have things your way?*"

Preferred outcome of pregnancy	Nonvirgin girls: All	Age 13–15	Age 16–19
Have an abortion	18%	3%	23%
Have the baby and give it up for adoption	7	4	7
Have the baby and count on the father to help me bring it up	15	3	20
Have the baby and bring it up by myself	18	29	14
Have the baby and get married	38	45	36
Tell my parents and let them decide what to do	4	16	0
TOTAL	100%	100%	100%

Table 456

"If you were to become pregnant, which *one* of the things listed below would you *most prefer* to do, *if you could have things your way?*"

Preferred outcome of pregnancy	Nonvirgin girls: All	Current intercourse experience	No current intercourse experience
Have an abortion	18%	24%	3%
Have the baby and give it up for adoption	7	5	10
Have the baby and count on the father to help me bring it up	15	20	3
Have the baby and bring it up by myself	18	13	30
Have the baby and get married	38	37	41
Tell my parents and let them decide what to do	4	1	13
TOTAL	100%	100%	100%

Table 457

"Sometimes people can have things their own way, and sometimes they can't. If you were to become pregnant, which *one* of the things listed below do you think you would *actually do?*"

Expected outcome of pregnancy	Nonvirgin girls: All	Age 13–15	Age 16–19
Have an abortion	18%	2%	23%
Have the baby and give it up for adoption	8	9	8
Have the baby and count on the father to help me bring it up	14	7	17
Have the baby and bring it up by myself	22	31	18
Have the baby and get married	31	31	31
Tell my parents and let them decide what to do	7	20	3
TOTAL	100%	100%	100%

Table 458

"Sometimes people can have things their own way, and sometimes they can't. If you were to become pregnant, which *one* of the things listed below do you think you would *actually do?*"

	Nonvirgin girls		
Expected outcome of pregnancy	All	Current intercourse experience	No current intercourse experience
Have an abortion	18%	23%	3%
Have the baby and give it up for adoption	8	4	19
Have the baby and count on the father to help me bring it up	14	18	6
Have the baby and bring it up by myself	22	17	35
Have the baby and get married	31	31	30
Tell my parents and let them decide what to do	7	7	7
TOTAL	100%	100%	100%

Table 459

"If you were to make a girl pregnant, do you think you would or would not . . . say that it was someone else who had made her pregnant?"

	Nonvirgin boys		
Would say that it was someone else who had made her pregnant	All	Age 13–15	Age 16–19
Yes	7%	12%	5%
Maybe	31	40	27
No	62	48	68
TOTAL	100%	100%	100%

Table 460

"If you were to make a girl pregnant, do you think you would or would not . . . say that it was someone else who had made her pregnant?"

	Nonvirgin boys		
Would say that it was someone else who had made her pregnant	All	Current intercourse experience	No current intercourse experience
Yes	7%	6%	9%
Maybe	31	24	40
No	62	70	51
TOTAL	100%	100%	100%

Table 461

"If you were to make a girl pregnant, do you think you would or would not . . . say that it was the girl's problem, and none of my business?"

	Nonvirgin boys		
Would say that it was the girl's problem, and none of my business	All	Age 13–15	Age 16–19
Yes	5%	2%	6%
Maybe	10	14	8
No	85	84	86
TOTAL	100%	100%	100%

Table 462

"If you were to make a girl pregnant, do you think you would or would not . . . say that it was the girl's problem, and none of my business?"

	Nonvirgin boys		
Would say that it was the girl's problem, and none of my business	All	Current intercourse experience	No current intercourse experience
Yes	5%	6%	2%
Maybe	10	14	5
No	85	80	93
TOTAL	100%	100%	100%

Table 463

"If you were to make a girl pregnant, do you think you would or would not . . . talk to her about it and help her decide what to do, but that's all?"

	Nonvirgin boys		
Would talk to her about it and help her decide what to do, but that's all	All	Age 13–15	Age 16–19
Yes	20%	38%	11%
Maybe	38	36	40
No	42	26	49
TOTAL	100%	100%	100%

Table 464

"If you were to make a girl pregnant, do you think you would or would not . . . talk to her about it and help her decide what to do, but that's all?"

	Nonvirgin boys		
Would talk to her about it and help her decide what to do, but that's all	All	Current intercourse experience	No current intercourse experience
Yes	20%	22%	17%
Maybe	38	38	40
No	42	40	43
TOTAL	100%	100%	100%

Table 465

"If you were to make a girl pregnant, do you think you would or would not. . . help to arrange and pay for an abortion?"

	Nonvirgin boys		
Would help to arrange and pay for an abortion	All	Age 13–15	Age 16–19
Yes	23%	22%	24%
Maybe	28	33	26
No	49	45	50
TOTAL	100%	100%	100%

Table 466

"If you were to make a girl pregnant, do you think you would or would not . . . help to arrange and pay for an abortion?"

	Nonvirgin boys		
Would help to arrange and pay for an abortion	All	Current intercourse experience	No current intercourse experience
Yes	23%	23%	25%
Maybe	28	31	24
No	49	46	51
TOTAL	100%	100%	100%

Table 467

"If you were to make a girl pregnant, do you think you would or would not . . . help her bring up the child?"

	Nonvirgin boys		
Would help her bring up the child	All	Age 13–15	Age 16–19
Yes	54%	38%	61%
Maybe	27	30	25
No	19	32	14
TOTAL	100%	100%	100%

Table 468

"If you were to make a girl pregnant, do you think you would or would not . . . help her bring up the child?"

	Nonvirgin boys		
Would help her bring up the child	All	Current intercourse experience	No current intercourse experience
Yes	54%	57%	50%
Maybe	27	23	31
No	19	20	19
TOTAL	100%	100%	100%

Table 469

"If you were to make a girl pregnant, do you think you would or would not . . . help her do whatever she decided to do?"

	Nonvirgin boys		
Would help her do whatever she decided to do	All	Age 13–15	Age 16–19
Yes	66%	50%	74%
Maybe	26	42	18
No	8	8	8
TOTAL	100%	100%	100%

Table 470

"If you were to make a girl pregnant, do you think you would or would not . . . help her do whatever she decided to do?"

	Nonvirgin boys		
Would help her do whatever she decided to do	All	Current intercourse experience	No current intercourse experience
Yes	66%	66%	66%
Maybe	26	24	28
No	8	10	6
TOTAL	100%	100%	100%

Table 471

"If you were to make a girl pregnant, do you think you would or would not . . . marry the girl?"

	Nonvirgin boys		
Would marry the girl	All	Age 13–15	Age 16–19
Yes	27%	15%	33%
Maybe	46	49	44
No	27	36	23
TOTAL	100%	100%	100%

Table 472

"If you were to make a girl pregnant, do you think you would or would not . . . marry the girl?"

	Nonvirgin boys		
Would marry the girl	All	Current intercourse experience	No current intercourse experience
Yes	27%	28%	26%
Maybe	46	39	54
No	27	33	20
TOTAL	100%	100%	100%

Table 473

"If you were to make a girl pregnant, do you think you would or would not . . . discuss it with your parents to see what they think?"

	Nonvirgin boys		
Would discuss it with parents to see what they think	All	Age 13–15	Age 16–19
Yes	29%	23%	32%
Maybe	30	28	31
No	41	49	37
TOTAL	100%	100%	100%

Table 474

"If you were to make a girl pregnant, do you think you would or would not . . . discuss it with your parents to see what they think?"

Would discuss it with parents to see what they think	Nonvirgin boys All	Current intercourse experience	No current intercourse experience
Yes	29%	31%	27%
Maybe	30	27	33
No	41	42	40
TOTAL	100%	100%	100%

Table 475

"Have you ever wanted to have sex with a girl but decided not to do so because you were afraid that the girl might become pregnant?"

Refrained from sex due to fear of pregnancy	Nonvirgin boys All	Current intercourse experience	No current intercourse experience
Yes	33%	29%	37%
No	67	71	63
TOTAL	100%	100%	100%

Table 476

"Have you ever wanted to have sex with a boy but decided not to do so because you were afraid that you might become pregnant?"

Refrained from sex due to fear of pregnancy	Nonvirgin girls All	Current intercourse experience	No current intercourse experience
Yes	44%	38%	58%
No	56	62	42
TOTAL	100%	100%	100%

Table 477

"Have you ever made a girl pregnant?"

Pregnancy experience	Nonvirgin boys All	Age 13–15	Age 16–19
Yes	13%	7%	16%
No	87	93	84
TOTAL	100%	100%	100%

Table 478

"Have you ever made a girl pregnant?"

Pregnancy experience	Nonvirgin boys All	Current intercourse experience	No current intercourse experience
Yes	13%	21%	3%
No	87	79	97
TOTAL	100%	100%	100%

Table 479

"Have you ever been pregnant?"

Pregnancy experience	Nonvirgin girls All	Age 13–15	Age 16–19
Yes	23%	11%	28%
No	77	89	72
TOTAL	100%	100%	100%

Table 480

"Have you ever been pregnant?"

Pregnancy experience	Nonvirgin girls All	Current intercourse experience	No current intercourse experience
Yes	23%	28%	7%
No	77	72	93
TOTAL	100%	100%	100%

Table 481

Pregnancy precautions taken in the past month

Pregnancy precautions taken	Nonvirgins with current intercourse experience All	Boys	Girls
Always	59%	55%	62%
Sometimes	27	33	22
Never	14	12	16
TOTAL	100%	100%	100%

Table 482

Male contraceptive practices in the past month: "I used a condom (rubber)."

Used a condom	Male nonvirgins with current intercourse experience
Never	60%
Sometimes, once or twice	15
Always	25
TOTAL	100%

Table 483

Female contraceptive practices in the past month: "The boy used a condom (rubber)."

Boy used a condom	Female nonvirgins with current intercourse experience
Never	76%
Sometimes, once or twice	15
Always	9
TOTAL	100%

Table 484

Male contraceptive practices in the past month: "I withdrew before ejaculating (coming)."

Withdrew before ejaculating	Male nonvirgins with current intercourse experience
Never	44%
Sometimes, once or twice	36
Always	20
TOTAL	100%

Table 485

Female contraceptive practices in the past month: "The boy withdrew before ejaculating (coming)."

Boy withdrew before ejaculating	Female nonvirgins with current intercourse experience
Never	66%
Sometimes, once or twice	17
Always	17
TOTAL	100%

Table 486

Male contraceptive practices in the past month: "The girl used birth control pills."

Girl used birth control pills	Male nonvirgins with current intercourse experience
Never	62%
Sometimes, once or twice	21
Always	17
TOTAL	100%

Table 487

Female contraceptive practices in the past month: "I used birth control pills."

Used birth control pills	Female nonvirgins with current intercourse experience
Never	65%
Sometimes, once or twice	2
Always	33
TOTAL	100%

Table 488

Male contraceptive practices in the past month: "The girl used an intrauterine device (coil, IUD)."

Girl used an intrauterine device	Male nonvirgins with current intercourse experience
Never	74%
Sometimes, once or twice	21
Always	5
TOTAL	100%

Table 489

Female contraceptive practices in the past month: "I used an intrauterine device (coil, IUD)."

Used an intrauterine device	Female nonvirgins with current intercourse experience
Never	98%
Sometimes, once or twice	0
Always	2
TOTAL	100%

Table 490

Male contraceptive practices in the past month: "The girl used a diaphragm."

Girl used a diaphragm	Male nonvirgins with current intercourse experience
Never	80%
Sometimes, once or twice	17
Always	3
TOTAL	100%

Table 491

Female contraceptive practices in the past month: "I used a diaphragm."

Used a diaphragm	Female nonvirgins with current intercourse experience
Never	100%
Sometimes, once or twice	0
Always	0
TOTAL	100%

Table 492

Male contraceptive practices in the past month: "The girl used a contraceptive foam."

Girl used a contraceptive foam	Male nonvirgins with current intercourse experience
Never	73%
Sometimes, once or twice	21
Always	6
TOTAL	100%

Table 493

Female contraceptive practices in the past month: "I used a contraceptive foam."

Used a contraceptive foam	Female nonvirgins with current intercourse experience
Never	92%
Sometimes, once or twice	0
Always	8
TOTAL	100%

Table 494

Male contraceptive practices in the past month: "The girl used a contraceptive jelly."

Girl used a contraceptive jelly	Male nonvirgins with current intercourse experience
Never	87%
Sometimes, once or twice	11
Always	2
TOTAL	100%

Table 495

Female contraceptive practices in the past month: "I used a contraceptive jelly."

Used a contraceptive jelly	Female nonvirgins with current intercourse experience
Never	100%
Sometimes, once or twice	0
Always	0
TOTAL	100%

Table 496

Male contraceptive practices in the past month: "The girl used a contraceptive douche."

Girl used a contraceptive douche	Male nonvirgins with current intercourse experience
Never	80%
Sometimes, once or twice	15
Always	5
TOTAL	100%

Table 497

Female contraceptive practices in the past month: "I used a contraceptive douche."

Used a contraceptive douche	Female nonvirgins with current intercourse experience
Never	99%
Sometimes, once or twice	1
Always	0
TOTAL	100%

Table 498

Male contraceptive practices in the past month: "The girl used the rhythm method."

Girl used rhythm method	Male nonvirgins with current intercourse experience
Never	69%
Sometimes, once or twice	22
Always	9
TOTAL	100%

Table 499

Female contraceptive practices in the past month: "I used the rhythm method."

Used rhythm method	Female nonvirgins with current intercourse experience
Never	86%
Sometimes, once or twice	9
Always	5
TOTAL	100%

Table 500

Male contraceptive practices in the past month: "I made sure that the girl was using something, but I don't know what it was."

Made sure girl was using something, but don't know what it was	Male nonvirgins with current intercourse experience
Never	71%
Sometimes, once or twice	27
Always	2
TOTAL	100%

Table 501

Male contraceptive practices in the past month: "I just assumed that the girl was using something, but I don't know what it was."

Assumed girl was using something, but don't know what it was	Male nonvirgins with current intercourse experience
Never	61%
Sometimes, once or twice	36
Always	3
TOTAL	100%

Table 502

Male contraceptive practices in the past month: "I just trusted to luck that the girl wouldn't become pregnant."

Trusted to luck girl wouldn't become pregnant	Male nonvirgins with current intercourse experience
Never	54%
Sometimes, once or twice	28
Always	18
TOTAL	100%

Table 503

Female contraceptive practices in the past month: "I just trusted to luck that I wouldn't become pregnant."

Trusted to luck I wouldn't become pregnant	Female nonvirgins with current intercourse experience
Never	63%
Sometimes, once or twice	18
Always	19
TOTAL	100%

Table 504

Male contraceptive practices in the past month: "I didn't think about whether or not the girl might become pregnant."

Thought about whether or not girl might become pregnant	Male nonvirgins with current intercourse experience
Never	51%
Sometimes, once or twice	33
Always	16
TOTAL	100%

Table 505

Female contraceptive practices in the past month: "I didn't think about whether or not I might become pregnant."

Thought about whether or not I might become pregnant	Female nonvirgins with current intercourse experience
Never	82%
Sometimes, once or twice	10
Always	8
TOTAL	100%

Table 506

"This very last time that you had sex with a girl, did either of you use any kind of contraceptive or birth control method, or do anything else to cut down the risk of the girl becoming pregnant?"

Use of contraception on occasion of most recent intercourse	Male nonvirgins with current intercourse experience		
	All	Age 13–15	Age 16–19
Yes, I did	30%	66%	22%
Yes, the girl did	17	0	20
I didn't, and I don't know whether or not the girl did	8	11	8
No, neither of us did	45	23	50
TOTAL	100%	100%	100%

Table 507

"This very last time that you had sex with a boy, did either of you use any kind of contraceptive or birth control method, or do anything else to cut down the risk of your becoming pregnant?"

Use of contraception on occasion of most recent intercourse	Female nonvirgins with current intercourse experience		
	All	Age 13–15	Age 16–19
Yes, I did	40%	23%	46%
Yes, the boy did	20	32	16
No, neither of us did	40	45	38
TOTAL	100%	100%	100%

Table 508

"Who was the very first girl with whom you ever had sexual intercourse?"

First intercourse partner	Nonvirgin boys		
	All	Age 13–15	Age 16–19
A girl I was going steady with and planned to marry	7%	0%	11%
A girl I was going steady with but had no definite plans to marry	18	14	19
A girl I knew well and liked a lot, even though we weren't going together	31	29	31
A girl I knew slightly and was more or less friendly with	19	30	14
A girl I had met only a little while before the time that we first had sex together	25	27	25
TOTAL	100%	100%	100%

Table 509

"Who was the very first boy with whom you ever had sexual intercourse?"

First intercourse partner	Nonvirgin girls		
	All	Age 13–15	Age 16–19
My husband, after we were married	2%	0%	3%
Someone who raped me	1	4	0
A boy I was going steady with and planned to marry	36	33	37
A boy I was going steady with but had no definite plans to marry	21	8	26
A boy I knew well and liked a lot, even though we weren't going together	25	35	21
A boy I knew slightly and was more or less friendly with	5	1	7
A boy I had met only a little while before the time that we first had sex together	10	19	6
TOTAL	100%	100%	100%

Table 510

Male: "Which of the words below accurately describe how you felt the first time that you had sex with a girl?"

Female: "Which of the words below accurately describe how you felt the first time that you had sex with a boy?"

Own reaction	Nonvirgins*		
	All	Boys	Girls
Excited	37%	46%	26%
Afraid	37	17	63
Happy	35	42	26
Satisfied	33	43	20
Thrilled	30	43	13
Curious	26	23	30
Joyful	23	31	12
Mature	23	29	14
Fulfilled	20	29	8
Worried	20	9	35
Guilty	17	3	36
Embarrassed	17	7	31
Tired	15	15	14
Relieved	14	19	8
Sorry	12	1	25
Hurt	11	0	25
Powerful	9	15	1
Foolish	8	7	9
Used	7	0	16
Disappointed	6	3	10
Raped	3	0	6

*Percentages add to more than 100% because most respondents reported more than one reaction.

Table 511

Male: "Of course, you weren't inside this girl's head at the time, and you can't know for sure how she felt then. But if you had to *guess*, which of the words below do you think might accurately describe how she felt when you had sex with her for the very first time?"

Female: "Of course, you weren't inside this boy's head at the time, and you can't know for sure how he felt then. But if you had to *guess*, which of the words below do you think might accurately describe how he felt when you had sex with him for the very first time?"

Reaction ascribed to first partner	Nonvirgins*		
	All	Boys	Girls
Excited	48%	43%	55%
Afraid	22	23	22
Happy	42	39	46
Satisfied	41	35	50
Thrilled	36	39	31
Curious	20	22	16
Joyful	25	30	19
Mature	19	17	22
Fulfilled	30	30	30
Worried	14	12	15
Guilty	9	8	10
Embarrassed	8	8	9
Tired	17	20	13
Relieved	12	16	8
Sorry	6	3	9
Hurt	3	3	3
Powerful	18	7	31
Foolish	5	7	2
Used	4	5	2
Disappointed	9	6	13
Raped	2	4	0

*Percentages add to more than 100% because most respondents reported more than one reaction.

Table 512

"Have you ever felt a girl's breast with your hand?"

Breast contact	Male beginners
Yes	95%
No	5
TOTAL	100%

Table 513

"Has a boy ever felt your breasts with his hand?"

Breast contact	Female beginners
Yes	98%
No	2
TOTAL	100%

Table 514

"Thinking back to *the very first time* that you felt a girl's breast with your hand, how old were you then?"

Age at first breast contact	Male beginners with breast contact experience
12 or under	8%
13	30
14	19
15	15
16	8
17 or over	20
TOTAL	100%

Table 515

"Thinking back to *the very first time* that a boy felt your breasts with his hand, how old were you then?"

Age at first breast contact	Female beginners with breast contact experience
12 or under	9%
13	7
14	24
15	28
16	25
17 or over	7
TOTAL	100%

Table 516

"When was the *most recent* occasion on which you felt a girl's breast with your hand?"

Most recent breast contact	Male beginners with breast contact experience
Within the past month	53%
More than a month ago	47
TOTAL	100%

Table 517

"When was the *most recent* occasion on which a boy felt your breasts with his hand?"

Most recent breast contact	Female beginners with breast contact experience
Within the past month	40%
More than a month ago	60
TOTAL	100%

Table 518

"Have you ever felt a girl's sex organ with your hand?"

Vaginal contact	Male beginners
Yes	56%
No	44
TOTAL	100%

Table 519

"Has a boy ever felt your sex organ with his hand?"

Vaginal contact	Female beginners
Yes	46%
No	54
TOTAL	100%

Table 520

"Thinking back to *the very first time* that you ever felt a girl's sex organ with your hand, how old were you then?"

Age at first vaginal contact	Male beginners with vaginal contact experience
13 or under	14%
14	22
15	44
16	6
17 or older	14
TOTAL	100%

Table 521

"Thinking back to *the very first time* that a boy ever felt your sex organ with his hand, how old were you then?"

Age at first vaginal contact	Female beginners with vaginal contact experience
13 or under	14%
14	11
15	12
16	26
17	26
18 or 19	11
TOTAL	100%

Table 522

"When was the *most recent* occasion on which you felt a girl's sex organ with your hand?"

Most recent vaginal contact	Male beginners with vaginal contact experience
Within the past month	43%
More than a month ago	57
TOTAL	100%

Table 523

"When was the *most recent* occasion on which a boy felt your sex organ with his hand?"

Most recent vaginal contact	Female beginner with vaginal contact experience
Within the past month	29%
More than a month ago	71
TOTAL	100%

Table 524

"Has a girl ever felt your sex organ with her hand?"

Penis contact	Male beginners
Yes	32%
No	68
TOTAL	100%

Table 525

"Have you ever felt a boy's sex organ with your hand?"

Penis contact	Female beginners
Yes	45%
No	55
TOTAL	100%

Table 526

"Thinking back to *the very first time* that a girl ever felt your sex organ with her hand, how old were you then?"

Age at first penis contact	Male beginners with penis contact experience
12 or under	22%
13	13
14	21
15	9
16	0
17 or older	35
TOTAL	100%

Table 527

"Thinking back to *the very first time* that you ever felt a boy's sex organ with your hand, how old were you then?"

Age at first penis contact	Female beginners with penis contact experience
12 or under	7%
13	13
14	11
15	0
16	27
17	24
18 or 19	18
TOTAL	100%

Table 528

"When was the *most recent* occasion on which a girl felt your sex organ with her hand?"

Most recent penis contact	Male beginners with penis contact experience
Within the past month	9%
More than a month ago	91
TOTAL	100%

Table 529

"When was the *most recent* occasion on which you felt a boy's sex organ with your hand?"

Most recent penis contact	Female beginners with penis contact experience
Within the past month	33%
More than a month ago	67
TOTAL	100%

Table 530

Male: "Where was it that you had sex with a girl for the very first time?"
Female: "Where was it that you had sex with a boy for the very first time?"

	Nonvirgins						
		Boys			Girls		
Place of first intercourse	All	All	Age 13–15	Age 16–19	All	Age 13–15	Age 16–19
In my home	19%	21%	12%	24%	18%	23%	16%
In a friend's home	10	9	12	8	10	11	10
In an automobile	20	16	7	20	24	25	24
In the girl's/boy's home	20	19	17	20	21	16	23
In a hotel or motel	2	0	0	0	5	0	8
Outdoors	20	26	34	23	13	12	12
Somewhere else	9	9	18	5	9	13	7
TOTAL	100%	100%	100%	100%	100%	100%	100%

Technical Appendix

Definition of Sexual Behavior Groups

VIRGINS: Adolescents who say they have never had sexual intercourse.

INEXPERIENCED: Virgins who deny having engaged in any of the three preintercourse activities (touching or being touched on the breast, the vagina, or the penis).

BEGINNERS: Virgins who affirm that they have engaged in one or more of the three preintercourse activities.

UNCLASSIFIED VIRGINS: Those few virgins whose reported sexual behavior did not clearly identify them for classification purposes.

NONVIRGINS: Adolescents who say they have had sexual intercourse one or more times.

MONOGAMISTS: *a.* Nonvirgins who have not had intercourse during the preceding month but have engaged in one or more preintercourse activities with only one person during the preceding month; *b.* Nonvirgins who have had intercourse during the preceding month with only one person and say that they never have sex with anyone else; and *c.* Nonvirgins who have had intercourse during the preceding month, say that they have sex mostly or only with one person, do *not* say that they never have sex with anyone else, but who have *not* during the preceding month engaged either in intercourse or any preintercourse activity with *more than two* different people.

ADVENTURERS: *a.* Nonvirgins who have had intercourse during the preceding month and deny that they have sex mostly or only with one person; *b.* Nonvirgins who have had intercourse during the preceding month, say that they have sex mostly with one person, deny that they never have sex with anyone else, and have engaged either in intercourse or in one or more preintercourse activities with *three or more* different people during the preceding month; and *c.* Nonvirgins who have not had intercourse during the preceding month, deny that they have sex mostly or only with one person, and have engaged in one or more preintercourse activities with *three or more* different people during the preceding month.

UNCLASSIFIED NONVIRGINS: Those few nonvirgins whose reported sexual behavior did not clearly identify them for classification purposes.

Sample Design and Execution

The adolescents whose questionnaire responses are reflected in the statistical findings of this study were selected from the national sample designed and maintained by Response Analysis Corporation (RAC), Princeton, New Jersey. Consisting of 103 primary areas in which there are 600 secondary areas or sample locations, this well-dispersed area probability sample has been used for a variety of survey research studies dealing with important social issues.

Selection of primary and secondary areas

Primary areas were selected as follows:

1. The entire area of the coterminous United States was divided into approximately 1,140 primary sampling units (PSUs). Each PSU is a well-defined geographic unit, usually a county or a group of counties with a minimum population of 50,000 in 1970. PSUs are of two general types: (1) metropolitan areas or parts of metropolitan areas and (2) nonmetropolitan areas.
2. Thirty-eight large PSUs were included in the sample as self-representing primary areas.
3. All other PSUs were grouped into sixty-five strata, with an average stratum population of approximately 2,000,000 persons in 1970.
4. Random numbers were used to select one PSU from each of the sixty-five strata that included two or more PSUs.

Each of the 103 primary areas (38 selected as self-representing areas, plus 65 selected as a result of the stratification procedure) is a relatively heterogeneous area. Most include city, town, suburban, and rural residents. Some are primarily small town or rural but are several counties in size.

Within the 103 primary areas 600 secondary areas or specific sample locations were defined and selected. Secondary areas in the RAC sample are areas of approximately 2,500 population in 1970. A secondary area may be as small as a block or two in a densely populated portion of a city, or it may be an entire county or even larger in a sparsely populated rural area.

Secondary areas usually consist of a number of administrative units used in the census, either enumeration districts or block groups. Census microfilm records were used to define and select secondary areas. These units were selected with probability proportionate to population size.

Metropolitan areas

In most cases, primary sampling units that are metropolitan areas are the same as Standard Metropolitan Statistical Areas (SMSAs) defined by the Bureau of the Census. In the census definition, each SMSA is a county or group of contiguous counties which contains at least one city of 50,000 inhabitants or more, or "twin cities" with a combined population of at least 50,000. In addition to the county or counties containing a central city or cities, contiguous counties are included in an SMSA if, according to certain criteria, they are essentially metropolitan in character and are socially and economically integrated with the central city.

In the RAC sample exceptions to the SMSA definitions were of three general types:

1. In New England, SMSAs consist of towns and cities rather than counties. In the RAC sample the county was retained as the basic level for formation of primary sampling units. Thus, primary sampling units may include all or parts of two or more SMSAs.
2. Some SMSAs include counties in two census geographic divisions (for example, the Cincinnati SMSA consists of counties in Ohio and Indiana, in the East North-Central Division, and in Kentucky in the East South-Central Division). In order to maintain a strict stratification of primary sampling units on a geographic division basis, these SMSAs were divided into two parts, corresponding to the geographic divisional classifications.
3. Seven very large metropolitan areas (New York, Boston, Philadelphia, Chicago, Detroit, Los Angeles, and San Francisco) were subdivided into two or more primary sampling units. Altogether, the seven SMSAs comprise twenty primary sampling units. The objective of these subdivisions was to create smaller areas as more efficient field assignment units.

Nonmetropolitan areas

Primary sampling units that are not metropolitan areas consist of a county or a group of contiguous counties and include a minimum population of 50,000 in 1970. The minimum-size condition was intended to create PSUs of sufficient population size to serve diverse survey needs, including sampling of special populations, over a long period of time.

A number of criteria were used in combining counties to form primary sampling units to meet the minimum size requirement:

1. Whenever possible, a city or large town serving as the central point for the PSU
2. Convenience of travel to different parts of the PSU from the central point
3. Heterogeneity of population characteristics (for example, whenever possible, entirely rural counties were added to other counties that were partly urban)

Self-representing areas

Thirty-eight large primary sampling units were included in the sample as self-representing primary areas. These range in 1970 population size from 1.1 million to 3.3 million persons and include the twenty-five largest

SMSAs in the United States. By "self-representing" is meant that because of their size, they automatically have a probability of 1.0 for inclusion in the sample.

Stratification of primary sampling units

All other primary sampling units were grouped into sixty-five strata, with an average stratum population of approximately 2,000,000 persons in 1970. Within a stratum, primary sampling units are as much alike as possible in terms of geography, metropolitan or nonmetropolitan areas, population density, and other characteristics. Actual criteria used in the stratification, and the order of priority assigned to them, were:

1. Geographic division—within a stratum, all PSUs are in the same census geographic division (see list of states below).
2. Metropolitan or nonmetropolitan (with the exception of a few counties, strata consist entirely of SMSAs or entirely of other counties). The few exceptions occurred when an SMSA was partly in each of two geographic divisions; in a few of these instances, a small part of the SMSA in one geographic division was grouped with one or more nonmetropolitan counties to form a primary sampling unit.
3. Further stratification criteria for metropolitan and nonmetropolitan areas were:

For SMSAs

Size of the SMSA
Population density
Percentage nonwhite (in the South only)
Percentage employed in manufacturing
Population growth in the 1960–1970 decade

For other than SMSAs

Percentage nonwhite (in the South only)
Population density
Percentage employed in manufacturing
Percentage of land in farms

Census geographic regions and divisions

Region	Divisions	
Northeast	New England Connecticut Maine Massachusetts New Hampshire Rhode Island Vermont	Middle Atlantic New Jersey New York Pennsylvania

Region	Divisions	
North Central	East North-Central Illinois Indiana Michigan Ohio Wisconsin	West North-Central Iowa Kansas Minnesota Missouri Nebraska North Dakota South Dakota
South	South Atlantic Delaware District of Columbia Florida Georgia Maryland North Carolina South Carolina Virginia West Virginia	East South-Central Alabama Kentucky Mississippi Tennessee West South-Central Arkansas Louisiana Oklahoma Texas
West	Mountain Arizona Colorado Idaho Montana Nevada New Mexico Utah Wyoming	Pacific California Oregon Washington

Selection of primary sampling units

One PSU was selected with probability proportionate to size (preliminary 1970 population count) from each of the sixty-five strata that included two or more PSUs. The selected PSUs are primary areas in the RAC national sample. Together with the thirty-eight self-representing PSUs, the RAC sample includes a total of 103 primary areas.

Selection of secondary sampling units

Secondary sampling units (SSUs) in the RAC sample are areas of approximately 2,500 population in 1970. An SSU may be as small as a block or two in a densely populated portion of a city, or it may be an entire county or even larger in a sparsely populated rural area.

Secondary sampling units were defined to be roughly equal in population size so that they would best serve the needs of general population studies. SSUs remain in the national sample for the same length of time.

Prior to defining secondary sampling units, land areas within PSUs were listed in the following general order:

1. Municipalities of 10,000 or more in order by population size*
2. Places of 2,500 to 9,999 in geographic order within county
3. Remaining minor civil division or census county divisions in geographic order within county

Primary areas (PSUs that were selected as part of the national sample) were then divided into "pairs" of secondary sampling units—that is, units of about 5,000 population. The pairs of SSUs are intended to provide for a convenient rotation of SSUs in the RAC sample. In effect, SSUs were selected for the RAC sample in pairs—then one member of each selected pair was selected as part of the initial sample. The other member of the pair was available for a systematic planned rotation of the sample. Because each unit of the pair came from the same general part of the listing, the two SSUs—the one selected for the sample now and the one that would replace it in the rotation cycle—usually have similar geographic location and city-size characteristics. The two members of the pair are often within the same municipality or are rural sections of the same county.

For the entire sample, the total number of secondary units to be selected was set at 600. This was based on expected needs of users of the sample for dispersion for regional studies, as well as for national studies.

To determine the number of SSUs to select, the primary area was divided into zones. For each primary area, the zone size (z) was:

$$z = \left(\frac{P}{S}\right)\left(\frac{\text{primary area population}}{\text{stratum population}}\right)$$

where P = total 1970 population (preliminary)
S = number of secondary sampling units to be selected = 600

One zone was created for each 1/600 of the 1970 population. In self-representing primary areas, the zone size was equal to the 1/600 population interval. In other than self-representing areas, the zone was adjusted proportionate to the probability of selection of the primary area.

For each primary area, the first zone started at the beginning of the area listing for that primary area, and continued for the first z people in the population listing. The second zone started at $z + 1$ and continued to $2z$ people; and so on. Incomplete zones at the end of the primary area listings were cumulated within a geographic division until the full zone size was reached.† Thus, some zones included portions of two or more primary areas within the same census geographic division. Zones cumulated in this way included similar population characteristics to the extent

* In practice, the types of units listed depended somewhat on the detail provided in preliminary census reports for 1970 from which the listings were made.

† Primary areas were taken in the order in which they were numbered—starting with self-representing primary areas, then other metropolitan areas, then nonmetropolitan areas.

that they were cumulated from "ends" of primary area listings and thus were primarily rural areas. Each census geographic division included one incomplete zone at the end of the primary area listing.

One SSU (actually a pair of secondary sampling units) was selected from each zone by selecting a random number within the zone interval and determining where it fell within the cumulated listing. The random number selected a previously defined pair of SSUs.

SSUs usually consist of a number of administrative units used in the census—either enumeration districts (EDs) or block groups (in areas for which block statistics are to be published). EDs and block groups average approximately 800 persons.

Two hundred SSUs were selected from the original 600 through a systematic random procedure which assured proper representation to all previously specified strata.

Identification of potential respondents

A systematic random procedure was used to select 2,042 households from these 200 SSUs. After completion of an unrelated interview, RAC interviewers enumerated by sex and age all persons thirteen to nineteen years old living in the sample households. 839 such adolescents were enumerated, and they became the sampling frame from which our respondents were drawn.

Securing parental consent

As described in Chapter 1, intensive efforts were made to secure parental consent for these adolescents to participate in our study. These efforts were successful (or, in a few cases involving older adolescents not living under parental supervision or control, deemed unnecessary) for 508 of the original 839 young people. The differences between these 508 eligible respondents and the original sampling frame are detailed in the following table:

	Total sample frame (839 = 100%)	Eligible respondents (508 = 100%)
Sex		
Male	53%	52%
Female	47	48
Age		
13–15	47	47
16–19	53	53
Geographic region		
Northeast	23	25
North Central	32	29
South	30	32
West	15	14

	Total sample frame (839 = 100%)	Eligible respondents (508 = 100%)
Locality size		
Large metropolitan areas	38%	37%
Small metropolitan areas	34	33
Nonmetropolitan areas	28	30
Race		
White	87	86
Nonwhite	13	14
Household income		
Under $5,000	17	20
$5,000–$9,999	28	29
$10,000–$14,999	25	23
$15,000–over	30	28
Number of people in household		
3 or less	20	20
4	19	22
5	27	26
6	16	14
7 or more	18	18

Actual respondents

RAC interviewers recontacted the eligible respondents and asked them to fill out our questionnaire. 393 adolescents (77% of all eligible respondents) agreed to participate. Differences between these 393 actual respondents and the 508 eligible respondents are detailed in the following table:

	Eligible respondents (508 = 100%)	Actual respondents (393 = 100%)
Sex		
Male	52%	54%
Female	48	46
Age		
13–15	47	49
16–19	53	51
Geographic region		
Northeast	25	26
North Central	29	28
South	32	31
West	14	15

	Eligible respondents (508 = 100%)	Actual respondents (393 = 100%)
Locality size		
Large metropolitan areas	37%	40%
Small metropolitan areas	33	31
Nonmetropolitan areas	30	29
Race		
White	86	86
Nonwhite	14	14
Household income		
Under $5,000	20	19
$5,000–$9,999	29	27
$10,000–$14,999	23	25
$15,000–over	28	29
Number of people in household		
3 or less	20	19
4	22	21
5	26	28
6	14	15
7 or more	18	17

These 393 adolescents plus 18 "invisible" adolescents constitute our national sample of 411 adolescents. Our definition of "invisible" adolescents is found in Chapter 1, Section 1.2.5.5.

Weighting and projecting the results

All questionnaire data were reduced to machine-readable form. Prior to tabulation, two sets of statistical weights were applied to each respondent's responses: (1) a "selection equalization" weight, which was applied to all of the questionnaires obtained from any given secondary sampling unit and which was equal to the reciprocal of the probability with which the secondary sampling unit was selected for inclusion in the national sample; and (2) a "recovery equalization" weight, which was applied by sex and age within each primary sampling unit in order to reflect the minor differences that occurred between primary sampling units in the rates at which questionnaires were recovered from eligible respondents of each sex and at each age level.

Sampling tolerances

The methods used for this survey assure close control over each step of the sampling procedure. All survey percentages, however, are subject to some error due to random sampling variation. Standard statistical techniques are used to calculate the range of possible sampling error. These ranges provide a general guide to the amount of possible variation between the sample result and the result that would have been obtained had the same survey procedures been used to study the entire population of young people. The principal factor affecting sampling variation is the size of the sample: the larger the sample, the smaller the range of sampling error.

Guides to the possible range of sampling error for percentages based on the total youth sample are as follows: (1) There are about 67 chances in 100 that the error due to sampling does not exceed three percentage points; and (2) There are about 95 chances in 100 that the error due to sampling does not exceed six percentage points.

For example, 48% of young people in the survey were classified as virgins. Suppose the entire population had been studied, using the same survey procedures. What result would have been obtained? The statistical measures of sampling variability tell us that there are 67 chances in 100 that the "true" population figure is somewhere in the range of 45% to 51% (48% plus or minus three percentage points). The range for the higher confidence level—95 chances in 100—is between 42% and 54% (48% plus or minus six percentage points).

The range of sampling error is somewhat dependent on the level of the survey percentage as well as on the size of the sample. The first table given here shows the approximate range of random sampling error for different survey percentages based on the total sample. The figures given in the example above are in the first row of the table for percentages "near 50%." Somewhat smaller sampling error ranges apply to other percentage levels.

Approximate random sampling error for percentages based on total sample

Survey percentages near	Error range in percentage points at	
	67 in 100 confidence level	95 in 100 confidence level
50%	3%	6%
40 or 60	3	6
30 or 70	3	6
20 or 80	3	5
10 or 90	2	4

Percentages based on subgroups of the youth sample (for example, results for boys, or results for younger teenagers) are subject to somewhat wider statistical tolerances. The second table shows the approximate range of sampling error for percentages based on about half of the total sample (for example, boys, or girls, separately) and for percentages based on one-fourth of the total sample (for example, younger boys, age 13–15).

Approximate random sampling error for percentages based on sample subgroups

Survey percentages near	Error range in percentage points at 67 in 100 confidence level	Error range in percentage points at 95 in 100 confidence level
Subgroups that are about one-half of total sample (200 interviews)		
50%	4%	8%
40 or 60	4	8
30 or 70	4	8
20 or 80	4	7
10 or 90	3	5
Subgroups that are about one-fourth of total sample (100 interviews)		
50%	6%	11%
40 or 60	6	11
30 or 70	5	10
20 or 80	5	9
10 or 90	4	7

A Note on the Methodology

JIRI NEHNEVAJSA, Ph.D.
Professor of Sociology, University of Pittsburgh

Any study that deals with a subject as sensitive as sexual behavior is likely to be controversial. Whatever its findings, it forces us to consider issues we might not want to think about and to reconsider our attitudes and beliefs. It is to be expected then that the reader will find aspects of this study on adolescent sexuality unsettling. But in assessing the validity of Sorensen's work, the reader may ask: Does the sampling procedure give accurate results? Were adolescents truthful in answering questions? What effects did the survey have on the respondents?

Sampling procedure

What can data on several hundred young people tell us about 27 million American adolescents? In other words, were the adolescents interviewed representative of the American adolescent population? To answer this question, we must examine the procedures by which these adolescents became part of the sample.

If a sample, regardless of its size, is drawn in such a way as to involve known probabilities of being included in it (and therefore also known probabilities for not being included), it *is* possible, and proper, to generalize from that sample to the population as a whole from which it was chosen. The Sorensen sample is, in fact, a probability sample of households (2,042 of them) around the nation. The probabilities of inclusion are known at each sampling stage. (See the Sample Design and Execution section.) For example, thirty-eight primary sampling units (PSUs) covering the largest metropolitan areas of the country were included in the sample with a probability of 1 = certainty. All other PSUs into which the nation was divided were stratified by a number of characteristics into sixty-five groupings. Selections were made from these with probabilities proportionate to size; hence, with probabilities not made explicit here, but known and calculable.

In the 2,042 selected households, 839 adolescents from thirteen to nineteen years of age were enumerated. Since the probability of household inclusion is known and since all adolescents became potential subjects of the study (that is, given the households, adolescent inclusion had odds of 1), these 839 potential interviewees represent a probability sample of the nation's adolescents. Then 508 of these youngsters became eligible for interviews because parental consent was secured. A comparison of the sample frame (839) with the eligible roster (508) along a number of important sociocultural and demographic characteristics showed that the differences between the potential and eligible respondents were statistically insignificant. Finally 393 young people were eventually interviewed (some two months after the enumeration). Again the differences between the eligible and actual participants were statistically insignificant.

There are some nonprobability elements in the last two stages of the process, and these should be made explicit. Going from the sample frame to the eligible category, the study-pertinent difference is the presence or absence of parental consent. But since this consent variable does not "behave" differently in different crucial categories of young people (sex, age, region, race, size of locality, household income, size of household), there are no reasons for assuming that bias has entered into the research. The reasoning linking the eligible and the actual subjects must be, in effect, identical. Here, the nonprobability element involves the inability to contact the otherwise eligible subject, the subsequent decision of the adolescent not to be interviewed, or other such factors. But the actual participants are not different from the eligible ones, and they are not different from the adolescents in the sample frame. Again, we have no reason to assume bias as a consequence of this final step in the data acquisition process in the Sorensen research.

To summarize, I have high confidence in Sorensen's results. The households are chosen by statistically valid means and the adolescents interviewed are representative, along several strategic lines, of the total roster of youngsters in these sampled households. It follows that it makes good sense to conclude that they are representative of the nation's young people.

There are, however, some groups or categories of young people to whom the generalizations cannot be legitimately applied. For example, institutionalized young people were not included in the original national sampling design, and the results therefore are not necessarily applicable to them. (This is discussed in Chapter 1.) The probability sample also includes only coterminous states of the Union. Hence, the results cannot be generalized to include Hawaii, Alaska, Puerto Rico, or Guam.

But what about the effect of sample size, even if the procedures for selection comply with the canons of valid probability sampling? The size of the sample has a bearing on the range within which the data (from the actual respondents) can be generalized to the population at large.

Sorensen reports, for example, that 48% of the young people in the study claim to be virgins. This is true (in terms of claims) for these particular young people. But given this datum, we could make the following statement:

$$C\,(42.2\% \leqq P \leqq 53.8\%) = .95$$

This simply says that 95 times in 100 (.95), we have confidence (C), that the true percentage of adolescent virgins (P) lies between 42.2% and 53.8%.

But what does it mean to say that we have confidence "95 times in 100"? It means that if we drew hundreds or thousands of samples (all the same size and based on the same design), we would find that only 5% or fewer of these samples would yield a percentage of virgins below 42.2% or above 53.8%.

Clearly, with the same (95%) confidence level, a larger sample would estimate the national percentage of adolescent virgins within a narrower range, the difference between the lower and the upper limits being smaller. And obviously, if we had data on *all* adolescents, the result would be P itself, the true percentage of adolescent virgins.

Percentages given for particular groups of adolescents should also be viewed in terms of variation. For example, Sorensen reports that 41% of adolescent boys are virgins; since the subsample of boys is smaller than the whole sample, we should expect the subsample percentage to be subject to greater variation than is that of the total sample. The *P* value for boys can be expected to lie, again with 95% confidence, between 33.1% and 48.9%—that is, 41% (as obtained in the study) $\pm$ 7.9%. These variations are not based on conjecture but on mathematical fact.

These are conservative estimates of statistical significance that do not take into consideration other significant indicators of the data's validity such as direction and consistency.

Truthfulness of respondents

But even if the results were generalizable and even if the sample size was adequate, is the information obtained true? In other words, were the adolescents honest about their sexual behavior and attitudes?

I am often asked this question by students, and my answer is usually another question: How often have *you* deliberately lied in response to a question? On occasion all of us fib (or even, heaven forbid, lie) to raise (or lower) our status, to brag (impress), to gain sympathy (or pity), and so on. But, on the whole, hardly anyone lies consistently and persistently. Hardly anyone volunteers to give answers and then deliberately presents false information.

The Sorensen subjects agreed to be interviewed in full knowledge of the subject matter under study. The motivation to cheat (I am not including the games that our memory, and sometimes our mood, may play with us) was not strong. There are, however, some adolescents who, while not intending to lie, may have exaggerated or minimized their sexual experience. But I believe there would be little reason for this behavior in answering an anonymous and impersonal questionnaire.

No absolute assurance of the participants' honesty can be given to the reader who thinks that the young people may have lied in large numbers about a large number of items. But survey research experience suggests that widespread dishonesty is not a very frequent or likely occurrence. And the young people who were interviewed cannot be assumed to be a national sample of liars.

Effects of survey

Many readers will feel concern about the respondents themselves. Did the questionnaire expose the participants to disturbing or perhaps harmful sexual material? Was the survey an invasion of privacy?

Speaking generally, our era is a permissive one, particularly in regard to sexual matters. It is also a period of increasing sex education in the classroom. It seems, under these circumstances, that it would take blindfolds and earmuffs to prevent young people from knowing about sex. Considering all the sex-related stimuli with which adolescents are bombarded, it seems unlikely that a straightforward questionnaire on sex behavior would have a great impact, let alone a harmful one.

More importantly, throughout this study Sorensen was concerned with protecting the sensibilities of the participants. He designed the questionnaire with extreme care; he fully disclosed its purposes and subject matter to the parents of potential participants and sought their consent. Thus, parents judged whether or not they felt the study might be harmful to their children. Some of them in fact did not want their youngsters to be exposed to the questionnaire.

Sorensen must be commended for his respect for the privacy of the participants. The young people were free to refuse to participate, and they were also free to refuse to answer any portion of the questionnaire. The interviewers never had access to the filled-out questionnaires: the participant completed the questionnaire, sealed it in an envelope, and walked with the interviewer to the nearest mailbox and deposited the envelope. I know of no research study that has been more careful in protecting the individual than this survey by Sorensen and his associates.

I hope that Sorensen's work will become the subject of national discussion, or perhaps controversy. Examination of his findings, and dialogue about them, will benefit us all by increasing our understanding of the mind of a generation.

Survey Questionnaires: Male and Female

WHAT YOUNG PEOPLE BELIEVE AND DO

A TOTALLY CONFIDENTIAL STUDY OF SOCIAL AND SEXUAL ATTITUDES AND BEHAVIOR

MALE QUESTIONNAIRE

We appreciate the help you are giving us by taking part in the first nationwide survey of this kind ever to be conducted in the United States. If you are like the many other young people who have tested out this questionnaire, you will find the questions both interesting and easy to answer.

THIS IS NOT A TEST. THERE ARE NO "RIGHT" ANSWERS AND NO "WRONG" ANSWERS. BUT WE ARE COUNTING ON YOU TO GIVE TRUTHFUL ANSWERS ABOUT WHAT YOU BELIEVE AND WHAT YOU DO. SOME OF THE QUESTIONS ARE VERY PERSONAL, BUT TO MAKE SURE THAT YOU CAN FEEL COMPLETELY FREE AND HONEST IN WHAT YOU SAY, THE INTERVIEWER WILL TELL YOU ABOUT THE FOOLPROOF SYSTEM WE ARE USING TO MAKE SURE THAT THESE QUESTIONNAIRES REMAIN ABSOLUTELY CONFIDENTIAL IN EVERY WAY.

Please remember:

You are in complete charge of handling this questionnaire. The interviewer is remaining only to answer questions that you may have about the meaning of words or instructions that may not be clear to you. Neither the interviewer nor anyone else who knows who you are will ever see the answers that you give.

You can make sure of this for yourself simply by doing the following three things as soon as you have finished filling out the questionnaire:

1. Immediately put the questionnaire in our postage-paid return envelope.
2. Seal the envelope yourself.
3. Go with our interviewer to the nearest mailbox, and mail the envelope. (If you prefer to have the interviewer mail it for you, he or she will be glad to do that. Either way, it will come directly to our Research Office.)

ABOUT FILLING IN THIS QUESTIONNAIRE

To make everything as easy as possible, all of the questions in this booklet have been carefully designed so that you can answer them with an absolute minimum of writing:

Either by marking an "X" in a box, like this -- /X/

or by writing a number on a line, like this -- NUMBER OF FINGERS ON MY LEFT HAND: 5

If you put an "X" in a box that has an arrow leading from it, follow the arrow to see where it goes. It will point either to the next question that you should answer, or to an instruction asking you to turn to another page.

If a question asks you to fill in a number, and you're not sure exactly what number to fill in, write in whatever number represents your best guess about what the answer really is.

There are only a few other things that you should try to keep in mind while filling out the questionnaire.

1. The interviewer is here only to answer any questions you may have about what different words mean, or to explain the meaning of any instructions that may not be clear to you.

   The interviewer is not supposed to explain any of the questions, or to suggest what answers you should give. Most important, the interviewer is not permitted to look at your answers.

2. If you are 13 or 14 years old, some of the questions may seem to be written for people who are older than you are. If you are 18 or 19 years old, some of the questions may seem to be written for people who are younger than you are. But almost all of the questions can be answered by almost anyone between the ages of 13 and 19.

   So please do your best to answer every question, even if the question doesn't seem to be serious, necessary, or applicable to your own experience or way of thinking. Each question does have a purpose, and unless we have your answer our study will be incomplete.

   Afterwards, if you want to tell the interviewer anything or write to us with any suggestions, by all means feel free to do so. But please do try to answer all of the questions.

3. All of the X-marks and numbers will be fed directly into a computer, and since the computer doesn't know your name or address it can't possibly tell anyone what your answers were. All it can do is add your answers in with the answers we get from hundreds of other young people all over the country, and print out the results as percentages.

How old were you on your last birthday?

13 /_7 14 /_7 15 /_7 16 /_7 17 /_7 18 /_7 19 /_7

- -

Are you male or female? Male /_7 Female /_7

PLEASE CHECK THE FRONT OF THIS BOOKLET TO MAKE SURE THAT YOU HAVE THE RIGHT QUESTIONNAIRE FOR A PERSON OF YOUR SEX

- -

Which of your parents is easier to talk to about sex?

My mother /_7 My father /_7

- -

If you had a serious problem that had to do with sex, which of your parents could you count on to stand by you the most?

My mother /_7 My father /_7

- -

Do you have any brothers who are older than you are? Yes /_7 No /_7

- -

Do you have any sisters who are older than you are? Yes /_7 No /_7

- -

Do you have any brothers who are younger than you are? Yes /_7 No /_7

- -

Do you have any sisters who are younger than you are? Yes /_7 No /_7

PLEASE GO ON TO THE NEXT PAGE

Are both of your parents still living?

Yes /_/ No /_/

Which of your parents is not still living?

My mother /_/ → How old were you when your mother died? AGE WHEN MOTHER DIED:_______

My father /_/ → How old were you when your father died? AGE WHEN FATHER DIED:_______

- -

Are your parents still married to each other, or are they divorced or separated?

They are still married /_/ They are divorced or separated /_/

How old were you when your parents were divorced or separated?

AGE WHEN PARENTS WERE DIVORCED OR SEPARATED:________

- -

What is (or was) your father's religious preference?

Protestant /_/ Catholic /_/ Jewish /_/ Other /_/ None /_/

- -

What is (or was) your mother's religious preference?

Protestant /_/ Catholic /_/ Jewish /_/ Other /_/ None /_/

- -

What is your own religious preference?

Protestant /_/ Catholic /_/ Jewish /_/ Other /_/ None /_/

PLEASE GO ON TO THE NEXT PAGE

Have you attended religious services or church activities this year?

Regularly /_7 Occasionally /_7 Hardly ever /_7 Never /_7

- -

How religious would you say you are?

Very religious /_7 Somewhat religious /_7 Not very religious /_7 Not religious at all /_7

- -

Are you attending school at the present time?

No /_7 Yes /_7

What grade are you in now?

5th Grade /_7 6th Grade /_7 7th Grade /_7

8th Grade /_7 9th Grade /_7 10th Grade /_7

11th Grade /_7 12th Grade (High School Senior) /_7

Secretarial, trade, or technical school ------------/_7

First year college /_7 Second year college /_7

Third year college /_7 Fourth year college /_7

How well are you doing in school?

Superior grades --------/_7 Good grades -----------/_7

Average grades ---------/_7 Poor grades -----------/_7

- -

Are you working at a job to earn money at the present time?

Yes, full-time /_7 Yes, part-time /_7 No, I'm not working /_7

PLEASE GO ON TO THE NEXT PAGE

The next few pages of this questionnaire contain statements about many different things. We would like you to read each statement, and then mark it as being either "True" or "False."

For instance, if there were a statement such as:

I am less than 35 years old --True /_7----False /_7

you would put an "X" in the box next to the word "True."

If there were a statement such as:

I think it would be fun to fall down and break my leg --------------------True /_7----False /_7

you would put an "X" in the box next to the word "False."

But please remember, this is not a "True-False" test such as the ones they give in school, because there are no "right" answers and no "wrong" answers. Most of the statements in this questionnaire are worded so that some people would think of them as being "True" for themselves while other people would think of them as being "False" for themselves -- AND THE ONLY THING THAT MATTERS IS WHAT YOU YOURSELF THINK.

For instance, there might be a statement such as:

I don't mind cold weather ---True /_7----False /_7

People who always like cold weather would mark the statement "True," while people who always hate cold weather would mark the statement "False." Some people, on the other hand, would think of the statement as being partly true and partly false.

IF YOU COME UPON A STATEMENT THAT YOU THINK OF AS BEING PARTLY TRUE AND PARTLY FALSE, try to decide whether you think it's more true than false or more false than true.

If, for you, a statement is more true than false, mark it as "True."

If, for you, a statement is more false than true, mark it as "False."

For instance, in the example about cold weather, you should mark the statement "True" if you usually like cold weather, even though sometimes you may not like it. If you usually don't like cold weather, then you should mark the statement "False," even though there may be times when you do like cold weather.

In other words, TRY TO MARK EACH STATEMENT AS EITHER "TRUE" OR "FALSE," depending on what you yourself think or feel most of the time, or under most circumstances. If you come upon a question that you really do not understand, cannot decide about (even after trying), or do not wish to answer, just go on to the next question.

= *START HERE* =

If I had to go out into the world on my own right now, I think I could get along pretty well ---True /_7----False /_7

Some day, I will probably want to get married and have children --------------------True /_7----False /_7

Sex education courses in school can't teach me anything ---------------------------True /_7----False /_7

I wouldn't use birth control or contraception because it's against my religion -----True /_7----False /_7

Sometimes I get sexually aroused from the music that I hear -----------------------True /_7----False /_7

I often ask my parents for advice about sexual matters ----------------------------True /_/----False /_/

I find it hard to accept the idea of obeying laws that I don't agree with ----------True /_/----False /_/

Some of the opinions that I express to my parents are opinions that I invent just to put them uptight --True /_/----False /_/

On one or more occasions, I've done sexual things mostly to show that I don't care what society thinks --True /_/----False /_/

If an organization came along wanting to sign up people to register and vote in this year's election, I wouldn't be interested in helping ----------------------True /_/----False /_/

I think my parents' ideas about sex are wrong, but they have a right to their own opinions --True /_/----False /_/

My parents and I sometimes talk about sex, but it makes them very uncomfortable ----True /_/----False /_/

I think like an adult, but I feel a lot younger ------------------------------------True /_/----False /_/

I wish my parents and I could agree more about what we think is right and wrong where sex is concerned --True /_/----False /_/

My parents don't really like me --True /_/----False /_/

I don't think that I would want to have sex with a person of another race ----------True /_/----False /_/

My parents and I talk pretty freely about sex in general, but we don't really say what's on our minds when it comes down to really personal things ---------------True /_/----False /_/

I don't pay any attention to what goes on in politics ------------------------------True /_/----False /_/

I wish my parents and I could agree more about social and political issues ---------True /_/----False /_/

I get a lot of satisfaction out of my sex life ------------------------------------True /_/----False /_/

I have a lot of respect for my parents' ideas and opinions -------------------------True /_/----False /_/

It's right that we have laws against homosexuality --------------------------------True /_/----False /_/

Most of the time I can't stand to be around my parents, and I have as little to do with them as possible ---True /_/----False /_/

A white girl and a black boy having sex together is something that I would consider immoral, even if both of them wanted to do it ------------------------------True /_/----False /_/

So far as sex is concerned, I have pretty much come to definite conclusions about what I think is right and wrong for other people -----------------------------True /_/----False /_/

Getting V.D. or venereal disease isn't really a very serious problem because one can always go to a doctor and get it cured ------------------------------------True /_/----False /_/

It doesn't make any difference who wins the Presidential Election this year --------True /_/----False /_/

I wish my parents understood that what I do sexually is pretty tame compared to some of the sexual things that go on today -------------------------------------True /_/----False /_/

In general, I think that my sex life is pretty normal for a person my age ----------True /_/----False /_/

I believe that my parents are still very much in love with each other -------------True /_/----False /_/

I think it's right that people should make their own moral code, deciding for themselves what's moral and what's immoral --True /_/----False /_/

The idea of two men having sex together is disgusting -----------------------------True /_/----False /_/

Smoking marijuana is an important thing in my life --------------------------------True /_/----False /_/

When I'm listening to the radio and they start talking about the news, I usually switch to another station ---True /_/----False /_/

A white boy and a black girl having sex together is something that I would consider immoral, even if both of them wanted to do it ----------------------------True /_/----False /_/

I have told my parents that I disagree with the way they think about sex ----------True /_/----False /_/

Two boys having sex together is something that I would consider abnormal or unnatural --True /_/----False /_/

I find it hard to accept the idea of conforming to society in matters of clothing and personal grooming --True /_/----False /_/

All in all, I think my head is pretty well together these days so far as sex is concerned --True /_/----False /_/

My parents believe that sex is immoral unless it's between two people who are married to each other ---True /_/----False /_/

My parents have told me the facts about birth control -----------------------------True /_/----False /_/

My parents believe that anything two people want to do sexually is moral, so long as they both want to do it and it doesn't hurt either one of them -----------------True /_/----False /_/

I wouldn't mind having a dictator in this country, if he would run things the way I would like to see them run --True /_/----False /_/

On one or more occasions, under the influence of alcohol, I've had sex with someone that I wouldn't have had sex with otherwise --------------------------------True /_/----False /_/

I don't talk about sex with my parents because their attitude is that I'm too young to know anything ---True /_/----False /_/

I would consider it abnormal or unnatural for a boy not to have sex until he gets married ---True /_/----False /_/

I think my parents' ideas about most things are wrong, but they have a right to their own opinions ---True /_/----False /_/

So far as sex is concerned, I still haven't really made up my mind what I think is right and wrong for other people ---True /_/----False /_/

I think that voting in elections is a waste of time ---True /_/----False /_/

If I go for a long time without having sex, I get to feeling uptight ---True /_/----False /_/

When talking with my parents about sex, I try to tell them only what I think they can accept ---True /_/----False /_/

A brother and sister having sex together is something that I would consider abnormal or unnatural, even if both of them wanted to do it ---True /_/----False /_/

I don't feel any strong affection for my parents ---True /_/----False /_/

So far as sex is concerned, what other young people do doesn't have any influence on what I myself do ---True /_/----False /_/

I have never read a serious educational book about sex ---True /_/----False /_/

When I talk with my parents about sex I try to tell them what is going on with young people today, even though they don't approve of it ---True /_/----False /_/

So far as sex is concerned, I wouldn't do anything that society would disapprove of ---True /_/----False /_/

My parents believe that it's immoral for two persons of the same sex to have sexual relations with each other ---True /_/----False /_/

I think it's important to re-elect President Nixon in this year's election ---True /_/----False /_/

Having sex helps me take my mind off some of the bad things that happen to me ---True /_/----False /_/

If I had to go out into the world on my own right now, I think I'd have a pretty hard time of it ---True /_/----False /_/

I don't talk with my parents about my sex life because I consider it a personal subject and nobody's business but my own ---True /_/----False /_/

I believe that this society is hell-bent on destroying the planet ---True /_/----False /_/

My parents practice what they preach about love and sex ---True /_/----False /_/

So far as sex is concerned, I have pretty much come to definite conclusions about what I think is right or wrong for myself ---True /_/----False /_/

My parents have talked to me about masturbation ---True /_/----False /_/

I don't think that God has any interest in my sex life ----------------------------True /_/----False /_/

I don't believe that there should be any laws against having sex with a girl under the age of 16 --True /_/----False /_/

My parents get along with each other very well ------------------------------------True /_/----False /_/

So far as sex is concerned, I think that what is morally right for boys is morally right for girls too ---True /_/----False /_/

When it comes to sex, my attitudes and my parents' attitudes are pretty much the same ---True /_/----False /_/

I still tend to think of myself as a child because there are a lot of things I can't do on my own ---True /_/----False /_/

I've never really gotten to know my father --True /_/----False /_/

Sometimes when I go to church I get to feeling guilty about my sexual behavior -----True /_/----False /_/

On one or more occasions, I've done sexual things mostly to spite my parents -------True /_/----False /_/

I think there are some kinds of sex acts that should be against the law ------------True /_/----False /_/

I don't much believe in planning for the future; life right now is the most important thing ---True /_/----False /_/

My parents and I talk pretty freely about sex -------------------------------------True /_/----False /_/

On one or more occasions, I've done sexual things mostly because the people I was hanging out with at the time expected me to ----------------------------------True /_/----False /_/

I believe that modern technology is a constructive force ---------------------------True /_/----False /_/

I agree that there should be laws against rape ------------------------------------True /_/----False /_/

Young people these days sometimes have sex mostly to take their minds off other things that are going down --True /_/----False /_/

I started experimenting with sex partly because it was such a forbidden topic around my house --True /_/----False /_/

Hassles about my sexual behavior cause a lot of bad vibes between myself and my parents --True /_/----False /_/

My parents and I sometimes talk about sex, but it makes me very uncomfortable ------True /_/----False /_/

There are some things that I wouldn't do because my conscience would bother me -----True /_/----False /_/

My parents don't understand what I want out of life --------------------------------True /_/----False /_/

I don't like it when older people think of me as an adolescent ---------------------True /_/----False /_/

In my family we're all very open with each other, so it's difficult or impossible to have any secrets about sex --True /_/----False /_/

Sometimes I take part in sexual activities that are not consistent with my religious beliefs ---True /_/----False /_/

I believe that LSD and other psychedelic drugs have had a beneficial effect on the spiritual development of many persons --------------------------------------True /_/----False /_/

I've pretty much given up on ever being able to get along with my parents ----------True /_/----False /_/

The American Indians had a life-style that I deeply admire -------------------------True /_/----False /_/

I've never taken part in any sex act, or been involved in any kind of sexual situation, that I myself would think of as being abnormal --------------------------True /_/----False /_/

There are serious flaws in our society, but the system is flexible enough to solve them ---True /_/----False /_/

Two girls having sex together is something that I would consider abnormal or unnatural --True /_/----False /_/

Violence is the only way to get the kind of changes that I would like to see in our society --True /_/----False /_/

I wish my parents and I could agree more about things in general -------------------True /_/----False /_/

In general, I think that my basic personal values are shared by most of the older people in this country ---True /_/----False /_/

My parents are anxious about whether or not I'm going to get married ---------------True /_/----False /_/

When deciding for myself what to do or not to do so far as sex is concerned, I don't pay any attention to what the laws say -------------------------------------True /_/----False /_/

If I like one of the candidates in this year's Presidential Election, I would seriously consider working to get people to vote for him ---------------------------True /_/----False /_/

My parents are always bugging me with questions about my sexual behavior -----------True /_/----False /_/

In general, I think that my basic personal values are shared by most of the younger people in this country ---True /_/----False /_/

My parents think that I pretty much agree with their ideas about sex, and I don't say anything that would make them think different ---------------------------True /_/----False /_/

My sexual behavior is pretty much the way my parents would want it to be -----------True /_/----False /_/

How important to you are each of the things listed below?

	Very Important	Somewhat Important	Not very Important
Getting along with other boys my own age	/_/	/_/	/_/
Having fun	/_/	/_/	/_/
Becoming independent so that I can make it on my own	/_/	/_/	/_/
Trying to change the system	/_/	/_/	/_/
Making out with girls	/_/	/_/	/_/
Keeping up with schoolwork	/_/	/_/	/_/
Learning about other people	/_/	/_/	/_/
Doing creative or artistic things	/_/	/_/	/_/
Preparing myself to accomplish meaningful things	/_/	/_/	/_/
Listening to music	/_/	/_/	/_/
Living according to my religion	/_/	/_/	/_/
Working for money	/_/	/_/	/_/
Getting along with my parents	/_/	/_/	/_/
Having a good relationship with one particular girl	/_/	/_/	/_/
Getting loaded and hanging out	/_/	/_/	/_/
Learning about myself	/_/	/_/	/_/
Sports and athletics	/_/	/_/	/_/
Eating good food	/_/	/_/	/_/
Preparing myself to earn a good living when I get older	/_/	/_/	/_/
Having sex with a number of different girls	/_/	/_/	/_/
Worshipping God	/_/	/_/	/_/

- -

Most people identify with (feel they have a great deal in common with) a lot of different groups. But they identify with some groups more strongly than with others. Which one of the groups listed below do you identify with most strongly?

PLEASE CHECK ONLY ONE

Young people of my own generation -- wherever they may live, whatever their race or religion, and regardless of whether they are boys or girls ---------- /_/

People who live in my community -- whatever their race or religion, and regardless of whether they are male or female, young or old ---------- /_/

People of my own religion -- wherever they may live, whatever their race, and regardless of whether they are male or female, young or old ---------- /_/

People of my own race -- wherever they may live, whatever their religion, and regardless of whether they are male or female, young or old ---------- /_/

Males -- wherever they may live, whatever their race or religion, and regardless of whether they are young or old ---------- /_/

Here are some statements that we would like you to agree with or disagree with.

If you agree with a statement more than you disagree with it, please check the "agree" box.
If you disagree with a statement more than you agree with it, please check the "disagree" box.

Remember, there are no "right" or "wrong" answers -- the only thing that matters is what YOU YOURSELF think.

- -

It's all right for young people to have sex before getting married, if they are in love with each other --Agree /_/----Disagree /_/

Our society's values concerning sex come from many generations of accumulated wisdom --Agree /_/----Disagree /_/

It's immoral for two persons of the same sex to have sex with each other -------Agree /_/----Disagree /_/

One of the most important tasks of growing up is to learn to live with one's parents' ideas and opinions about sex ----------------------------------Agree /_/----Disagree /_/

A girl who goes to bed with a boy before marriage will lose his respect --------Agree /_/----Disagree /_/

Two people shouldn't have to get married just because they want to live together --Agree /_/----Disagree /_/

Churches could do things that would help older people understand young people's ideas --Agree /_/----Disagree /_/

Young people who get married without ever having had sex together are foolish Agree /_/----Disagree /_/

Some boys use sex to reward or punish their girl friends ----------------------Agree /_/----Disagree /_/

Churches could do things that would be a big help in keeping down V.D. among young people who have sex --Agree /_/----Disagree /_/

Young people these days understand more about honesty than most older people in their forties or fifties ---Agree /_/----Disagree /_/

Sex is immoral, unless it's between two people who love each other ------------Agree /_/----Disagree /_/

A girl should stay a virgin until she finds the boy she wants to marry ---------Agree /_/----Disagree /_/

If I found out that a girl had had sex for money, even once, I would lose respect for her ---Agree /_/----Disagree /_/

Organically grown food is much healthier than the food you get in most supermarkets ---Agree /_/----Disagree /_/

Sexual activities that society is opposed to are immoral ----------------------Agree /_/----Disagree /_/

In some ways, I still think and act somewhat like a child ----------------------Agree /_/----Disagree /_/

Young people these days tend to be more idealistic than most older people in their forties or fifties --Agree /_/----Disagree /_/

There's nothing wrong with paying a girl for sex, if a boy can't get sex in any other way --Agree /_/----Disagree /_/

When it comes to sex, some young people do the things they do mostly to spite their parents ---Agree /_/----Disagree /_/

It's immoral for a boy to force a girl to have sex, no matter what the circumstances --Agree /_/----Disagree /_/

I believe that most young people can go directly from childhood to adulthood without being forced to go through a period of years that society defines as adolescence ---Agree /_/----Disagree /_/

Young people these days understand more about sex than most older people in their forties or fifties --Agree /_/----Disagree /_/

It's right that we have laws saying people have to be married in order to live together ---Agree /_/----Disagree /_/

Sex is immoral, unless it's between two people who like each other and have something in common ---Agree /_/----Disagree /_/

Some girls use sex to reward or punish their boy friends ----------------------Agree /_/----Disagree /_/

My generation is going to do a better job of running things than the last generation has done --Agree /_/----Disagree /_/

Anything two people want to do sexually is moral, as long as they both want to do it and it doesn't hurt either one of them --------------------------------Agree /_/----Disagree /_/

If two people are really in love, that love should last for life ---------------Agree /_/----Disagree /_/

When a President does something that's bad for the country, it's mostly the fault of the people who let him get elected --------------------------------Agree /_/----Disagree /_/

Sex is immoral for people who are too young to understand what they are getting out of it ---Agree /_/----Disagree /_/

Young people these days tend to be less materialistic than most older people in their forties or fifties --Agree /_/----Disagree /_/

A person who truly loves God doesn't have sexual relationships outside of marriage --Agree /_/----Disagree /_/

Young people these days tend to be less considerate of others than most older people in their forties or fifties --Agree /_/----Disagree /_/

Churches teach that enjoyment of sex is sinful --------------------------------Agree /_/----Disagree /_/

Young people these days understand more about what is really important in life than most older people in their forties or fifties ---------------------Agree /_/----Disagree /_/

Sex is immoral, unless it's between two people who are married to each other --Agree /_/----Disagree /_/

The government shouldn't be allowed to censor magazines or books, no matter how extreme they may be about sexual matters ----------------------------Agree /_/----Disagree /_/

The sexual behavior of most young people today would not be acceptable to society as a whole ---Agree /_/----Disagree /_/

Churches could be a big help to young people who are trying to find themselves --Agree /_/----Disagree /_/

It's possible for love to be very real and very strong, but still not last for more than a few weeks ---Agree /_/----Disagree /_/

The most important thing in a love relationship is sex ------------------------Agree /_/----Disagree /_/

Sex is one of the few human activities where there is always something new to be discovered ---Agree /_/----Disagree /_/

Over a period of time, I think it's better to have sexual relationships with several different people, rather than just one person --------------------Agree /_/----Disagree /_/

The laws against prostitution (having sex for money) should continue to remain in force --Agree /_/----Disagree /_/

Where sex is concerned, anything people want to do is all right so long as they want to do it and it doesn't hurt them --------------------------------Agree /_/----Disagree /_/

A lot of young people are leaving home these days because they are seeking sexual freedom --Agree /_/----Disagree /_/

One of the reasons why many young girls these days don't use birth control pills is that they're afraid their parents will find them ---------------------Agree /_/----Disagree /_/

Hurting another person is wrong --Agree /_/----Disagree /_/

Showing that young people have sexual freedom is one way of making the older generation realize that things are really changing in the world ----------------Agree /_/----Disagree /_/

One of the reasons why young people stop going to church is because churches teach that enjoyment of sex is sinful --------------------------------Agree /_/----Disagree /_/

Young people these days understand more about friendship than most older people in their forties or fifties ---Agree /_/----Disagree /_/

It's not wrong for a girl to have sex with someone for money, if that's what she wants to do --Agree /_/----Disagree /_/

Young people these days understand more about love than most older people in their forties or fifties ---Agree /_/----Disagree /_/

When it comes to sex, a lot of young people these days do the things they do just because everyone else is doing it -------------------------------------Agree /_/----Disagree /_/

The government shouldn't try to keep people from seeing any kind of sex movies that they want to see -- even if they're so dirty I wouldn't want to see them myself ---Agree /_/----Disagree /_/

Most boys sometimes play with themselves sexually while they are growing up. If a boy does this and has an erection, it is called masturbation.

How old were you the very first time that you masturbated?

IF YOU HAVE NEVER MASTURBATED, PLEASE SKIP TO THE NEXT YELLOW PAGE

AGE WHEN I FIRST MASTURBATED:__________

Sometimes masturbation results in a climax, or orgasm -- what most young people refer to as "coming."

How old were you the very first time that you masturbated until you had a climax or orgasm?

AGE WHEN I FIRST MASTURBATED TO CLIMAX OR ORGASM:________

I've never had a climax or orgasm from masturbating ---------------/ /

When was the most recent occasion on which you masturbated?

Since this time yesterday-----------------/ /

Since this time last week-----------------/ /

Since this time last month ---------------/ /

More than a month ago ------------/ /

PLEASE SKIP TO THE NEXT YELLOW PAGE

Since this time last month, approximately how many times have you masturbated until you had a climax or orgasm?

NUMBER OF TIMES IN THE PAST MONTH THAT I MASTURBATED TO CLIMAX OR ORGASM:________

Since this time last month, approximately how many times have you masturbated without having a climax or orgasm?

NUMBER OF TIMES IN THE PAST MONTH THAT I MASTURBATED WITHOUT HAVING A CLIMAX OR ORGASM:________

PLEASE GO ON TO THE NEXT PAGE

When you masturbate, do you daydream or think about things most of the time, only some of the time, rarely, or never?

Most of the time /_/ Some of the time /_/ Rarely /_/ Never /_/

How often do you look at pictures while you are masturbating -- most of the time, only some of the time, rarely, or never?

Most of the time /_/ Some of the time /_/ Rarely /_/ Never /_/

In general, do you usually enjoy masturbating a great deal, somewhat, a little, or not at all?

A great deal /_/ Somewhat /_/ A little /_/ Not at all /_/

How about feelings of guilt, anxiety, or concern about masturbation? Do you have such feelings often, sometimes, rarely, or never?

Often /_/ Sometimes /_/ Rarely /_/ Never /_/

If you had to guess, would you say that you masturbate more often or less often than most other boys of about your own age?

More often /_/ About the same /_/ Less often /_/

Here are some more "True-False" statements...

- -

If I were to make a girl pregnant and she had an abortion, I wouldn't feel guilty about it ---True /_7----False /_7

It isn't healthy for someone my age to go for a long time without having sex -------True /_7----False /_7

Sometimes I feel guilty about my sexual behavior ------------------------------------True /_7----False /_7

If I heard that a girl had had V.D., I would avoid having sex with her even after she was completely cured --True /_7----False /_7

I've never had sex with a girl, because I haven't yet met a girl who I would want to have sex with --True /_7----False /_7

If I were married and my wife had sexual relations with someone else, I would be angry about it but it would not in itself be enough reason to get divorced ---True /_7----False /_7

On one or more occasions, another boy or a grown man has tried to get me to have sex with him --True /_7----False /_7

I wouldn't want to marry a girl who isn't a virgin at marriage --------------------True /_7----False /_7

I would be embarassed about having sex with a girl if there were anyone else in the same room ---True /_7----False /_7

I've never had sex with a girl, because I'm not really ready for it ----------------True /_7----False /_7

It's just possible that sometime, if I really needed the money very badly, that I might have sex with a man who would pay me to do it -------------------------True /_7----False /_7

There's nothing wrong with telling a girl that you love her -- even if you don't -- if that's what it takes so she will have sex with you --------------------True /_7----False /_7

I would never pay a girl money to have sex with me ---------------------------------True /_7----False /_7

I've never had sex with another boy, but it's possible that sometime in the future I might want to ---True /_7----False /_7

If you really dig a girl, it's all right to have sex with her even if you've only known her for a few hours ---True /_7----False /_7

I've never had sex with a girl, because I haven't yet met a girl who wants to have sex with me ---True /_7----False /_7

I rarely if ever go to religious services, but I still think of myself as being a fairly religious person --True /_/----False /_/

Politically, I tend to think of myself as being a Republican ----------------------True /_/----False /_/

I would consider it abnormal or unnatural for a girl not to have sex until she gets married --True /_/----False /_/

I have a lot of respect for my parents' ideas and opinions about sex --------------True /_/----False /_/

I think that young people and many American business firms could work together to make things better --True /_/----False /_/

Making money is more important to me than being creative --------------------------True /_/----False /_/

About the time I became able to have sex, I started to feel more grown up ---------True /_/----False /_/

My parents trust me to use my own best judgment when it comes to sex --------------True /_/----False /_/

I wouldn't want to have anything to do with any sex acts that are against the law --True /_/----False /_/

The only reason young people these days have sex is for physical enjoyment ---------True /_/----False /_/

Living at home with my parents doesn't interfere with my sex life -----------------True /_/----False /_/

I wish that churches would talk more about the really important things that we need to get done in this country ---True /_/----False /_/

When I was a child, I was taught that sex was natural and healthy -----------------True /_/----False /_/

My parents and I find it easy to talk with each other about sex -------------------True /_/----False /_/

I like to smoke marijuana sometimes ---True /_/----False /_/

My parents have told me the facts about V.D. --------------------------------------True /_/----False /_/

I wish my parents could overcome their own early training, so they could realize that sex is natural and beautiful ---True /_/----False /_/

Ever since I was 12 or 13 years old, my parents have encouraged me to go out on dates --True /_/----False /_/

Whether or not to use marijuana should be up to each person to decide for himself, like with alcohol and tobacco --True /_/----False /_/

I don't like it when older people think of me as a child --------------------------True /_/----False /_/

The fact that I have to conceal my sexual activities from my parents makes it hard for me to be close to them ---True /_/----False /_/

So far as sex is concerned, I still haven't really made up my mind about what I think is right and wrong for myself --------------------------------------True /_/----False /_/

There isn't anything in sex that I wouldn't want to try, at least once ------------True /_7----False /_7

My parents and I have heavy disagreements about what is right and wrong in regard to sex, but this doesn't bother me --True /_7----False /_7

I think it's important to defeat President Nixon in this year's election -----------True /_7----False /_7

My parents think that my sexual activities are pretty much my own personal business --True /_7----False /_7

Politically, I tend to think of myself as being a Democrat ------------------------True /_7----False /_7

I believe that drugs are much more harmful than alcohol ---------------------------True /_7----False /_7

When I talk with my parents about sex I try to make them think I've had more sexual experience than I've actually had --True /_7----False /_7

A parent and child having sex with each other is something that I would consider abnormal or unnatural, even if both of them wanted to do it --------------True /_7----False /_7

I've never really gotten to know my mother --True /_7----False /_7

Politically, I tend to think of myself as being a revolutionary -------------------True /_7----False /_7

My parents think that the only reason young people have sex is for physical enjoyment --True /_7----False /_7

I would like to be able to talk with my parents about sex -------------------------True /_7----False /_7

In general, I feel pretty self-confident about sex --------------------------------True /_7----False /_7

If I had children and any of them turned out to be homosexual, I would be very upset --True /_7----False /_7

Oral sex is something that I would consider abnormal or unnatural -----------------True /_7----False /_7

I have a lot of respect for my parents as people ----------------------------------True /_7----False /_7

I have never read a serious magazine article about sex ----------------------------True /_7----False /_7

So far as I know, my parents have never really gotten sexually passionate about each other --True /_7----False /_7

I would not want to have children in the kind of world we live in today -----------True /_7----False /_7

I've never taken part in any sex act, or been involved in any kind of sexual situation, that I myself would think of as being immoral --------------------------True /_7----False /_7

The only reason I would get legally married would be to satisfy my parents ---------True /_7----False /_7

I go to religious services fairly often ---True /_7----False /_7

I don't think it would be possible for a boy to be really in love with more than one girl at the same time --True /_/----False /_/

I won't tell a girl that I love her unless I really do ----------------------------True /_/----False /_/

My parents are anxious that before I get too old I should find the right girl to marry --True /_/----False /_/

I'd like to ask my parents for information about V.D., but I'm afraid to because they would ask whether I'm having sex with girls --------------------------True /_/----False /_/

My parents tell me that I'm too young to have sex with girls ----------------------True /_/----False /_/

If I were married and my wife had sexual relations with someone else, I would divorce her --True /_/----False /_/

I wouldn't want to have sex with a girl only for the physical enjoyment of doing it, and nothing else --True /_/----False /_/

I usually think of myself as being sexually attractive to girls -------------------True /_/----False /_/

I've never had sex with another boy, and I'm sure I'd never want to ---------------True /_/----False /_/

I wouldn't want to have sex with a girl unless I liked her as a person ------------True /_/----False /_/

I think it would be wrong for me to have sex with a girl I'd just met and hadn't gotten to know --True /_/----False /_/

I'd like to ask my parents for information about birth control, but I'm afraid to because they would ask whether I'm having sex with girls ----------------True /_/----False /_/

My parents assume that I have had sex with girls ----------------------------------True /_/----False /_/

I wouldn't want to have sex with a girl unless she loved me -----------------------True /_/----False /_/

I wouldn't want to marry a girl unless I'd lived with her first -------------------True /_/----False /_/

I don't think it would be possible for a boy to have a real relationship with more than one girl at the same time ---True /_/----False /_/

My parents think that if I have to have sex before getting married, they would rather I do it with a girl I don't love -------------------------------------True /_/----False /_/

My parents wouldn't want me to marry a girl unless I'd lived with her first --------True /_/----False /_/

My parents assume that I haven't had sex with girls ------------------------------True /_/----False /_/

I wouldn't want to have sex with a girl unless I loved her -----------------------True /_/----False /_/

I wouldn't want to have sex with a girl unless she liked me as a person -----------True /_/----False /_/

Some people I know are so much involved in sex that it's the most important thing in their lives ---True /_/----False /_/

Because of the problem of over-population, I would not want to have more than two children --True /_/----False /_/

My parents try to seem broad-minded about sex, but actually they're pretty uptight when it comes down to what I myself want to do ----------------------True /_/----False /_/

I believe that many people who live in communes are finding meaning and brotherhood in their way of life ---True /_/----False /_/

Some day, I will probably want to have children -- but it won't matter whether or not I get married first ---True /_/----False /_/

When talking to my parents about sex, I try to persuade them to my way of thinking --True /_/----False /_/

I sometimes worry about whether God would approve of my sexual activities ----------True /_/----False /_/

So far as sex is concerned, I do what I want to do, regardless of what society thinks ---True /_/----False /_/

My parents don't get along with each other very well -------------------------------True /_/----False /_/

If a girl uses birth control pills or other methods of contraception, it makes it seem as if she were planning to have sex ----------------------------------True /_/----False /_/

My parents believe that it's all right for young people to have sex before getting married, if they are in love with each other -------------------------------True /_/----False /_/

When I was a child, I was taught that sex was wrong --------------------------------True /_/----False /_/

I don't think I will want to have children, because I don't like the idea of having all that responsibility ---True /_/----False /_/

One of the reasons I stopped going to church is because churches teach that sex is sinful --True /_/----False /_/

Some of my sexual activities are probably harmful to my relationship with my parents ---True /_/----False /_/

Birth control pills can be physically harmful to a girl ----------------------------True /_/----False /_/

I have no personal values of my own --True /_/----False /_/

I can't see myself getting married until I know it will last for the rest of my life ---True /_/----False /_/

I am comfortable talking with my parents about sex in general, but I avoid telling them what I myself do ---True /_/----False /_/

Some of my sexual activities are probably harmful to me ----------------------------True /_/----False /_/

Sometimes, people of the same sex do things together that result in sexual stimulation or satisfaction for either or both of them. When this happens, it is called "homosexuality."

Have you ever heard of homosexuality?

Yes /_/ No /_/ → *IF YOUR ANSWER IS "NO," PLEASE SKIP TO THE NEXT PAGE*

- -

Have you yourself ever done anything with another boy, or with a grown man, that resulted in sexual stimulation or satisfaction for either or both of you?

Yes /_/ No /_/ → *IF YOUR ANSWER IS "NO," PLEASE SKIP TO THE NEXT PAGE*

- -

How old were you <u>the very first time</u> that you did this?

AGE WHEN I FIRST DID THIS:__________

- -

The very first time that you did this, who did you do it with?

A boy younger than I was -----------------/_/

A boy my own age -------------------------/_/

A boy older than I was ----------------/_/

A grown man --------------------------/_/

- -

When was the <u>most recent</u> occasion on which you did this?

Since this time yesterday ----------------/_/

Since this time last week ----------------/_/

Since this time last month ---------------/_/

More than a month ago -----------------/_/

PLEASE GO ON TO THE NEXT PAGE

Have you ever had sexual intercourse with a girl?

Yes /_/ No /_/ → *IF YOUR ANSWER IS "NO," PLEASE SKIP TO THE NEXT BLUE PAGE*

- -

Thinking back to the very first time that you had sex with a girl, how old were you then? AGE:______

- -

Where was it that you had sex with a girl for the very first time?

In my home ------------------------/_/

In a friend's home ----------------/_/

In an automobile ------------------/_/

At school -------------------------/_/

In the girl's home --------------------/_/

In a hotel or motel -------------------/_/

Outdoors ------------------------------/_/

Somewhere else ------------------------/_/

- -

Which of the words below accurately describe how you felt the first time that you had sex with a girl? *(PLEASE CHECK ALL THAT APPLY)*

Afraid ------------/_/

Thrilled ----------/_/

Hurt --------------/_/

Fulfilled ---------/_/

Raped -------------/_/

Powerful ----------/_/

Sorry -------------/_/

Excited ------------/_/

Guilty -------------/_/

Happy --------------/_/

Foolish ------------/_/

Relieved -----------/_/

Worried ------------/_/

Curious ------------/_/

Embarassed ------------/_/

Joyful ----------------/_/

Used ------------------/_/

Mature ----------------/_/

Disappointed ----------/_/

Satisfied -------------/_/

Tired -----------------/_/

- -

This first time that you had sex with a girl, did either you or the girl make use of any birth control method, or do anything else to cut down on the risk of the girl's becoming pregnant?

Yes /_/ No /_/ I didn't, and I don't know whether the girl did or not /_/

- -

If you had it to do all over again, do you wish that you had waited until you were older before having sex with a girl for the first time, are you glad you did it when you did, or do you wish that you had done it when you were younger?

I wish I had waited until I was older before having sex with a girl for the first time --/_/

I'm glad I did it when I did --/_/

I wish I had done it when I was younger ------------------------------------/_/

Who was the very first girl with whom you ever had sexual intercourse?

A girl I had met only a little while before the time that we first had sex together ---------/__/

A girl I was going steady with, and planned to marry ----------------------/__/

A girl I was going steady with, but had no definite plans to marry -----------/__/

A girl I knew slightly, and was more or less friendly with -----------------/__/

A girl I knew well and liked a lot, even though we weren't going together ----------/__/

A prostitute --------------------------/__/

My wife, after we were married ------------/__/

- -

How old was this girl when you first had sex together? AGE:__________

- -

Of course, you weren't inside this girl's head at the time, so you can't know for sure how she felt then. But if you had to <u>guess</u>, which of the words below do you think might accurately describe how she felt when you had sex with her for the very first time? *(PLEASE CHECK ALL THAT APPLY)*

Afraid -------------/__/	Excited -------------/__/	Embarassed -------------/__/
Thrilled -----------/__/	Guilty --------------/__/	Joyful -----------------/__/
Hurt ---------------/__/	Happy ---------------/__/	Used -------------------/__/
Fulfilled ----------/__/	Foolish -------------/__/	Mature -----------------/__/
Raped --------------/__/	Relieved ------------/__/	Disappointed -----------/__/
Powerful -----------/__/	Worried -------------/__/	Satisfied --------------/__/
Sorry --------------/__/	Curious -------------/__/	Tired ------------------/__/

- -

So far as you know, were you the first boy that she had ever had sex with, or had she ever had sex before with one or more other boys?

I know for sure that I was the first boy she'd ever had sex with ------------------------/__/

I think that I was probably the first boy she'd ever had sex with -----------------------/__/

I really don't know whether or not she'd ever had sex before ----------------------------/__/

I think that she'd probably had sex with one or more other boys before me ---------------/__/

I know for sure that she'd had sex with one or more other boys before me ----------------/__/

PLEASE GO ON TO THE NEXT PAGE

Still thinking about this very first girl that you ever had sex with, what happened to your relationship with her after the first time you had sex together?

Did the relationship become stronger or weaker as a result of having had sex together?

The relationship became stronger --------------/ / The relationship became weaker ----------/ /

There wasn't any relationship to begin with ---/ / The relationship stayed about the same---/ /

- -

After the first time, did you ever have sex with this girl again?

No / / Yes / /

On about how many more occasions did you have sex together, after the first time?

NUMBER OF OCCASIONS AFTER THE FIRST TIME:________

- -

Looking back at it now, are you glad that this particular girl was the first one you ever had sex with? Or if you had it to do over again, would you rather have had sex for the first time with a different girl?

I'm glad it was this particular girl ----/ / I wish it had been a different girl ----/ /

- -

Since this first girl, have you ever had sexual intercourse with any other girls?

Yes / / No / / → *IF YOUR ANSWER IS "NO," PLEASE SKIP TO THE NEXT PAGE*

- -

All in all, how many different girls (counting the first one) have you ever had sex with?

TOTAL NUMBER OF DIFFERENT GIRLS I'VE EVER HAD SEX WITH:_______

PLEASE GO ON TO THE NEXT PAGE

There are a number of different things that can be done to cut down the risk of a girl becoming pregnant.

When you have sex with a girl, how often do you do each of the things listed below?

	Always	Usually	Sometimes	Never
I use a condom (rubber)	/_/	/_/	/_/	/_/
I withdraw before ejaculating (coming)	/_/	/_/	/_/	/_/
I make sure that the girl is using birth control pills or some other method of contraception	/_/	/_/	/_/	/_/
I just assume that the girl is using birth control pills or some other method of contraception	/_/	/_/	/_/	/_/
I just trust to luck that the girl won't become pregnant	/_/	/_/	/_/	/_/
I don't think about whether or not the girl might become pregnant	/_/	/_/	/_/	/_/

Do you ever worry about the possibility that you might cause a girl to become pregnant?

Often /_/ Sometimes /_/ Hardly ever /_/ Never /_/

If you were to make a girl pregnant, which one of the things listed below would you most prefer that she do, if you could have things your way?

PLEASE CHECK ONLY ONE

Have an abortion	/_/
Have the baby and give it up for adoption	/_/
Have the baby and count on me to help bring it up	/_/
Have the baby and bring it up herself	/_/
Have the baby and get married	/_/
Tell her parents and let them decide what to do	/_/

If you were to make a girl pregnant, do you think you would or would not do each of the things listed below?

	Yes	Maybe	No
I would say that it was someone else who had made her pregnant	/_/	/_/	/_/
I would say that it was the girl's problem, and none of my business	/_/	/_/	/_/
I would talk to her about it and help her decide what to do, but that's all	/_/	/_/	/_/
I would help to arrange and pay for an abortion	/_/	/_/	/_/
I would help her bring up the child	/_/	/_/	/_/
I would help her do whatever she decided to do	/_/	/_/	/_/
I would marry her	/_/	/_/	/_/
I would discuss it with my parents to see what they think	/_/	/_/	/_/

Have you ever wanted to have sex with a girl but found yourself unable to do so because you couldn't get an erection?

Yes /_/ No /_/

- -

Have you ever wanted to have sex with a girl but decided not to do so because you were afraid of catching V.D., or venereal disease?

Yes /_/ No /_/

- -

Have you ever wanted to have sex with a girl but decided not to do so because you were afraid that the girl might become pregnant?

Yes /_/ No /_/

- -

When was the most recent occasion on which you had sex with a girl?

Since this time yesterday ----------------/_/

Since this time last week ----------------/_/

Since this time last month ---------------/_/

More than a month ago -----------/_/

PLEASE SKIP TO THE NEXT PAGE

- -

This very last time that you had sex with a girl, did either of you use any kind of contraceptive or birth control method, or do anything else to cut down the risk of the girl becoming pregnant?

No, neither of us did --------------------/_/

Yes, I did -------------------------------/_/

I didn't, and I don't know whether or not the girl did ----------------/_/

Yes, the girl did ------------------/_/

- -

Since this time last month, approximately how many occasions have there been on which you have had sex with a girl?

NUMBER OF OCCASIONS IN THE PAST MONTH ON WHICH I HAD SEX WITH A GIRL:________

- -

And how many different girls have you had sex with since this time last month?

NUMBER OF DIFFERENT GIRLS I'VE HAD SEX WITH IN THE PAST MONTH:________

On those occasions during the past month on which you had sex with a girl, what -- if anything -- was done to cut down the risk of the girl becoming pregnant?

	Always	Sometimes	Once or twice	Never
I used a condom (rubber)	/_7	/_7	/_7	/_7
I withdrew before ejaculating (coming)	/_7	/_7	/_7	/_7
The girl used birth control pills	/_7	/_7	/_7	/_7
The girl used an intrauterine device (coil, IUD)	/_7	/_7	/_7	/_7
The girl used a diaphragm	/_7	/_7	/_7	/_7
The girl used a contraceptive foam	/_7	/_7	/_7	/_7
The girl used a contraceptive jelly	/_7	/_7	/_7	/_7
The girl used a contraceptive douche	/_7	/_7	/_7	/_7
The girl used the rhythm method	/_7	/_7	/_7	/_7
I made sure that the girl was using something, but I don't know what it was	/_7	/_7	/_7	/_7
I just assumed that the girl was using something, but I don't know what it was	/_7	/_7	/_7	/_7
I just trusted to luck that the girl wouldn't become pregnant	/_7	/_7	/_7	/_7
I didn't think about whether or not the girl might become pregnant	/_7	/_7	/_7	/_7

- -

Have you ever made a girl pregnant?

Yes /_7 No /_7 → IF YOUR ANSWER IS "NO," PLEASE SKIP TO THE NEXT PAGE

- -

What happened? *(PLEASE CHECK ALL THAT APPLY)*

I said that it was someone else who had made the girl pregnant -------- /_7

I said that it was the girl's problem, and none of my business -------- /_7

I talked to her about it and helped her decide what to do -------- /_7

I helped her arrange and pay for an abortion -------- /_7

I discussed it with my parents to find out what they thought should be done -------- /_7

I married the girl and am helping to bring up the baby -------- /_7

I am helping to bring up the baby, without marrying the girl -------- /_7

The girl had the baby and married someone else -------- /_7

The girl had the baby and gave it up for adoption -------- /_7

The girl had an abortion -------- /_7 The girl had a miscarriage -------- /_7

At the present time, do you have sex mostly (or only) with just one particular girl?

Yes /_7 No /_7 → IF YOUR ANSWER IS "NO," PLEASE SKIP TO THE NEXT PAGE

Would you say that you have a close relationship with this girl, a casual relationship, or no real relationship at all?

No real relationship /_7 A casual relationship /_7 A close relationship /_7

For how long have you had such a relationship with this girl?

NUMBER OF WEEKS:______ NUMBER OF MONTHS:______ NUMBER OF YEARS:______

And for how long have you been having sex with this girl?

NUMBER OF WEEKS:______ NUMBER OF MONTHS:______ NUMBER OF YEARS:______

Do you love this girl? Yes /_7 No /_7 I'm not really sure /_7

Does she love you? Yes /_7 No /_7 I'm not really sure /_7 She says she does /_7

Do you plan to get married? Yes /_7 Probably /_7 Probably not /_7 No /_7

We haven't decided /_7 We haven't talked about it /_7

Do you have sex with other girls?

Frequently /_7 Occasionally /_7 Very rarely /_7 Never /_7

Does she have sex with other boys?

Frequently /_7 Occasionally /_7 Very rarely /_7 Never /_7

I don't think so, but I'm not sure /_7 I think so, but I'm not sure /_7

PLEASE GO ON TO THE NEXT PAGE

Here are some more "True-False" statements...

- -

It bothers me that I can't seem to be satisfied sexually --------------------------True /_/----False /_/

If I were to have sex with another girl, just occasionally, it wouldn't really put my girl friend uptight --True /_/----False /_/

I have never had V.D. or venereal disease --True /_/----False /_/

If I were to make a girl pregnant, I wouldn't want her to have an abortion because taking the life of an unborn child is wrong --------------------------------True /_/----False /_/

I've never had sex with a person of another race -----------------------------------True /_/----False /_/

On one or more occasions, under the influence of marijuana, I've had sex with someone that I wouldn't have had sex with otherwise --------------------------True /_/----False /_/

On one or more occasions, I've refused to ball a girl unless she would do something that I wanted her to do --True /_/----False /_/

Having sex doesn't make my life any more meaningful --------------------------------True /_/----False /_/

There are many times when I get horny but don't have anyone to ball ---------------True /_/----False /_/

On one or more occasions, I've had sex with a girl mostly because people would have put me down if I hadn't ---True /_/----False /_/

If I were to get a girl pregnant, I wouldn't want her to have an abortion because it's against my religion --True /_/----False /_/

If my girl friend were to have sex with another boy, just occasionally, it wouldn't really put me uptight --True /_/----False /_/

I don't like to have sex with a girl when she's having her period -----------------True /_/----False /_/

It really bothers me a lot if I have sex with a girl and she doesn't seem to be completely satisfied ---True /_/----False /_/

Sometimes I think that I am addicted to sex, the way some people are addicted to drugs ---True /_/----False /_/

I don't get as much physical enjoyment out of sex as I think I should be getting ---True /_/----False /_/

Abortions are so easy to get these days that I don't really worry about getting a girl pregnant --True /_/----False /_/

On one or more occasions, a girl has refused to ball me unless I would do something that I didn't want to do ---True /_/----False /_/

IF YOU DON'T WANT TO ANSWER THE QUESTIONS ON THIS PAGE, PLEASE GO ON TO THE NEXT PAGE

Have you ever felt a girl's breast with your hand?

Yes /_/ No /_/ → *IF YOUR ANSWER IS "NO," PLEASE SKIP TO THE NEXT PAGE*

Thinking back to the very first time that you felt a girl's breast with your hand, how old were you then?

AGE AT WHICH I FIRST FELT A GIRL'S BREAST WITH MY HAND:_______

When was the most recent occasion on which you felt a girl's breast with your hand?

Since this time yesterday --------------/_/

Since this time last week --------------/_/

Since this time last month -------------/_/

More than a month ago -------------/_/ → *PLEASE SKIP TO THE NEXT PAGE*

Since this time last month, approximately how many times have you felt a girl's breast with your hand?

NUMBER OF TIMES IN THE PAST MONTH THAT I FELT A GIRL'S BREAST WITH MY HAND:_______

And how many different girls have you done this with in the past month?

NUMBER OF DIFFERENT GIRLS WHOSE BREASTS I HAVE FELT IN THE PAST MONTH:_______

PLEASE GO ON TO THE NEXT PAGE

IF YOU DON'T WANT TO ANSWER THE QUESTIONS ON THIS PAGE, PLEASE GO ON TO THE NEXT PAGE

Have you ever felt a girl's sex organ with your hand?

Yes /_/ No /_/ → *IF YOUR ANSWER IS "NO," PLEASE SKIP TO THE NEXT PAGE*

Thinking back to the very first time that you ever felt a girl's sex organ with your hand, how old were you then?

AGE AT WHICH I FIRST FELT A GIRL'S SEX ORGAN WITH MY HAND:________

When was the most recent occasion on which you felt a girl's sex organ with your hand?

Since this time yesterday --------------/_/

Since this time last week --------------/_/

Since this time last month -------------/_/

More than a month ago ------------/_/ → *PLEASE SKIP TO THE NEXT PAGE*

Since this time last month, approximately how many times have you felt a girl's sex organ with your hand?

NUMBER OF TIMES IN THE PAST MONTH THAT I FELT A GIRL'S SEX ORGAN WITH MY HAND:________

And how many different girls have you done this with in the past month?

NUMBER OF DIFFERENT GIRLS WHOSE SEX ORGAN I HAVE FELT IN THE PAST MONTH:________

PLEASE GO ON TO THE NEXT PAGE

IF YOU DON'T WANT TO ANSWER THE QUESTIONS ON THIS PAGE, PLEASE GO ON TO THE NEXT PAGE

Has a girl ever felt your sex organ with her hand?

Yes /_/ No /_/ → *IF YOUR ANSWER IS "NO," PLEASE SKIP TO THE NEXT PAGE*

- -

Thinking back to the <u>very first time</u> that a girl ever felt your sex organ with her hand, how old were you then?

AGE AT WHICH A GIRL FIRST FELT MY SEX ORGAN WITH HER HAND:_______

- -

When was the <u>most recent</u> occasion on which a girl felt your sex organ with her hand?

Since this time yesterday -------------/_/
Since this time last week -------------/_/
Since this time last month ------------/_/

More than a month ago -----------/_/ → *PLEASE SKIP TO THE NEXT PAGE*

- -

Since this time last month, approximately how many times has a girl felt your sex organ with her hand?

NUMBER OF TIMES IN THE PAST MONTH THAT A GIRL FELT MY SEX ORGAN WITH HER HAND:_______

- -

And how many <u>different</u> girls has this happened with in the past month?

NUMBER OF DIFFERENT GIRLS WHO HAVE FELT MY SEX ORGAN IN THE PAST MONTH:_______

- -

Sometimes, when a girl feels a boy's sex organ with her hand, it results in the boy having a climax or orgasm -- what most young people refer to as "coming." Has this ever happened to you?

Yes /_/ No /_/ → *PLEASE SKIP TO THE NEXT PAGE*

- -

When was the <u>most recent</u> occasion on which you had a climax or orgasm because a girl was feeling your sex organ with her hand?

Since this time yesterday--------------/_/
Since this time last week -------------/_/
Since this time last month ------------/_/

More than a month ago -----------/_/

PLEASE GO ON TO THE NEXT PAGE

Here are some more statements that we would like you to agree with or disagree with.

If you agree with a statement more than you disagree with it, please check the "agree" box.
If you disagree with a statement more than you agree with it, please check the "disagree" box.

Remember, there are no "right" or "wrong" answers - the only thing that matters is what YOU YOURSELF think.

- -

If a girl has led a boy on, it's all right for the boy to force her to have sex ----------Agree /_/----Disagree /_/

The politicians are the only ones to blame for the mess this country is in ----------Agree /_/----Disagree /_/

Twenty years from now, most of the people in my generation are going to be living happier lives than most older people in their forties or fifties live now ----------Agree /_/----Disagree /_/

After election time is over, most candidates who win pay no attention to the desires of the people who supported them ----------Agree /_/----Disagree /_/

Churches are really doing their best to understand young people's ideas about sex ----------Agree /_/----Disagree /_/

I'm not a child any more, but I'm not an adult yet, either ----------Agree /_/----Disagree /_/

If two boys want to have sex together, it's all right so long as they both want to do it ----------Agree /_/----Disagree /_/

The American system of the representative democracy can still respond effectively to the needs of the people ----------Agree /_/----Disagree /_/

Physical attractiveness of the other person is more important in love than it is in sex ----------Agree /_/----Disagree /_/

It is up to public officials, not me, to say what is necessary for the good of this country ----------Agree /_/----Disagree /_/

A lot of the pleasure in sex would be lost if it did not seem to be such a forbidden activity ----------Agree /_/----Disagree /_/

The kind of people who could really do a good job in government are not interested in trying to get themselves elected ----------Agree /_/----Disagree /_/

When it comes to morality in sex, the important thing is the way people treat each other, not the particular things that they do together ----------Agree /_/----Disagree /_/

If two girls want to have sex together, it's all right so long as they both want to do it ----------Agree /_/----Disagree /_/

A young person who has sex only for physical enjoyment and nothing else is doing something immoral ----------Agree /_/----Disagree /_/

There is no kind of sex act that I would think of as being abnormal, so long as the people involved want to do it ----------Agree /_/----Disagree /_/

If two people are in love, it's only natural for them to want to get married ---Agree /_/----Disagree /_/

The way I'm living right now, most of my abilities are going to waste ----------Agree /_/----Disagree /_/

It's not so important that a child live in a home with both of his parents, so long as he has a good relationship with each of his parents individually -------Agree /_/----Disagree /_/

Marriage would make sex even more enjoyable, because both people would know that they really belong to each other ------------------------------------Agree /_/----Disagree /_/

The most important thing in a sexual relationship is just the sheer physical pleasure of having sex --Agree /_/----Disagree /_/

The cancer scare about cigarette smoking has been exaggerated ------------------Agree /_/----Disagree /_/

The Women's Liberation Movement has been a good thing for women ----------------Agree /_/----Disagree /_/

Alcohol increases sexual pleasure --Agree /_/----Disagree /_/

My sexual behavior would not be acceptable to society --------------------------Agree /_/----Disagree /_/

It would be wrong to take advantage of a girl who was stoned or drunk by having sex with her --Agree /_/----Disagree /_/

The only good reason for getting married is if a baby is on the way ------------Agree /_/----Disagree /_/

In general, I think that so far I've been able to achieve most of the things that I've set out to achieve --Agree /_/----Disagree /_/

When it comes to deciding how far a boy and girl should go where sex is concerned, it is up to the girl to decide ---------------------------------Agree /_/----Disagree /_/

Most girls these days have sexual intercourse before they are married ----------Agree /_/----Disagree /_/

When a boy has sex for the first time, it should be with a girl who is sexually experienced ---Agree /_/----Disagree /_/

Young people don't really want independence from society; they only want independence from their parents --Agree /_/----Disagree /_/

If two people are going to have a baby that neither person really wants, it is all right for the girl to have an abortion -------------------------------Agree /_/----Disagree /_/

Having sex together is a good way for two people to become acquainted ----------Agree /_/----Disagree /_/

PLEASE GO ON TO THE NEXT PAGE

Politically, there is no way that young people can ever beat "the silent majority" ---Agree /_/---Disagree /_/

It's possible for love to be very real and very strong, but still not last for more than a few years ---Agree /_/---Disagree /_/

It's all right for married people to have sexual relations with other people once in a while for the sake of variety ---Agree /_/---Disagree /_/

It's all right for a person to have sexual relations with both males and females, if that's what the person wants to do ---Agree /_/---Disagree /_/

It is really a tragedy if a couple that has children breaks up ---Agree /_/---Disagree /_/

If a boy finds out that he has V.D., he should immediately tell any girl he has recently had sex with ---Agree /_/---Disagree /_/

Sex education courses in school are valuable for young people ---Agree /_/---Disagree /_/

Marijuana increases sexual pleasure ---Agree /_/---Disagree /_/

If a girl truly doesn't want to have a baby, she won't get pregnant even though she may have sex without taking any birth control precautions ---Agree /_/---Disagree /_/

It's important that I try to develop my own set of personal values ---Agree /_/---Disagree /_/

Too many young people these days are irresponsible where sex is concerned ---Agree /_/---Disagree /_/

If older people would only remember what they were like when they were young, they would understand how young people think today ---Agree /_/---Disagree /_/

If two people love each other and are living together, getting married is just a legal technicality ---Agree /_/---Disagree /_/

Most boys these days have sexual intercourse before they are married ---Agree /_/---Disagree /_/

When a girl has sex for the first time, it should be with a boy who is sexually experienced ---Agree /_/---Disagree /_/

If parents no longer love each other, it's better for their children that the parents break up rather than continue to live together unhappily ---Agree /_/---Disagree /_/

The main reason why people are more casual about sex these days is because birth control is easily available to everyone ---Agree /_/---Disagree /_/

It's immoral to bring an unwanted child into this over-populated world, especially now that abortions are so easy to get ---Agree /_/---Disagree /_/

THANK YOU VERY MUCH FOR YOUR COOPERATION IN ANSWERING THESE QUESTIONS

Now that you have finished --

1. Please put the questionnaire in our brown postage-paid return envelope.

2. Seal the envelope yourself, making sure that it is tightly sealed.

3. Go with our interviewer to the nearest mailbox, and mail the envelope. (If you prefer to have the interviewer mail it for you, he or she will be glad to do that. Either way, it will come directly to our Research Office.)

WHAT YOUNG PEOPLE BELIEVE AND DO

A TOTALLY CONFIDENTIAL STUDY OF SOCIAL AND SEXUAL ATTITUDES AND BEHAVIOR

FEMALE QUESTIONNAIRE

We appreciate the help you are giving us by taking part in the first nationwide survey of this kind ever to be conducted in the United States. If you are like the many other young people who have tested out this questionnaire, you will find the questions both interesting and easy to answer.

THIS IS NOT A TEST. THERE ARE NO "RIGHT" ANSWERS AND NO "WRONG" ANSWERS. BUT WE ARE COUNTING ON YOU TO GIVE TRUTHFUL ANSWERS ABOUT WHAT YOU BELIEVE AND WHAT YOU DO. SOME OF THE QUESTIONS ARE VERY PERSONAL, BUT TO MAKE SURE THAT YOU CAN FEEL COMPLETELY FREE AND HONEST IN WHAT YOU SAY, THE INTERVIEWER WILL TELL YOU ABOUT THE FOOLPROOF SYSTEM WE ARE USING TO MAKE SURE THAT THESE QUESTIONNAIRES REMAIN ABSOLUTELY CONFIDENTIAL IN EVERY WAY.

Please remember:

You are in complete charge of handling this questionnaire. The interviewer is remaining only to answer questions that you may have about the meaning of words or instructions that may not be clear to you. Neither the interviewer nor anyone else who knows who you are will ever see the answers that you give.

You can make sure of this for yourself simply by doing the following three things as soon as you have finished filling out the questionnaire:

1. Immediately put the questionnaire in our postage-paid return envelope.

2. Seal the envelope yourself.

3. Go with our interviewer to the nearest mailbox, and mail the envelope. (If you prefer to have the interviewer mail it for you, he or she will be glad to do that. Either way, it will come directly to our Research Office.)

ABOUT FILLING IN THIS QUESTIONNAIRE

To make everything as easy as possible, all of the questions in this booklet have been carefully designed so that you can answer them with an absolute minimum of writing:

Either by marking an "X" in a box, like this -- [X]

or by writing a number on a line, like this -- NUMBER OF FINGERS ON MY LEFT HAND: 5

If you put an "X" in a box that has an arrow leading from it, follow the arrow to see where it goes. It will point either to the next question that you should answer, or to an instruction asking you to turn to another page.

If a question asks you to fill in a number, and you're not sure exactly what number to fill in, write in whatever number represents your best guess about what the answer really is.

There are only a few other things that you should try to keep in mind while filling out the questionnaire.

1. The interviewer is here only to answer any questions you may have about what different words mean, or to explain the meaning of any instructions that may not be clear to you.

   The interviewer is not supposed to explain any of the questions, or to suggest what answers you should give. Most important, the interviewer is not permitted to look at your answers.

2. If you are 13 or 14 years old, some of the questions may seem to be written for people who are older than you are. If you are 18 or 19 years old, some of the questions may seem to be written for people who are younger than you are. But almost all of the questions can be answered by almost anyone between the ages of 13 and 19.

   So please do your best to answer every question, even if the question doesn't seem to be serious, necessary, or applicable to your own experience or way of thinking. Each question does have a purpose, and unless we have your answer our study will be incomplete.

   Afterwards, if you want to tell the interviewer anything or write to us with any suggestions, by all means feel free to do so. But please do try to answer all of the questions.

3. All of the X-marks and numbers will be fed directly into a computer, and since the computer doesn't know your name or address it can't possibly tell anyone what your answers were. All it can do is add your answers in with the answers we get from hundreds of other young people all over the country, and print out the results as percentages.

How old were you on your last birthday?

13 /_/ 14 /_/ 15 /_/ 16 /_/ 17 /_/ 18 /_/ 19 /_/

- -

Are you male or female? Male /_/ Female /_/

PLEASE CHECK THE FRONT OF THIS BOOKLET TO MAKE SURE THAT YOU HAVE THE RIGHT QUESTIONNAIRE FOR A PERSON OF YOUR SEX

- -

Which of your parents is easier to talk to about sex?

My mother /_/ My father /_/

- -

If you had a serious problem that had to do with sex, which of your parents could you count on to stand by you the most?

My mother /_/ My father /_/

- -

Do you have any brothers who are older than you are? Yes /_/ No /_/

- -

Do you have any sisters who are older than you are? Yes /_/ No /_/

- -

Do you have any brothers who are younger than you are? Yes /_/ No /_/

- -

Do you have any sisters who are younger than you are? Yes /_/ No /_/

PLEASE GO ON TO THE NEXT PAGE

Are both of your parents still living?

Yes /_7 No /_7

Which of your parents is not still living?

My mother /_7 → How old were you when your mother died? AGE WHEN MOTHER DIED:______

My father /_7 → How old were you when your father died? AGE WHEN FATHER DIED:______

- -

Are your parents still married to each other, or are they divorced or separated?

They are still married /_7 They are divorced or separated /_7

How old were you when your parents were divorced or separated?

AGE WHEN PARENTS WERE DIVORCED OR SEPARATED:________

- -

What is (or was) your father's religious preference?

Protestant /_7 Catholic /_7 Jewish /_7 Other /_7 None /_7

- -

What is (or was) your mother's religious preference?

Protestant /_7 Catholic /_7 Jewish /_7 Other /_7 None /_7

- -

What is <u>your own</u> religious preference?

Protestant /_7 Catholic /_7 Jewish /_7 Other /_7 None /_7

PLEASE GO ON TO THE NEXT PAGE

Have you attended religious services or church activities this year?

Regularly /_7 Occasionally /_7 Hardly ever /_7 Never /_7

- -

How religious would you say you are?

Very religious /_7 Somewhat religious /_7 Not very religious/_7 Not religious at all /_7

- -

Are you attending school at the present time?

No /_7 Yes /_7

What grade are you in now?

5th Grade /_7 6th Grade /_7 7th Grade /_7

8th Grade /_7 9th Grade /_7 10th Grade /_7

11th Grade /_7 12th Grade (High School Senior) /_7

Secretarial, trade, or technical school ------------/_7

First year college /_7 Second year college /_7

Third year college /_7 Fourth year college /_7

How well are you doing in school?

Superior grades --------/_7 Good grades -----------/_7

Average grades ---------/_7 Poor grades -----------/_7

- -

Are you working at a job to earn money at the present time?

Yes, full-time /_7 Yes, part-time /_7 No, I'm not working /_7

PLEASE GO ON TO THE NEXT PAGE

The next few pages of this questionnaire contain statements about many different things. We would like you to read each statement, and then mark it as being either "True" or "False."

For instance, if there were a statement such as:

I am less than 35 years old ---True /_7----False /_7

you would put an "X" in the box next to the word "True."

If there were a statement such as:

I think it would be fun to fall down and break my leg --------------------True /_7----False /_7

you would put an "X" in the box next to the word "False."

But please remember, this is not a "True-False" test such as the ones they give in school, because there are no "right" answers and no "wrong" answers. Most of the statements in this questionnaire are worded so that some people would think of them as being "True" for themselves while other people would think of them as being "False" for themselves -- AND THE ONLY THING THAT MATTERS IS WHAT YOU YOURSELF THINK.

For instance, there might be a statement such as:

I don't mind cold weather --True /_7----False /_7

People who always like cold weather would mark the statement "True," while people who always hate cold weather would mark the statement "False." Some people, on the other hand, would think of the statement as being partly true and partly false.

IF YOU COME UPON A STATEMENT THAT YOU THINK OF AS BEING PARTLY TRUE AND PARTLY FALSE, try to decide whether you think it's more true than false or more false than true.

If, for you, a statement is more true than false, mark it as "True."

If, for you, a statement is more false than true, mark it as "False."

For instance, in the example about cold weather, you should mark the statement "True" if you usually like cold weather, even though sometimes you may not like it. If you usually don't like cold weather, then you should mark the statement "False," even though there may be times when you do like cold weather.

In other words, TRY TO MARK EACH STATEMENT AS EITHER "TRUE" OR "FALSE," depending on what you yourself think or feel most of the time, or under most circumstances. If you come upon a question that you really do not understand, cannot decide about (even after trying), or do not wish to answer, just go on to the next question.

= *START HERE* =

If I had to go out into the world on my own right now, I think I could get along pretty well ---True /_7----False /_7

Some day, I will probably want to get married and have children --------------------True /_7----False /_7

Sex education courses in school can't teach me anything ---------------------------True /_7----False /_7

I wouldn't use birth control or contraception because it's against my religion -----True /_7----False /_7

Sometimes I get sexually aroused from the music that I hear ------------------------True /_7----False /_7

I often ask my parents for advice about sexual matters ----------------------------True /_/----False /_/

I find it hard to accept the idea of obeying laws that I don't agree with ----------True /_/----False /_/

Some of the opinions that I express to my parents are opinions that I invent just to put them uptight ---True /_/----False /_/

On one or more occasions, I've done sexual things mostly to show that I don't care what society thinks ---True /_/----False /_/

If an organization came along wanting to sign up people to register and vote in this year's election, I wouldn't be interested in helping -----------------------True /_/----False /_/

I think my parents' ideas about sex are wrong, but they have a right to their own opinions ---True /_/----False /_/

My parents and I sometimes talk about sex, but it makes them very uncomfortable ----True /_/----False /_/

I think like an adult, but I feel a lot younger ----------------------------------True /_/----False /_/

I wish my parents and I could agree more about what we think is right and wrong where sex is concerned ---True /_/----False /_/

My parents don't really like me ---True /_/----False /_/

I don't think that I would want to have sex with a person of another race ----------True /_/----False /_/

My parents and I talk pretty freely about sex in general, but we don't really say what's on our minds when it comes down to really personal things ---------------True /_/----False /_/

I don't pay any attention to what goes on in politics -----------------------------True /_/----False /_/

I wish my parents and I could agree more about social and political issues ---------True /_/----False /_/

I get a lot of satisfaction out of my sex life ------------------------------------True /_/----False /_/

I have a lot of respect for my parents' ideas and opinions ------------------------True /_/----False /_/

It's right that we have laws against homosexuality --------------------------------True /_/----False /_/

Most of the time I can't stand to be around my parents, and I have as little to do with them as possible ---True /_/----False /_/

A white girl and a black boy having sex together is something that I would consider immoral, even if both of them wanted to do it -----------------------------True /_/----False /_/

So far as sex is concerned, I have pretty much come to definite conclusions about what I think is right and wrong for other people -----------------------------True /_/----False /_/

Getting V.D. or venereal disease isn't really a very serious problem because one can always go to a doctor and get it cured --True /_/----False /_/

It doesn't make any difference who wins the Presidential Election this year --------True /_/----False /_/

I wish my parents understood that what I do sexually is pretty tame compared to some of the sexual things that go on today --True /_/----False /_/

In general, I think that my sex life is pretty normal for a person my age ----------True /_/----False /_/

I believe that my parents are still very much in love with each other --------------True /_/----False /_/

I think it's right that people should make their own moral code, deciding for themselves what's moral and what's immoral --True /_/----False /_/

The idea of two men having sex together is disgusting ------------------------------True /_/----False /_/

Smoking marijuana is an important thing in my life ---------------------------------True /_/----False /_/

When I'm listening to the radio and they start talking about the news, I usually switch to another station --True /_/----False /_/

A white boy and a black girl having sex together is something that I would consider immoral, even if both of them wanted to do it -----------------------------True /_/----False /_/

I have told my parents that I disagree with the way they think about sex -----------True /_/----False /_/

Two boys having sex together is something that I would consider abnormal or unnatural ---True /_/----False /_/

I find it hard to accept the idea of conforming to society in matters of clothing and personal grooming --True /_/----False /_/

All in all, I think my head is pretty well together these days so far as sex is concerned --True /_/----False /_/

My parents believe that sex is immoral unless it's between two people who are married to each other --True /_/----False /_/

My parents have told me the facts about birth control ------------------------------True /_/----False /_/

My parents believe that anything two people want to do sexually is moral, so long as they both want to do it and it doesn't hurt either one of them ------------------True /_/----False /_/

I wouldn't mind having a dictator in this country, if he would run things the way I would like to see them run --True /_/----False /_/

On one or more occasions, under the influence of alcohol, I've had sex with someone that I wouldn't have had sex with otherwise --------------------------------True /_/----False /_/

I don't talk about sex with my parents because their attitude is that I'm too young to know anything ---True /_/----False /_/

I would consider it abnormal or unnatural for a boy not to have sex until he gets married ----------True /_/----False /_/

I think my parents' ideas about most things are wrong, but they have a right to their own opinions ----------True /_/----False /_/

So far as sex is concerned, I still haven't really made up my mind what I think is right and wrong for other people ----------True /_/----False /_/

I think that voting in elections is a waste of time ----------True /_/----False /_/

If I go for a long time without having sex, I get to feeling uptight ----------True /_/----False /_/

When talking with my parents about sex, I try to tell them only what I think they can accept ----------True /_/----False /_/

A brother and sister having sex together is something that I would consider abnormal or unnatural, even if both of them wanted to do it ----------True /_/----False /_/

I don't feel any strong affection for my parents ----------True /_/----False /_/

So far as sex is concerned, what other young people do doesn't have any influence on what I myself do ----------True /_/----False /_/

I have never read a serious educational book about sex ----------True /_/----False /_/

When I talk with my parents about sex I try to tell them what is going on with young people today, even though they don't approve of it ----------True /_/----False /_/

So far as sex is concerned, I wouldn't do anything that society would disapprove of ----------True /_/----False /_/

My parents believe that it's immoral for two persons of the same sex to have sexual relations with each other ----------True /_/----False /_/

I think it's important to re-elect President Nixon in this year's election ----------True /_/----False /_/

Having sex helps me take my mind off some of the bad things that happen to me ----------True /_/----False /_/

If I had to go out into the world on my own right now, I think I'd have a pretty hard time of it ----------True /_/----False /_/

I don't talk with my parents about my sex life because I consider it a personal subject and nobody's business but my own ----------True /_/----False /_/

I believe that this society is hell-bent on destroying the planet ----------True /_/----False /_/

My parents practice what they preach about love and sex ----------True /_/----False /_/

So far as sex is concerned, I have pretty much come to definite conclusions about what I think is right or wrong for myself ----------True /_/----False /_/

My parents have talked to me about masturbation ----------True /_/----False /_/

I don't think that God has any interest in my sex life ----------------------------True /_7----False /_7

I don't believe that there should be any laws against having sex with a girl under the age of 16 --True /_7----False /_7

My parents get along with each other very well -------------------------------------True /_7----False /_7

So far as sex is concerned, I think that what is morally right for boys is morally right for girls too ---True /_7----False /_7

When it comes to sex, my attitudes and my parents' attitudes are pretty much the same ---True /_7----False /_7

I still tend to think of myself as a child because there are a lot of things I can't do on my own --True /_7----False /_7

I've never really gotten to know my father ---True /_7----False /_7

Sometimes when I go to church I get to feeling guilty about my sexual behavior -----True /_7----False /_7

On one or more occasions, I've done sexual things mostly to spite my parents -------True /_7----False /_7

I think there are some kinds of sex acts that should be against the law -----------True /_7----False /_7

I don't much believe in planning for the future; life right now is the most important thing ---True /_7----False /_7

My parents and I talk pretty freely about sex --------------------------------------True /_7----False /_7

On one or more occasions, I've done sexual things mostly because the people I was hanging out with at the time expected me to ------------------------------------True /_7----False /_7

I believe that modern technology is a constructive force --------------------------True /_7----False /_7

I agree that there should be laws against rape ------------------------------------True /_7----False /_7

Young people these days sometimes have sex mostly to take their minds off other things that are going down ---True /_7----False /_7

I started experimenting with sex partly because it was such a forbidden topic around my house --True /_7----False /_7

Hassles about my sexual behavior cause a lot of bad vibes between myself and my parents ---True /_7----False /_7

My parents and I sometimes talk about sex, but it makes me very uncomfortable ------True /_7----False /_7

There are some things that I wouldn't do because my conscience would bother me -----True /_7----False /_7

My parents don't understand what I want out of life --------------------------------True /_7----False /_7

I don't like it when older people think of me as an adolescent --------------------True /_7----False /_7

In my family we're all very open with each other, so it's difficult or impossible to have any secrets about sex --True /_7----False /_7

Sometimes I take part in sexual activities that are not consistent with my religious beliefs ---True /_7----False /_7

I believe that LSD and other psychedelic drugs have had a beneficial effect on the spiritual development of many persons --------------------------------------True /_7----False /_7

I've pretty much given up on ever being able to get along with my parents ----------True /_7----False /_7

The American Indians had a life-style that I deeply admire ------------------------True /_7----False /_7

I've never taken part in any sex act, or been involved in any kind of sexual situation, that I myself would think of as being abnormal -------------------------True /_7----False /_7

There are serious flaws in our society, but the system is flexible enough to solve them ---True /_7----False /_7

Two girls having sex together is something that I would consider abnormal or unnatural --True /_7----False /_7

Violence is the only way to get the kind of changes that I would like to see in our society ---True /_7----False /_7

I wish my parents and I could agree more about things in general -------------------True /_7----False /_7

In general, I think that my basic personal values are shared by most of the older people in this country ---True /_7----False /_7

My parents are anxious about whether or not I'm going to get married ---------------True /_7----False /_7

When deciding for myself what to do or not to do so far as sex is concerned, I don't pay any attention to what the laws say --------------------------------------True /_7----False /_7

If I like one of the candidates in this year's Presidential Election, I would seriously consider working to get people to vote for him ---------------------------True /_7----False /_7

My parents are always bugging me with questions about my sexual behavior -----------True /_7----False /_7

In general, I think that my basic personal values are shared by most of the younger people in this country ---True /_7----False /_7

My parents think that I pretty much agree with their ideas about sex, and I don't say anything that would make them think different ----------------------------True /_7----False /_7

My sexual behavior is pretty much the way my parents would want it to be -----------True /_7----False /_7

How important to you are each of the things listed below?

	Very Important	Somewhat Important	Not very Important
Getting along with other girls my own age	/_/	/_/	/_/
Having fun	/_/	/_/	/_/
Becoming independent so that I can make it on my own	/_/	/_/	/_/
Trying to change the system	/_/	/_/	/_/
Making out with boys	/_/	/_/	/_/
Keeping up with schoolwork	/_/	/_/	/_/
Learning about other people	/_/	/_/	/_/
Doing creative or artistic things	/_/	/_/	/_/
Preparing myself to accomplish meaningful things	/_/	/_/	/_/
Listening to music	/_/	/_/	/_/
Living according to my religion	/_/	/_/	/_/
Working for money	/_/	/_/	/_/
Getting along with my parents	/_/	/_/	/_/
Having a good relationship with one particular boy	/_/	/_/	/_/
Getting loaded and hanging out	/_/	/_/	/_/
Learning about myself	/_/	/_/	/_/
Sports and athletics	/_/	/_/	/_/
Eating good food	/_/	/_/	/_/
Preparing myself to earn a good living when I get older	/_/	/_/	/_/
Having sex with a number of different boys	/_/	/_/	/_/
Worshipping God	/_/	/_/	/_/

- -

Most people identify with (feel they have a great deal in common with) a lot of different groups. But they identify with some groups more strongly than with others. Which one of the groups listed below do you identify with most strongly?

PLEASE CHECK ONLY ONE

Young people of my own generation -- wherever they may live, whatever their race or religion, and regardless of whether they are boys or girls ---------- /_/

People who live in my community -- whatever their race or religion, and regardless of whether they are male or female, young or old ---------- /_/

People of my own religion -- wherever they may live, whatever their race, and regardless of whether they are male or female, young or old ---------- /_/

People of my own race -- wherever they may live, whatever their religion, and regardless of whether they are male or female, young or old ---------- /_/

Females -- wherever they may live, whatever their race or religion, and regardless of whether they are young or old ---------- /_/

Here are some statements that we would like you to agree with or disagree with.

If you agree with a statement more than you disagree with it, please check the "agree" box.
If you disagree with a statement more than you agree with it, please check the "disagree" box.

Remember, there are no "right" or "wrong" answers -- the only thing that matters is what <u>YOU YOURSELF</u> think.

- -

It's all right for young people to have sex before getting married, if they are in love with each other ----Agree /_/----Disagree /_/

Our society's values concerning sex come from many generations of accumulated wisdom ----Agree /_/----Disagree /_/

It's immoral for two persons of the same sex to have sex with each other ----Agree /_/----Disagree /_/

One of the most important tasks of growing up is to learn to live with one's parents' ideas and opinions about sex ----Agree /_/----Disagree /_/

A girl who goes to bed with a boy before marriage will lose his respect ----Agree /_/----Disagree /_/

Two people shouldn't have to get married just because they want to live together ----Agree /_/----Disagree /_/

Churches could do things that would help older people understand young people's ideas ----Agree /_/----Disagree /_/

Young people who get married without ever having had sex together are foolish---Agree /_/----Disagree /_/

Some boys use sex to reward or punish their girl friends ----Agree /_/----Disagree /_/

Churches could do things that would be a big help in keeping down V.D. among young people who have sex ----Agree /_/----Disagree /_/

Young people these days understand more about honesty than most older people in their forties or fifties ----Agree /_/----Disagree /_/

Sex is immoral, unless it's between two people who love each other ----Agree /_/----Disagree /_/

A girl should stay a virgin until she finds the boy she wants to marry ----Agree /_/----Disagree /_/

If I found out that a girl had had sex for money, even once, I would lose respect for her ----Agree /_/----Disagree /_/

Organically grown food is much healthier than the food you get in most supermarkets ----Agree /_/----Disagree /_/

Sexual activities that society is opposed to are immoral ----Agree /_/----Disagree /_/

In some ways, I still think and act somewhat like a child ----Agree /_/----Disagree /_/

Young people these days tend to be more idealistic than most older people in their forties or fifties ----Agree /_/----Disagree /_/

There's nothing wrong with paying a girl for sex, if a boy can't get sex in any other way --Agree /_7----Disagree /_7

When it comes to sex, some young people do the things they do mostly to spite their parents --Agree /_7----Disagree /_7

It's immoral for a boy to force a girl to have sex, no matter what the circumstances --Agree /_7----Disagree /_7

I believe that most young people can go directly from childhood to adulthood without being forced to go through a period of years that society defines as adolescence ---Agree /_7----Disagree /_7

Young people these days understand more about sex than most older people in their forties or fifties --Agree /_7----Disagree /_7

It's right that we have laws saying people have to be married in order to live together ---Agree /_7----Disagree /_7

Sex is immoral, unless it's between two people who like each other and have something in common --Agree /_7----Disagree /_7

Some girls use sex to reward or punish their boy friends ----------------------Agree /_7----Disagree /_7

My generation is going to do a better job of running things than the last generation has done ---Agree /_7----Disagree /_7

Anything two people want to do sexually is moral, as long as they both want to do it and it doesn't hurt either one of them -------------------------------Agree /_7----Disagree /_7

If two people are really in love, that love should last for life --------------Agree /_7----Disagree /_7

When a President does something that's bad for the country, it's mostly the fault of the people who let him get elected --------------------------------Agree /_7----Disagree /_7

Sex is immoral for people who are too young to understand what they are getting out of it ---Agree /_7----Disagree /_7

Young people these days tend to be less materialistic than most older people in their forties or fifties --Agree /_7----Disagree /_7

A person who truly loves God doesn't have sexual relationships outside of marriage ---Agree /_7----Disagree /_7

Young people these days tend to be less considerate of others than most older people in their forties or fifties ---------------------------------------Agree /_7----Disagree /_7

Churches teach that enjoyment of sex is sinful --------------------------------Agree /_7----Disagree /_7

Young people these days understand more about what is really important in life than most older people in their forties or fifties ---------------------Agree /_7----Disagree /_7

Sex is immoral, unless it's between two people who are married to each other --Agree /_7----Disagree /_7

The government shouldn't be allowed to censor magazines or books, no matter how extreme they may be about sexual matters ---------------------------Agree /_7----Disagree /_7

The sexual behavior of most young people today would not be acceptable to society as a whole --Agree /_7----Disagree /_7

Churches could be a big help to young people who are trying to find themselves ---Agree /_7----Disagree /_7

It's possible for love to be very real and very strong, but still not last for more than a few weeks --Agree /_7----Disagree /_7

The most important thing in a love relationship is sex ------------------------Agree /_7----Disagree /_7

Sex is one of the few human activities where there is always something new to be discovered --Agree /_7----Disagree /_7

Over a period of time, I think it's better to have sexual relationships with several different people, rather than just one person --------------------Agree /_7----Disagree /_7

The laws against prostitution (having sex for money) should continue to remain in force ---Agree /_7----Disagree /_7

Where sex is concerned, anything people want to do is all right so long as they want to do it and it doesn't hurt them --------------------------------Agree /_7----Disagree /_7

A lot of young people are leaving home these days because they are seeking sexual freedom --Agree /_7----Disagree /_7

One of the reasons why many young girls these days don't use birth control pills is that they're afraid their parents will find them ---------------------Agree /_7----Disagree /_7

Hurting another person is wrong --Agree /_7----Disagree /_7

Showing that young people have sexual freedom is one way of making the older generation realize that things are really changing in the world ---------------Agree /_7----Disagree /_7

One of the reasons why young people stop going to church is because churches teach that enjoyment of sex is sinful ----------------------------------Agree /_7----Disagree /_7

Young people these days understand more about friendship than most older people in their forties or fifties ---Agree /_7----Disagree /_7

It's not wrong for a girl to have sex with someone for money, if that's what she wants to do --Agree /_7----Disagree /_7

Young people these days understand more about love than most older people in their forties or fifties ---Agree /_7----Disagree /_7

When it comes to sex, a lot of young people these days do the things they do just because everyone else is doing it -----------------------------------Agree /_7----Disagree /_7

The government shouldn't try to keep people from seeing any kind of sex movies that they want to see -- even if they're so dirty I wouldn't want to see them myself --Agree /_7----Disagree /_7

Most girls sometimes play with their sex organ while they are growing up. If a girl does this in order to experience a pleasant sensation, it is called masturbation.

How old were you the very first time that you masturbated?

IF YOU HAVE NEVER MASTURBATED, PLEASE SKIP TO THE NEXT YELLOW PAGE

AGE WHEN I FIRST MASTURBATED:_________

Sometimes masturbation results in a climax, or orgasm -- what most young people refer to as "coming."

How old were you the very first time that you masturbated until you had a climax or orgasm?

AGE WHEN I FIRST MASTURBATED TO CLIMAX OR ORGASM:_______

I've never had a climax or orgasm from masturbating----------------/_/

When was the most recent occasion on which you masturbated:

Since this time yesterday----------------/_/

Since this time last week----------------/_/

Since this time last month---------------/_/

More than a month ago-------------/_/

PLEASE SKIP TO THE NEXT YELLOW PAGE

Since this time last month, approximately how many times have you masturbated until you had a climax or orgasm?

NUMBER OF TIMES IN THE PAST MONTH THAT I MASTURBATED TO CLIMAX OR ORGASM:_______

Since this time last month, approximately how many times have you masturbated without having a climax or orgasm?

NUMBER OF TIMES IN THE PAST MONTH THAT I MASTURBATED WITHOUT HAVING A CLIMAX OR ORGASM:________

PLEASE GO ON TO THE NEXT PAGE

When you masturbate, do you daydream or think about things most of the time, only some of the time, rarely, or never?

Most of the time /_/ Some of the time /_/ Rarely /_/ Never /_/

How often do you look at pictures while you are masturbating -- most of the time, only some of the time, rarely, or never?

Most of the time /_/ Some of the time /_/ Rarely /_/ Never /_/

In general, do you usually enjoy masturbating a great deal, somewhat, a little, or not at all?

A great deal /_/ Somewhat /_/ A little /_/ Not at all /_/

How about feelings of guilt, anxiety, or concern about masturbation? Do you have such feelings often, sometimes, rarely, or never?

Often /_/ Sometimes /_/ Rarely /_/ Never /_/

If you had to guess, would you say that you masturbate more often or less often than most other girls of about your own age?

More often /_/ About the same /_/ Less often /_/

Here are some more "True-False" statements...

- -

If I had an abortion, I wouldn't feel guilty about it ------------------------------True /_7----False /_7

It isn't healthy for someone my age to go for a long time without having sex -------True /_7----False /_7

Sometimes I feel guilty about my sexual behavior ----------------------------------True /_7----False /_7

If I heard that a boy had V.D., I would avoid having sex with him even after he was completely cured ---True /_7----False /_7

I've never had sex with a boy, because I haven't yet met a boy who I would want to have sex with --True /_7----False /_7

If I were married and my husband had sexual relations with someone else, I would be angry about it but it would not in itself be enough reason to get divorced --True /_7----False /_7

On one or more occasions, another girl or a grown woman has tried to get me to have sex with her --True /_7----False /_7

I don't use birth control pills or other contraceptives because my parents might find them ---True /_7----False /_7

I would be embarassed about having sex with a boy if there were anyone else in the same room ---True /_7----False /_7

I've never had sex with a boy, because I'm not really ready for it yet -------------True /_7----False /_7

There isn't any place where I could go to get birth control pills or contraceptives ---True /_7----False /_7

If I have sex with a boy, making sure that I don't get pregnant is <u>his</u> responsibility ---True /_7----False /_7

I would never have sex with a boy for money --True /_7----False /_7

I've never had sex with another girl, but it's possible that sometime in the future I might want to --True /_7----False /_7

If you really dig a boy, it's all right to have sex with him even if you've only known him for a few hours --True /_7----False /_7

I've never had sex with a boy, because I haven't yet met a boy who wants to have sex with me ---True /_7----False /_7

I rarely if ever go to religious services, but I still think of myself as being a fairly religious person --True /_/----False /_/

Politically, I tend to think of myself as being a Republican -----------------------True /_/----False /_/

I would consider it abnormal or unnatural for a girl not to have sex until she gets married --True /_/----False /_/

I have a lot of respect for my parents' ideas and opinions about sex --------------True /_/----False /_/

I think that young people and many American business firms could work together to make things better ---True /_/----False /_/

Making money is more important to me than being creative --------------------------True /_/----False /_/

About the time I became able to have sex, I started to feel more grown up ---------True /_/----False /_/

My parents trust me to use my own best judgment when it comes to sex --------------True /_/----False /_/

I wouldn't want to have anything to do with any sex acts that are against the law --True /_/----False /_/

The only reason young people these days have sex is for physical enjoyment ---------True /_/----False /_/

Living at home with my parents doesn't interfere with my sex life -----------------True /_/----False /_/

I wish that churches would talk more about the really important things that we need to get done in this country --True /_/----False /_/

When I was a child, I was taught that sex was natural and healthy -----------------True /_/----False /_/

My parents and I find it easy to talk with each other about sex -------------------True /_/----False /_/

I like to smoke marijuana sometimes ---True /_/----False /_/

My parents have told me the facts about V.D. --------------------------------------True /_/----False /_/

I wish my parents could overcome their own early training, so they could realize that sex is natural and beautiful --True /_/----False /_/

Ever since I was 12 or 13 years old, my parents have encouraged me to go out on dates --True /_/----False /_/

Whether or not to use marijuana should be up to each person to decide for himself, like with alcohol and tobacco ---True /_/----False /_/

I don't like it when older people think of me as a child --------------------------True /_/----False /_/

The fact that I have to conceal my sexual activities from my parents makes it hard for me to be close to them --True /_/----False /_/

So far as sex is concerned, I still haven't really made up my mind about what I think is right and wrong for myself --True /_/----False /_/

There isn't anything in sex that I wouldn't want to try, at least once ------------True /_7----False /_7

My parents and I have heavy disagreements about what is right and wrong in regard to sex, but this doesn't bother me --True /_7----False /_7

I think it's important to defeat President Nixon in this year's election -----------True /_7----False /_7

My parents think that my sexual activities are pretty much my own personal business --True /_7----False /_7

Politically, I tend to think of myself as being a Democrat ------------------------True /_7----False /_7

I believe that drugs are much more harmful than alcohol ----------------------------True /_7----False /_7

When I talk with my parents about sex I try to make them think I've had more sexual experience than I've actually had --True /_7----False /_7

A parent and child having sex with each other is something that I would consider abnormal or unnatural, even if both of them wanted to do it --------------True /_7----False /_7

I've never really gotten to know my mother ---True /_7----False /_7

Politically, I tend to think of myself as being a revolutionary --------------------True /_7----False /_7

My parents think that the only reason young people have sex is for physical enjoyment ---True /_7----False /_7

I would like to be able to talk with my parents about sex --------------------------True /_7----False /_7

In general, I feel pretty self-confident about sex ---------------------------------True /_7----False /_7

If I had children and any of them turned out to be homosexual, I would be very upset ---True /_7----False /_7

Oral sex is something that I would consider abnormal or unnatural ------------------True /_7----False /_7

I have a lot of respect for my parents as people -----------------------------------True /_7----False /_7

I have never read a serious magazine article about sex -----------------------------True /_7----False /_7

So far as I know, my parents have never really gotten sexually passionate about each other ---True /_7----False /_7

I would not want to have children in the kind of world we live in today ------------True /_7----False /_7

I've never taken part in any sex act, or been involved in any kind of sexual situation, that I myself would think of as being immoral --------------------------True /_7----False /_7

The only reason I would get legally married would be to satisfy my parents ---------True /_7----False /_7

I go to religious services fairly often ---True /_7----False /_7

I don't think it would be possible for a girl to be really in love with more than one boy at the same time --True /_7----False /_7

I won't tell a boy that I love him unless I really do ----------------------------True /_7----False /_7

My parents are anxious that before I get too old I should find the right boy to marry --True /_7----False /_7

I'd like to ask my parents for information about V.D., but I'm afraid to because they would ask whether I'm having sex with boys ---------------------------True /_7----False /_7

My parents tell me that I'm too young to have sex with boys -----------------------True /_7----False /_7

If I were married and my husband had sexual relations with someone else, I would divorce him ---True /_7----False /_7

I wouldn't want to have sex with a boy only for the physical enjoyment of doing it, and nothing else --True /_7----False /_7

I usually think of myself as being sexually attractive to boys --------------------True /_7----False /_7

I've never had sex with another girl, and I'm sure I'd never want to --------------True /_7----False /_7

I wouldn't want to have sex with a boy unless I liked him as a person -------------True /_7----False /_7

I think it would be wrong for me to have sex with a boy I'd just met and hadn't gotten to know --True /_7----False /_7

I'd like to ask my parents for information about birth control, but I'm afraid to because they would ask whether I'm having sex with boys -----------------True /_7----False /_7

My parents assume that I have had sex with boys -----------------------------------True /_7----False /_7

I wouldn't want to have sex with a boy unless he loved me -------------------------True /_7----False /_7

I wouldn't want to marry a boy unless I'd lived with him first --------------------True /_7----False /_7

I don't think it would be possible for a girl to have a real relationship with more than one boy at the same time --True /_7----False /_7

My parents think that if I have to have sex before getting married, they would rather I do it with a boy I don't love --True /_7----False /_7

My parents wouldn't want me to marry a boy unless I'd lived with him first ---------True /_7----False /_7

My parents assume that I haven't had sex with boys --------------------------------True /_7----False /_7

I wouldn't want to have sex with a boy unless I loved him -------------------------True /_7----False /_7

I wouldn't want to have sex with a boy unless he liked me as a person -------------True /_7----False /_7

Some people I know are so much involved in sex that it's the most important thing in their lives --True /_/----False /_/

Because of the problem of over-population, I would not want to have more than two children --True /_/----False /_/

My parents try to seem broad-minded about sex, but actually they're pretty uptight when it comes down to what I myself want to do ---------------------True /_/----False /_/

I believe that many people who live in communes are finding meaning and brotherhood in their way of life ---True /_/----False /_/

Some day, I will probably want to have children -- but it won't matter whether or not I get married first --True /_/----False /_/

When talking to my parents about sex, I try to persuade them to my way of thinking ---True /_/----False /_/

I sometimes worry about whether God would approve of my sexual activities ----------True /_/----False /_/

So far as sex is concerned, I do what I want to do, regardless of what society thinks --True /_/----False /_/

My parents don't get along with each other very well ------------------------------True /_/----False /_/

If a girl uses birth control pills or other methods of contraception, it makes it seem as if she were <u>planning</u> to have sex ---------------------------------True /_/----False /_/

My parents believe that it's all right for young people to have sex before getting married, if they are in love with each other -------------------------------True /_/----False /_/

When I was a child, I was taught that sex was wrong --------------------------------True /_/----False /_/

I don't think I will want to have children, because I don't like the idea of having all that responsibility --True /_/----False /_/

One of the reasons I stopped going to church is because churches teach that sex is sinful ---True /_/----False /_/

Some of my sexual activities are probably harmful to my relationship with my parents --True /_/----False /_/

Birth control pills can be physically harmful to a girl --------------------------True /_/----False /_/

I have no personal values of my own --True /_/----False /_/

I can't see myself getting married until I know it will last for the rest of my life --True /_/----False /_/

I am comfortable talking with my parents about sex in general, but I avoid telling them what I myself do ---True /_/----False /_/

Some of my sexual activities are probably harmful to me ----------------------------True /_/----False /_/

Sometimes, people of the same sex do things together that result in sexual stimulation or satisfaction for either or both of them. When this happens, it is called "homosexuality."

Have you ever heard of homosexuality?

Yes /_/ No /_/ → *IF YOUR ANSWER IS "NO," PLEASE SKIP TO THE NEXT PAGE*

Have you yourself ever done anything with another girl, or with a grown woman, that resulted in sexual stimulation or satisfaction for either or both of you?

Yes /_/ No /_/ → *IF YOUR ANSWER IS "NO," PLEASE SKIP TO THE NEXT PAGE*

How old were you <u>the very first time</u> that you did this?

AGE WHEN I FIRST DID THIS: ________

The very first time that you did this, who did you do it with?

A girl younger than I was ----------------/_/
A girl my own age ------------------------/_/
A girl older than I was ---------------/_/
A grown woman -------------------------/_/

When was the <u>most recent</u> occasion on which you did this?

Since this time yesterday ----------------/_/
Since this time last week ----------------/_/
Since this time last month ---------------/_/
More than a month ago -----------------/_/

PLEASE GO ON TO THE NEXT PAGE

Have you ever had sexual intercourse with a boy?

Yes /_/ No /_/ → IF YOUR ANSWER IS "NO," PLEASE SKIP TO THE NEXT BLUE PAGE

Thinking back to the very first time that you had sex with a boy, how old were you then? AGE:______

Where was it that you had sex with a boy for the very first time?

In my home ------------------------------/_/
In a friend's home ---------------------/_/
In an automobile -----------------------/_/
At school ------------------------------/_/
In the boy's home --------------------/_/
In a hotel or motel ------------------/_/
Outdoors -----------------------------/_/
Somewhere else -----------------------/_/

Which of the words below accurately describe how you felt the first time that you had sex with a boy? *(PLEASE CHECK ALL THAT APPLY)*

Afraid -------------/_/
Thrilled -----------/_/
Hurt ---------------/_/
Fulfilled ----------/_/
Raped --------------/_/
Powerful -----------/_/
Sorry --------------/_/
Excited -------------/_/
Guilty --------------/_/
Happy ---------------/_/
Foolish -------------/_/
Relieved ------------/_/
Worried -------------/_/
Curious -------------/_/
Embarassed -------------/_/
Joyful -----------------/_/
Used -------------------/_/
Mature -----------------/_/
Disappointed -----------/_/
Satisfied --------------/_/
Tired ------------------/_/

This first time that you had sex with a boy, did either you or the boy make use of any birth control method, or do anything else to cut down on the risk of your becoming pregnant?

Yes /_/ No /_/

If you had it to do all over again, do you wish that you had waited until you were older before having sex with a boy for the first time, are you glad you did it when you did, or do you wish that you had done it when you were younger?

I wish I had waited until I was older before having sex with a boy for the first time --/_/

I'm glad I did it when I did --/_/

I wish I had done it when I was younger --/_/

Who was the very first boy with whom you ever had sexual intercourse?

A boy I had met only a little while before the time that we first had sex together ------------/ /

A boy I was going steady with, and planned to marry ---------------------/ /

A boy I was going steady with, but had no definite plans to marry ---------/ /

A boy I knew slightly, and was more or less friendly with ----------------/ /

A boy I knew well and liked a lot, even though we weren't going together -------/ /

Someone who raped me -----------------/ /

My husband, after we were married ------/ /

- -

How old was this boy when you first had sex together? AGE:________

- -

Of course, you weren't inside this boy's head at the time, so you can't know for sure how he felt then. But if you had to <u>guess</u>, which of the words below do you think might accurately describe how he felt when you had sex with him for the very first time? *(PLEASE CHECK ALL THAT APPLY)*

Afraid -------------/ /
Thrilled -----------/ /
Hurt ---------------/ /
Fulfilled ----------/ /
Raped --------------/ /
Powerful -----------/ /
Sorry --------------/ /

Excited -------------/ /
Guilty --------------/ /
Happy ---------------/ /
Foolish -------------/ /
Relieved ------------/ /
Worried / /
Curious -------------/ /

Embarassed -------------/ /
Joyful -----------------/ /
Used -------------------/ /
Mature -----------------/ /
Disappointed -----------/ /
Satisfied --------------/ /
Tired ------------------/ /

- -

So far as you know, were you the first girl that he had ever had sex with, or had he ever had sex before with one or more other girls?

I know for sure that I was the first girl he'd ever had sex with ------------------------/ /

I think that I was probably the first girl he'd ever had sex with ----------------------/ /

I really don't know whether or not he'd ever had sex before ----------------------------/ /

I think that he'd probably had sex with one or more other girls before me --------------/ /

I know for sure that he'd had sex with one or more other girls before me ---------------/ /

PLEASE GO ON TO THE NEXT PAGE

Still thinking about this very first boy that you ever had sex with, what happened to your relationship with him after the first time you had sex together?

Did the relationship become stronger or weaker as a result of having had sex together?

The relationship became stronger --------------/_/ The relationship became weaker -----------/_/

There wasn't any relationship to begin with ---/_/ The relationship stayed about the same ---/_/

After the first time, did you ever have sex with this boy again?

No /_/

Yes /_/

On about how many more occasions did you have sex together, after the first time?

NUMBER OF OCCASIONS AFTER THE FIRST TIME:________

Looking back at it now, are you glad that this particular boy was the first one you ever had sex with? Or if you had it to do over again, would you rather have had sex for the first time with a different boy?

I'm glad it was this particular boy ----/_/ I wish it had been a different boy ----/_/

Since this first boy, have you ever had sexual intercourse with any <u>other</u> boys?

Yes /_/

No /_/ → *IF YOUR ANSWER IS "NO," PLEASE SKIP TO THE NEXT PAGE*

All in all, how many <u>different</u> boys (counting the first one) have you ever had sex with?

TOTAL NUMBER OF DIFFERENT BOYS I'VE EVER HAD SEX WITH:________

PLEASE GO ON TO THE NEXT PAGE

There are a number of different methods of contraception, or birth control, that can be used to cut down the risk of a girl becoming pregnant.

Which of the methods listed below -- if any -- have you heard about?

Which -- if any -- have you yourself ever used?

	Heard about and used	Heard about but never used	Never heard about
Birth control pills	/_/	/_/	/_/
Intrauterine device (coil, IUD)	/_/	/_/	/_/
Diaphragm	/_/	/_/	/_/
Contraceptive foam	/_/	/_/	/_/
Contraceptive jelly	/_/	/_/	/_/
Contraceptive douche	/_/	/_/	/_/
Rhythm method	/_/	/_/	/_/

- -

Do you ever worry about the possibility that you might become pregnant?

Often /_/ Sometimes /_/ Hardly ever /_/ Never /_/

- -

If you were to become pregnant, which <u>one</u> of the things listed below would you <u>most prefer</u> to do, <u>if you could have things your way</u>?

PLEASE CHECK <u>ONLY ONE</u>

Have an abortion -- /_/

Have the baby and give it up for adoption -- /_/

Have the baby and count on the father to help me bring it up -- /_/

Have the baby and bring it up by myself -- /_/

Have the baby and get married -- /_/

Tell my parents and let them decide what to do -- /_/

- -

Sometimes people can have things their own way, and sometimes they can't. If you were to become pregnant, which <u>one</u> of the things listed below do you think you would <u>actually do</u>?

PLEASE CHECK <u>ONLY ONE</u>

Have an abortion -- /_/

Have the baby and give it up for adoption -- /_/

Have the baby and count on the father to help me bring it up -- /_/

Have the baby and bring it up by myself -- /_/

Have the baby and get married -- /_/

Tell my parents and let them decide what to do -- /_/

Some girls sometimes reach a climax, or orgasm when they have sex. Other girls don't, or do so only on rare occasions. Do you yourself ever have a climax or orgasm when having sex with a boy?

Never yet ----------------------------/_/ Only once or twice so far --------------/_/

Every once in a while -----------------/_/ Fairly often ----------------------------/_/

Usually ------------------------------/_/ Almost always --------------------------/_/

- -

Have you ever wanted to have sex with a boy but decided not to do so because you were afraid of catching V.D., or venereal disease?

Yes /_/ No /_/

- -

Have you ever wanted to have sex with a boy but decided not to do so because you were afraid that you might become pregnant?

Yes /_/ No /_/

- -

When was the most recent occasion on which you had sex with a boy?

Since this time yesterday -------------/_/ →

Since this time last week -------------/_/ →

Since this time last month ------------/_/ →

More than a month ago -----------/_/

PLEASE SKIP TO THE NEXT PAGE

- -

This very last time that you had sex with a boy, did either of you use any kind of contraceptive or birth control method, or do anything else to cut down the risk of your becoming pregnant?

No, neither of us did -----------------/_/

Yes, the boy did ----------------------/_/ Yes, I did --------------------------/_/

- -

Since this time last month, approximately how many occasions have there been on which you have had sex with a boy?

NUMBER OF OCCASIONS IN THE PAST MONTH ON WHICH I HAD SEX WITH A BOY:________

- -

And how many different boys have you had sex with since this time last month?

NUMBER OF DIFFERENT BOYS I'VE HAD SEX WITH IN THE PAST MONTH:________

Thinking back over those occasions in the past month on which you had sex with a boy, on how many of these occasions did either you or the boy you were with use any contraceptive or birth control method, or do anything else to cut down the risk of your becoming pregnant?

NUMBER OF OCCASIONS IN THE PAST MONTH WHEN CONTRACEPTION OR BIRTH CONTROL WAS USED:________

- -

On these occasions in the past month, what was it that was done to cut down the risk of your becoming pregnant?

	Always	Sometimes	Once or twice	Never
The boy used a condom (rubber)	/_7	/_7	/_7	/_7
The boy withdrew before ejaculating (coming)	/_7	/_7	/_7	/_7
I used birth control pills	/_7	/_7	/_7	/_7
I used an intrauterine device (coil, IUD)	/_7	/_7	/_7	/_7
I used a diaphragm	/_7	/_7	/_7	/_7
I used a contraceptive foam	/_7	/_7	/_7	/_7
I used a contraceptive jelly	/_7	/_7	/_7	/_7
I used a contraceptive douche	/_7	/_7	/_7	/_7
I used the rhythm method	/_7	/_7	/_7	/_7
I just trusted to luck that I wouldn't become pregnant	/_7	/_7	/_7	/_7
I didn't think about whether or not I might become pregnant	/_7	/_7	/_7	/_7

- -

Have you ever been pregnant?

Yes /_7 ↓ No /_7 ⟶ *IF YOUR ANSWER IS "NO," PLEASE SKIP TO THE NEXT PAGE*

- -

What happened?

I'm still pregnant right now ------------/_7

I had the baby and got married ----------/_7

I had the baby and gave it up for adoption ----------------------------/_7

I had an abortion -----------------------/_7

I had a miscarriage ---------------------/_7

I had the baby and am bringing it up myself ----------------------------/_7

- -

Did your parents know about your being pregnant?

Yes, I told them about it --------------/_7

No, they never found out ----------------/_7

I didn't tell them about it, but they found out anyway --/_7

Here are a few more "True-False" statements...

- -

Getting pregnant is something that happens to <u>other</u> girls; I just can't believe that it could really happen to <u>me</u> --True /_7----False /_7

Sometimes when I have sex, I just get careless and forget to do anything to cut down the risk of my becoming pregnant --------------------------------------True /_7----False /_7

Except for birth control pills, most other birth control methods are just too much trouble to use ---True /_7----False /_7

Once I asked a doctor for birth control pills or other contraceptives, and his attitude put me very uptight ---True /_7----False /_7

Sometimes I don't really care whether or not I get pregnant -----------------------True /_7----False /_7

I don't know where to get birth control pills or any other kind of reliable contraceptive --True /_7----False /_7

I have a boy friend who doesn't approve of birth control pills or other contraceptives --True /_7----False /_7

Sometimes I just get careless and forget to take my birth control pills ------------True /_7----False /_7

I can't afford to buy birth control pills or any other reliable kind of contraceptive --True /_7----False /_7

At the present time, do you have sex mostly (or only) with just one particular boy?

Yes /_/ No /_/ → *IF YOUR ANSWER IS "NO," PLEASE SKIP TO THE NEXT PAGE*

Would you say that you have a close relationship with this boy, a casual relationship, or no real relationship at all?

No real relationship /_/ A casual relationship /_/ A close relationship /_/

For how long have you had such a relationship with this boy?

NUMBER OF WEEKS:_______ NUMBER OF MONTHS:_______ NUMBER OF YEARS:_______

And for how long have you been having sex with this boy?

NUMBER OF WEEKS:_______ NUMBER OF MONTHS:_______ NUMBER OF YEARS:_______

Do you love this boy? Yes /_/ No /_/ I'm not really sure /_/

Does he love you? Yes /_/ No /_/ I'm not really sure /_/ He says he does /_/

Do you plan to get married? Yes /_/ Probably /_/ Probably not /_/ No /_/

We haven't decided /_/ We haven't talked about it /_/

Do you have sex with other boys?

Frequently /_/ Occasionally /_/ Very rarely /_/ Never /_/

Does he have sex with other girls?

Frequently /_/ Occasionally /_/ Very rarely /_/ Never /_/

I don't think so, but I'm not sure /_/ I think so, but I'm not sure /_/

PLEASE GO ON TO THE NEXT PAGE

Here are some more "True-False" statements...

- -

It bothers me that I can't seem to be satisfied sexually --------------------------True /_7----False /_7

If I were to have sex with another boy, just occasionally, it wouldn't really put my boy friend uptight --True /_7----False /_7

I have never had V.D. or venereal disease ---True /_7----False /_7

I would never want to have an abortion, because taking the life of an unborn child is wrong --True /_7----False /_7

I've never had sex with a person of another race ----------------------------------True /_7----False /_7

On one or more occasions, under the influence of marijuana, I've had sex with someone that I wouldn't have had sex with otherwise -------------------------------True /_7----False /_7

On one or more occasions, I've refused to ball a boy unless he would do something that I wanted him to do --True /_7----False /_7

Having sex doesn't make my life any more meaningful -------------------------------True /_7----False /_7

There are many times when I get horny but don't have anyone to ball ---------------True /_7----False /_7

On one or more occasions, I've had sex with a boy mostly because people would have put me down if I hadn't ---True /_7----False /_7

I would never want to have an abortion, because it is against my religion ---------True /_7----False /_7

If my boy friend were to have sex with another girl, just occasionally, it wouldn't really put me uptight --True /_7----False /_7

I usually experience a lot of pain or discomfort when I have my period ------------True /_7----False /_7

When I have sex, it's very important to me that I reach a climax or orgasm ---------True /_7----False /_7

Sometimes I think that I am addicted to sex, the way some people are addicted to drugs --True /_7----False /_7

I don't get as much physical enjoyment out of sex as I think I should be getting ---True /_7----False /_7

Abortions are so easy to get these days that I don't really worry about getting pregnant --True /_7----False /_7

On one or more occasions, a boy has refused to ball me unless I would do something that I didn't want to do ---True /_7----False /_7

IF YOU DON'T WANT TO ANSWER THE QUESTIONS ON THIS PAGE, PLEASE GO ON TO THE NEXT PAGE

Has a boy ever felt your breasts with his hand?

Yes /_/ No /_/ → *IF YOUR ANSWER IS "NO," PLEASE SKIP TO THE NEXT PAGE*

- -

Thinking back to the very first time that a boy felt your breasts with his hand, how old were you then?

AGE AT WHICH A BOY FIRST FELT MY BREASTS WITH HIS HAND:________

- -

When was the most recent occasion on which a boy felt your breasts with his hand?

Since this time yesterday -------------/_/

Since this time last week -------------/_/

Since this time last month -------------/_/

More than a month ago -------------/_/ → *PLEASE SKIP TO THE NEXT PAGE*

- -

Since this time last month, approximately how many times has a boy felt your breasts with his hand?

NUMBER OF TIMES IN THE PAST MONTH THAT A BOY FELT MY BREASTS WITH HIS HAND:________

- -

And how many different boys has this happened with in the past month?

NUMBER OF DIFFERENT BOYS WHO HAVE FELT MY BREASTS IN THE PAST MONTH:________

PLEASE GO ON TO THE NEXT PAGE

IF YOU DON'T WANT TO ANSWER THE QUESTIONS ON THIS PAGE, PLEASE GO ON TO THE NEXT PAGE

Has a boy ever felt your sex organ with his hand?

Yes /_/ No /_/ → *IF YOUR ANSWER IS "NO," PLEASE SKIP TO THE NEXT PAGE*

Thinking back to the very first time that a boy ever felt your sex organ with his hand, how old were you then?

AGE AT WHICH A BOY FIRST FELT MY SEX ORGAN WITH HIS HAND:________

When was the <u>most recent</u> occasion on which a boy felt your sex organ with his hand?

Since this time yesterday --------------/_/

Since this time last week --------------/_/

Since this time last month -------------/_/

More than a month ago ------------------/_/ → *PLEASE SKIP TO THE NEXT PAGE*

Since this time last month, approximately how many times has a boy felt your sex organ with his hand?

NUMBER OF TIMES IN THE PAST MONTH THAT A BOY HAS FELT MY SEX ORGAN WITH HIS HAND:________

And how many <u>different</u> boys has this happened with in the past month?

NUMBER OF DIFFERENT BOYS WHO HAVE FELT MY SEX ORGAN IN THE PAST MONTH:________

Sometimes, when a boy feels a girl's sex organ with his hand, it results in the girl having a climax or orgasm -- what most young people refer to as "coming." Has this ever happened to you?

Yes /_/

No /_/ → *PLEASE SKIP TO THE NEXT PAGE*

I'm not sure /_/ → *PLEASE SKIP TO THE NEXT PAGE*

When was the <u>most recent</u> occasion on which you had a climax or orgasm because a boy was feeling your sex organ with his hand?

Since this time yesterday --------------/_/

Since this time last week --------------/_/

Since this time last month -------------/_/

More than a month ago ----------------/_/

IF YOU DON'T WANT TO ANSWER THE QUESTIONS ON THIS PAGE, PLEASE GO ON TO THE NEXT PAGE

Have you ever felt a boy's sex organ with your hand?

Yes /_/ No /_/ → *IF YOUR ANSWER IS "NO," PLEASE SKIP TO THE NEXT PAGE*

Thinking back to the very first time that you ever felt a boy's sex organ with your hand, how old were you then?

AGE AT WHICH I FIRST FELT A BOY'S SEX ORGAN WITH MY HAND:_______

When was the most recent occasion on which you felt a boy's sex organ with your hand?

Since this time yesterday --------------/_/

Since this time last week --------------/_/

Since this time last month -------------/_/

More than a month ago -------------/_/ → *PLEASE SKIP TO THE NEXT PAGE*

Since this time last month, approximately how many times have you felt a boy's sex organ with your hand?

NUMBER OF TIMES IN THE PAST MONTH THAT I FELT A BOY'S SEX ORGAN WITH MY HAND:_______

And how many different boys has this happened with in the past month?

NUMBER OF DIFFERENT BOYS WHOSE SEX ORGAN I HAVE FELT IN THE PAST MONTH:_______

Sometimes, when a girl feels a boy's sex organ with her hand, it results in the boy having a climax or orgasm -- what most young people refer to as "coming." Has this ever happened while you were feeling a boy's sex organ with your hand?

Yes /_/ No /_/ → *PLEASE SKIP TO THE NEXT PAGE*

When was the most recent occasion on which a boy had a climax or orgasm because you were feeling his sex organ with your hand?

Since this time yesterday --------------/_/

Since this time last week --------------/_/

Since this time last month -------------/_/

More than a month ago -------------/_/

Here are some more statements that we would like you to agree with or disagree with.

If you agree with a statement more than you disagree with it, please check the "agree" box.
If you disagree with a statement more than you agree with it, please check the "disagree" box.

Remember, there are no "right" or "wrong" answers - the only thing that matters is what YOU YOURSELF think.

- -

If a girl has led a boy on, it's all right for the boy to force her to have sex ---------- Agree /_/----Disagree /_/

The politicians are the only ones to blame for the mess this country is in ---------- Agree /_/----Disagree /_/

Twenty years from now, most of the people in my generation are going to be living happier lives than most older people in their forties or fifties live now ---------- Agree /_/----Disagree /_/

After election time is over, most candidates who win pay no attention to the desires of the people who supported them ---------- Agree /_/----Disagree /_/

Churches are really doing their best to understand young people's ideas about sex ---------- Agree /_/----Disagree /_/

I'm not a child any more, but I'm not an adult yet, either ---------- Agree /_/----Disagree /_/

If two boys want to have sex together, it's all right so long as they both want to do it ---------- Agree /_/----Disagree /_/

The American system of the representative democracy can still respond effectively to the needs of the people ---------- Agree /_/----Disagree /_/

Physical attractiveness of the other person is more important in love than it is in sex ---------- Agree /_/----Disagree /_/

It is up to public officials, not me, to say what is necessary for the good of this country ---------- Agree /_/----Disagree /_/

A lot of the pleasure in sex would be lost if it did not seem to be such a forbidden activity ---------- Agree /_/----Disagree /_/

The kind of people who could really do a good job in government are not interested in trying to get themselves elected ---------- Agree /_/----Disagree /_/

When it comes to morality in sex, the important thing is the way people treat each other, not the particular things that they do together ---------- Agree /_/----Disagree /_/

If two girls want to have sex together, it's all right so long as they both want to do it ---------- Agree /_/----Disagree /_/

A young person who has sex only for physical enjoyment and nothing else is doing something immoral ---------- Agree /_/----Disagree /_/

There is no kind of sex act that I would think of as being abnormal, so long as the people involved want to do it ---------- Agree /_/----Disagree /_/

If two people are in love, it's only natural for them to want to get married ---Agree /__/----Disagree /__/

The way I'm living right now, most of my abilities are going to waste ----------Agree /__/----Disagree /__/

It's not so important that a child live in a home with both of his parents, so long as he has a good relationship with each of his parents individually -------Agree /__/----Disagree /__/

Marriage would make sex even more enjoyable, because both people would know that they really belong to each other ------------------------------------Agree /__/----Disagree /__/

The most important thing in a sexual relationship is just the sheer physical pleasure of having sex ---Agree /__/----Disagree /__/

The cancer scare about cigarette smoking has been exaggerated ------------------Agree /__/----Disagree /__/

The Women's Liberation Movement has been a good thing for women ----------------Agree /__/----Disagree /__/

Alcohol increases sexual pleasure --Agree /__/----Disagree /__/

My sexual behavior would not be acceptable to society --------------------------Agree /__/----Disagree /__/

It would be wrong to take advantage of a girl who was stoned or drunk by having sex with her --Agree /__/----Disagree /__/

The only good reason for getting married is if a baby is on the way -----------Agree /__/----Disagree /__/

In general, I think that so far I've been able to achieve most of the things that I've set out to achieve ---Agree /__/----Disagree /__/

When it comes to deciding how far a boy and girl should go where sex is concerned, it is up to the girl to decide ---------------------------------Agree /__/----Disagree /__/

Most girls these days have sexual intercourse before they are married ----------Agree /__/----Disagree /__/

When a boy has sex for the first time, it should be with a girl who is sexually experienced ---Agree /__/----Disagree /__/

Young people don't really want independence from society; they only want independence from their parents --Agree /__/----Disagree /__/

If two people are going to have a baby that neither person really wants, it is all right for the girl to have an abortion -------------------------------Agree /__/----Disagree /__/

Having sex together is a good way for two people to become acquainted ----------Agree /__/----Disagree /__/

PLEASE GO ON TO THE NEXT PAGE

Politically, there is no way that young people can ever beat "the silent majority" --Agree /_7----Disagree /_7

It's possible for love to be very real and very strong, but still not last for more than a few years ---Agree /_7----Disagree /_7

It's all right for married people to have sexual relations with other people once in a while for the sake of variety --------------------------------Agree /_7----Disagree /_7

It's all right for a person to have sexual relations with both males and females, if that's what the person wants to do ---------------------------------Agree /_7----Disagree /_7

It is really a tragedy if a couple that has children breaks up -----------------Agree /_7----Disagree /_7

If a boy finds out that he has V.D., he should immediately tell any girl he has recently had sex with --Agree /_7----Disagree /_7

Sex education courses in school are valuable for young people ------------------Agree /_7----Disagree /_7

Marijuana increases sexual pleasure --Agree /_7----Disagree /_7

If a girl truly doesn't want to have a baby, she won't get pregnant even though she may have sex without taking any birth control precautions ---Agree /_7----Disagree /_7

It's important that I try to develop my own set of personal values ------------Agree /_7----Disagree /_7

Too many young people these days are irresponsible where sex is concerned --Agree /_7----Disagree /_7

If older people would only remember what they were like when they were young, they would understand how young people think today ---------------------Agree /_7----Disagree /_7

If two people love each other and are living together, getting married is just a legal technicality --Agree /_7----Disagree /_7

Most boys these days have sexual intercourse before they are married ----------Agree /_7----Disagree /_7

When a girl has sex for the first time, it should be with a boy who is sexually experienced ---Agree /_7----Disagree /_7

If parents no longer love each other, it's better for their children that the parents break up rather than continue to live together unhappily --Agree /_7----Disagree /_7

The main reason why people are more casual about sex these days is because birth control is easily available to everyone ---------------------------------Agree /_7----Disagree /_7

It's immoral to bring an unwanted child into this over-populated world, especially now that abortions are so easy to get ------------------------------Agree /_7----Disagree /_7

THANK YOU VERY MUCH FOR YOUR COOPERATION IN ANSWERING THESE QUESTIONS

Now that you have finished --

1. Please put the questionnaire in our brown postage-paid return envelope.

2. Seal the envelope yourself, making sure that it is tightly sealed.

3. Go with our interviewer to the nearest mailbox, and mail the envelope. (If you prefer to have the interviewer mail it for you, he or she will be glad to do that. Either way, it will come directly to our Research Office.)

HB2C